DATE DUE

LIVING AUTHORS
A Book of Biographies

The H. W. Wilson Company
960 University Avenue
New York

———

W. & R. Holmes, Glasgow C.1
G. Hedeler, Leipzig

Copyright 1931   Probably Jan 1931
by The H. W. Wilson Company

—————

Set up and published at the press of
The H. W. Wilson Company
in April 1931

LIVING AUTHORS

A Book of Biographies

Edited by DILLY TANTE, *pseud*

and ILLUSTRATED with 371 PHOTOGRAPHS and DRAWINGS

Apr 1931

THE H. W. WILSON COMPANY

NEW YORK   1931

PREFACE

RUNNING thru this alphabet of authors, one snatches random scraps of knowledge from their lives. Sherwood Anderson, manager of a paint factory, halted his dictation in the middle of a letter, uttered one cryptic sentence, and went away; Henri Barbusse's mother was English; Algernon Blackwood is a convert to Buddhism; E. F. Benson's father was Archbishop of Canterbury; Karel Capek has been influenced most by American philosophy; Willa Cather cried in the French wheat fields because she was homesick for the prairies; Paul Claudel calls himself a moron in his prayers; A. E. Coppard did not begin to write till he was forty; Walter De La Mare was a bookkeeper for eighteen years; Theodore Dreiser was the conservative editor of a woman's magazine; Lord Dunsany is six feet, four inches, in height; T. S. Eliot became a British subject in 1927; Ford Madox Ford was gassed in the war; E. M. Forster lives with his mother; David Garnett discovered a new species of mushroom; André Gide wears a skull cap and a shawl in the Mallarmé tradition; Gorky's name is a pseudonym, meaning "the bitter one"; Ernest Hemingway served in the Italian army during the World War and was twice decorated by the Italian government; A. E. Housman spent 30 years editing the Latin poet Manilius; Aldous Huxley, who might have been a doctor but for an attack of blindness, writes his novels in Italy; Robinson Jeffers built with his own hands the tower in which he writes; James Joyce cultivated his voice for the concert stage; Margaret Kennedy began her literary career with a textbook on European history; Rudyard Kipling married an American girl; Sinclair Lewis was the janitor of Helicon Hall, Upton Sinclair's Utopian colony in New Jersey; John Livingstone Lowes has read everything that Coleridge read; William McFee was born at sea; Maeterlinck thinks that most Americans are hypocrites; Thomas Mann has six children; H. L. Mencken was destined for the tobacco business; Edna St. Vincent Millay wrote *Renascence* at nineteen; George Moore still has trouble with grammar and spelling; Sean O'Casey did not learn how to read till he was twelve years old; Eugene O'Neill has sketched the plots of thirty plays to come; Julia Peterkin is mistress of a plantation; Pirandello taught in a girls' school for thirty years; Llewelyn Powys has fought tuberculosis since he was twenty-five; Erich Remarque's *All Quiet on the Western Front* was rejected by several publishers; Edwin Arlington Robinson's favorite reading is detective stories; Bertrand Russell inherited an earldom in 1931; Siegfried Sassoon won a Military Cross for heroism in the World War, but threw it into the sea; Edith Sitwell is an accomplished pianist and her favorite sport is "reviewer-baiting"; Frank Swinnerton eats a plum pudding every time he finishes writing a novel; Arthur Symons was insane for a year and a half and wrote a book about it; H. M. Tomlinson spent his youth as a clerk, making out bills of lading for the *Cutty Sark* and other now "legendary" clipper ships; Sigrid Undset dresses in the costume of a Viking matron of the Middle Ages; Paul Valéry writes essays only on order; Rebecca West (née Cecily Isabel Fairfield) took her name from an Ibsen play; Jakob Wassermann was once forced to steal a small sum of money to keep from starving; the wife of William Butler Yeats is a medium; Arnold Zweig has translated Poe and Kipling.

In themselves these facts are trivial and meaningless. If they concerned the man in the brown hat next door or the discreet lady across the way, they might be dismissed as idle gossip, both inexcusable and dull. But in the world of art, where talent is primarily a consolidation of personality, we have a right to be curious. Our desire to know the artist is matched by his desire to reveal himself, for the art of the modern world is fundamentally autobiographical, and Goethe, described by Spengler as "the man who forgot nothing, the man whose works, as he avowed himself, are only fragments of a *single great confession,*" may well stand as the type of the Western artist. In our own time the impulse behind the work of James Joyce, the representative genius of the twentieth century, is to be found in the absolving confession of the Catholic Church.

It is with living authors, men and women alive on the first of January 1931, that these miniature biographies, some four hundred in number, are concerned. Their object is not critical, but expository. They have nothing to do with "psychographs." If they are found to be concise and pleasant introductions, or desirable supplements, to the works of the authors represented, their modest purpose will have been entirely fulfilled. The collection makes no pretension to comprehensiveness, its object being rather to present, within its scope, a selective survey of contemporary literary personalities, ranging from the great figures of our age down to the young poet or novelist with his first ("promising") book. The bias of the editor has been in favor of youth, and some older writers of merit have been, perforce, excluded to make room for young men and women with more work ahead of them, God willing, than behind. Poets, novelists, dramatists, essayists, biographers, critics, writers of children's books, and those philosophers whose personalities seem definitely to have encroached upon the literary scene, have been considered eligible for inclusion. The selection has been made from the living writers of all countries whose works are available in English. France, Germany, Spain, Italy, Austria, Hungary, Russia, India, Czechoslovakia, Norway, Sweden, Belgium, Holland, Great Britain, Ireland, Australia, Canada, and the United States are among the countries represented.

Posterity, no doubt, will forget many of these "living authors," but we need not be apologetic for our interest in them today. A mediocre living author is likely to impinge on our consciousness more than a good dead one. "The great works of past ages seem to a young man," observed Coleridge, who need not have restricted his observation to youth, "things of another race, in respect to which his faculties must remain passive and submiss, even as to the stars and mountains. But the writings of a contemporary, perhaps not many years older than himself, surrounded by the same circumstances, and disciplined by the same manners, possess a reality for him, and inspire an actual friendship as of a man for a man."

An effort has been made in these pages not only to publish a passable likeness of each author, but also to describe his appearance, for there is nothing about which the reader is more persistently curious, as if he hoped somehow to wrest from the body or the body's image the quintessential soul that the works themselves seem reluctant to yield. It is good Platonic doctrine to relate body to soul, but since not all our authors are equally handsome, it may be judicious to reflect, with Montaigne, that "in a face which is none of the best, there may dwell some air of probity and trust." Socrates, it will be remembered, said that his unprepossessing features betrayed how ugly his soul would have been if he had not corrected it by education.

It should be added that any marked variations from the average length of the biographies should be attributed to the paucity or abundance of available information, as the case may be. Certain authors have been omitted regretfully because either photographs or sufficient biographical data were unobtainable.

Newspapers, magazines, books, publishers, and authors have been consulted in the preparation of these biographies. All statements have been carefully verified whenever possible, but it is perhaps vain to hope that, in the multiplicity of details, no inaccuracies occur.

Acknowledgment is gratefully made to the four hundred authors, particularly those consulted personally, who put their "lives," as it were, in our hands; to the publicity representatives of some thirty publishers, who patiently gave of their time and invaluable data; and to the members of the American library profession, who practically demanded the publication of this work.

To fill in the gaps, both considered and inadvertent, of the present volume, another volume of at least equal size would be required and may be forthcoming, should the occasion arise. A continuous series of such volumes might constitute a valuably intimate record of the contemporary literary scene for the benefit of a neglectful posterity. Another generation will have its own "living authors." Much that is recorded here will scatter irretrievably to the winds; the original photographs will have cracked and faded. Here, then, are our four hundred men and women.

April 10, 1931

LIVING AUTHORS

Léonie Adams

LÉONIE ADAMS, one of the leading younger American poets, was born December 9, 1899, in Brooklyn, New York. With one exception her immediate ancestry is of Maryland and Virginia stock. But in that exception there may be justification for those romanticists who speculate upon the value of an inherited exotic strain in developing poetic genius, for Miss Adams' paternal grandmother was a Venezuelan.

After attending the New York public schools Miss Adams was graduated from Barnard in 1922, and then proceeded to teach and do editorial work in New York City. In 1924 she was on the editorial board of *The Measure,* one of the most important poetry magazines at that time. A Guggenheim fellowship for creative writing was awarded her in 1928, and this fellowship was renewed in 1929. She lived for a year in London, Oxford, and Paris, the three places where all good poets should go sooner or later, if they can.

As a personality Miss Adams has charm and wit. Altho she has the reputation of being both shy and reserved, those who know her well say that she is a witty talker and at her best as a raconteur. It has almost become a law of nature that poets do not read poetry well, particularly their own. If it is a law Miss Adams has broken it. She reads poetry aloud delightfully. In the spring of 1930 she read the annual Phi Beta Kappa poem for the Columbia Chapter. She has given a reading of her poems at one of the meetings of the Poetry Society of America, to which she belongs.

The poetry of Léonie Adams is distinguished for its mysticism and its

LÉONIE ADAMS

sophisticated rhythm. Her verses are sensuous but they also have a reserve that such verse usually does not possess.

She began publishing verse early. While an undergraduate Miss Adams' first poems appeared in *The New Republic.* In 1925 her first book of poems, *Those Not Elect,* came out. Her second collected volume of verse, *High Falcon,* was published in 1929. In 1930 Miss Adams edited for the Limited Editions Club a collection of translations from François Villon's lyrics that included a number of translations by herself. Many a poet has broken his lance in a technical tourney with Villon. One must have a complete knowledge of poetic technique in addition to a thoro mastery of Old French.

At present Miss Adams lives in the Ramapo Hills above Hillburn, New York, coming to New York City several times a week to lecture on Victorian poetry at New York University.

Conrad Aiken

CONRAD POTTER AIKEN was born in Savannah, Georgia, August 5, 1889, and was reared in New England.

He attended Harvard University (1907-1911), his schoolmates including T. S. Eliot, John Hall Wheelock, Alan Seeger, Van Wyck Brooks, Walter Lippmann, Robert Edmund Jones, Kenneth MacGowan, Robert Benchley, John Reed, and Heywood Broun. He was class poet.

Unlike some of these, Aiken held firm to the resolve to devote himself entirely to letters. Many of those contemporaries wandered off into the pleasant bypaths— editing, feature-writing, advertising. Aiken did not. Even during the war he kept to his own course. He was, in fact, the occasion for the interesting verdict of a draft board by which men of letters in general and poets in particular were declared to be engaged in a useful occupation.

Since 1912, when he was graduated from Harvard, Conrad Aiken has lived in Boston rooming houses, Roman *pensions,* among the English lakes, on a New Hampshire farm, in Sussex on the Channel, and on the south shore of Cape Cod. For the last few years he has lived in Cambridge, Massachusetts, but in the summer of 1930, after receiving the Pulitzer award for his *Selected Poems,* he left for England, where he says that he will live permanently because he can write better there.

He is a shy person, unhappy in public appearances, but capable, when aroused, of ironic utterance. It is told of him that on board a trans-Atlantic liner, when an insistent fellow-traveler attempted to engage him in conversation, finally asking the inevitable question, "What's your line?"—Mr. Aiken replied curtly, "Blank verse!"

In an analysis of his own poetry, Mr. Aiken has written: "Here I give myself away as being in quest of a sort of absolute poetry, a poetry in which the intention is not so much to arouse an emotion, or to persuade of a reality, as to employ such emotion or sense of reality (tangentially struck) with the same cool detachment with which a composer employs notes or chords." He is essentially a lyric poet whose emphasis has been—thru a series of influences, modifications, and evolving rhythms—on sound, overtone, and suggestions. His verse as a whole is sensuous, psychological, musical, the long cadence dissolving into a vague poignance.

The single poem by which he is best known is the celebrated "Morning Song of Senlin." Mr. Aiken married in 1912 and has three children, alliteratively christened John, Jane, and Joan.

The Jig of Forslin (1916) which followed the less mature *Earth Triumphant* (1914) and *Turns and Movies* (1916), relates the vicarious experiences of a man who, sitting alone in his room at night, passes in imagination thru all manner of adventures in other men's lives—some sordid, some beautiful. *A Nocturne of Remembered Spring* (1917), *The Charnel Rose* (1918), and *The House of Dust* (1920), characteristic in their slow music and subtle analysis, develop further this poet's unique gift. In *Mr. Punch, the Immortal Liar* (1921) we have a study of a typical character. *The Pilgrimage of Festus* (1923) and *Priapus and the Pool and Other Poems* (1925), were his next volumes. *Scepticisms* (1919), a collection of essays on contemporary poetry; *Bring! Bring!*

CONRAD AIKEN

(1925), a volume of stories; *Blue Voyage* (1927) his first novel; *Costumes by Eros* (1928), a collection of short stories; *Selected Poems* (1929), the Pulitzer Prize winner; and *John Deth and Other Poems* (1930), followed.

He has also compiled two anthologies, *Modern American Poets* (1922) and *American Poetry, 1671-1928* (1929), and edited the *Selected Poems of Emily Dickinson* for publication in England in 1924.

Richard Aldington

R ICHARD ALDINGTON was born in 1892 in Hampshire, England, of English parents. He received the usual education then given the children of well-to-do middle class persons in England, was at Dover College for several years and spent a year or more at London University. He had begun to write verse and prose—chiefly verse—at fifteen, and has never since had any doubts about what sort of a career he wanted.

His first poems appeared in 1909; in 1915 he published *Images Old and New*. Aldington married "H.D." in October 1913, and the two poets were soon recognized as leaders among the Imagists, both of them appearing in Amy Lowell's three issues of *Some Imagist Poets*.

Thru the influence of Pound he became literary editor of the *Egoist,* where he published a good deal of modern French and American poetry. All sorts of plans for his own work, for modern poetry, for intellectual cooperation between England, America and the Continent were knocked on the head by the war. Early in 1916 he became an infantry soldier in the British Army.

Dawn of the 11th November, 1918, found him an infantry officer, aged 26, standing on the Mons-Maubeuge road, utterly worn out, shattered in nerves, depressed—and as penniless as when he had left home eight years before.

Within a few days of demobilisation he had to sell his dress clothes for food, since the War Office delayed the payment of money due to him and he was too proud to borrow. Altho suffer-

RICHARD ALDINGTON

ing from shell-shock he began to work the day after he returned to England. A millionaire offered him money. Aldington said: "I don't want charity, I want work. Give me an introduction." In this way he got the job of critic of French literature for the London *Times* Literary Supplement. After a few months in London, he was told that he must go to the country, as the one chance of recovering from the effects of war. In 1919 he went to Berkshire, and found a workman's cottage, which he filled with books.

In the meantime he had published *War and Love* (1918) and *Images of Desire* (1919). Among the volumes of his verse that followed were *Exile and Other Poems* (1923), *A Fool i' the Forest* (1925), *Collected Poems* (1928), *Love and the Luxembourg* (1930).

After the war he spent a good deal of time in Italy and some in France and Switzerland. About the end of 1927 he felt he had really recovered from the shell-shock, and became increasingly dissatisfied with mere translation and criticism. An American, Crosby Gaige, paid him handsomely for a volume anthology of romance poems. With this money Aldington pulled himself out of the rut, escaped to Paris, Florence, Rome, Naples, the Riviera. Almost immediately he became again creative. At Port-Cros he began to write a novel of the war, but put it aside to make a translation of Boccaccio. He showed the first 30,000 words of *Death of a Hero* (1929) to an American publisher, who promptly bought the American rights, and told him to finish it at once. The English rights of the novel were bought by cable, five days after the manuscript was submitted. *Roads to Glory* (1930) is a book of thirteen war and post-war stories.

Mr. Aldington is one of our most accomplished as well as one of our busiest translators. Among his numerous translations (about twenty-five volumes at the close of 1930) are *The Poems of Meleager,* Cyrano de Bergerac's *Voyages to the Moon and the Sun,* Boccaccio's *Decameron, Letters of Voltaire and Frederick the Great, Medallions* (Greek and Latin poems). He has also edited and translated *Latin Poems of the Renaissance, Eighteenth Century French Literature,* and *Fifty Romance Lyric Poems.*

HERVEY ALLEN

Hervey Allen

HERVEY ALLEN, christened William Hervey Allen, Jr., was born in Pittsburgh, Pennsylvania, December 8, 1889. He received his early elementary training in that city, and attended the United States Naval Academy at Annapolis 1910 and 1911, resigning before he was graduated. He entered the University of Pittsburgh immediately and received a B. S. in Economics in 1915.

In 1916 Allen was a Second Lieutenant in the Pennsylvania Infantry on the Mexican Border, and in 1917 and 1918 he was a First Lieutenant in the 111th Infantry, 28th Division, A. E. F. In August of 1918 he was seriously wounded during active service, and was sent back to America later in the year.

Mr. Allen drifted South and lived in Charleston, South Carolina, for a year before going to Harvard where he took special courses in 1921 and 1922. While in the South he made the friendship of Du Bose Heyward, and in 1922 *Carolina Chansons* was published, a collaboration of the two men. They founded the Poetry Society of South Carolina, and were active in awakening interest in poetry thruout the South. Mr. Allen was an English Instructor in the Charleston High School from 1922 to 1924, and a member of the Department of English of Columbia University in 1924 and 1925. He lectured at Vassar in 1926 and 1927.

He was married to Miss Ann Hyde Andrews in 1927. They have one daughter, Marcia Andrews Allen.

Mr. Allen has been a frequent contributor to several periodicals. His published books of poetry include: *Wampum and Old Gold* (1921) containing the distinguished war ballad, *The Blindman,* which the Poetry Society of South Carolina commemorated for five years (1922-1926) by the annual award of the Blindman Prize for poetry; *Earth Moods and Other Poems* (1925); and *New Legends* (1929). *New Legends,* an epic divided into three parts, is the result of five years' research in the Bermuda Islands. *Toward the Flame* (1926) is a novel.

Allen's *Israfel: The Life and Times of Edgar Allen Poe* (1926), a two-volume biography and critical study, is regarded as one of the most authoritative works on Poe.

Serafín and Joaquín Álvarez Quintero

SERAFÍN and JOAQUÍN ÁLVAREZ QUINTERO were born in 1871 and 1873, respectively, in a small town in Spain not far from Seville. They began writing together when they were school boys, and their first play was produced in 1888 when Serafín was seventeen and Joaquín fifteen. It was the first of a long series of successes—indeed, in the number of plays published and produced (over one hundred and fifty) their only rival seems to be the American, Owen Davis.

The two are devoted brothers and their harmonious collaboration over a long period of years has never been interrupted. An older brother, Pedro, altho not a writer himself, was their adviser and critic from the first, and no play was produced, no final decisive dress rehearsal ever passed on, without his approval. When he died, two years after the death of his young wife, the two younger brothers grew even closer —neither one has ever married. They lived for years in their native Andalusia, the background of so many of their plays, and tho they have now moved to the capital, Seville has done them homage; for, as Helen Granville-Barker says, "they have enshrined Andalusia in drama." A charming faience fountain has been placed in the park of Seville, and there by the tiled space, square basin, everlastingly running water, flowers, and low-arching trees, is a bench inscribed with the names of chosen plays, and shelves to hold the books themselves. The inscription round the fountain reads:

"A Serafín y Joaquín Álvarez Quintero, gloriosos autores dramaticos, Sevilla, su madre adoptiva, consagra este monumento en testimonio de gratitud, porque infandieron en cien comedias, gala de la scena española, el alma de la reina del Guadalquivir."

Four of the plays were translated into English by Helen and Harley Granville-

S. AND J. ÁLVAREZ QUINTERO

Barker, and published here in 1928 under the title, *Four Plays: The Women Have Their Way, A Hundred Years Old, Fortunato,* and *The Lady from Alfaqueque.* They have been widely produced in England and America. *Fortunato* and *The Lady from Alfaqueque* met with success in London—a success which was repeated when Eva Le Gallienne produced the latter play at the Civic Repertory Theatre in January 1929, and Otis Skinner took the title rôle in *A Hundred Years Old* at the Lyceum the following year.

The Spanish critic Azorin calls *The Women Have Their Way* the brothers' masterpiece. It is the story of a young man who, coming from Madrid to an Andalusian town, is forced into a betrothal by the gossip of the place. Technically admirable, the play is remarkable for its economy of exposition, and, as Azorin says, for "a sort of lucid simplicity in the dialogue."

Jo Van Ammers-Küller

JO VAN AMMERS-KÜLLER, the Dutch novelist, writes of her life:— "I was born and passed my youth in the little quiet town of Delft, the only child in a family of doctors and lawyers which had resided in the town for many generations. I published a little love story

JO VAN AMMERS-KÜLLER

written from it which had 150 performances in one winter. It has been translated into German, Danish, English, and Polish, and several other translations are planned."

The *Rebel Generation* was published in the United States in 1928. It is a discussion of the emancipation of women and covers three generations. *The House of Joy* which was issued here in 1929 concerns a girl's desire to go on the stage and the complications involved. *Jenny Heysten's Career,* published late in 1930, is a continuation of this. The theatre as a career has always attracted the author and she shows her intimate knowledge of it in these books.

She has lectured in London and in Hamburg; she can speak several languages fluently. She has visited America and uses the first-hand information she obtained in *Tantalus,* published here January 1930, wherein the "new freedom" of this country is a foil for the authoritarian attitude of such older countries as Holland.

Maxwell Anderson

MAXWELL ANDERSON, the author of several Broadway successes, was born in Atlantic, Pennsylvania, on December 15, 1888. His father was a minister in this village in the northwestern corner of the state. Anderson spent his boyhood in the Middle West and divided his college days between the University of North Dakota and Leland Stanford.

in a weekly when fifteen and my family was so shocked that I was sent to boarding school. I wrote a few short stories and sketches but stopped writing when I married in my twentieth year and during the time my two boys were babies. While living in London where my husband was director of the gas and electric works, I began to write again and published several novels, which had a considerable success from the first. Three plays were written and produced during those years (1912-1921)."

Continuing her account, she speaks of *The House of Joy,* her first success, the stage novel which was a best seller in Holland and was also published in Germany. Then: "I came to Amsterdam and published *The Rebel Generation* in 1925, which is said to be the most popular book published in Holland in fifty years. Half a dozen people lectured about it, meetings were held where it was publicly discussed, and a play was

For several years he taught in schools in North Dakota and in California, and for a time worked on the San Francisco *Call-Bulletin* and the *Chronicle,* remaining in San Francisco until 1918. He had begun to contribute poems and articles to various magazines, and, on the strength of these was engaged by *The New Republic.* He was one of the founders of *The Measure* with Padraic Colum, George O'Neil, Genevieve Taggard, Frank Ernest Hill and others. He was also associated with the *New York Globe* for some time, and later with the *World.*

Anderson wrote his first play, *White Desert*, in 1923. Altho this drama of the Northwest ran only a few nights it did not alter his prediction that "some day he would write a great play." *What Price Glory*, written in collaboration with Laurence Stallings, came near to fulfilling this prophecy. This play was one of the earliest and most successful realistic dramatizations of the World War, the forerunner of *Journey's End* and many lesser plays.

Outside Looking In, based on *Beggars of Life*, by Jim Tully, was Anderson's next play, and was also well received. It needed only *Saturday's Children* and *Gods of the Lightning* to establish him as one of America's foremost playwrights.

Elizabeth the Queen, produced by the Theatre Guild in the fall of 1930, with Lynn Fontanne as Elizabeth and Alfred Lunt as Essex, was one of the outstanding features of the 1930-1931 season in New York.

Anderson's first book published was a volume of lyrics, *You Who Have Dreams* (1925). His others are *Saturday's Children* (1927), *Gods of the Lightning* and *Outside Looking In* (in one volume, 1928), and *Elizabeth the Queen* (1930). His collaborations with Laurence Stallings were published in

MAXWELL ANDERSON

1926 under the title *Three American Plays;* these were *What Price Glory, First Flight*, and *The Buccaneer*.

Mr. Anderson, six feet tall, proportionately broad-shouldered and with a massive head, has a gentle friendliness of manner. With his wife and three children he lives on their farm in the country about thirty miles from New York. He is a hard worker, and takes his chief recreation in walking, driving a car, and hearing old American songs.

Sherwood Anderson

SHERWOOD ANDERSON, almost entirely a self-made writer, was born in the little town of Camden, Ohio, September 13, 1876. The family ancestry is somewhat uncertain; his father, Irwin Anderson, came from a Southern family, probably Scotch-Irish in origin; his mother, Emma Smith Anderson, was said to be half Italian.

The family was a wandering, gypsy sort of tribe. Irwin Anderson, whom his son describes as "a lovable, improvident fellow, inclined to stretch the truth in statement . . . colorful, no-account, who should have been a novelist himself," moved from place to place in Ohio whenever debts became too pressing. No two of the children were born in the same town.

At the time Sherwood, the third of a family of five boys and three girls, was born, his father was running a small harness shop. Most of Sherwood's boyhood was spent in Clyde, Ohio, where his schooling was naturally irregular, as it was necessary for him to go to work when he was twelve to add to the family income. He got a job as timekeeper on some public construction work, attended school infrequently, and drifted about barrooms and stores. At the death of his mother when he was fourteen, all formal schooling ceased and Sherwood worked in factories and did odd jobs.

He went to Chicago when he was about seventeen and drifted from job to job for four years. The Spanish-American War gave him the opportunity for adventure and he served in Cuba. He returned to Ohio after the war, and

SHERWOOD ANDERSON

genius." Dell undertook to place the novel, and a publishing house accepted it on the condition that it be revised and censored. This Anderson refused to do, and it was some time before the book found another publisher.

Shortly before its publication in 1916 the author had a nervous breakdown and spent some months in an isolated cabin in the Ozarks. He wrote a novel there, but became so disgusted with it at the beginning of the trip back to Chicago that he threw the entire manuscript out of the train window.

Marching Men was published in 1917, a novel on factory conditions. *Mid-American Chants,* a book of verses, followed in 1918. By this time Anderson had aroused considerable attention, altho much of it was unfavorable. *Winesburg, Ohio* (1919) won him recognition, and critics began to compare him with Dostoievsky and Chekhov, neither of whom he had ever read. His chief reading until this time had been George Borrow's *Lavengro* and *The Bible in Spain,* and the *Old Testament.* Dreiser interested him in D. H. Lawrence, and he became an admirer of Lawrence's works.

Paul Rosenfeld arranged a trip abroad for Anderson in 1921. On his return Anderson went to New Orleans where he lived for a year. He found much to interest him there and New Orleans found much of interest in him; there were particularly cordial relations with the *Double Dealer* group.

After living in New York for some time, and returning to New Orleans for two or three shorter periods he bought a home in Marion, Virginia. Since then he has been editing simultaneously two newspapers there, one Democratic and one Republican. He is contented in the Smyth County Virginia mountains, and maintains that he has no desire to live elsewhere or to do other than edit his two papers. He lives directly above "the shop" because he enjoys going to the press room at all hours of the night.

Mr. Anderson has been married three times. His second wife was Tennessee Mitchell, the sculptor. He has three children, two sons and a daughter.

The Little Review was one of the first periodicals to publish him, and later *The*

to his surprise was greeted as a hero. Mr. Anderson married at that time, and after a series of events became manager of a paint factory in Elyria, Ohio. He began to write during this period, and became so dissatisfied with industrialism and the problems of capital and labor that one day, in the middle of a letter he was dictating, he turned to his stenographer and said: "I am walking in the bed of a river." He put his hat on, walked out of the factory and out of the town, never to return. His words had the effect he desired, and it was rumored that he was mentally unbalanced.

Sherwood's brother, Karl Anderson, who is now a well known portrait painter, had become a magazine illustrator in Chicago. Sherwood joined him there, secured a hall bedroom, and found a position with an advertising agency.

Thru his brother he came in contact with Theodore Dreiser, Carl Sandburg, Ben Hecht, Floyd Dell, Llewellyn Jones and others of the now dispersed "Chicago group." *Windy McPherson's Son* was written at this time, and was read to his group of friends, who listened enthusiastically. Ben Hecht and Floyd Dell were particularly convinced as to its value, and the former tried to interest "Papa Mencken" in this new "American

Dial and other magazines accepted his offerings eagerly. He won the *Dial* award in 1921 for the best original work by an American.

Mr. Anderson's publications include: *Windy McPherson's Son* (1916); *Marching Men* (1917); *Mid-American Chants* (1918); *Winesburg, Ohio* (1919); *Poor White* (1920); *Triumph of the Egg;* (1921); *Many Marriages* (1922); *Horses and Men* (1923); *A Story Teller's Story,* an autobiography (1924); *Dark Laughter* (1925); *Sherwood Anderson's Notebook* (1926); *Tar, a Midwest Childhood* (1926); *Hello Towns* (1929).

Gabriele D'Annunzio

GABRIELE D'ANNUNZIO, Prince of Monte Nevoso, has lately been described as "a man old in figure, small, thin, stooped, but young in the buoyant elasticity of his movements, young in the ever-changing expressions which play constantly over his pale, thin, mocking face, ageless in the malicious—impishly malicious—animation of the pale eyes under the exaggeratedly high forehead."

The Italian poet, novelist, dramatist, soldier, hero, who is living out his days in the mock-garb of a Franciscan father, a hermit of imperial luxury, was born at Pescara (Abruzzi) on March 12, 1863. Educated at the College of Prato in Tuscany and at the University of Rome, he published a volume of verse, *Primo Vere* (1880), while still a youngster at school. At the age of twenty he had published five volumes of poetry and created a national sensation, being stigmatized by many critics as an enemy of public morals. Others welcomed him as a startling and invigorating newcomer to Italian letters.

Under the pseudonym of "Duca Minimo" he did some brilliant journalism on the staff of the *Tribuna* in Rome. His first novel, *Il Piacere,* 1889 (English translation, *The Child of Pleasure,* 1898), was followed by *L'Innocente* (English translation, *The Intruder*), and by *Giovanni Episcopo.* Then came *Il Trionfo della Morte,* 1894 (English translation, *The Triumph of Death*), *Le Vergini delle Rocce,* and his glorification

GABRIELE D'ANNUNZIO

of Venice, *Il Fuoco* (1900). His finest poetry, such as *Il Poema Paradisiaco* (1893), was written in this fertile period.

Among his most famous plays are those he wrote in 1898 for the two greatest actresses of the modern stage: *Città Morta* for Sarah Bernhardt, and *Sogno d'un Tramonto d'Autumno* and *La Gioconda* for Eleonora Duse. In the following years he wrote many dramatic pieces and, in 1910, *Forse che si, forse che no,* a long novel in which many of the episodes have to do with aviation.

Having left Italy because of financial difficulties, D'Annunzio was in France when the World War broke out. Returning to Italy in the spring of 1915, he transformed himself from an esthete to a man of action and a politician, touring the country and delivering inspiring patriotic addresses. Volunteering for active service, he served successively in the cavalry, the infantry, and the navy, and finally in the air service, where he won international fame for his sensational exploits as an aviator, piloting his plane thru storms of bullets time and time again, receiving a wound in his wrist, and losing the sight of an eye. Flying over Vienna in August 1918 at the head of a fleet of planes, he dropped propaganda pamphlets over the enemy's city. He published ten war poems during his service. The sensations of his blindness were later described in *Notturno* (1921).

His most fantastic post-war adventure was his occupation of the city of Fiume in defiance of the Italian government. D'Annunzio was indignant at President Wilson's attitude toward Italy and wrote many bitter invectives against him. The terms of the Armistice did not satisfy him. When the Italian garrison at Fiume was reduced because of the anti-French riots, D'Annunzio at the head of an expedition of grenadiers and other troops marched on the city from Ronchi and on the night of September 11-12, 1919, triumphantly entered Fiume. Much to the astonishment of the world he created a new state, proclaiming himself ruler and "reigning" for fifteen months. The Italian government, bound to carry out the terms of the Rapallo Treaty, was at length forced to send out its troops in order to expel the defiant poet. Submitting in January 1921, D'Annunzio left the city and went to live at Gardone on the lake of Garda.

In 1924 D'Annunzio published the first volume of *Le Faville del Maglio,* which might be translated "Sparks from the Hammer," an autobiography in poetic prose. He is an ardent Fascist. In 1924 he was awarded the title of Prince of Monte Nevoso by the King in recognition of his efforts in securing Italy's new eastern frontier, of which Monte Nevoso is the highest point. The Italian Government undertook the publication of a collected edition of his works in 1927. died 1938.

Michael Arlen

MICHAEL ARLEN (originally Dikran Kuyumjian), the child of Armenian parents, was born in Roustchonk, Bulgaria, on the Danube in 1895.

He was sent to school at Malvern, England, and later studied medicine for three months at Edinburgh University. Settling in London after a sojourn in Switzerland, he wrote, at eighteen, what he calls his book of confessions, *The London Venture.* Next came *The Romantic Lady,* a book of short stories, and

his first novel, *Piracy,* written at twenty-three. Altho *Piracy* enabled him to pay his debts, he admitted in an interview that so far he had been playing scales in public. Then another book of short stories: *These Charming People.*

It took him a year to write a novel called *The Dark Angel,* but it did not satisfy him and he destroyed it. If he suffered any discouragement, the overwhelming success of *The Green Hat* in 1924 must surely have ended it. The younger generation became infatuated with his heroine, Iris March, whom Katharine Cornell later represented on the stage, and Greta Garbo in the motion-pictures. Arlen's royalties from *The Green Hat* amounted altogether to over half a million dollars.

A friend writes of Arlen: "Michael is like no other writer there ever has been. I hate to call him by that beastly word—immaculate—but I will say it and have done with it. He is. His slim, perfectly-proportioned figure is the joy of his tailor. His dress shirts and waistcoats are by Hawes and Curtis, his shoes by Lobb. His ties and socks are a gracefully subdued symphony. His barber is the best in town. He has a gold cigarette case which Mr. Asprey was a fool to part with. His Rolls-Royce is at least six inches longer than any other Rolls-

MICHAEL ARLEN

Royce. With evening dress he wears a gardenia, one white pearl and one black." He has dark hair, rather thick and wavy, and a light red mustache that bristles and turns up at the ends.

In May 1928 Arlen married the Countess Atalanta Mercati, daughter of Count Mercati of Athens and an American mother. A son, John Michael, was born to them late in 1930.

Arlen's recent books are *May Fair* (1925), a collection of short stories; *Young Men in Love* (1927), a novel which he calls "a flop"; *Lily Christine* (1928), a more serious novel; *Babes in the Wood* (1929), a volume of short stories subtitled "a relaxation intended for those who are always traveling but never reaching a destination"; and *Men Dislike Women* (1931), which he regards as his best novel.

Gertrude Atherton

GERTRUDE FRANKLIN ATHERTON was born in San Francisco, California, on October 30, 1857. She is the daughter of Thomas L. and Gertrude (Franklin) Horn. She received her education at private schools and under private teachers. She married George H. Bowen Atherton, of Menlo Park, California (died 1887). She has lived abroad much of her time. The French Chevalier Legion of Honor was awarded to her in 1925. She is the author of over thirty-five books.

The following is an extract of a letter received from Mrs. Atherton:

"I was born in San Francisco and educated there and in Lexington, Kentucky. Before I finished school I married, and was widowed a few years later. I immediately started for New York, to enter upon my career. I did not know much at that age but at least I knew enough to know that I could learn little of the world in California; and know the world I must if I would be a novelist. I have been studying the world ever since. The small town interests me occasionally, and I was deeply interested in visiting the old California towns—I returned for the purpose some years after I had left to find out all I could about the life of the old Spanish era—which

GERTRUDE ATHERTON

I embodied in *Rezanov, The Doomswoman,* and *The Splendid Idle Forties.* But life at its highest pitch of civilization interests me most—altho I do not suppose I ever took more pleasure in writing a novel than in *Tower of Ivory,* which was laid for the most part in Munich.

"As to ancestry: my mother's name was Franklin, she was descended from a brother of Benjamin Franklin, and her grandfather Amos Franklin founded the town of Oxford, New York. My father Thomas Lyman Horn was also of a revolutionary Nordic family, and his ancestor was one of the founders of Stonington, Conn. My grandfather, Stephen Franklin, went to San Francisco in the fifties and was one of the formative influences of the young city. My father went later, as well as his two brothers. I was educated by my grandfather, and as he had the finest private library in the state, and was determined I should be well-read, I owe the more serious turn of my mind to him, altho I rebelled bitterly at the time."

California, her native state, has a strong hold on Mrs. Atherton's heart. Beginning with *Rezanov,* a tale of 1806, she has covered over a hundred years of its social history in novel after novel:

*The Californians, Patience Sparhawk,
American Wives and English Husbands,
The Traveling Thirds, Ancestors, The
Avalanche, The Sisters-in-Law.* She
has also written a *History of California.*
Yet she cannot be identified solely as a
novelist of California, for her cosmopolitan interests are revealed in such novels
as *Senator North, Rulers of Kings, The
Gorgeous Isle, Tower of Ivory, Julia
France, The Living Present, Black Oxen,*
with scenes set in America, Austria, the
West Indies, Germany, and France,
countries which she knows at first hand.
The Conqueror, centering round Alexander Hamilton, is regarded by many as
her greatest success in the field of the
historical novel. It was suggested by a
line in Bryce's *American Commonwealth*
that Mrs. Atherton was reading as background for *Senator North.*

Recently Mrs. Atherton announced
that she had lost interest in the modern
scene. When she was in Monte Carlo
in 1925, a chance remark sent her off to
Greece, where she visited Athens, Cor-
inth, and Mycenae. Returning to San
Francisco with a great load of books,
she began *The Immortal Marriage*
(1927), the story of Aspasia, for which
she read over two hundred volumes.
Two more novels of ancient Greece followed: *The Jealous Gods* (1928), the
romance of Alcibiades, and *Dido, Queen
of Hearts* (1929), which she wrote in
celebration of the Virgil bimillenium.
The Sophisticates, her first modern novel
in five years, appeared in 1931.

Of Mrs. Atherton's "classic Colonial
profile," Isabel Paterson has written: "It
might have been drawn by Peale or Gilbert Stuart. Her eyes are very blue,
her hair pale gold; she is of middle
height, and of that erect carriage one
associates with an earlier generation
which used straight backed chairs as a
matter of self respect."

Joseph Auslander

JOSEPH AUSLANDER was born
in Philadelphia October 19, 1897.
He attended St. Catherine's School in
Philadelphia, the Eastern District High
School in Brooklyn, and was graduated

with honors from Harvard. He did
graduate work in English at Harvard
and was sent abroad as a Parker Traveling Fellow to pursue studies at the Sorbonne. In 1922 he was appointed to
teach English composition and literature
at Harvard and Radcliffe. He was for
a time editor of *The Measure.* He has
reviewed poetry for the *New York
World* and the *New York Sun,* and contributed poems and critical articles to the
leading periodicals. In 1924 he was
awarded the Blindman Prize for Poetry.

Mr. Auslander is the author of several
volumes of poetry—*Sunrise Trumpets*
(1924), *Cyclop's Eye* (1926), *Hell in
Harness* (1929), *Letters to Women*
(1929). With Frank Ernest Hill he has
written *The Winged Horse* (a story of
poetry, 1927), and *The Winged Horse
Anthology* (1929); and with Jacques Le
Clercq translated the *Fables of La Fontaine* (1930). He has also translated
Lazy Teddy Bear (1930), a picture book
by Willy Plunck, from the German.

In 1930 Mr. Auslander went to Europe
to write a new kind of travel book, the
account of a poet's pilgrimage thru the
Old World. Following the trail of the
poets from Homer to the present day,
Mr. Auslander visited those places in

JOSEPH AUSLANDER

Europe that by romantic association or residence have called forth great poems. After the pilgrimage was completed, he settled down to finish his manuscript in a tower built by the Emperor Justinian overlooking the Adriatic Sea.

Mary Austin

BORN of Revolutionary stock in Carlinville, Illinois, on September 9, 1868, Mary Hunter moved to California at the age of eighteen. She received a B. S. degree from Blackburn University in 1888.

For sixteen years she lived in the California desert, working like an Indian woman, studying Indian lore and the nature and properties of the desert. She was married in 1891 to S. W. Austin and had one child. It was not until after the loss of this child that her literary career was begun.

After abandoning the desert, Mrs. Austin lived for some time at Carmel where with George Sterling, Jack London, and Michael Williams she was an important member of the literary colony. She made several trips abroad where she was recognized by many of the leading writers of England, France, and Italy. Each year she spent part of her time in New York. Finally in 1918 she selected Santa Fe, New Mexico, as affording the best facilities for her work, and has since built a house there.

Mrs. Austin's home, Casa Querida, at Santa Fe, is in the old Spanish Colonial style and is furnished with the plunder of the desert accumulated thru thirty years. Lately she has undertaken the revival of Spanish colonial arts and the reestablishment of the annual Spanish market at Santa Fe. Her recreations are gardening and cooking. Between finishing one piece of work and beginning another, she goes on what she describes as "jam-borees," in which she makes jams and jellies and pickles in enormous quantities, much to the delight of her friends. All the natives know that when flowers are wanted for weddings or funerals or the altars of the Saints, they can get them from Mary Austin's garden.

Mary Austin has written a score of books, several of which will not be over-

MARY AUSTIN

looked by future historians of our Southwest—not because these books are histories, but because they accurately and with penetration describe in fiction, fact, and drama, phases of Western development that are rapidly passing away. Among her works are a life of Jesus; the only dramas of Indian life with Indian characters that have had professional performance on the American stage; distinguished translations of Indian poetry and collections and translations of old Spanish plays; a standard book on genius and talent; and, recently, a volume of poems of the Southwest for children. Carl Van Doren says that the degree, M.A.E. (Master of the American Environment) should be invented and conferred upon her. She has been called "a great person who happens to be a woman."

Mary Austin's books include: novels, *Isidro* (1905), *A Woman of Genius* (1912), *The Green Bough* (1913), *No. 26 Jayne Street* (1920), *Starry Adventure* (1931); short stories, *The Basket Woman* (1904), *The Trail Book*

(1918); a play, *The Arrow-Maker* (1911); a book of poems, *Outland* (1910, under pseudonym, Gordon Stairs); essays and studies, *The Land of Little Rain* (1903), *California* (1914), *The Man Jesus* (1915), *The American Rhythm* (1923), *Everyman's Genius* (1925), *The Children Sing in the Far West* (1928). Mrs. Austin contributed the chapter on Aboriginal Literature to the *Cambridge History of American Literature*. She is at work now on her autobiography.

Irving Babbitt

IRVING BABBITT, leader of the "Humanist" school, was born in Dayton, Ohio, on August 2, 1865. After graduation from Harvard College in 1889, he studied at the Sorbonne in Paris for two years in 1891 and 1892, and took his master's degree at Harvard in 1893. After teaching French at Williams College in 1893-94, he returned to Harvard, where he was appointed assistant professor in 1902. Ten years later, in 1912, he was given the chair of professor in French which he has kept ever since. His distinction as professor and author spread abroad and in 1923 he was asked to give a series of lectures on the French romantic school of literature at the Sorbonne.

He has edited four French books to be used in colleges and universities. These are Taine's *Introduction à l'Histoire de la Littérature Anglaise* (1898), Renan's *Souvenirs d'Enfance* (1902), Voltaire's *Zadig* (1905), Racine's *Phèdre* (1910). These books are fully annotated by Professor Babbitt.

Professor Babbitt is better known for his philosophical criticisms, and his contribution in this field is one of the best of our time. If his books have gained him many admirers, they have also been the subject of passionate controversy.

Professor Babbitt's point of view, which he developed in five volumes, each one complete in itself, but each a part of a complete whole, is essentially a humanistic, but not a humanitarian one. His idea is that the world at large has been permeated by the romantic ideas originated by Rousseau and his school, that our conception of government, ethics, education, and general conduct of life is extreme, sentimental, and in direct opposition to the requirement of modern life, and that the world needs to face these facts and revert to a more humanistic equilibrium.

He began by analyzing the Romantic Movement with special reference to literature and education. *Literature and the American College* (1908) is a defense of the Humanistic in the Liberal Arts course and an essay upon the influence of Romanticism on education theories.

The question of the confusion of the arts both on the pseudo-classic and on the Romantic side is treated in the *New Laokoön* (1910). As a study in comparative literature the book is important.

Masters of French Criticism (1912) is a thoro study of the leading French critics of the nineteenth century as well as a discussion of the problem of modern criticism and its aim.

Professor Babbitt's strongest attack on Romanticism and clearest definition of modern life and wants is found in his *Rousseau and Romanticism* (1919). His *Democracy and Leadership* (1924) deals chiefly with the Romantic influence on the theory of government and with the logical development of Romantic

IRVING BABBITT

practice in modern governments. It is the book that comes closest to the ordinary reader. He has also contributed a chapter defining Humanism to the symposium, *Humanism and America* (1930).

"His appearance," writes Harry Salpeter, "gives the clue to his character. It is that of a strong man touched by age . . . but sustained by something like faith. He is rather above medium height, a fact that is not obvious because of his inclination to walk with a slight stoop, and his arms give the impression of hanging loosely from his shoulders. His face is rather long and concave. He has a strong jaw and the thin hard line of his lips seconds the impression of decision. He has a large forehead from beneath which his eyes look out clearly and coldly. He speaks deliberately, forcefully, not harshly, but as one who might be impatient of interruption or disagreement."

ISAAC BABEL

Isaac Babel

ALTHO Isaac Babel is the author of but one published book, this book has given him a place among the important writers who have come from the new Russia.

Born in 1894 in Odessa, he is the son of a Jewish merchant and a Moldavian Jewess. His Jewish heritage has been at all times important in his career. When he was three years old his family moved to Nikoliev, but during the violent Czarist pogroms of 1905 they were forced to flee for their lives and returned to Odessa, where young Babel lived for the next nine years.

During his boyhood Babel read and studied practically all of Maupassant, Flaubert, and Rabelais. In 1914 he was graduated from the University of Saratov and returned to Odessa.

In 1916 he went to Petrograd. He was in daily danger there as this city had exiled and banned all Jews, but by living under false passports and remaining somewhat in seclusion in the house of a waiter he was safe temporarily. His

first published stories were written here; these appeared in Gorki's famous paper, *Annals*. These articles and stories did not escape the notice of Czarist officials and Babel was indicted for pornography and for inciting class hatred, two severe charges. Because of the revolution, the cases were never heard.

In 1920 he joined the Cossacks, a regiment which until the revolution was noted for its bitter anti-Semitic tendencies. He was probably the first Jew to serve in the Cossacks. Babel, a bespectacled lawyer with an air of lofty intellectualism, was at first the subject of contempt and ridicule of his comrades. Finally one of them took pity on him and advised him to commit some daring rascalities, which he did so successfully that he won the respect and admiration of the regiment.

Red Cavalry (translated 1929) is a collection of stories based on the experiences of the Russian cavalry, and is said to describe Cossack life better than any book since Gogol's *Taras Bulba*. It was published in Russia, Germany, and France before it appeared in America. Many of the scenes described are almost unspeakably brutal, yet the writing has such poetic quality that one of the stories in the book, *Salt*, has been learned by heart by many Russians.

Irving Bacheller

IRVING BACHELLER was born in Pierpont, New York, September 26, 1859. He speaks of his childhood as an unhappy time; he was not robust, his family was poor, and life seemed to him a painfully serious prospect. Yet he sees also richness in his background and his contact with lonely people on the edge of the forests of northern New York, hunters, rivermen and lumberjacks, French, Irish, and Yankees.

At the age of thirteen he went to work in a country store with the aim of learning the mercantile business. His first train ride was to Burlington, Vermont, which impressed him as no other city has since. He was graduated from Canton Academy, in Canton, New York, and in 1882 received a B. S. degree from St. Lawrence University. He received an M. S. there in 1892, and this university conferred the degree of A.M. and Ph.D. on him in 1901 and 1911 respectively.

When Bacheller was twenty-one he went to New York, "the slimmest, most solemn-faced youth who ever came to New York to make his fortune," he says of himself. He married Miss Anna Detman Schultz, of Brooklyn, in 1883.

IRVING BACHELLER

Just before Sir Henry Irving's American tour Bacheller wrote a sketch of him which pleased the actor so much that he asked the young reporter to visit him immediately upon his arrival in New York. Thru Irving, Bacheller met Joseph Hatton, an English novelist and critic who was responsible for his becoming a pioneer in the newspaper syndicate business. He took over one of Hatton's novels and later a series of interviews with famous men in England. Authors of international fame, including Conan Doyle, became contributors to his syndicate.

Bacheller sold his first short story which had been sent to a magazine under a pseudonym, at this time; a short time later a ballad was accepted and published by Bliss Carman. The result was that he left the *Brooklyn Times* and, when he found himself insolvent not long later, began to write seriously. *Eben Holden* was begun in a small apartment in Tarrytown where he and Mrs. Bacheller were living, but before it was finished Joseph Pulitzer offered him an editorial position on the *New York World*. He was on the editorial staff of the *World* from 1898 to 1900; he obtained a six months' leave of absence in order to finish his novel, and did not return to newspaper work again.

Mr. Bacheller's present homes are in Riverside, Connecticut, during the summer, and Winter Park, Florida, in the winter. His home in Florida is called "Gate o' the Isles." He is one of the directors of Rollins College in Winter Park.

He enjoys at least two hours and a half of exercise daily. He is described as being large of frame, slow-motioned yet athletic. He is fond of singing old fashioned ballads and is a successful orator.

Mr. Bacheller has published a number of novels; among his early ones are *Eben Holden* (1900), *D'ri and I* (1901) and *Darrel of the Blessed Isles* (1903); his latest are *The House of Three Ganders* (1928) and *A Candle in the Wilderness* (1930), the latter being exhibited at the New England Tercentenary which was celebrated in 1930. He has also published two autobiographical books,

Opinions of a Cheerful Yankee (1926) and *Coming up the Road,* memories of a north country boyhood (1928).

Henri Barbusse

HENRI BARBUSSE was born in Paris on May 17, 1874. His father was French, his mother English. He was educated at the Collège Rollin and became a successful journalist, editing eventually the periodical *Je Sais Tout.* On his fortieth birthday, in 1914, just before the outbreak of the World War, he had only a small literary reputation, having published a volume of poetry, *Pleureuses* (1895); two novels, *Les Suppliants* (1903) and *L'Enfer* (1908); and a volume of short stories, *Nous Autres* (1914). He was in contact, however, with French literary circles, having married the daughter of Catulle Mendès.

The war in a way marked his regeneration. A common soldier in the trenches, he was invalided to the rear and wrote his book, *Le Feu (Under Fire)*, which made him famous overnight on its publication in 1916. By the following year *Le Feu* had received the *Prix Goncourt,* soon it had run thru more than two hundred editions in France and had been translated into practically every language of Europe and some outside of Europe. It echoed the conviction of the people that the war *must* end.

After peace had been declared, Barbusse became passionately interested in politics and social reform, writing numberless articles, especially as correspondent of the socialist journal *L'Humanité,* and preaching over and over again his message against war.

Barbusse does not like to be called a propagandist. "I never intended *Under Fire* for propaganda," he asserts. "My enemies made it political, and not my friends." But a book, he believes, must have direct relevance to contemporary ideas: "The sort of literature that exists in a fourth dimension and has no connection with modern life: 'pure literature,' as people call it, is dead. But the literature of ideas is always living." New experiments in prose and poetry interest

HENRI BARBUSSE

him exceedingly. "It is ridiculous," he says, "to try to cast the present age into molds which we have inherited from the eighteenth century."

Among the books that Barbusse published after the war are *Clarté* (translated here as *Light* in 1919), in which is evident the faith he somehow found in the possibility of a better world; *La Lueur dans l'Abîme* (1920); *Les Enchaînements (Chains,* tr. 1925), which tells of man's bondage thru the ages; *Jesus* (tr. 1927); *Manifeste aux Intellectuels* (1927); *I Saw It Myself* (tr. 1928); and *Thus and Thus* (tr. 1929), a collection of short stories in which he denounces the evils that follow on a great war.

Soon after the armistice Barbusse organized an international group of intellectuals in opposition to all forms of tyranny and violence. Lately he founded an anti-Fascist league in Paris. Malcolm Cowley describes him as having inherited much from his English mother, "for he is as tall and cadaverous as a typical Englishman of letters, but his hands are long and eloquent and French. His practical grey eyes—English eyes—are framed by two long wisps of hair. He has an abnormally high French forehead and an English chin. The same combination is apparent in his conversation; it has an uncompromising French logic, but unlike some Latin conversations it never deserts hard fact. There is a charm about his talk; when under its spell one believes that Henri Barbusse has succeeded in combining the virtues of two races."

In 1931 Barbusse was at work on a new volume, a denunciation of war, to be called *Ce Qui Fut Sera.*

Maurice Baring

HON. MAURICE BARING, the fourth son of the first Lord Revelstoke and brother to the present one, was born April 27, 1874. He was educated at Eton and Trinity College, Cambridge, going abroad for some years afterward to finish his education in languages.

Entering the Diplomatic Service in 1898, he became attaché to the British Embassy in Paris. A year later he published his first book in Paris, *Hildesheim, Quatre Pastiches,* a parody of the great masters of French style. For his theme he chose the old city of Hildesheim and treated it in the manner of Ernest Renan, Pierre Loti, Anatole France, and Paul Bourget. This first volume was reprinted

MAURICE BARING

in England in 1924, more than a quarter of a century after its initial appearance.

Before he resigned from the foreign service in 1904, Baring had been transferred from Paris to Copenhagen and subsequently to Rome. He began his career, as it were, of following the wars in 1904 when he took the long trip to Manchuria as war correspondent of the *Morning Post.* He knows Russia intimately, having been special correspondent there from 1905 to 1908. His next journalistic posts were in Constantinople (1909) and in the Balkans (1912).

In the *Puppet Show of Memory,* A Book of Recollections (1922), Baring gives an autobiographical account of these days of his life, of his studies at school, his sojourn in Germany, his activity in the Foreign Office. There is a chapter on diplomatic life in Copenhagen, and another of his impressions of the Russo-Japanese War, and of the first outbreak of revolutionary disorders in Russia (1904-1906). In conclusion he describes his two journeys to Turkey, one during the unrest in Constantinople and the other during the Balkan war of 1912.

During the World War Baring served in various capacities in the Royal Flying Corps, attaining the rank of major in 1917. He is a Chevalier of the Legion of Honor. He is a prominent figure in the social life of London, Paris, and Rome, and his literary productions, which show his cosmopolitan culture, are known in many countries. He speaks five or six languages fluently.

Maurice Baring is devoted to the theatre and has written many essays on the stage. He is also the author of several dramas. He is a prolific writer, having published close to fifty volumes, including essays, dramas, travel impressions, poems, short stories, translations, reminiscences, criticism, and an outline of Russian literature.

His prose bespeaks his love of what he calls "the line of divine simplicity, where there is nature and nothing else, no style, no ornament, no effort, just the ordinary simple thing said in the simplest possible way with the result that it is sublime, inimitable, and unapproachable."

Among the recent publications of Maurice Baring are *A Triangle* (1923),

C (1924), *Half a Minute's Silence* (1925), *Collected Poems* (1925), *Cat's Cradle* (1925), *Daphne Adeane* (1926), *Tinker's Leave* (1927), *Comfortless Memory* (1928), *The Coat Without Seam* (1929), and *Roger Peckham* (1930).

Larry Barretto

LARRY BARRETTO was born at Larchmont, N. Y. on May 30, 1890. His full name, he confesses, is Laurence Brevoort Barretto, and he is a descendant of one of New York's oldest families. One of his ancestors was Francesco Barretto, for whom Barretto Street was named, and another was Hendrick Brevoort, upon whose farm the present Greenwich Village stands.

He was educated at Hoosac School, Hoosick, N. Y. During the World War he served with the U. S. Ambulance Corps attached to the French Army and was awarded the Croix de Guerre.

Mr. Barretto has engaged in a variety of occupations, but these were mainly to acquire a background for the literary career which he started in 1920 as assistant editor of *Adventure Magazine.* He also spent two years as dramatic critic on *The Bookman.*

In 1924 Barretto began his free lance writing. His first novel, *A Conqueror Passes,* was one of the first stories of the returned soldier to result from the World War. This was followed by *To Babylon* (1925) and *Walls of Glass* (1926).

In 1928 was published *Old Enchantment,* a story of the modern age in conflict with a disintegrating aristocracy.

In 1929 Mr. Barretto's fifth novel, *Horses in the Sky,* made its appearance. It is based on his own war experience, and in an interview granted shortly before the book was published, Mr. Barretto made a parenthetical acknowledgment of his personal indebtedness to the chances of war:

"Because of the war, I married the girl I married.

Louis Bromfield and I were ambulance drivers in the same outfit. We were merely acquaintances until one fearfully dark night we smashed into each other.

LARRY BARRETTO

We both got out and swore, and each of us said the collision was the other's fault. Finally, we decided to share the blame, and after that we were friends. I married his wife's first cousin. If it hadn't been for the war, and the accident, I should never have met her."

The Indiscreet Years (1931) is the story of a woman who must live down her early indiscretions.

Besides his novels, Mr. Barretto has written short stories for various publications.

He makes his home in Goshen, N. Y., in the summer and in New York City in the winter, with occasional trips, usually to Europe.

James Barrie

SIR JAMES MATTHEW BARRIE was born in one of the most Scottish parts of Scotland, Kirriemuir, Forfarshire, May 9, 1860. He was "a queer, solemn-looking baby, with enormous eyes and an apparent sense of grievance."

Barrie's inheritance was purely Scotch and during his early years he absorbed

JAMES BARRIE

what little Scottishness might have been left out of his nature to such an extent that those characteristics are still wholly intact. During that time also he unconsciously accumulated rich material which he was later to use in stories and plays.

He attended Dumfries Academy where he was an indifferent pupil, seldom opening his books except to draw pictures in them. His literary career was inaugurated there by accounts of cricket matches he wrote for the Dumfries newspapers, and letters signed "Paterfamilias," his most frequent theme being the desirability of longer vacations from school.

Barrie's first play, *Bandelero the Bandit,* was written for and presented by the Dumfries Academy Dramatic Society. His only appearance as an actor was in this play, in which he was, as he describes himself, "a young lady with her hair attached to her har." He also wrote a novel while in the Academy, an ambitious one hundred thousand word opus entitled *A Child of Nature.* Fortunately for Barrie's literary reputation he had the good judgment to destroy it, "just in case it should fall into the wrong hands, you know," as he said.

From Dumfries Academy Barrie went to the University of Edinburgh where he received an M.A. and also took honors in English Literature. This University conferred the degree of Doctor of Letters on him in 1922.

Five months after his graduation he began as a "leader-writer" on a Nottingham newspaper. He started writing stories at this time which he unsuccessfully tried to sell to London papers and periodicals. Barrie says that it was a long time before he became conscious of the quaintness of his native town and its possibility as material.

The young Scot who came to London in 1885 was "a very little man with a ragged black mustache, a notably bulging brow, a large, reflective, luminous eye— shy, sensitive, chaste, a dry, making his first tentative experiments with a pipe."

Under the name "Gavia Ogilvy" he began writing for the *British Weekly*. *Better Dead* (1887), his first book, was a satirical "shocker" that fell dead from the press. His second book, *Auld Licht Idylls* (1888), was favorably received, however, delighting readers with its fresh character sketches against an unfamiliar landscape.

A Window in Thrums (1889), a sequel to *Auld Licht Idylls,* confirmed his literary reputation. Thrums was the name Barrie had chosen for his birthplace, Kirriemuir.

The Little Minister (1891) raised Barrie from the rank of an admirable sketch writer to that of a first-class novelist. In 1896 *Margaret Ogilvy* appeared, a touching biography of and tribute to his mother. *Sentimental Tommy* (1896) and its sequel, *Tommy and Grizel* (1900), and *The Little White Bird* (1902) practically complete the list of Barrie's novels.

Barrie's marriage with Mary Ansell, an actress, ended quietly, after fourteen years, in the divorce court.

Barrie was knighted in 1913. Altho he is very wealthy now, he lives modestly in a flat overlooking the river at Adelphi Terrace, London. Travel is not to his taste. He likes to dine and talk with one or two friends and occasionally play a game of billiards.

From 1900 to 1920 Barrie wrote almost nothing but plays, and with such success that he is now considered preeminently a playwright. Since 1920 he has practically stopped writing. Of his many plays the most important are *The Admirable Crichton* (1902); *Peter Pan* (1904), a dramatization of *The Little White Bird; Alice-Sit-By-The-Fire* (1905); *What Every Woman Knows* (1908); *A Kiss for Cinderella* (1916); *Dear Brutus* (1917); *Mary Rose* (1920); *Shall We Join The Ladies?* (1922).

There have been various sets of Barrie's plays published, but not until 1929 was there a complete one-volume edition.

PHILIP BARRY

Philip Barry

PHILIP BARRY, the dramatist, was born in Rochester, New York, June 18, 1896. After attending the schools of his native city he went to Yale, from which he received an A.B. degree in 1919. In the meantime he had become connected with the Department of State, Washington, D.C., and from May 1918 to February 1919 was attached to the American Embassy in London. His next three years were spent at Harvard, where he acquired an excellent early discipline in the drama under Professor George Pierce Baker of 47 Workshop.

You and I, a three-act comedy, chosen as the Harvard Prize Play in 1922, established Barry's reputation when it was produced in New York in 1923. A year later his second play, *The Youngest,* was produced, followed in rapid succession by *In a Garden, White Wings, John, Paris Bound, Cock Robin* (with Elmer Rice), *Holiday, Hotel Universe, Tomorrow and Tomorrow.*

It is curious that the play which many critics regard as Barry's best—*White Wings,* a clever whimsical piece, with an undercurrent of pathos, satirizing the displacing of the horse by the automobile—should have been a commercial failure. But in general one can agree with the commentator who remarked that Barry has been a child of fortune in the American theatre. "Without exception his plays have been presented by first line producers, including Winthrop Ames and Arthur Hopkins [and the Theatre Guild]. They have been interpreted by such experienced, competent,

and well known players as Laurette Taylor, Henry Hull, Madge Kennedy, Genevieve Tobin, Katharine Alexander, and Jacob Ben-Ami. They have been furnished with settings designed by talented stage artists including Norman Bel-Geddes and Robert Edmond Jones. They have been produced outside of New York more frequently than the plays of any other American except Eugene O'Neill. Now they have been published in a uniform edition."

Barry aims to write sparkling and intelligent comedy, with sincere and serious motivations. Altho his earlier plays brought him favor among discriminating followers of the drama, Barry's first great popular success came with *Paris Bound,* a comedy about divorce, which was produced in 1927. *Holiday,* a comedy contrasting the people whose end and aim in life is to make more and ever more money with those people who look at life and find it good without the aid of millions, had an equally favorable reception. *Hotel Universe,* produced by the Theatre Guild in 1930, is an interesting experiment in psychological drama that provoked much dispute among the critics. *Tomorrow and Tomorrow,* the romance of a fine woman's adjustment to life, was produced in 1931. This modern play is based on the Biblical story of

Elisha and the Shunemmite woman (II Kings, IV, 8-37).

Mr. Barry spends most of the year on the French Riviera in his villa at Cannes, but from September to January he is usually to be found at home in Mount Kisco, New York. He is married and is the father of two boys.

The published plays of Mr. Barry, with publication dates, include: *You and I* (1923), *The Youngest* (1925); *In a Garden* (1926), *White Wings* (1927), *Paris Bound, John, Holiday* (1929), *Hotel Universe* (1930), *Tomorrow and Tomorrow* (1931).

Vernon Bartlett

VERNON BARTLETT was born in England on April 30, 1894, and was educated at Blundells School, Tiverton. (This is the school that was made famous by R. D. Blackmore in *Lorna Doone*.)

He left school, however, at the age of sixteen, and traveled abroad to study languages for the Consular Service. At this time he lived for a while with a German family in Bromberg, and *Calf Love* (1929), a novel of adolescence, is

VERNON BARTLETT

a result of this part of his experience. He later lived in Florence, Madrid, and Paris. His next venture was a position in London, translating foreign correspondence in an office, but he left this after one morning's work. He next tried a position teaching English in a language school and had just begun to study at the Sorbonne University when the war broke out.

He joined up in August 1914 and went to France as second lieutenant early the next year. He spent five months at the front, much of the time in command of his company, and then as he was slightly wounded, he spent his twenty-first birthday in a hospital train. He was invalided home and spent two years of severe illness. When he recovered he drifted into journalism, first on the *Daily Mail* and then at *Reuter's*. He attended the Paris Peace Conference for *Reuter's* and was for three weeks first Paris correspondent of the *Daily Herald*. He then transferred to the *Times*, where he was private secretary to the editor.

He traveled all over Europe as special correspondent for the *Times*, covering revolutions, etc. This period of travel brought forth his novel, *Topsy Turvy* (1927). He was with the Polish army in 1920 in the war against the Bolshevists and was in various upheavals in Germany. He then represented the *Times* as correspondent in Rome, leaving a few days after Mussolini came into power after spending two years there. He returned to England to become Director of the London Office of the League of Nations Secretariat which post he still holds. In connection with his war and post-war experiences, Mr. Bartlett has written the following books: *Mud and Khaki* (1916), *Behind the Scenes at the Peace Conference* (1919), *The Brighter Side of European Chaos* (1925). In the fall of 1930 Mr. Bartlett visited the United States on a lecture tour under the auspices of the Foreign Policy Convention.

When he is in England, he talks each week on the radio from all British Stations on international affairs, and in recent ballots heads the list as the most popular English radio speaker. *The World Our Neighbor* (1931) is a collection of his radio addresses.

He collaborated with R. C. Sherriff in the novelization of Sherriff's famous war play, *Journey's End* (1930). His own novel, *No Man's Land* (1930, American title: *The Unknown Soldier*), exposes the consciousness of a young Englishman, Stevenson, as he lies with death wounds in a shell-hole in No Man's Land.

H. E. Bates

HERBERT ERNEST BATES was born in the spring of 1905 in Rushden, England. Of the incidents of his early life none now seem to be so impressive and significant as those with which his maternal grandfather was concerned. Bates' earliest memories are full of his grandfather's white-haired, brown-skinned, slightly stooping and strong figure going about the smallest of poor farms which he worked a mile or two from his home on the bare edge of the river valley. There he spent day after day of his childhood. From the little windows one could see miles of the green

H. E. BATES

passage where the river came down. In the winter that passage was flooded, sprinkled with flocks of gulls and full of a sort of sad, cold beauty. There was little for them to do but watch and wonder, tho in hot weather Bates would lie and read under haystacks, and in harvest sleep in a wheat-stack. When it rained he sat in a little, dirty, gloomy hovel smelling of straw and potatoes, watching and listening to his grandfather. There was a rusty shot-gun in one corner, mice ran about and sickly grass grew in the dark corners. His grandfather was full of gestures all the time. One of his thumbs was like the knobbish end of a stick. He was friendly with gypsies, had known prize fighters and for some reasons always began his stories of them in the middle, giving them an air of

mystery. He had read nothing. At the same time he seemed to Bates full of strange, humorous and arresting ideas to which he never failed to respond and which even now move him in the profoundest way. Bates is deeply in debt to his grandfather.

At fifteen he began to write. Two years later he left school and took up journalism but was oppressed by its prosaic bondage and left it for what might seem worse—a clerkship in a warehouse, but there he had time to spare and wrote a rambling novel. During that time he had the most violent quarrels with church elders, threw his doctrines into their astonished mouths, and was, as a result, regarded with apprehension. At 18 he wrote a play, *The Best Bread;* at 19 *The Two Sisters* (1926). This was followed by *Day's End* (1927), a volume of short stories; *Catherine Foster* (1929), a novel; *Seven Tales and Alexander* (1930); *Charlotte's Row* (1931), a novel.

Bates reads much and has always had a passionate desire "to create some really beautiful thing such as the stories of Turgenev, the music of Beethoven and Tchaikowsky and the poetry of Shelley." He remembers no day for a long time when he hadn't such a longing.

Lately he claims to owe much to Miss Mary L. Pendered, a novelist who read some of his earliest work, and later still to Mr. Edward Garnett, who inspired him, he feels certain, towards a deeper art, and whose friendship has already filled him with hope, determination, and wholly new sensations.

L. Adams Beck

BEFORE 1919 Mrs. Lily Adams Beck had not written a line for publication. Ten years later she had published approximately twenty-five volumes . . . and under three different names! She was an Englishwoman of distinguished family, the daughter of late Admiral John Moresby and the grand-daughter of late Admiral-of-the-Fleet Sir Fairfax Moresby. Before taking up her residence in Canada in 1919 she went to the Orient with her father, who was stationed there, and lived in India, Ceylon, China, Java, Egypt,

L. ADAMS BECK

Burma, and Japan, crossing the great Himalayan Pass and sojourning in Little Tibet among the strange Mongolian people, meanwhile studying manners and customs. In 1930, after several years in Canada, Mrs. Beck took up residence again in the East, living in Kyoto, Japan, where she died on January 3, 1931.

"I have had long and deep experiences in the East," she said, "which have revealed to me the true, the lovable side with which so few Europeans care to come in contact. . . . It is because of this lack of comprehension of the Oriental modes of thought that I was first moved to write. . . . I have had most interesting work with Buddhist priests in translating ancient Buddhist psalms never before done in England, and some of my stories have appeared in Japanese vernacular magazines as representing the thought of the people themselves."

It was on a trip thru Canada, shortly after the war, in the lobby of a Victoria hotel, that the idea for her first short story came to her. Others followed, and they were published in her first volume, a collection of short stories, *The Ninth Vibration* (1922). She began and continued to write at an amazing pace: short stories, magazine articles, novels of the Orient, English historical novels, a history of philosophy.

Her stories of the Orient were published under the name of L. Adams Beck; for her historical romances she adopted the *nom de plume* of E. Barring-

ton; and another pseudonym, Louis Moresby, stands on the title-page of three miscellaneous books. In connection with her historical romances it is interesting to learn that her grandfather, Admiral Moresby, served as a midshipman in Lord Nelson's fleet; and that her grandmother had known Lord Byron when she was a girl. At the time of her death Mrs. Beck was reported to have completed a novel based on the family history of the Moresbys.

As an explanation of her threefold prolific output, Mrs. Beck said, "I write with the quickest speed my hand will allow. Thus *Glorious Apollo* was begun on the twenty-third of November, 1924, and finished on the twenty-sixth of December, 1924, taking just over a month. . . . There is no weariness of mind in writing any of my books. I never know weariness either of mind or of body and I attribute this to the fact that I have learned from high Oriental thought that the body has its share in mental and spiritual training, and must itself be trained. I eat only twice a day and rise very early and take a long walk before breakfast."

Her house in Victoria was described by a visitor as a veritable museum of the Orient, altho set in a secluded and lovely English garden. Mrs. Beck herself was rather little, rather frail, yet quietly lively with a sort of smoldering spiritual fire. She was one of those women who have no age. She looked a little worn and faded; yet she spoke with a youthful sparkle, and her restless eyes and hands were alert with young vivacity.

Mrs. Beck's last publications included: *Captain Java* (1928), *Empress of Hearts* (1928), *Story of Oriental Philosophy* (1928), *Garden of Vision* (1929), *Laughing Queen* (1929), *Duel of the Queens* (1930), *Openers of the Gate* (1930).

William Beebe

WILLIAM BEEBE, scientist and author, was born in Brooklyn, New York, July 29, 1877. He received his B.S. degree at Columbia in 1898, remaining at the University for another year to take a post-graduate course. In 1899 Beebe became Curator of Ornithology of the New York Zoological Society, of which he is also Director of the Department of Scientific Research. He is a member of the chief ornithological and zoological societies in New York, London, and Paris. His first expedition was into the heart of Mexico.

Since then Beebe has followed the trails of strange and rare animals, birds, and insects into the remote parts of the earth. "The *Isness* of facts," he explains, "is boring and futile, the *Whyness* is the chief reason for going on living." An abnormal curiosity about the ways and forms of living things has motivated his expeditions into the jungles of Borneo, Brazil, and British Guiana, thru the waters of a half dozen seas, across the deserts of Mexico and Mongolia. It explains why, for example, he has lain for hours in the thick grass of Sarawak to watch the mating dance of the Argus Pheasant, tho tortured by an army of ants and in momentary danger of discovery by head-hunting Dyaks. He has gained an intimate knowledge of the last living links between birds and reptiles; he loves to study a whole world teeming with life in a pailful of sea water, or in a square yard of jungle floor to examine another complex and fascinating world in which is enacted day by day the whole cycle of nature's law.

When he is not in the jungle or at the bottom of the sea, Beebe lives in the midtown section of New York City. Elswyth Thane, the novelist, is his wife. It takes him only a day, he says, to become acclimated to the clamor of the city after returning from one of his expeditions, which last from five to ten months. He believes that his scientific labors are the most enchanting in the world, and cannot imagine a more dreadful punishment than to be wholly without work to do.

When he was a boy the tales of Jules Verne and Henty made a great impression on him. Now his favorite piece of fiction is *Alice in Wonderland,* and his favorite author, Lord Dunsany. He is also fond of Kipling, Milne, Buchan, and Wells. He speaks and reads French, German, and Spanish.

Beebe is six feet tall and extremely

WILLIAM BEEBE

thin, weighing only 135 pounds. His adventures in the field have not affected his health, for in thirty years he has been ill for only three days. He looks younger than his actual age.

His publications include *Two Bird Lovers in Mexico* (1905), *The Bird* (1906), *Log of the Sun* (1906), *Our Search for a Wilderness* (1910), *Tropical Wild Life* (1917), *Monographs of the Pheasants* (1918), *Jungle Peace* (1918), *Edge of the Jungle* (1921), *Galapagos; World's End* (1923), *Jungle Days* (1925), *The Arcturus Adventure* (1925), *Pheasants—Their Lives and Homes* (1926), *Pheasant Jungles* (1927), *Beneath Tropic Seas* (1928). He is also the author of many scientific papers and monographs relating to birds and evolution.

Thomas Beer

THOMAS BEER was born in Council Bluffs, Iowa, November 22, 1889. But he once amended this fact and said, "I was born in a library." At an early age young Thomas moved with his family to Bucyrus, Ohio, the home of his grandfather, Judge Thomas Beer, in whose house his grandson spent many

THOMAS BEER

summers reading all the books he could lay his hands on.

As he neared manhood, Mr. Beer moved into the vicinity of New York, and first went to Yale, and then to the Columbia Law School. At Yale, a member of the class of 1911, he was very active on the undergraduate publications and became class poet. He received his law degree from Columbia in 1913, thus upholding the tradition of his family, which for five generations had contributed its males to the adornment of the American Bar.

"Then as now," writes Waldo Frank of Beer's Columbia days, "he was a boy in body as in mind. His plumpness had an ursine grace, as if this paddling walk across the Campus or across Broadway were just the thing to gain him secret access to some Reminiscence. A disdain was on his solemn face, from which the keen words shyly parted. His eyes had a brave cleanliness of distance. You felt that some betrayal had already made his thought heir to the anguish of delusion. And there he stood, barbed and plagued by the experience to which he was devoted."

After he had spent a few years as a clerk in his father's law office and sold his first stories, "The Brothers" and "On-

nie," to the *Century Magazine*, the United States entered the War, and Beer tried to enlist, first in the army and then in the navy, finally succeeding in having himself inducted into the field artillery as a private in 1917. He became a first lieutenant on the staff of the 87th Division and served for six months in France. He seems to have been uninterested in war as a patriotic enterprise, but irritated when he was not amused by the contemplation of human grandeur and imbecility in a concentrated and panoramic form.

After the War he continued to write for magazines, such as *Smart Set*, the *Century*, and the *Saturday Evening Post*. He published his first novel, *The Fair Rewards* (1922), which won him immediate attention; followed it with his biography of Stephen Crane (1923), which established his reputation; wrote his next novel, *Sandoval* (1924), a picture of New York in the gas-light era, and then the book by which he is perhaps best known, a psychological presentation of a faded American epoch, *The Mauve Decade* (1926). More recently he has written *The Road to Heaven* (1928), a novel; *Hanna* (1929), a history of American politics in the latter half of the nineteenth century; and *Form, Color and Desire*.

Mr. Beer is unmarried and lives in Yonkers, outside of New York, in "a monument of mid-Victorian architecture." He does his writing in a turret whose windows open over the Hudson. A stiffness of movement, a detached manner, a formality of address characterize him in society. "When he talks with you," reports Mr. Frank, "he has a way of turning from you: his eyes glance, sidewise; and altho his words are most appositely for you, his attention close upon your mood, the man himself is remote from this perhaps too painful present."

Max Beerbohm

MAX BEERBOHM, whom the *Encyclopaedia Britannica* describes as "a caricaturist and parodist of genius," was born in London, August 24, 1872. He was the half-brother of Sir Herbert Beerbohm Tree (1853-1917), one of the most celebrated actors and stage managers in London in the early part of the twentieth century.

Max Beerbohm, commonly called Max, attended Charterhouse School and later Merton College, Oxford University. Before leaving Oxford he had attained considerable reputation as an essayist and wit of polish and as early as 1892 the *Strand Magazine* had published in obscure pages in three different months thirty-six "Club Types," drawn by H. Maxwell Beerbohm, his first public appearance as a caricaturist. From boyhood he had been fond of making sketches of friends, not from life but imaginatively from memory. He says that he read a great deal of Bergson and Schopenhauer and it was from the latter he learned the art of humor, which he portrays both in his caricatures and in his essays.

The Yellow Book, the famous magazine of the '90s, welcomed Beerbohm, and soon after his graduation from Oxford his name and that of Aubrey Beardsley were much discussed in connection with this periodical. Max became a frequent contributor to *Vanity Fair* and to *Pick-me-up,* and other well-known magazines of that period.

He traveled in the United States for a short time in 1895, and after his return to England succeeded George Bernard Shaw as dramatic critic of *The Saturday Review.* He was married in 1910 to Miss Florence Kahn, of Memphis, Tennessee, and he and his wife went to Italy to live the same year. They have maintained their permanent residence there from that time, at the Villino Chiaro, Rapallo. Gordon Craig, who occupies the Villa Reggio, is their nearest neighbor.

Many descriptions are given of this most famous living caricaturist. He is considered a British Institution, in the same category as Parliament, afternoon tea, Dean Inge, and the Oxford accent— Max, "the irrepressible, the light of touch, the inimitable, the insouciant, and the impertinent." When he was very young he wrote: "For my own part, I am a dilettante, a *petit-maître.* I love best in literature delicate and elaborate

Caricature by Bohun Lynch
MAX BEERBOHM

ingenuities in form and style." And in 1921 he wrote: "My gifts are small. I've used them very well and discreetly, never straining them, and the result is that I've made a charming little reputation."

Rather short of stature, with a round head, prominent forehead, very blue eyes and black eyelashes, small hands and feet, skin as clear as a child's, white hair, an air of cherubic modesty, except for his cavalry-moustache he looks like a choir boy on Easter morning. Rebecca West compares him to a little white Chinese dragon, "obviously precious and not of this world, a museum piece." He has a gentle, courteous voice.

Mr. Beerbohm is consistent in his art and his personality, a caricaturist in speech and writing, with pencil and with water color and wash, "a sophisticated commentary on the social and literary life of his time." His art is, he says, to caricature strength by picking out its weak points.

Mr. Beerbohm's published works are in two series, his collected caricatures and his writing. The first include: *Caricatures of Twenty-Five Gentlemen* (1896); *The Poet's Corner* (1904); *Fifty Caricatures* (1913); *Seven Men* (1919); *A Survey* (1921); *Rossetti and*

His Circle (1922); and *Observations* (1925). His other works are: *A Christmas Garland,* a collection of parodies; *Works of Max Beerbohm* (1896); *The Happy Hypocrite* (1897); *More; Yet Again* (1909); *Zuleika Dobson,* a novel full of ironic humor (1911); *And Even Now* (1920); *Defense of Cosmetics* (1922); *Variety of Things* (1928); *Around Theatres* (1930), a collection of his early dramatic reviews.

Hilaire Belloc

JOSEPH HILAIRE PIERRE BELLOC was born at La Celle, near Paris, July 27, 1870, the son of Louis Swanton Belloc, a well-known French barrister. He has been described aptly as "a Frenchman, an Englishman, an Oxford man, a country gentleman, a soldier, a satirist, a democrat, a novelist, and a practical journalist." It might be added that he is an historian, a poet, an essayist and an economist, a traveler, a writer on military affairs, and a writer of children's verses.

After attending the Oratory School, at Edgbaston, Mr. Belloc enlisted in the 8th Regiment of French Artillery and served as a driver at Toul Meurthe-et-Moselle

HILAIRE BELLOC

for a short time. Subsequent to this military service he entered Balliol College, Oxford University, in 1892. He was graduated in 1895, taking honors and receiving the Brackenbury History Scholarship.

Belloc's literary career began immediately and he quickly achieved success as a newspaper and magazine writer. A trip to the United States in 1896 resulted in his marriage with the late Elodie Agnes Hogan, of Napa, California.

Upon his return to England Mr. Belloc was naturalized as a British citizen. He represented South Salford as a Liberal Member of the House of Commons from 1906 to 1910, but refused to serve a third term because, in his own words, he was weary of the party system and thought he could attack politics better from without Parliament than from within. Since that time he has been one of the most active and prolific of English writers. He is named with Chesterton and Shaw as one of the three cleverest men in London. Like Chesterton, Belloc is a staunch Roman Catholic and has devoted years to the study of the Catholic influences in Europe, and unlike Shaw, bitterly opposed to Socialism. Belloc and Chesterton are considered in England as "halves of one rather stupendous whole," and Shaw describes "the Chesterbelloc" as an animal with four legs, capable of doing infinite harm."

Because of his antagonism to a number of English doctrines and his criticism of them Belloc is not the most popular man in England. His enmity is not confined to ideals and ideas, but extends itself vociferously toward other persons. The most outstanding example of this is his disagreement with H. G. Wells in 1927, a year after the publication of a revised edition of Wells' *Outline of History.* Mr. Belloc wrote *A Companion to H. G. Wells' "Outline of History"* in which he pointed out "the principal popular errors, most of them now out of date." He resented among other things Wells' consigning Catholicism to a minor position, saying that "the foundation and career of the Catholic Church is the chief event in the history of mankind." Wells countered with a

pamphlet entitled *Mr. Belloc Objects to
"The Outline of History."*

Because Shaw is a freethinker and a
Socialist he and Belloc are frequently in
conflict. Belloc is opposed to Communism. He believes that an extension
of peasant-proprietorship, rather than
collectivism, is necessary.

Belloc lives at King's Land, Shipley,
Horsham, about twenty miles south of
London. He has two sons and two
daughters. Burton Rascoe describes him
as "a stocky man of middle height in
romeos and imprecise tailoring, with a
cetic midriff, a rubicund face, belligerent
eyes, a tired and rather sulky mouth,
closely cropped sandy hair, a small head
with no slope to the back and a brogue
which at times becomes wholly incomprehensible. . ."

Mr. Belloc is the author of over fifty
books. The following titles illustrate his
versatility and the range of his ability
and interests: *Verses and Sonnets*
(1895); *The Bad Child's Book of Beasts*
(1896); *On Nothing* (1908), *On Everything* (1909), *On Anything* (1910), *On
Something* (1911), and *On* (1923), a
series of essays; *Book of the Bayeaux
Tapestry* (1914); *Cruise of the Nona*,
the story of a cruise from Holyhead to
the Wash (1925); *History of England*,
four volumes (1925-1927); *Robespierre*
(1927); *James the Second* (1928);
Richelieu (1929); *Wolsey* (1930), a
biography of the famous Cardinal who
was at the head of the Church in England when it broke from Rome under
Henry the Eighth; *The Man Who Made
Gold* (1931), fiction.

Jacinto Benavente

JACINTO BENAVENTE, one of the
greatest living dramatists in Spain,
was born in Madrid August 12, 1866, into
a family of the upper middle-class. His
father, a successful and eminent physician who specialized in diseases of children, had come from the most African
of European cities, Murcia.

Since boyhood Jacinto Benavente's
chief interest has been in people of all
classes and conditions, but particularly
those whose lives are uncouth and prim-

itive in their surroundings and whose
natures are simple and childlike. He
studied law with little enthusiasm at the
University of Madrid until the death of
his father, immediately whereupon he
left the University without completing
his course and traveled thru France, Germany, and Russia as manager of a circus. It is said that he even enjoyed
performing in the ring occasionally.
Since that period he has continued to
travel extensively and is familiar with
the language, customs, and literature of
all the countries of western Europe and
America.

In 1892 his first work was published,
Teatro Fantastico, a volume of several
plays not intended for the stage. A volume of verse and a book of prose, *Cartas
de Mujere,* were published in 1893.

Practically all the rest of Benavente's
work is drama. His love for Spain is
one of the most obvious features, as
most of his one hundred plays deal
with one phase or another of Spanish
life. Peasant drama and the tragedy of
blood, which is always associated with
Spain in the mind of the foreigner, satires of provincial and metropolitan society, and of the middle-class and the
aristocracy, are all within his range and
have been encompassed by his plays. He
handles tragedy, comedy, farce, musical

JACINTO BENAVENTE

comedy, dialog, and monolog with equal power.

At the beginning of Benavente's career Echegaray was the most popular playwright in Spain and the unquestioned dictator of the stage. Benavente, in breaking away from this school and introducing forms foreign to the traditional was at first so unsuccessful that it is said he produced thirty-eight plays before the public was friendly toward him. Oddly enough, Madrid society, which he had satirized unflatteringly, was the first to recognize him.

His first play, *Thy Brother's House* (*El Nido Ajeno*), was produced in Madrid in 1894. His second play, *In Society* (*Gente Conocida*), fared a little better than the first but it was not until 1905 with *The Evil-Doers of Good* that he attained popularity. He has translated several foreign plays, and has been particularly influenced by Shakespeare and Molière.

A great fondness for children led to his organizing a children's theater a few years ago. He has written a number of plays for this theater.

The Passion Flower and *Bonds of Interest* have been produced on the English stage. The latter is his most popular play both in Spain and America.

Four series of his works, including about twenty plays, have been translated into English by John Garrett Underhill (1917-1924). *Saturday Night* (1926), and *Bonds of Interest* (1929), both of which are included in the preceding series, have been published separately. *Smile of Mona Lisa* (1915) is also available in English, having been translated by John Armstrong Herman.

Benavente was awarded the Nobel Prize in 1922. He still lives in Madrid for which city his life-long attachment has not lessened.

Julien Benda

JULIEN BENDA was born December 28, 1867, in Paris. Originally a pupil of the Central School of Arts and Manufactures, he became a graduate of the Faculty of Letters.

JULIEN BENDA

Benda made his literary debut in the *Revue Blanche* in 1898 with some philosophical commentaries on the Dreyfus case. Himself a Jew, he found in the *Affaire* a revelation of how people are ruled by their passions instead of their ideas. All his life he has been an enemy of beliefs that are induced by sentiment rather than by reason.

After this first commentary Benda discontinued writing for practically ten years. He resumed interest as the result of his renewed contact with the literary life of Paris thru his visits to the little bookshop of his friend, the late Charles Péguy, at No. 8 Rue de la Sorbonne, now a celebrated site because of its associations with modern French men of letters. In 1907 Benda wrote a preface to the pamphlet of Georges Sorel on the metaphysical preoccupations of modern physicians. In 1910, when he was forty-three years old, he published his first book, which he appropriately called *Mon Premier Testament*. This volume, as well as the Sorel book, appeared as one of those "Cahiers de la Quinzaine" which made Péguy famous. *Mon Premier Testament* is concerned with ideas, chiefly with the classifying of existing political and religious ideas in respect to the sentiments that they satisfy.

Benda does not regret having waited until his maturity before publishing seriously. "As he pointed out," writes Montgomery Belgion, "before settling down to write, he had lived; and whereas many writers seek ideas because they have to write, he was seeking to write because he had ideas."

After *Dialogue d'Eleuthere* (1911) and *L'Ordination* (1912), an analytical novel in the tradition of Benjamin Constant's *Adolphe,* Benda became celebrated as a pamphleteer with the first of his series of attacks on the philosophy propagated by Henri Bergson at the Collège de France. *Le Bergsonisme ou Une Philosophie de la Mobilité* (1912) and *Sur le Succès du Bergsonisme* (1914) assailed Bergsonism because it was an attempt, in the field of philosophy, to substitute sentiments for ideas, emotion for reason, and he explained its astonishing popularity by the readiness of French society to exploit emotionalism. *Belphegor* (1919)—Belphegor is another name for Moloch—analyzed the cravings of French society for emotional satisfaction in the sciences as well as in the arts, and its horror of the rational. *Belphegor* was a great success and spread Benda's influence abroad to such critics as T. S. Eliot and Wyndham Lewis. *La Trahison des Clercs* (1927), his most ambitious work, asserts that the scholars, the "clerks," whose kingdom is rightfully not of this world, have betrayed their trust by assuming temporal interests and contaminating themselves with political passions.

Benda's other works include: *Les Sentiments de Critias* (1917), *Le Bouquet de Glycere* (1918), *Les Amorandes* (1922), *La Croix des Roses* (1923), *Lettres à Melisande pour Education Philosophique* (1924), and *La Fin de l'Eternel* (1929). The articles he wrote during the war for *Le Figaro,* consisting of philosophical commentaries on current events, have been published under the title *Billets de Sirius.*

Two of Benda's books have been translated into English: *La Trahison des Clercs,* by Richard Aldington (1928, American title: *The Treason of the Intellectuals;* English title: *The Great Betrayal*); and *Belphegor,* by Sarah J. I. Lawson (1929). A competent study of Benda's ideas is given in *Julien Benda and the New Humanism* (1930), by H. E. Read.

Stephen Vincent Benét

STEPHEN VINCENT BENÉT was born in Bethlehem, Pennsylvania, July 22, 1898. He probably assimilated the art of writing from his family for his elder brother and sister, William Rose and Laura, are both poets and critics.

The name Benét is Spanish, which may explain his dark hair and brown eyes. He is tall, six feet or over, and has a slight stoop due to hours spent at writing. The Benét family came originally from the Island of Minorca and settled in St. Augustine several generations ago. Stephen Vincent cherishes the belief that he is related to Black Pedro, the Mexican bandit.

"From a rather early age," writes his brother William Rose Benét, "there was a distinct tendency in the author of *John Brown's Body* to grit his teeth. In human relationships both mild and amiable, poetry was yet from the first a bright valour in his blood. It was a direct inheritance from a father whose love of

STEPHEN VINCENT BENÉT

the ringing line was well known to the evening circle in a certain home."

Benét's father, grandfather and great-grandfather were army officers and, like the children in most military families, Stephen Vincent had many homes. His father was transferred from New York to Benicia Arsenal, California, just in time for the seven-year old boy to see the red glow of San Francisco burning thirty miles away. After having lived and gone to school in California for several years, and then in Georgia, Benét entered Yale, from which he was graduated in 1919.

While in France studying at the Sorbonne on a scholarship, he met Rosemary Carr of Chicago, who was on the staff of the Paris edition of the *Chicago Tribune*. They were married later in Chicago.

"My brother," continues William Rose Benét, "depended upon his typewriter for a living and there came a certain fairly straitened season during which the short stories he was writing failed more and more to satisfy him, tho they happened to pay the rent. The opportunity to go to Paris again, this time on a fellowship, was a welcome turn of fortune... He wished to concentrate all his powers upon a longer work which would either be better poetry than he had ever written, or a failure... That he suddenly knew his theme was to be the American Civil War did not seem at all extraordinary to his immediate family. Books in his father's library, the *Battles and Leaders*, old Army records, had from the time he was very young helped to ruin his eyesight quite as much as Ferrero on the Roman emperors."

In the two years of writing *John Brown's Body*, which won the Pulitzer prize in 1929, Mr. and Mrs. Benét and their two children, Stephanie Jane and Thomas Carr, lived at Neuilly on a Guggenheim Memorial Foundation Fellowship. On their return from France they lived in Rhode Island until late in 1930, when they moved to New York City.

Mr. Benét, altho still a young man, has been publishing for years. When he was only seventeen his first volume of poetry, *Five Men and Pompey*, was published (1915). Critics considered this collection of six dramatic monologs remarkable for so young a writer and the book was given favorable attention. It was followed by other books of poetry, *Young Adventure* (1918), *Heavens and Earth* (1920), *Young People's Pride* (1922), *Ballad of William Sycamore, 1790-1880* (1923), *Tiger Joy* (1925), his long narrative poem *John Brown's Body* (1928), and *Ballads and Poems, 1915-1930* (1931).

Mr. Benét has written three novels, *The Beginning of Wisdom* (1921), *Jean Huguenot* (1923), and *Spanish Bayonet* (1926).

William Rose Benét

WILLIAM ROSE BENÉT, the elder brother of Stephen Vincent Benét, was born at Fort Hamilton, New York Harbor, February 2, 1886. For at least two generations the family had been military, and his father and grandfather were graduates of the United States Military Academy at West Point. His father was naturally transferred from post to post, and young Benét lived in Springfield, Massachusetts; Bethlehem, Pennsylvania; and Buffalo, New York, during the first few years of his life.

WILLIAM ROSE BENÉT

Benét was graduated from the Albany Academy, a preparatory school, in 1904. His proclivities not being particularly militaristic, he then went to the Sheffield Scientific School of Yale University, probably as a compromise between a military and an arts education. Henry Seidel Canby was at "Sheff" at the same time as an instructor, and was Benét's proctor. As a Scientific School undergraduate, Benét was barred from the editorial board of the *Yale Literary Magazine,* but he was chairman of the *Yale Courant* and an editor of the *Yale Record.*

After graduating from Yale in 1907 Benét went to Benicia Arsenal, California, where his father was then stationed. He "lived off the family," he says, while establishing himself as a writer. Correspondence with the editor of *Century Magazine* led to the offer of a position. His first two weeks in New York after entering the *Century* offices were spent in addressing envelopes. He soon was made a reader and later became associate editor, which position he held from 1910 to 1917.

Benét received a commission as second lieutenant in the Air Service in 1918, after instruction at Kelly Field, Texas, and Columbus, Ohio. He spent the next year or so as a Ground officer at Fort Worth, Texas, and later at Washington, D. C.

The organization of *Century* had been changed when he returned to New York after the war, and Benét worked for an advertising agency for six months. There are still some advertising slogans in use which he is said to have originated. He next went to Washington on *The Nation's Business,* the magazine of the United States Chamber of Commerce.

With Henry Seidel Canby and Christopher Morley, Benét started the *Literary Review* of the *New York Evening Post* in 1920. In 1924 this group organized the *Saturday Review of Literature,* an independent weekly. Mr. Benét is still one of the editors of this magazine and is "The Phoenician," the conductor of *The Phoenix Nest.*

Mr. Benét is a poet, a critic, and a novelist. His earliest published works are verse, *Merchants from Cathay* (1912), *Falconer of God, and Other*

Poems (1914), *Great White Wall* (1916), *Burglar of the Zodiac, and Other Poems* (1918), *Perpetual Light, a Memorial* (1919), and *Moons of Grandeur* (1920).

His first novel was published in 1922. Most of it was written in the garage of the family home in Scarsdale, New York. He owed his father $400, he says, and agreed to have the house repapered in payment. This also came to $400, so, after receiving that sum as advance royalties he proceeded to write *The First Person Singular.*

He assisted his first wife in translating *East I Know,* by Paul Claudel (1914); he contributed to *Saturday Papers,* essays selected from the *Literary Review* of the *New York Evening Post* (1921); he edited *Poems for Youth* (1925). His other books are *The Flying King of Kurio,* a story for children (1926); *Wild Goslings,* fugitive essays, (1927); *Man Possessed,* selected poems, (1927). *Twentieth Century Poetry,* an anthology, was edited by John Drinkwater, Henry Seidel Canby, and William Rose Benét in 1929.

Mr. Benét has been described as "long and lean and lissom with spidery legs. He speaks slowly and smiles readily at bad and pointless jokes. This is courtesy, however, not stupidity. He is brown and smooth faced and guileless. One has to look twice before discovering his eyebrows. His eyes are small. He is aggravatingly patient. He loves poetry and that is all there is to it. Wherever it may be and in whatever guise, he will willingly recognize it if it be there."

His voice is soft and his manner is gracious, but he gives the impression of having definite opinions and an independent point of view.

His first wife was a sister of Kathleen Norris, and the Norrises have the three Benét children with them in their Palo Alto home. The oldest, James Walker Benét, will probably enter Leland Stanford University in the fall of 1931. The two younger are girls, Frances Rosemary and Kathleen Anne.

Elinor Wylie, who at the time of her death in 1928 was generally regarded as our finest contemporary woman poet, was Mr. Benét's second wife.

Arnold Bennett [1]

"I HAVE written between seventy and eighty books," reads a late entry in Arnold Bennett's diary, "but also I have only written four: *The Old Wives' Tale* (1908), *The Card* (1911, American title: *Denry the Audacious*), *Clayhanger* (1910), and *Riceyman Steps* (1923)."

He is a heavy-set man, with large liquid eyes, a military mustache, and a great mop of hair.

Enoch Arnold Bennett was born at North Staffordshire near Hanley, called "Hanbridge" in his novels of the Five Towns, on May 27, 1867. His scholastic education terminated at his graduation from the Newcastle Middle School. The events of the next few years are best summarized in his own words: "I began to write reports for the Staffordshire newspapers, and then I came to London and began as a clerk in a lawyer's office. That lasted six years. The law bored me, and at night in my room I used to write. When I was about twenty-six, I escaped via journalism and became editor-in-chief of a weekly magazine, feminine and fashionable, called *Woman*, where I remained until I was thirty-two. From then on I was a free-lance journal-

ARNOLD BENNETT

ist." Bennett reduced a bad impediment in speech to a slight stammer.

As a boy, and even as a young man, Bennett had no literary ambitions. He became interested in writing merely as a means of earning a living, receiving his first awards, the handsome sum of twenty guineas, for a humorous condensation of a cheap serial novel in a competition conducted by a popular weekly. At 31 his first novel, *A Man from the North* (1898), containing many autobiographical incidents, was published. Then began his astonishingly frequent and regular production of books. A year later he could record in his diary:

"This year I have written 335,340 words, grand total; 224 articles and stories, and four instalments of a serial called *The Gates of Wrath* have actually been published and also my book of plays, *Polite Farces*. My work includes six or eight short stories not yet published, also the greater part of a 55,000 word serial, *Love and Life,* for Tilliotsons, and the whole draft, 80,000 words, of my Staffordshire novel *Anna Tellwright*." "*Anna Tellwright*" was later published as *Anna of the Five Towns*.

It was in 1900 that Bennett threw up his editorial job and withdrew to the country in order to devote his entire time to literature. Soon afterwards he was occupying a cottage at Fontainebleau. The idea for his most famous novel, *The Old Wives' Tale* (1908), came to him in the autumn of 1903, when he sat in a Paris restaurant and observed the eccentric behavior of a fat old woman who, he reflected, was once young and perhaps lovely. *The Old Wives' Tale* is the story of two sisters, girls of the Five Towns, from girlhood to old age and death. The sisters' temperaments are as different as their respective experiences. Much of Sophia's life is passed in Paris. In the five years of writing *The Old Wives' Tale* Bennett studied as his model Maupassant's *Une Vie.*

"French literature," he says, "has been the great passion of my life, and the chief influence of my literary youth. I can never say enough about what I owe to Stendhal. *La Chartreuse de Parme* was my bedside book for a long time." Flaubert, Rimbaud, Huysmans, and Gide

[1] Arnold Bennett died in London on March 27, 1931, of typhoid fever.

are among his other enthusiasms. Russian literature has also had an enormous influence on him. "I have read the stories of Chekhov, Tolstoi, Dostoievsky —the last a giant, probably the greatest novelist that has ever appeared in the world. My favorite book is *The Brothers Karamazov.*" Bennett has also a great admiration for Thomas Hardy.

Bennett's manuscripts are beautiful specimens of calligraphy. He is proud of the fact that in the writing of *The Old Wives' Tale* he did not blot a line. "I do all my work in my head," he says. "I never begin to write until everything is ready and all is in order."

Here is Bennett's modest analysis of himself: "I have nothing to say. I have no ideas. I am not an intellectual. I am a man who spends his life telling little stories. The American and English public is so good as to get some pleasure out of them."

Bennett's genius has its basis in his remarkable grasp of details. He spends years of research before writing such a novel as *Imperial Palace,* a book of some 240,000 words with 85 speaking characters, in which a great modern "luxury hotel" is the real protagonist.

In addition to his tremendous creative activity Mr. Bennett finds time to conduct a weekly column on books for the *London Evening Standard.* He is always ready to praise deserving newcomers, and he is so powerful an influence that his praise alone, it is said, is almost sufficient to insure the success of a book in England. He married Marguerite Hebrard, a gifted French actress, in 1912.

Bennett has written many plays and books of essays. His principal works of fiction are: *Anna of the Five Towns* (1902), *The Grand Babylon Hotel* (1902), *Leonora* (1903), *The Truth About an Author* (1903, an autobiographical account first published anonymously), *Sacred and Profane Love* (1905, American title: *The Book of Carlotta*), *Whom God Hath Joined* (1906), *Buried Alive* (1908), *The Old Wives' Tale* (1908), *Clayhanger* (1910), *Hilda Lessways* (1911), *The Card* (1911, American title: *Denry the Audacious*), *The Matador of the Five Towns* (1912), *These Twain* (1916), *The Pretty Lady* (1918), *Mr. Prohack* (1922), *Riceyman Steps* (1923), *Lord Raingo* (1926), *The Woman Who Stole Everything* (1927), *The Vanguard* (1927), *Accident* (1929), *Imperial Palace* (1930).

John Bennett

JOHN BENNETT was born on May 17, 1865, in Chillicothe, Ohio, a quaint charming old town. His boyhood in that town reads like some chapters out of *Tom Sawyer.* He went to the public schools there but says, "I was a dull and plodding student with a painfully ineffective memory." He gave up high school to attend art school—Matt Morgan's School of Design in Cincinnati and the Art Students' League in New York—but the necessity for him to earn his own living compelled him to cut short his studies.

The first position John Bennett held was on a country newspaper at $3.00 a week, docked for time off. On this large salary young Bennett lived and clothed himself. After two years, his salary was raised to $5.00. Mr. Bennett, himself, declares the only reason why the proprietor hired him in the first place was because the owner needed one sober member on his staff of reporters.

JOHN BENNETT

As a boy John Bennett had but one ambition and that was to contribute to *St. Nicholas.* And at this point in his career that ambition seemed further off than ever before. Besides working on the newspaper, Bennett did other work on the side. By turns, he was a taxidermist, a cartoonist, member of a minstrel troupe, painter of paper dolls and of scenery for theatrical barnstormers, and his was the odd experience of illuminating obituary memorials and of writing letters for medicine men.

From 1884 to 1890 Mr. Bennett edited the *Daily News* in Chillicothe. For a while he contributed to the *Cincinnati Commercial-Gazette* what would now be called a "column." In 1891 the ambition of his boyhood was achieved. Mary Mapes Dodge, then editor of *St. Nicholas,* recognized John Bennett's talent and published his *Barber of Sari-Ann.* The year 1897 marked the publication of *Master Skylark* which later on ran into thirty editions and now is ranked as a children's classic.

Then Mr. Bennett was ordered south because of his health. It was almost inevitable that he should have chosen Charleston, South Carolina, to live in. That picturesque old town with its wrought-iron gateways was like a collection of Bennett's own silhouettes come to life. There, Mr. Bennett met his future wife. They married in 1902 and Charleston has been their home ever since.

Barnaby Lee was published in 1900 and after that came *The Treasure of Peyre Gaillard* (1906) and *Madame Margot, A Grotesque Legend of Old Charleston* (1921).

Shortly after the World War, Mr. Bennett and some other writers began to realize the mass of literary treasure that lay in the South waiting to be discovered. For three years Hervey Allen and DuBose Heyward met every Wednesday evening at John Bennett's house in Charleston and from those meetings resulted the Poetry Society of South Carolina.

Besides his writing and illustrating, Mr. Bennett is interested in tree culture, cabinet-making and repairing old furniture.

After a long silence, Mr. Bennett appeared in 1928 as author and artist in *The Pigtail of Ah Lee Ben Loo,* a collection of humorous verses, ballads, and stories illustrated with 250 silhouettes.

E. F. Benson

EDWARD FREDERIC BENSON, English author, was born July 24, 1867, at Wellington College, the son of the headmaster of the college who later became Bishop of Canterbury. He was one of six children and had two brothers who became distinguished men. One of them was the Very Reverend Monsignor Hugh Benson, a priest in the Catholic Arch-Diocese of Westminster, the author of several religious books, articles and pamphlets. He died in 1914. The other brother, Arthur Christopher Benson, was Master of Magdalene College, Cambridge, from 1915 until his death in 1925. He wrote numerous biographies and poems.

E. F. Benson recalls some events of his busy childhood in *Our Family Affairs* (1920). The family moved in 1873 from Wellington to Lincoln where his father was Chancellor, and they moved again four years later to Truro where his father presided as Bishop. During these early days, he writes, "we were all of us draughtsmen, ornithologists,

E. F. BENSON

conchologists, geologists, poets and literary folk: we all drew and wrote and collected shells and birds' eggs, and smashed stones in order to discover fossils. . . . Never can I sufficiently admire or be sufficiently thankful for the encouragement my father and mother both gave to these multitudinous hobbies."

An important influence of this early home life was a joint literary effort called the *Saturday Magazine,* to which every member of the family contributed when the children were home for holidays. The requirement of each was "at least four pages of prose or one page of verse" written on the elder Mr. Benson's sermon paper. "This habit gave us all a certain ease in expressing ourselves if only because we expressed ourselves so freely," he writes. The enterprise was continued for years, even after the children were in college and began to extend their literary efforts beyond its pages.

After his preliminary education at private schools, young Benson was sent to Marlborough where, among many activities, he edited *The Marlburian.* In the pages of this publication can be seen his imitations of Addison and Tennyson. The latter, he recalls, was a guest at the Benson household after his father had attained the dignity of Bishop of Canterbury. Distinguished guests on other occasions were Robert Browning and the Duke of York (George V).

E. F. Benson completed his formal education at King's College, where he continued his literary activities and published *Sketches From Marlborough.* The latter was done without his father's knowledge for fear of disapproval. While still a student at Cambridge, he discovered remains of Roman monuments to soldiers of the tenth legion embedded in the wall of the city of Chester, and it was no less a person than William Gladstone who showed him how to make blotting paper "squeezes," or casts, of the inscriptions.

He was now deeply interested in archaeology and after pursuing it for a while at King's College thru a scholarship, he set out in 1892 for Athens to study and work at the British Archaeological School. En route he travelled with his family thru Algiers. He continued his work in Athens until 1895, making numerous trips back to England.

Meanwhile, in 1893, his first novel, *Dodo,* was published. The manuscript had been lying in a drawer for years, coming out now and then for revision. The germ of the book actually went back to the days of the *Saturday Magazine* when Benson and his sister Maggie started a joint story in which, he said in retrospect, he could "perceive the infancy" of *Dodo.* The criticisms of Henry James and Lucas Malet were a helpful guide in the preparation of the manuscript for publication. When Benson returned to England later for a visit, he found the book had won him recognition. His second novel, *The Rubicon,* appeared in 1894.

In the years 1895 to 1897 Benson spent his winters in Egypt doing work for the Hellenic Society, returning to Greece for the rest of the time. During these years he produced another novel, *The Babe, B. A.* (1897). Then he gradually settled into writing as a career.

Mr. Benson now lives in London, but from October to June each year he goes down to the old town of Tye in the Romney Marsh and writes. He spends his summer leisure on the golf course and the tennis court. In winter his favorite diversion is skating.

Among his best known works besides those mentioned are: *David Blaize* (1916), *Mike* (1916), *Queen Lucia* (1920), *Colin* (1923), *Paying Guests* (1929), *Life of Alcibiades* (1929), and *Ferdinand Magellan* (1929). Volumes published in 1930 were: *Lovers and Friends, The Inheritor,* and *As We Were,* The last, labeled a "Victorian peep show," contains his memoirs in which he makes public new facts in the Oscar Wilde case, the Tranby Croft affair, and other scandals of the impeccable Victorians.

Stella Benson

STELLA BENSON was born January 6, 1892, in Much Wenlock, Shropshire, her father being " a sort of squire down there." She is a niece, thru her mother of Mary Cholmondeley, author of *Red Pottage.* Because she was a deli-

STELLA BENSON

cate child she never went to any school,
but spent most of her girlhood in Southern France, Germany, and Switzerland.
Just before the war she became a militant
suffragette, well known in London, and
did social work in London's East End as
a member of the staff of the Charity
Organization in Hoxton. But not being
altogether pleased with the methods of
the society and wishing to get closer
to the people about her, she opened a
little shop in partnership with a woman
of the district, where she sold "paper
bags for costers to put their bananas in."
During her residence in Hoxton, 1914-
1917, she wrote her first two novels, *I
Pose* (1915) and *This is the End*
(1917). For a year or so she worked
in the ranks of the Land Army, but
the weakness of her lungs forced her to
leave England for America in June 1918.

Having "spent all her substance" in
New England and New York, she set
out for California whither she had been
ordered by her physician. That was how
it came about that she worked on a ranch
in Colorado as a "chore boy." A few
days before Christmas, 1918, she finally

arrived in San Francisco with five dollars in her pocket, and on Christmas Day
completed her third novel, *Living Alone*
(1919), on a beach near the Golden Gate.
California was not very kind to her at
first. She tried earning her living as a
lady's maid, a bill collector, and a book
agent, without much success. Then her
luck turned and she secured a position
first as tutor in the University of California and later as editorial reader for
the University Press. During the rest of
her year and a half in the state she had
many delightful experiences.

By January 1920 she had saved enough
money for the trip back to England, going by way of the Orient. Even illness
in Japan could not spoil her adventurous
spirit. Among other unusual experiences
in the East she dined with a Maharajah,
taught a class of fifty Chinese boys in
a mission school, had an encounter with
yellow pirates and smugglers, and worked
as X-Ray assistant at the American Hospital in Peking during a thrilling month
of war between rival Chinese factions.
It was the summer of 1921 before she
saw England again. *The Poor Man*
(1922) was written on her return. In
1921 she married J. G. O'Gorman Anderson, of Bally David, Waterford, Ireland, whom she had met in China. They
came to America for their honeymoon
and traveled across the continent to California in their Ford, "Stephanie." Miss
Benson tells the entertaining story of
their adventures in *The Little World*
(1925). She is now living in Manchuria,
where her husband holds a position in
the Chinese Customs Service, and where
she does most of her work during the
long and severe winters. She is a fine
horsewoman and does pen-and-ink drawings. She describes herself as the world's
worst needle-woman, and collects "only
dogs."

Tolstoy is Miss Benson's literary god.
She considers *War and Peace* and *Anna
Karenina* the two greatest books ever
written. As to art she says, "The artist
has no mission in life except to tell the
truth," and as to sexes: "There is a
difference—in kind, not in degree. Men
know more, women feel more; that's all
there is to it."

Among Miss Benson's books not previously mentioned here are a volume of

poems, *Twenty* (1918); *Pipers and a Dancer* (1924) and *Goodbye, Stranger* (1926), two novels of character; a book of travel, *Worlds Within Worlds* (1929); and *The Faraway Bride* (1930, English title: *Tobit Transplanted*), a novel that deals with a family of White Russians, driven out of their own country, who settle down haphazardly in upper Manchuria; *Hope Against Hope* (1931), short stories.

Konrad Bercovici

KONRAD BERCOVICI

KONRAD BERCOVICI was born in Roumania in 1882, the son of Jackot and Mirel Bercovici. His youth was spent much among the tents of the gypsies who poured into Roumania from the borders of Hungary, sleeping by their campfires at night, listening to their songs, and learning their language, until they came to accept him as one of them, for "there is not a gypsy in the world who cannot tell you who I am. I am a gypsy by choice and not by blood, by temperament and not race," he writes. From such a background, enriched by years of travel thru Greece and Turkey, Palestine, Egypt, Persia and India, his books have come.

In Paris, where he received his later education, he spent much time studying music and playing the organ. When he came to New York some years later, one of his first positions here was that of organist at the Grace Episcopal Church of New York. Since he has become a novelist he has kept up this study of music and is particularly interested in symphonic composition. He arranged a group of gypsy songs for his daughter, Rada Bercovici, to sing at her debut as a concert singer recently. During his stay in France he married Naomi Librescu, a Roumanian, and they now have four children.

In 1916 he came to America, and altho he had studied English assiduously, even memorizing Samuel Butler's novel, *The Way of All Flesh,* word for word, to perfect his speech, he found that he had so much difficulty in making himself understood that he pretended to be a mute.

Today he speaks fluently in English, Roumanian, French, German, Greek, Yiddish, Italian, and Spanish. A year after he arrived in this country he had become proficient enough in speaking and writing English to sell his first story to an American magazine.

Bercovici does most of his work in the morning, rising at 6 a. m. and writing until noon. He never sets a sentence down on paper until he believes he has it so expressed that it will be clear to anyone. Consequently his revisions have only to do with major aspects of literary construction.

Bercovici's works include *Crimes of Charity* (1917), *Dust of New York* (1918), *Around the World in New York* (1918), *Ghitza* (1919), *Murdo* (1921), *Iliana* (1924), *Marriage Guest* (1925), *On New Shores* (1925), *Singing Winds* (1926), *Alexander* (1928), *Nights Abroad* (1928), *The Story of the Gypsies* (1928), *The Crusades* (1929), *For a Song* (1931), *That Royal Lover* (1931), and numerous stories and articles about gypsies. His literary productions have been translated into many languages. In Russia, one of the few countries in which he has never lived, editions of his work run into many thousands.

J. D. Beresford

JOHN DAVYS BERESFORD was born March 7, 1873, son of the late Reverend J. J. Beresford, Rector of Castor, near Peterborough. He was seriously injured thru the carelessness of a nurse and was made permanently lame. He was educated at Oundle, the well known public school near Peterborough. At the age of eighteen he came to London and was articled to Lacey W. Ridge, architect. After practising architecture for some years, he began to write for publication in 1906.

As literary adviser to Messrs. Collins and Company, in Pall Mall, he inaugurated the idea of publishing the Collins group of "First Novels" and introduced many young writers to the English public. Mr. Beresford, who has written numerous novels, is a busy man. In the morning he writes; after luncheon he walks or rests until teatime; then he is at his work again until dinner. In the evening he smokes, reads, or chats with his family—he is married and has three sons and one daughter—and then reads again, something in manuscript perhaps. He is interested in the development of the modern novel, particularly in the work of Dorothy Richardson. His home is in Cornwall.

In general it is realistic experiment that interests him most. "The romantics seldom, and the classicists never," he says, "enter the ranks of the experimenters. If I sit down to tell you a story out of my head, I shall choose inevitably an accepted traditional form for the telling of it. By that means my task will be made easier and you will more quickly understand. That road has been well laid and hedged, and why should we not follow it? But if I want to give you a nearer and nearer transcript of life as I have seen it, I find that it cannot be done by following the old signposts. And the more ardent the realism, the greater the necessity to experiment with new methods."

Mr. Beresford is a student of the occult and has participated in theosophical discussion.

Among the many novels he has written are *Jacob Stahl* (1911), *God's Counterpoint* (1919), *The Monkey Puzzle* (1925), *Love's Illusion* (1930); belles lettres, *H. G. Wells* (1915); plays, *A Royal Heart* (with the late Arthur Scott Craven), *Howard and Son* (with Kenneth Richmond). He has also written short stories and critical articles for the leading English periodicals.

J. D. BERESFORD

Henri Bergson

HENRI BERGSON, French philosopher, was born October 18, 1859, in Paris, of Anglo-Jewish parents. He became a naturalized Frenchman during his youth. After a brilliant school career at the Lycée Condorcet and the École Normale Supérieure he became professor of philosophy at the Lycée d'Angers in 1881. He served there two years and then occupied a similar post at the Lycée de Clermont from 1883 to 1888. From 1888 to 1889 he was a professor at the Collège Rollin.

In 1889 Bergson published his first work. It was entitled *Essais sur les Données Immédiates de la Conscience*. He served from 1889 to 1897 at the Lycée Henri IV, meanwhile publishing *Matière et Mémoire* in 1896. The École Normale

Supérieure then claimed his services until the year 1900 when he published *Le Rire*, an essay on the meaning of the comic. Bergson was professor of philosophy at the Collège de France from 1900 to 1921. During that period his major work, *L'Evolution Créatrice*, appeared in 1907. All fashionable Paris flocked to his lectures and all philosophical England was engaged in criticizing him.

The furore he had created exasperated Bergson. He was swamped with social invitations, letters from admirers, and requests for opinions and interviews. He realized that as long as he held office he would be subject to this fuss and hullabaloo, so he resigned his chair at the Collège de France in 1921. He devoted himself for a while to politics and international affairs as head of a mission to America and after the war as president of the committee of intellectual cooperation.

Bergson continued publishing his works with *l'Énergie Spirituelle* (1919), a collection of relatively early lectures and essays, and a critique of Einstein in 1922. He was awarded the Nobel Prize for Literature for 1927. He is a commander of the Légion d'Honneur, an officer of l'Instruction Publique, a member of the Academie Française and of l'Institut.

He has changed his residence in Paris numerous times in his search for tranquility and freedom from interruption. His frequent movings have caused him to be politely dubbed "the wandering Jew." The most recent change brought him to a small private hotel in the Passy quarter where he now lives with his daughter in complete seclusion. He refuses to see anyone except a few intimate friends, declines to answer letters, and keeps his name out of the telephone directory.

A sufferer from rheumatism, Bergson rarely leaves his room, which he has transformed into a study. There he seeks the intellectual concentration he has gone to great pains to allow himself. His friends believe he is working on a treatise on morals for which he is summoning his diminished physical strength to a final effort.

HENRI BERGSON

Despite his aloofness Bergson is a meticulous dresser and at seventy he is as fastidious as when he was twenty. He wears a close-buttoned cutaway, derby hat and straight standing collar with cushion cravat, round cuffs, the white *passe poil* and congress gaiters. He keeps his hair and moustache close-cut. People remark that his eyes are keen, distant, pensive, brilliant and unforgettable. His manner is gentle.

Among the English translations of Bergson's writings are: *Creative Evolution* (1911), *Laughter* (1911), *Introduction to Metaphysics* (1912), *Matter and Memory* (1913), *Time and Free Will* (1913), *Dreams* (1914), and *Mind-energy* (1920).

Elsa Beskow

ELSA BESKOW, whose books for children are read around the world, lives in Djursholm, a beautiful residential suburb of Stockholm, Sweden, where she writes the stories and draws the illustrations that have made her known to boys and girls in so many different lands. She is the wife of Dr. Nathaniel Beskow, an eminent clergyman, writer, and pioneer social worker, who has won a national reputation by his preaching and writing on religious themes. As a pastor, with Mrs. Beskow's vital cooperation, he has enriched the life of the community in which they live and work. Their home is a gift from Dr. Beskow's parishioners. The Beskows have six sons.

Elsa Beskow's father, Bernt Maartman, was born in Flekkefjord, on the southwestern coast of Norway. Her mother, Augusta Fahlstedt, from whom she inherits her artistic talent, bore a name honored in the history of Finland. At an early age Elsa Beskow began to tell stories to her younger brothers and sisters and to illustrate them with her own drawings.

Her schooling began at the Anna Whitlock School for girls. After completing her course at the so-called high industrial art school, where she prepared for a teacher's career, she returned to the Anna Whitlock School as instructor in drawing. There she prepared her popular *Will You Paint?* books, consisting of outline drawings to be colored in by the children.

In 1897, the year of her marriage to Dr. Beskow, her first picture book was published, *The Tale of the Wee Little Old Woman*, which is still in great demand. *Putte's Adventures in the Blueberrywood* (1901) extended her popularity outside of her own country. Today Mrs. Beskow has had her books translated into French, Finnish, Polish, German, Czech, Russian, Danish, Norwegian, Dutch, and English.

Many of Mrs. Beskow's stories were conceived in association with her own six sturdy boys, who served as models for her drawings, receiving, it is sa' the hourly wage of about half a penny One of the sons is now an engineer in the Orient.

"Ekeliden," the Beskow home, was formerly the residence of Victor Rydberg, the famous Swedish poet. "In one corner," reports Marion Bromley Newton in the *Horn Book*, "stood a piano with the quaint Swedish candle holder on either side of the music rack; in another, the tall tile stove, or 'kakelugn,' which warms the Swedish rooms on the coldest winter days. On the walls hung pictures in oils, in water color, and in pastel, the work of various members of the family. Portraits, landscapes, studies of children—colorful, exquisite in execution—effected an ensemble peculiarly charming in the subdued light of a northern winter afternoon."

Mrs. Beskow is described as follows: "There is a light of kindness and understanding in her clear, blue eyes, a smile plays readily upon her face, her manner is gracious and sincere, with a certain shyness and modesty when her work is mentioned. She is true to the traditional Norse type, even Wagnerian in stature, and altogether there is a sweet womanliness about her of indescribable charm."

Among her books available in English are *Olle's Sky Trip; Aunt Green, Aunt Brown and Aunt Lavender; Pelle's New Suit; Aunt Brown's Birthday;* and *The Tale of the Wee Little Old Woman.*

Margery Williams Bianco

MARGERY WILLIAMS BIANCO was born July 22, 1881, in London. She was the daughter of Robert and Florence (Harper) Williams. Much of her early life was spent in the United States, where she was educated privately at Sharon Hill, near Philadelphia. Re-

ELSA BESKOW

turning to Europe, she married Captain Francesco Bianco of Turin, Italy, in 1904. Their two children, Cecco and Pamela, were born in England, but during their childhood the family lived, for the most part, in France and Italy.

Mrs. Bianco's first two books, *The Late Returning* (1902) and *The Price of Youth* (1904), were novels, published fore her marriage in her twenties. Another novel, *The Bar*, followed in 1906. She did not publish then for sixteen years. It was with *The Velveteen Rabbit* (1922), a book for children, that she broke her silence, and all her books since then have been for young people: *Poor Cecco* (1925), *The Little Wooden Doll* (1925), *The Apple Tree* (1926), *The Skin Horse* (1927), *The Adventures of Andy* (1927), *Candlestick* (1929), *All About Pets* (1929), a handbook for aspiring young pet fanciers. Mrs. Bianco has always had many pets and her information about rabbits, frogs, dogs, white mice, and lizards is reliable and pragmatic.

Two of Mrs. Bianco's books, *The Little Wooden Doll* and *The Skin Horse*, have been illustrated by her daughter Pamela. The drawings for the former book were made by Pamela when she was fourteen years old. Pamela was born in London in 1906. Six months later the family moved to Paris, then the United States, Paris again, London, Italy, and finally the United States once more. Pamela began to draw rabbits and guinea pigs, elves and fairies, when she was five. "She has never," says her father, "had a teacher of drawing or painting. We did not wish Pamela to lose any of her originality thru the influence of others." When she was fourteen, in 1919, her drawings and paintings were exhibited at the Leicester Galleries in London. Walter de la Mare, who strolled in to see them, was so impressed that he wrote a series of verses to accompany them, and both drawings and verses were published in book-form under the title, *Flora*. Since that sensational debut, Pamela Bianco has illustrated *Natives of Rock* (1925), poems by Glenway Westcott; *The Land of Dreams* (1928), poems by William Blake; *The Birthday of the Infanta* (1929), by Oscar Wilde; *Three Christ-*

MARGERY WILLIAMS BIANCO

mas Trees (1930), by Juliana H. Ewing; and the two books by her mother already mentioned. She has recently exhibited some work in oils, as well as lithographs and woodcuts. In 1930 she received a Guggenheim fellowship and went abroad —back to the Italy of her childhood— to continue her painting.

Mrs. Bianco is described as a quiet dark-haired woman, while her daughter has blue eyes and "shoulder-length brown hair."

Laurence Binyon

LAURENCE BINYON says that he has never belonged to any special group of writers, altho Robert Bridges, W. B. Yeats, Henry Newbolt, T. Sturge Moore, and Maurice Hewlett have been among his oldest friends. He was born in Lancaster, England, on August 10, 1869, and he was educated at St. Paul's School and Trinity College, Oxford. He won the Newdigate Prize in 1890, and, in the same year, published a volume of poems, *Primavera*, together with his cousin Stephen Phillips. He entered the

LAURENCE BINYON

Department of Printed Books in the British Museum in 1893, and two years later was transferred to the Department of Prints and Drawings. He is now Deputy Keeper of the collection of Oriental prints—the most important collection of its kind in Europe.

He says: "Being poor, I had to choose between journalism and some such post as I have at the Museum. I am glad I chose as I did, but I have never had any real leisure, or I should have produced far more. I now have a house in the Museum, which perhaps suggests a mummified existence, but is far from being so."

The poet has visited the United States three times and had "a glorious time." During the war he worked in an English hospital for French soldiers in Eastern France, and his poem "Fetching the Wounded" echoes his experience there.

He was invited to represent English men of letters at the great Molière celebration in Paris a few years ago, and he has received a French honor that gives him the rank of *Officier de l'Instruction Publique.*

As a schoolboy, Binyon wrote verse which was praised by Browning and

Matthew Arnold, but he says that his talent developed slowly, and he considers his latest work his best.

He has written several books on art, including *Painting in the Far East* (1908), *The Drawings and Engravings of William Blake* (1922), and *Chinese Paintings in English Collections* (1926); some critical work, *English Poetry in its Relation to Painting and the Other Arts* (1919), and *Tradition and Reaction in Modern Poetry* (1926); poetic dramas; and numerous volumes of poetry. *Selected Poems* (1922) contains his best work up to that time. Since then he has published *The Sirens* (1927) and *The Idols* (1928), and "described" the poems of Nizami, a 12th century Persian poet. Mr. Binyon also edited *The Golden Treasury of Modern Lyrics,* which carries on the idea of the original *Golden Treasury* thru the Victorian age to the present day.

Algernon Blackwood

ALGERNON BLACKWOOD was born under the sign of Pisces in 1869, the second son of Sir Arthur Blackwood, K. C. B., gentleman-usher to Queen Victoria, and Sydney, widowed Duchess of Manchester. His father was somewhat of a religious fanatic and Algernon was brought up in a home excessively pietistic where drink, tobacco, cards, the theatre, and dancing were all frowned upon as paths to Hell, and in which people were taken aside and asked whether they had given their "souls to Jesus."

Algernon attended four or five "horrible" private schools. He was a dreamy boy and dreaded the practical world. His head was full of wild fancies and he believed in ghosts. He used to slip out of his room at night and on a nearby pond in a boat he would practice incantations he had written. Nature was the strongest influence on his life.

His childhood reading consisted of Longfellow and countless religious tracts. At the age of seventeen, when he came home after a year and a half at the Moravian School in the Black Forest, he began to revolt against the strict home atmosphere. He got his hands on Pantanjali's *Yoga Aphorisms*, translated from the Sanscrit, and he read it thru three times in the middle of the night. Then he secured numerous books on spiritualism, theosophy, magic, and Buddhism, which he called his "Eastern books." Secretly he became a convert to Buddhism. A period at Wellington College, Cambridge, followed, but at the age of twenty he was packed off to Canada to learn dairy-farming. He reached Toronto with his fiddle and "a unique ignorance of life."

Blackwood describes his experiences of the nine years that followed in *Episodes Before Thirty* (1923). During the year and a half spent in Canada he worked in an insurance office at nothing a week, apprenticed himself to the editor of the *Methodist Magazine* at four dollars a week, sank the bulk of his money in an unsuccessful dairy farm, and the rest of it in a Toronto hotel that quickly went bankrupt. After six months on the lakes of North Ontario, he and his last business partner went to New York with a hundred dollars between them.

The money was soon gone. They paid $8 a week for a dingy room which they shared with a "pleasant" English youth. Blackwood experienced three horrors for the first time in his life: "the horror of loathsome vermin running over my body night after night, the horror of hunger, and the horror of living at close quarters with a criminal and degraded mind." The new friend eventually swindled Blackwood out of money and clothes, deserted him when he was sick, and took advantage of his illness to borrow money from Blackwood's sympathetic friends for his own indulgences.

During the period in New York Blackwood learned to make use of the "free lunch" counters where food could be had with a five cent glass of beer; to sleep on benches in Central Park; to pawn his clothes; to cook porridge over the gas jet in his room; and to eat dried apples followed by swallows of hot water to make them swell in the stomach and kill the pangs of hunger so one could sleep.

He worked on the *New York Sun* and the *New York Times*, gave violin les-

ALGERNON BLACKWOOD

sons at twenty-five cents an hour, posed as an artist's model, acted on the stage, instructed in shorthand, entered the dried milk business, gave French and German lessons, and served as private secretary to a financier, James Speyer. After seven years in New York he returned to England, just before he was thirty. In the years of hard living he had found mental freedom, but he had lost his faith in humanity.

A chance meeting with Angus Hamilton caused him to start writing books in 1906. He had no literary ambitions but he felt the need of a safety-valve for expression of his thoughts. Entirely without his knowledge, a friend carried a group of his first stories to a publisher who accepted them at once. So he took up literature as a profession. His first book was *The Empty House* (1906).

Blackwood's adventurous spirit led him to further travels. He journeyed the length of the Danube in a canoe; explored the temples of Egypt on foot and camel-back, and tramped thru the remote regions of the Caucasus with a Georgian guide, a mule, and a sack of flour. A two years residence in Switzerland furnished the inspiration for *The Education of Uncle Paul* (1909) and *A Prisoner in Fairyland* (1913).

Each one of his books contains a definite theme. For example, The *Human Chord* (1910) is a daring and fanciful exposition of the possibilities of vibration in color, light, sound, and human attraction. *The Centaur* (1911), which is largely autobiographical, is a plea for a return to the simple, inner life from the shams and vulgarities of the day.

Many of Blackwood's short stories are reminiscent of Poe, inducing an atmosphere of mystery that carries one to the verge of terror.

Among Blackwood's publications are: *The Listener* (1907), *John Silence* (1908), *The Lost Valley* (1910), *Incredible Adventures* (1914), *Julius Le Vallon* (1916), *The Promise of Air* (1918), *Through the Crack* (1921), *Tongues of Fire* (1924), *Sambo and Snitch* (1927), and *Full Circle* (1929).

Jean-Richard Bloch

JEAN-RICHARD BLOCH was born in Paris in 1884, of Alsacian Jewish parentage. His childhood was precocious. At the age of seven he was composing plays, imitations of Molière; at ten he was writing poems based on Musset; at twelve he was already dreaming of writing a history of Macedonia;

JEAN-RICHARD BLOCH

at thirteen, inspired by Buffon, he began to write an enormous zoological work.

After completing his secondary studies and military service, he entered the Sorbonne and began advanced researches in history and geography, started a novel, a play, wrote some poems and some stories, but without any idea of ever seeing them in print. At twenty he married and became a professor in a little high school in the Jura region.

Bloch's career as a writer really started in 1910. In that year he finished a play which the famous Antoine of the Odéon Theatre in Paris accepted and produced. In the same year he founded *L'Effort*, a "technical review of art and humanity," which he wished to be "less sympathetic than combative." Bloch has since collected his articles, "first essays for a better understanding of my time," under the title of his manifesto, *Carnaval est mort*. Carnival is dead, he says, because there is no longer any faith.

A series of tales, published as the *Premier Livre de Contes*, was Bloch's first book. André Gide and Jacques Copeau admired the tales and became interested in Bloch's career.

Et Cie, Bloch's Balzacian novel on a Jewish family and business house, was finished just before the war, but its publication was deferred until August 1917, at which time the author was engaged in military service. In 1925 the author revised the entire novel and published a definitive edition. The English translation,—*& Co.* (1929), with an introduction by Romain Rolland, was made by the late Mr. Scott-Moncrieff from the revised French edition. Among Bloch's other books are *La Nuit Kurde, Sur un Cargo,* and *Cacaouettes et Bananes,* of which the first, a novel expressing the author's nostalgia for Asia, which he calls "the continent of passion," has been translated into English by Stephen Haden Guest as *A Night in Kurdistan* (1931).

Bloch was wounded again and again at the Marne, in Champagne, and at Verdun, before his demobilization in 1919. The war, he says, "left me broken in body and spirit," but he continued with his writing. His play, *Le Dernier Empereur,* enjoyed great success in Paris, Berlin, Geneva, Stockholm, and other European capitals.

In 1926 a re-opening of one of his war wounds threatened him with loss of sight, but again he recovered. In 1930 he announced that he had in preparation eight volumes, including *Faiseur de Fédérations,* a social novel in continuation of *—& Co.; Sous le Genou des Amazones,* a novel or a play—maybe both—concerning the revolt of men against women; another novel; three plays; a collection of essays; and a volume of poems. Bloch also finds time to act as director of one of the leading Paris publishing houses and assistant editor of *Europe,* a noted review.

Of himself Bloch has said: "I live in the country for most of the year, where my favorite sports are bicycling, motorcycling, motoring, and all other modes of transportation including walking and cargo-boating. I do not know what boredom means; I like struggle, I like peace; I like society and solitude; I like traveling and tranquillity; I like the city and the revolt against the city; I like to see my friends and to refrain from seeing them; I dislike work and I work enormously. I have just passed my forty-third year and feel that my *Wanderjahren* are now over and that my *Lehrjahren* are just beginning. I feel myself at the beginning of the second stage of my life and work. A first cycle of books has just been closed. The second is just begun." He adds that he writes for his own pleasure, that he hates to follow a straight line, and that he is afflicted with an incurable love for intellectual vagabondage.

Bloch is described as a person made up of contraries, a strange marriage between the man of action and the oriental dreamer. He has a smiling keen face, and his gestures are nervous and awkward. One interviewer was reminded of the albatross of Baudelaire, so ill at ease when it does not fly.

Louise Bogan

LOUISE BOGAN was born at Livermore Falls, Maine, on August 11, 1897, of Irish-American parents. Her father's people came from Londonderry and her mother's from Dublin. Her

LOUISE BOGAN

paternal grandfather, James Bogan, was a sea-captain out of Portland Harbor. She was educated in New England schools and at the Girls' Latin School in Boston.

Except for a year spent in Vienna in 1922 and another in Santa Fe, New Mexico, she has lived in New York City for the most part during the past ten years.

Miss Bogan's work was first published in *The New Republic,* to which she has also contributed book reviews and other criticisms. *Body of This Death,* a book of poems, was published in 1923. Her second book is *Dark Summer* (1929). She was married in 1925 to Raymond Holden, himself a poet of distinction, and lived on a small farm in upper eastern New York State until a fire that destroyed their home recently forced them to return to the city.

Louis Untermeyer says of her first book that it displays "an intellect which, for all its burden of thought, expresses itself best in the lyric." Of her second collection, that "the accents, deep, bell-like, vesperal, are more her own. The metaphysical note has strengthened, the beat of measured blood has become more pronounced."

Johan Bojer

JOHAN BOJER, who was born at Orkedalsoren, near Trondhjem, Norway, March 6, 1872, describes his own boyhood:

"The fisherman's hut where I grew up was grey like the sea and the sand on the beach—like the rocks around. But if I kneeled upon the wooden seat under the window I saw far away the red, yellow, and white painted houses of the well-to-do. It was like a bit of Paradise to stare at, and it was evident to my mind that the people living in those bright houses must be bright and beautiful and that I must have a house like that when I grew up. Out there near the sea the soil was poor, few families possessed more than a cow or two and milk was a costly thing. But from the window seat I saw large farms in front of the forest, and there would be flocks of cattle and sheep and horses. There the people would drink milk with their porridge, not water sweetened with treacle, they would have enough wool to weave good clothes for themselves, and need not shiver with cold. And just imagine the quantities of meat and bacon and real butter there must be—these people surely did not eat fish and fish and fish again every day of their lives as we did.

"I began my life as a literary tramp. I lived for five years in Paris as a correspondent for Norwegian newspapers, three years were spent in Italy, two years in Germany. I have frequently visited England, wandered thru Holland and Belgium and tried everywhere to profit by what I saw. The time in Paris from 1902 to 1907 appears to me the richest. I was at an age when there is no limit to one's activity. I wrote newspaper articles and books, read incredible amounts in various languages, at the same time living a merry Bohemian life with artist friends. There were so many hours in a day and a night, and everything which made an impression is so easily recalled; my heart was still full of dreams and of youth.

"At the moment I recall the first half-century of my life with gratitude, because the kindly fates have filled my life with such varied experiences, and have little by little given me what I glimpsed far, far away standing at the window of a grey cottage."

It is interesting to go a little more into detail about the publication of his first novel, that was notably successful. Having written it—it was entitled *Et Folketog*—he set out from a little Norwegian town where he was working to go to Christiania to find a publisher. He was, literally, so poor that he was compelled to pawn his few belongings piece by piece as he went along. But he got to Christiania and found a publisher.

In 1899, when he was twenty-seven, Bojer married Ellen Lange, the daughter of Colonel Lange. Their children were Thora, Randi Faetten (named after Bojer's beloved foster-mother) and Halvard, the one boy.

In 1907 he returned with his family to Norway, and has since lived there almost continuously, bringing up his children, and striking roots deep into his native soil.

The novel by which the name of Johan Bojer became established in this country was *The Great Hunger*, published in English in 1919. Since then ten other novels from his pen have been published in America: *Life, The Face of the World, Treacherous Ground, The Power*

JOHAN BOJER

of a Lie, (the novel which was crowned by the French Academy), *The Last of the Vikings, The Prisoner Who Sang, A Pilgrimage, The Emigrants* (1925), *The New Temple* (1928)—a sequel to *The Great Hunger—,* and *The Everlasting Struggle* (1931).

Mary Borden

A LTHO since her marriage to Brigadier-General E. L. Spears in 1918 Miss Borden has lived in France and England with occasional visits to the United States, she still has an extraordinarily strong feeling of belonging to America, particularly the West. Her childhood in Chicago and holidays at the family homestead in Indiana left vivid impressions upon which she has drawn in several of her books. The ample old farmhouse in Indiana was the scene of many a jolly Thanksgiving. It belongs to the grandfather, John Borden, a Rhode Islander who in his adventurous youth sailed down the Ohio in search of silver mines. He found no silver, but very good farm land, so he settled on the Kentucky border of Indiana and built the friendly old homestead which his grandchildren made a place of delightful memories.

Mary Borden was born in Chicago in 1886. Most Chicago families of the nineties were deeply religious and it was not unusual for children to attend the services of some of the more violently evangelical creeds and to experience emotional upheavals which they mistook for religious experiences, upheavals which left a powerful and disquieting memory. Mary Borden has never been able to free herself from a distaste amounting to horror for any form of emotionalism in religion.

After graduation from Vassar College and a trip around the world, Miss Borden sojourned pleasantly in France and England. The war found her in France, and it is these four years that she will

MARY BORDEN

probably look upon as the most intensely interesting period of her life. She organized and ran a large field hospital for the French army. After the Armistice she found herself the possessor of five war medals, the Legion of Honor, the Croix de Guerre, the French gold medal of the Service de Santé, and two British war medals.

Miss Borden lives in one of the most beautiful old houses in London, a house designed by Lutyons in Little College Street, just behind Westminster Abbey and well within the sound of Big Ben. The great hallway and main staircase are of veined, cream-colored marble and the library is finished in the beautiful, natural panelling for which many old English houses are famous. Here Miss Borden maintains her reputation of being one of the most smartly dressed and brilliant of London's hostesses.

Among her works are *Jane—Our Stranger* (1923); *Three Pilgrims and a Tinker* (1924); *The Romantic Woman* (1925); *Jericho Sands* (1925); *Four O'Clock* (1926); *Flamingo* (1927); *Jehovah's Day* (1929); *The Forbidden Zone* (1929), sketches and poems of her own experiences as a nurse in the World War; and *A Woman With White Eyes* (1930).

Phyllis Bottome

PHYLLIS BOTTOME was born in England, and her mother was English, but her father was an American clergyman. Rev. William MacDonald Bottome brought his family to the United States when Phyllis was nine, in order to accept the pastorate of Grace Church, Jamaica, Long Island. They remained for six years before returning permanently to England. "My father," she says, "was a brilliant preacher, but had the tastes of a gypsy, and we never stayed more than two or three years in the same place. Rochester, Berkshire, and Somerset were all our homes."

As a girl, she did every conceivable sort of parish work, short of actually preaching in the pulpit. In her leisure moments she nursed an aspiration for the stage. Later a serious physical breakdown caused her to abandon her plans for a dramatic career, and she found herself a patient in a Swiss sanitarium, fighting for her life, at Davos.

Phyllis Bottome did not serve a discouraging apprenticeship as a writer. Her first novel, completed when she was seventeen, fell into the hands of Andrew Lang and was immediately accepted for publication. Three other novels were promptly issued in London.

PHYLLIS BOTTOME

Until the War she wintered regularly in Rome, which she came to know nearly as well as London. She feels very much at home in France and Switzerland and has known intimately many Russians, Dutch, and Austrians. Her work has been translated into Norwegian, Swedish, French, German, and Dutch; and in many ways Phyllis Bottome can rightly lay claim to being a cosmopolitan. "I have never been back to America," she says, "but in many happy and constant intimacies with Americans I feel as if I had never altogether left it."

In many respects the War served as a turning point in her career. She had become engaged when very young but had been forced to break off her engagement on account of ill health. However, just before the War, she again met her former fiancé, A. E. Forbes Dennis, and married him in 1916. He served with distinction in France for three years, was dangerously wounded, and upon his recovery was made Intelligence Officer at Marseilles and put in charge of all English shipping from that port. During these war years, Miss Bottome was brought into intimate contact with people of many nationalities, types, and professions.

Captain Forbes Dennis carried his work at Marseilles thru with such success that after the armistice he was immediately offered an important post as Passport Control officer in Vienna. His wife meantime resumed her relief work in the Austrian capital, throwing her energies into the feeding of the hordes of people who were literally starving in Vienna before the stabilization of the krone. Out of this experience grew her *Old Wine,* a story of the Austrian breakdown.

Altho the winter months are frequently spent in Italy, Mr. and Mrs. Forbes Dennis have, for several years, lived in a chalet at Kitzbuhel in the heart of the Austrian Tyrol, midway between Innsbrook and Salzburg on the main line to Vienna. Kitzbuhel is one of the healthiest and most picturesque spots in the Tyrol, and Phyllis Bottome is particularly happy in these stimulating surroundings. Of her life there and of her interests she says, "Our chalet is a large farmhouse, surrounded by rows of balconies which look over a beautiful valley filled with flowers in spring. We are so situated that we are able to keep in constant touch with the intellectual life of Vienna, Paris, and Berlin."

Phyllis Bottome's publications include *Broken Music, The Dark Tower, Crystal Heart, Old Wine, Belated Reckoning, Strange Fruit* (short stories, 1928), *Plain Case* (1928), *Windlestraws* (1929), and *Tatter'd Loving* (1930).

Ernest Boyd

ERNEST BOYD was born in Dublin June 28, 1887. His grandfather was a Scot who had been sent to Ireland in the diplomatic service and had remained there. His father, half Irish and half Scotch, was also in governmental service. His mother, a racial mixture of Spanish and Irish, was a brilliant woman who had been educated in Germany.

Ernest Boyd is described as the most striking looking figure in present day literary circles in New York. He has a copper colored beard, and always dresses harmoniously in brown; even his dinner clothes are of a brown tone—like his beard and complexion—from hat to shoes. His expression is gentle and benign; when a boy he posed for the Christus in a well known series of paintings hanging in the stations of the Dublin Cathedral.

Until he was sixteen Mr. Boyd was taught at home by a French tutor and absorbed French literature thoroly, particularly Molière and Racine. He then attended school in Switzerland and Germany, where he learned Italian, Spanish, German, and modern Greek. He has added the knowledge of several other tongues to these, and is now conversant with a dozen languages.

In 1910 he became a member of the editorial staff of the *Irish Times* in Dublin and contributed articles both on political subjects and on the Irish theatre to London papers; some of these also appeared in translation in French newspapers.

Mr. Boyd married Mlle. Madeleine Reynier in London in 1913; she had gone from her native Paris to Dublin to teach and to attend Trinity College. Mr. Boyd had taken Civil Service examinations

some time prior to this event, and had entered the British consular service. As British Vice-Consul, he and Mrs. Boyd came to the United States immediately after their marriage. From 1913 until 1920 he served in this capacity in Baltimore (Maryland), Barcelona (Spain), and Copenhagen (Denmark). During the World War he was accused of being a Sinn Feiner, and was involved in some difficulty with the government.

Mr. Boyd resigned from political service in 1920 and since that time has lived in New York. When he was in Baltimore he made the friendship of Henry L. Mencken, editor of the *American Mercury,* and began to write critical articles and to contribute translations to various magazines here. From 1920 to 1922 he wrote the editorials on foreign politics for the *New York Evening Post,* and also contributed to the *Literary Review* which was under the editorship of Dr. Canby. In 1922 and 1923 he was a reader and adviser on foreign literature for the publishing house of Alfred A. Knopf. He has subsequently read plays for the Theatre Guild for a year, conducted the "Readers and Writers Section" in the *Independent,* and is now literary editor of the *New Freeman.*

The number of Mr. Boyd's translations, criticisms, and essays is large.

ERNEST BOYD

Aside from his many magazine articles, he has published the following books: *Contemporary Drama of Ireland* (1917); *Appreciations and Depreciations,* Irish literary studies (1918); *Ireland's Literary Renaissance* (1922); *Portraits: real and imaginary* (1924); *H. L. Mencken* (1925); *Studies from Ten Literatures* (1925); *Guy de Maupassant,* a biographical study, (1926); *Literary Blasphemies* (1927). A volume of essays on books and life is to be published in 1931. *The Sacred Ego,* which was published anonymously in Dublin and attributed to Darrell Figgis, is also by Mr. Boyd.

Mr. and Mrs. Boyd have individually translated many books, particularly from the French.

James Boyd

JAMES BOYD was born on July 2, 1888, in Dauphin County, Pennsylvania, but moved to North Carolina, the home of his earlier ancestors, when he was thirteen. He was graduated from Princeton in 1910, and afterwards spent two years at Trinity College, Cambridge. In 1917 he married Katharine Lamont of New York City. He has two sons and one daughter.

As to early literary activity, Mr. Boyd says he was "a journalist for one summer,"—between his graduation from Princeton and departure for Cambridge —on the *Harrisburg Patriot.* "All the regular fellows were away on vacation, and I was dramatic critic one week; sporting editor another; then human interest writer; and finally I drew the cartoons. They did tell me they'd keep me on as a cartoonist if I'd learn how to draw!"

Looking at him now—lean, brown and muscular, Master of Hounds at Southern Pines, North Carolina—it is difficult to realize that doctors' orders to go South and live on his grandfather's plantation really transformed James Boyd, just discharged from the army, into an author. Mr. Boyd had never believed he had sufficient ability to write, and, before the war, had been in the publishing business, with Doubleday Page, as the "next best thing."

"I had to do something when I got down South," he says, simply, "so I decided to try writing short stories. I tried all kinds—character, description, everything—I believe now that anybody with reasonable ability can *learn* to *write;* that *imagination* has to be born, but style is pure craftsmanship. I had no conviction that I could do it, but I thought I would spend five years gaining an apprenticeship before I either succeeded or gave up. Then the trial balloons I sent out started selling—to the *Pictorial Review, Scribner's,* and other magazines. I didn't really expect them to, and wasn't particularly proud of them. You can see your mistakes so much better in print and you realize that thirty or forty thousand other people are seeing them also!"

A few years ago, thru a friend and fellow writer, Hugh McNair Kahler, Mr. Boyd met John Galsworthy, who with Mrs. Galsworthy was stopping in Southern Pines on his way up from New Orleans. Galsworthy got him to show him some of his stories, put a number of notes on the margin, and helped him "plan out a way of attacking the business." On his return to New York, he gave his verdict, "Keep your eye on

JAMES BOYD

James Boyd." Since then, Mr. Boyd's first novel, *Drums* (1926), his second, *Marching On* (1927), and his third, *Long Hunt* (1930), have been published. *Drums* is a novel of the American Revolution; *Marching On* is a Civil War novel; *Long Hunt* is a re-creation of frontier America.

James Boyd explains the natural talk of the characters in *Drums,* which differs from the artificial Revolutionary War jargon disfiguring so many historical novels, by saying: "I had a tremendous advantage because I live in North Carolina and could just take the local speech. North Carolina is almost entirely Anglo-Saxon—98½ per cent American born— and in the back districts has an almost pure Colonial dialect, as I discovered by checking it up as much as I could with old diaries and letters, etc., of the Revolutionary period. For instance, they say *stub* for *stake*, *Egyptians* for *gypsies*, *nearabout* for *almost*. I chose North Carolina as a setting for a Revolutionary novel because there is a better picture of the American Colonies there than in any other state; its character has changed less than any other, since it has no important seaport."

Mr. Boyd is now a permanent resident of Southern Pines, having built there a fine home patterned largely after "Westover" in Virginia, the famous home of William Byrd, the father of Richmond and prominent in Virginia history. Southern Pines now boasts a literary colony embracing among others, the Struthers Burts, Holworthy Hall, Hugh McNair Kahler, and Donald Herring.

Gamaliel Bradford

GAMALIEL BRADFORD, eighth direct descendant of Governor William Bradford of the Plymouth Colony, was born in Boston October 9, 1863. His early life was spent in Wellesley Hills, thirteen miles from Boston where he was educated in the public schools. He entered Harvard College in 1882 but was obliged to leave almost immediately on account of ill-health. Altho handicapped by illness ever since, he managed to secure a Litt. D. degree at Washington and Lee University, and produce

GAMALIEL BRADFORD

numerous works of a biographical nature. On October 30, 1886, he married Helen Hubbard Ford of Wellesley Hills, where he still makes his home.

Bradford considers the term biographer inadequate to describe himself. He calls himself, instead, a psychographer. In describing psychography, a word which he has borrowed from Sainte-Beuve, he says, in *A Naturalist of Souls* (1917): "As a portrait-painter I could present a man at only one moment of his career, and depict his character in only one phase, one situation, one set of conditions and circumstances. Now the aim of psychography is precisely the opposite to this. Out of the perpetual flux of actions and circumstances that constitutes a man's whole life, it seeks to extract what is essential, what is permanent and so vitally characteristic." His portraits are highly analytical of the inner motives and characters of his subjects.

His method is well illustrated by *Damaged Souls* (1923), one of his best known books, in which he portrays Aaron Burr, Thomas Paine, P. T. Barnum, Randolph and other historical figures of generally unsavory reputations. In *American Portraits, 1875-1900,* (1922), appear nationally famous Americans such as Henry Adams, Mark Twain,

James G. Blaine, Joseph Jefferson and Grover Cleveland, "psychographed" in the Bradford style.

Women have been sketched in four of Bradford's books: *Portraits of Women* (1916), *Portraits of American Women* (1919), *Wives* (1925), and *Daughters of Eve* (1930). The last includes psychographs of seven fascinating women, including Catherine the Great, George Sand, and Sarah Bernhardt. The volume which preceded *Daughters of Eve* in publication was entitled *As God Made Them* (1929), in which he characterizes some nineteenth century Americans, among them the political triumvirate, Webster, Clay, and Calhoun, as well as Horace Greeley and Edwin Booth.

Most of Bradford's books contain collections of seven or eight sketches, none of them long. His scheme of psychographic portraiture seems to have proven better adapted to small than to large canvasses. Several volumes, however, have been devoted to single characters, among them *Lee, the American* (1912), *The Soul of Samuel Pepys* (1924), *Darwin* (1926), and *D. L. Moody—A Worker in Souls* (1927). Altho lately Bradford scarcely passes a year without the publication of a book, he spent ten years preparing *Lee, the American*.

Some other Bradford works are: *Union Portraits* (1916); *Confederate Portraits* (1918); *Bare Souls* (1924); *Haunted Biographer* (1928), containing dialogs of the dead; *Life and I* (1928), "an autobiography of humanity"; *The Quick and the Dead* (1931), including studies of Roosevelt, Wilson, Edison, Ford, Lenin, Mussolini, and Coolidge.

Roark Bradford

ROARK BRADFORD had already received moderate recognition for his Negro stories when *The Green Pastures* opened in a New York theatre in February 1930. Honors for *The Green Pastures*, which won the Pulitzer award for the best play of the year, went chiefly to Marc Connelly, but Mr. Connelly, critics, and the public acknowledge readily the debt due Mr. Bradford for his *Ol'*

ROARK BRADFORD

Man Adam an' His Chillun on which the play was based.

Altho Roark Bradford is a descendant of Governor William Bradford of Massachusetts he is closely connected with the South. His ancestors moved to Virginia shortly after the Queen Anne wars, and his grandfathers and great-uncles fought in the Confederate Army with Morgan, Forrest, and Beauregard.

Roark Whitney Wickliffe Bradford, as he admits his full name to be, was born August 21, 1896, in Laureldale County, Tennessee. His birthplace was fifteen miles from a railroad, but very near the Mississippi River. He studied at home and in public schools before attending the University of California where he received, in his words, "a freakish LL.B. degree in the last half of the senior year in order to enter training camp at the outbreak of the war." He was a first lieutenant of coast artillery when the Armistice was signed, but served various post-war assignments until March 1920.

He was discharged in Atlanta, Georgia, and went to work immediately on a

Hearst newspaper there. Two years later he went to Louisiana to edit a country daily paper, and then to New Orleans to the *Times-Picayune*. After a few months on the *Times-Picayune*, as copy reader, night city editor, and Sunday editor successively, he left the paper to spend his entire time writing. In his spare moments he built up a unique collection of phonograph records of Negro and mountain songs.

Child Of God, practically his first short story, won the O'Brien Prize Story award in 1927. *Ol' Man Adam an' His Chillun*, a collection of negro Bible stories which are "the stories they tell about the time when the Lord walked the earth like a natural man," was published in 1928. *This Side of Jordan*, a full-length novel, was published in 1929; and *Ol' King David and the Philistine Boys*, a continuation of *Ol' Man Adam*, in 1930. Mr. Bradford next wrote *John Henry* (1931), based on the legendary super-Negro of the Lower Mississippi.

Mr. Bradford is a genial person and talks with the same rich humor that is found in his written stories. He differs from many authors of humorous stories in that he is generous with his material in conversation. He is a slightly bald, stocky, grey-eyed man of medium height.

While in New Orleans Mr. and Mrs. Bradford live in the historic Pontalba building, facing Jackson Square in the Vieux Carré. This building was built by the Baroness Pontalba, and is said to be the earliest apartment house in the United States.

Louis Bromfield

LOUIS BROMFIELD represents the anomaly of a novelist born in the middle West—which he interprets in *The Green Bay Tree, Possession*, and *A Good Woman*—yet familiar enough with New England to achieve the Pulitzer Prize-winning novel, *Early Autumn;* a novelist also who during several years' residence abroad has been imbued with the Continental feeling and tradition which is so strongly a part of *The Strange Case of Miss Annie Spragg*. He feels that living and writing in France gives him a far better perspec-

tive on American life than he could possibly have if he were in the middle of New York. He says, moreover, that he has been much influenced by "the French point of view of seeing things as they are."

Born December 27, 1896, in Mansfield, Ohio, of Boston-Maryland stock, Bromfield was educated in public schools and took his first job on a local newspaper at the age of fifteen. At sixteen he entered the Cornell School of Agriculture, intending to settle on the family farm but this idea was soon superseded by a wish to write and see the world. His next project was to spend a year at each of four different colleges but it was shattered by the World War in which he served with the French army, touching in turn every sector of the front from Switzerland to the North Sea. After the war he lived for six months in Paris, and traveled for some time where only French was spoken.

When at length he returned to New York—it was New York and not Ohio to which he returned—he wrote news stories for the New York City News Association and later for the Associated Press. He left newspaper work to serve as Foreign Editor on the staff of *Musical America*. Then he worked with a lead-

LOUIS BROMFIELD

ing theatrical producer and afterwards with a publisher. At this period he also conducted the department of "The New Yorker" in *The Bookman.*

In 1924, after having written four unpublished novels, Louis Bromfield published his "first" novel, *The Green Bay Tree,* a story of life in a great American steel town, of a beautiful, eager and lawless woman, of labor troubles, of changing social ideas. This was the first of four novels of American life—each a complete story in itself—which group themselves under the general name of *Escape.* The three others that followed were *Possession* (1925); *Early Autumn,* the Pulitzer Prize novel (1926); and *A Good Woman* (1927). A novel of a very different type appeared in 1928— *The Strange Case of Miss Annie Spragg.* It concerns the lives of a dozen strange characters, each seized at a moment of crisis on the night Miss Annie Spragg, an American spinster, died in an Italian palace under miraculous circumstances. In 1929 Bromfield published a volume of short stories, *Awake and Rehearse,* including three prize stories. *The House of Women,* a play made from *The Green Bay Tree* was produced in New York in 1927.

His novel, *Twenty-Four Hours,* published in September 1930, is a story of New York that begins at a Sutton Place dinner one evening and ends at a Murray Hill tea the following day.

Bromfield is back in France with his wife and two children, after a sojourn in New York and Hollywood.

He is described as tall, spare, broad-shouldered, with legs and arms that are loosely but powerfully articulated, quick to smile and given to vivacious gestures. His leisurely manner is deceptive, for by nature he is alert and eager. Of his own novels he likes best *The Green Bay Tree,* and least of any *Early Autumn,* which is strongly influenced, he says, by Virginia Woolf.

Van Wyck Brooks

VAN WYCK BROOKS, one of America's most respected critics and literary scholars, was born in Plainfield, New Jersey, February 16, 1886. He re-

VAN WYCK BROOKS

ceived his secondary education there and was graduated from Harvard in 1907.

Mr. Brooks had already found that his interests lay in critical and editorial work, and joined the editorial staff of Doubleday, Page and Company immediately after receiving his A. B. degree, remaining with this publishing company until 1909.

He published his first book in 1909, *The Wine of the Puritans,* in which American civilization and institutions are considered from the point of view of two expatriated citizens. This book was pronounced a brilliant study for so young a critic, and led to the author's giving a series of lectures at Leland Stanford University from 1911 to 1913. He was married in 1911 to Miss Eleanor Kenyon, at Carmel, California.

In 1913 a second book was published, a study of Obermann, Amiel, and Maurice de Guerin, entitled *The Malady of the Ideal. John Addington Symonds,* another critical analysis, followed in 1914, and *The World of H. G. Wells* in 1915.

America's Coming-of-Age (1915), still a timely cultural study, is a competent analysis of the American mind, which in Mr. Brooks' opinion is made up of two attitudes, one the theoretical and the idealistic and the other the utilitarian and the practical, which are rarely blended satisfactorily in the individual.

Mr. Brooks was associated with the Century Company in an editorial capacity from 1915 to 1918. In 1920 he became associate editor of *The Freeman,* which position he held until 1924. He was editor, with Alfred Kreymborg, Lewis Mumford, and Paul Rosenfeld, of the first *American Caravan,* in 1927. Due to poor health he was forced to resign from the editorial board of this annual for its subsequent editions. He lives with Mrs. Brooks and their two sons, Charles Van Wyck and Oliver Kenyon Brooks, in Westport, Connecticut.

In his personal manner as well as his writing he is persuasive, considerate, urbane and dignified. He is reticent with strangers, and lives in comparative seclusion. The definition of criticism which he follows is that it is "the intellectual study of origins and relations. It regards the work of art, not as a record personal to the critic, but as a specimen to be investigated dispassionately, intellectually, and in its relation both to art and life." Personally, he is interested particularly in frustrated artists such as Amiel.

The 1923 *Dial* prize of $2,000 was given to Mr. Brooks, in recognition of his having created a new point of view in criticism in this country. This award, which had been won by Sherwood Anderson in 1921 and T. S. Eliot in 1922, was not given for a single work but for the cumulated achievements of a writer.

Mr. Brooks has also published the following: *Letters and Leadership* (1918); *The Ordeal of Mark Twain* (1920); *The Pilgrimage of Henry James* (1925); and *Emerson and Others* (1927).

He has edited *The History of a Literary Radical and Other Essays* (1920) by R. S. Bourne, and *Journal of the First Voyage to America* (1924) by Christopher Columbus.

Mr. Brooks has also translated a number of books, among them: *Philine* (1930) by Henri Frédéric Amiel, and several novels by André Chamson.

Mr. and Mrs. Brooks translated *Some Aspects of the Life of Jesus* (1923) by Georges Berguer. Mrs. Brooks is also the translator of Romain Rolland's *Game of Love and Death* (1926).

John Buchan

JOHN BUCHAN was born at Perth, Scotland, August 26, 1876 of an old Border family. His mother was a cousin of Mr. Gladstone. He was educated at Glasgow University and Brasenose College, Oxford, and won the Stanhope Historical Prize and the Newdigate prize for English verse. His future eminence as a historian was hinted when he took first class honors at Oxford in history and philosophy. At Oxford he was also president of the Union, that great debating society.

In 1901 he was called to the English bar, and the same year went to South Africa and up to the Zambesi where he shot big game, fell eternally in love with the country and became a convert to Cecil Rhodes' dream of a United British Empire. At the end of 1903 he returned to England and the English bar, working with Sir Robert Finlay. In 1907 he became a partner in Thomas Nelson and Sons, Ltd., publishers.

The war brought to him one of his greatest opportunities for service. The London *Times* sent him to the front as

JOHN BUCHAN

a correspondent in the spring of 1915 and he was present at the second battle of Ypres. In 1916 he joined Sir Douglas Haig's staff as intelligence officer, was present at the battle of the Somme and was recalled in January 1917 to take the supremely important post of Director of Information.

It was this war service, joined to his gifts as narrator and historian, which enabled him to write *John Buchan's History of the Great War* (1921-22).

As a romancer, Mr. Buchan has written many volumes, including *Greenmantle, The Three Hostages, The Dancing Floor, Witchwood,* and *Castle Gay.* He has also written biographies, poems, essays, and memoirs.

John Buchan is an indefatigable worker, and he apparently finds much of his recreation in turning from one variety of work to another. He combines the activities of lawyer, soldier, business man, novelist, historian, essayist, poet, and member of Parliament. To absorb his leisure time, he resorts to riding to hounds, mountain climbing, and the sports of rod and gun.

"I have to live on a very strict schedule. From Monday to Friday noon I put everything out of my head but politics and business and limit my activity to four major interests: Parliament, my publishing connection with Thomas Nelson, and my work with the British film and radio industries.

"Over the week-ends I am out in the country, near Oxford, and when not gardening, I am generally writing. Then I have two months in Scotland every summer, with absolutely no interruptions save an occasional telegram. I write very quickly after I start because I compose my stories to myself before I begin—when riding on the top of a bus or lathering my face in the morning.

"I regard business as my profession, writing as my amusement, and it looks as if some kind of politics was going to be my duty," he wrote some time ago. "I have three ambitions, one in each sphere: to write a full life of General Robert E. Lee; to make the best literature accessible to the poorest purse, and in any language; and to do a little to help bring about the full understanding of America and the British Empire."

Thornton W. Burgess

THORNTON WALDO BURGESS was born in Sandwich on Cape Cod on January 14, 1874, the son of Thornton W. and Caroline F. Burgess. His father died when he was a small child and as a young boy it was necessary for him to help his mother eke out the family income by doing odd jobs—mowing lawns, picking berries, shoveling sidewalks in winter, driving cows, carrying milk—in fact anything at all that a bright eager little boy could turn his hand to, and when he was twelve years old he was earning enough money to buy his own clothes. He had little time for recreation, and no money to spend on a small boy's conventional good time. But when he could, he used to wander over the fields and woods and the salt marshes of Cape Cod.

He went to school in Sandwich and lived there until 1891 when, unable to go to college, as he wished, he went to Boston and took a course in bookkeeping at a commercial college. He entered the business world as a cashier and assistant bookkeeper in a large shoe store, a position which he hated but which necessity forced him to accept. In those days he wanted to write novels—an ambition which he has given up—and since dealing in shoes (no less than in ships and

THORNTON W. BURGESS

sealing wax) is hardly conducive to creative writing, he resigned his position when he heard of an opening in the editorial rooms of the Phelps Publishing Company in Springfield, Massachusetts. With a salary of five dollars a week, he was glad enough to be office boy in a business in which he was constantly in touch with books, proofs, ink, and pencils.

For fifteen years he remained here, and became household and literary editor of the earlier *Good Housekeeping Magazine*. His wife died when their son was born—the "blue-eyed little boy" who was responsible for the first of the Bedtime Stories. The child was in the habit of having his father tell him a story before he went to sleep every night, and once when he went to visit his grandmother, his father wrote him a story— a "Peter Rabbit" or "Reddy Fox" or "Jerry Muskrat" story—and sent it every day in his letter.

Good Housekeeping was sold to another firm and moved to New York. Mr. Burgess wrote advertising for a while, and occasionally sold a story for a small price. A friend of his saw the *Old Mother West Wind* stories one day and disposed of them for book publication. "I never thought of having them published," Burgess said. "They were written for my son." In 1911 he married again. His first book had gone well, and his publishers wanted another collection of animal stories. "I've written or told my last animal story," the author (who was to write his 2000th story in 1925) said. "I haven't got another one in me." But he found some more stories "in him" and the second book went better than the first. In 1912 he sold a story for six dollars to a newspaper syndicate and thus inaugurated what has been one of the great successes of recent times in American journalism. Every day since then (except Sundays) this feature has been running in newspapers, seventy of which, in the United States and Canada, now use it.

With the advent of the radio, came the Bedtime Story hour—and Burgess, with his daily newspaper audience of ten million people, started in 1924 his Radio Nature League. Its members now include nearly 50,000 people, ranging in age from nine months to ninety-four years.

The Bedtime Stories originated, Burgess says, "from a desire to inculcate early in a certain laddie who calls me 'Dad' something of the love of nature and the little people of meadow and forest which was my birthright." These stories have been published in book form in six series, in addition to his popular volumes of nature lore—*The Burgess Bird Book for Children* (1919), *The Burgess Animal Book for Children* (1920), *The Burgess Flower Book for Children* (1923), and *The Burgess Sea Shore Book for Children* (1929).

Besides his Radio Nature League (one purpose of which is to preserve wild life), Mr. Burgess earlier organized the Bird Sanctuary plan, and in three years there were nearly three million acres of land in the United States where bird life was safe. He was awarded the Distinguished Service Medal of the Permanent Wild Life Protection Fund.

Struthers Burt

MAXWELL STRUTHERS BURT was born in Baltimore, October 18, 1882, of a Philadelphia family. He was educated in private schools in Philadelphia. Before entering college he was for two years a reporter on the old *Philadelphia Times,* under Col. A. K. McClure. Altho he had been writing since he was nine years old, Burt was first set definitely on the path of fiction by Philip Keats Speed, his city editor, grand nephew of John Keats.

He was graduated from Princeton, 1904. While in college he followed the usual undergraduate literary pursuits: served as Managing Editor of the *Princeton Tiger,* wrote two Triangle Club plays, and was on the board of the *Nassau Literary Magazine*.

Upon leaving Princeton he entered Merton College, Oxford University, but did not stay for his degree. He was called back to take a job as instructor in English at Princeton where he taught for three years.

Meanwhile, hunting antelope one summer in western Wyoming, Burt saw the Jackson Hole country, fell in love with

STRUTHERS BURT

McClure's Magazine, literary editor of McClure, Phillips & Company, and subsequently advisory editor with Small, Maynard & Company. In 1918-1919 he was instructor of English at the University of California.

Bynner's first volume of verse, *Young Harvard* (1907), in praise of his *alma mater,* was followed by two plays and a long poem, *The New World* (1915), celebrating the ideals of democracy. In 1916, under the pseudonym "Emanuel Morgan," Bynner was co-author with Arthur Davison Ficke ("Anne Knish") of a sensational hoax, *Spectra,* a volume of verses so successfully burlesquing the futuristic poetic tendencies of the period that many poets and critics in the vanguard of the new movement were deluded into praising it enthusiastically. Bynner used his pseudonym again in 1920 when he published *Pins for Wings,* a series of five-or-six word caricatures of some two hundred of the author's contemporaries, chiefly poets.

Bynner's lyric gift manifested itself in *Grenstone Poems* (1917), *The Beloved Stranger* (1919), *A Canticle of Pan* (1920), and *Caravan* (1925).

Bynner has lectured frequently on poetry, traveled in the Orient, and spent much of his time in recent years in collecting and studying Chinese and

it, and immediately bought a partnership in a ranch. Giving up teaching at the end of three years he settled permanently in Jackson Hole, where he has been a citizen ever since. Recently he has been coming East in the winters to Princeton.

In 1913 Mr. Burt married Katherine Newlin, author of *The Branding Iron, Hidden Creek,* etc. They have two children, a son and a daughter. Mr. Burt now has a home at Southern Pines, North Carolina, but is still faithful to his Wyoming ranch which he visits every year He served as a private in the Air Service, U. S. A., in 1918.

His publications include: *In the High Hill* (1914), *John O'May, and other Stories* (1918), *Verse and Short Stories* (1918), *Songs and Portraits* (1920), *Chance Encounters* (1921), *Interpreter's House* (1924), *The Diary of a Dude Wrangler* (1924), *The Delectable Mountains* (1927), *They Could Not Sleep* (1928), *The Other Side* (1928), *Festival* (1931).

Witter Bynner

WITTER BYNNER was born in Brooklyn, New York, August 10, 1881. After graduation from Harvard in 1902, he became assistant editor of

WITTER BYNNER

American-Indian art and poetry. His house in Santa Fe, New Mexico, is a museum of Chinese carvings in wood and jade, long scrolls of Chinese paintings, together with Indian jars, Mexican serapes, and Navajo rugs. Two books of verse published in 1929 reflect these interests. One of the books, prepared in collaboration with Kiang Kang-Hu, is *Jade Mountain*, a Chinese anthology in English translation, being three hundred poems of the T'ang dynasty; the other, *Indian Earth*, in which he transcribes the spirit of the ritual of the American Indian.

Mr. Bynner has also translated Euripides' *Iphigenia in Tauris* (1915) and Charles Vildrac's *Book of Love* (1923). *A Book of Plays* was published in 1922 and *Cake*, a play, in 1926. He edited in 1931 *The Sonnets of Frederick Goddard Tuckerman*, a forgotten New England poet, 1821-1877.

He is described as a tall man with a high shining bald forehead, sparkling eyes, and a loud infectious laugh. He is adept at the piano, playing and singing with a refreshing gusto.

JAMES BRANCH CABELL

James Branch Cabell

JAMES BRANCH CABELL was born in Richmond, Virginia, April 14, 1879. His family had been residents of Virginia since colonial days. After attending private school he entered William and Mary College; he was an instructor in Latin and Greek there from 1896 to 1898, and was graduated in 1898 with a Phi Beta Kappa key and other awards of high scholarship.

Cabell's first position was on the *Richmond Times*. The following year he went to New York and reported on the *New York Herald* from 1899 until 1901, when he returned to Richmond and worked on the *News*. He spent the period from 1902 to 1910 in writing, and his first magazine stories and books appeared in these years. He worked in the coal mines of West Virginia from 1911 to 1913, and upon his return to Virginia interested himself in genealogical and historical research and in his writing. He was appointed Genealogist of the Virginia chapter of the Sons of the Revolution, and subsequently has held several other offices as genealogist or historian of various clubs and organizations.

Cabell and Miss Priscilla Bradley, also of Virginia, were married in 1913; they have one son, Ballard Hartwell Cabell.

The Cabell family live quietly in Richmond. Cabell is regarded by Richmond as an enigma; he is genuinely shy, blushes easily, and maintains a distinct aloofness toward all except a few close friends. He consented to join the Virginia Writers' Club when it was founded, and was president from 1918 to 1921, but he attended few meetings and could never be prevailed upon to speak at banquets or any social gatherings.

Mr. Cabell says that no one can decipher his handwriting and therefore he does his own typing. He makes no carbon copy, and the one which goes to the printer is the only manuscript complete with revisions. *The Silver Stallion* fell out of the mail-bag when the bag was put on the train at the small station of Dumbarton, and the manuscript lay unnoticed in the ditch for thirty-six hours before it was discovered.

Most of Cabell's books belong to a

series which is referred to collectively as the *Biography of Manuel.* It is the history of an imaginary but perfectly constructed medieval country, Poictesme, seen in Cabell's mind so minutely that he has drawn maps of the country and has given it the traditions and the trappings of a royal state. The characters, allegorical, symbolic, philosophic figures, trace the lineage of the nobility of the country from Dom Manuel, Count of Poictesme, to his Virginia descendants. The scheme of the novels is built round the author's conception of human life, that it is a comedy perpetually reënacted in the birth, aspirations, successes, failures and death of man and his progeny.

Altho a number of books had appeared before *Jurgen* (1919), it was not until the suppression of this book that Cabell was nationally known. Immediately his works were attacked, and strong antagonists and champions were created who bitterly attacked and defended "Cabellianism." Cabell said at the time of the book's suppression: "Should *Jurgen* be remembered ten years hence, it will, thru being remembered be amply exonerated: whereas if *Jurgen* be forgotten, the book will then of course be violating nobody's moral sensibility."

The chronological history of Cabell's Poictesme does not follow the sequence of the publication of the books: *The Eagle's Shadow* (1904); *The Line of Love* (1905); *Gallantry* (1907); *Chivalry* (1909); *The Cords of Vanity* (1909); *The Soul of Melicent* (1913) (reissued in 1920 as *Domnei*); *The Rivet in Grandfather's Neck* (1915); *From the Hidden Way* (verse, 1916); *The Certain Hour* (1916); *The Cream of the Jest* (1907); *Beyond Life* (1919); *Jurgen* (1919); *Figures of Earth* (1921); *The High Place* (1923); *Straws and Prayerbooks* (1924); *The Music from behind the Moon* (1926); *The Silver Stallion* (1926); *Something about Eve* (1927); *The White Robe* (1928); *Way of Ecben* (1929); and *Some of Us* (1930).

The Way of Ecben was announced as Cabell's swan song in the writing of novels; *Some of Us* is subtitled *An Essay in Epitaphs,* and contains appreciations of other writers, including Elinor Wylie, Frances Newman, H. L. Mencken, Sinclair Lewis, and Joseph Hergesheimer.

Morley Callaghan

MORLEY CALLAGHAN was born in Toronto. He is of Irish descent, several generations away from Ireland. He is short and sturdy, and frequently smiles. He has thick black curling hair and blue eyes.

MORLEY CALLAGHAN

He went to school in Toronto and was graduated from St. Michael's College of the University of Toronto. Later he was a reporter on the *Toronto Daily Star,* and later still the proprietor of a lending library in his native city. He was graduated from the law school there and has become a member of the Canadian Bar.

He first encountered and was encouraged by Ernest Hemingway when the latter was on the *Star.* Callaghan later sent one of his stories to Hemingway in Paris. Four months later the story was returned with an encouraging note from Ford Madox Ford, who was then editing the *Transatlantic Review* in Paris.

Some time later *transition* published a story entitled "Last Spring They Came Over." His next story was published in *This Quarter.* Ezra Pound, at the time editing *The Exile* in Italy, published one of Callaghan's stories. His next stories were published in *The American Caravan.* It was these stories that attracted the attention of his publishers-to-be.

Two stories were printed in *Scribner's Magazine* and aroused great interest. Then his first novel, *Strange Fugitive* (1928), was published, followed by a collection of his stories, *A Native Argosy* (1929), and a second novel, *It's Never Over* (1930). *No Man's Meat* (Paris, 1931) is a series of long-short stories.

At school Mr. Callaghan boxed, played football, and forsook cricket in order to pitch on a baseball team. At college he was interested in public speaking and debating. He won a debate on free speech. In the summers during college he worked, sometimes selling subscriptions for magazines. His wandering about Canada gave him the opportunity to exercise his talent for observation.

Henry Seidel Canby

HENRY SEIDEL CANBY was born September 6, 1878, in Wilmington, Delaware, where his family, which came to America with William Penn, settled several generations before. He says of himself that he "is a Quaker by inherited temperament, an Epicurean by taste and desire." Spiritually he resembles his ancestors, who "wore plain clothing for the soul's sake, but bought expensive books and admirable furniture."

After attending Friend's School, a famous old preparatory school in Wilmington, Delaware, he went to Yale. An early interest in mining engineering determined his entering the Sheffield Scientific School at Yale. He attended the academic department also, and later added graduate work English to his scientific training. He taught composition while in the graduate school, and after receiving a Ph.D. from Yale had charge of Freshman English.

He is still on the Yale faculty altho on a temporary leave of absence, but expects to conduct a course there again beginning in the fall of 1931.

Dr. Canby spent 1918 in England. He had gone abroad in governmental service during the war and was in England, France, and Ireland for some time. Being in Ireland for a few weeks when it was at its worst in political upheaval, he wrote some keenly analytical criticisms of the situation there. *Education by Violence* was written as the result of his experiences during the war.

He has lectured at Cambridge and other universities abroad, as well as at the University of California and a number of American colleges.

Dr. Wilbur Cross, former Dean of the Graduate School of Yale who was elected Governor of Connecticut in November 1930, started the *Yale Review* in 1911, with Dr. Canby as Assistant Editor; Dr. Canby held this position until 1920 when he was asked to edit the *Lit-*

HENRY SEIDEL CANBY

erary Review of the *New York Evening Post* at its inception.

In 1924 Dr. Canby and his editorial staff on the *Literary Review,* including Christopher Morley and William Rose Benét, organized the *Saturday Review of Literature,* of which Dr. Canby is still editor-in-chief and Mrs. Canby editor of the Children's Book Department.

Dr. Canby's policy, as shown in the *Saturday Review of Literature,* is "catholic in criticism, comprehensive in scope, sound, stimulating and accurate." In starting the *Saturday Review* he was meeting the need he felt for a journal, not of opinion but of authority and honesty of perception in regard to literature, which would bridge the gulf between the academic and the literary world.

Dr. Canby's many books include *Definitions;* essays in contemporary criticism (1923), 2d series, (1924); *Better Writing* (1926); and *American Estimates* (1929). He is joint editor of *Winston's Simplified Dictionary* (1928), and, with John Drinkwater and William Rose Benét, edited *Twentieth-Century Poetry* in 1929.

Dr. Canby has also edited volumes of Masefield's poems and Shakespeare's works. In 1921 he and Mr. Benét edited

Saturday Papers, essays on literature from the *Literary Review.*

Dr. and Mrs. Canby live in New York most of the winter months and divide the rest of the year between Hamden, just outside of New Haven, and a home in northern Connecticut. One son is in Yale University and the other in preparatory school.

Dorothy Canfield

DOROTHY CANFIELD'S books are about the experiences all of us go thru but which many writers don't think worth writing about. She is a Ph.D. of romance languages, has had the advantages of much international travel, and was the first woman on the Vermont State Board of Education, but her values are always the ordinary human values of universal experience.

She is an American of New England descent. Her family came to America in 1636, moved to Vermont in 1764 and have owned land there ever since. Her father, James Hulme Canfield, was an educator, a college professor, and President of two State Universities. A Vermonter by birth and New Yorker by residence, he went west after graduating from Williams College, and was profes-

DOROTHY CANFIELD

sor at the State University of Kansas, where on February 17, 1879, his daughter Dorothea Francis was born. When ten years old she was sent to Paris for a year's schooling, and from that time on her education was partly carried on in France and partly in this country. She got her A.B. at Ohio State University in Columbus, during the time her father was President there. She studied for her doctor's degree at the Sorbonne and Columbia University.

In 1907 she married John R. Fisher and they went to live on one of the Canfield farms at Arlington, Vermont. The small old house is on the side of Red Mountain, two miles from the village, with a spring at the front door. Below the house to the south stretches the valley of the Battenkill, with the Green Mountains beyond, up behind it the steep slope of Red Mountain on part of which Mr. Fisher has planted many acres of pine trees. On the farms up and down the valley are people still living, as Mrs. Fisher does, on land which has belonged for many generations to the same family, to many of whom she is distantly related by blood and closely by ties of inherited, faithful friendship.

Her first book was a study of Corneille and Racine; her second, a text book for English classes, written with Professor George Carpenter of Columbia.

The Squirrel-Cage, a novel about middle-western life, was published in 1912. The following winter Mr. and Mrs. Fisher and their little daughter Sally spent in Rome. She became very much interested in Dr. Montessori's work, and on her return to America she wrote, at Dr. Montessori's request, *A Montessori Mother,* which told American mothers and teachers just what this system of child training was and how it could be applied in American homes and schools. It filled such a need that mothers all over the country wrote to her asking for advice and help in this or that particular case. As a sort of round robin answer to these letters, she wrote *Mothers and Children.*

In 1915 *Hillsboro People,* a collection of stories about Vermont people, and her second novel, *The Bent Twig,* were published; the following spring, *The*

Real Motive, another collection of short stories.

Both Mr. and Mrs. Fisher had been so intimately associated with France that the outbreak of the war was as terrible to them as if the United States had been invaded. Early in 1916 Mr. Fisher entered the ambulance service and sailed for France. Mrs. Fisher stayed in the United States for a few months during which she wrote *Understood Betsy.* In August 1916, she, with her two children, went to Paris and immediately became absorbed in war relief work. As her little daughter had been very ill with typhoid fever, Mrs. Fisher spent most of the year of 1918 in southern France. It was here, while Sally was convalescing, that the stories published in *Home Fires of France* and *The Day of Glory,* stories of the French people who kept the daily life of France going on during the war, were written. Her house was always open for refugees, and under the greatest difficulties she established, during that year, a large Convalescent Home for delicate children which a French charitable organization took over later.

In the spring of 1919, the family returned to the United States, tired mentally and physically from the strain of life in France. But the Arlington home, the gardening, the planting of new pine trees brought the needed rest, and after a good many months, Mrs. Fisher began her novel, *The Brimming Cup* (1921).

During 1921 and 1922, Mrs. Fisher was working on a translation from the Italian (Papini's *Life of Christ*—published 1923) and on *Rough-Hewn* (1922). In the spring of 1923 the family went to Europe and spent the following year in France and Switzerland. *Raw Material* was published in the fall of 1923; *The Home-Maker* in 1924; *Made-to-Order Stories* in 1925; *Her Son's Wife* in 1926; *Why Stop Learning?* a book about adult education, in 1927; and *The Deepening Stream* in 1930. The title of this last novel sounds the key-note. The stream of ordinary average unsensational life deepens as it is lived by an inherently fine woman.

Karel Capek

KAREL CAPEK was born in 1890 in the mountains of Northern Bohemia, and his father, a physician, encouraged him in his studies, especially in natural science. He studied philosophy in Prague, Berlin, and Paris, and read William James and John Dewey. He says: "American philosophy influenced me most." He published a book on philosophy, translated French poetry, wrote, in collaboration with his brother Joseph, short stories and humorous articles, and then in 1911 began his first play, *The Robber,* a drama of young love and adventure, which was not completed until 1920. His next play was *R. U. R.,* depicting the rebellion of the mechanical "robots," and then came *The Life of the Insects,* a satirical presentation of the human comedy, written in collaboration with his brother, and produced in New York as *The World We Live In.* Capek's next play was *The Makropoulos Secret,* an amusing drama dealing with the possibility of prolonging human life. But his own opinion is, "A short life is better for mankind, for a long life would deprive man of his optimism."

KAREL CAPEK

He has written two novels which have been published in America—*The Absolute at Large,* a satirical romance showing how a marvelous scientific discovery throws into confusion the industrial, political, and religious life of modern times; and *Krakatit,* the fantastic story of a man who discovers an explosive of such horrible potentialities that he endures persecution and peril rather than give up his secret. He is also the author of *A Criticism of Words, Letters from England, Letters from Italy, Money and Other Stories,* etc.

Capek's home is in Prague and there he is preeminently the great producer. He was at first associated with the National Art Theater of Prague, the greatest of Czech institutions, which was built with money gathered in every town and hamlet of Bohemia. Capek, as art director, put on ambitious productions at this theater which attracted notice thruout Europe. Then he broke away and established his own playhouse, the Vinohradsky Art Theater, and here he continues making dramatic history, producing Shakespeare, Byron, Molière, Ibsen, Strindberg, Goethe, Hauptmann, and many of the young Czech authors, also.

Capek has won recognition, then in several fields—as short story writer, novelist, dramatist, manager and producer, but he says, "I think I have more ahead of me than behind me." He is described as dark, slender, and wiry, modest and rather hesitating in manner, but vigorous and biting in speech.

Willa Cather

WILLA SIBERT CATHER was born near Winchester, Virginia, December 7, 1876. Her books deal with the west, however, and her association with the west is so strong that she has been described by an Englishman as a "characteristic" American, because over twenty years of residence in New York City have not robbed her of her western accent and bearing.

Her family, originally English, had been granted lands in Ireland by the crown in appreciation for its loyalty to

WILLA CATHER

the Stuart cause. Her great-grandfather emigrated to America from there and settled in Frederick County, Virginia, where her grandfather, her father, and herself were born.

At the age of eight Willa Cather was taken from this strictly English community and "transplanted" to a ranch in Nebraska. The new land fascinated the girl, "a tomboy with a charming open face, obstinate blue eyes, and shingled red-brown hair." Her days were spent roaming the prairie, riding her pony twelve miles over the rough red grass of the Divide to get the mail for her family and the other settlers. She grasped the opportunity to play with the other children, Scandinavian, Bohemian, German, French or Russian, and to learn the ways of the foreigner and the pioneer; there was also the excitement of constant danger from prairie fires, droughts, or blizzards.

There was no elementary school near and she was taught at home. She was fond of reading the English classics to her two grandmothers at night; she learned Latin early and easily, and enjoyed Virgil particularly.

Miss Cather attended high school in Red Cloud, Nebraska, a little town named for the famous Sioux warrior, when her family removed there. After graduation she went to the University of Nebraska, where she partially supported herself by working on a newspaper. She was graduated in 1895 and a desire to live in a more highly civilized community where she would have greater advantages and be able to attend concerts brought her east. Music has always been one of Miss Cather's principal pleasures.

Having friends in Pittsburgh, Miss Cather went there and was appointed telegraph editor and dramatic critic of the *Daily Leader*. She held this position until 1901 when she accepted that of head of the English department of the Allegheny high school. She began to write for publication at this time, and poems appeared from time to time in magazines. A book of verse, *April Twilights*, was published in 1903. *The Troll Garden* (1905), a collection of prose stories, received such favorable notice that Miss Cather was offered an editorship on *McClure's Magazine* in 1906; she was managing editor from 1908 to 1912.

During the years she was on *McClure's* she travelled extensively abroad and in southwestern United States. Conscious of a great homesickness for the flat stretches of the prairies when away from this country, she returned to Wyoming and Nebraska on all vacations. She relates that she tried to live in France, but her nostalgia was so great that she haunted the wheatfields and cried silently when she watched the harvesting.

Since leaving *McClure's*, Miss Cather has written a number of books, each of which has added to her prestige and brought her, quietly but surely, to her present high place in American letters. She lives a retired life among her books, paintings of Italy and the Southwest, autographed photographs of singers and writers of international fame, and lithographs of Czechoslovakia. She is unmarried.

Miss Cather's spirit and personality are as distinct and vivid as when she was a child, and her eyes still as blue and fearless. She is known for her gentle frankness in speech, and for her loyalty to her friends. She regards among her closest friends the ones she knew in childhood in the West.

Many of Miss Cather's books have been translated into French and Czech; her complete works, which are as follows, have been translated into Swedish: *April Twilights* (1903); *The Troll Garden* (1905); *The Bohemian Girl* (a novelette, 1912); *Alexander's Bridge* (1912); *O Pioneers!* (1913); *The Song of the Lark* (1915); *My Antonia* (1918); *Youth and the Bright Medusa* (1920); *One of Ours*, which won the Pulitzer Prize for 1922; *A Lost Lady* (1923); *The Professor's House* (1925); *Death Comes for the Archbishop* (1927).

Maristan Chapman

WITH a background that other novelists might envy, Maristan Chapman joins the pioneers who are making literature out of native American material. She was born in Chattanooga, Tennessee, in the edge of the mountain land of which she writes, in 1895. Her father entered the ministry at Sewanee a few years later, and her childhood was spent in many parishes. In her teens she taught in a Blue Ridge mission school which she helped her mother to conduct. When the War came, she was suddenly transplanted to England. There she

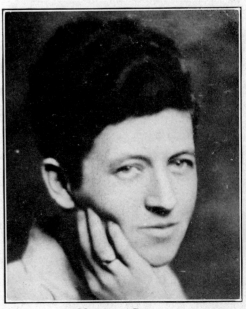

MARISTAN CHAPMAN

served as secretary to a member of Parliament, engaged in nursing, lectured on business science in war training schools, became a secretary in the British aircraft service, married an engineer, and was sent to America to inspect airplane motors at Dayton.

It was not until after the War that she returned to the Hills of Tennessee and formed the friendships which were to give her the materials for *The Happy Mountain* (1928) and *Homeplace* (1929). Already writing had been her secret preoccupation for years, and during the period that followed, which was spent in camping among the mountains and roaming about the South in a Ford, her articles for papers and magazines added materially to the Chapman resources. In 1924 the Ford became a house-car, which she and her engineer husband designed and built themselves; they named it The Nomad and spent two years on the road in it, writing and doing odd jobs. Finally they returned to Sewanee and bought Neverland, "a downgone barn of a house surrounded by seven acres of unkempt land," where *The Happy Mountain* was written.

Explaining the basic motivation of her work, she writes:

"Born in the east Tennessee mountains, on the edge of the Cumberlands, and forever coming back to them in the intervals of a miscellaneous life, I have been haunted always by the southern highlanders' need of a recorder. Driven to frenzy of outland interpretation, I at last took up the work of their defense.

"I try to get soundness and sureness into the simple stories of the mountain people as they are. They have strength and simplicity and much fun, self-reliance, and complete lack of self-pity. Mostly they have fun, and no happening of life can disturb them. My object is to show a class of people, too long looked upon only *as* a class, to be live and knowing individuals; to make their eyes the eyes thru which the outlander may see their world, and, thus seeing, experience an understanding kinship with them, and at the same time feel a sense of adventure for himself in seeing an unexplored corner of life."

Miss Chapman's *Imperial Brother*, the Life of the Duc de Morny (1931), a statesman of the Second Empire, will be followed by a new mountain novel.

Sheldon Cheney

SHELDON WARREN CHENEY is a Californian, born in Berkeley on June 29, 1886. This lean stooped gentleman with the kindly blue eyes somewhat resembles those portraits of "the absent-minded professor" of the undergraduate magazines; but here the comparison ends. Far from being a dusty pedant, Mr. Cheney is one of the most vigorous champions of the 20th century Renaissance.

After graduation from the University of California in 1908, Mr. Cheney became dramatic and art critic for various newspapers and magazines. He married Maud Meurice Turner of Berkeley in 1910. They have three children.

Founder of the *Theatre Arts Magazine* in 1916, Mr. Cheney served also as its editor until 1921 when he became a dramatic critic and free lance writer for other journals and magazines. He is the author of some half dozen books, dealing with the theatre. He is the friend of Gordon Craig and Max Reinhardt.

Believing that the drama traces the courses of various civilizations, Mr. Cheney advises the student of world history not to neglect this phase of social development. He contends that we are

SHELDON CHENEY

approaching a new era in the world theatre, similar to the classic and Elizabethan periods. His research into world stage craft has recently concentrated his interest on the relation of architecture to the theatre.

Mr. Cheney's *The New World Architecture* (1930) is a volume containing some 300 illustrations of modern world architecture, from samples of our own Frank Lloyd Wright's creations to the work of the Vienna Secessionists. Mr. Cheney argues the cause of the moderns in opposition to the architectural traditions of the past 500 years.

A list of the author's works includes: *The New Movement in the Theatre, The Open Air Theatre, The Art Theatre,* and *Stage Decoration.* His *Modern Art and the Theatre* was published in 1921 and *A Primer of Modern Art* appeared two years later. In 1929 Mr. Cheney's *The Theatre: 3000 Years of Drama, Acting and Stagecraft* was published. It is considered one of the most comprehensive surveys known upon the subject.

During the past few years, Mr. Cheney has been traveling in Europe, gathering material on the theatre, and studying production methods and architecture.

G. K. Chesterton

"**I** AM one of those people," says Gilbert Keith Chesterton, "who believe that you've got to be dominated by your moral slant. I'm no art-for-art's-sake man. I am quite incapable of talking or writing about Dutch gardens or the game of chess, but if I did, I have no doubt that what I would say or write about them would be colored by my view of the cosmos."

Gilbert Keith Chesterton, English author and journalist, poet, pamphleteer, propagandist, was born in London May 29, 1874. He attended St. Paul's where, he says, much of his time was spent in writing poor poetry rather than in working.

Chesterton thought his interests lay in art rather than in literature, and in 1891 enrolled in the Slade School of Art. As a result he has illustrated at least half a dozen of his books with cartoons, and

G. K. CHESTERTON

his first book was a collection of jingles and sketches, *Greybeards at Play.* On being asked to write art criticism for the London *Bookman,* G. K. C. found that he enjoyed the expression of his ideas by pen rather than by paint and brush. He began to contribute also to the *Speaker,* and since that time has contributed scores of articles to periodicals in both England and America; from 1905 to 1930 he wrote an essay a week for the *Illustrated London News,* missing only two numbers in the quarter-century.

Miss Frances Blogg and Chesterton were married in 1901. They lived in London for a short while, then moved to a cottage at Beaconsfield in Buckinghamshire, some thirty miles from the metropolis. One of the author's earliest memories is a theater that his father constructed with his own hands. The main part of Chesterton's own home, "Top Meadows," consists of a huge living room probably a hundred feet long, with a raised stage at one end.

Chesterton has retained the enthusiasm and the frankness of a child. His frame is massive, and he easily dominates any company. He gives the impression of complete disregard for personal appearance, with his unkempt curly hair, his shaggy reddish-brown moustache, and his careless clothes. With G. B. S. he shares the distinction of being known almost everywhere by his initials alone.

Chesterton began his career as a pamphleteer during the Boer War. At that time he considered himself a Liberal in politics. During the struggle from 1898 to 1901 in Ireland, Hilaire Belloc, his lifelong friend and collaborator, Chesterton's brother Cecil, and G. K. C. founded the *New Witness* for the purpose of attacking political corruption. Reacting from Socialism, they later propagated theories which they named Distributism. *G. K. C.s' Weekly* is the official voice of the Distributist League, which advocates the small farmer system, the "widest possible ownership of property, more particularly the ownership and actual use of agricultural land."

The event of most significance in Chesterton's life was his conversion to the Roman Catholic Church in 1922. This did not indicate a change in his views in any respect, but rather a confirmation of the spiritual and intellectual development of his doctrines as expressed in his writings from *Heretics* (1905), in which his religious views are negative, and its positive complement, *Orthodoxy* (1908), to date.

From February to June 1930 Chesterton lectured at the University of Notre Dame, South Bend, Indiana. The university conferred an honorary LL.D. on him at its graduation exercises.

The sheer volume of Chesterton's works is amazing. His versatility is shown in the following titles, which include poetry, biography, history, detective stories and other fiction, and political and critical essays: *The Wild Knight* (1900), poetry; *Robert Browning* (1903) and *Charles Dickens* (1906); *The Man Who Was Thursday* (1908), fiction; *Magic* (1913), a play which had a successful run in London; the *Father Brown* series (1911, 1914, 1926, 1927), detective stories; *A Short History of England* (1917); *The Everlasting Man* (1925), a literary and controversial outline of history; *The Judgment of Dr. Johnson* (1927), a play; *New and Collected Poems* (1929); *Generally Speaking* (1929), essays; and *Come to Think of It* (1930), essays.

A. B. Chrisman

ARTHUR BOWIE CHRISMAN'S ancestors made the first permanent settlement west of the Blue Ridge mountains. He is a Virginian by birth and choice, farming at White Post in the Shenandoah Valley, "in Stonewall Jackson's Granary, as we call it." He is very proud of the massive oak trees that surround his house. The old road from Winchester to Alexandria—Braddock's Road, now in disuse—runs thru his family's woods.

He was born near White Post on July 16, 1889. For two years he studied electrical engineering at Virginia Polytechnic Institute (1906-1908).

In his youth he went to Los Angeles, lured by the moving-pictures. This escapade was to exert a great influence on the course of his life, chiefly because he lived next door to a Chinese boarding house in a poor section of the city, where he made friends with "a wise and kindly man of China," who awoke his interest in Chinese life and literature.

"Movie extra" is listed among Mr. Chrisman's occupations; he was also draftsman, farmer, lecturer, story teller, and a school teacher for two years. He is unmarried.

Soon after Mr. Chrisman began to write humorous and children's stories for magazines and newspapers, he was at

A. B. CHRISMAN

work on a book. It was a children's book, because "there are too many books for grown-ups; not enough for children." The book, published in 1925, was called *Shen of the Sea*, a volume of Chinese legends. It was illustrated by Else Hasselriis of Copenhagen, who revived the art of the silhouette in Europe, and it was awarded the Newbery Medal at the American Library Association convention in Atlantic City the following year, with Fenton T. Newbery (a great-grandson of "the father of children's books") in attendance.

The Wind That Wouldn't Blow (1927), "stories of the merry Middle Kingdom for children, and myself," was his second collection of Chinese tales, again illustrated by Else Hasselriis.

Mr. Chrisman wants to tell stories in the way he remembers he liked to have stories told to him. "Goodness only knows how well I succeeded," he says. "But anyhow I spent many pleasant hours in writing my books. Say what you please, I made the world a trifle merrier for *one* person. Now then, the question is who'll say 'Two' ? "

Mr. Chrisman is studying American folk stories and intends some day to explore this fertile territory in his books for children.

Paul Claudel

ON Christmas Day, 1886, a French youth of eighteen entered the cathedral of Notre Dame in Paris and became converted to the Catholic religion. He was Paul Claudel, who had spent his childhood among people indifferent to religion at Villeneuve-sur-Fère, where he was born August 6, 1868. He had recently been forced to watch the lingering death of his grandfather whose body was undermined by cancer and Claudel's soul had been stirred and torn by pity. When he attended the Christmas mass he experienced a revelation: "In one moment," he says, "my heart was touched and I believed. God exists, He is here. He is Somebody, He is just as personal a being as I." This experience inspired his credo: "Be thanked, O Lord, Who have delivered me from the idol and

PAUL CLAUDEL

made me to adore You alone and not Isis and Osiris, or justice or progress or truth or divinity or the laws of nature or art or beauty. . ." And because he had been brought so near to God he felt he could even joke with him: "Heroes, saints, martyrs, virgins, You have galore, O Lord. But if you want to save a lazybones and a moron, an unclean, ungrateful, overweening, low-minded fellow, here am I, take me!"

Claudel took a law degree, receiving his education at the Lycée Louis-le-Grand, and at the age of 24 entered the French diplomatic service, assuming his first post in 1893 as vice-consul at New York. His service continued with a period spent at Boston, and thence he was transferred in 1899 to Fou-Tchéou, where he became a consul. In 1906 he was appointed First Secretary at Pekin and three years later he was sent to Prague. He was made Consul-General at Frankfurt in 1911 and was moved to Hamburg in 1913. His next appointment, which came in 1916, was as Minister at Rio-de-Janeiro, and three years later he was sent to Copenhagen in the same capacity. Claudel was made Ambassador to Japan in 1921 and he remained at Tokio until 1926, when he was appointed Ambassador to the United States.

In the course of his diplomatic career,

Claudel has found time for considerable writing. His chief works are ten dramas, referred to as "musical prose poems endowed with symbolic meaning." These dramas, however, have not been successfully produced; only three of them have reached the stage. One of these is *L'Annonce Faite à Marie* (1912), which was the rewritten version of *La Jeune Fille Violaine,* an early work. *L'Annonce* has been translated into English (*The Tidings Brought to Mary*) and was produced by the Theatre Guild in 1922.

Claudel began his literary career with a drama, *Tête d'Or,* written before his conversion. This work had a pagan quality. Following the conversion his work assumed a profoundly religious tone and he wrote *La Ville,* a drama which expresses the theory that every society which is not based on divine law must be miserable. The works that followed are all inspired by his own Catholic faith. Each drama has a specific idea underlying it, yet the same general thought underlies them all: that modern society errs in destroying the Catholic unity at the pleasure of individual caprices. The other plays are: *L'Échange,* written in 1893-94 while Claudel was in New York and Boston; *La Repose du Septième Jour,* written in China; *Le Partage du Midi* (1906), *L'Otage* (1911), and *Le Père Humile.*

As a youth Claudel was strongly influenced by Arthur Rimbaud, a French writer who was an abnormal neurotic. Two other factors in moulding his life and writings were the Bible and Æschylus. A mystic, he sees God, but being a poet, he sees nature, too. He writes: "Every tree has its character, every little animal its task, every voice its part in the symphony; as one says that one understands music, do I understand nature. Years ago I discovered with delight that all things are bound together in a certain harmony and my eye proves to me the secret relationship by which the black of this pine is married to the light green of that maple, and insofar as I re-establish the primordial plan, I call my visit a supervision. I am the inspector of creation, I examine everything that exists; the steadfastness of the world is my beatitude."

Claudel has a verse and a metre of his own which, he explains, is based on breathing. He is rich in metaphors. Fed on the Bible and Rimbaud, he constructed his "verse paragraph," a highly flexible medium which is "plastic enough to serve at once the dramatist and the poet." Like Rimbaud he is objective; he thinks with his senses. Claudel is rather difficult; a critic even called that trait his great merit, "for the Anglo-Saxon public likes books over which it can ruminate." He is not unaware of the fact that he is difficult: "I lay great stress on my *Art Poétique,* which has not been understood by anybody, so to say."

Other Claudel works include: *La Connaissance de l'Est, Cinq Grandes Odes, Vers d'Exil, La Nuit de Noël, Poemes de Guerre.* Claudel is married and has five children. He has been the recipient of many awards, including the French Legion of Honor. His residence is still the French Embassy, Washington, D.C.

Robert M. Coates

R OBERT M. COATES was born in New Haven, Connecticut, in 1897. His father was an inventor and engineer, whose profession sent him and his family to all parts of the country. Robert began his travels at the age of seven.

ROBERT M. COATES

Coates was graduated from Yale College in 1919. *The New Republic* published a sonnet by him when he was still an undergraduate, and he had visions of being a poet, but after graduation he became instead a writer of publicity. He managed to get across to Europe, and for a year or so his great frame with its shock of red hair was one of the sights of Paris. He is over six feet tall. "His great, baggy, flapping clothes, his barge-like figure, his gentle blue eyes and his red hair impinge unforgettably upon the most jaded retinas," reads one impression.

His first book, *The Eater of Darkness,* was published in Paris and later (1929) republished in this country. It has been described as the first Dada novel in English.

The Outlaw Years (1930), the history of the land pirates of the Natchez Trace, was begun in 1927, and Coates expected to complete it in six months. It took him three years, in the course of which he went over the Natchez Trace, the overland trade route running thru Kentucky, Tennessee, and Mississippi, where the famous outlaws operated from about 1800 to 1835.

Coates has been writing "Profiles" and "Talk of the Town" articles for *The New Yorker.* He contributed an essay called "Leviathan, or the Future of Ocean Travel," to *Whither, Whither, or After Sex What?* (1930), a symposium to end symposiums. He is married to the well known medallist, Elsa Kirpal. They live in New York City and in the country near Brewster, New York, where he built his own house.

James Thurber contributes this potpourri of additional information about Mr. Coates, who "doesn't like to talk about himself": He was on the Lit Board at Yale; flew planes during the war; boxed with Ernest Hemingway; discussed Henry James with Gertrude Stein (and incidentally introduced Hemingway to Miss Stein); is an authority on modern French writers; has read Gerard de Nerval but not Willa Cather; likes the *Saturday Evening Post,* Bach fugues, Negro blues, Jimmy Durante, the poetry of Hart Crane, Mahonri Young; enjoys reading dictionaries, histories of Ireland, Flaubert, trade journals, the printing on cans of preserved vegetables, the *Graphic,* old clippings about Gerald Chapman, and interviews with Sam Langford; loves calamai (octopus), stewed plums, and strega; haunts five-and-ten cent stores and factories; explores the basements of state-houses and the dim back-stage regions of puppet shows; and spends whole afternoons throwing an ice-pick at a bull's-eye on a barndoor, hitting it regularly."

Elizabeth J. Coatsworth

ELIZABETH J. COATSWORTH was born in Buffalo, New York, in 1893. All her life she has been an indefatigable traveler. Her childhood was spent in Buffalo, where she received her early education; she was graduated from Vassar in 1915 and did graduate work at Columbia and the University of California; in 1929 she married Henry Beston, author of *Outermost House* and other books; they live in Hingham, Massachusetts, in an old house overlooking the sea.

A detailed account of the travels Miss Coatsworth has squeezed into her years would make a long story in itself. She knows, as a leisurely visitor, not as a tourist, England, France, Spain, Italy, Greece, Egypt, Morocco, Japan, China, Mexico, Yucatan, the Philippines. Her writing is full of the memories of these places. She has tramped over a good deal of New England and motored thru southern California and Arizona. Her

ELIZABETH J. COATSWORTH

studio in Hingham is full of evidences of her varied friendships and interests: Chinese statues, Indian carvings, old maps, modern wood prints. Besides all this, she is very fond of dogs and cats and horses and gardens.

Despite her wanderings round the world, Miss Coatsworth has done a remarkable amount of work. It is said that she has had more poetry printed in current magazines than any young poet alive today. She has also published several books of poems, several books for boys and girls, short stories in the *Atlantic Monthly* and elsewhere, and travel writings in *Asia* and other periodicals.

Miss Coatsworth began as a poet with *Fox Footprints* (1923), a collection of imagistic poems that show an Oriental influence. *Atlas and Beyond* (1924) contains a number of poems inspired by Miss Coatsworth's travels abroad. *Compass Rose* (1929) was her third book of verse, a miscellaneous group of poems about many lands, episodes, and moods.

As a writer of books for children, Miss Coatsworth has produced *The Cat and the Captain* (1927); *Toutou in Bondage* (1929), the adventures of a fox-terrier in Morocco; *The Boy with the Parrot* (1929), a story of Guatemala; and *The Cat Who Went to Heaven* (1930), a tale of Japan. *The Sun's Diary* (1929) is "a book of days for any year."

Irvin S. Cobb

IRVIN SHREWSBURY COBB was born in Paducah, Kentucky, on June 23, 1876, and spent most of his early days there. "In my youth," he says, "I was the Younger Bohemian Set of Paducah." He began his journalistic career in his home town, reporting on the local papers, and writing for comic weeklies on the side, and by the time he was nineteen years old had become the editor of the *Paducah News*.

He was married to Laura Spencer Baker of Savannah, Georgia, in 1900, and after a few more years of reporting he began to hear the inevitable voice of the city that every small town boy knows, and so one day he packed up his trunk and set out for New York, sending his wife and small daughter to stay with her parents in Savannah until he should be settled. It was she, more than anyone else, who "pushed him over the edge," as it were, when he was undecided about leaving for New York. "She had ten times my nerve," Mr. Cobb has since remarked.

Every small-town newspaper worker who ventures to New York expecting to gain new laurels finds the first six months the most trying. Irvin S. Cobb was no exception. He had, in fact, more trouble than most. Arriving in New York on an August evening in 1904, Cobb spent the first two weeks calling at newspaper offices in search of reportorial work.

Mr. Cobb left Paducah with two hundred dollars in his pocket, a tidy sum for expenses a quarter century ago. But this steadily decreased as he walked the streets seeking a job. He stayed at a hotel the first night, but the next morning, upon making inquiry about the rates, removed his trunk to a hall bedroom on West Fifty-Seventh Street.

While sitting on a bench in Madison Square at noontime pondering what he had best do, the thought passed thru his mind that he might write a plain

IRVIN S. COBB

letter to the editor of each paper; for he had been kept in the ante room of the big offices and denied the opportunity of meeting the chief scribes personally. Accordingly, he addressed the editors of thirteen leading papers tersely and with candor. He wrote each editor the same letter, neatly typewritten, saying among other things that he was in dead earnest and "had grown tired of studying the wall paper design in the anteroom." The whole letter was nothing short of a frank tho flippant statement of facts, couched in the soon-to-be-popular Cobb style. The recipients in each case weren't nearly so much shocked as they were amused, and five of the lot thought the note was clever enough to warrant an offer of a job. All of the propositions looked good to Cobb as they came rolling into his rooming house. He accepted the *Evening Sun* from the list.

As a tryout, he was given a place on the telegraph desk editing dispatches, at fifteen dollars a week. This was just half of what he received in Paducah. He wired his wife that he had a job, but refrained from telling her at what salary, reserving this blow for a letter. "Then I treated myself to a good cigar and sat in City Hall Park and smoked it," the Genial Paducan reminisced. Later he was put on the eight o'clock morning edition with a five-dollar-a-week raise. Shortly afterward he received a murder story over the telephone.

Instead of turning his notes over to a re-write man, he wrote and edited the story himself. It went on the first page and held that position in subsequent editions of the day. Editors of other New York dailies read it and inquired the author's name, and Mr. Cobb was given reason to be flattered by offers of two positions on the strength of its popularity.

He was sent to Portsmouth, N. H., as a representative of the *Evening Sun* at the Russo-Japanese Peace Conference held there in 1905. It lasted three weeks. Believing those already on the ground could "cover" the proceedings sufficiently well and knowing the public craving for something different, Mr. Cobb shrewdly set about writing sidelights which his paper syndicated thruout the country. These articles bore the title "Making

Peace at Portsmouth," and held the nation's interest.

Returning to New York, Cobb chose the Evening and Sunday *World* from among the many offers prompted by his handling of the Portsmouth affair. There, on Joseph Pulitzer's chief organ, he struck his full stride and made newspaper history. The laurels came fast, tumbling over each other. In 1914-15 and 1917-18 he represented the *Saturday Evening Post* as war correspondent in Europe. He is a major of the Officers' Reserve Corps, U. S. A., and has received The Chevalier Legion of Honor from the French government.

Cobb has written several plays and among his many books, humorous and serious, are *Back Home* (1912), *Old Judge Priest* (1915), *Speaking of Operations* (1916), *The Thunders of Silence* (1918), *Snake Doctor* (1923), *Ladies and Gentlemen* (1927), *To Be Taken Before Sailing* (1930), *Incredible Truth* (1931).

Jean Cocteau

JEAN COCTEAU has been called "the most charming young man in Paris." As a French poet, novelist, playwright and artist, he has trodden successfully the highways and byways of all the arts and has been credited with attracting "more attention to himself and his works than all the immortal members of the Académie Française banded together."

But Cocteau's name is impressed upon his generation not so much by what he has created as by what he is. Critics have termed him the "eternal schoolboy," the "eternal debutant," because he has the prodigious gift of always being ready to start afresh. He does not lean on his own past, let alone the past of his generation. "If you want to remain young, you must always be making a fresh start," is the way he sums it.

Born in 1891, Cocteau sought means of self-expression at an early age. "When I was seventeen," he writes, "and charged with electricity—I mean the spirit of poetry—of a poetry without form—for which I was incapable of forging a transmitting apparatus; bewildered too by praise of a doubtful value, and the reading of bad books, I

JEAN COCTEAU, a self-portrait

he had definitely settled into the tradition of poetic form. In his volume of essays, *Le Rappel à l'Ordre,* Cocteau explains how he came to abandon his first manner of writing: "To say, 'let us be modern' is senseless. . . . It is absurd to try to make poetry modern by confounding the letter and the spirit and to overemphasize the 'décor.'"

Cocteau has been brought to American readers in four English translations: *A Call to Order* (1926), *Grand Écart* (1925), *Thomas the Imposter* (1925), and *Enfants Terribles* (1930). The last three are novels. *A Call to Order* is a collection of essays, including *Cock and Harlequin* and *Professional Secrets.* *Enfants Terribles* concerns the furious and jealous attachment of a brother and sister for each other which culminates in double suicide.

All photographs of Cocteau are inadequate to picture his personal appearance. Margaret Anderson writes: "His face is so delicate, so constantly in transition, that only the cinema could register its nuances. His hands are even more expressive than his face. They would be merely grotesque—too long, too veined—except that he uses them like words. With every phrase of his talk their gesture changes. The rhythm of their movement is extraordinary. He wears his coat sleeves short, his cuffs tight and turned back."

Cocteau, in his writings, is an irritant but invariably proves a stimulus. He is a champion of the fresh-air-even-if-that-of-the-street movement in realistic art. Among his varied works are several ballets, and *Parade,* one of these, is a fresh air fantasy depicting mob melancholy at a fair. *Les Mariés de la Tour Eiffel,* another poetical fantasia in ballet form, baits the Paris bourgeois. In this piece, he commences with wild absurdity and emerges with a nightmare logic. A third ballet, *Le Boeuf sur le Toit,* is a satire on American prohibition. One of Cocteau's chief joys is using his pen to irritate the music fundamentalist. He has displayed his versatility by not only writing ballets but designing back cloths for them. Among his other artistic efforts are his amusing drawings after the manner of Picasso, who is a close friend.

spent all my time turning over and over on the same spot, like a sick person trying to fall asleep. I dragged myself about, absurdly puffed up with pride; I was sick of myself and would have been glad to die. It was Comtesse de Noailles who imparted to me her love of life. . . . Gradually I fell into the sleep of a somnambulist. This became my normal state, and no doubt I shall continue to sleep until the end. Then I set out in search of myself. The first person I met was Gide. How I envied him his Protestant childhood! I watched him, Bible in hand, skating strangely on Russian waters, and writing his name there in a fine English hand. Our friendship gave me strength."

When the war came, Cocteau entered the service of his country and he flew with the aviator Garros. His emotional frame was shaken by the war and he turned to Catholicism, in revolt from the machine-god to the Virgin.

He published *Discours du Grand Sommeil,* poems of the war written during the war, translated, he says, "from that dead speech, that dead land in which my friends are dead." His *Poésies* (1920) showed fuller musical quality than his early formless works, and then came *Plain-Chant* (1923), which indicated that

Cocteau has discussed style in *Le Secret Professionel* (1922), an essay criticizing contemporary ideas: "What I propose is to dispense with a style. Let us have style instead of having a style. No one, as a matter of fact, gets rid of a certain gait which, to the eye of a delicate observer, gives a family likeness to all his works. But let us carry our style next the skin instead of wearing it on our sleeve, let us bother about having good stuff to our coat rather than about putting smart patterns on it."

Other Cocteau works include: *Romeo and Juliet* and *Antigone,* two drama adaptations; *Orphée* (1926), a play; *Potomak; Lettre à Jacques Maritain* (1926).

Dale Collins

DALE COLLINS

D ALE COLLINS was born at Sydney, Australia, on April 7, 1897. He was an ailing child and spent months of each year in bed. He never thought of any career but writing. At the age of eleven he had a story, "A Kangaroo Hunt," printed in the English comic paper *Puck.* His father was an Irish doctor who had been a ship's surgeon. He died when Dale was two years old as a result of a night ride to a mining camp to save a prospector's life. Mrs. Collins, whose family had supplied several generations of English clergymen, was left alone to rear a family of five children.

At fourteen Dale went on the staff of a suburban paper near Melbourne and showed such aptitude as office boy, proofreader, leader-writer, and "Evangeline" of the woman's page, that he was soon graduated to a metropolitan paper as dramatic critic and chief special writer. The back files of the *Sydney Bulletin* and other Australian papers hold many of his youthful efforts in the writing of verse and short stories.

When the Chicago millionaire, A. Y. Gowen, came to port in his motor-yacht, *The Speejacks,* in which he was making his celebrated circumnavigation of the globe, the first motor-boat voyage of its kind, Collins joined up on twenty-four hours' notice, and said goodbye to Australia. At the end of the 35,000-mile trip he went to London, anticipating aid from Lord Northcliffe, since he had been writing the story of the voyage for the *Daily Mail.* But Northcliffe died a fortnight before he landed.

It was an Irish palm-reader who advised Collins to cease wasting his time on small things. Collins' way of following this advice was to write his first novel, *Ordeal,* a harsh straightforward tale of the sea. His second novel, *The Haven,* is an imaginative romance of the South Seas. In these early books, as well as in his later ones, his scenes are set in the exotic ports of the world which he knows from long acquaintance, and his characters are drawn from the sea captains, stokers, planters, and chance companions he has happened upon in the course of a roving career that has taken him from Sydney to Monte Carlo and from New York to Singapore. He met the present Mrs. Collins in Monte Carlo, altho she is an Australian by birth and in fact lived within a few doors of Collins' home in Melbourne when they were both children.

Mr. Collins and his wife recently boarded a round-the-world freighter for an eighteen months' cruise, signing on as steward and stewardess at a shilling a month. It is the ideal life, he says, for a writer of his temperament.

The books of Dale Collins, with dates of American publication, are: *Sea-Tracks of the Speejacks Round the World* (1923), *Ordeal* (1924), *The Haven* (1925), *The Sentimentalists* (1927), *Vanity under the Sun* (1928), *Idolaters* (1929), *Rich and Strange* (1931). *Ordeal*, dramatized by the author, was produced in London in 1924.

Padraic Colum

ONCE a certain Irish writer who was among the pilgrims at a Holy Well in Donegal was asked his name by one of the devotees. He gave it, and the name was received with a certain courteous incredulity. It seemed indeed as if it had been made up to be in harmony with the place and the occasion; for it joined together in the Christian and family name the two greatest of the Irish saints—Patrick and Colum-cille. The name was Padraic Colum.

Padraic Colum typifies the best in the Irish Renaissance. The mixture of gaiety and shadow which is so much a part of the Irish heart is his, and with that subtle twist of English speech which only the Irish give it, he writes poetry, dramatic legends, fantasies, and stories for children which have won him a high place in English literature.

Born in county Longford on December 8, 1881, he was brought up in the

PADRAIC COLUM

counties of Longford and Cavan, and as he grew up he absorbed folk-lore and popular songs until he became fairly steeped in the traditional native culture of the Irish people. The county he was born in, incidentally, was the birthplace of Oliver Goldsmith; it was there that Maria Edgeworth began to write her Irish stories; and it was the same county that produced John Keegan Casey, the writer of the most stirring of Irish ballads, *The Risin' o' the Moon.*

Colum entered the ranks of the writers in his youth. One of his loveliest lyrics came into the boy's head as he returned late from a dance in an old farmhouse, "to climb over the crooked limbs of a testy great-uncle in whose bed he slept." He joined the National Theatre movement in Dublin, and learned to know and admire George Russell (AE), William Butler Yeats, and Lady Gregory. It was at this time that his first poems and essays appeared in the journal which Arthur Griffith was conducting. His plays were among the first to be produced by the Irish Theatre. *Broken Soil* (1903) was given when he was only twenty-one. He intended to write a series of plays for the Irish Theatre—a sort of Human Comedy of Ireland—but a disagreement on the question of policy led to his withdrawal from the group that directed the theatre. Meanwhile he was writing verse (published in the volume called *Wild Earth*, 1907) that marked a new departure in Irish poetry.

He was one of the founders of the *Irish Review* in 1911, and its sole editor during 1912-1913. In 1912 he married Mary Gunning Maguire of Dublin; his wife has decided literary ability herself, and is a very able critic. For some years the Colums have made their home in America, and this country is richer for having acquired even by adoption a poet so full of whimsy and the feeling of Ireland. To hear him talk on Irish poetry, or give a reading from his own poems or tales, is to fall under the spell of all Ireland.

In the presence of this "faëry cardinal," writes Llewelyn Powys, "I never failed to feel that particular spiritual elation which authentic poets are able to arouse in the hearts of those of us who value imagination more highly than anything else in the world. I could never set eyes on Mr. Colum without longing to go out into a cornfield to gather for him an armful of red poppies."

In 1923 Mr. Colum went to Hawaii at the invitation of the Hawaiian Legislature to make a survey of native myth and folk-lore. After his return, two volumes of Hawaiian folk-lore, showing the influence of this trip, were published: *At the Gateway of the Day* (1924) and *The Bright Islands* (1925).

The Colums live in New Canaan, Connecticut. Colum and his wife, who was the recipient of a Guggenheim Fellowship in 1930, sailed for France late in that year, following the appearance of Mr. Colum's three most recent books. They were: *Cross Roads in Ireland,* a travel volume describing his country from three points of view, visual, historical, and psychic; *Old Pastures,* a group of poems; and *Orpheus: Myths of the World,* containing folk-legends from all nations. Among his other books are: *The Boy Who Knew What the Birds Said* (1918), *Dramatic Legends and Other Poems* (1922), *Castle Conquer* (1923), and *The Road Round Ireland* (1926).

Marc Connelly

MARCUS COOK CONNELLY, familiarly known as Marc, was born December 13, 1890, in McKeesport, a small city in southwestern Pennsylvania at the junction of the Monongahela and the Youghagheny Rivers. Until shortly before his birth his father was manager for Richard Mansfield, the most famous actor of the last quarter of the nineteenth century. Mr. Connelly recalls an incident of his childhood, when Mansfield came to Pittsburgh in *Cyrano de Bergerac.* Mr. and Mrs. Connelly and Marc went to Pittsburgh to see the show, but, because the train was late, arrived at the theater between the first and the second act. The audience was applauding loudly, and Mansfield came to the footlights to say that he could repay its appreciation in only one way, and, with its permission, the first act would be repeated. This event is noteworthy to Marc; it was his first visit to a theater, and it is probably

MARC CONNELLY

the only time an act was performed a second time under such circumstances.

Mr. Connelly attended Trinity Hall, a private school in Washington, Pennsylvania, until his graduation in 1907. Desiring to write, he went to Pittsburgh in 1910 and secured a position as a reporter on the *Pittsburgh Sun.* He later transferred to the *Dispatch,* and subsequently conducted a column for the *Gazette-Times.* At the same time Mr. Connelly was doing this writing his future collaborator, George Kaufman, was writing a similar humorous column for the *Washington Times.*

In 1915, when he was twenty-four, Mr. Connelly sold some lyrics to a musical comedy producer, and decided to go to New York to see this show and to hear his songs. The play was not a success, and he found himself stranded in Manhattan, jobless and without the fare to Pittsburgh. He did miscellaneous writing for the next few years, wrote verse for *Life,* covered newspaper and magazine assignments, and occasionally contributed lyrics and sketches to musical comedies.

The meeting of Mr. Connelly and Mr. Kaufman was a fortunate coincidence, and resulted in their collaboration on the following plays, all of which have been decidedly successful: *Dulcy* (1921); *To*

the Ladies (1923) ; *Beggar on Horseback*
(1924) ;*Merton of the Movies,* a dramatization of Harry Leon Wilson's story by
the same name. *Helen of Troy, N.Y.;
The Deep Tangled Wildwood,* a satire on
small town apings of city life; and a
musical comedy libretto, *Be Yourself,*
also came from the Kaufman-Connelly
partnership.

The Wisdom Tooth, one of the successful plays of 1926, was Mr. Connelly's
first solo-show. In 1927 he collaborated
with H. J. Mankiewicz in the writing of
The Wild Man of Borneo, which failed.

Mr. Connelly's talents are not confined to writing alone, and he directed
Berkeley Square, one of the most popular
plays of the 1929-1930 season in New
York. He is versatile also in his writing,
was one of the founders of *The New
Yorker* and is still a frequent contributor,
as well as appearing in numerous other
magazines. Altho he has written few
short stories, his *Coroner's Inquest* won
the 1930 O'Henry Memorial award.

The Green Pastures, which opened in
New York in February 1930 received
the 1930 Pulitzer prize as the best play
of the year. Mr. Connelly based his play
on Roark Bradford's Old Testament
stories of the southern Negro in *Ol' Man
Adam and His Chillun,* and spent considerable time with Mr. Bradford in
Louisiana while working on this "divine"
comedy. He is also the director of the
play. *The Green Pastures* was published
in 1930, with illustrations by Robert
Edmond Jones.

A collection of miscellaneous articles,
both humorous and serious, by Mr.
Connelly will be published in 1931.

Miss Madeline Hurlock and Mr.
Connelly were married in October 1930.
Their permanent home is in New York.
Altho extraordinarily successful, Mr.
Connelly has retained his modesty, his
interest in people of all types, his con-
sideration of others. He is of medium
height, with keen blue eyes.

M. Constantin-Weyer

MAURICE CONSTANTIN-WEYER
was introduced to English-speaking
countries thru his Goncourt prize novel,
A Man Scans His Past. His novels deal
with Canadian pioneer life. In order to
understand his interest in and knowledge
of this territory, it is necessary to know
something about his life, which is filled
from beginning to end with adventure.

He was born in 1881 in the Haute
Marne, France. His father was an army
officer and badly disabled in the war of
1870, just as he himself became an officer and was badly disabled in the World
War. He learned three languages besides his own while still a child: Provençal, German, and English. The last-
named stood him in good stead when
he later went to live in Canada. He has
always been interested in English literature and it was his habit in the Canadian
wilds always to carry a volume of
Shakespeare with him. He also read
Fielding, Hazlitt, and others, and eventually made several translations from the
English.

After studying in several schools in
the provinces, he arrived in Paris to
work for a degree in sciences. At this
time he met the literary men who later,
after his Canadian and War experiences,
urged him to write. But the product of
his own pen at that Paris period was
small: a slender volume of verse,
Images, of which even he himself has no
copy today.

M. CONSTANTIN-WEYER

In 1901, when he was twenty, his mother lost her fortune and that accident turned his thoughts to Canada, to which he went to win a new fortune.

"I had scarcely arrived," he says in a recent interview in the *Nouvelles Litteraires*, "before I was thrown rudely into the midst of the life. I was in turn farmer, cowboy, woodcutter, trapper, horse trader in the summer, fur trader in winter, occasionally journalist, reporting this or that for the English papers, but I was too caught by the fever of the fast-moving life to think of translating it to paper."

In 1912, having gathered together a little money, he established a horse and cattle ranch in the north of Manitoba. It was an era of prosperity, and of broad and easy life. He had books, good saddle horses, game and fish in abundance, and magnificent health. The daily work was not unpleasant, and he had amusement that would satisfy the most exigent hunter: hunting wolves on horseback, tracking moose in the forest, and fishing in the magnificent rivers.

With the outbreak of the war, M. Constantin-Weyer dropped everything and rushed to France to enlist. At the front he was repeatedly sighted for bravery, notably on the Macedonian front, where he was wounded in fifty-three places by a bursting shell. Pronounced "inapt" in 1918, he nevertheless insisted on re-entering the fray with the tanks, and participated, while still dependent upon two crutches, in several attacks.

When at last he returned to Manitoba to his stock farm, there was no stock farm. Everything had gone to ruin during his six years' absence. He had no money to go to law and his crippled condition made it impossible for him to earn any at his strenuous pre-war occupations. So he re-embarked for France and turned to writing for a living.

From his short stories and travel sketches, M. Constantin-Weyer has been called the French Jack London.

A Man Scans His Past (tr. 1929), *The Half-Breed* (tr. 1930), and *Towards the West* (tr. 1931), are all novels of the Canadian Northwest.

A. E. Coppard

UNKNOWN at the age of forty, Alfred Edgar Coppard commenced at about that time to write verse and short stories. That was in 1919, in England. With the publication in 1921 of his first book, a collection of tales entitled *Adam and Eve and Pinch Me,* he immediately sprang into prominence as a writer.

Born January 4, 1878, at Folkstone, England, Coppard was sent to the Lewes Road Board School to commence his education. It was only a beginning, however, for he was abruptly withdrawn at the age of nine because of ill-health. For a cure he was put to work and he was never able to return to school. His education, thus, has been practically self-acquired. After following numerous occupations, among them that of a professional sprinter, he finally became a clerk in London. This work he continued until 1919, moving meanwhile to Oxford where he came within the inspiration of that city of learning. His decision to become a writer was followed by retirement to a great woods where he plunged into deep thinking accompanied by meager living.

A. E. COPPARD

Adam and Eve and Pinch Me appeared on April Fool's Day of 1921. Besides being Coppard's first book it was the initial product of the Golden Cockeral Press, a communal society of craftsmen. The make-up of the book betrayed the beginner's hand—even the author shared the work of printing and binding—but in spite of that fact every one of the 550 copies claimed an owner. Much of his subsequent work has appeared in limited editions.

Hips and Haws was published just a year later—the first collection of Coppard's verse—and along with it appeared his second book of tales, called *Clorinda Walks in Heaven.* Three more books of tales followed: *The Black Dog* (1923), *Fishmonger's Fiddle* (1925), and *The Field of Mustard* (1926); and two volumes of verse: *Pelagea and Other Poems* (1926), and *Yokohama Garland* (1926).

In point of view and style of writing Coppard is essentially a poet; even his prose has a rhythm and a glow which make it verge on poetry. In his verse Coppard employs both the irregular and conventional forms. Altho a poet in spirit, Coppard has won his public rather as a teller of unusual and fanciful tales. He says that folk tales are the best model for good writing. He dislikes pretension of any kind.

First editions of Coppard's books are priced high, but he has been forced to live on a scanty income, even turning occasionally to his clerical work for a livelihood. His home is at Long Wittenham, Abingdon, Berks.

Ford Madox Ford has written: "Mr. Coppard is almost the first English writer to get into English prose the peculiar quality of English lyric poetry. I do not mean that he is metrical; I mean that hitherto no English prose writer has had the fancy, the turn of imagination, the wisdom, the as it were piety and the beauty of the great 17th century lyricists like Donne or Herbert—or even Herrick. And that peculiar quality is the best thing that England has to show."

Later books by Coppard include: *Silver Circus* (1928), *Count Stefan* (1928), *Collected Poems* (1928), *The Gollan* (1929), *Pink Furniture* (1929).

Donald Corley

DONALD CORLEY is a native of Georgia. He was born and grew up in Covington.

He and his brother lived with an aunt in a house set in an overgrown tangle of trees that had been an arboreal nursery about 1860. Mr. Corley recalls with pleasure his aunt's vast library full of antique atlases and books of all description. Long before the books were read they were used to build palaces which stimulated an already active imagination. Many of the illustrations in *The House of Lost Identity* come from Mr. Corley's memory of these books,—djinn, temples in the sky, and Palaces of Ind.

Mr. Corley attended Emory College, in Georgia. After a visit abroad he lived in New York, and was with the architectural firm of McKim, Mead and White for seven years. Among the buildings he worked on are the Municipal Building, the fabulous Deering house in Miami, Florida, and buildings for the Panama-Pacific Exposition which was held in San Francisco in 1915.

He has also worked in the theatre, from writing plays and acting to constructing stage sets, and was one of the charter members of the Provincetown Players. During the war he was a camofleur in the Port of New York.

DONALD CORLEY

Altho he began to write short stories when he was sixteen, he did not submit one for publication until 1919. *Harper's* immediate acceptance of the first story he sent to a magazine led him to continue writing; his stories have appeared in *Harper's, Scribner's, Pictorial Review,* and other periodicals.

In 1920 during a siege of influenza Mr. Corley began drawing for his own amusement. He was so successful with pen and ink sketches that a collection, *22 Drawings in Black and White,* was published in 1921. He designed the jacket and did the illustrations for *The House of Lost Identity* (1927), which is prefaced by James Branch Cabell. *The Fifth Son of the Shoemaker,* a fairy tale of New York (1930), is not illustrated, but the jacket was done by the author. Mr. Corley's other publications are *The Haunted Jester* (1930), tales and drawings, and *Preface to an Unwritten Novel* (1931).

Mr. Corley's artistry is not confined to writing and drawing. He builds ship models, "without rhyme or reason," he says, which have such romantic names as "The Caravel of Lüllüme, the Extravagant" and "The Pleasure Ship of Pergamon." These ships, he explains, are not orthodox ships. He prefers "to build little ships whose like has never existed . . . dream ships, out of this and that beautiful thing." He also composes music, "for pleasure, not profit."

Mr. Corley is tall and slender. He is an excellent conversationalist and on all subjects the whimsicalities of his mind and his devotion to whatever is romantic and beautiful, particularly in hurried New York where he lives, are strikingly evident.

Noel Coward

NOEL COWARD, the brilliant young English playwright, composer, lyricist, actor, director, and producer, was born in Teddington December 16, 1899.

He was educated privately and at Croydon, and received his dramatic training at the Italia Conti Academy, the foremost dramatic school in Great Britain. His stage debut was made in 1910 at the Gaiety Theater, Manchester. Ger-

NOEL COWARD

trude Lawrence, who later starred in *Charlot's Revue,* for which Mr. Coward wrote most of the words and lyrics, played in this show. Later as a child actor with Charles Hawtrey's players, young Coward was cast with Estelle Winwood, who is now a popular comedienne in London and New York.

After serving in the army during the World War Coward returned to London and had an important rôle in Cosmo Hamilton's *Scandal.* Besides writing the book, lyrics, and music for *London Calling,* this Jack-of-all-trades of the theater next was leading song-and-dance man of the production.

Mr. Coward abandoned acting for a time and devoted his energies to writing. *The Rat Trap,* written when he was eighteen, was his first play. *I'll Leave it to You,* produced in 1920 with the author in the lead, was a failure. *The Young Idea* was his next play, and was followed by *The Vortex* in 1921, which was one of the successes of the season in London and later in New York, and won Mr. Coward praise both as a playwright and an actor. *Hay Fever,* a comedy which had been written earlier, was his next stage success.

In 1927 *The Queen Was in the Parlor, Home Chat, Sirocco, The Marquise,* and

Fallen Angels were running simultaneously in London, and the last two in New York. Of these, the first three were practically failures, but *The Marquise* and *Fallen Angels* fared better. Billie Burke had the lead in the New York cast of *The Marquise*, the scenes of which were laid in early eighteenth century France; Fay Bainter and Estelle Winwood were the two Fallen Angels.

On With the Dance was the first revue for which Mr. Coward was entirely responsible. The very successful musical comedy *This Year of Grace*, with the author in the cast, followed. *Bitter Sweet*, an operetta with the English actress Evelyn Laye in the lead, charmed New York during the 1929-1930 season. Mr. Coward directed the play but did not act in it. *Private Lives*, a comedy in which the author played a leading rôle, was no less successful in 1930 and 1931 in New York and London.

After the completion of the New York run of *Bitter Sweet*, Mr. Coward took a trip around the world before returning to his country home near London.

Modesty is said to be one of the most outstanding of this versatile young man's characteristics. Altho success and lack of it have alternated with him, he has had more than enough in any of his lines of endeavor to turn the head of a less sensible person. He is tall and slim, not handsome, yet strikingly attractive, with neatly parted black hair, clear blue eyes, sensitive hands, and an engaging smile. His clothes are unobstrusive, but chosen with a nice discrimination in things sartorial. His accent is London, his conversation easy and sometimes witty. He moves and thinks quickly, and enjoys acting. He is able to work practically anywhere, and says that he composed one of his most popular melodies while riding in a taxi up 8th Avenue in New York city. Travel fascinates him more than anything else. He is unmarried.

Coward writes his plays at teriffic speed, first in longhand, then on the typewriter. The writing of *Bitter Sweet*, score and all, took three months. He considers this his best musical piece, *Hay Fever* (which took him three days to write) his best comedy, and *The Vortex* his best drama. He says that he has written three novels—"all of them terrible"—of which only one was published, tho no one seems to have suspected its existence. He is anxious to write another. At thirty-one he has had sixteen plays produced.

His plays are: *I'll Leave It To You; The Rat Trap* (1924); *The Young Idea* (1924); *The Vortex* (1924); *Easy Virtue; Fallen Angels; Hay Fever* (1925); *The Queen Was in The Parlor* (1926); *This Was a Man; The Marquise* (1927); *On With the Dance* (revue); *Home Chat* (1927); *Sirocco* (1927); *This Year of Grace* (revue); *Bitter Sweet* (operetta); *Private Lives* (1930); *Post Mortem* (1931).

Malcolm Cowley

MALCOLM COWLEY was born August 24, 1898, in Belsano, Pennsylvania, a village in the central western part of the state. After attending public school there and in Pittsburgh he went to Harvard where he received his A.B. in 1920. He edited the *Harvard Advocate* and participated in all the literary activities of the University.

His studies at Harvard were interrupted by the war in 1917. At that time he went to France in the American Ambulance Service, which he calls the "university for the present generation of writers," referring to others who had

MALCOLM COWLEY

also served in the Ambulance Service in France—Ernest Hemingway, Louis Bromfield, John Dos Passos, W. B. Seabrook, E. E. Cummings, and Slater Brown, to mention a few.

From 1921 to 1923 he studied at the University of Montpellier in France on an American Field Service Fellowship; he concentrated particularly on French literature and history.

Mr. Cowley settled in New York when he returned to America, doing free lance writing, translating, and book reviewing. He has contributed poetry and critical essays frequently to *The New Republic, Harper's, The Nation, Forum,* and other magazines, and is a member of the editorial staff of *The New Republic.*

Mr. Cowley has been married several years, and divides his time between his sixty acre farm near Patterson, New York, and New York City. The incidents connected with the purchase of his farm are rather unique: it was bought with a down payment of $75, after Mr. Cowley had won a $100 prize from the magazine *Poetry.* The reward was a surprise to him, he says, and he decided that he could do nothing better with the money than buy a farm; he decided further to keep part of the amount for some personal items.

Blue Juniata, a book of poems, was published in 1929. The poems are divided into groups either according to the year or period when written or according to the mood or idea. The book is a representative "record kept by a member of this generation who broke with the past, witnessed the moral collapse of Europe, and returned to make the best of the confused intellectual life of post-war New York."

The Lost Generation (1931) is a psychological history of the war generation of American writers, including Hemingway, Cummings, Westcott, Dos Passos, and Cowley himself. It illuminates the emotional and rational background of "the sad young men."

Mr. Cowley contributed *Oedipus, or The Future of Love,* to *Whither, Whither, or After Sex What?* (1930).

He has translated many books from French into English, including *Variety,* by Paul Valéry; *Catherine-Paris,* by Princess Marthe Lucie Bibesco; *The*

Sacred Hill, by Maurice Barrès; and *The Count's Ball,* by Raymond Radiguet. In 1928 he edited *Adventures of an African Slaver,* by Theodore Canot, "being a true account of the life of Theodore Canot, trader in gold, ivory, slaves, on the coast of New Guinea, his own story told in the year 1854 to Brantz Mayer."

Edward Gordon Craig

EDWARD GORDON CRAIG was born on January 16, 1872, the son of Ellen Terry. In 1889 he went on the stage and acted in Sir Henry Irving's company for about eight years, also playing Shakespearean parts in the provinces. Giving up acting in 1896, he turned his attention to the study of stage management.

Early in the nineties he ventured to show his work, and produced Alfred de Musset's *On ne badine pas avec l'amour* near London, after which, for several years, he continued his study of stage management. Then followed seven important productions in quick succession, for all of which he designed and supervised every scene and every dress, and acted as stage manager: *Dido and*

EDWARD GORDON CRAIG

Æneas in 1900; *The Masque of Love* and a revival of *Dido and Æneas* in 1901; Handel's opera *Acis and Galatea* and a revival of *The Masque of Love* in 1902; Laurence Housman's Nativity play *Bethlehem,* part of *Sword and Song,* Ibsen's *Vikings,* and *Much Ado About Nothing* in 1903.

Much Ado About Nothing was Gordon Craig's last production in England, and he now began to turn his attention to the Continent, where, especially in Germany theatrical people had already begun to alter their style and make it more decorative and, in so doing, to adopt most of his technique.

After producing a German version of Otway's *Venice Preserved* in Berlin in 1904, Craig designed *Electra* for Eleonora Duse a year later. Isadora Duncan's enthusiasm gained for him his commissions to design Ibsen's *Rosmersholm* for Duse in Florence (1906) and *Hamlet* for the Moscow Art Theatre in 1912. Since then his commissions have been infrequent. His chief production in recent years was *The Pretenders,* by Ibsen, at Copenhagen in 1926. In 1928 he made a few designs for a production of *Macbeth* in New York.

Early in 1908 Gordon Craig founded *The Mask,* a sumptuous journal devoted to the art of the theatre, published and printed in Florence, Italy. To this journal, he has contributed numerous designs and writings.

In March 1913 Gordon Craig opened his School for the Art of the Theatre in Florence, but as support was withdrawn from it in August 1914 within 14 days notice, and no provision whatever made by its supporters to preserve the valuable works already commenced, half done, or completed, the entire enterprise ceased, the works were broken up and burnt, and the ideal of a life-time was for some years thus rendered useless.

Craig has been called egocentric, impractical, contentious, and even lazy, by his critics. No one, however, has questioned his devotion to the theatre, and his friends protest that he is neither self-centered nor *difficile.* Alfred Kreymborg, reporting a visit to Craig's villa at Rapallo, Italy, in 1921, describes Craig as "tall, erect, handsome, a younger edition of Franz Liszt in appearance and a descendant of Till Eugenspiegel in his fondness of the world of play. . . The little villa on the hill overlooking the sea was permeated with the warmth, at all times, of Craig's family: his wife, a small, energetic Italian woman, and the two children, Nelly, named after her grandmother, and Teddy, named after his father."

In 1930 the Cranach Press, under the direction of Count Kessler, published *Hamlet,* translated by Gerhart Hauptmann and containing some 70 wood-engravings by Gordon Craig.

He has written and published several books in which his ideas are elaborated. Among these publications, the following may be mentioned:

A Programme for *Dido and Æneas* (1900), a booklet with engraved designs; An Illustrated Souvenir Booklet of *Acis and Galatea* (1902); *The Art of the Theatre* (1905), published also in German, Russian, and Dutch; *A Portfolio of Etchings* (1908); *A Second Portfolio of Etchings* (1910); *On the Art of the Theatre* (1911), translated into Russian, French, and Italian; *Towards a New Theatre* (1912); *The Theatre-Advancing* (1919); *Scene* (1922); *Woodcuts and Some Words* (1923); *Books and Theatres* (1925); *A Production, 1926* (1930); *Henry Irving* (1930).

Hart Crane

O F hardy New England stock is Hart Crane—New England stock which, three generations back, dug up the stakes and moved to Ohio. It was there, in Garrettsville, on July 21, 1899, that Hart (really Harold) was born, the only son of Grace Edna Hart and Clarence A. Crane.

He began writing verse at thirteen, and published his first poem (in *Bruno's Bohemian*) two years later. Mrs. William Vaughn Moody became interested in his work when he was sixteen.

Crane lived in Ohio, chiefly Cleveland, where his father was a prosperous candy manufacturer, until 1922. Then, he took up his permanent residence in New York where he began doing advertising copywriting. He has done his

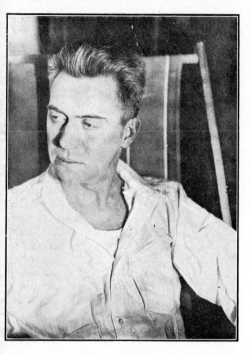

HART CRANE

share of traveling, having spent six months on the Isle of Pines in Cuba, and eight months in France (Paris and Marseilles).

He has admired, with varying fidelity, the Elizabethans, Donne, Blake, Waldo Frank, Ouspensky, Melville, Whitman, Dostoievsky, Sherwood Anderson, and T. S. Eliot. He paints and draws with a natural talent.

Crane collected the best of his early poems in *White Buildings* (1926). It was followed by *The Bridge* (1930), a group of fifteen poems unified by a symbolic concept of The Brooklyn Bridge. Mr. Crane, himself, tells how *The Bridge* came to be written:

"During 1924, while living in an old house (110 Columbia Heights, Brooklyn), I conceived the idea of writing a long poem about America and the modern consciousness that its development has given rise to. This poem was largely inspired by the magnificent architectural sweep of Brooklyn Bridge, which I could see from my window, along with the panorama of the harbor and the lower Manhattan skyline. (I did not know until years after I had left this house that one of its earliest owners had been Washington Roebling, builder of Brooklyn Bridge, and that the identical chamber I had occupied had been his observation point, after he became paralysed, for watching the completion of that structure.) By the autumn of 1925, this plan had attained a definite pattern. Then, owing to the kindly interest and material assistance of Mr. Otto H. Kahn, I was given the leisure to proceed with its uninterrupted composition. *The Bridge* was not finished, however, until December 1929, during which five years the work continued, much interrupted by various handicaps in such widely separated places of residences as Patterson, N. Y.; Isle of Pines, Cuba; Pasadena, Calif.; Paris and Marseilles— finally to reach completion at Columbia Heights, Brooklyn, in the latter months of 1929."

Crane is often difficult to comprehend as a poet, because (to quote his own declaration) he is "more interested in the so-called illogical impingements of the connotations of words on the consciousness (and their combinations and interplay in metaphor on this basis) than . . . in the preservation of their logically rigid significations at the cost of limiting [the] subject matter and perceptions involved in the poem."

Crane was awarded the Helen Haire Levinson prize by *Poetry* magazine in 1930. He contributed an essay on poetry in the machine age to the symposium, *Revolt in the Arts* (1930), edited by Oliver Sayler.

Benedetto Croce

BENEDETTO CROCE, Italian philosopher, was born February 25, 1866, in Pescasseroli, a remote village in the province of Aquila. He came of an Abruzzese family whose members had often won distinction as lawyers and magistrates. When he was very young his parents moved to Naples, where the family seat had been established by his grandfather. There he was educated at a Catholic school.

When Croce was seventeen, his parents and his sister were killed in an earth-

BENEDETTO CROCE

quake and he was seriously injured himself, having lain for several hours under the ruins. He went to live in Rome with an uncle, Silvio Spaventa. The tragedy made the following years gloomy ones, and after a slow recovery he emerged a stoic in his attitude towards pain and suffering, accepting the inevitability of sorrow in life. He entered the University of Rome but left in 1886 to return to Naples, where he occupied himself for several years as an independent student of Italian literature and Neapolitan history.

Croce's contributions to philosophy began with two essays on the nature of history and the method of literary criticism, published in 1893. Between 1896 and 1900 he published a group of essays on points of Marxian economic doctrine.

When Croce was thirty-three, his study of philosophy precipitated in himself an intellectual crisis which he describes in his *Autobiographie* (1918): "I read almost nothing, walked for hours and hours, spent half my days and all my nights lying on a couch, searching assiduously within myself, and putting down on paper notes and ideas, each a criticism of the other." At length he established his philosophical bearings "with an awakened and sure understanding of almost all the principal problems

with which classical philosophers have toiled, an understanding which cannot be acquired by merely reading their books, but only by repeating within oneself, under the stimulus of life, their mental drama."

In 1902 Croce began his exposition of *Filosofia dello Spirito* (Philosophy of the Spirit) and in that year the first volume, *Estetica,* was published. Two other volumes followed: *Logica* (1905) and *Filosofia della Pratica* (1908). In *Estetica,* which he calls the science of intuitive knowledge, he defines art as a purely spontaneous imaginative form, rather than the product of reflection or skill. *Logica* treats the science of intellective knowledge, of concepts scientific and philosophical. In *Pratica* he discusses the two kinds of knowledge as men possess and make use of them. A fourth volume was added to the group in 1916 called *Teoria della Storiografia* (Theory of History). In 1903 Croce founded the journal *La Critica,* in which he reviewed the literature of Italy and its contributions to historical literature.

Croce has been called the guiding star of Italian culture from about the death of Carducci in 1907 to the outbreak of the war. His writings during that period included *Problemi di Estetica* (1910) and *La Filosofia di Giambattista Vico* (1911). He was nominated to the senate of the kingdom in 1910 and remained until 1917. During the war he took no sides, retaining his philosophic impartiality and viewing events without passion in what he considered the true light. In June 1920, when Giolitti came into power in Italy, Croce became Minister of Education but comparatively little of his program of reform could be carried out before the defeat of the Giolitti government in July of 1921. Croce returned to his life of thought.

In 1920 Croce received the great gold medal of Columbia University, and in 1923 he was given an honorary degree at Oxford. The University of Freiburg in Baden has made him an honorary Doctor of Philosophy. He is Secretary of the Historical Society of Naples, where he resides. Altho actively interested in educational administration, he has never sought or occupied any university office. Professor Giuseppi Gen-

tile, "the Fascist philosopher," has been a close associate and collaborator with Croce. The collected works of Croce, published in 1926, filled twenty volumes.

Several of Croce's works have been translated into English, his chief translator being Douglas Ainslie. The translations include: All four books of the *Philosophy of the Spirit—Aesthetic, Logic, Philosophy of the Practical,* and *Theory of History; Historic Materialism and Marxian Economy* (1914); *On Hegel; Aristotle, Shakespeare and Corneille* (1920); *The Poetry of Dante* (1922); *Goethe* (1924); *European Literature in the 19th Century* (1924); *The Conduct of Life* (1924); *Autobiography* (1927); *History of Italy from 1871 to 1915* (1928); and *Moral Aspects of Political Life* (1930).

COUNTÉE CULLEN

Countée Cullen

COUNTÉE CULLEN was born in New York city in 1903, the son of the Rev. R. A. Cullen, minister and founder of Salem M.E. Church. He was educated in New York public schools, being graduated from DeWitt Clinton High School in 1922, and he received the degree of Bachelor of Arts from New York University in June 1925 after being elected to Phi Beta Kappa. He entered Harvard University in the fall of 1925 and received his A.M. in English literature in 1926.

Cullen began to write when he was fourteen years old. A teacher in DeWitt Clinton High School gave an assignment to his class to write some verse and Cullen handed in *To A Swimmer* (the only free verse poem he has ever done). He thought no more of writing until a year later when he saw this poem published in *The Modern School Magazine* issue of May 1918. Cullen then became ambitious to write and his first verse appeared in *The Crisis,* official magazine of the National Association for the Advancement of Colored People. While still in high school he was awarded first prize in a contest conducted by the

Federation of Women's Clubs with his poem, *I Have A Rendezvous With Life.*

In November 1923 Cullen's verse appeared in a white magazine for the first time when *To A Brown Boy* was published in *The Bookman.* In 1928 he went abroad on a Guggenheim Fellowship.

When Cullen began to write, he was a great admirer of Tennyson. Later he was influenced by Edna St. Vincent Millay, Housman, Robinson, and, most of all, Keats. He is essentially an emotional and lyrical poet. His only present tendency towards free verse is limited to experimental attempts and he finds himself more and more inclined towards rigid forms. "Most things I write," he says, "I do for the sheer love of the music in them. A number of times I have said I wanted to be a poet and known as such and not as a Negro poet. Somehow or other, however, I find my poetry of itself treating of the Negro, of his joys and his sorrows—mostly of the latter—and of the heights and depths of emotion which I feel as a Negro."

Cullen has published: *Color* (1925), *Copper Sun* (1927), *Caroling Dusk,* a comprehensive anthology of Negro verse, (1927), *The Ballad of the Brown Girl* (1927), and *The Black Christ* (1929).

E. E. Cummings

EDWARD ESTLIN CUMMINGS was born in Cambridge, Massachusetts, October 14, 1894. His father was the late Reverend Edward Cummings (1861-1926), who had taught English at Harvard and Radcliffe, was subsequently assistant professor at Harvard, and from 1900 until his death was pastor of the famous South Congregational Church in Boston (succeeding Edward Everett Hale), and of the First Congregational church after the union of the two. He was also well known as a lecturer on sociological subjects and on problems of world peace.

Cummings received his A. B. from Harvard in 1915, and his A. M. in 1916. The following year he and Slater Brown, a close friend who was in Harvard with him and shared many of his literary activities, enlisted in the ambulance service. After driving ambulances in France for six months and spending three months in a French prison for some epistolary indiscretion (see *The Enormous Room*), Cummings served as a private in the American Infantry.

BACHRACH

E. E. CUMMINGS

After the Armistice he returned to th United States and lived in New Yor for two years. He then went to Pari where he lived in comparative poverty gradually winning recognition for bot his writing and painting. Burton Rasco describes a visit to him during thi period: "His mouth was taut and sulle under a blond tooth-brush moustach His head was thrown back challengingl as always except when he is bein courteous to a lady. There was the fir of passionate conviction in his eye. Altho usually reserved, Cummings ha his moments of inspired conversatio when he speaks in "a coruscating cascad of unrelated or only slightly relate images, poetic tags, remembered lines i Greek, French, Latin, German, and Eng lish." He regards poetry ironically as a "idiotic disease."

Cummings returned to New York an reestablished his residence there. Th *Dial* award, that admirable prize give for distinguished service to America literature, was won by Cummings i 1925. He has contributed frequently t various magazines devoted to the ac vanced movements in arts and letters. I 1928 he married Ann Barton.

His sketches also have appeared i *The Dial* and other periodicals, and th Society of Independent Artists and th Salons of America have exhibited h paintings.

him, a phantasmagoric play in twent one scenes, was presented by the Pro incetown Players in New York in 192 Altho not entirely successful either as business venture or as a dramatic pr duction, it added to the already enviab reputation of this group for its sincerit in producing experimental plays, and al to that of the author for "the vagra heat and flying image, that rich textu of detail and idea, that superb irony ar mordant boldness, and that wide ar passionate beauty and intensity for whi we follow him."

The Enormous Room (1922), his fir book, is a record of his impressions du ing his war imprisonment. Four boo of poetry followed: *Tulips and Chimne* (1923), *XLI Poems* (1925), *&* (1925 *Is 5* (1926). *him* was published in 192 and "———" (a book without a title, t content of which had appeared in th 1929 *New American Caravan*) in 193

C I O P W (1931) derives its curious title from the initials of the five forms of pictorial art of which it is composed: Charcoal drawings, Ink drawings, Oil paintings, Pencil drawings, and Water colors. Cummings has lately divided his time between painting and poetry.

His lyrics and satirical verses have placed him in the first rank of our poets. An experimental poet, considered radical because of his omission of capital letters, an individual structural style and the breaking up of words and sentences to obtain certain unorthodox typographical effects and new relative values for the component parts of his conceits, he has incited animated discussion of his writing and methods.

In Paris in 1931 Cummings was preparing a new volume of poems for publication.

S. Foster Damon

SAMUEL FOSTER DAMON, poet, Blake scholar, and biographer, was born February 22, 1893, at Newton, Massachusetts, the only son of Joseph N. and Sarah (Pastorius) Damon. "The Damon family," he writes, "was founded by Deacon John Damon, who simultaneously founded Reading, Mass., in the 17th century; the Pastorius family was founded by Francis Daniel Pastorius, who also simultaneously founded Germantown, Pennsylania in the 17th century. All my progenitors, in all families, have reached this country as early as the 18th century, at least; and none earlier than the 17th, as far as I know. Consequently, I feel entitled to call myself of old American stock; and if you want more facts about witch-defenders, alchemists, Boston tea-party persons, Bunker Hill heroes, and the like, I can furnish it.

"I was educated at the public schools, and later at Harvard University, from which I hold the degrees of A.B. and A.M. As an undergraduate, I was President of the *Harvard Musical Review* and captain of the fencing team. My first poems were published in the *Harvard Monthly* and the *Harvard Advocate* (1915 on); my first poems to appear in professional periodicals came out in 1918.

"In the volume called *Eight Harvard Poets* (N.Y., 1917) I published nine poems; the other seven poets were: E. E. Cummings, J. R. Dos Passos, Robert Hillyer, R. S. Mitchell, William A. Morris, Dudley Poore, and Cuthbert Wright. The eight of us are sometimes known as the 'Eight Original Harvard Poets.'

"There is nothing to be said about my war experience, as I never got into the army. My highest job was bayonet-instructor and corporal in the Harvard camp; after that I was twice rejected from the draft.

"In 1920-1921, I was a traveling Fellow of the American-Scandinavian Foundation: I spent a year in Copenhagen, Denmark. Hillyer and I there translated together a *Book of Danish Verse,* which the foundation published in 1922."

Mr. Damon was assistant in English at Harvard, 1921-27, and is now assistant professor in English at Brown University. At the Boston Beethoven Centenary Festival, March 28, 1927, Mr. Damon, who spends much of his leisure time at the piano, read a memorial ode on Beethoven in Symphony Hall. His most important book, to date, is *William Blake: His Philosophy and Symbols* (1924), which has been the subject of much discussion and controversy. He has published two volumes of verse, *Astrolabe* (1927) and *Tilted Moons*

S. FOSTER DAMON

(1929); a biography of *Thomas Holley Chivers*, friend of Poe (1930); and a children's story, *The Day After Christmas* (1930), illustrated by Vera Bock.

Clemence Dane

CLEMENCE DANE, English novelist and playwright, whose name in private life is Winifred Ashton, has tried her hand at various professions and met with success in all of them. After being brought up in rural England and attending several schools in that country, she left school at the age of sixteen and became a teacher of French at Geneva, Switzerland. Soon she became interested in painting and abandoned her teaching to study at the Slade School of Art, where she remained three years, and later in Dresden for one year. In spite of a certain amount of success and optimistic prophesies for her as a portrait painter, she gave it up. The next year found her teaching school in Ireland, and then she startled everybody by going on the stage, playing every sort of part. She continued her theatrical activities for four or five years.

The World War came and, because of overwork, Miss Dane's health began to

CLEMENCE DANE

give way. She had long thought of writing and now began a novel which resulted in *Regiment of Women* (1917), her first published work. This was followed by two other novels in quick succession, *First the Blade* (1918) and *Legend* (1919). The latter is a piece of dramatic fiction in which a few friends, accustomed to meet in a sort of literary circle, hear the news of the illness and later the death of the most brilliant of their number. They discuss her genius, temperament, and personality and give a real picture of the woman who never appears at all in the story.

The insistence of friends that *Legend* would have made a good play led Miss Dane to dramatize it under the name, *Bill of Divorcement* (1921). This play, her first, met with instant success in London and New York, and Katharine Cornell rose to prominence in the leading rôle. It opened in New York in October of 1921. A post-war play, *Bill of Divorcement* made use of the supposition that certain amendments to the English divorce law (then being considered) had been put into effect. The action took place in 1932, on Christmas Day. Three more of Miss Dane's plays have been produced in this country: *Will Shakespeare* (1921), *The Way Things Happen* (1923), and *Granite* (1926).

Miss Dane has retained her early attachment for rural England and lives in the depths of Devonshire where she feeds her guests cold ham for breakfast. Some day she wants to give an old-fashioned house party at which the guests will include Shakespeare, Solomon, Baron Münchausen, and the Recording Angel.

Recently Miss Dane has been writing in conjunction with Helen Simpson, and three books have resulted from this collaboration: *Enter Sir John* (1928), *Printer's Devil* (1930), and *Author Unknown* (1930). The last is a light satire on London's literary circles and its lions and lambs, into which a murder-mystery is woven. Other novels by Miss Dane include *Wandering Stars* (1924); *The Babyons* (1928), the chronicle of a family; *Broome Stages* (1931).

Her plays include: *Naboth's Vineyard* (1925), *Mariners* (1926), and *Adam's*

Opera (1928). *Tradition and Hugh Walpole* (1929) is a literary biography of the English novelist with a guide to his works. *The Woman's Side* (1927) is an essay.

W. H. Davies

WILLIAM HENRY DAVIES was born April 20, 1871, in a public-house at Newport, Wales. He attended school for a few years but while still a small boy organized a robber gang among his schoolmates, and being caught stealing from merchants in the neighborhood, was forced to quit school. He was apprenticed to a picture-frame maker and as soon as his apprenticeship was completed he crossed the Atlantic.

Arriving in New York at the age of twenty-four with ten dollars, he became acquainted with a professional tramp who introduced him to the ways of hoboes and beggars. During the next six years he led the life of a vagabond, riding the rails from coast to coast, working occasionally as a berry picker and begging food from farmsteads. He made eight or nine trips with cattle to England. His tramping career came to an abrupt close in his thirtieth year, however, when he was about to head for the Klondike gold region. In boarding a Canadian train he slipped under the wheels and had his right foot cut off at the ankle, it later becoming necessary to amputate the leg at the knee.

Resolved to become a poet, Davies returned to England and lived in common lodging-houses while he peddled laces, pins, and needles for a livelihood, sometimes singing or begging in the streets. But he spent some of his time in the free libraries, reading and writing. "I was determined," he wrote later, "that, as my body had failed, my brains should now have the chance they had longed for, when the spirit had been bullied into submission by the body's activity." A tragedy he had written in blank verse was rejected by one publisher after another. Finally he bargained with a printer to publish a volume of his poems which he called *The Soul's Destroyer* (1905) and he sent copies to

Portrait by Harold Knight
W. H. DAVIES

various persons with the request that they buy them for half a crown or return them. One of these fell into the hands of Bernard Shaw, who relates the incident in his preface to Davies' *The Autobiography of a Super-Tramp* (1906): "....before I had read three lines I perceived that the author was a real poet. His work was not in the least strenuous or modern; there was no sign of his ever having read anything otherwise than as a child reads." Shaw bought some spare copies and recommended to Davies that they be sent to several critics, who at once recognized Davies as a poet of worth and introduced him to the public.

His reputation established, Davies wrote rapidly and between 1905 and 1930 published twenty volumes of poetry and eight books of prose. Three of the poetry volumes are his *Collected Poems*, which appeared in 1916, 1923, and 1929. The last edition contains more than four hundred poems. Practically everything he has written reflects in some way those early hardships, that life of the road and contact with raw earth.

Davies derived something in his reading from Defoe, Bunyan, and, more especially, the Bible. But a more obvious model for his poetic and prose style is his own experience with nature. "My heart has many a sweet bird's song," he writes in one of his lyrics, "and one that's all my own." His verses are naïve and spontaneous.

In October of 1921, Davies made his first appearance in the rôle of an editor when he took charge of the newly resuscitated magazine, *Form*. In 1926 the University of Wales gave him the honorary degree of Doctor of Literature. He is married and lives at Oxted, Surrey, where his chief recreation is walking, mostly alone.

Davies' poetry editions include: *Songs of Joy* (1917), *Farewell to Poesy* (1917), *Foliage* (1917), *Nature Poems, New Poems, True Travellers: a Tramp's Opera* (1923), *Captive Lion* (1921), *Secrets* (1924), *A Poet's Calendar* (1927), *Ambition* (1929), and *Forty-nine Poems* (1929). His prose works include: *Beggars, A Weak Woman, A Poet's Pilgrimage, Later Days* (1925), *Dancing Mad* (1927).

Owen Davis

OWEN DAVIS says that his ultimate ambition is to find out the difference between a good play and a bad one. And it seems that by this time he certainly ought to know. He is the author

OWEN DAVIS

of nearly two hundred plays which range in quality from one of the most perfectly bad plays of its era, *Nellie the Beautiful Cloak Model,* to *Icebound,* which won the Pulitzer Prize for the best American play produced in 1923.

It has been suggested by a somewhat malicious press that Owen Davis wrote *Icebound* with his tongue in his cheek— a "sop to the sophisticated." A consumate master of the craft of play writing, it was said that Mr. Davis, after writing over a hundred melodramas unaffectedly designed to please the more lurid and less discriminating taste of his audiences, and hence enormously profitable (A. H. Woods often paid Davis as much as $20,000 a year in royalties for things like *Chinatown Charlie* and *The Creole Slave's Revenge*), wrote *Icebound* in the spirit of the realism of Eugene O'Neill just to show how easy it was.

In view of Owen Davis's entire career, the whole supposition seems most unlikely. He was born in Portland, Maine, January 29, 1874, educated at Harvard, and after graduation in 1894 acted with a stock company for several years until his first play was produced in 1898. The period in the American theatre was one of extraordinary literary poverty. The renaissance of the English drama, after being in a comatose state for nearly half a century, was marked in England by the successful production of Pinero's *The Second Mrs. Tanqueray* in 1893. But it was some time before the American theatre was to feel the influence of the new realism which was gaining ground on the Continent, and made itself evident in England in 1889 by the production (which ran for three weeks) of *The Doll's House.* The theatre of Owen Davis was still devoted to adaptations of French operettas, to blood-and-thunder melodramas (such as Gilbert satirized in *Ruddigore* in 1887) and to Shakespeare. Since he could not pretend to vie with the last, Mr. Davis fell in naturally with the fashion of the first, and turned out farces at a tremendous and highly remunerative rate, and melodramas of the most satisfactorily gory variety—*The Queen of the Opium Ring, The Convict's Sweetheart,* etc.

In 1902 Mr. Davis married Elizabeth Breyer of Chicago, who played the lead

in *My Lady Nell,* produced several years
after their marriage. Between the years
1902 and 1910 he wrote fifty melodramas.
But after this there appeared a tendency
toward realism in his work. He refused
to allow *Nellie* to be revived. At this
time he wrote *An Everyday Man, The
Family Cupboard, Sinners, Opportunity,*
and *The Detour*—the last being, according to Heyward Broun, "among the five
or six best plays written by Americans,"
and in the opinion of Mr. Davis himself,
"far better than *Icebound.*" Both *The
Detour* and *Icebound* are published in
book form.

"The uneven but ascendant Owen
Davis," as Alexander Woollcott calls
him, or "our dramatic laureate," according to *The New York Tribune,* has two
sons, Owen and Donald. He used to
enjoy taking them to the circus. He
plays golf, a rather uneven game; lives
in New York; has been President of the
Authors' League of America, and American Dramatists; and he heartily believes
in the future of the motion pictures.

Mr. Davis's memoirs were published
in 1931 under the title *I'd Like to Do It
Again.*

Warwick Deeping

WARWICK DEEPING

WARWICK DEEPING likes to
think of his life in terms of the
Phoenix, that is to say, as one who "rises
on the stepping stones of his dead selves
to better things." He was born at
Southend, Essex, England, in 1877. He
was educated at Merchant Taylor's
School and Trinity College, Cambridge,
where he took his B.A. degree in 1898,
and his M.A. and M.B., in 1902. He
studied then at Middlesex Hospital and
began to practice medicine. But he had
begun to write while still a medical student. Soon after receiving his degree,
the success of his first book enabled him
to give up the profession which his
father and grandfather had pursued, and
to embrace at the same time a literary
and a marital career. Both have rewarded him. He returned to the practice of medicine, however, during the
war, joining the R.A.M.C. in 1915. He
served thru the Gallipoli Campaign,
and afterwards in France, where he was
for a time, a liaison officer for a New
York Division.

Mr. Deeping wrote for years, and had
a large number of novels, upwards of
twenty, behind him, before he wrote
Sorrell and Son. He somewhat deplores
his earlier works, which did not exactly
set the world afire. "I wish the work
I did before the war had never been
written," he once said. "I was living
a self-absorbed, dreamy life. The war
pulled me out of that. I think I came
back with bigger, more human enthusiasms. I felt I had to make a fresh
start. I began in France—I scribbled in
dug-outs, huts, and billets. I came back
feeling I had not got anywhere near
where I wanted to get, but that I had
to get there. I was after humanity, and
the life of the day, and how it would
express itself thru me." Here is
where the Phoenix analogy comes in, for,
beginning with *Sorrell and Son,* Mr.
Deeping began an almost new career.
Since then all his books have appeared
on the best seller lists, as soon as they
have been published. His books have
usually originated out of a meeting
with striking characters. At different
times Mr. Deeping met Sorrell and
old Pybus at country inns, and was so
struck by their qualities as men that
in each case a novel resulted. He lives
with his wife at his home at Wey-
bridge, where Fanny Kemble and Mrs.
Siddons spent their childhood. Here

Warwick Deeping works three hours a day in the absolute quiet that he needs for results. Mr. Deeping does not hesitate to admit that his wife has constantly been a pillar of encouragement during his entire career. He lives a regular, secluded life, cherishing his garden and his golf. He very much dislikes to be interviewed, and attending literary dinners is one of his aversions. He prefers carpentering and all out-of-door work.

Mr. Deeping's recent publications, since the beginning of his "new career," are *Sorrell and Son* (1925) *Doomsday* (1928), *Roper's Row* (1929), *Exiles* (1930), *Stories of Love, Courage and Compassion* (1930).

E. M. Delafield

E. M. DELAFIELD is the pen name chosen by Mrs. Arthur Paul Dashwood, who was born with the imposing name of Edmée Elizabeth Monica de la Pasture. For the purpose of a convenient pseudonym, "Pasture" became "field" and the name was shortened to E. M. Delafield. Her maiden name was nevertheless a distinguished one, for her father was Count Henri de la Pasture

E. M. DELAFIELD

of Llandogo, Monmouthshire. Her grandfather, Comte et Marquis de la Pasture came to England after the French Revolution. Miss Delafield's mother is now Lady Clifford. Miss Delafield was the eldest daughter, born in 1890.

During the war Miss Delafield served as V. A. D. in Exeter from 1914 to 1917, then she was offered an appointment under the Ministry of National Service in the Southwestern Region at Bristol. She remained there until the end of the war. "My first novel," she relates, "was written at the age of 24, during the war, in the intervals of Red Cross work, and since then I have been writing steadily." The novel was *Zella Sees Herself*, published in 1917.

In 1919 Miss Delafield married Major Arthur Paul Dashwood, O. B. E., late Royal Engineers, and the second surviving son of Sir George Dashwood and Lady Mary Dashwood. They have a son and a daughter. She writes: "For two years after our marriage my husband and I were in the Federated Malay States, but we now live in my native county of Devon, in the depths of the country.... It is one of my greatest ambitions to visit the U. S. A. and I hope one of these days to do so; when my two children have grown old enough to be left."

Miss Delafield hints at the way she writes her novels: "To me the most interesting study in the world is psychology, and naturally it is on that plane that I approach both the books that I read and those that I write. I have profound admiration for such writers as Edith Wharton, Anne Douglas Sedgwick, and Fannie Hurst. Sinclair Lewis is of course a great joy."

Miss Delafield's full address is Croyle, Cullompton, Devon. Her chief recreations, she says, are reading other people's books and studying criminology. In 1925 she was appointed Justice of the Peace in the county of Devon.

Her earlier works include *The Optimist* (1922), *Consequences, A Reversion to Type* (1923), *Messalina of the Suburbs* (1924), *Mrs. Harter* (1924), *The Chip and the Block* (1925). *Jill* (1926), the study of a rootless but essentially virginal girl, helped to establish Miss Delafield's reputation as a novelist. It was followed by *The Way Things Are* (1928), the story of an average woman who seeks an ideal love; *First Love* (1929), a novel of the young post-war generation in England; *Women Are Like That* (1930), seventeen short stories portraying the typical behavior of women; *Turn Back the Leaves* (1930), the story of an English Catholic family; *House Party* (1931), the portrait of a woman who knows exactly what she wants and has a way of getting it.

Walter De La Mare

WALTER JOHN DE LA MARE was born in Charleston, a village of Kent in England, in April 1873, a descendant of the famous Huguenot De La Mares and related to Browning. A dreamy child, loving to sit and read and think, he spent his literary adolescence at St. Paul's Cathedral Choir School, and then, without a college education, at Easter, in 1890, he stepped into the London office of The Anglo-American Oil Company, where he remained for eighteen years, spending his youth in the compilation of statistics. But even his tedious post as bookkeeper did not prevent him from being a poet. He wrote at his desk; he thought of himself as a poet, dressing in imitation of the French students of the Latin Quarter in Paris, with wavy abundant black hair. The drabness of his daily life perhaps made more urgent that love for fantastic beauty which has always been characteristic of his work.

His first public literary enterprise was in connection with the company house organ, which lived thru only two issues, a modest publication bound in brown paper. De La Mare was editor and publisher and wrote nearly all the contents of both issues. *Songs of Childhood* (1902), his first volume, was published under the pseudonym of "Walter Ramal," an anagram of part of his name. *Henry Brocken,* a novel (1904), was the first book to bear his own name on the title page. *Poems* followed in 1906.

Mr. De La Mare's pecuniary fortunes took a turn for the better when, under the government of Herbert Asquith, he

WALTER DE LA MARE

was placed on the Civil List for a pension of one hundred pounds a year. This official income, together with certain periodical literary work, enabled him at last to step out of the business world and devote himself entirely to writing. *The Three Mulla-Mulgars* (1910) was the first result of his added leisure.

By 1930 Mr. De La Mare had written over twenty-five volumes, which fall, according to Louis Untermeyer, into four categories: (1) The poetry of metaphysical phantasy; (2) the poems to and of children; (3) the mixture of prose and verse achieved in *Ding Dong Bell* (1924); (4) the introspective prose.

Among Mr. De La Mare's later books are the following: *The Return* (1910); *Peacock Pie* (1913); *Flora,* a book of drawings by Pamela Bianco with illustrative poems by the author; *Collected Poems, 1902-1918,* (1920); *Down-adown -Derry* (1921); *Memoirs of a Midget* (1921), which won the James Tait Black Memorial Prize, the most important literary award in England; *Come Hither* (1923), an anthology of English poetry "for the young of all ages"; *The Connoisseur, and Other Stories* (1926); *Told Again* (1927), a retelling of the world's favorite fairy tales for children; *Stories from the Bible* (1929); *Desert Islands and Robinson Crusoe* (1930), a discursive essay on the desert island as symbol and in literature; *Poems for Children* (1930); *On the Edge* (1930), a book of short stories; *The Eighteen-eighties* (1931).

A poem, he believes, is "a transfiguration of an emotion. . . It seems to me that our one hope is to get away from realism, in the accepted sense. . . To me it is utter nonsense to assume that an imaginative piece of poetry is lacking in reality. An imaginative experience is not only as real but far realer than an unimaginative one."

Mr. De La Mare lives quietly in a suburb of London with his wife and four children. He is a retiring man, "more at home in a garden than in a club."

Margaret Deland

MARGARET WADE DELAND was born in Allegheny, Pennsylvania, February 23, 1857. Her parents died when she was very young and she was brought up by an uncle and his wife, Mr. and Mrs. Benjamin Campbell, who lived in Manchester, then a suburb of Allegheny. She was educated in private schools. This spot is the original "Old Chester" of Mrs. Deland's stories and

MARGARET DELAND

the childhood associations with it have colored most of her subsequent works.

"Our home," she writes, "was a great old-fashioned country house, built by English people among the hills of western Pennsylvania more than a century ago. There was a stiff, prim garden, with box hedges and closely clipped evergreens. In front of the garden were terraces, and then meadows stretching down to the Ohio River, which bent like a shining arc about the circle of the western hills." In this old garden the little girl romped and played and became an ardent lover of nature.

The child was not allowed to read anything without Mrs. Campbell's approval. Scott, Hawthorne, Irving, Shakespeare, parts of the *Spectator* and the *Tatler,* and most of all the Bible, were put into her hands and these formed her literary taste. Mrs. Campbell helped her in her youthful writings by what might be called a judicious neglect. Everything the little girl wrote was shown to her aunt, not because Mrs. Campbell had told her she wanted to see the little stories or verses, but "because," she said, "I want to know whether you are improving in your spellings."

Mrs. Campbell wrote to a relative during this period: "Margaret is very anxious to send some of her productions to a magazine, and if I were perfectly sure they would be rejected I would allow her to do so." Mrs. Deland now feels that it is a serious mistake to allow a child to suppose that anything it writes is to be taken seriously, and she is convinced that Mrs. Campbell's wisdom was of great assistance to her in her future work.

Mrs. Deland commenced her literary activities as a poet. Her first offering, entitled "The Succory," appeared in *Harper's Magazine.* It is an out-of-door poem of twelve lines. Mrs. Deland has always been an out-of-door person, wandering amongst the trees or grubbing in a flower garden. She can name all the flowers.

Her first book, *The Old Garden* (1886), is her one and only volume of verse. It was followed by a long succession of novels, beginning with *John Ward, Preacher* (1888) and *A Summer Day* (1889). She turned intermittently from the novel to the short story as a means of gathering, little by little, the impressions of her childhood, her best volume of this kind being *Old Chester Tales* (1899).

Altho in her long career she has produced numerous works, Mrs. Deland is not a prolific writer. Her work is slow and painstaking. Her first draft of a story is only a beginning and she makes numerous subsequent revisions to exclude whatever hinders or mars the clear intuition and to reinforce the natural current of the story's life. She makes extensive changes even after a story is in type, to the dismay of compositors.

Mrs. Deland was married in 1880 to Lorin Fuller Deland. Of late years she has resided at Kennebunkport, Maine, and Cambridge, Mass. Her most recent work is *The Kays* (1926). Only two other books have appeared since 1920: *New Friends in Old Chester* (1924) and *The Vehement Flame* (1922). Among her many titles are: *Dr. Lavendar's People* (1903), *The Awakening of Helena Richie* (1906), *The Iron Woman* (1911), *Partners* (1913), *The Hands of Esau* (1914), *Around Old Chester* (1915), *The Rising Tide* (1916).

Mazo de la Roche

"**W**E were a horsey (and a doggy) family," writes Mazo de la Roche out of her memories. An only child born in 1885, she spent many years on her father's fruit farm in Ontario, near the Niagara Peninsular, and perhaps it was in those years that she grew to love the solitary ways of life in the forest country of her native Canada. For she was alone during much of her childhood—until her cousin Caroline Clement came to live with her and be her adopted sister. Surrounded by dogs and horses, a cat—Christopher—, chickens, and white pigeons, Mazo grew up in an atmosphere of gentle and deep family affection. "Shy and sensitive" she calls herself as a child.

This early life, which developed the shy, introspective side of her nature, was, no doubt, one of the contributing causes of her natural early development as a

MAZO DE LA ROCHE

writer (short stories of hers were published when she was eighteen) and of her deep, sure maturity. She was educated at home, and later took courses at the University of Toronto. Her family had French, English, and Irish ancestors—an enthnological recipe which often results (as in this case) in character with some of the diversity, the richness, and the unexpectedness of a French peasant's *pot-au-feu*. And, for a dash of garlic and red pepper, Mazo's first name is Spanish, after a friend of her father's. "My father promised my mother that if she would let him name the first, she should be allowed to name all the others. There were no others."

Her life has not been an easy one. Her father—her "broad-shouldered father," she says, with her appreciation of the overtones of the single salient adjective—died after a long illness and the family was forced to sell the old house and farm. To anyone of Mazo de la Roche's temperament, this uprooting must have been painful and terrible. The family, three members now, spent their winters in Toronto and their summers in a little house on a lake in the woods— "the lake was a dark blue bowl, its ruffled surface touched by shadows of flocking birds flying southward." Here Mazo wrote every morning: reviews, short stories, plays—*Low Life and Other Plays*, a collection published in this country in

1929 which won first prize in two competitions held in 1925 by the Imperial Order of the Daughters of the Empire, and the Dramatic Section of the Montreal Branch of the Canadian Authors' Association—and novels—*Explorers of the Dawn* (1922), *Possession* (1923), *Delight* (1926). Here, too, she began to work on *Jalna*. The lives of the three women flowed on in a deep and quiet serenity. "We wanted no outsiders. We sat together enthralled by old books. We read aloud a very old copy of *Don Quixote*—strange print and stranger pictures. Nearly a thousand pages of it."

After the influenza epidemic of 1918 the family was reduced. Mazo and her adopted sister, "my only, my dearest possession," she calls her, and her beloved Scottie, Bunty, lived on in a harmony only endangered by the narrowing, unhappy effects of poverty. Caroline had a position in the Civil Service and they were obliged to live in the city. Mazo hated it. She cannot, she says, abide "telephones, department stores, lifts, comic supplements, noisy patriotism, speeches, lectures, helpful information of any kind."

Still, with a strange intractable determination animating her long thin body with its powerful individual features—copper colored hair, glowing brown eyes, and tremendous beak of a nose—and with an unyielding self-confidence strangely at odds with her nervous and terrible fears in the face of the common crises of everyday life (catching trains, boats, or crossing streets crowded with traffic) she continued to write on the old drawing board on her knee, which she had used years before when she studied to be an illustrator, and whose "dingy surface, covered with grotesque drawings and caricatures of the people about whom I am writing, has become a veritable nightmare."

Then *Jalna* won the $10,000 Atlantic prize in 1927 for "the most interesting novel of any kind, sort or description, submitted by any writer whether born in London or Indianapolis"—"breaking," as she says, "the chains that bound me." A sequel to *Jalna*, *Whiteoaks of Jalna*, was published in the fall of 1929, and *Portrait of a Dog* in the fall of 1930. This last book was written, in part, in "the lovely Devon landscape . . . green and sunlit . . . the thick rounded clumps of trees, the hedges outlining the curious shapes of the fields . . . the song of the finch, the smell of the moss rose," and in part in Taormina, Sicily, where Mazo fled after the award, to escape what she calls the "iron Canadian winters" which try her thin, highly strung body too severely. It is the story of Bunty, her dog, her late beloved companion and friend.

Grazia Deledda

GRAZIA DELEDDA, of Italy, was the second woman to receive the Nobel Prize for achievement in literature. This was in 1926. (Selma Lagerlöf received the prize in 1909.)

The most important one of her novels which has so far been published in America is *The Mother*. It is the tragedy of a priest who is tempted from his spiritual office by the demands of love; but the keynote of the book is the mother-love that has placed a halo on his head. Pirandello called *The Mother* the greatest story written in Italy in recent times.

Grazia Deledda was born in 1872, the daughter of humble peasants, in the

GRAZIA DELEDDA

island of Sardinia, which she has used as the background for almost all of her twenty or more published novels. The little town of Nuoro was her home and here, among peasants, mountaineers, and shepherds such as she so faithfully depicts in her books, she grew up loving the wild and melancholy beauty of Sardinia. Up to the age of twenty-five years she had never left the island, but her literary career had begun when she was fifteen, her first article being published in a fashion magazine in Rome. "Then," she says, "I wrote for literary and political magazines in Sardinia. One day I wrote a romance of my home and sent it to *La Tribuna,* at Rome, trembling at my own daring. To my joy it was accepted. Before I was twenty-one I had written half a dozen Sardinian novels."

Her education was scanty; after she finished elementary school she took a few lessons in Italian and French, but aside from this she has educated herself by reading. When she was twenty-five she married a civil officer of the Ministry of War—Signor Madesani. The young couple moved to Rome, and there they still live, tho Signor Madesani retired from the public service in 1927.

Grazia Deledda is modest and retiring, and has always devoted herself to her home and her children, and even now when her children are grown, and she is recognized and honored as one of Italy's foremost writers, she still finds her greatest happiness in her own family circle. A friend of Deledda's says that her recent election to the Italian Academy of Immortals did not seem to thrill her so much as the attainment by her children of the degrees of doctor of philosophy and doctor of science, the result of the educational advantages she had secured for them by her writing and which she in her youth could not have.

She is described as "a timid little woman, her thick dark hair threaded with grey; great luminous brown eyes, a sensitive face with rather heavy features— the face of a woman of deep feeling and extreme reticence."

Among her books are *Nell Azzuro, Elias Portolu, Cenere* (tr. *Ashes*), *Il Nostro Padronne, Marianna, Sirca,* and *La Fugo in Egitto.*

Floyd Dell

FLOYD DELL was born in Barry, Illinois, June 28, 1887. His literary career began as a poet and his economic career as a factory-hand when he was forced to leave high school to earn his living at sixteen. "It was made inevitable that I should become a writer," Mr. Dell confesses, "by my gradual expulsion at an early age from most of the other available ways of making a living."

A journalistic career was the opening, and from 1905 to 1908 he was a reporter on newspapers in Davenport, Iowa, and in Chicago. When Francis Hackett became editor of the Friday Literary Review of the *Chicago Evening Post* in 1909, Dell was chosen as his assistant. At the age of twenty-three, in 1911, Dell became literary editor, building the book section into one of the livest and most stimulating that any newspaper has ever published.

Three years later he was in New York, writing principally for the radical papers. He was associate editor of the *Masses* from 1914 to 1917 and of the *Liberator* from 1918 to 1924. During this time he wrote several plays, which were first produced at the Liberal Club in Green-

FLOYD DELL

wich Village, an offshoot of which was
the Washington Square Players, which
led in turn to the Provincetown Players
and to the Theatre Guild.

In 1919 Mr. Dell married Berta-Marie
Gage of Pasadena, California. They
have two children, Anthony and Christopher. Ever since he left Greenwich Village to live at Croton-on-Hudson, Dell
has been mourned as a lost soul to the
radical cause, altho his interests remain
liberal.

After such sporadic publications as
Women as World-Builders (1913), *The
Angel Intrudes,* a one-act play (1918),
and *Were You Ever a Child?* (1919),
Mr. Dell published his first novel, *Moon-
Calf* (1920), which made him the voice
of what was then the younger genera-
tion. Since then he has published a number of volumes, among them *The Briary-
Bush* (1921), *Janet March* (1923), *This
Mad Ideal* (1924), *Looking at Life*
(1924), *Runaway* (1925), *Intellectual
Vagabondage-An Apology for the Intelligentsia* (1926), *An Old Man's Folly*
(1926), *An Unmarried Father* (1927),
The Outline of Marriage (1926-27), *Upton Sinclair* (1927), *Souvenir* (1929),
and *Love in the Machine Age* (1930).
He has also edited, together with Paul
Jordan-Smith, an all-English edition
of Burton's *Anatomy of Melancholy*
(1927). His novel *An Unmarried Father*
was successfully dramatized for a long
Broadway run as *Little Accident.*

Mr. Dell is tall, slender, rather shy.
It is reported that when he was editing
the literary section of the *Chicago Evening Post* as a mere boy, he was regarded
in some quarters as "a highly offensive
person whose brilliancy only increased
his objectionableness." Yet he is, according to Sinclair Lewis, "a faun at
the barricades," with "a valiant gentleness, a robust sensitiveness."

Viña Delmar

"**I** WAS born in New York City in the
winter of 1905," writes Viña Delmar. My father and mother were both
theatrical people and my infancy was
spent in seeing America. I went to San
Francisco at the age of three weeks and

VIÑA DELMAR

while my mother was out of her dressing
room I slept in the top tray of her trunk.

"When I was eight my mother left
the stage and settled in Flatbush where
I was sent to Public School. Mother
died when I was thirteen and my father
and I left Flatbush. We moved to the
Bronx. I did not continue my schooling. I've been working since I was sixteen. I've been on the stage. I was not
a good actress. I have an unquenchable
thirst for experience so I tried the other
side of the footlights. I was a notable
success as an usher. I have been a typist,
a switchboard operator, assistant manager of a movie picture theatre in Harlem; but none of my successes is comparable to that of my ushering days.

"I've been writing stories since I was
nine years old and had the first one published in 1922. I met my husband while
I was on the stage. We have lived most
of our married life in Inwood, New
York city, where the scene of *Bad Girl*
is almost completely laid."

Miss Delmar's first novel *Bad Girl*
(1928), a Literary Guild selection, is
the story of a typist and a mechanic.
It was praised for its realism, the honesty of the story, and the straightforward accuracy of the writing. In *Loose
Ladies* (1929) she gives eleven portraits

of American city girls. Many of these stories were mentioned for the O. Henry Memorial Award. *Kept Woman*, a novel, was published in 1929. A dramatic version of *Bad Girl* was produced on Broadway in the fall of 1930.

Babette Deutsch

BABETTE DEUTSCH was born in 1895 in New York City. She was educated there, receiving her A. B. at Barnard College in 1917. Her literary career may be said to have begun while she was still a sophomore, one of her poems having then been published in *The North American Review*. After taking her degree she was for a time assistant to the editor of *The Political Science Quarterly,* and then secretary to the late Thorstein Veblen. In 1921 she was married to Avrahm Yarmolinsky. They have two sons, Adam and Michael. Shortly after her marriage she went abroad with her husband, visiting several capitals in Western Europe, but spending the better part of her time in Russia, where Dr. Yarmolinsky was engaged in research.

Miss Deutsch's first book of poetry, *Banners* (1919), appeared two years after she left college. The second book, which was published in 1925, is entitled *Honey out of the Rock*. It was followed by *Fire for the Night* (1930), a third collection of verse, and *Epistle to Prometheus* (1931), a long philosophical poem about the Prometheus spirit thru the ages.

With her husband she has edited and translated three collections of foreign verse, entitled respectively: *Modern Russian Poetry, Contemporary German Poetry,* and *Russian Poetry*. They also co-operated in 1931 on an English version of *The Twelve*, an epic of the Russian revolution, by Alexander Blok, for a de luxe edition, illustrated with lithographs by George Biddle. Miss Deutsch has also published two novels: *A Brittle Heaven*, (1926) and *In Such A Night* (1927). The latter was published in England as well as here, and was also translated into Dutch. She has in addition written a little book of criticism:

BABETTE DEUTSCH

Potable Gold, Some Notes on Poetry and This Age (1929). This volume was the result of the first of two series of lectures which she delivered under the auspices of The People's Institute.

Miss Deutsch has contributed extensively to current periodicals, both as poet and prose writer. Many of her poems have been reprinted in various anthologies, here and in England. She won *The Nation* Poetry Prize in 1926. Three years later she was Phi Beta Kappa poet at Columbia University, reading on that occasion her sonnet sequence: "Time and Spirit," which is included in *Fire for the Night.*

Ernest Dimnet

THE Very Reverend Abbé Ernest Dimnet, canon of Cambray Cathedral, was born in 1869 in the little town of Trélon in French Flanders, the wheat-raising lowlands of the Nord, close to the Channel and the Belgian border. He grew up in stormy times, when the Monarchists and Republicans were engaged in an intense political struggle for supremacy in France. In his very first years came the terror of the Prussian invasion.

ERNEST DIMNET

As a young man he became interested in English life and literature, growing so familiar with the English tradition that he was invited to teach English at the Collège Stanislas in Paris, where he remained for many years. As early as 1898 he was writing articles for the English magazines, serving as French correspondent to *The Pilot* (1899-1903) and to the *North American Review* (1904-1909). Many of his articles have appeared in *The Nineteenth Century and After* and in the leading French, English, and American periodicals. His religious education and later his religious duties as a priest in the Roman Catholic Church seem to have promoted rather than thwarted his cultural interests. His early publications were in French and revealed both his ecclesiastical and literary persuasions. Their titles were *La Pensée Catholique dans l'Angleterre Contemporaine* (1905) and *Figures de Moines* (1908), which was crowned by the French Academy.

It is a commentary on his cosmopolitan tolerance that his next book was the study of an English Protestant family of geniuses, *Les Soeurs Brontë* (1910), the first book in French on the Brontës and an acknowledged authority in any language. Translated from the French, *The Brontë Sisters* was published in this country in 1928.

Abbé Dimnet's subsequent publications constitute a varied shelf of books: *Paul Bourget,* a literary biography (1913); *France Herself Again* (1914); *French Grammar Made Clear* (1923); *From a Paris Balcony* (1924); *Latine de Romanis* (1924); *France and Her Problems* (1924); and the spectacularly popular *Art of Thinking* (1928), by which his name is known everywhere in the United States.

Abbé Dimnet was the Lowell Lecturer at Harvard University in 1919 and French Lecturer at the Williamstown (Mass.) Institute of Politics in 1923. There he did much to promote understanding between France and the United States in that difficult and suspicious time of the parleyings over war debts and reparations.

He has a deep-rooted and fervent love for his native France, balanced by a temperamental fairness and a scholarly sense of justice. "The good Abbé" is described as "charming to meet, kindly, serene, with the white hair of his sixty-odd years, and humor in his dark eyes. He speaks with a cultivated voice. . . The qualities of mind which appear both in his conversation and in his writings are those which we are accustomed to find with delight in the French classics,— clarity, a kind of astringent simplicity, tolerant wisdom, vigor, tonic wit, firm uprightness." He is at work on a study of morals.

Hilda Doolittle (H. D.)

HILDA DOOLITTLE, whose pen name is "H.D.," was born September 10, 1886, at Bethlehem, Pennsylvania, the daughter of Charles L. Doolittle, professor of mathematics and astronomy at Lehigh University, and his second wife, Helen Eugenia Wolle.

When she was nine years old, the family moved to Philadelphia, where Professor Doolittle became Director of the Flower Astronomical Observatory at the University of Pennsylvania, a position that he held until he retired in 1912.

Her education was varied. In Bethlehem she attended a public school; in Philadelphia she entered the Gordon School, where she studied until 1902;

next she attended the Friends' Central School to prepare for entrance to Bryn Mawr College; in 1904 she matriculated at Bryn Mawr, but ill health forced her to withdraw in her sophomore year.

She began to write stories soon after leaving Bryn Mawr. It is rather surprising to learn that they were children's stories and that some of them were published in a Presbyterian paper in Philadelphia. This was her first published work.

In 1911 she went to Europe, intending to stay only for the summer, but on reaching London after a trip thru Italy and France she became interested in the literary movements and resolved to stay. When she showed some of her poetry to Ezra Pound, at that time leader of the Imagist movement, he was delighted with her work and sent it to *Poetry: A Magazine of Verse* in Chicago. In the January 1913 number of *Poetry* appeared a group of her poems, the first of hers to be published. She was soon regarded as a unique and valuable addition to the group of Imagist poets, and her work began to appear in several periodicals. Her first book, *Sea Garden,* was published in England in 1916.

She was married to Richard Aldington, likewise known then as an Imagist poet, on October 18, 1913. In the winter of 1913 they made several translations of Greek and Latin poets. The next great event in their lives was the war, of which Aldington was to write many years later in *Death of a Hero.* When her husband joined the army, H.D. assumed her duties on *The Egoist,* the London magazine which he was editing.

In 1920, following an absence of nine years, H.D. returned to the United States, but after a few months in California she took passage for Europe. Since 1921 she has lived in a small Swiss town by Lake Geneva.

A second volume of poetry, *Hymen,* was published in 1921. Her other publications are *Heliodora and Other Poems* (1924); *Collected Poems* (1925); *Palimpsest,* a novel (1926); *Hippolytus Temporizes,* a lyrical tragedy (1927); and *Hedylus,* a novel (1928).

John Dos Passos

JOHN RODERIGO DOS PASSOS was born in Chicago, January 14, 1896. He received his A. B. degree *cum laude* from Harvard in 1916 and since then has lived in Chicago, New York, Washington, Cambridge (Mass.), London, Brussels, Madrid, and Paris.

During the war Dos Passos served with the Harjes Volunteer Ambulance Service in 1917, the Red Cross Ambulance Service in Italy in 1918, and the U. S. A. Ambulance Service in 1918 and 1919. He was honorably discharged as a private in Gievre, France, July 11, 1919. After the war he married Miss Kate Smith of Chicago.

Dos Passos is so near-sighted he wears glasses about a quarter of an inch thick. One time when he went to a bull-fight abroad with Ernest Hemingway, he got into the ring to try his own hand. When the bull charged he moved the red sash instead of leaping aside and was caught between the animal's horns. Disaster was averted by Hemingway.

Recently Dos Passos has developed a strong social consciousness. He is not a Communist, but sympathizes in every way with Soviet Russia and the workers

Courtesy of Covici, Friede

H. D.

JOHN DOS PASSOS

of the world. During the Sacco-Vanzetti demonstrations, Dos Passos was arrested in the picket line in front of the Boston State House and incarcerated in the same cell with Michael Gold, editor of the *New Masses*. Dos Passos contributes frequently to the *New Masses* and other radical periodicals.

An interviewer wrote of him: "John Dos Passos isn't like his books at all. You'd rather expect the man who won renown by his championship of the private soldier and his other ultra-sophisticated volumes to be a cynical citizen who has seen thru the thin shams of existence eons ago. But quite to the contrary. Don Passos is brimming with youthful enthusiasm. When he wrote *Three Soldiers* (1921) he was hardly more than a beardless fledging. He's still too shy to speak in public or even over the radio."

Dos Passos himself once explained that he writes for "historical" accuracy and in "low moments" consoles himself with the thought that if his work should prove otherwise worthless, it at least gives an exact picture of an epoch—not necessarily in detail (altho he likes his details exact) but in spirit. Knuckling down to censorship makes him extremely uneasy, he says, because he believes that accuracy is the historian's only virtue.

Manhattan Transfer (1925) has been called the "Rhapsody in Blue of contemporary American fiction." Sinclair Lewis describes the book as presenting "the panorama, the sense, the smell, the sound, the soul, of New York. It is a long book—nearly two hundred thousand words, no doubt... The book covers some twenty-five years of growth and decay of not only the hundred or more characters, but of the whole mass of the city—the other millions of characters whom you feel hauntingly behind the persons named and chronicled." He has managed this by omitting transitions. "It is indeed, the technique of the movie, in its flashes, its cut-backs, its speed."

The 42nd Parallel (1930) is a novel of the same type as *Manhattan Transfer*, but more intricate. It deals with the rise of industrial democracy in America from three different angles simultaneously— that of a child growing up in it, from the dramatic-historical point of view, and from the critical-interpretative point of view. Nine biographical sketches include such American leaders as Carnegie, Rockefeller, Edison, and Burbank.

Dos Passos' other works include: *One Man's Initiation* (1917), a novel; *A Pushcart at the Curb* (1922), verse; *Rosinante to the Road Again* (1922), essays; *The Garbage Man* (1926), a play; *Orient Express* (1927), travel diary of a flying trip thru the Near East; and *Airways, Inc.* (1928), another play. *Orient Express* has illustrations in color from paintings by the author. Being as adept with the brush as with the pen, he has also designed scenery for the production of his plays.

In 1931 he will publish a book of fiction, called *1919,* and a translation, with illustrations, of Blaise Cendrars' *Panama.*

Norman Douglas

"A RUGGED, sensitive figure" with one of the most iridescent male voices I have ever heard" is the impression of Norman Douglas written by Muriel Draper. "He spoke rapidly but very distinctly, with a slight shaping of his words on his under-lip that just escaped a lisp. The infinitely varied inflections of his voice rose and fell on a constantly sliding scale, so that even his pauses were a vibrating sound bridge between words."

And his chuckle "was the most satisfactory sound one could hear. It was focussed in his throat, drawing into itself all the reinforcement that could be extracted from every different part of the . . . body."

This man, whom she describes as having a "terrifyingly intelligent humorous gleam in his eye" and an "indescribably rich 'know' flowing from him," was born in 1868. The first twelve years of his life were spent in "growing up," the second twelve were devoted to music, and the next twelve, between the ages of twenty-four and thirty-six, were spent in diplomatic service which took him to many countries and acquainted him with many languages. The fourth twelve-year period was devoted to study and investigations in geology, zoology, and archaeology, and the writing of treatises on these subjects. He lived on the island of Capri where he had his geological specimens fenced in for observation.

That brings him to the age of forty-eight. At this point in his career he turned from his special studies and writings to the production of short stories and thence the creation of books. At the age of sixty, in 1928, he expressed an apprehension lest the twelve-year myth which he had built up about his life should mean a turn from the productive period of writing. "The twelve years are up, you know," he said, "I'm sixty." But he has continued his vigorous writing.

"At the age," Miss Draper writes, "when most men are retiring on a special diet, spending half their lives in curing their bodies of ills that come from not having used them, to say nothing of their minds, he is at present walking about the surfaces of the earth, watching his fellowman and woman, the world they live in, the animal and vegetable life that exists upon it, and, with his unique wisdom, humour, and ageless vitality, forming his own conclusions. He returns to Florence occasionally, to look

at his mail, collect whatever modest sums accrue to his credit, drink a bottle of wine with a friend, and starts off again."

Douglas first appeared in print in 1886 with a series of articles on animal observations for *The Zoologist,* journal of natural science. Then, at intervals between 1889 and 1895, he published several more zoological treatises. In 1901 came his first attempt at creative writing with *Unprofessional Tales,* which, he says, "were published, thank God, under a pseudonym, and eight copies were sold." Signed "Normyx," they were a group of short stories and sketches with a poem or two. Most of his literary efforts between the years 1904 and 1915 consisted of numerous monographs reflecting his scientific studies.

In 1911, however, Douglas' first book, *Siren Land* was published. The manuscript, he says, "was hawked about for more than a year without success," and Joseph Conrad and Edward Garnett were instrumental in finally getting a publisher to accept it. The first edition, numbering fifteen hundred copies, sufficed for twelve years and the author's royalties amounted to less than sixty dollars. *South Wind,* which appeared in

NORMAN DOUGLAS

1917 when Douglas was forty-nine, made his reputation as a novelist but did badly by him financially. "*South Wind*, indeed!" he comments, "Do you know what I got for that? Seventy-five pounds. I sold the book outright—too hard up to make terms. Haven't received another penny for it."

In 1930 Douglas published *Goodbye to Western Culture*. It is a series of about a hundred brief essays, notes, and marginal jottings which present a scathing indictment of European and especially British culture, occasioned by Katherine Mayo's *Mother India*. Other books by Douglas include: *They Went* (1921), *Together* (1923), *Fountains in the Sand* (1923), *Experiments* (1925), *Old Calabria* (1928), *Birds and Beasts of the Greek Anthology* (1929), *One Day* (1929), and *Three of Them* (1930).

At the age of sixty, Douglas looked back over his career: "Haven't made five hundred pounds by this damned writing you talk so much about since I first began it. . . But friends—that's another matter. Sometimes friends are kind, you know, just as sometimes God is not stupid."

William A. Drake

WILLIAM A. DRAKE, one of the most versatile and prolific of the younger writers in New York, was born in Dayton, Ohio, December 9, 1899. His education has been entirely informal; he has never attended school in the rôle of a student, and holds no academic diploma or degree from any institution. He received instruction at home from a tutor for a time, but is largely self-taught. Yet he was a member of the faculty of Antioch College, at Yellow Springs, Ohio, teaching comparative literature, and has given a series of lectures at Columbia University.

Mr. Drake was engaged in newspaper work, chiefly as an editorial writer, from 1916 to 1918. Until 1922 he was in direct mail advertising work, also in the middle west, and served as a merchandising consultant.

Shortly after his arrival in New York in 1922 he became managing editor of

WILLIAM A. DRAKE

Vanity Fair. From 1924 when he left this magazine until 1929 when he gave up his position as assistant supervisor of production for Paramount Famous Lasky Corporation to do his own writing, he was executive secretary of the New York Stage Society, Inc., associate editor of *The Art News*, and general press representative of Charles Frohman, Inc. In addition to these activities, he contributed the entire page "Books Abroad" to *Books*, the literary supplement of the *New York Herald Tribune* from 1924 to 1927.

Mr. Drake and Miss Ethel Lewis were married in 1922. Mrs. Drake is an interior decorator and a writer of articles on that subject.

Mr. and Mrs. Drake and their three-year old son have homes both in New York City and on Long Island. The son, incidentally, has never been given a first name; he is to be allowed to select his own when he reaches the age of discretion. For the sake of convenience, however, he is called "Bill" or "Young Bill."

Mr. Drake is small, energetic, alert, with black hair, and keen, intelligent eyes. Many anecdotes are told about him because of his extremely youthful looks, one being that soon after he had joined the staff of *Vanity Fair* as managing editor he was accosted in the hall and asked to join the office boys' baseball team. That Mr. Drake is an extremely hard worker is proved by the bulk of his production; he frequently works from sixteen to eighteen hours a day.

He has contributed verse, short stories, translations, literary criticism and essays to a number of periodicals. The bulk of his published work consists of translations from French, German, Italian, Spanish, Hungarian, Russian, Roumanian, Czech, Latin, Greek, and Hebrew. He admits having dropped three languages because he was a little hard pressed for time.

He is author of *The War Poetry* (1920) and *Contemporary European Writers* (1928). The latter is a critical study of some forty of the most notable European writers; some of these essays were reprinted from his page in *Books* of the *Herald Tribune*. These in revised form with at least fifty additional are to be published under the title *Studies in Contemporary Literature* in the fall of 1931. *George Bryan Brummell, Beau and Hypocrite,* is also in preparation for 1931 publication.

The following books have been edited by Mr. Drake: *The Memoirs of Carlo Goldoni* (1926); *American Criticism* (1926); *Il Pentamerone,* by Giovanni Batiste Basile (1927); *The Memoirs of Prince Metternich,* in two volumes (1931).

Among Mr. Drake's translations are *Daybreak* (1927) and *Theresa* (1928) by Arthur Schnitzler. He is co-translator of *The Book of Marriage,* by Count Hermann Keyserling (1926), and other books.

Mr. Drake is also the translator and adapter of several plays which have been successful on Broadway, among them the outstanding hit of the 1930-31 season, *Grand Hotel,* by Vicki Baum. Others include *Schweiger,* by Franz Werfel, in which Ann Harding and Jacob Ben Ami had the leads in the 1925 season. His adaptation of Maurice Donnay's version of *Lysistrata* has been announced for production by the Theatre Guild.

Mr. Drake also finds time to publish a few finely printed books in limited editions under the imprint of The Golden Drake Press.

Theodore Dreiser

THEODORE DREISER, American novelist, was born in Terre Haute, Indiana, August 27, 1871. His father was a strict Catholic. "I never knew," says Dreiser, "a narrower, more hidebound religionist nor one more tender and loving in his narrow way." Dreiser's mother was "a happy, hopeful animal; an open, uneducated, wondering, dreamy mind; a pagan mother taken over into the Catholic Church at marriage." The first books he really liked were Goldsmith's *Deserted Village* and *The Vicar of Wakefield.*

After attending the public schools of Warsaw, Indiana, Dreiser went to Chicago at sixteen and worked for a hardware company at five dollars a week. At eighteen he attended Indiana University, but after about a year of study he was forced to leave because of the economic pressure. Back in Chicago, he became a clerk in a real estate office and later a collector for a furniture house. "But my

THEODORE DREISER

daily work seemed trivial to me and I felt I was no good at it." He longed to be a newspaperman and haunted newspaper offices till he was "as well known as a lost dog."

Dreiser entered newspaper work in June 1892, on the *Chicago Daily Globe*. He was dramatic editor and travelling correspondent for *The St. Louis Globe-Democrat* in 1892 and 1893, and travelling correspondent for *The St. Louis Republic*, 1893-94. In 1894 he went to New York. The following year he became editor of *Every Month*, a musical magazine, which position he held until 1898. Subsequently he worked on a number of special assignments, articles and series of articles, interviews, and sketches. He read Herbert Spencer and lost "every shred of belief."

Dreiser edited *Broadway Magazine*, and was for a time editor-in-chief of the Butterick publications, including *The Delineator*. As an editor for this woman's magazine, he is said to have been cautious and conservative. In 1898 Dreiser married a "very lovely" St. Louis girl, "religious, thoughtful, well-read," but the marriage was not a success. "It was a binding state and I was not to bound. . . I begged her to set me free and she did."

Dreiser is tall, broad and blond, quiet, deliberate, and apparently phlegmatic. His forehead is powerful, his eyes keen; the lower part of his face he terms "lumpy." He speaks slowly, in a soft, well-modulated voice. He has known rebuffs and criticism; an air of humility and equally of pride is stamped on him, producing the same impression as his books, that of dogged persistency, honesty, and curiosity about life. He is slow to anger, but has slapped a Nobel Prize winner in resentment of a charge of plagiarism.

"Theodore Dreiser," writes Llewelyn Powys, "is one of those who are utterly incapable of swallowing the world as a young cuckoo swallows the grub that its wagtail mother has brought to it. He must look under every leaf, turn over every stone. His great lumbering imagination, full of divine curiosity, goes roaring thru the prairie-lands of the Cosmos with the restless heavy-shouldered force of an old bull *wildebeest*. Whenever I am with him and can watch his cumbersome intellect at work upon any one of the manifold subjects that occupy his attention, subjects like 'the trickiness of women,' the breeding of pigeons, the reasoning-power of a spider he studied once in his bed-chamber, or the electronic basis of the Universe, I never fail to be amazed, never fail to feel awe at the struggles of this ungainly giant, whose limbs are still half buried in clay."

Sister Carrie (1900) was Theodore Dreiser's first novel. It is generally thought that he was entirely obscure until the publication of his first book, but this is disproved by his inclusion in the first volume of *Who's Who in America* (1899). With the other biographical details is given: "Author: *Studies of Contemporary Celebrities; Poems*." This has caused many people to attempt to trace these two books, but as neither was ever published, it is naturally hopeless. Both were projects which did not materialize. He had published some forty articles before *Sister Carrie* appeared.

Some one has said that Dreiser has always been fortunate in his enemies. *Sister Carrie* was withdrawn immediately by the publishers after only a few copies had been distributed. *Jennie Gerhardt* (1911), *The Financier* (1912), *A Traveller at Forty*, an autobiography (1913), and *The Titan* (1914) followed.

The Genius (1915) met the same fate as *Sister Carrie* and was banned in 1916. Other books followed, including *A Book About Myself* (1922), devoted largely to the author's journalistic career. *An American Tragedy* was published in 1925, the disturbance over which has not yet entirely ceased; it was brought into the Boston courts and is still banned there, altho a number of colleges in various parts of the country have it on their reading lists for students.

Dreiser visited Russia recently "to revive my understanding of America." "Life is life," he said. "It may be a lolling, fat, disgusting thing, but in the hand of a master it would become a very sardonic thing. The life of America today, fast verging as it is on social tragedy, should lend itself to satire and irony. Or perhaps, we might have a literature of despair like that of Dostoievsky."

Dreiser's recent books include: *Dreiser Looks at Russia* (1928); *A Gallery of Women* (1929); *Dawn* (1931), subtitled "An Autobiography of Early Youth."

John Drinkwater

JOHN DRINKWATER was born June 1, 1882. "When I was nine," he writes, "I was sent off to the High School at Oxford, where I stayed for six years. I cannot remember that I took any particular interest in anything in the class-rooms, or that anybody took any particular interest in me. But I acquired an enthusiasm for games which I have never lost. I was, I think, the youngest boy to get colors in both the cricket and football elevens of my time, and I am quite unreasonably proud of the fact that I made a record for the junior long jump that has stood for over thirty years. I was under fourteen; the jump was 15 ft., 8 ins. But in school, so far as my credit to the masters was concerned, I was a total loss. I once got a form prize; but as I had stayed in the form two years over my time, they couldn't help giving it to me. I also, quite unaccountably, got a chemistry prize. How that could have happened I cannot conceive."

He had to begin to earn his living as soon as possible and his father put him into an insurance office hoping to discover in him some business ability. But all his interests were in books and he was desperately anxious to go on the stage. However, he stuck to his insurance work for twelve years, keeping himself to begin with on thirty-five pounds a year, and he remembers how two of them at lunch time would subscribe 1½d between them and he would go to the market place in Nottingham and "come back with a large bag full of bad fruit from which he would cut out the good parts."

In 1903, at the age of 21, he published his first book, *Poems*, followed by another collection of verse, *The Death of Leander* (1906). These he refers to as "two books of unbelievably bad verse, which I have been trying to escape ever since; tho I might have spared myself

anxiety, as, happily, no one ever took any notice of them. An uncle to whom I sent the first book, with a request that he should buy it, sent a postal order for half-a-crown, with the advice that I should give up the writing, as one should say 'the drink.'"

In 1907, he met Barry Jackson in Birmingham and with him and some other kindred souls formed an amateur society known as the Pilgrim Players, finding an outlet for self-expression in producing as well as writing plays. Here his first play *Cophetua* was acted. In 1913, the movement had made sufficient heading in the town to persuade Barry Jackson to build the Repertory Theatre. It was then that his distasteful business career was given up and he became manager of the Birmingham Repertory Theatre. In 1918 *Abraham Lincoln* was produced at Birmingham and John Drinkwater came into his own.

Mr. Drinkwater is perhaps best known as a poetic dramatist, altho his lyrics are also popular. Besides *Abraham Lincoln*, he has written several plays about historical figures: *Mary Stuart* (1921), *Oliver Cromwell* (1921), *Robert E. Lee* (1923), *Robert Burns* (1925). In writing his biographical plays Mr. Drinkwater absorbs a great

JOHN DRINKWATER

deal of material and familiarizes himself from many sources with the people and their environment. Then having made a great many notes he puts them aside and does the actual writing of the play in as short a time as possible. "I have an idea," he says, "that by doing this one ought to get behind a simplified expression a great pressure from all the material in the background."

Mr. Drinkwater's *Collected Poems* were published in 1923; his *Collected Plays* in 1925. He is a remarkably prolific writer, having published close to fifty volumes of verse, drama, and prose by 1931. His critical prose includes monographs on Morris and Swinburne, essays on *The Lyric*, *The Nature of Drama*, and many miscellaneous papers. Turning his hand to biography, he has written a life of Byron, *The Pilgrim of Eternity* (1925); *Mr. Charles, King of England* (1926); *Charles James Fox* (1928); *Pepys: His Life and Character* (1930); *The Life of Carl Laemmle, motion-picture producer* (1931). He is also the author of *All About Me* (1928), a book of verses for children; and *American Vignettes* (1930). His comedy, *Bird in Hand* (1929), has been a great popular success on the stage in both London and New York.

Mr. Drinkwater devotes most of his spare moments to philately, specializing in Confederate stamps, of which he has a fine collection. He married in 1924 and has one daughter.

Lord Dunsany

LORD DUNSANY, the 18th Baron Edward John Moreton Drax Plunkett, was born July 24, 1878, and educated at Cheam School and Eton.

In a letter to Frank Harris, Dunsany wrote: "I think I owe most of my style to the reports of proceedings in the divorce court; were it not for these my mother might have allowed me to read newspapers before I went to school; as it was she never did. I began reading Grimm and then Andersen. I remember reading them in the evening with twilight coming on. All the windows of rooms I

LORD DUNSANY

used in the house in Kent where I was brought up faced the sunset. . . When I went to Cheam School I was given a lot of the Bible to read. This turned my thoughts eastward. For years no style seemed to me natural but that of the Bible and I feared that I never would become a writer when I saw that other people did not use it. When I learned Greek at Cheam and heard of other gods a great pity came on me for those beautiful marble people that had become forsaken and this mood has never quite left me."

In 1904 Dunsany married Lady Beatrice Villiers, the youngest daughter of the 7th Earl of Jersey. They have one son, the Hon. R.A.H. Plunkett. Lord Dunsany served in both the South African War and, as Captain of the Royal Inniskilling Fusiliers (wounded April 25, 1916), in the World War.

He is six feet, four inches, in height, and he adds: "Our trenches were only six feet deep. I shall never fear 'publicity' again." According to his calculations, 97 per cent of his life has been spent out of doors in athletic activities, following the hounds, hunting big game, playing cricket, and soldiering. The other 3 per cent he has devoted to writing.

William Butler Yeats first produced a play by Lord Dunsany, *The Glittering Gate*, at the Abbey Theater. Other plays by him were soon being staged in Moscow and the United States. His chief interest is in the writing of plays and tales, but in 1929 he added *Fifty Poems* to the long list of his books.

"One should never write literature except to please oneself," is his judgment. "Writing to please popular fancy should never be done. Then one is attempting to tell what the other person thinks; what his ideas of and reactions to life are. It is impossible to know another man's mind. That is why so much literature does not ring true."

His method of writing he describes as follows: "I begin with anything, or with next to nothing. Then, suddenly, I get started, and go thru in a hurry. The main point is not to interrupt a mood. Writing is an easy thing when one is going strong and fast; it becomes a hard thing only when the onward rush is impeded. Most of my short plays have been written in a sitting or two."

He believes that altho people may not be good judges of poetry they are excellent judges of the drama, "for all art is simply essence of life, but the drama is life itself."

Lord Dunsany is described as excessively tall, loose-jointed, raw-boned, rather awkward, with a large head and "enormous" hands and feet. His gait is shambling; he talks fluently and well, being friendly and conversable. His fine Celtic blue eyes reflect the boyish frankness of his nature. He has traveled much in foreign countries, including the United States.

This is a selected list from Lord Dunsany's numerous books: *The Gods of Pegana, Time and the Gods, A Dreamer's Tales, Five Plays, Fifty-One Tales, Tales of Wonder, Plays of Gods and Men, The Laughter of the Gods, Unhappy Far-Off Things, The Chronicles of Rodriguez, If, Plays of Near and Far, The Charwoman's Shadow* (1926), *The Blessing of Pan* (1928), *Seven Modern Comedies* (1929), *Travel Tales of Mr. Joseph Jorkens* (1931).

T. S. Eliot

THOMAS STEARNS ELIOT, poet and critic, was born in St. Louis, Missouri, in 1888, the son of Henry Ware Eliot and Charlotte Chauncey Eliot. Mrs. Eliot is the author of a poetic drama, *Savonarola*, for which her son wrote the introduction. The Eliots come of a long line of New Englanders and are connected with the family of which the late Charles W. Eliot, president of Harvard University, was a distinguished member. T. S. Eliot went East after receiving his secondary training in the Middle West. He received his A. B. from Harvard in 1909, his A. M. in 1910, and entered the Sorbonne the following year.

He subsequently studied at Merton College, Oxford University, and in 1914 went to London where he has lived since that time. He married Miss Vivienne Haigh-Wood, of London.

Eliot was a bank clerk for a short time in London, and for several years taught and lectured. He became assistant editor of *The Egoist* before he helped found the *Criterion*, of which he still is editor. He is on the editorial and advisory board of Faber and Faber, a London publishing house.

Altho in some ways a typical product

Pen and ink sketch by Powys Evans
T. S. ELIOT

of the New England civilization, with "all of the Puritan fastidiousness, scrupulousness, prudence, and preoccupation with moral questions," Mr. Eliot has completely expatriated himself from this country and has never returned to the United States since he first went abroad. In doing so, he has "escaped from contemporary America . . . and evolved for himself an aristocratic myth out of English literature and history." He became a British citizen in 1927 and recently joined the Anglo-Catholic church. In *For Lancelot Andrewes,* essays on style and order (1929), he announces that he is "an Anglo-Catholic in religion, a classicist in literature, and a royalist in politics." Such views have identified Eliot with the humanists, who desire a return to the classical ideal in literature.

Alfred Kreymborg describes an evening with Eliot at the latter's apartment in Clarence Gate Gardens, London. "The man was as clearly the expression of the artist as the artist was of the man. The suave intelligence was given over to the pursuit of a refinement of experience from which unnecessary details dropped away with an ironical tho almost imperceptible smile. The man was beautiful to look at as well as to listen to, and one could readily give credence to the rumor that he had become the idol of the most exclusive set in Mayfair. Always a little more subtle than the subtlest Englishman, Eliot was the high priest of the best of the younger English poets and essayists."

An anecdote, told by Burton Rascoe, concerns Eliot ("who looks like an Arrow Collar man") at a tea party given by Lady Rothermere at which a great number of literary and artistic lions were present. Eliot was asked by a much impressed American visitor if he didn't think the party was very interesting. "Yes," he replied, "if you concentrate on the essential horror of the thing." His poems often concentrate on that "essential horror."

The volume of work published by Mr. Eliot is exceedingly small in comparison with the influence he has exerted over the younger writers both in America and England. "The Love Song of J. Alfred Prufrock," a poem which had been writ-

ten when he was a student in Harvard, was published in England in 1917 in *Prufrock and Other Observations.* It was reprinted in *Poems* (London 1919, New York 1920), a book of sixty-three pages containing twenty-four poems, five of them in French. "Portrait of a Lady" and "Sweeney Among the Nightingales" are among the other familiar poems in this volume. *Ara Vos Prec* (1919) is a slim volume of verse.

The Sacred Wood (1920), a collection of essays, established Eliot's position as a critic. By 1922, when *The Waste Land* was published, Eliot's reputation was considerable in advanced literary circles. This poem occasioned probably the most violent literary controversy in the '20s, no two critics agreeing as to its interpretation or merit. The reading public as a whole considered that it was being duped by clever (perhaps) but meaningless (certainly) utterances. Edmund Wilson, who championed Eliot, reviewed it in *The Dial,* giving a readable summary. "Mr. Eliot uses the Waste Land as the concrete image of a spiritual drought. His world takes place half in the real world—the world of contemporary London, and half in a haunted wilderness— the Waste Land of the medieval legend; but the Waste Land is only the hero's arid soul and the intolerable world about him." Assembled in this poem are classical allusions, quotations (without quotation marks) from thirty-one sources, a mixture of Shakespeare, Baudelaire, the Bible, vaudeville ballads, Swinburne, Eliot's own poems, the Upanishads, etc. There are obscurities in the poem, but critics now agree to this extent: that the poem is successful in the development of its tragic theme. The *Dial* award was given to Eliot primarily for *The Waste Land,* in 1922.

Eliot has been influenced by the French symbolist poets, to whom he was introduced by Arthur Symons' *Symbolist Movement in Literature.* "I myself owe Mr. Symons a great debt," he has written. "But for having read his book I should not, in the year 1908, have heard of Laforgue and Rimbaud; I should probably not have begun to read Verlaine; and but for reading Verlaine, I should not have heard of Corbière. So the Symons book is one of those which

have affected the course of my life."
Ezra Pound's poems also influenced Eliot
in his early work.

Since the publication of *The Waste
Land*, Eliot's work has been mostly
critical. *Homage to John Dryden*
(1924); *Shakespeare and the Stoicism
of Seneca* (1928), an address read before the Shakespeare Association; *An
Essay of Poetic Drama* (1928); *For
Lancelot Andrewes* (1928); and *Dante*
(1929), an introduction to the appreciation of the Italian poet's work, have
confirmed his high position among English critics.

An edition of Eliot's collected poems,
Poems 1909-1925, appeared in 1925. In
1930 he published *Ash Wednesday*, a
short series of poems, testifying to the
progress of his religious faith.

HAVELOCK ELLIS

Havelock Ellis

HENRY HAVELOCK ELLIS was
born February 2, 1859, in a small
flint-built house close to a picturesque
old church in Croydon, Surrey. Altho
his family on both sides had been closely
connected with the sea for generations,
his ancestry also traces back thru both
his father and his mother to prominent
17th and 18th century churchmen.

When the boy was six he accompanied
his father, a sailor for fifty years and
then Captain of *The Empress,* to Sydney, Peru, Chile, and elsewhere. This
trip lasted a year and upon his return
Ellis was enrolled in a boys' school in
London, where he studied until the age
of twelve. Between the years he was
twelve and sixteen he received private
instruction. His chief interests were
literature and music, and he was fond
of playing Beethoven's sonatas. He had
also commenced writing poetry.

Ellis made a second trip to Australia
for his health at the age of sixteen, and
thru accidental circumstances began to
teach. The following year he tutored
a family in the Bush; in 1877 he conducted a private school of his own; and
in 1878 he was in charge of a government school under the Board of Education at Sparkes Creek, New South
Wales, (the Kanga Creek of his short

novel by that title, written in 1892 but
not published until 1922).

Ellis' "conversion" was begun during
this four-year period, and his ideas
changed radically from the typically Victorian ones which his training had led
him to have. He was influenced by Hinton's *Life in Nature* and by Hopkins'
Life and Letters of James Hinton. His
conclusion was that it was necessary for
him, fundamentally, to have a complete
knowledge of biology in order to understand himself and other persons. He
returned to London and enrolled at St.
Thomas's Hospital.

Olive Schreiner, author of *The Story
of an African Farm*, and Ellis became
friends in 1884. She had experienced a
similar indecision between medicine and
writing, and was influential in his abandoning the active practise of medicine
which he had just begun.

When Ellis was still at St. Thomas's
he had contributed an essay on Hardy
to *The Westminster Review,* and he now
decided to apply his scientific attitude to
literary criticism. Consequently in 1886-
87 he was in charge of the theology section of *The Westminster Review,* and
thru certain of the books reviewed at
that time became interested in the Chinese ideals of culture.

In 1886 Ellis edited two volumes of Landor's *Imaginary Conversations* for the Camelot Series, under the editorship of Ernest Rhys, and the following year he edited Ibsen's plays. His next enterprise was the editorship of the Mermaid Series, 1887-1889, which has made Elizabethan and Restoration Drama accessible to the general public since that time.

Ellis was becoming more absorbed in psychology, and turned his knowledge of biology into a special study of sexual psychology. *The New Spirit* (1891), his first book, was a group of literary essays. He then began his series, *Studies in the Psychology of Sex.*

Ellis's contributions to this branch of science are inestimable, altho at the present time the more popular researches of the Freudian school to a considerable degree overshadow the methods of Ellis, in which more emphasis is laid on biology and less on clinical experience.

Ellis's best known book is *The Dance of Life* (1923), in which he conceives of life as an art, and the dance its symbol, signifying the rhythm of the entire universe. His other works include *Affirmations* (1897), *A Study of British Genius* (1904 and 1926), *The Soul of Spain* (1908), *The Philosophy of Conflict* (1919). He has also translated Zola's *Germinal* (1925) and published a book of poems, *Sonnets, with Folk Songs from the Spanish* (1925).

Ellis and Miss Edith Lees were married in 1891. She died in 1916 directly after their return to England from a lecture tour in the United States. Ellis's way of living has changed little since 1891. His tastes are simple, and he spends spring and fall in London, the winter by the sea, and the summer in some inland country. His home in London is a four-room-and-kitchen apartment in Brixton, far enough from the center of the city to be economical as well as peaceful. He is an excellent cook, and his friends speak highly of the dinners prepared by him, served with claret or Burgundy.

Ellis is described as looking like a sailor with his fine head, high forehead, deep eyes, white hair, white moustache and beard, and clear ruddy complexion.

John Erskine

"**A** HUGE mast of a man with a bright rudder of a nose, a humorous diagonal mouth, a sabre wit, the manner of a Sidney" is the way Henry Morton Robinson describes John Erskine, "poet, novelist, scholar, musician, and teacher."

John Erskine's lectures are popular events at Columbia and students even cut other classes to hear him. "His manner of lecturing is unique," Mr. Robinson writes. "I have never seen him refer to notes. I am sure he does not 'study up' on a poet before a lecture; he is always revolving his poets in his mind. Professor Erskine speaks casually, intimately, as tho he had just been lunching with the man he is talking about."

Born in New York City on October 5, 1879, John Erskine attended Columbia Grammar School and entered Columbia College, where he received his A. B. degree in 1900. A year later he was granted an A. M. and in 1903 a Ph. D. His other degrees are LL. D. (Norwich, 1919), Litt. D. (Amherst, 1923), and L. H. D. (Hobart, 1927). He taught English at Amherst from 1903 to 1909 before returning to Columbia.

During the war Erskine served in France as chairman of the Army Edu-

JOHN ERSKINE

cation Commission and as chief of the A. E. F. University at Beaume. For his work, France made him Chevalier of the Legion of Honor and his own country gave him the Distinguished Service Medal. When he returned to Beaume on a vacation he was the center of an enthusiastic demonstration, so well had he impressed the citizens.

Actaeon, his first volume of poetry, appeared in 1907. In 1915 he published a volume of essays, *The Moral Obligation to be Intelligent.* A second book of verse, *The Shadowed Hour,* made its appearance in 1917. Numerous essays and poems followed in the succeeding years up to 1925. Until the publication of *The Private Life of Helen of Troy* in that year, Erskine's works had been mostly for the scholarly reader. But within a month that book attained a larger sale than any other book in the country and Erskine returned from Europe in the fall to find himself both celebrated and prosperous.

He was prompted to write *Helen of Troy* because he felt she was a popular personage who had been neglected and about whom people knew too little. "The reason *Helen of Troy* was popular," he says, "is not so much my fault as it is that since Homer she has been consistently celebrated—an eternal favorite." The same motive prompted him to produce *Galahad* (1926).

"I cannot remember that I ever cherished a desire to be a novelist," Erskine says. "At five or six years I began studying the piano, and even in college I maintained the decision to be a pianist." Then he abandoned the piano for twenty-six years, but took it up again about 1923. "I had to," he says. "The urge returned with such ferocity that I felt I'd go mad if I didn't play again." One season he toured with the New York Symphony Orchestra as soloist, "just for fun." He is chairman of the administrative committee of the Juilliard School of Music.

"This man is a great furnace of energy," Mr. Robinson writes, "yet his outward demeanor is leisurely and calm, as tho he were on a perennial week-end in the country." Erskine makes use of his odd moments. If he has ten minutes

here or half an hour there, he will sit down at the piano or plunge into a novel where he left off work the night before. He follows no set routine. He spends his days lecturing, conferring in seminars and committees, accessible always to students, carrying on a tremendous correspondence, and writing in the quiet hours at night. *Helen of Troy* was written between the hours of eleven P. M. and one A. M. from January to June 1925.

Other books by Erskine are: *Adam and Eve* (1927), *Penelope's Man* (1928), *Sincerity* (1929), *Uncle Sam* (1930), *Cinderella's Daughter* (1930), *Jack and the Beanstalk* (1931). His essays and poems include: *The Kinds of Poetry* (1920), *The Literary Discipline* (1923), *Sonata and Other Poems* (1925), and *Prohibition and Christianity* (1927). He wrote a play called *Hearts Enduring* (1920).

Susan Ertz

A COSMOPOLITAN training, with opportunities to study people, is the background which serves Susan Ertz in writing her novels dealing with the problems of modern men and women. She was born in England of American parents, both New Yorkers. At a very early

SUSAN ERTZ

age she was brought to America, but returned to England at the age of seven and remained there five years. When she was twelve years old she crossed the Atlantic again and spent the six following years in the Sierra Nevada mountains of California.

"In the company of brothers and a sister," she says, "I sat at the feet of an English governess who had a liking for adventure. Our studies were pursued in a small cabin, at desks made of rough hewn pine. The mountain winters were so severe that we went down to the milder climate of San Francisco until the snows were melted. I was in that city at the time of the disaster of 1906. But those long, happy summers in the pine forests of the Sierras are unforgettable."

At eighteen Miss Ertz had a taste of New York life and then returned to England in May 1914 "to the enjoyment of a few perfect months before the World War." She did war work in London, "a spectator of every kind of heroism except the actual heroism of the battle-fields." During the war she was six months in New York, returning to England to do canteen work for American soldiers from late in 1917 until after the armistice.

Her first novel, *Madame Claire,* appeared in 1922. Its success was not instantaneous but it grew steadily to popularity. She asserted her strength with *Nina* (1924), the story of a woman's hopeless infatuation for an unfaithful husband. Her next novel was *After Noon* (1926), the tale of a middle-aged man, his well-founded skepticism on the subject of marriage, his upbringing of two daughters abandoned in infancy by their faithless mother, and his middle-aged marriage. In *Now East, Now West* (1927), Miss Ertz explains, in the form of a novel, the chief differences between the English and the American mentality. *The Galaxy* was published in 1929. It is the story of one woman's life from her birth in 1862 to her death in London after the war.

Unlike many women writers, Miss Ertz does not number other women writers among her most intimate friends. She prefers knowing all sorts and conditions of men and women, which prefer-ence keeps her from remaining in any little coterie. To meet, she is a calm young woman, quietly dressed. She is bored by movies and would rather talk to anybody, or listen to anybody talking. She is fond of the prose of Max Beerbohm and the singing of Paul Robeson. Her favorite amusements, besides conversation, are fishing, dancing, and travel. She is of the opinion that women merely follow where men lead. At present she is living in London and says: "I would rather have a new idea, even if it is given to me by somebody else, than a diamond wrist watch, any day."

The novels by Miss Ertz are: *Madame Claire* (1922), *Nina* (1924), *After Noon* (1926), *Now East, Now West* (1927), and *The Galaxy* (1929). Among her other works is a collection of short stories, *The Wind of Complication* (1927).

St. John Ervine

"AN Irishman who never hesitates to speak his mind"—that describes St. John Ervine, dramatist, critic and novelist. He has been pictured further as "a cheerful and enthusiastic soul with a sanguine nature. Red-headed and

St. John Ervine

salmon-pink complexioned, he has more of a military than of a literary look." And he walks with a limp.

Mr. Ervine was born in Belfast, Ireland, December 28, 1883. The year 1907 marked the publication of a one-act play, *The Magnanimous Lover,* and in 1910 appeared a play in four acts, *Mixed Marriage.* The latter was produced at the Abbey Theatre, Dublin, in 1911, the year of his own marriage to Leonora Mary Davis of Birmingham. His *Jane Clegg* (1911) made its appearance at the Gaiety Theatre, Manchester, in 1912; and the next year *The Magnanimous Lover* was produced at the Abbey Theatre, of which Mr. Ervine became manager in 1915. Meanwhile his play, *John Ferguson* (1914) had been written, and it was played at the Abbey in 1916.

The war brought a halt to Ervine's dramatic activities and he served as a trooper in the Household Battalion from October 1916 to April 1917. He went to France as a lieutenant with the First Battalion of the Royal Dublin Fusiliers in October of 1917 and saw active service until May 1918 when he was wounded, resulting in the loss of a leg.

Following his recovery Mr. Ervine resumed writing, and three plays were published in successive years: *The Ship* (1922), *Mary, Mary, Quite Contrary* (1923), and *The Lady of Belmont* (1924). The plays that followed were: *Anthony and Anna* (1925), *The First Mrs. Fraser* (1928), and *The Wonderful Visit,* the last done in collaboration with H. G. Wells.

This Irishman's plays have been acted all over the English-speaking world, and have been translated into German, French, and Japanese. Two of them were performed by the Theatre Guild of New York in its early days. The first of them, *John Ferguson,* established the fortunes of that organization, while the second, *Jane Clegg,* consolidated it.

Mr. Ervine has made several visits to America, and in 1928 and 1929 he spent seven months in New York as visiting dramatic critic on the *World.* His independence and plain speaking offended some of his readers, but he soon found that he had more friends than enemies and he said he would never forget the

kindness he received here. When he was ready to leave in March of 1929, he said: "the disquieting thing about your theatre, and largely this is the fault of your managers, is that you still depend upon Europe for your plays of quality." He said he was tired of plays "about gunmen, gangsters, noble crooks, bootleggers, hijackers, young women who drink cocktails and are raped, young women who wish to lead their own lives and can't stop yammering about it," but most of all he was sick of plays with foul speech. His conclusion was that the American theatre, as well as the English theatre, was on the downward path.

The First Mrs. Fraser was produced in London in 1929 and 1930 and in America in 1930. It is a comedy, the scene of which is present-day England. Mr. Fraser goes to his ex-wife, the first Mrs. Fraser, for advice about the second Mrs. Fraser's proposed divorce. From that moment the first Mrs. Fraser, clever, canny woman that she is, dominates the situation.

Mr. Ervine's novels are: *Mrs. Martin's Man* (1914), *Alice and a Family* (1915), *Changing Winds* (1917), *Foolish Lovers* (1920), *The Wayward Man* (1927). His other works include two books on theatrecraft, *The Organized Theatre* and *How to Write a Play.*

He has a house in London and one in Devonshire.

Jeffery Farnol

JEFFERY FARNOL was born February 10, 1878, in Warwickshire, and acknowledges with affection the debt to his father who guided his taste and first roused his interest in literature. The elder Mr. Farnol was in the habit of reading aloud to his wife, and Jeffery and his brother, having been sent to bed, used to creep down stairs again and listen, sitting in their nightshirts, outside the door. Perhaps their pleasure came from a sense of conscious naughtiness as well as from hearing *The Count of Monte Cristo,* Cooper, Scott, Dickens, Thackeray, and Dumas, read beautifully aloud.

JEFFERY FARNOL

Jeffery was privately taught at home, and when the time came for him to go up to the University, the family funds were not sufficient to send him. To his reiterated pleas that he wanted to write for a living, his father said, sensibly enough, "Nonsense, you haven't a University education and you don't know how to write." So Jeffery was sent as an apprentice to a brass foundry in Birmingham—partly to give him a means of earning his living, and partly, no doubt, to put out of his head all notions of a literary career. The work in the foundry was not very congenial to him—indeed it is doubtful if he learned to do anything at all except to use his fists adeptly, and when he was summarily discharged the foreman sent a note back to his parents—"No good for work, always writing."

He had some little talent for drawing, and his family, seeing him so bent upon some sort of artistic work, sent him to London to the Westminster School of Art, with the hope that he might become an illustrator. But his artistic gift being very slight and his literary one very pronounced, he soon gave this up and took a job in his father's business, writing short stories on the side—and occasionally getting one published.

His favorite recreation at this time was cycling. All the little lanes, the twisting, turning narrow ways of Kent, Surrey, and Sussex became familiar to him. And after hours of wheeling between the sweet hedgerows, he used to stop at the old taverns, then still untouched by motor tourists, still full of the incomparable flavor of English country inns, and eat enormous meals, washed down with good brown ale.

It was a change from this leisurely life and the green shaded Kentish lanes to a New York garret and scene painting at the Astor theatre. The change came about when, at the age of twenty, with no resources at all, Jeffery Farnol married Blanche Hawley, a daughter of Mr. F. Hughson Hawley, an artist of New York. This precipitous step (which shows in his nature a sort of endearing romanticism) resulted in his trying his luck in New York in 1902, while his wife lived with her parents until Jeffery could find something to do that would support them both—for the short stories and articles which he managed to get published afforded a meager income. After painting scenery (a job which his father-in-law got him) all day, he used to come back to his rat-infested room in Hell's Kitchen, and with the aid of a pot of strong tea, write most of the night, seeing with nostalgic intensity the scenes of his childhood, and the green beauty of the Kentish countryside. So he wrote *The Broad Highway*.

It was an enormous manuscript, and American publishers were not very hospitable to it. One said it was "too long and too English"—a criticism which assumes a certain irony in the light of later happenings when it appeared that part of the book's success was due to the charm of its peculiarly *English* quality, both in scene and in character.

One New York publisher after another turned it down. Farnol, in despair, was of a mind to consign it to the flames, but his wife retrieved it and sent it to his mother in England, who forthwith found a publisher to take it. Published in America in 1911, it was, from the day of its appearance, immediately and tremendously successful, and has continued in popularity ever since. Meanwhile, in 1910, before the book appeared in America, the Farnols returned to England, to settle in Kent, later moving to Sussex. They have one daughter.

A stream of novels and other books has continued to flow from Mr. Farnol's pen, including *The Amateur Gentleman* (1913), *The Quest of Youth* (1927), *Famous Prize Fights* (1928), *The Shadow and Other Stories* (1929), *Over the Hills* (1930).

William Faulkner

WILLIAM FAULKNER was born in Ripley, Mississippi, in October 1897. In his family background are governors, statesmen, and generals. His great-grandfather, whose name he bears, was the author of *The White Rose of Memphis,* one of the most popular romantic novels of its days, the pages of which are filled with descriptions of lovely ladies and gallant swains and magnolia-scented moments.

When he was a child William Faulkner's family moved to Oxford, Mississippi, where his permanent home has been ever since. He attended the University of Mississippi for two years, leaving early in the war to join the Canadian Flying Corps. When the armistice was signed he was a Lieutenant, with wounds resulting from a plane crash. He returned to Mississippi for a short time and then spent several months tramping thru Europe.

Upon his return to the United States he went to New Orleans and took an apartment with Sherwood Anderson on St. Peter Street, in the Vieux Carré. Most of his time was spent on his first novel, *Soldier's Pay,* but he also wrote a number of sketches for the magazine section of the Sunday *Times-Picayune.* New Orleans remembers him particularly for his frequent quarrels with Sherwood and their immediate reconciliations.

Mr. Faulkner and Miss Estelle Oldham Franklin were married in the spring of 1929. Mr. Faulkner has found it necessary to do occasional odd jobs to supplement the income from his books, and has painted several of the houses in Oxford. It is said also that at one time he stoked a furnace for a manufacturing plant.

Mr. Faulkner lives very quietly; he dislikes crowds and cities, and has particular antagonism toward New York. He is slightly below medium height, but sturdily built. His eyes are black and keen, his mustache dark, and his hair, formerly black, is prematurely grey. His forehead is high and straight, and his nose aquiline. He has a ready wit and is a brilliant conversationalist, with the talent for inventing spontaneously extraordinary and imaginative stories.

Mr. Faulkner first published a small volume of poems, *The Marble Faun* (1924).

Soldier's Pay (1926) aroused interest in the author, and marked him as a writer to be watched. It is the story of the homecoming of a young man who was reported to have been killed in battle. It attracted little attention here on publication, but the English edition in 1930 was widely praised abroad. *Mosquitoes* was published in 1927, and *Sartoris* in 1929.

The Sound and the Fury (1929) startled critics and confused many readers. It is the record of the decay of a

WILLIAM FAULKNER

Southern family, partly given thru the eyes of the idiot son Benjy. The author's interest in the morbidly psychological aspect of humanity was defended by one critic who said: "If Faulkner is obsessed with futility and insanity so is Fyodor Dostoevsky."

As I Lay Dying (1930) is in the same style as *The Sound and the Fury*. The children in a family of poor whites, accompanied by their dazed father, carry the body of their mother, enclosed in a home-made coffin, for days across a rain-swept country to her old home.

In *Sanctuary* (1931) Faulkner employs his bitter talent to relate the tragic and horrible experiences of an eighteen-year old college girl who enters a Tennessee moonshiner's hut in search of liquor. Here, as always, the world of Faulkner's vision is full of vicious and abnormal persons. *Sanctuary* was written before *As I Lay Dying*.

EDNA FERBER

Edna Ferber

EDNA FERBER was born August 15, 1887, in Kalamazoo, Michigan, of Jewish parents. Her mother was an American, born in Milwaukee, and her father was Hungarian. Mr. Ferber kept a general merchandise store in Appleton, Wisconsin, where Edna Ferber spent her childhood. She went to public school there and was graduated from the high school at the age of seventeen.

Her graduating essay attracted the attention of the local editor and she got a reporting job on the *Appleton Daily Crescent* at three dollars a week. She continued her reportorial experience with the *Milwaukee Journal* and later the *Chicago Tribune*. When she was twenty-three years old and earning her living in this manner, she wrote a short story which was published in *Everybody's*. It was called *The Homely Heroine*. Then she set to work on a novel which she threw away when finished because she didn't like it. Her mother retrieved the manuscript from the wastebasket and *Dawn O'Hara* was published (1911).

Miss Ferber writes about life in the Middle West, and her characters are commonplace middle-class people. "No other kind of person fascinates and excites my writing sense," she explains. She cannot enthuse over the leisured wealthy folk, neither is she moved to compassion for the poor. People who are workers fill her pages. And she is one of them herself, for she practices the doctrine of hard work in her writing. "They who say that work hardens one," she remarks, "or wearies or dulls, have chosen the wrong occupation, or have never really tasted the delights of it. It's the finest freshener in the world."

This busy woman does her work in a bare studio in her apartment facing Central Park in New York City. Here, away from her telephone, she sits down before a well-worn typewriter and a pad of copy paper at nine in the morning and concentrates, usually until four in the afternoon. In this same apartment she meets her friends, breakfasts, lunches, dines, and sleeps. She chose the furniture, the color scheme—planned everything herself.

Altho Miss Ferber lives in New York her heart is in Chicago and she frequently goes there to freshen her acquaintance with it. She says she has two ambitions and one of them is to "sit in a rocking chair on the curb at the corner of State and Madison streets and watch the folks go by." The other is to "live on a houseboat in the Vale of Cashmere." Chicago is the setting for many of her stories.

Miss Ferber knows how to play as well as work. On social errands she enters the room almost with a rush, with a quick, firm step. She is short, scarcely more than five feet three. Her rather large head with its thick black hair, cropped so one may see the shape of her skull, is held erect. She greets one with a cordiality that is sometimes disarming and she speaks with a curious drawl that seems quite out of character with her forthright nature.

Miss Ferber's best selling novels have been: *The Girls* (1921), *So Big* (1924), *Show Boat* (1926), *Cimarron* (1930). Of *So Big* she remarks: "Not only did I not plan to write a Best Seller when I wrote *So Big* but I thought, when I had finished it, that I had written the world's worst seller. Not that alone, I thought I had written a complete Non-seller. I didn't think anyone would ever read it. And that's the literal truth." *Show Boat* was adapted into a musical comedy by Ziegfeld and was one of the outstanding theatrical successes of its time.

Two of Miss Ferber's plays have been successfully produced on Broadway: *Minick* (1924) and *The Royal Family* (1928). They were written in collaboration with George S. Kaufman. With George V. Hobart she wrote *Our Mrs. McChesney*, and with Newman Levy she wrote *$1,200 a Year* (1920). All the plays are comedies.

Miss Ferber has periodically collected her short stories in book form. The volumes include: *Buttered Side Down* (1912), *Emma McChesney & Co.* (1915), *Cheerful, By Request* (1918), *Half Portions* (1920), *Gigolo* (1922), and *Mother Knows Best* (1927).

Her novels are: *Dawn O'Hara* (1911), *Fanny Herself* (1917), *The Girls* (1921), *So Big* (1924), *Show Boat* (1926), and *Cimarron* (1930). The last is a departure from her "indoor" stories of the Midwest to the wild Oklahoma out-of-doors. The novel begins with the land rush of 1889, when Oklahoma was still Indian territory, and traverses the pioneer statehood days up to the present. Both *Show Boat* and *Cimarron* were made into motion pictures.

Harvey Fergusson

HARVEY FERGUSSON was born at Albuquerque, New Mexico, January 28, 1890. At the age of nine he had a gun of his own; at eleven, and until he was eighteen, he roamed the mesas and mountains of his native state on his own horse, shooting deer and riding range with the cattle-men. He took his preparatory schooling at the New Mexico Military Institute and then divided his college career between Washington D. C., the University of New Mexico, and Washington and Lee University.

He passed an examination to become a forest ranger and was waiting for an appointment when his father, who was lone Representative from New Mexico, offered him a government job in the House Office Building. The job paid $75 a week and gave him a chance to go to law school, but he abandoned it at the end of three weeks, sold his law books, and became a reporter on the *Washington Herald*. Subsequently followed brief periods with the *Savannah Morning News* and the *Richmond Times-Dispatch*. Then, in 1913, he joined the Washington bureau of the *Chicago Record-Herald*. "My chief duty," he writes, "was to keep in touch with all the members of one state delegation in Congress, and I

HARVEY FERGUSSON

achieved an intimate and disillusioning knowledge of these gentlemen and their activities."

The following year, 1914, Fergusson became editor of the F. J. Haskin newspaper syndicate, where he remained until 1922. During that time he wrote about a thousand articles about the government and had occasion to visit the Panama Canal, the West Indies, and Canada. He began writing fiction to "make money as a free lance so that I could spend half the year in the Rockies." But after ten years, he found that he had sold four short stories and a few articles, so he decided to write a novel.

His first novel, *The Blood of the Conquerors* (1921), is a picture of the modern Southwest and his second book, *Capitol Hill* (1923), is a satire on the social and political life of Washington. Then followed *Women and Wives* (1924) and *Hot Saturday* (1926). With *Wolf Song* (1927), Fergusson began a series of stories about the Southwest; continued it with *In Those Days* (1929); and concluded it in *Footloose McGarnigal* (1930).

In the first book of the group, a restless youth grows to manhood among the hunters and trappers of New Mexico, chiefly engrossed in feasting, drinking, loving, and fighting. The second book is the story of a man who goes down into the Southwest in those days when the wagon trains were pouring into the land. Thru all the phases of the pioneering he stays and works and prospers. In *Footloose McGarnigal* a tenderfoot wanders west from New York with his head full of romantic ideas about "the great open spaces" but soon tires of the adventure and returns.

Lion Feuchtwanger

LION FEUCHTWANGER was born in 1884 in Munich, Germany. He is not in love with his native city. "Except for its location, its beautiful public art galleries and libraries, its Carnival, and its beer," he says, "the city possessed little of real value. Altho it placed much emphasis on its tradition as an art center, its art really did not go very far.

LION FEUCHTWANGER

It was embodied in a narrow-minded, pompous, academic institution maintained for the tourist trade by a mouldy, stuffy, and alcoholic population."

He received in the schools "a dreary and pedantic education—conservative, patriotic, unaware of sport—in fact, entirely detached from life." Young Feuchtwanger wrote a play to celebrate the birthday of a prince, and it was performed by his schoolmates. The classics were read in carefully purified editions.

Feuchtwanger studied literature and philosophy in Munich and Berlin under Erich Schmidt, Müncker, and Count Hartling, who later became Prime Minister. In 1905 to 1910 he founded a literary society in Munich which, in the face of hidebound opposition, tried to foster modern literature. During those years he wrote "a pretentious tho very artistic novel describing the gay and lurid life of an unscrupulous young society man," a play about a Renaissance artist and "a thoroly demoniacal lady," and many brilliant and combative reviews.

In 1912 he married Martha Löffler of Munich. The young couple went abroad and, as long as they had money, lived very well on the Riviera. After their money disappeared, Feuchtwanger wrote articles and waited for money. They were in Calabria and Sicily now. When they had money again, they went to Tunis. The war broke out and he was made a prisoner of war by the French in Tunis, but his wife smuggled him on to an Italian boat, and soon he was in Germany and in the army. He served for only a short time in the military force.

During the war his works were constantly suppressed: *Warren Hastings; Jud Süss* (Power) ; a daring translation of Aristophanes' *Peace;* a play, *Die Kriegsgefangenen* (Prisoners of War), repeatedly forbidden by the authorities, which has been translated into French ; a revolutionary dramatic novel, *Thomas Wendt,* which the reactionary white wing strenuously opposed.

Feuchtwanger is proud of the fact that he wrote the "first pronouncedly revolutionary poem" to be published in Germany during the war period. It appeared in the October 1914 issue of the magazine *Die Schaubühne* and had as refrain, "We are waiting."

Feuchtwanger's greatest dramatic success was with his poetic version of *Vasantasena,* which was produced more than a thousand times within eight years in Germany. *Warren Hastings* was also produced successfully, abroad as well as in his native country. He won international reputation with his novel *Jud Süss,* published here under the title of *Power* in 1926. This was followed by the translation of *Die Hässliche Herzogin (The Ugly Duchess)* in 1928; *Two Anglo-Saxon Plays* (1928), containing *The Oil Islands* and *Warren Hastings;* and *Pep, J. L. Wetcheek's American Song Book* (1929)—Wetcheek being the literal translation of Feuchtwanger. These satirical poems translated by Dorothy Thompson (Mrs. Sinclair Lewis) were directed against the American scene, altho Feuchtwanger had never been here. His answer to the charge of prejudging the United States without direct knowledge of it is that he never lived in the 18th century and yet wrote *Jud Süss.*

Late in 1930 Feuchtwanger's *Success* was published simultaneously in Germany and the United States. This is his first modern novel, laid in contemporary Munich, altho even here he introduces an historical element by writing from the standpoint of one who is living in the future and looking back at the past.

In appearance Feuchtwanger is thin and short with a sharp, intelligent face, "tremulous as a rodent's." The Feuchtwangers live at the top of a tall building in the Wilmersdorf section of Berlin. From its windows Feuchtwanger can look across to the tennis courts on the opposite side where his beautiful young wife often plays. When he does research for any of his historical novels he consults the city library. He makes detailed notes of his books and then dictates the more or less final form to his secretary, an efficient young woman who keeps a card index of all his characters, their appearance and idiosyncrasies, so that a character will not be grey-eyed at the beginning of a novel and blue-eyed at the end. He works in a queer sort of costume that is a cross between sports pajamas and a French mechanic's corduroys. When he talks, his whole face talks : his eyes twinkle behind the glasses and his black eyebrows jerk nervously.

Rachel Field

RACHEL FIELD, author of numerous children's books and plays, and the first woman to win the John Newbery Medal, was born in Stockbridge, Massachusetts, in 1894. Her childhood was spent in this village in the western part of the state and in Springfield, Massachusetts. After graduation from the local schools she entered Radcliffe College. Her early literary interests were in poetry.

Miss Field came to attention first with a one-act play, *Three Pills in a Bottle,* written while a student at Radcliffe College. She worked under Professor Baker when he was head of the department of drama and director of the workshop theater there and at Harvard. Many of her one-act plays are produced yearly in Little Theatres all over the United States.

Her first five years in New York were spent with a leading moving picture company in an editorial position. Since then she has devoted all of her time to the writing of fiction and poetry. Her books

RACHEL FIELD

the year she lives in New York; the three summer months are spent on Sutton Island, off the Maine Coast, where she has a large house.

Miss Field draws and paints, and has illustrated many of her own books with silhouettes and sketches. These include her first book, a collection of poems entitled *The Pointed People* (1924); another book of verse, *Taxis and Toadstools* (1926); a series of small, tho charming books: *An Alphabet for Boys and Girls* (1926), *A Little Book of Days* (1927), *Polly Patchwork* (1928), and *Pocket-Handkerchief Park* (1929); and *Little Dog Toby* (1928), a story of Victorian England.

are known primarily as juveniles, but Miss Field, believing that children hate having their books written down to them, has carefully avoided, in verse and prose, this form of insult to the young intelligence. Adult readers have been known to like her books almost as much as children do.

Miss Field's interest lies chiefly in American stories, as illustrated by *Hitty: Her First Hundred Years* (1929), the biography of a wooden doll, a piece of genuine Americana, which Miss Field and Miss Dorothy Lathrop, who made the drawings for the book, found in a shop on 8th Street in New York.

Thru the experiences of Hitty the history of the past hundred years is told. The book was awarded the John Newbery Medal in 1930 by the American Library Association as the best children's book for 1929. *American Folk and Fairy Tales* (1929) is another example of Miss Field's use of American source material. *Points East* (1930), narratives of New England in verse, is her first book written exclusively for adults.

Miss Field is described as a gracious and charming person, with a delightful sense of humor and an infectious, chuckling laugh. Her hair is brown and curly. She gives the impression of kindliness without sentimentality. Nine months of

Charles J. Finger

CHARLES JOSEPH FINGER has led a varied life of travel and adventure, and from his experiences he has written numerous books for children. He was awarded the Newbery Medal for the most distinguished contribution to juvenile literature in 1924, and five years later received the $2,000 Longmans, Green Juvenile Fiction Prize. The former was awarded for his *Tales From Silver Lands* (1924), a collection of nineteen South American folk tales, and the latter for *Courageous Companions* (1929), the tale of a lad who sailed with Magellan on his first trip round the world.

Mr. Finger was born in Willesden, England, on Christmas Day, 1871. He attended private schools, went to King's College, London, and then studied music at Frankfort-on-the-Main, Germany. He came to the United States in 1887, when he was sixteen, and began his life of exploration and travel. He served before the mast, traveling to South America, Africa, and the Antarctic. He followed Magellan's trail, crossed and re-crossed Patagonia, sailed the Straits and twice rounded Cape Horn. In Tierra del Fuego he served as guide to an ornithological expedition and he explored in the Andes. His wanderings led him to the Klondike gold fields and he also had adventures in Canada, Mexico, and

Texas. He lived among Indians, sailors, and miners.

On June 7, 1902, Mr. Finger married Nellie B. Ferguson of Crockett County, Texas, and his life became more stationary. He was made director of the Conservatory of Music at San Angelo, Texas, in 1903. From 1906 until 1920 he served as general manager for a group of railways in Ohio, acting as receiver for several roads. Meanwhile, in 1919, he had begun his literary activities, assuming the editorship of *Reedy's Mirror* and also writing stories for boys' magazines. In 1920 he became editor and proprietor of the magazine, *All's Well*.

It was Cunninghame Graham and W. H. Hudson who advised Finger to write about his adventures, and his first book, *Choice of the Crowd,* appeared in 1921. Since then his volumes have been published frequently. He lives with his wife and five children at Fayetteville, Arkansas, in the Ozark Mountains, where, besides writing, he raises sheep, goes hiking, holds archery contests, and does revolver shooting. His other hobbies are boxing, cutting down trees, breaking in horses, sheep-shearing, and playing bagpipes on the hills. He is enthusiastic about his children's outdoor theatre, their libraries, their music, and the natural beauty all about.

Mr. Finger seems possessed of inexhaustible vitality and he makes innumerable friends. He has a sturdy appearance, wears home-spun suits, laughs frequently, and has a knack for telling unusual anecdotes. He says about children's stories: "Experience with all kinds of people, savage and civilized, leads me to believe that the chief thing to be achieved by the story teller is a sense of reality; without that it is not possible to interest boys and girls. A story-teller who tries to talk either up or down to children will fail."

Among Mr. Finger's books are: *In Lawless Lands* (1923); *Highwaymen* (1923); *Bushrangers* (1924); *Spreading Stain* (1927); *David Livingstone* (1927); *Frontier Ballads* (1927); *Ozark Fantasia* (1927); *Romantic Rascals* (1927); *Man For A' That* (1929), a story of Robert Burns; *Seven Horizons* (1930), a romantic autobiography in

CHARLES J. FINGER

which he describes his adventures, actual and spiritual, in the seven most important phases of his career; *Adventures Under Sapphire Skies* (1931); *Paul Bunyan Geography* (1931). Nearly all the books are illustrated with woodcuts by Paul Honoré.

F. Scott Fitzgerald

FRANCIS SCOTT KEY FITZGERALD—named after the author of "The Star Spangled Banner," a distant connection—has a sturdy figure, wavy blond hair and blue eyes, and is good-looking—altogether, perfectly made up to step in or out of one of his own novels. He was born in St. Paul, Minnesota, on September 24, 1896, and remembers always wanting to write. At the age of twelve, while attending the St. Paul Academy, he wrote in the back of geography and Latin books and on the margins of themes and declensions and mathematic problems, until finally, in an effort to get him to study, his family sent him to the Newman School, Hackensack, N. J. Here, however, he developed a passion for writing musical comedy, and two years later, at Princeton, spent his entire Freshman year writing an operetta for the Triangle Club. "To do this," he says, "I failed in algebra, trigonometry, co-ordinate geometry, and hygiene. But the Triangle Club accepted my show, and by tutoring all thru a stuffy August I managed to come back a sophomore and act in it as a chorus girl."

Fitzgerald left college to join the army in 1917, but did not get over-seas. He served as Second Lieutenant and then as First Lieutenant in the Forty-fifth and Sixty-seventh Infantry Regiments and as Aide-de-Camp to General J. A. Ryan, Seventeenth Infantry Brigade. And it was in the Army that Fitzgerald wrote his first novel—certainly under circumstances cramping to any one's style!—"Every Saturday at one o'clock when the week's work was over," he says, "I hurried up to the Officer's Club, and there, in a corner of a room full of smoke, conversation, and rattling newspapers, I wrote a one hundred and twenty thousand word novel on the consecutive weekends of three months." His heart was completely in this book, but the publishers wrote him that tho *The Romantic Egotist* was the most original manuscript they had received for years they couldn't publish it. Six months afterward, when he got out of the army, he tried to get a job as reporter with seven New York city editors, planning to "trail murderers by day and do short stories by night," but was conspicuously unsuccessful in this quest. He finally became an advertising man at ninety dollars a month, writing the slogans that while away the weary hours in trolley-cars. He stayed at this three months, during which time he wrote satires constantly and sold one for thirty dollars. Then, disgusted with himself and all the editors, he gave up his job and went home to St. Paul to write a novel. The novel was *This Side of Paradise* (1920). Accepted by special delivery, it sold well as soon as it was off the press. Fitzgerald immediately got married to the girl to whom he had been engaged for a year and a half— Zelda Sayre, an Alabama girl, in appearance the brilliant counterpart of the heroines of his novels.

Since then, things have continued to happen to Fitzgerald. For one thing, he has become the father of Patricia Scott Fitzgerald, somewhat resembling a pocket edition of himself. After *This Side of Paradise* came two books of short stories—*Flappers and Philosophers* (1920) and *Tales of the Jazz Age* (1922), and a second novel, *The Beautiful and Damned* (1922). Then a satirical play called *The Vegetable; or, From President to Postman* (1923); and a novel, *The Great Gatsby* (1925), part of which was written in Rome and on the Riviera, tho he collected the material for it when he was living on post-war Long Island; and another book of short stories, *All the Sad Young Men* (1926). The courage which is one of Fitzgerald's most pronounced characteristics was clearly shown when his play, *The Vegetable,* was produced in Atlantic City and was a flat failure. The success of the play had been a cherished dream and he had counted on it financially and in every other way. Many people insisted that it would have succeeded if it had been more carefully produced; but Fitzgerald rejected all excuses, and simply set to work writing short stories again to pay back the heavy debts he had incurred.

Ford Madox Ford

FORD MADOX FORD was born in Merton, England, in 1873. His father, Dr. Francis Hueffer, a German, was at one time musical editor of *The*

F. SCOTT FITZGERALD

FORD MADOX FORD

collaboration and for ten years they worked together intermittently, evolving jointly *The Inheritors* (1901) and *Romance* (1903).

In 1908 Mr. Ford started the *English Review*, an extraordinary periodical, which numbered among its contributors Thomas Hardy, Joseph Conrad, William James, W. H. Hudson, and John Galsworthy. Another of his famous periodicals, several years later, was *The Transatlantic Review*, which was the rallying point of "Ford's boys" in 1924.

In July 1914 Ford finished what was to have been his last book, *The Good Soldier*, joined a Welch regiment as lieutenant and went to the front. Returning from the War with health impaired he wrote two novels in anger, which were not published. He intended to write no more, but changed his mind and in 1922 commenced his celebrated series of novels dealing with England and the War, *Some Do Not* (1924), *No More Parades* (1925), *A Man Could Stand Up* (1926), and *The Last Post* (1928).

Mr. Ford, one of the last Tories, lives in the United States and Provence, feeling that England, because of the War, will not be normal until another generation has grown up. His paternal name, Hueffer, was changed for family reasons to Ford in 1919.

He has written novels, poems, monographs, critical commentaries, essays, reminiscences. His earlier books include several brilliant historical novels.

Mr. Ford is Roman Catholic. He is described as looking like a cartoonist's drawing of a beef-eating English Tory. He is solidly built, about six-feet tall, with fair skin, yellow hair, a walrus-like grey moustache. His eyes are a pale lustreless blue. He wears rough unpressed tweeds and smokes cheap French cigarettes. As a result of having been gassed in the War he speaks in a wheeze. His chief impatience is with stupidity. He was one of the first to recognize Joyce and praise *Ulysses*. He also admires Henry James, Stephen Crane, Ezra Pound, Ernest Hemingway.

Among his recent books are: *A Mirror To France* (1926), *New Poems* (1927),

Times; his English grandfather was Ford Madox Brown, the painter. He was born into the midst of the pre-Raphaelite group, his aunt having married William Rossetti. He says that he loathes pre-Raphaelite art, but he is very fond of Christina Rossetti.

Prior to the war he lived for a few months out of every year in Germany; German poetry, particularly Heine, appeals to him. At the same time, however, he inherited from both his father and grandfather a deep love of French culture, and he himself has said that he thinks his novels in French before writing them in English.

Ford wrote verses at the age of fifteen which, he says, are contained in his *Collected Poems* (1914). His first book, a fairy story called *The Brown Owl*, was written when he was seventeen. Two years later he wrote *Shifting of Fire*, his first novel. When Ford was twenty-two he had four books to his credit and had begun a biography of his grandfather. His first volume of poems, called *Poems for Pictures*, was printed in 1897. The next year, when Ford was twenty-five, Joseph Conrad suggested a

New York Is Not America (1927), *Little Less Than Gods* (1928), *The English Novel* (1929), *No Enemy* (1929), *When the Wicked Man* (1931).

E. M. Forster

EDWARD MORGAN FORSTER is an English novelist who lives in retirement and writes when he pleases. His intermittent writing has brought this remark from a critic: "So erratically and spasmodically has he worked that one cannot think of his genius as in course of development; it comes and goes, apparently as it wills." He resides with his mother in a Surrey village, not far from London, and on rare occasions appears in the big city with a newly completed manuscript.

Mr. Forster is a slender man of middle height, his slight stooping figure giving the impression of being smaller than it really is. A low forehead, a prominent hooked nose and pointed chin lend his face an almost bird-like aspect, which is further accentuated by his curious way of crooking his head to one side as he speaks. His brown hair and moustache complete the picture of this simple, unobtrusive man, who would not look out

E. M. FORSTER

of place perched on a high stool in an old-fashioned London counting house.

He was born in 1879, the eldest son of Edward Morgan Llewellyn and Alice Clara Forster. He received a gentleman's education at Tonbridge public school as a day boy, and later at King's College, Cambridge. When he completed his schooling he leisurely set about the business of writing.

The first product of his efforts was a group of four novels: *Where Angels Fear to Tread* (1905), *The Longest Journey* (1907), *A Room With A View* (1908), and *Howards End* (1910). These four novels by Forster have been called an attempt, four times repeated, to deliver his own soul from what seemed an eternal argument on good and evil. He carefully detailed both sides of the argument, to be weighed in the balance. All four books had, at bottom, the same setting and the same theme. The last book, *Howards End,* was the final statement for which the others were only trial drafts, and with it he came to a stop. These pre-war novels reflect the quarter century preceding 1914 and give a full picture of the upper middle classes.

The period of silence that followed lasted ten years. Some college friendships with Indian students led him to make a trip to India. Then, during the war, he was stationed for a long time in Egypt. After the war Mr. Forster turned to the short story and in 1920 he published *The Story of the Siren,* a queer tale laid on the Italian coast of the Mediterranean. It was printed in a booklet of about a dozen pages. A volume of short stories, *The Celestial Omnibus,* was published in 1923. The sojourn in India then bore fruit with two books containing sketches of Alexandria and its history: *Alexandria: A History and A Guide* and *Pharos and Pharillon* (1923).

Meanwhile Mr. Forster had returned to India, this time to remain two years. His best-known novel, *A Passage to India* (1924), was an outgrowth of that visit. It is about the British in India and the Indians who come in contact with them. This book was awarded the *Prix Femina Vie Heureuse* and the James Tait Black Prize in 1925.

In 1927 Mr. Forster's *Aspects of the Novel* appeared. In 1928 he published *The Eternal Moment,* a collection of short stories which he says "represent together with those in *The Celestial Omnibus* volume all that I am likely to accomplish in a particular line. Fantasy can be caught in the open here by any who care to catch her."

Mr. Forster's list of novels is: *Where Angels Fear to Tread* (1905), *The Longest Journey* (1907), *A Room With A View* (1908), *Howards End* (1910), and *A Passage to India* (1924).

Bruno Frank

THE author of *Trenck* and *The Days of the King* has reached his position among the foremost of Germany's "middle" generation of writers by a steady development from his childhood. His earliest ambition was to be an author and from that aim he has never swerved. His first book, in fact, was published when he was eighteen—a collection of verses entitled *Aus der Goldenen Schale* —and the entire edition (we are not informed as to its size) was sold out within a few weeks. His entire canon of work is not large, but his few books have won him high praise from his colleagues, among them Thomas Mann, Emil Ludwig, and Lion Feuchtwanger.

He was born at Stuttgart, June 13, 1887, and received the imposing education characteristic of Germany, attending successively the universities of Munich, Leipzig, Strasbourg, and Tübingen, from which last he received his doctorate in literature and philosophy in 1912. The history of the eighteenth century has been his major interest and his exhaustive studies in that period have resulted in his book on Frederick the Great, *The Days of the King* (translated 1927), so individual in its point of view that it aroused the furious resentment and condemnation of the German diehards and nationalists. Herr Frank's interpretation of the bizarre monarch is nevertheless finding many adherents, and his novel, *Trenck* (1928), based on the career of Frederick's ill-starred favorite, developed the portrait already painted in

BRUNO FRANK

the earlier work. His play, *Twelve Thousand,* is laid in the same period and is in the repertory of 150 German theatres. It was produced in New York with some success in 1928. Bruno Frank's other interests are in international affairs and have found expression in his political romance, *The Persians Are Coming* (1929), a fictional presentation of the trend of thought among the finest minds of contemporary Germany and France.

Mrs. Frank is the daughter of Fritzi Mazary, perhaps the best known of Viennese operetta stars, and her stepfather is Max Pallenberg, Germany's foremost comic actor. The Franks live at Munich, where he alternately works and plays with his four black poodles, whose literary prototypes are to be found in *The Days of the King.*

Leonhard Frank

LEONHARD FRANK was born in 1882 in Wurzburg, Germany. The son of a carpenter, he himself tasted the hunger, the misery, the humiliation, which were the lot of the German workman's child in the closing decades of the last century. At the age of thirteen, he

LEONHARD FRANK

was sent to work in a cycle factory, was later attendant in a hospital-laboratory, and chauffeur to a country doctor, but in all these humble pursuits he was haunted by an ideal that demanded expression. An art student in Munich, living somehow on the few coppers he had saved, he strove to capture his vision in paint; but a natural bent drove him to literature, and his first novel, *The Robber Band*, published in 1914, marked him out as the possessor of a rare and original talent. This early promise was realized in the works that followed, and reached its full fruition in *Carl and Anna*, which was the immediate cause of his election to the German Academy of Letters.

Carl and Anna is available here in the short novel form in which it was originally written, as well as in its dramatic version (produced by the Theatre Guild in 1929). There is also a translation of the novel into "basic English," in which a vocabulary of a few simple and elementary forms is employed. *Carl and Anna* is the story of two prisoners of war, who spend four years together in a prison camp. Richard describes his wife Anna so intimately to Carl that the latter grows to love her and, when he escapes, seeks her out and tells her he is her husband. She is not convinced, but their life together is happy until Richard returns. Anna explains that she loves Carl. They pity Richard's misery, but leave his house together.

After the translations of *The Robber Band* and *Carl and Anna*, English and American readers were introduced to *Brother and Sister* and *Clamoring Self* in 1930.

Mr. Frank makes his home in Germany. His hobby is motoring.

Waldo Frank

WALDO DAVID FRANK has ventured into nearly every field of writing. He is the author of critical and informal essays, novels, plays, biographical sketches, travel works, and translations, in addition to magazine and newspaper articles. He was born August 25, 1889, in Long Branch, N. J., the son of Julius J. Frank and Helene Rosenberg Frank. His father was a lawyer and participated in political reform movements in New York. His mother came from Alabama and was musically gifted.

He attended the public grammar schools and De Witt Clinton High School in New York City. At four he had written a brief play and at sixteen a novel which a New York publisher accepted, but which his father judiciously withdrew. In 1906 he attended a school in Lausanne, Switzerland. At Yale Mr. Frank was a rebel. In his senior year he wrote dramatic criticism for the New Haven *Journal-Courier*. He received his A.B. and A.M. degrees in 1911 and was elected to Phi Beta Kappa.

In the two years following graduation Mr. Frank ranched in Wyoming, worked on the New York *Evening Post* and the *Times,* and wrote plays which were too unconventional for Broadway managers. He spent 1913 in Europe, principally in Paris and Germany. Back in New York in 1914, he lived in an East Side block similar to the one in *City Block* (1922), and free-lanced as a writer.

Mr. Frank founded *The Seven Arts,* with James Oppenheim, in 1916. During its one year of existence he published his first novel, *The Unwelcome Man* (1917). On December 20, 1916, he married Margaret Naumburg, founder of the Walden School of New York City and a pioneer in applying psychoanalysis to education. They are now divorced. Their son is named Thomas. When the World War broke out in 1917, Mr. Frank registered as a conscientious objector and wrote *Our America* (1919), an essay, and *The Dark Mother* (1920), a second novel.

He is now American correspondent for *La Nouvelle Revue Française* and for *Europe,* both Parisian publications. He is also a contributing editor of *The New Republic* and *New Masses,* and a lecturer on modern art and literature at the New School for Social Research, New York City. His home is in New York City. His second wife, whom he married in 1927, was Alma Magoon.

Frank's critical estimates of America, its life in the present and its prospective life in the immediate future, have been widely appreciated abroad, especially in South America. At one time he made a lecture tour of several South American countries where he was enthusiastically received and was even lent a government airplane. In Buenos Aires he became almost a popular figure. The subjects he discussed appealed to the intellectual tastes of the Argentines and he attracted large audiences. The lectures he delivered were immediately published in Spain.

Waldo Frank is a handsome, dark, intense man "with a lyrical, testamental quality of speech permeated with a new mysticism and prophecy."

In *Our America* (1919), his first book to be translated into French, he gives a painfully acute description of the present state of America, and of what he calls the American reality. The book was greeted in France with every mark of sympathy. His criticism of American life and culture in *The Re-Discovery of America* (1929) analyzes its European background, its gods and cults, art, leaders, and the spirit of the people. Out of the confusion of the "American jungle" he tries to discover a direction for the growth of a creative American life. He condemns the fragments European civilization in America but he believes a new America is being born.

Mr. Frank edited a book called *Tales From the Argentine* (1930), containing seven stories by the most important writers of Argentina, translated by Anita Brenner from the Spanish. This book is the first of a series of Spanish translations Mr. Frank is editing. He has written introductions to *Adventures in the Arts* by Marsden Hartley (1921), *Cane* by Jean Toomer (1923), and *Plays of Molière* in the *Modern Library* (1924). He is co-author of *The Novel of To-morrow* (1922). His translations include *Lucienne* by Jules Romains (1925).

His play, *New Year's Eve* (1929), is done in the modernistic manner in seven scenes. In it he experiments with staging, the time element, and the employment of a chorus at the close of the scenes. It is designed for presentation on three stage levels and the action begins in 1901 and culminates eighteen years later.

Mr. Frank's other works include: *Salvos* (1924), an informal work about books and plays; *Virgin Spain* (1926), "scenes from the spiritual drama of a great people"; *Time Exposures* (1926), biographical sketches under the pseudonym of "Search-Light"; and six impres-

WALDO FRANK

istic novels: *The Unwelcome Man* (1917), *The Dark Mother* (1920), *Rahab* (1922), *City Block* (1922), *Holiday* (1923), and *Chalk Face* (1924).

Gustav Frenssen

GUSTAV FRENSSEN, German author, was born October 19, 1863, in the small village of Barlt on the North Sea coast of Holst, where his father was the local carpenter. His humble parents worked hard to send him away to good schools because they wanted him to become a clergyman. He was educated in the Universities of Tübingen, Berlin, and Kiel.

The parental wish was fulfilled. Frenssen took orders and served a pastorate at Hemme from 1892 to 1902. The year he went to Hemme he married the youngest daughter of Lehrers Walter in Meldorf. During the period of his pastorate he published three volumes of village sermons: *Dorfpredigten* (1899-1902). They were read with interest by both Protestants and Catholics. He also wrote fiction during his pastorate and published *Die Sandgräfin* (1895), *Die Drei Getreuen* (1898), and *Jörn Uhl* (1901). The success of the last novel

GUSTAV FRENSSEN

caused him to give up his clerical duties in 1902 and devote all his time to literature.

Frenssen's next work was a play, *Das Heimatsfest* (1903). Then he wrote a novel, *Hilligenlei* (1906). The other books that followed were: *Peter Moors Fahrt nach Südwest* (1906); *Eine Feldzugsgesch* (1906); *Klaus Hinrich Baas* (1909); *Anna Hallmann* (1911); *Sönke Erichsen* (1912), another play; *Bismarck* (1914); *Die Brüder* (1917); and *Grübeleien* (1920).

During the World War Frenssen returned to the village in which his family had dwelt for five hundred years, and inhabited the simple thatched cottage in which his parents used to live. He has traveled considerably but his affections are centered on the region on the northern bank of the Elbe estuary where his home is. This region provides the settings for most of his books. Of the world's writers Dickens is his favorite, but he reads Hardy with pleasure.

The Anvil (translated 1930) is frankly autobiographical. It depicts a generation of people in a country district of Schleswig bordering on the North Sea. Every incident in the book either happened to the author or came within the scope of his personal experience. His characters are ordinary villagers and farmers and simple townsfolk. Frenssen's books about the peasantry of the countryside in north Germany have identified him with a school of writers of the *Heimatkunst* (literature of special regions).

Ludwig Lewisohn writes: "Gustav Frenssen is a peasant of the ancient Saxon stock. His words gain authority from that depth of human life whence his inspiration is drawn. Out on the heath and dunes here, he seems to say, the moral perversions of historic Christianity never struck to the roots of life. We have wastrels and drunkards and brutes, but the ancient Germanic peasantry has always been sound at the core. We can draw from it our examples and borrow from it those moods that we need for the fuller life of a new age."

English translations of Frenssen's works include: *Jörn Uhl* (1905); *Holyland* (1906); *Three Comrades* (1907);

Peter Moor's Journey to Southwest Africa, a narrative of the German campaign (1908); *Klaus Hinrich Baas,* the story of a self-made man (1911); *Village Sermons by a Novelist* (1924); *The Anvil* (1930).

Robert Frost

ROBERT LEE FROST was born in San Francisco, March 26, 1875, where his father, a New Englander by birth in a long line of New Englanders, was editing a newspaper. When Robert Frost was ten years old, his father died. Mrs. Frost and her son came east to settle in Lawrence, Massachusetts, where her husband's father lived.

The boy disliked grammar school, but found high school more interesting. When he entered Dartmouth College in 1892, the routine of college life and some of the required courses were distasteful to him, and he stayed only a few months. His first job was as a millhand in a factory in Lawrence.

Miss Elinor Miriam White and Robert Frost were married in 1895, and in 1897 he entered Harvard with the idea of taking a complete college course and receiving a degree. He left at the end of two years, however, and turned his hand to various kinds of work, including shoemaking and reporting on a newspaper. His grandfather bought him a farm near Derry, New Hampshire, in 1900, which Frost managed until 1905. To supplement his income he secured a position as English teacher in the Pinkerton Academy at Derry that year, remaining there until 1911. He taught psychology in the New Hampshire State Normal School in Plymouth in 1911-12. Tired of both teaching and farming, he sold his farm in 1912 and with his wife and four children went to England.

A Boy's Will, his first book, was published in England in 1913. *North of Boston* (1914), also published in England, established his reputation as a poet both abroad and in America. In 1914 Frost and his family moved from the little country town of Beaconsfield where they had settled on their arrival in England to Ledbury, Gloucestershire, near the homes of two English poets, Lascelles Abercrombie and W. W. Gibson.

When Frost returned to America in 1915 he went to live near Franconia, New Hampshire. From 1916 to 1920 he taught at Amherst College, giving informal seminar courses for students interested in writing prose or poetry. Then, jealous of the time taken by his classroom work, he gave up teaching and moved with his family to a new farm at South Shaftsbury, Vermont. But a year later the University of Michigan offered him its newly established fellowship in creative art, which entailed no academic duties, and from 1921 to 1923 he was "poet in residence" at Ann Arbor. He returned to Amherst in 1923; in 1925-26 he went back to the University of Michigan as a Fellow in Letters; since 1926 he has been teaching at Amherst again, dividing his time between the college and his South Shaftsbury farm. It would seem as tho Mr. Frost, who couldn't bear colleges in his youth, can't get away from them now.

The Frosts live simply in their rough stone house. Mr. Frost is a quiet soft-voiced man with kind, yet keen, eyes and grey hair, liking young people and friendly with his neighbors. He works late into the night and sleeps far into

ROBERT FROST

the morning. Walking is his favorite recreation.

He does not force himself to write, preferring to wait until he can write at his best. "It takes me two days to unscrew and two to screw up again," he says. He does not believe in fancy esthetics. "A poem," he explains, "begins with a lump in the throat; a homesickness or a love-sickness. It is a reaching-out toward expression; an effort to find fulfilment. A complete poem is one where an emotion has found its thought and the thought has found the words."

Mr. Frost received the Pulitzer prize for poetry in 1924. The titles of his published works are as follows: *A Boy's Will* (1913); *North of Boston* (1914); *Mountain Interval* (1916); *New Hampshire* (1923); *West-running Brook* (1928); *A Way Out* (1929), a play. *Selected Poems* appeared in 1923 and 1928, and *Collected Poems* in 1930.

René Fülöp-Miller

RENÉ FÜLÖP-MILLER was born March 17, 1891, in the picturesque little Carpathian town of Caransebes, in the romantic Banat, which was formerly part of Hungary.

RENÉ FÜLÖP-MILLER

At the age of fourteen, a poet and dreamer, with long flowing hair, he was editor of one of the most widely-read liberal-democratic newspapers, the chief organ of news in the Banat. He edited and wrote the paper under various pseudonyms, and even conducted the editorial policy.

René's father was a well-known and respected chemist, and at the same time the equivalent of doctor, psychologist, spiritual advisor, and even confessor for the whole surrounding district. His mysticism, and the conflicting influences in his nature, in the long run were bound to be at variance with his father's rigid code, which had selected him for the practice of chemistry. At that time he was very much under the influence of Swedenborg, Paracelsus, and Jakob Böhme, altho in literature, Balzac, Stendhal, and Dostoievsky were his masters. His father frowned upon these mystical and literary studies, so that it was not long before he made up his mind to run away. He arrived in Vienna with scarcely any money, and took up his first quarters, for the sake of economy, in a shabby little laundry, still consumed with the one idea of writing his book. As his money was fast diminishing, he went on from bad to worse, tasting the utmost poverty. His difficulty was to keep his nerves under a sufficient stimulus so that he could finish his book. At night, he slept on the benches on the Rinstrasse. During all this time, he was living in a heightened state of nerves, with every one of his senses sharpened to a painful intensity beneath the stimulus of caffeine. His hearing, sight, and touch were all abnormal, tuned to an unearthly pitch. After some time, his parents discovered him, ill and delirious, in a Vienna hospital. His money was at an end, the coffee had run out, his strength had failed, and his book was all but finished. They took him home again to the Banat where, in his father's house, beneath friendly skies and in the familiar surroundings, he slowly recovered.

It seemed inevitable that he was destined for the pharmacy and chemistry which he had so long tried to escape, and for which his father was now determined that he should definitely prepare.

After having finished high school and failed in literature with his paper on *Don Quixote,* he completed his studies in the Universities of Vienna and Lausanne, and in Paris at the Sorbonne. At the age of 21 he received his diploma in Pharmaceutical Chemistry. At the same time he was doing extensive medical research work. He studied anatomy with Professor Tandler in Vienna, psychiatry with Babinsky in Paris and with Forel in Switzerland, and psychoanalysis with the Vienna specialists. Upon his return to Siebenburgen, there ensued a period during which he was comparatively well-to-do, living in splendid style and consorting with the prideful, landed gentry. He lived and traveled extensively in the Near East, visiting strange places and peoples, off the beaten track. The following years were devoted to various interests. He threw himself enthusiastically into journalism in Berlin, Paris, Vienna and elsewhere, and for some time was correspondent of several of the foremost German and Hungarian newspapers.

In 1916, he met and married the well-known Hungarian soprano, Heddy Bendiner, of the Budapest Opera. An exceptional musician with great dramatic talents, she nevertheless gave up her own career to be a companion to her husband thru the dark shadow of the war years. Together with her, his life was transformed into one of serious and systematic labour, during which all his important works have been produced.

Thru his previous books on Lenin and Gandhi, Rasputin, Bolshevism, and the Russian Theatre, the author is known for his uncanny powers of research and his ability to portray his findings. *Rasputin, The Holy Devil,* which was published here in 1928, was one of his greatest successes, followed by *The Power and Secret of the Jesuits* (1930). In 1930 translations of his *Unknown Tolstoi* and of *The Ochrana: the Russian Secret Police* (prepared in collaboration with A. T. Vassilyev) were also published in this country; in 1931, *Tolstoy: New Light on His Life and Genius.* He edited *Under Three Czars: Memories of Elizabeth Narishkin-Kurakin* (1931).

He is at work on a book on America which will not appear for a while since Herr Fülöp-Miller, a recent visitor to these shores, wants to live here for some time before writing the book.

Rose Fyleman

ROSE FYLEMAN, writer and lecturer known to the British public as "R. F.," was born in Nottingham in 1877 of Jewish parentage. She first attracted attention as a writer at the tender age of nine when one of her school compositions was published in the local newspaper. But she had the firm intention of becoming a school teacher. After finishing private school she entered the University College at Nottingham where she failed in Greek and mathamatics. She thought she had been disgraced forever and that her life was ruined.

But it was discovered that Miss Fyleman had an exceptionally good voice, so she went to Paris for training. There she studied with Sir Henry Wood for about two years, then went to Berlin for a period, and finally received a diploma at the Royal College of Music in London. She made her debut as a profes-

ROSE FYLEMAN

sional singer at Queen's Hall, London, in 1903, and set about her career of singing in public and teaching music.

Miss Fyleman, however, began to write articles for London magazines and newspapers and in 1916 she started to contribute poems to *Punch,* above the signature, R. F. The acclaim her verse received caused her to take her writing seriously and she settled into writing as a career. She has been a regular contributor to *Punch* since. Her first book was *Fairies and Chimneys,* published in 1918, and other tales for children have followed regularly since. She was the founder of *The Merry Go Round,* a magazine for children which she edited for two years.

R. F., her friends say, has the heart of a child and she is able to project herself into the feelings of a child. She is pictured by Lady Adams as a believer in fairies, which she sees everywhere: "R. F. has her own particular brand of fairies; fairies who hop in and out of pumpkin coaches, who flit through the air like butterflies. Take a walk down Fleet Street with her and she sees them sitting daintily on the window-sills of the solemnest London daily newspapers; more surprising, she makes you see them too. R. F. is a second Tinker Bell. She will never grow up."

R. F. has travelled extensively, both on the Continent and in America. She speaks fluent French, German, and Italian. She has a keen sense of humor. Miss Fyleman is far from temperamental, in the broad sense, for she writes at all sorts of odd times and in equally odd places. She is of the opinion that her knowledge of music has been exceedingly beneficial to her in her verse writing, for when she has trouble with a line, she thrashes it out in just the same manner she would readjust a faulty note.

Miss Fyleman lives in London in a quaint old house boasting of bowed windows of a venerable age, which, she says, she passed for years, always hoping that some day she would make it her own.

Among her books are: *The Fairy Green* (1919), *The Fairy Flute* (1921), *Eight Little Plays for Children* (1924), *Forty Good Morning Tales* (1926), *A Princess Comes to Our Town* (1927),

Round the Mulberry Bush (1928), *Gay Go Up* (1929), *Twenty Tea-Time Tales* (1929) and *The Katy Kruse Play Book* (1930). She wrote a Christmas play that was performed at the Old Victoria in December 1926.

Zona Gale

ZONA GALE is the daughter of the late Charles Franklin Gale of Ohio and Eliza (Beers) Gale of New York State. She is the eighth generation in America on her father's side, in direct descent from Richard Gale who came to Watertown, Mass., in 1640. His name was spelled Gael, and there is also Scotch-Irish descent thru the women of the family. The village of Waltham, Mass., stands on a part of the "Oldham Farm" purchased by Richard Gale in 1661, and remaining in the family until 1864 when it passed to Governor Banks. Her great-great-grandfather, Captain Henry Gale, was in Shay's Rebellion and marched on the Supreme Court at Worcester demanding the repeal of the law for imprisonment for debt, for which he was sentenced to death for treason, and reprieved. On her mother's side, she is the third generation in America,

ZONA GALE

thru Brown, Billinghurst, and Beers families. Her great-grandfather, Edward Beers of Pittsford, N. Y., whose house and farm with its family "burying-ground" have changed family ownership but once since he came there about 1795, was an occasional fervent and scholarly writer on Universalism, in Universalist magazines. Tradition on both sides of the family is liberal. Of her great-great-grandfather Billinghurst, the first Baptist preacher in Monroe County, N. Y., the Monroe County history says that "he came to the United States from England in 1798 out of sympathy for Republican ideas, then in great disfavor in England on account of the French Revolution."

Zona Gale was born in Portage, Wisconsin, on August 26, 1874. She has always written. Printed and bound in ribbon, her first book of fiction and verse was illustrated by herself at seven. In high school she wrote a play which nobody ever saw. She was educated in the public schools of Portage and at the University of Wisconsin, where she was graduated in 1895. Four years later she received her Master's degree. Recently, in 1929, the University bestowed on her the honorary degree of Litt. D. In college she was poor in mathematics and language, but took three prizes in fiction and verse.

From 1899 to 1901 she worked on Milwaukee newspapers, writing plays in her spare time. She was ambitious, and her thoughts turned eastward. From 1901 to 1904 she was in New York, where she worked on the staff of the *New York World*. All this time she was writing stories and submitting them persistently to the magazines, but not one was accepted until 1904. She wrote plays too, and one of them, called *A Garret in Gotham*, was thrown out by a chambermaid before its time. The magazine *Success* was the first to publish a story by her; *The Smart Set* printed her early verses.

As a reporter for the *World*, Miss Gale (who was "as beautiful as any girl could be") received assignments that might well have terrified "one as fragile and flowerlike and feminine as she." But she did everything that she was asked to do, and every day she sent a letter to her mother in Wisconsin, and while waiting for interviews she would pull out a pad and pencil and write as much as she could on a short story or lyric.

Just as soon as she felt that she had absorbed all she could from New York, Zona Gale made up her mind to return to her quiet village of five thousand souls in order to do the work she wanted to do. So one day in 1904, "having set that determined jaw of hers, she packed her trunks and fared back to little Portage— which is presumably Burage and Friendship Village (of her books) rolled into one." She has lived in Portage ever since.

"And how she did work!" commented an anonymous biographer in 1923. "She writes everything by hand, first, and then copies it herself on the typewriter, roughly, having it recopied by an expert. When she is deep in the throes of composition her mother, whom she worships, knows better than to disturb her; and she acts as a Cerberus when small town callers come, as they sometimes do, of a morning. Se has even been known to put a bone on a tray outside her daughter's door, tap lightly, and slip down the stairway again. Thus is the genius of Portage guarded, looked after, protected."

Zona Gale's first novel, *Romance Island*, was published in 1906. More than a score of books have followed since that date. These books include poems (*The Secret Way*, 1921), plays, short stories, essays, and novels. The novels are her most important work, and the best of these are: *Birth* (1918), the story of Marshall Pitt, an insignificant, humiliated traveling salesman of Burage, Wisconsin; *Miss Lula Bett* (1920), a short novel, "as spare as the virgin frame of Lulu Bett," about an obscure drudge in the house of her foolish sister; *Faint Perfume* (1923), the study of a "poor relation"; *Preface to a Life* (1926), the life-story of a Wisconsin business man, frustrated in his real love, and his long search for reality; and *Borgia* (1929), the portrait of a morbid egocentric girl who thinks of herself as a modern Lucrezia Borgia. The imaginative substance of Miss Gale's later work borders on the mystical.

Miss Gale has dramatized two of her novels. *Miss Lulu Bett* was produced by Brock Pemberton at the Belmont

Theatre, New York, in 1920 and received the Pulitzer award for the best play of the year in 1921. *Mr. Pitt,* her dramatization of *Birth,* was produced in 1923.

Her volumes of short stories include: *Friendship Village* (1908), *Yellow Gentians and Blue* (1927), and *Bridal Pond* (1930). In 1911 she won *The Delineator* prize of $2,000 for a 3000 word story. *When I Was a Little Girl* (1913) and *Portage, Wisconsin* (1928) are books of reminiscences and impressions.

Miss Gale is chairman of the Wisconsin Free Library Commission, of which she has been a member since 1923. She was for six years (1923-29) a member of the board of regents of the University of Wisconsin. She has lectured at Columbia, Chicago, Minnesota, and Wisconsin universities. On June 12, 1928, she married William L. Breese, manufacturer and banker of Portage.

John Galsworthy

JOHN GALSWORTHY was born in a Victorian mansion amid the woods of Coombe, in Surrey, now a suburb of London. The year was 1867. The Galsworthys had lived in Devonshire as far

JOHN GALSWORTHY

back as the records go, and his mother came of an old Worcestershire family named Bartleet. His father was an attorney practicing successfully in London.

John Galsworthy attended Harrow, an expensive school, where he captained the football team and ran and jumped. His youthful characteristics were earnestness and tenacity. He was not surprisingly brilliant, but sure and steady. In 1886 he went up to New College, Oxford, and three years later was graduated with an honor degree in law. He was called to the bar in 1890.

"I read," he says, "in various chambers, practised almost not at all, and disliked my profession thoroly." He was not required to earn money so he travelled for two years, reading meanwhile in Dickens, Turgenev, Maupassant, Anatole France, and Tolstoy. On one of his sailing voyages he met Joseph Conrad, then still a sailor, and formed a fast friendship with him. Conrad showed him a manuscript which Galsworthy recognized as worthy and he advised his friend to devote himself to writing.

Galsworthy himself had no idea of becoming a writer, but when he returned to England his wife-to-be encouraged him in it. He relates: "If one has been brought up at an English public school and university, is addicted to sport and travel, has a small independent income, and is a briefless barrister, one will not take literature seriously, but one might like to please her of whom one was fond. I began. In two years I wrote nine tales. They had every fault."

He was twenty-eight when he started. His first novel, *Jocelyn,* was published in 1899. *Villa Rubein* followed in 1900. His first four or five novels appeared under the pseudonym, "John Sinjohn." The first suggestion of the *Forsyte Saga* novels came in *Salvation of a Forsyte* (1901). In 1903 he began writing *A Man of Property,* which was published in 1906. This began the series of stories, yet unplanned, which was to follow the Forsyte family thru three generations and occupy twenty-six years of the author's life.

Between 1906 and 1918, however, the Forsytes were silent and the author occupied himself with plays and other stories. His first play, *The Silver Box,* appeared in 1906. Then followed *Joy* (1907), *Strife* (1909), *Justice* (1910), and seven other plays before the Forsytes reappeared. "I never meant to go on with them," he recalls, "but after 1918 they began to liven up again and the whole thing then came on with a rush—six books and four interludes full of them. The interludes were long short stories and all that sort of thing."

So the family narrative was resumed with *Indian Summer of a Forsyte, In Chancery* (1920), *Awakening,* and *To Let* (1921). (The undated titles are interludes.) These stories, together with *A Man of Property,* were collected in *The Forsyte Saga* (1922). Meanwhile Galsworthy returned to his plays and published *The Skin Game* (1920), *A Family Man* (1921), *Loyalties* (1922), *Windows* (1922), and *Old English* (1924). He could not leave his family alone and the Forsyte group continued with *The White Monkey* (1924), *Silent Wooing, The Silver Spoon* (1926), *Passerby, The Swan Song* (1928), and *On Forsyte 'Change* (1930). *Silent Wooing* and *Passersby* were later published together in *Two Forsyte Interludes.*

In the fall of 1930 Galsworthy came with his wife to the United States where he secluded himself for the winter in Arizona "as near the desert as possible" to work on a new novel. He has definitely given up the Forsytes. "One can't keep on with that sort of thing indefinitely," he remarks, "especially after one has killed one's principal character." The novel "begins the story of another family. It may continue on to be another saga. One never knows."

In England Galsworthy now spends most of his time at his new country home, a reproduction Tudor manor house at the foot of a big hill in Sussex, Kipling's country. He shares the house with his wife, his nephew, and a large family of dogs and cats. His nephew is the artist, Rudolph Sauter, whose paintings adorn most of the rooms. Galsworthy is passionately fond of music and likes to listen to his wife play the piano. The works of Bach and Chopin especially please him. He is fond of horses and still rides occasionally. Now and then he goes to London for a dinner of the

P.E.N. Club or a rehearsal of one of his plays. His house there is "Grove Lodge," in Hampstead, the quarter where many literary men have lived.

Galsworthy "is about medium height," writes Frank Harris, "spare of habit and vigorous, his head long, well-shaped; his features fairly regular, a straight nose, high forehead; he is almost completely bald and wears glasses. . . Seen close to, his face becomes more interesting; the serious blue eyes can laugh; the lips are large and well-cut, promising a good deal of feeling, but the characteristic expression of the face is seriousness and sincerity."

Galsworthy's manner is easy and courteous. He does most of his work sitting in a close armchair, legs crossed, and a big pad on his knee. He usually writes rapidly and in a bold hand. Subsequently he corrects extensively. His manuscripts are not tidy ones. He never makes scenarios for his plays or outlines for his novels, and never knows quite how they will work out. Galsworthy does not write under the pressure of necessity. He waits, rather, until the inspiration comes. He writes under all sorts of conditions and in all sorts of places. He has a special fondness for the Tyrol. *Escape* (1926) was written in the sun of California.

Hamlin Garland

HAMLIN GARLAND was born on September 16, 1860, at West Salem, Wisconsin, in the heart of the middle west of which he writes. His people were Yankees from Oxford County, Maine, and his father, Richard Garland, was a clerk, as a youth, for three years in Amos Lawrence's warehouse in Boston.

When he was still a youngster his family migrated to Iowa, and when he was sixteen he became a pupil at Cedar Valley Seminary, Osage, Iowa, working on the farm six months out of every school year.

After a short period of teaching school in Illinois, he took up a claim in McPherson County, North Dakota, in 1883, but the next year he mortgaged his claim

HAMLIN GARLAND

for $200 and went to Boston, wearing a queer Gopher-prairie outfit of store clothes, to embark on a career of letters.

Joseph Edgar Chamberlin, of the *Boston Transcript*, has created for us a picture of him at this period:

"He lived in bleak little attic rooms, breakfasted on eight cents, dined on fifteen and supped on ten; wore his prairie-born coat to a shine and his cuffs to a frazzle, and was shrunken thin by low fare; but his head was up and his manner, tho grave, was confident. . . . He would not equivocate or compromise or deny anything that he really believed in. He would not write anything that his heart was not in. When he was earning eight dollars a week, and sent a part of that to support his father and mother, whose crops on their claim in Dakota had for two years running been entirely eaten up by grasshoppers and chinch bugs, he refused to write anything for a newspaper that he was not willing to sign with his name, or to write romantic love stories for a magazine. 'We have had enough of those lies,' he said . . . and went off and dined on a dime."

For the next few years he studied, taught private classes in English and American Literature, and lectured in and about Boston.

In 1887 he visited Dakota, Iowa and Wisconsin. This trip marks an epoch in his life, for it led to his Mississippi Valley stories. Writing was now very definitely his "work." *Main-Travelled Roads* (1891), short stories; *A Spoil of Office* (1892), his first novel; *Crumbling Idols* (1894), a volume of essays; *Rose of Dutcher's Coolley* (1895); and his *Ulysses S. Grant* (1898), all were published within a period of eight years. Garland returned to the West in 1893.

In 1899 he married Zulime Taft, the sister of Lorado Taft, the sculptor, and in the sixteen years following his marriage eleven books, widely different in theme and showing a marked development in style, gave evidence of his creative power. It was, however, with *A Son of the Middle Border*, published in 1917, after he had brought his family to New York and established a home there, that Hamlin Garland came to be recognized as a typically American author.

In 1918 Hamlin Garland was elected to the American Academy of Arts and Letters, and in 1921 *A Daughter of the Middle Border*, which carries on the tale of the Garlands, was published and awarded the Pulitzer Prize for the best biography of that year.

Trail Makers of the Middle Border followed in 1926, and *Back Trailers from the Middle Border,* his final chronicle of his family, was published in the fall of 1928. Mr. Garland applied the name of *Back Trailers* to himself and his family when they sold their Wisconsin home and came back East to live.

Roadside Meetings, a book of reminiscences, which tells the story of his literary life and encounters, was published in 1930.

David Garnett

DAVID GARNETT was born into literary tradition in 1892 and he has spent a good part of his life trying to evade it. He recollects the early parental advice: "Never try to write, but above all never have anything to do with publishing or the book trade." The maxim was spoken by his father, Edward Garnett, critic and writer, and it was seconded by his mother, Constance Garnett, translator of the great Russians. It probably would have been echoed by his grandfather and great-grandfather, the two Richard Garnetts who were in turn Assistant Keeper and Keeper of Printed Books in the British Museum Library and who had written a score of books between them.

So David Garnett set out to become an economic botanist and there was joy among the literary Garnetts. He studied botany for five years and discovered a new species of mushroom. The war put an end to these activities and altho he was a conscientious objector he joined the Friends' War Victims Relief Expedition with Francis Birrell.

The close of the war brought an end to Garnett's adherence to the family wishes and he succumbed to the book lure. He writes: "Birrell and I were both at a loose end, and it was natural that we should think of starting a bookshop together." They encountered hardships in their chosen trade but they prospered steadily and "learned where to buy string and kraft paper and how to do up parcels."

In the evenings of those days Garnett wrote his first book, *Lady Into Fox*, which was published in 1923. It is a fantasy in which a woman is changed into a fox while walking with her husband in a wood. He takes her home and cares for her tenderly. As her nature becomes that of the animal into which she has been transformed he continues to love her and deals gently with her vixenish ways. Finally, hunted down by the hounds, she dies in his arms where she springs for protection. The story, unlike most fables, is told without attempt at allegorical significance. It was immediately successful and Garnett had the rather embarrassing pleasure of selling it himself.

In the meantime the two friends had let the back room of their shop to Francis Meynell, who was then engaged in launching the Nonesuch Press, of which Garnett soon became a partner. Later he sold out his share of the bookshop in order to have more time to write, but he retained his connection with

DAVID GARNETT

Nonesuch. "The three partners in the concern settled down," Meynell recalls, "in a cellar under the bookshop of Francis Birrell and David Garnett in Gerrard Street, Soho, and there tackled the donkey work of book production and the mule work of book distribution. It was an uncomfortable cellar, but a bottle of whiskey and two decks of cards warmed some of its bleakest hours."

Garnett produced three other books, more or less in the same vein as the first. Then he suddenly turned aside from fantasy to write a full-length "straight" novel of modern life, and in 1929 he published *No Love*, the story of two English families of widely different backgrounds, tastes and habits who become neighbors on a tiny island off the coast of Sussex. The relations of these two families, chiefly in the friendship of the two sons, make the story.

Garnett is married and has two children. His wife, who was Rachel Marshall, has made woodcut illustrations for several of his books, as well as the jacket design and title page for *No Love*. They live at St. Ives, Huntingtonshire. Garnett's translation from the French of *Voyage to the Island of the Articoles*, by André Maurois, was published in 1929

His books are: *Lady Into Fox* (1923), *A Man In The Zoo* (1924), *The Sailor's Return* (1925), *Go She Must!* (1927), *No Love* (1929), *The Grasshoppers Come* (1931).

William Gerhardi

WHEN H. G. Wells first met young William Gerhardi he refused to pass thru a door before him. "No, you go first," he said, "You are tomorrow; I am yesterday." Gerhardi has been described as "good-looking, well-dressed, nervously agile, a svelte blond with deep eyes and a sensuous mouth." He looks even younger than he is. He has been further characterized as a "polyglot, educated, cynical, indiscreet, and erratic."

William Gerhardi was born in St. Petersburg, November 22, 1895. His father was a wealthy British cotton-spinning manufacturer who had settled in Russia. The boy went to school at St. Annen Schule and the Reformierte Schule in St. Petersburg. He learned Russian from his nurse, German and French in school, and English from his parents. "When I was fourteen", he recalls, "I started a monstrous novel on Tolstoyan lines—in Russian." And he kept on writing from that time. He finally journeyed to England where he

WILLIAM GERHARDI

took his Bachelor's degree at Worcester College, Oxford.

During the war Gerhardi served in the British Cavalry as cadet, lieutenant, and captain, from 1915 to 1916. In 1917 he was attached to the British Embassy in Petrograd where he was an eye-witness to the Russian Revolution in all its stages. From 1918 to 1920 he served on the staff of the British Military Mission to Siberia. He has been awarded the Czecho-Slovakian Croix de Guerre and the Russian Order of St. Stanislas.

Gerhardi's first book, *Futility*, appeared in 1922. Then he wrote a critical work, *Anton Chekhov*, which was published in 1923. Chekhov is Gerhardi's god among modern writers. Wells is his hero. "Chekhov!" he exclaims. "There's a man who takes you into the middle of life. There is no tedious introduction; no beating around the bush. . . As for Wells—he's vastly underrated. It's the fashion right now to read only his earliest books. But they're all good. . . Chekhov and Wells are vivid. Vividness is everything. A talented man can make anything vivid—even tediousness. Look at *The Three Sisters*. . ."

His second novel, *The Polyglots*, appeared in 1925. It was followed by *Jazz and Jasper* (1927). Gerhardi says of *Jazz and Jasper*: "The American publisher wouldn't have that title so I finally called it *Adam and Eva*. It's about Lord Beaverbrook, who's a friend of mine. In the book his name is Lord Ottercover, and what do you think, your American publishers gave the show away and printed a 'Who's Who' on the jacket. But you know, he didn't seem to mind at all. He was rather flattered."

In 1927 Gerhardi published a play, *Perfectly Scandalous*, and a book of five short stories, *Pretty Creatures*. His fourth novel, *Pending Heaven*, came out in 1930.

Gerhardi is called a realist, a pitiless realist—with an astonishing sense of humor. He writes with his brain and his eyes, with acute objective vision and with witty mockery. He writes about people who are introspective, whose emotions are easily touched, who are by turns gay and amorous and melancholy, who are eager for happiness, and who have queer traits. His is the European point of view. A reviewer said: "His short stories read as tho they had been translated into excellent English from a foreign language."

This young writer loves Wagner's *Tristan* but he abhors mysticism. Shakespeare is his favorite classic. He calls Byron "overestimated," Anatole France "sentimental," Shaw "old-fashioned," and Hardy "crude." His recreations are riding, dancing, and tennis. He has been around the world twice and has lived in practically every country. He is a popular guest. Lord Beaverbrook entertained him uninterruptedly for a year and the Princess of India lavished super-hospitality upon him. He is unmarried.

Gerhardi uses a dictaphone in his work. "You see", he comments, "I design my novels like a carpet or a tapestry, and I go on enriching the design here and there. Whenever I have an inspiration—when I'm shaving maybe—I take this up (the dictaphone) and speak. Then, in the morning my secretary comes and types it out. . . , leaving wide margins, and files it where it belongs. . ." His first book he wrote on a card index.

The *Memoirs of a Polyglot* (1931) is Gerhardi's autobiography to date.

A. Hamilton Gibbs

A. HAMILTON GIBBS

ARTHUR HAMILTON GIBBS was launched on his literary career by his brother, Cosmo Hamilton, who, finding himself too busy one week-end editing the London *World* and writing a novel to play tennis with his young brother who was visiting him, gave him pen and paper and the outline of a plot, and told him to go ahead and amuse himself. And, writing being a form of amusement that no Gibbs can withstand, Arthur *did* amuse himself and got a guinea and something in print for his pains.

He was seventeen at the time. He was born in London on March 9, 1888. He was the youngest member of a big family and was sent at the age of thirteen to the Collège de St. Malo, Brittany, where, he says, "I was a French boy, in a French uniform with brass buttons and a peaked cap, thinking, fighting, eating, smoking—all in French." Shortly after he came home from school, his father died and he set about to earn his living. It was his brother, Sir Philip Gibbs, who found him a job with a firm of assayers and refiners of gold and precious metals.

For three years he worked here until he was sent up to Oxford by Cosmo who played a decisive part in his young brother's career at every turn. At Oxford, Arthur boxed, won his Blue, rowed for his college, and decided that he could never become a barrister, the career which his family expected him to adopt. He wanted to write—was already writing for the *Isis,* the Varsity paper, had helped start the *Tuesday Review,* and when he left Oxford became sub-editor of a magazine which Cosmo Hamilton was launching in London. In two weeks it (the magazine) blew up, for financial reasons, and Arthur found himself jobless.

His first book, *The Compleat Oxford Man,* was published when he was twenty-one. He came to America in 1912, and 1913, playing a small part in Cosmo Hamilton's play *The Blindness of Virtue.* In 1914 he enlisted in the artillery division of the British Army and saw service until the Armistice, in Egypt, Greece, Serbia, Malta, Mudros, Ireland, and was for more than a year in France, where he was gassed. After demobilization in 1919 he wrote the story of his experiences in *Gun Fodder* —in two months, "working twenty-three hours a day," he says, with pardonable exaggeration.

His four and a half years of war left him with the rank of Major, the M.C., a distinctly international attitude—with a deep conviction that war, for whatever cause at all, must be avoided—and a feeling that the West, and not England, was where he wanted to live. "I like the bigness of it," he says of the United States. "It has breathing spaces. I like the idea that if you happened to feel like it you could get up in the morning and drive like fury for five hundred miles. In England you'd land in the ocean long before you got that far."

In 1919 Major Gibbs married Jeannette Phillips of Lynn, Massachusetts, a practising lawyer in Boston and a member of the New York and Massachusetts bars. Mrs. Gibbs, who, before her marriage, had contributed stories and articles to the magazines, has written three novels, *Portia Marries,* (1926), *Humdrum House* (1929), and *French Leave* (1930), while Major Gibbs has produced four consecutive best sellers, *Soundings* (1925), *Labels* (1926), *Harness* (1928), and *Chances* (1930). The Gibbses lived for a time in New York, "but," Major Gibbs says, "cities are prisons to me," and they decided that they would either have to take out their telephone (and still be at the mercy of the doorbell) or move to the country for peace. An old farm, belonging to Mrs. Gibbs's family, with a colonial house on the property, at Lakeville, Massachusetts, seemed the very solution.

They live here for eight or nine months of the year, making sallies to Boston and New York whenever necessary.

Major Gibbs's workroom is in the top of an old stone tower, on a hilltop a quarter of a mile from the house. Thru its thirteen windows, framed with ivy, he can look out over a green rolling country of pasture and woodland, and a blue, sun-flecked expanse of lake. The lake is generally sun-flecked for him because the Gibbses fly to the Riviera during the grey months. "Some people collect antiques, first editions, or Paul Revere silver," Major Gibbs says, his tanned face corroborating his words: "I prefer to collect sun the year round."

Philip Gibbs

SIR PHILIP HAMILTON GIBBS, son of Henry Gibbs, a departmental chief of the Board of Education in London, and eldest brother of the literary trio composed of Cosmo Hamilton (Gibbs), Arthur Hamilton Gibbs, and himself, was born May 1, 1877.

He was educated privately. In 1898 he and Miss Agnes Rowland were married. Their son, Anthony Gibbs, following the literary traditions of the family, is now a successful young novelist; his first book, *Peter Vacuum,* was published in 1925.

In the year of his marriage Philip Gibbs became associated with an educational publishing firm in London. In 1901 he was editor of Tillotson's Fiction Bureau at Bolton, in Lancaster, but, finding Lancaster too dull, he returned to London and served successively as a literary editor of the *Daily Mail,* the *Daily Chronicle,* and the *Tribune,* afterwards being special correspondent for these papers.

PHILIP GIBBS

The name of Philip Gibbs became known on both sides of the Atlantic when, along with other newspaper men, he was sent to Copenhagen to get Dr. Cook's story of his discovery of the North Pole on his return from the Arctic regions. The young English reporter suspected the hoax, and in spite of warnings that he was ruining his future career by challenging the statements of a man of Dr. Cook's standing, he persevered with his accusations until an official investigation exposed the fraud.

When war broke out in the Balkans in 1912 Gibbs was sent as correspondent for the *Daily Graphic* with the Bulgarian Army. Later he was war correspondent with the French and Belgian armies in 1914, and the British armies in the field, 1915-18. His journalistic services were so brilliant and distinctive that the English government conferred a title on him in 1920.

Sir Philip was editor of *The Review of Reviews* in 1921 and 1922. Since then he has traveled widely, visiting America several times, given a number of lectures, and written many books, articles, and essays.

Sir Philip Gibbs, Cosmo Hamilton, and A. Hamilton Gibbs differ widely in appearance and in talents. Philip Gibbs is a tallish, thin man with a face at once ascetic and gentle. Cosmo Hamilton has the handsomeness, suavity, and urbanity of the polished man about town. A. Hamilton Gibbs resembles Philip more in appearance, but is more swarthy and of a more athletic build. Despite the exquisite neatness of his appearance, Sir Philip, according to his wife, is one of the most absent-minded men alive: "Always losing his money, or being robbed; never has any matches, and (tho he is an inveterate traveler) always forgets to look up a train."

Sir Philip Gibb's works include novels, historical studies, and essays. A partial list of his books follows: *The Street of Adventure* (published early in 1900. American edition 1920); *Beauty and Nick* (1914); *The Soul of the War* (1915); *Battles of the Somme* (1916); *Now It Can Be Told* (1920); *Adventures in Journalism* (1923); *Young Anarchy* (1926); *Darkened Windows*

(1928); *Since Then* (1930), the disturbing story of the world at peace; *The Wings of Adventure and Other Little Novels,* a collection of ten stories (1930); *The Winding Lane* (1931), a novel.

W. W. Gibson

WILFRED WILSON GIBSON was born on October 2, 1878, in the ancient town of Hexham, Northumberland. He attended private schools and traveled occasionally as a boy. He showed an early interest in poetry and has devoted his time almost uninterruptedly to it since. There are 791 pages in his *Collected Poems, 1905-1925.*

While still in his teens Mr. Gibson made his first important appearance in print when his poem, *Blind,* was printed in *The Spectator* of September 4, 1897. A slim volume, *Urlyn the Harper,* appeared in 1902, and his second book of poems, *The Queen's Vigil,* was published in the same year. Then followed *The Golden Helm* (1903), *The Nets of Love* (1905), and *Stonefolds* (1907). These early books were pseudo-Tennysonian; imitative in manner and sentimentally romantic in tone.

Sherrill Schell
W. W. GIBSON

With *Daily Bread* (1910) Mr. Gibson changed his manner and began writing poems that dramatize the primitive emotions of ordinary people—ferrymen, berry-pickers, stone-cutters, farmers, printers, circus-men, carpenters.

In 1912 Mr. Gibson removed to London, where he was married. The following year, however, he went to reside in the country again, this time in the west of England, in the Malvern Hills. When the World War broke out he volunteered for service four times and was rejected each time.

From January to July of 1917, he made a tour of the United States, giving lectures and reading his poems in the principal cities and towns. For three months of that time he lived in Chicago. He has written poems that recall Lake Michigan, Indiana, and Broadway.

When he returned to England, Mr. Gibson once more offered himself for military duty and was accepted in October 1917. He served in the Army Service Corps as a private until January 1919. Now he resides at Letchworth, in Hertfordshire.

Wilfred Gibson is prolific, producing an enormous amount of poetry. He still takes his subjects from common life and his characters from the humblest of the obscure millions who perform menial tasks. His aim is to present human life in its normal guise, never exalting or refining it. He is a realist. In his gallery of varied portraits may be found the London tramp, the unemployed soldier, the rural teacher, the gypsy horse-coper, and the farm servant.

His volumes since 1910 include: *Fires* (1912), *Thoroughfares* (1914), *Border-lands* (1914), *Battle* (1915), *Friends* (1916), *Livelihood* (1917), *Whin* (1918), *Home* (1920), *Neighbours* (1920), *Krindlesyke* (1922), *Kestral Edge* (1924), *I Heard a Sailor* (1925), *Collected Poems, 1905-1925* (1926), *The Golden Room* (1928), and *Hazards* (1930). *Krindlesyke* and *Kestral Edge* contain poetic dramas. *Whin* was published in the United States under the title *Hill Tracks* because the shrub, whin or gorse, is known only to Europeans.

Mr. Gibson is the author of a prose play: *Between Fairs* (1928).

André Gide

A NDRÉ GIDE was born at Paris, November 21, 1869. Much has been made of the fact that his father, from the south of France, was a Protestant, while his mother, altho herself a Protestant, came from a Catholic family of Normandy.

He began his formal studies at the École Alsacienne de Paris; ill health forced him, at the age of twelve, to live in the country, and for several years his education was fragmentary and intermittent. Later he returned to the École Alsacienne, and there he met Pierre Louÿs, who became his daily companion and who later dedicated to him several of his early books. At eighteen, Gide was already preparing his own book, *Les Cahiers d'André Walter*, which appeared anonymously in 1891, as a posthumous work. It attracted little attention and few readers; nevertheless, it was noticed by Marcel Schwob and Maurice Barrès; and Maeterlinck, completely taken in by the hoax, announced in an interview that André Walter, whom he thought really dead, was one of his favorite authors.

At this time, and for the next few years, Gide was an ardent member of the Symbolist group whose center was Mallarmé, and he was one of the faithful who came each Tuesday evening, to sit at the feet of the Master. In 1893, he made his first journey to Africa, which he has several times revisited. He fell seriously ill at Tunis, and the winter of 1894 found him back in Paris. His African trip, bringing as it did the contact with a new people and a new religion, was destined profoundly to influence his later work. Its immediate fruit, however, was more apparent. The air of the Paris *salons* had become stifling to him and the pallid theorizing of the Symbolists no less so. *Paludes*, the first of his *soties* (farce is the closest English equivalent), was written and published in 1895; *Les Nourritures Terrestres* in 1897. Symbolism knew him no more—in truth, he had become incomprehensible to the Symbolists, and Henri de Régnier has since stated so in a vigorous repudiation of Gide and all his works.

In 1902 he published *The Immoralist*, the earliest of his studies of the Puritan

Berenice Abbott

ANDRÉ GIDE

conscience, a book which is today placed in the first rank of his work but which was a complete failure at the time. So pronounced a failure, in fact (as had been all of his previous books), that for the next seven years, discouraged and in doubt, he produced nothing save desultory magazine work, and thought seriously of abandoning literature. A newspaper interview with Octave Mirbeau made public that writer's admiration for *L'Immoraliste*. Gide took fresh heart and set about the composition of *Strait is the Gate*, published in 1909. This book, too, which, until the appearance of *The Counterfeiters*, was considered by many critics to be his masterpiece, made no appreciable stir and was apparently kept in print by its publishers only because of an appreciative essay on Gide's work by Edmund Gosse in the *Contemporary Review*.

With the exception of one *récit, Isabelle*, the next few years were given over to criticism. He published a second volume of critical essays as well as his first studies of Dostoievsky. *Les Caves du Vatican* appeared in 1914, on the eve of the war. Unquestionably one of his greatest books, its success was seriously handicapped by the war. During the war he devoted himself to translations. He

had learned English when he was forty, and has since been an ardent propagandist for the cause of English literature, translating Shakespeare, Conrad, and Whitman, besides other works. *La Symphonie Pastorale*, the third of the "Puritan" narratives, appeared in 1919. In 1921 he began the writing of *The Counterfeiters,* to be completed, finally, in 1925. Since 1921, he has published also his autobiography (written in large part simultaneously with *The Counterfeiters*), *Travels in the Congo,* and *The School for Wives.*

The Immoralist was published here in 1930, followed by translations of *Isabelle* and *La Symphonie Pastorale* in 1931.

Gide is the most powerful figure in French letters today, altho he asserts that he has done everything possible to discourage his "disciples." His appearances and movements are mysterious and theatrical. A soft black hat habitually shades his lean and clever face. (In his youth he wore a loose moustache, but now he believes in exposing the "natural" physiognomy.) He often wears a skull cap to cover his bald head and a shawl over his shoulders in the Mallarmé tradition. His eyes are brown, his skin yellow.

When *Si le Grain ne Meurt* was published some years ago the frankness of his confessions shocked some of the French public. The translation of the axiom "nature abhors a vacuum" is "la nature a l'horreur du vide." Gide's shocked compatriots turned it into "la nature a l'horreur du Gide."

His dominant trait is curiosity. In Africa he once followed a native marriage ceremony, literally entranced by the throbbing drums, the weird costumes and gyrations of the celebrants, down a dusty village street into the forbidden chamber where no white man had ever gone. A moment later he was to be seen dashing for his life, pursued by a howling pack of indignant natives, back to the party of friends whom he had deserted.

The following books by Gide are available in English translation: *Strait is the Gate* (1924), *The Vatican Swindle* (1925, reissued in 1928 as *Lafcadio's*

Adventures), *Dostoicvsky* (1926), *The Counterfeiters* (1927), *The School for Wives* (1929), *Travels in the Congo* (1929), *The Immoralist* (1930), *Two Symphonies: Isabelle* and *La Symphonie Pastorale* (1931).

Ellen Glasgow

ELLEN GLASGOW, in her novels, has broken the sentimental tradition of the South—the tradition in which she herself was raised. She was born in Richmond, Virginia, April 22, 1874. Because she was a delicate child she was not sent to school. "Her mother taught her the alphabet from one of Scott's novels, and she grew up in her father's fine library, studying with tutors when her health permitted, and reading voraciously whatever she chose. Browning became her favorite poet." When she came of college age she attended the University of Virginia and made Phi Beta Kappa.

Miss Glasgow's revolt against her environment began very quietly. She was a part of that environment herself and she did not like to be disloyal to her friends, so wrote anonymously. None of her family was aware that she was writing a novel until her first one, *The Descendant,* was finished. The first quarter of the book was rewritten on the

ELLEN GLASGOW

advice of Walter Hines Page and it was published in 1897.

Her first success came in 1900 when *The Voice of the People* was published. While writing this novel Miss Glasgow defied feminine tradition of the South and persuaded a friend to smuggle her into the Virginia state convention where she got a description she needed. This novel, dealing with the 1880's, was the first of a series which was to record much of the social history and political atmosphere of Virginia from the 1850's to the present. In *The Battle Ground* (1902), she went back to Civil War times.

Adherence to reality was the core of Miss Glasgow's revolt. She insisted on picturing people as they actually were and not just as they had always been pictured by others. Furthermore, she wished to break away from the false sentiment and romanticism of the traditional novel of the South.

Miss Glasgow protested against the old system of chivalry in which a woman's education "was designed to paralyze her reasoning faculties" in *Virginia* (1913) and *Life and Gabriella* (1916). Two more novels about women followed: *The Builders* (1919) and *Barren Ground* (1925).

In 1925 Miss Glasgow said "What the South needs now is—blood and irony." And she proceeded with social satire. The wit she had laid aside in *Barren Ground* appeared full and sparkling in *The Romantic Comedians* (1926) and later in *They Stooped to Folly* (1929).

Altho she has travelled extensively Miss Glasgow confesses she has always been a home person. She lives at Number One, West Main Street, Richmond, in a dwelling a hundred years old that is proudly resisting the oncoming of industrialism. It has a self-sufficing air. In the heart of the city, its iron fence encloses flowering shrubs and a garden securely hidden behind. In this garden Miss Glasgow writes in perfect seclusion. The square old house has big rooms with open fireplaces and many ancient furnishings. She entertains such famous writers as James Branch Cabell, Mary Johnston, Joseph Hergesheimer, and Hugh Walpole.

Miss Glasgow is of good height, altho not tall, with wavy dark hair and lively brown eyes. She finds life agreeable and amusing. She suffers from a slight deafness which she does not allow to become a handicap in life. Rather, she dismisses the difficulty and enters into conversation, becoming a part of everything that goes on.

Following the publication of *The Romantic Comedians* she told how, during the long months of waiting for *The Descendant* to be published after acceptance, she had said to herself that if only this one book would be published she could die of happiness. "And now," she said with characteristic irony, "I've had seventeen published and I've never been happy and have not died."

Among Miss Glassgow's other novels are: *The Wheel of Life* (1906), *The Ancient Law* (1908), *The Romance of a Plain Man* (1909), *The Miller of Old Church* (1911), *One Man in His Time* (1922), and *The Shadowy Third* (1923).

Susan Glaspell

SUSAN GLASPELL is an Iowan, born in Davenport July 1, 1882. Like many another writer she gained her training thru newspaper work. "We lived in Davenport but I spent my summers with an aunt, on a farm not unlike the Kelloggs' (in *Brook Evans*). Later I would go to Colorado in the summer, and one year stayed all winter at Monte Vista, in a vast mountain valley, about nine thousand feet above sea level."

Miss Glaspell was educated at Drake University, Des Moines, where, in 1899, she was an unsuccessful candidate for the editorship of the *Delphic*. The day after receiving her Ph.B. she got a job on the *Des Moines Daily News* where she was State House and Legislative reporter. After continuing her reportorial experience with the *Des Moines Capital*, she went to Chicago where she took postgraduate work at the University of Chicago. The background for her first novel, *Glory of the Conquered* (1909), was inspired by Chicago. The book was sufficiently successful to finance a year in the Latin Quarter of Paris.

SUSAN GLASPELL

The desire to live life at its fullest and to experience all its varieties took her thereafter to a ranch in Idaho and later to Provincetown, Massachusetts, where she spent a number of years. Here she married George Cram Cook in 1913 and with him identified herself with the Little Theatre movement as actress, producer, and author for the Provincetown Players. Among the plays she wrote for this group were *Suppressed Desires* (1914), in collaboration with her husband, and *Trifles* (1917).

Of the community of artists and writers there she says: "We were a particularly simple people, who sought to arrange life for the thing we wanted to do, needing each other as protection against complexities, yet living as we did because of an instinct for the old, old things, to have a garden and neighbors, to keep up the fire, and let the cat in at night. None of us had much money. We worried together thru illnesses, ate together when the cook had left, talked about our work. Each could be himself. That was perhaps the real thing we did for each other." Mr. Cook was responsible for the first production of Eugene O'Neill's plays on an old wharf which had been built into a theatre by the Provincetown Players.

Miss Glaspell and her husband moved in 1917 to Greenwich Village, New York City, where he was manager and she chief playwright for a theatre. Several more of her plays were produced: *Woman's Honor* (1918), *Bernice* (1919), *The Inheritors* (1921), and the *Verge* (1922). In 1922 Miss Glaspell and her husband travelled to Greece, where he died in 1923 and was buried in Delphi.

In 1925 Miss Glaspell married Norman Matson, author and critic. The next year *The Road to the Temple* was published. It contains the story of her married life with George Cram Cook, their trip, and his death. It is a living picture of the man who realized the dream of his life in Greece where he lived among his Greek friends and dressed like a shepherd.

Miss Glaspell collaborated with Mr. Matson on her play *The Comic Artist* (1927). They now live in a secluded old farm house at Truro, Cape Cod. There Miss Glaspell has a hut up in the pines, which, she says, is her workshop "and nothing else. It is over the hill from our house, and from every house, and gives a sense of being in the woods."

Brook Evans (1928) was Miss Glaspell's first novel in thirteen years. Its setting is in three different parts of the world in which she has lived: the banks of the upper Mississippi; Colorado; and "France, at Senlis, the old walled cathedral town, looking across rich fields to the forest of Chantilly." *The Fugitive's Return* (1929) reflects Miss Glaspell's experience in Greece. It is the story of a woman who is stunned by the loss of her husband and child and who is saved from suicide and sent to Greece where she regains her hold on life.

The drama, *Alison's House*, based on the life of Emily Dickinson, appeared in 1930 in *Six Plays*, an English publication. The play was published separately in the United States in 1931. It concerns a poet, twenty years after her death, and the question as to whether her unpublished love poems should be revealed to the world. The play was produced by Eva Le Gallienne and her Civic Repertory Company during the season of 1930 and 1931. The company had previously presented *The Inheritors*.

Miss Glaspell's novels are: *The Glory of the Conquered* (1909), *The Visioning* (1911), *Fidelity* (1915), *Brook Evans* (1928), *The Fugitive's Return* (1929), and *Ambrose Holt and Family* (1931). *Lifted Masks* (1912) is a book of short stories.

Isa Glenn

ISA GLENN'S father, John Thomas Glenn, was at one time mayor of Atlanta, Georgia, where she was born. Her mother was Helen Garrard, sister of Louis F. Garrard. She is a member of the Urquhart family of New Orleans, and has the red hair of Cora Urquhart Potter. Her grandmother was a sister of the two Confederate generals, Howell Cobb and T. R. Cobb.

Miss Glenn showed a youthful interest in art. She was educated privately in Atlanta and in New York City before she was sent to Paris at the age of ten. There she studied art in the studio of her cousin, James MacNeill Whistler. At the end of a year Whister, who was never notable for his guarded speech, told her in so many words that she was no artist and had better take to "scrib-

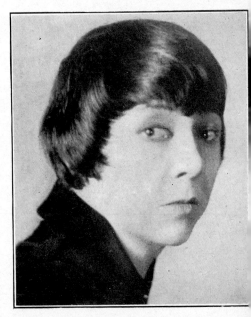

ISA GLENN

bling." Such was the inglorious end of her first career.

She returned to America and while still in her teens married a West Pointer, Brigadier General S. J. Bayard Schindel. She accompanied him when he was stationed in the Philippines and subsequently in the South Sea Islands, South America, and all over the Orient. On these travels she soaked up material and experiences which served her in good stead later in her novels. Her husband died March 11, 1921.

Their son, John Bayard Schindel, born in 1908, published his first novel, *Golden Pilgrimage,* in 1929.

Miss Glenn began her "scribbling" and wrote short stories for a number of years. Once she was awarded the O. Henry Prize. Her first full-length novel appeared in 1926. It was *Heat,* a story of the Philippines, laid in Manila. Indo-China and Brazil furnished the background for *Little Pitchers* (1927), a study of the moral disintegration of Americans in the enervating climate and alien social organization of the Orient. *Southern Charm* (1928) goes back to the rural Georgia of her childhood days. In it she turns her attention to the task of debunking a traditional Southern legend and a mythical state of living by the experiences of a family that moves north after the oldest daughter marries a Northerner. The action of *Transport* (1929) takes place at sea between San Francisco and Manila.

A Short History of Julia was published in 1930. In it a Georgia girl loses the man she loves to her younger sister, and accepting the fact that "the pattern of her life had been laid down at her birth," passes with all outward serenity into spinsterhood.

Miss Glenn is painstakingly methodical in the writing of her novels. She details her studied method of writing *A Short History of Julia* as follows: She began with comprehensive sketches of her twenty-three characters. Then she drew up a chart of chapters, with brief notes on each chapter. The chronology of events listed the birth, deaths, and marriages from 1836 to 1928 of persons who influence the story. Miss Glenn then proceeded to write a detailed account, chapter by chapter, of the unfolding of the narrative. All this covered ninety pages, closely typewritten. After that, the writing of the novel in its final form took comparatively little time.

She says it usually takes her "six months in my head, two months on the typewriter" to complete a novel. "I always have to write a book in my head before I put it on paper—I have to know everything about my characters. In the case of *Southern Charm,* I got to know the old lady intimately—even to the kind of underwear she wore—before I wrote down a word. When I came to the actual writing, it was almost like copying, for the book was already written in my mind."

Miss Glenn lives at present in a New York apartment surrounded by an interesting collection of Whistler photographs, etchings, and mementoes. She is a member of the National Arts Club of New York and the Georgia chapter of the Society of Colonial Dames.

The list of her novels is: *Heat* (1926), *Little Pitchers* (1927), *Southern Charm* (1928), *Transport* (1929), and *A Short History of Julia* (1930).

Michael Gold

"**I** WAS born on April 12, 1896, on the East Side, on a street that was only one block removed from the Bowery," writes Michael ("Mike") Gold, apostle of the proletariat and of proletarian literature. "The East Side was then the red light district of the city. The immigrant Jews had to live in its moral and physical filth and bring up children there. My father was a shiftless, easy-going Roumanian Jew, who was fond of wine and song. He worked at many trades here, from street peddling to operating a machine in a cloak and suit sweatshop, and finally opened a little suspender shop of his own, in back of which we lived and worked with him. I remember long, miserable hours of work almost since the cradle. My mother toiled from dawn till midnight. I myself went to work at the age of twelve, in a factory for making incandescent gas mantles. Then I worked for the Adams Express Com-

MICHAEL GOLD

pany for several years, as a driver's helper and night watchman.

"My father died when I was nineteen. I had been the chief support of our family, and now I became restless and escaped from New York. My first stop was Boston, where I spent several years. I don't know why, but Boston has always seemed to me to be the most interesting city in America. I became a radical there. I got in with an anarchist group, and with a friend issued a little anarchist weekly, which was soon suppressed by the Boston cops. I did my first writing for this paper. Then I joined the I. W. W., and helped organize a strike of textile workers and one of Negro longshoremen in Providence, R. I. Then I came back to New York, and worked for several years on the old *Call* as copy-reader. After that I drifted across the U. S. A., working on section gangs, newspapers, etc. I spent some time in Chicago and vicinity, and then headed south for Mexico, where I rambled for over two years. In Mexico I became a Communist, and have been one ever since.

"After some more tramping I came back to New York again, and got a job as editorial assistant to Max Eastman on the *Masses*. When Max grew tired of a perpetually bankrupt magazine, Claude McKay, the Negro poet, and I took it over. The paper failed.

"About three years ago, Hugo Gellert and I founded the *New Masses,* of which I am now editor. I have had two plays produced, *Hoboken Blues,* a Negro fantasy, and *Fiesta,* a romantic comedy-tragedy of the Mexican revolution. Both were flops.

"All in all, I have worked on about thirty-six jobs entailing manual labor, and on about twelve newspapers as a reporter and copyreader. I have been chased by the cops in about forty street demonstrations, and have helped in about twenty strikes. I now believe that writing is the one way in which I, as an individual, can best contribute to the world revolutionary movement."

Mr. Gold has published *120 Million* (1929), sketches of the American worker; *Jews Without Money* (1930), a book of East Side memories; and *Charlie Chaplin's Parade* (1930), a book for children.

Louis Golding

LOUIS GOLDING was born in November 1895 in Manchester, England. His schooling began at the famous Manchester Grammar School where he carried off from his surprised classmates all the honors and prizes obtainable for literature, history, and other subjects.

At the age of six he had developed a passion for literature which manifested itself in an epigrammatic poem about a boy who

". . . got a big smack
And said he'd go back
To school
The fool."

Thruout his early school days he seems to have followed this bent more or less, one of his extant works written at the age of nine being *The Adventures of Three on Bloody Island,* which was published in his elementary school magazine.

But when his grammar school days were over the business of getting along in the world had to be considered at the expense of his literary production. Golding was poor and had to make his own way. From the time he was 12 until he was graduated from Oxford, he supported himself by scholarships. The war having broken out, he left Queen's College, Oxford, to go to Macedonia with the English troops, but returned after the hostilities were over to finish his course.

While at college, he was one of the editors of the Oxford books of verse, and conducted the *Queen's College Miscellany,* an undergraduate magazine. His first volume of verse, *Sorrows of War* (1919), and his first novel, *Forward from Babylon* (1920), both appeared while he was at Oxford.

After taking his degree he was ordered to spend the greater part of each year abroad on account of his health, and his travels began again. He crosses the ocean in tramp steamers, and with a knapsack on his back and a stick in his hand he tramps thru countries, living with the people—an easy matter since he speaks French, German, Italian, and Spanish as fluently as English, and he knows modern Greek and Arabic. He has achieved the reputation of being the most widely traveled English author of his time. He lists his recreations as "wandering, reading, talking, listening, net-play at tennis."

When he left Oxford he began his wanderings among the enchanted isles of the Mediterranean. He has pursued and recreated the adventures of Odysseus from the Island of the Sirens to the Island of the Lotus Eaters and home again to Ithaca. He has made his bed on the quaking sides of the volcanic Stromboli and among beds of rosemary in Corfu. He has traveled steerage in Greek steamers and on the decks of Sicilian sailing boats. He has tramped thru Sicily and Greece.

He made a short visit to America in 1927 and entertained large audiences with accounts of his journeys into foreign lands and with acute and vivid descriptions of literary personalities and movements.

His works include: verse, *Sorrows of War, Shepherd Singing Ragtime, Prophet and Fool* (Collected Poems, 1923); books of travel, *Sunward, Sicilian Noon, Those Ancient Lands;* novels, *Forward from Babylon* (1920), *Seacoast of Bohemia* (1923), *Day of Atone-*

LOUIS GOLDING

ment (1925), *Store of Ladies* (1927), *The Miracle Boy* (1927), *Give Up Your Lovers* (1930), *Magnolia Street* (1931).

Maxim Gorky

ALEXEI MAXIMOVICH PYESH-KOFF was born at Nijni Novgorod on March 14, 1868. Maxim Gorky is his adopted pen-name. At the age of four he contracted cholera and was cured, but his father caught the disease from him and died. His mother took him to the home of her parents, where the family lived in two dark cellar rooms. The lad gathered rubbish and old bits of iron in the streets when he was not in school to help support the poor household. The other children would not sit near him because he smelled so strongly; they called him "the ragpicker."

Gorky's mother died when he was nine, and his schooling came to an end. His grandfather told him there was no longer any room for him and sent him "out into the world." For fifteen years he wandered about as a cobbler's apprentice, an errand boy, a draftsman's assis-

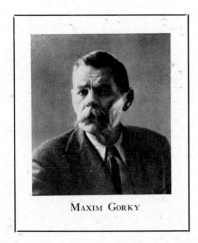

MAXIM GORKY

tant, dishwasher on a Volga steamer, clerk to a lawyer, a day laborer, and a tramp on the steppes.

At nineteen he tried to shoot himself. The bullet passed thru his lung and his life was despaired of, but an operation saved him. He found solace in the friendship of Korolenko, who recognized in the youth a fresh talent and encouraged him to write. When he was working in the railway shops at Tiflis, he published a story in the local newspaper, using the signature, "Maxim Gorky," and he became a provincial journalist. His name is derived from "gor'kii," which means "the bitter one."

Gorky began to write about his experiences and the poor people he had encountered on his extensive journeys over Russia. In 1895 a leading St. Petersburg journal printed his tale, *Chelkash*. Two years later he collected his stories in book form. Among the best-known of these tales is *My Fellow-traveler* and *Twenty-Six Men and a Girl*. After 1899 he turned to the writing of novels and plays which picture Russian life and attempt a solution of the social problems. He came under the influence of Chekhov and Tolstoy, and it was Chekhov who urged him to write dramas.

From his boyhood Gorky had been interested in the revolutionary movement. He now devoted himself to the Labor cause, becoming a member of the Russian Social Democratic Party, and later joining the Bolshevist wing of that party. In January 1905, on the Bloody Sunday in St. Petersburg which marked the beginning of the first Russian Revolution, Gorky was imprisoned.

In 1906 he went abroad to conduct an anti-Czarist campaign. He visited Berlin, Paris, and New York. Expelled from the United States, he went to the island of Capri, off the coast of Italy, where he settled down to continue his writing. In 1907 he was a delegate to the Congress of the Russian Social Democratic Party in London. He spent the period of his exile on Capri working in behalf of the labor movement and keeping up a steady exchange of friendly letters with Lenin. He helped found a school in Capri to educate Russian workers and professional revolutionists.

Gorky was allowed to return to Russia in 1913, and following the Revolution he dedicated himself to cultural work among the proletariat. But his health forced him to return to the mild climate of Capri, where he is still actively engaged in his writing. He received great ovations upon his return to Russia in 1928 for the dedication of the Gorky Museum and again in 1929 for the twelfth anniversary of the revolution.

At present he is working on a trilogy that has for its scope the period from the death of Alexander II to the Revolution of 1917. The first volume, *The Bystander* (1930), ends with the coronation of Czar Nicholas. The second volume is *The Magnet* (1931). Altho he is still suffering from consumption as he has most of his life, the author's prodigious energy enables him to work from six o'clock in the morning until one in the afternoon, and again late into the night.

Gorky, despite his ill-health, is tall, erect, and youthfully slender. He speaks in a booming bass. His interests and tastes are catholic and he is tolerant of individuals and nations. He is drunk with the joy of living, and is capable of abandoning himself for hours to Kuzka, his devoted terrier.

This Russian author is considered a master of the short story. His novels and plays are technically imperfect, but his characters, in any medium, are real creations, as in *Foma Gordyeeff*, *Mother*, *Three of Them*, and *Decadence*. Of his plays, *The Lower Depths* (1903) had a successful run on Broadway in a modernized version called *At the Bottom*, and it ran nearly two years in Berlin. Of his other writings, the contemporary reminiscences are outstanding, such as *Reminiscences of Tolstoy* (1920).

Among Maxim Gorky's other translated works are: *The Outcasts,* (1902), *Comrades* (1907), *The Spy* (1908), *Children of the Sun* (1912), *Night Lodgings* (1920), *Fragments from My Diary* (1924), *Reminiscences of My Youth* (1924).

Edwin Granberry

EDWIN GRANBERRY was born April 18, 1897, at Meridian, Miss. of a family connected for generations with the educational and professional life of the South. Until the World War, in which he served in the U.S. Marines, his training was for the career of a concert pianist. During the interruption of the War, he began to write and has never resumed concert work.

As a child, he lived for five years in the Indian territory and has almost too vivid recollections of prairie fires, roaming bands of Indians, and prairie wolves howling at night.

When he was ten, the family moved to Florida, and Mr. Granberry still calls Florida his home, altho spending the greater part of his time recently in and near New York City. It is the Old World atmosphere of Florida, combined with its varied wild forests, plains, and sea coasts, that excite most of his writing. His hobby is deep-sea fishing among the keys south of the peninsula. He is currently engaged on the first volume of a trilogy unfolding against the early Spanish and English background of this country.

Mr. Granberry was educated at the University of Florida, Columbia University, and Harvard, at the latter being a graduate of Professor Baker's famous 47 Workshop. In 1924 he married Mabel Leflar of Cincinnati, Ohio. He has two small sons.

Mr. Granberry is primarily a stylist. The effectiveness of his narrative and characterization lies in the literary investiture. The quality of his prose is rhythmic and melodious. He is at present on

EDWIN GRANBERRY

the faculty of Ancient Languages at Stevens.

He has published *The Ancient Hunger* (1927), *Strangers and Lovers* (1928), and *The Erl King* (1930).

H. Granville-Barker

HARLEY GRANVILLE-BARKER has distinguished himself as actor, producer, playwright, and translator. He was born in London in 1877, the son of Albert James Barker and Mary Elizabeth Bozzi-Granville. His great grandfather, a Dr. Bozzi, moved from Milan to England in 1821.

Young Granville-Barker was educated at a private school, learned elocution from his mother, and at the age of thirteen made his first appearance on the stage. For several years he acted in a great variety of plays, many of them Shakespearean. He showed an early interest in the intellectual drama and soon became an ardent adherent of the Elizabethan Stage Society and the Incorporated Stage Society.

In May 1905, with Vedrenne, Granville-Barker assumed management of the Court Theatre to produce unconventional plays that could not find production on

H. GRANVILLE-BARKER

the commercial stage. These plays were chiefly by Ibsen and Shaw. The project helped particularly to raise Shaw to popularity. Granville-Barker was actor as well as manager in the enterprise, and he was the original Eugene, Brassbound, Napoleon, and Frank in Shaw's plays. He made significant tests of new stage methods and experimented with Gordon Craig in top lighting and impressionistic scenery.

Meanwhile Barker was writing plays, having commenced at the age of twenty-two. *The Marrying of Ann Leete* (1901) has for its theme the upsetting of social convention. *The Voysey Inheritance* (1905) adopts Shaw's argumentative method in working out a moral problem in a comedy of business. *Waste* (1907) is a realistic tragedy. *The Madras House* (1910) discusses the position of women in modern civilization.

The story of Granville-Barker's producing experiences and his American tour is set forth in *The Contemporary Drama of England* by Thomas H. Dickinson. In 1907 he married Lillah McCarthy, who played in his American tour.

To quote Dickinson: "Barker is like Shaw in liking discussion, in feeling that ideas are among the most important things in the world. . . He takes as his theme the topics of intellectualism, the social, political, or sex interests of men

and women. But he treats the mental lives of men and women at their purest and best. . . His plays are like reminiscences of passionate things after emotion has cooled, for they are aloof and cynical."

In 1918 Barker married again. Helen Huntington Gates of New York is his second wife. To the distress of many theatrical admirers he turned his attention from playwriting to translation. With his wife's aid he produced translations of: *The Romantic Young Lady, Wife to A Famous Man, The Kingdom of God, The Two Shepherds* (1923), and *A Lily Among Thorns* (1927), all by G. Martinez Sierra; and *The Women Have Their Way, A Hundred Years Old, Fortunato,* and *The Lady From Alfaqueque* (1927), by Joaquin and Serafín Alvarez Quintero.

Besides the Spanish plays, he has adapted *Anatol* from the German of Arthur Schnitzler (1916) and *Doctor Knock* from the French of Jules Romains (1923). He publishes occasional magazine articles and his wife contributes poetry to periodicals. Their home is in Devon.

His other plays include: *Three Plays: The Marrying of Ann Leete, The Voysey Inheritance,* and *Waste* (1909); *Three Short Plays: Rococo, Vote By Ballot,* and *Farewell to the Theatre* (1917); *The Secret Life* (1923); *His Majesty* (1928).

In collaboration he has written *Prunella* with Laurence Housman (1906) and *The Harlequinade* with Dion Clayton Calthorop (1918).

Critical works on the theatre by H. Granville-Barker include: *A National Theatre*, with William Archer (1907); *The Exemplary Theatre* (1922); *Prefaces to the Players' Shakespeare* (1923, 1928), and *Henry V to Hamlet,* British Academy Lecture (1925).

Robert Graves

ROBERT GRAVES, English poet, was born in London July 26, 1895, into a distinguished family. His father is Alfred Percival Graves, poet and folk-song writer, son of a Protestant Bishop of Limerick. His mother is Amalie von Ranke, daughter of Heinrich Ritter von Ranke, professor of medicine in the University of Munich. The elder Graves has published numerous books of ballads, songs, and poetry. His autobiography, *To Return to All That* (1930), may be construed as a reply to his son's more pessimistic autobiographical work, *Goodbye to All That* (1929).

Robert Graves was the third of five children by Alfred Percival Graves' second wife. His first wife had died of consumption, leaving five children, so there were ten in all. As a youth Robert saw practically nothing of his father because the latter was inspector of schools.

The boy had an opportunity to read more books than most children do, for there were four or five thousand volumes in the home. The library consisted of an old-fashioned scholar's library bequeathed to the elder Mr. Graves by a friend of Wordsworth; Mr. Graves' own collection of books, mostly poetry; devotional works contributed by Mrs. Graves; text books sent to the father by publishers in the hope that he would recommend them for school use; and novels of adventure brought into the house by the older brothers and sisters.

Robert attended six preparatory schools in all, starting at the age of six. During vacations his mother would take the children to Germany, France, or later to Harlech in North Wales where she had built a house. In 1914 Robert went to Charterhouse where he began to write poetry. His education was interrupted by the war. A day or two after the outbreak he enlisted and in a few months he was in the trenches with the Royal Welch Fusiliers, serving in the same regiment with Siegfried Sassoon.

While in the battlefields Graves began to write poetry in earnest and he became conspicuous in France among the group of young English war poets which included Sassoon, Brooke, and Nichols. In 1916 his first two volumes were published: *Over the Brazier* and *Goliath and David*. *Fairies and Fusiliers* appeared in 1917. He was wounded and was sent to a hospital at Oxford for convalescence. In January 1918 he married Nancy Nicholson, whom he had met on leave in 1916. After the war, when he was

well enough to travel, he and his wife went to Harlech where they lived for a year. Their first of four children, a girl, was born in January 1919.

In October 1919 Graves went up to Oxford where he entered St. John's College and took his degree seven years later. For a while he and his family lived in a cottage at the bottom of John Masefield's garden. Graves published several volumes of poetry during this period: *The Treasure Box* (1919), *Country Sentiment* (1920), *The Pier-Glass* (1921), *Whipperginny* (1923), *The Feather Bed* (1923), *Mock Beggar Hall* (1924), *Welchman's Hose* (1925), and *The Marmosite's Miscellany* (1925) under the pseudonym of "John Doyle."

His wife's ill health forced them to spend the winter in Egypt, so in 1926 Graves secured an appointment as professor of English literature at the newly-founded Egyptian University at Cairo. They returned to England in 1927 and since then Graves has been hand-printing in partnership with Laura Riding as *The Seizin Press*, which publishes modern limited editions.

Most of Graves' writings now were

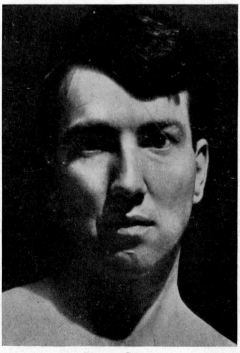

ROBERT GRAVES

critical prose and his poetry became analytical and philosophical in constrast to the playful gaiety of his early verse. His first collected poetry appeared in 1927 with *Poems, 1914-1926*. He wrote an autobiographical account of his war and domestic experiences in *Good-bye to All That* (1929). Graves and his wife separated in 1929. *Ten Poems More* was published in 1930.

Prose works by Graves include: *The Meaning of Dreams* (1924), *My Head! My Head!* (1925), *The English Ballad* (1927), *John Skelton* (1927), *Mrs. Fisher* (1928), *The Shout* (1929), and *But It Still Goes On* (1930), a miscellaneous continuation of *Goodbye to All That*.

Anna Katharine Green

ANNA KATHARINE GREEN was born in Brooklyn, New York, November 11, 1846, the daughter of a widely known criminal lawyer. She was graduated from Ripley Female College, Poultney, Vermont, in 1867. When she was a girl she wanted more than anything else to be a poet and continually wrote verses. After a meeting with Ralph Waldo Emerson she sent him some verse, and he in turn wrote a long letter of encouragement.

ANNA KATHARINE GREEN

Her treasures are few but the Emerson letter is chief among them. Emerson wrote to her: "If our thoughts come in such wealth and with such heat that we have no choice, but must watch and obey and live for them, the question is answered for us."

Anna Katharine Green would have preferred to be known as a poet and has tried to make people agree with her that she could write good verse. E. D. Stedman was among those who agreed; but the great mass of readers and the press have long ago settled the question for her, and she is very glad to be the author of twenty-five or more stories of mystery.

Anna Katharine Green became famous on the publication of her first mystery story, *The Leavenworth Case*, which she wrote during an interval of tedious inactivity after her graduation from the Ripley Female College. She traces her inspiration to Gaboriau and Poe, but the story itself, on which she wrote hundreds of thousands of words in a long fever of activity, was conceived and bred "entirely in my imagination." The author started with these two main ideas: the murderer should be the first one to announce the crime; and second, some one passing a door should hear a conversation and attribute it to a wrong person.

One of the things that give the writer of American detective stories no little perplexity is, according to Anna Katharine Green, the necessity of conforming to actual conditions. American procedure is very different from that of other countries. The American detective, under police control, cannot be a free lance in the land of mystery. If his work is convincing it must be natural and be done in conformity to well-known conditions, and necessarily be restricted and within the law. He cannot make his case and solve it too, and in his efforts to solve the problem he naturally proceeds as if he were human, and being human, can and does make mistakes. All her police detectives, she explains, have made mistakes.

In 1884 Miss Green married Charles Rohlfs, and she is the mother of three children. Her home is in Buffalo, New York.

In her eighty-third year she was described as "gentle, courteous, gracious—even shy. She sat in a high-backed chair surrounded with books and dark oak furniture, distilling mellowness and wisdom. Particularly in her eyes is that expression of eager curiosity which seems more effective than any 'treatment' in holding Youth captive. Her interest in life is unquenchable."

Among the books that Anna Katharine Green wrote after *The Leavenworth Case* are *A Strange Disappearance, The Mill Mystery, Behind Closed Doors, That Affair Next Door, The Circular Study, The Millionaire Baby, The Woman in the Alcove, The House of the Whispering Pines, The Mystery of the Hasty Arrow,* and *The Step on the Stair.*

ANNE GREEN

Anne Green

ANNE GREEN is the sister of Julian Green. Unlike him, she was born in the United States—Savannah, Georgia—in 1899, six months before her Virginian father and Georgian mother sailed for France, taking their small daughter with them. Julian was born about a year later, after the family had settled in Paris.

Anne's education, at home and for a few years in a large French school, was that of the typical Parisian child. Her mother died at the beginning of the World War. Anne became a war nurse before she was quite eighteen and spent four years in military hospitals, tending to the wounded.

After the war she traveled in Europe and America, finding her southern relatives in this country as agreeable as she had been taught to expect them. She had no serious idea, at first, of pursuing a literary career, but began by writing fashion and technical articles for a group of newspapers.

It was her cousin, John Macrae, President of E. P. Dutton & Company, who suggested that she should write a novel. *The Selbys* (1930), a light-hearted comedy about Americans in Paris, was the result. It was followed by *Reader, I Married Him* (1931), another amusing story of the American colony.

Anne and Julian Green present an interesting contrast in personalities. Both of them are bi-lingual, but whereas the brother writes his novels in French, the sister writes hers in English. Julian's books are dark and probing; Anne's are gay, with a bright touch of satire. Julian himself is serious, meditative, "with great calm eyes, a proud shyness"; she, on the contrary, is vivacious and bright-eyed. In brief, Anne is a light Green; Julian, a dark Green. They have a strong family affection and have lived quietly, for several years, in an apartment in Paris.

Julian Green

BOTH parents of Julian Green, the French novelist, were Americans, members of distinguished Virginian and Georgian families of Scotch-Irish ancestry. Green père brought his wife to the French capital when he became Paris agent of an American business firm. Julian was born in Paris on September 6, 1900.

As a boy, sensitive, lonely, uprooted, he spent much time in drawing, writing, and reading. He was more interested in French literature than in English, and it is said that his mother had to offer him a reward for each English book that he

JULIAN GREEN

read. The result was that he read widely in both literatures, becoming especially fond of Dickens, Jane Austen, Eugène Sue, and ghost stories. He was a good Latin student, but hated mathematics and science. Brought up as a typical young Frenchman, educated at a French *lycée*, Green to this day speaks English, really his native language, with just the hint of a French accent.

During the war, altho he was only a boy in his teens, he saw active service. In 1917 he was in the American Field Service near Verdun. Afterwards he joined the Morgan Harjes organization, which took him to the Italian front. In 1918 he enlisted in the French artillery.

After the armistice a year passed in which he accomplished nothing. Then an uncle persuaded him to visit the United States for the first time. At nineteen he crossed the ocean to spend two important years at the University of Virginia at Charlottesville. He did not study for a degree, but took the subjects which interested him most,—English and American literature, Latin and Greek. In his spare time he taught French. His first appearance in print was a long story called *The Apprentice Psychiatrist*, published in the college magazine. This is the only published piece by Green composed in English. On his return to France he rewrote the tale in French, calling it *Le Voyageur sur la Terre*; it was published in *La Nouvelle Revue Française* and later brought out in book form, receiving an enthusiastic critical reception. A strong Poe influence is apparent in this strange tale of Daniel O'Donovan, a young college student in southern United States, who is driven to his death by persistent hallucinations. In 1929 a limited de luxe edition of the tale, entitled *Pilgrim on the Earth*, was published in English.

Green was not certain that literature was to be his career when he returned to Paris. He thought of being a painter and studied art at La Grande Chaumière, applying himself also to music. But he was soon writing again. From his contributions to an ephemeral French magazine of this period came *Suite Anglaise*, a collection of essays on such well known English literary figures as Samuel Johnson, Lamb, Charlotte Brontë, and William Blake. During this time he also wrote a pseudonymous *Pamphlet contre les Catholiques de France*, already a rare collector's item.

His first full length novel appeared in France as *Mont Cinère* (1926) and in the English translation as *Avarice House* (1927). It was the result of an agreement in the spring of 1925 with a perspicacious publisher, who demanded a novel from Green in six months' time. The book was an immense success. Green says that the house which he describes in *Mont Cinère* is a real house belonging to a relative in northern Virginia, where the action of the novel occurs.

Green has strengthened his position in modern French letters with his subsequent publications. *Adrienne Mésurat*, a novel of French provincial life, translated into English in 1928 as *The Closed Garden*, was awarded the Femina-Bookman prize awarded annually for the best French work suitable for English translation. *Léviathan*, translated here as *The Dark Journey*, was the Harper prize novel in 1929. "You could see, across the night," writes André Maurois of this book, "a little town, commonplace yet somehow terrible,—very ordinary people, the patrons of a provincial boarding house, yet the prey of appalling passions."

Green's next volume was *Christine and Other Stories* (1930).

Edmond Jaloux describes Julian Green as "a slender young man with the bearing, the grace, and the reserve of a young girl—and a young girl of former days. His regular features are delicately modeled, and lighted by handsome eyes. He has an extreme modesty and a high integrity to his art."

André Maurois tells of a long walk with Green thru the streets of Paris, during the course of which the young writer explained "the profound inner sources of his inspiration. I asked him if he would continue to write in this 'dark manner.' He replied that he did not believe so. His vision of life was growing wider; he had felt the invincible need to paint those sombre pictures; he hoped now for a more evenly distributed light and different characters. I noticed the tranquil assurance with which he spoke of his future work; it was the calm of complete strength."

Paul Green

PAUL GREEN writes plays about the Southern Negro he learned to know on the farm in North Carolina where he grew up "and for twenty-three years saw nothing else." Paul Eliot Green was born on March 17, 1894, near Lillington, N.C. "My first memories", he says, "are of Negro ballads ringing out by moonlight and the rich laughter of the resting blacks, down by the river bottom. I started out very close to life—in the elemental. . . We were landowners, a class distinguished from the tenant farmers, but for all that we earned our living by labor in the fields—my father and brothers and I. As a child I worked out of doors, spring, summer, and fall, and went to school a few months each winter."

One year young Green was proclaimed one of the champion cotton pickers of Hartnett County. He was one of the first to introduce tobacco-farming in his vicinity. "I spent $300 on making my crop," he relates, "and sold it for $19. After paying warehouse charges and cartage, I had $8 left over, which I spent for three or four books. So ended my tobacco farming."

He loved the Negroes. "The smell of their sweaty bodies, the gusto of their indecent jokes, the knowledge of their twisted philosophies, the sight of their feet entangled among the pea vines and grass, their shouts, grunts and bellyachings, the sun blistering down upon them and the rim of the sky enclosing them forever, all took me wholly, and I was one of them—neither black nor white, but one of them, children of the moist earth underfoot."

Green attended Buie's Creek Academy where he bought a few extra books with his farm wages to augment his small library which included Milton, Stevenson, books on veterinary surgery, and monographs on Latin syntax. He was graduated from the Academy in 1914. He then taught school for two years before entering the University of North Carolina at Chapel Hill, N.C. The money he saved as a teacher helped defray his university expenses and during the summers he played semi-professional baseball near home.

Green's first play, written when he was a freshman at the University, won the prize in class competition. It was called *Surrender to the Enemy* (written 1917), and had to do with "a Southern gal's

PAUL GREEN

heart surrender to a Yankee captain, in opposition to her father's wishes."

The year after he entered the university, Green's first published work made its appearance. It was called *Trifles of Thought by P.E.G.*, published "by some local printer in Greenville, S.C., in 1917, I think. I don't know who he was." It was a collection of eulogies, epitaphs, war verses, and a few Negro dialect pieces. This booklet was occasioned by the World War. "Chances are I'll never come back", he reasoned. "I've wanted to be a writer. Maybe I never shall. Still, I'll set up this little gesture, crude as it may be, as a signpost to tell of the way I wished to go." So he spent seventy dollars, paying for thirty copies.

Green enlisted in the army in 1917. He served as private, corporal, sergeant, and sergeant-major with the 105th Engineers, 30th Division. Later he was second lieutenant with the Chief of Engineers at Paris. He served four months on the Western front.

In 1919 Green returned to the University of North Carolina, graduating in 1921. He did graduate work there the following year and on July 6, 1922, he married Elizabeth Atkinson Lay of Chapel Hill. In 1922-23 Green engaged in graduate study at Cornell University and then returned to Chapel Hill where he has been assistant professor of philosophy at the University of North Carolina since 1923.

In Abraham's Bosom (1927) was written in 1925. It was produced by the Provincetown Players of New York December 30, 1926, but was forced to close in the early spring. Altho not a Broadway hit, it was awarded the Pulitzer Prize. After the Pulitzer Award in May the play was revived with success. Green protested against the revival: "Let Abraham rest with dignity in his grave."

The Field God (1927) was first played in Brooklyn in April, 1927, and it later had brief runs in New York City and London. *Tread the Green Grass*, a folk fantasy, appeared in 1929. *The House of Connelly* is on the production schedule of the Theatre Guild.

Among the volumes of Green's plays are: *The Lord's Will and Other Carolina Plays* (1925), *Lonesome Road* (1926), *The Field God and In Abraham's Bosom* (1927), and *In the Valley and Other Carolina Plays* (1928). He has published many one-act plays of Negro life. *Wide Fields* (1928) is a book of short stories.

Graham Greene

GRAHAM GREENE was born in 1906, the son of Charles Henry Greene, retired head master of Berkhamsted School, and the nephew of Sir W. Graham Greene, K. C. B. who was Permanent Secretary to the Admiralty during the greater part of the war. He is also the cousin of the present Dean of Lincoln and of Robert Louis Stevenson.

Even before he went to Oxford he had begun to contribute prose, fantasies, and verse to the *Saturday Westminster*, then edited by Naomi Royde-Smith. At Oxford he edited the *Oxford Outlook*, founded by Beverly Nichols, and had his verse published in *Oxford Poetry*. His first publication was a volume of verse called *Babbling April* in 1925.

After coming down from Oxford, young Greene worked for ten days on the staff of the British American Tobacco Company and very nearly went to China. After that he became a subeditor on the *Nottingham Journal*, the

GRAHAM GREENE

paper of which both Sir James Barrie and Cecil Roberts were editors. He threw this up in March 1926, came to London, and joined the staff of the *Times,* with which he has been connected ever since.

Recently Mr. Greene sailed from England on a cruise to the Near East to visit Athens, Troy, Delos, and the ruins of Knossos in Crete.

Nothing helps a young man with a wanderlust so much as publishers' royalties, he says. And he hopes to be received more cordially in hotels than he was during school days when the absence of funds forced him to satisfy his fondness for travel by barrel-organing his way thru England disguised as a tramp.

The Man Within (1929) achieved an unusual success in England for a first novel. It was frequently compared by critics with *Treasure Island.* The scene is laid in the period of the older novel and the story deals with the smuggling traffic ; but as to character it is described as being a psychological study of a coward who justified himself in a flare of courage.

Mr. Greene's second novel, *The Name of Action,* appeared in 1930. It is the story of a young English millionaire who, as a relief from boredom, goes to a small Rhineland republic to finance a revolution against the dictator. He falls in love with the dictator's wife, realizes she doesn't love him, and reveals her secret about her husband's impotency. The dictator is crushed by the ridicule which follows; the youth's mission is accomplished. He has had his adventure, but it ends in disillusionment. In this novel Greene combines Graustarkian romance with psychological analysis.

The works by Graham Greene are *The Man Within* (1929) and *The Name of Action* (1930).

Philip Guedalla

PHILIP GUEDALLA was born March 12, 1889, the oldest son of the late David Guedalla and Louise Soman Guedalla. He was educated first at Rugby and then at Balliol College, Ox-

ford. In 1911 he was president of the Oxford Union Society, the debating group from which have come some of England's most eminent statesmen. While still an undergraduate at Oxford he published two books, *Ignes Fatui, a Book of Parodies* (1911) and *Metri Gratia, Verse and Prose* (1911). He took a First in Modern History in 1912.

PHILIP GUEDALLA

Immediately upon receiving his Master of Arts degree in 1913, Guedalla began practicing law at Inner Temple, London. In 1914 his book, *The Partition of Europe 1715-1815,* was published. During the war his energies were absorbed by his legal work. He served as legal adviser to the Contracts Department, the War Office, and Ministry of Munitions. He organized the Flax Control Board in 1917 and acted as its secretary until 1920. He was married in 1919 to Nellie Maude Reitlinger.

Guedalla resumed his writing in 1920 and in that year published *Supers and Supermen.* Then came *The Industrial Future* (1921) and *The Second Empire* (1922). In the year the latter book appeared he was unsuccessful as the Liberal candidate for North Hackney and in 1923 he failed to secure a seat in North-East Derbyshire.

The year 1923 marked Guedalla's retirement from law and his devotion exclusively to writing. In that year he published *Masters and Men.* This was followed by *A Gallery* (1924), sketches of British authors and statesmen; *A Council of Industry* (1925), *Napoleon and Palestine* (1925), and *Independence Day* (1926). In *Fathers of the Revolution* (1926) the author writes about eminent English, French, and American men. *Palmerston* (1926) is the result of prodigious research which included the study of much unpublished material. The book, a satire, is written with charm and wit. The next two years brought *Conquistador* (1927) and *Gladstone and Palmerston* (1928).

In *Bonnet and Shawl* (1928), which Guedalla calls an "album", he gives sketches of Jane Welsh Carlyle, Catherine Gladstone, Mary Arnold, Mary Anne Disraeli, Emily Tennyson, Emily Palmerston, and three portraits of the imaginary wives of Henry James, Swinburne, and the Goncourt brothers (one sketch for both). *Missing Muse* (1929) is a group of essays.

Guedalla discusses the work of the historian: "He is, when all is said, one cell in the world's memory of itself; he, too, like the lamented Proust, rides off *à la recherche du temps perdu.* And if the quest is to succeed, he must reconstruct the past, set old breezes stirring once again, and—most elusive miracle of all—bring the dead back to life. His business is to write about dead men; but if he is to do his duty, he should remember that they were not always dead. For he is not concerned to embalm them, but to resurrect, to set them moving, catch the tone of their voices, tilt of their heads, and posture of the once living men. . . The past should, for the historian, be his present. He must never write from the angle of today, but almost always from the angle of contemporaries with the events that he describes. . . When his reader is set dreaming of the past, the historian has done his work, only provided that the dream be true. For then *temps perdu* has become *temps retrouvé*, and the quest is ended."

Arthur Guiterman

ARTHUR GUITERMAN was born in Vienna on November 20, 1871, of American parents. When he was two years old the family returned to New York, and his earliest recollections are of that city. He was educated mainly at Grammar School No. 69—with an interval of two early years at Bridgeport, Conn.—and at the College of the City of New York, from which he was graduated in 1891 with the degree of Bachelor of Arts. During his college years he was active in lacrosse, tennis, and rowing, was captain of the bicycle club, class secretary and poet, and leading lady of the dramatic club.

After graduation, he went into newspaper work. He writes, "I have been editor of two trade papers, was two or three years on the editorial staff of the *Woman's Home Companion*, and every now and then I have run a department or otherwise assisted on *The Literary Digest;* but I have been a free-lance, devoting myself almost entirely to writing verse. I believe I was the first regular contributor of verse to *The New York Times*, I have written many historical and legendary ballads and many lyrics, but am probably best known as a writer of humorous verse."

ARTHUR GUITERMAN

He continues, "Since 1909 I have been the principal contributor of verse to *Life*, in which publication I originated 'Rhymed Reviews' and other features. In 1912, I established a course in the writing of verse in The School of Journalism in New York University, which I conducted several terms, eventually turning it over to Joyce Kilmer."

Mr. Guiterman was married in 1909 to Vida Lindo of New York and Panama, and lives in an old house in the old Stuyvesant Square section of New York. He is still considered a good skater. tennis and hockey player, is fond of canoeing, fishing and tramping, and he and Mrs. Guiterman usually manage to spend a month or two each summer deep in the Maine woods or on country roads and mountain trails with their packs on their backs.

How is his family name pronounced? Several years ago one of his editorial friends tried to enlighten an anxious inquirer on this point by printing the explanatory couplet,

> There ain't no better, fitter man
> Than Mister Arthur Guiterman.

Among his many volumes are *Chips of Jade* (1920), *A Poet's Proverbs* (1924), *I Sing the Pioneer* (1926), *Wildwood Fables* (1927), *Song and Laughter* (1929).

Francis Hackett

FRANCIS HACKETT

FRANCIS HACKETT, novelist, historian, editor, was born in Kilkenny, Ireland, January 21, 1883. He was the son of John Byrne Hackett and Bridget Doheny Hackett. After spending his childhood in Ireland and attending the Clongowes Wood College at Kildare, he came to America in 1900.

He worked for a New York law firm in 1902. Then he went to Chicago where he was editorial writer for the *Chicago Evening Post* from 1906 to 1909. He assumed charge of the literary section of the paper, called the *Friday Literary Review,* in 1909 and was its editor until 1911. He gave the review an impetus and authority which placed it among the foremost literary reviews in the country.

Hackett was an associate editor of *The New Republic* from 1914 to 1922. He wrote many articles and reviews which made him known on both sides of the Atlantic. His wide knowledge and clear style made his editorship memorable. During this time he commenced publishing his writings and the first two appeared in 1918: *Ireland, A Study in Nationalism* and *Horizons.* That same year, on September 5, he married Signe Toksvig of Denmark. Two more works followed: *The Invisible Censor* (1920) and *The Story of the Irish Nation* (1922).

At the close of his period of editorship Hackett began research for a biography of Henry the Eighth which lasted six years. He spent most of that time in Europe on the track of data for what was to be his most important literary production. Meanwhile his novel, *That*
Nice Young Couple, was published in 1924. *Henry the Eighth, A Personal History,* made its appearance in 1929. It is a scholarly volume which follows the life of the monarch from youth to old age and includes intimate portraits of his many wives.

Letters to Hackett's friends reveal his life during his research on Henry as a pilgrimage from one spot to another, sometimes in search of the most authentic material, sometimes only in search of a quiet spot where a writer could concentrate—with the lumbering Henry always at his elbow. "Henry shall be finished if the gasoline holds out," he wrote from the south of France; and again he and Henry must move from a London flat because the roof leaks. Finally the pilgrimage ends in his own little house by the sea in Ireland, where he completes the bulk of his book.

So voluminous was the material he found that it was not necessary for him to invent a single word of conversation. "No vividness excuses infidelity to the facts," he explains, "and I have sought to base this history entirely on the material provided by the unselfish labor of a host of scholars." His own task, as he saw it, was "to be then-minded, to use intuition and imagination, to suggest life."

Radclyffe Hall

THE daughter of Radclyffe Radclyffe-Hall was born at Bournemouth, Hants, and educated at King's College, London, and in Germany. Poetry was Miss Hall's first form of expression. In fact, she confesses that her maiden effort was dictated at the age of three. This was a stanza of four brief lines which her proud mother wrote down carefully in a note book. Here they are:

"No wonder the birdies love you,
  No wonder the butterflies hover near,
No wonder the roses grow above you,
  No wonder the birdies love you, dear!"

From which it would seem that she was a rank sentimentalist at that tender age. During her childhood, a fond American grandmother, who thought the little girl a heaven-born genius, wrote down many pages of long and rambling verse with which the young poet's calligraphy was too immature to cope. "If a parent today were to bring me such poems as emanating from her offspring and were to ask me for my candid opinion," says Miss Hall, "well, I should hate to have to give it."

RADCLYFFE HALL

A little later, the child learned to play the piano and thereafter composed her verse to music. And the habit remained. All her collected poems have a markedly singing lyric quality. Many of them have been set to music by well known composers, notably "The Blind Ploughman," set by Coningsby Clarke; and several by Coleridge Taylor, Liza Lehmann, Mrs. Woodforde Finden, and Mrs. George Batten. Some of her own settings have become favorites as concert songs. Her first five volumes, published at intervals from 1906 to 1915, were collections of verse.

Meanwhile she was publishing numerous short stories in the English magazines. William Heinemann became interested in her work and urged her to write a novel, promising to consider it for publication. It was her wish to justify his faith in her that kept Radclyffe Hall at work for three years on her first novel, *The Unlit Lamp,* which was published in 1924, after a period of nine years in which she published no books at all. *The Unlit Lamp* is the story of an English girl of talent who is kept from normal love by her devotion to an older girl, as well as by an excessive sense of filial duty. It foreshadows the fuller statement of the theme which shocked English society in *The Well of Loneliness.* *The Forge* was also published in 1924.

A Saturday Life (1925) is a novel in somewhat lighter vein than Miss Hall's other works, being the story of flighty Sidonia, daughter of Lady Shore, who "reveals successively exceptional talent in every line of artistic endeavor; drops each one for the next one, and drops the last to marry and have a baby."

For many years Miss Hall had intended to write the story of those who all day long serve their fellows; and when the idea finally took shape in her mind it so obsessed her that she had to abandon another book on which she was engaged in order to write *Adam's Breed* (1926), the story of a waiter who, frustrated in his desire to be a poet, poured all the love of beauty of his sensitive Italian soul into the restaurant in which he gradually fought his way until he became headwaiter. This novel was awarded the Femina-Vie Heureuse prize and the James Tait Black Memorial Book Prize for 1926.

The sensation created by Miss Hall's next novel, *The Well of Loneliness* (1928), is already a part of literary history. Altho several of England's most famous writers appeared in court to testify in favor of the book, which deals seriously with the unhappy life of a woman of perverse tendencies, the London magistrate, Sir Chartres Biron, ruled that altho the book was dignified and restrained in manner it presented an appeal for the recognition by decent people that sexual inversion exists and is not the fault of the person who suffers from it; therefore he judged the book an obscene libel and ordered all copies of it destroyed. On its publication in the United States the book was temporarily suppressed because of charges brought against it by Mr. Sumner of the Society for the Suppression of Vice, but was finally triumphantly vindicated in the American courts. The verdict, which was celebrated by the publication of a Victory Edition, disagrees with the English ruling that the theme of homosexuality is *per se* undiscussable and indecent.

When Miss Hall is moved to write, she writes anywhere. The top of a trunk in a noisy hotel bedroom is quite as acceptable to her as the desk in her own quiet study in London. *The Unlit Lamp*, for example, was written abroad in hotel bedrooms in Florence, northern Italy, Normandy, and Paris. She is an irregular worker. For several days together she will not write at all, but when she starts, ten or twelve hours at a stretch are quite usual, and meals and appointments go by the board.

Of hobbies Miss Hall has two, the breeding and showing of dogs, some of which have found their way to show-benches in America, and the collecting of early oak furniture. She is a fellow of the Zoological Society and devoted to animals. Wherever she is, she accumulates many and various pets. She is also intensely interested in psychical research, having been for some time a member of the council of the Society for Psychical Research.

Knut Hamsun

KNUT HAMSUN published his first two books in his very young manhood with money saved penny by penny during the years of his apprenticeship to a cobbler. In 1921, when he was awarded the Nobel Prize for Literature, his works had been translated into twenty-three languages, and the published editions of his books covered 65,000,000 pages. That was at the threshold of his introduction to America.

Hamsun—Knut Pedersen Hamsun—was born on August 4, 1860, the son of Peder Pedersen and Tora Olsdatter, in a deep valley of northern Norway. From the age of four he grew up under the care of an uncle in one of the relatively bleak and grim Lofoten Islands. Following the publication of the books just referred to—a long poem and a short novel, both forgotten—he spent twelve years wandering; and not only from place to place, but from one makeshift occupation to another. He was by turns longshoreman, coal-trimmer, tutor, and court messenger—these on his determined way to Christiania and the university. But his enrollment as a student simply made him a candidate for

KNUT HAMSUN

starvation; and he was shortly bound for America as a steerage passenger.

Here again his dream yielded to the conditions of a harsher reality. Intending to become a Unitarian clergyman— a curious goal for the man who was to be the author of *Growth of the Soil*—he actually became a farm hand, and later a dairyman, in Dakota. He lectured on French literature in Minneapolis; and he worked as a conductor on the old Halsted Street line of horse-cars in Chicago —where, according to a legend which has every mark of authenticity, he infuriated patrons of the company by being so deep in a pocket Euripides that he carried them past their stops, and was duly discharged therefor. He then returned to Norway; failed as abysmally as ever to strike a bargain with life; and once more came to America, where, after renewed fruitless attempts as a lecturer in the Northwest, he spent three years as a fisherman off the Grand Banks of Newfoundland.

And now, as if suddenly, he was ready for his work. Ostensibly a mere prolonged bout with hardship and waste, his twelve years had really been a groping for self-knowledge and for the meaning of life. They had brought him, these years, as much of both as was needed to make him the author of *Hunger*. This first of his considerable books was in substance the record of Hamsun's own earlier experiences in Christiania. But he wrote it, marvelously, without bitterness, in a way which showed that he had assimilated and got beyond the experience. He was thru for ever with being a wanderer and a failure: he was a European writer now. And the rest of his story is a quiet chronicle of mounting fame, of more than thirty books in a variety of forms, of placid domesticity and fatherhood, and of a retired life with his wife and five children near to the soil on an estate at Norholm near Grimstad (the town of Ibsen's unhappy youth), in a "white two-story house at the end of a quiet bight of the sea." His chief interest is in the cultivation of his farm and he takes part in the labor himself. But when he is writing he shuts himself away in a little cottage in a lonely section of the estate and lives apart from his family.

Among his books recently translated into English are: *Women at the Pump* (1928), *Chapter the Last* (1929), and *Vagabonds* (1930). The last is a curiously joyous book for Hamsun to have written. *August,* a continuation of *Vagabonds,* and written in the same vein, was published in Norway in 1930.

Frank Harris

READERS have accused Frank Harris of unnecessary frankness in his books and of weaving promiscuous fabrications under the guise of biography. Burton Rascoe calls him "a swashbuckling, sanguine, cavalier sort who, by all rules of law and order, ought long ago to have been strung up by due process of law or shot down by some pernickety observer of the code." Yet he has gusto; he compels interest. "They've treated me scandalously," Harris complains.

His long life of "misfortune" began in Galway, Ireland, on February 14, 1856. At the age of fourteen he came to the United States, where he was an immigrant bootblack in New York, a clerk in Chicago, and a cattle puncher in the Southwest and West. He worked his way thru college and law school at the University of Kansas. He became a naturalized citizen, and was admitted to the Kansas bar in 1875. His education continued abroad at the Universities of Paris, Heidelberg, Strasbourg, Göttingen, Berlin, Vienna, and Athens, but he took no degrees. His interest in literature was awakened in Paris. He began to seek out writers and artists. His later *Contemporary Portraits* are the result of his meetings with practically all the famous men of letters in England and the United States (and some in France) since the Victorian age.

Harris finally drifted to England where he became editor of the *Evening News,* and subsequently the *Fortnightly Review,* the *Saturday Review,* and *Vanity Fair.* He mingled in the political and financial circles of London and demonstrated a rare ability to envisage and resolve their problems. H. G. Wells once called him the best editor in England.

Because his life of *Oscar Wilde* contained revelations too frank for English publishers, Harris returned to America and printed and sold it himself in a bookshop on Washington Square in New York City. He took over the editorship of *Pearson's Magazine*, but his pro-German views forced him to suspend publication when America entered the World War. "I left America as I left England," he says, "because they treated me badly!"

Harris sought freedom in France, where he settled down in a villa at Nice with his second wife. He has no children. He encountered difficulty in publishing the first volume of the uninhibited story of his life. His original plan was to devote one volume to each ten years of his life. No publisher would risk his reputation with the book, so Harris was forced to have it published in Germany. It was printed in English under the title, *My Life and Loves* (1923). Several copies of the book were seized by police upon their arrival in New York. The author forthwith issued a pamphlet in which he protested the injustice that had been done him and attacked the authorities who had forbidden the book to be sent thru the mails.

Then he seemed to regret his audacity. "A year or two ago I was honored on all hands," he complained. "Wherever I came I felt that men and women spoke of me with interest, curiosity at least; since the first volume of *My Life* appeared, everywhere I feel the unspoken condemnation and see the sneer or the foul sidelong grin. I have paid dearly for my boldness." He published a second volume of his autobiography, less discursive about the "loves," in 1925. A third volume appeared in 1927.

Harris lives in constant expectation of arrest because the police have "marked passages in the book (*My Life and Loves*) to which the English might take exception." The passages dwell at length upon the privacies of two celebrated Englishmen; Harris also suggests that Browning might have been inspired to his passionate lines by another than his wife. "The French police are on my track," he says. "They come up here to my villa, armed with revolvers and permission to search thru all my papers.

FRANK HARRIS

I give them a drink, and a hundred francs, and they leave me in peace, without having seen a thing. But it's all very worrying, and I'm obliged to hold myself ready for trial at any moment."

If thwarted in further attempts to tell the whole truth about his life, Harris threatens to publish the story in French: "The French people won't cavil at anything I've said."

Of his *Joan la Romée* (1926), a play about Joan of Arc, he says: "I wrote my play before I read Shaw's. I wrote it because I knew Joan: I'd lived with her for years just as I'd lived with Jesus and Shakespeare." A series of caustic letters passed between the two authors. Shaw claimed the "Joan ground" for his own, and Harris pointed out that his was much the better play. Regardless of his tiffs with Shaw, Harris calls him "the chief figure from 1895 to 1900," and he regards Shaw and Mencken as the only two righteous people in the English-speaking world. Shaw calls Harris "a scoundrel and a monster," but admiringly.

In spite of his advanced age, Harris maintains an attitude of aggressive attack rather than defeat. His hair and walrus moustache are now grey, but his serious face is a healthy red. His bright eyes gleam fiercely when he speaks of his "persecution." He spends the mornings writing in his bedroom which is in perpetual disorder with books strewn on the floor and piled on chairs, and the bed littered with papers.

Biographical studies by Frank Harris include: *The Man Shakespeare* (1909), *The Women of Shakespeare* (1911), *Contemporary Portraits,* in four series (1915-23), *Oscar Wilde* (1916), and *Latest Contemporary Portraits* (1927). Among his plays are: *Mr. and Mrs. Daventry* (1900), *Shakespeare and His Love* (1910), *Joan la Romée* (1926). *My Reminiscences as a Cowboy* (1930) recalls the author's experiences on the Western plains in 1870-71.

Volumes of short stories by Harris include: *Elder Conklin* (1894), *Montes the Matador* (1900), *Unpath'd Waters* (1913), *The Veils of Isis* (1915), *A Mad Love* (1920), and *Undream'd of Shores* (1924). Among his novels are: *The Bomb* (1908), *Great Days* (1914), and *Love in Youth* (1916).

Gerhart Hauptmann

GERHART JOHANN ROBERT HAUPTMANN, was born in the Silesian village of Obersalzbrunn on No-

GERHART HAUPTMANN

vember 15, 1862, the same year that three other distinguished German dramatists were born, Arthur Schnitzler, Johannes Schlaf, and Ludwig Fulda. By descent he springs from the common people of his native province. His grandfather, Ehrenfried Hauptmann, had been a weaver and thru energy and good fortune changed his trade to that of a waiter; by 1824 he was an independent innkeeper. Robert Hauptmann, at the time of the birth of Gerhart, the youngest of his four children, was proprietor of the prosperous hotel *Zur Preussischen Krone.* He was unfortunately forced to sell his property before the discovery of a new and valuable mineral water spring on it.

From the village school in Obersalzbrunn, where he was an idle pupil, Gerhart went to the *Realschule* at Breslau in 1874. He lived here with his older brothers, Carl, who later achieved a considerable literary reputation, and Georg. Gerhart's chief interests seemed to lie in poetry and sculpture, both of which he played with in a desultory way. His father's change of fortune necessitated his removal from school in 1878 and he was placed in the home of a pious uncle, with the idea that he should become a farmer. In 1880 he entered the Royal College of Art in Breslau; three weeks later he received a disciplinary warning and early in 1881 he was rusticated for eleven weeks. Nevertheless he studied there until 1882 when he joined his brother Carl at the University of Jena. He studied zoology under Haeckel and philosophy under Professor Rudolph Eucken. Tiring of academic life, he went to Hamburg as the guest of his future parents-in-law, and thence made a tour thru Spain and Italy; out of this came his poem *Promethidenlos,* modeled on *Childe Harold.*

Hauptmann went to Italy in 1884 and had a sculptor's studio in Rome for a time. Overcome by typhoid fever, he was nursed back to health by Marie Thienemann and returned to Germany with her to recuperate in the Thienemann country home. He and Fraülein Thienemann were married later that same year.

Hauptmann decided to abandon the art of sculpture for that of the stage, and he and his wife went to Berlin. An interest in writing began to dominate all other thoughts and *Promethidenlos* was written and published in 1885. A collection of poems was issued under the title *Das Bunte Buch* soon after. An episodic story *Bahnwarter Thiel* was published in 1887.

A meeting with Arno Holz, the exponent of "consistent naturalism," brought Hauptmann into a political and social circle interested in social reform and in the development of realism in literature and on the stage. Hauptmann's home in the Berlin suburb of Eckner became a center for activities.

In 1889 the poet became the dramatist, and Hauptmann began his series dealing with the protests of the working classes and the poverty-stricken middle classes against the tyranny of society. *Vor Sonnenaufgang* (*Before Dawn*), presented in 1889, aroused a storm of criticism such as had descended on Ibsen. It was produced by the Free Stage Society of Berlin, so-called in that it could ignore censorship and economic needs.

Hauptmann persevered, and two more plays were given. In 1892 the most famous of all his plays, *Die Weber* (*The Weavers*), was given privately; public performances were prohibited until the following year. The scene is Silesia, where the weaving conditions of the '40s and '50s, such as his grandfather had known, were notoriously outrageous; it represents the rise, outbreak, development, and failure of a miniature revolution.

Hauptmann turned temporarily from uncompromising realism and his next play, *Hanneles Himmelfahrt* (*Hannele*) (1893), combined realism with the poetic mysticism of a child's dream. *Die Versunkene Glocke* (1896, *The Sunken Bell*) is a poetic allegory.

Other social dramas followed, including *Der Biberpelz* (*The Beaver-cape*), *Der rote Hahn* (*The Red Cock*) and *Ratten* (*The Rats*). By 1910 German naturalism was fully established. Hauptmann's beliefs and their expression have on more than one occasion infuriated political parties and brought trouble on him.

Oxford University conferred an honorary degree on Hauptmann in 1905. He received the Nobel Prize for Literature in 1912, the year his famous novel *Atlantis* was published. His only dramatic work of the war period was *Winterballade,* issued in 1917, the dramatization of a short story by Selma Lagerlöf. After the war he published two verse-dramas, *Der Weisse Heiland* (*The White Redeemer,* the story of the conquest of Mexico) and *Das Opfer* (*The Sacrifice*).

Ludwig Lewisohn translated and edited Hauptmann's *Dramatic Works,* in eight volumes (1912-1924). *Atlantis* was translated and available in America the year of its German publication, 1912.

Hauptmann's sixtieth birthday anniversary (in 1922) was celebrated by a dramatic festival in Breslau, to which friends and admirers from all parts of the world came. Many people also make pilgrimages to his home in Agnetendorf in the Riesen-Gebirge mountain range in western Germany. He is a large man, with a broad, high forehead and fluffy white hair. He is quite active, and enjoys long walks alone or preferably with a friend. He mentions Tolstoi frequently, and expresses profound admiration for him. Hauptmann's dominant characteristic is his love for humanity and for individual men. When he was only a small child he planned to write a diary of Judas Iscariot because there was nothing in the Bible outside the character of Jesus himself that so interested him as the question: "What evil powers made this disciple of the Savior a traitor?"

Ben Hecht

BEN HECHT, "an iconoclast, a smasher of idols," "an intellectual mountebank, an insincere fiddler," or, as Harry Hansen has aptly dubbed him, "Pagliacci of the Fire Escape," was born in New York City on February 28, 1893. He moved to Racine, Wisconsin, when quite young, and was graduated from high school there. He did not go to college, because he believed that it represented classicism, puritanism, and a didactic dogmatism.

BEN HECHT

After leaving school he went with Costello's road show as an acrobat, and played the small towns thruout Wisconsin. At the age of seventeen he went to Chicago, intending to be a violinist, but instead of joining an orchestra as he had planned he became a reporter on the *Chicago Journal.* From 1910 until 1923 he was with the *Chicago Daily News,* being correspondent in charge of the Berlin office from December 1918 until December 1919.

Hecht was one of the best known of the "Chicago group" during its heyday, that group made up of Carl Sandburg, Sherwood Anderson, Keith Preston, Llewellyn Jones, Vincent Starrett, Lew Sarett, and Edgar Lee Masters. Ben's vivacious cynicism, his plans for making a million dollars which changed daily, his dreams and philosophies, his poems and criticisms, endeared him to the group and made him one of its most influential members. Then, as now, he was famous for his ability to talk "volubly, incessantly, fascinatingly—holding all who came to hear him with his subtle innuendoes, his philosophical observations, his penetrating irony, his vehement indignation, his gentle persuasiveness, his dubious facts."

He was one of the first contributors to Margaret Anderson's *Little Review;* it was in the office of this magazine that he first met Maxwell Bodenheim, and was attracted to him. Differences arose soon, and the Hecht-Bodenheim debate and controversy which has been waged continuously since then has become legendary. Bodenheim is said to be the dubious hero of one of Hecht's picaresque novels.

Reading has always interested and influenced Hecht, and very early he fell under the romantic and pagan spell of Théophile Gautier and to an even greater degree Huysmans. Arthur Machen aroused such a personal fondness that, altho Hecht is in most cases violently opposed to hero worship, the one pilgrimage he made when he was in London in 1918 was to the humble rooms of this author who was as yet unpublished in America. Altho Hecht is not an imitator of H. L. Mencken he is an admirer, and many of the latter's opinions coincide with his own.

It was Dostoievsky who made the most profound impression on him, and he considers *The Idiot* the greatest novel ever written. Hecht says that "there is only one plot in the world and that is the human mind."

With his careless air of wearing clothes that hang loosely on him, his necktie recklessly knotted, his soft dark hair frequently disheveled and falling over his forehead, his kind brown eyes, and sensitive cynical mouth, Hecht is pictured best as a nonchalant reporter roving thru the Chicago streets, studying passersby and shop windows with almost equal interest. He has always used city themes in his stories, and the conglomerate life of an industrial center is portrayed in his experiences entitled *1001 Afternoons in Chicago* (1922) and *Tales of Chicago Streets* (1924), selections from his contributions to the *Daily News.*

Bodenheim and Hecht wrote several plays in collaboration. A subsequent meeting with Kenneth Sawyer Goodman resulted in several comedies. *The Wonder Hat,* described by Hecht as "one of those sweet little plays about Pierrot and Pierrette," is still played frequently by amateur groups. Another collaboration, *The Hero of Santa Maria,* had a short run in New York.

Hecht's work includes: *Erik Dorn* (1921); *Fantazius Mallare* (1922); *Gargoyles* (1922); *The Florentine Dagger* (1923); *Humpty Dumpty* (1924); *The Kingdom of Evil* (1924); *Count Bruga* (1926); *Broken Necks* (1926); and *A Jew in Love* (1931). He and Charles MacArthur are authors of one of the most successful plays of 1928-1929, *The Front Page.* They were said, early in 1931, to be collaborating on another play. Hecht was then at work on a book, *Journalese,* to be illustrated by Peter Arno, which has as its basis the *Chicago Literary Times,* a violently independent literary sheet founded by Hecht in 1923 and edited by him until 1925. Hecht is also preparing a book of short stories, called *The Champion From Far Away.*

Hecht and Miss Marie Armstrong, a writer and dramatic critic, were married in Chicago in 1915 and divorced in 1925. They have one daughter. He and Miss Rose Caylor, a writer and translator who adapted Checkov's *Uncle Vanya* for its successful 1929-1930 production, were married in 1925. Their home is in Nyack, near New York City.

Ernest Hemingway

ONE of the most popular spokesmen of the young post-war generation is Ernest Hemingway, born in Oak Park, Illinois, July 21, 1898. His father was a doctor, and during his boyhood Hemingway used to accompany him frequently on his visits; many of these experiences are reflected in his short stories, particularly in *In Our Time.* Most of his boyhood was spent in Michigan. He attended public schools, where he was popular for his prowess as a football player and a boxer. After graduation he reported on the *Kansas City Star* for a few months.

Hemingway went to France, before America entered the war, as a volunteer in an American ambulance unit. He later went to Italy and enlisted in the Italian Arditi, served at the Italian front, and was seriously wounded; he will always carry a silver plate in one shoulder be-

ERNEST HEMINGWAY

cause of an injury received. He was decorated with two of the highest medals of the country, the *Medaglia d'Argento al Valore Militare* and the *Croce di Guerra.*

When he returned to the United States after the Armistice, Hemingway married and reentered newspaper work. The following year he was "star" reporter for the *Toronto Star,* and became its European correspondent. He reported a few battles in the Near East and some of the activities of the Greeks, who at that time were in the midst of revolution and disorder, and went to Paris as a correspondent for William Randolph Hearst's syndicated news.

By the time he was twenty-five Hemingway had become almost a myth and a tradition. He was a well-known figure in Paris and had many friends. He had attained unusual success, was popular personally, and even then had many imitators in his writing.

During this Paris period he played tennis almost daily. He is naturally fond of sports, is a rabid fisherman, and enjoys spending vacations on long bicycle tours. He talks to bull-fighters whenever possible, and likes to go to fights. Several anecdotes are told about him; one is that he and some friends entered the arena at a bull-fight and, not proving as good toreadors as they had thought, eventually ran for their lives. Another story is told in connection with his boxing ability; at a middleweight championship fight in the Salle Wagram in Paris Hemingway became incensed by the foul blows the winning contestant was giving his opponent, jumped into the ring, and knocked out the champion.

Hemingway, "Hem" as he is known to all his friends, is referred to by them as a "swell guy." He is tall, broad shouldered and handsome, with a firm chin, a dark moustache, clear eyes, and short hair which is slightly curly. He has a somewhat arrogant but not unpleasant slouch, and walks with his elbows crooked a little and his arms swinging from his shoulders, like a boxer.

Hemingway was married for a second time in the summer of 1927. He has lived for some time in Key West, Florida, and was living in Wyoming temporarily in 1930-31. Mr. Hemingway dislikes New York, and cannot be persuaded to stay there longer than is necessary in passing thru. He keeps himself aloof particularly from quarrels, cliques, and the curiosity of the New York literary circles. His recreations are "skiing, fishing, shooting, and drinking."

The volume of Hemingway's published work is very small in comparison with the influence it has had. His writing typifies this generation, at once "hardboiled" and tender-hearted, disillusioned and optimistic. His themes are simple, and his style direct, pungently colloquial with clear-cut, staccato sentences.

A complete bibliography of his books follows: *Three Stories and Ten Poems* (Paris, 1923); *In Our Time* (Paris, 1924, New York, 1925, 1930 with introduction by Edmund Wilson); *The Torrents of Spring* (New York, 1926); *The Sun Also Rises* (New York, 1926); *Today is Friday* (Englewood, N. J., 1926; an eight page pamphlet); *Men Without Women* (New York, 1927); *A Farewell to Arms* (New York, 1929). Hemingway has also contributed to *Transatlantic Review, This Quarter, Scribner's,* and other magazines.

He is at work on a new novel which will deal with "bulls, bull-fighting, and bull-fighters."

A. P. Herbert

ALAN PATRICK HERBERT, author and barrister, was born on September 24, 1890, the eldest son of P. H. Herbert of the India Office. He was educated at Winchester and at New College, Oxford, where he took a First Class in Jurisprudence in 1914. He began writing for *Punch* in 1910. In 1914 he married Gwendolen Quilter. They have one son and three daughters.

Mr. Herbert served with the Royal Naval Division in the Hawke Battalion from 1914 to 1917, took part in the Gallipoli campaign, and was wounded in France. Following the war, he was admitted to the bar in 1918, but has never practiced. For two years he acted as private secretary to Sir Leslie Scott, King's Counsel and Member of Parliament.

He wrote one of the first realistic war books to appear in England, *Secret Battle* (1920), the novel of a sensitive lad who distinguishes himself at Gallipoli and later in France, only to be shot for cowardice. Mr. Herbert resumed his writings for *Punch* and collected his humorous and satirical sketches of London life in *Light Articles Only* (1921) and *A Man About Town* (1923). In 1924 he became a member of the staff of *Punch,* and the next year he represented that magazine at the Third Imperial Press Conference at Melbourne, Australia.

As a resident of Hammersmith, Mr. Herbert met Sir Nigel Playfair, who was looking for some attraction to sandwich between the eighteenth and nineteenth revivals of *The Beggar's Opera.* The result was their collaboration in the revue, *Riverside Nights.* The originality of his libretto placed Mr. Herbert on the theatrical map. Subsequent comic operas by him include *The Blue Peter* and *Tantivy Towers.* The latter was the success of the 1930-31 London season.

There is scarcely a day on which Mr. Herbert does not write to the *London Times* about something or other. The serious passion of his life is to secure the "Freedom of the Thames" for pleasure craft. Tradition confines the lower part of the river, below Richmond, to the water transport of timber and coal. In one of his letters to the *Times* he set forth his doctrine that the River Thames was the heritage of the British race and not the close preserve of the Gas Light and Coke Company. Elaborating his theory, he suggested that a service of water buses should ply from the Tower Bridge to Hammersmith, in order that the tired business man might go to and from the City in comfort.

But Mr. Herbert, who is well-known for his whimsical essays in *Punch*, is regarded as a humorist. When he saw that his plan was not taken seriously, he decided on direct action. He bought an old barge, built a house on it, and called it "The Ark." Then, dressed in red trousers and a blue jacket, he proceeded down the Thames into forbidden territory—past Burlingham, the Tate Gallery, Westminster, and the Savoy, to the Pool of London. Nothing happened. He wrote ten more letters to the *Times*. Then, swearing a great oath that he would bring London to her knees or perish in the Thames estuary, he moved his entire possessions on to "The Ark," closed his home in Hammersmith Terrace, and proceeded to cruise up and down the river.

The first fourteen months of the trip he occupied with writing *The Water Gipsies* (1930). It is a novel about a girl who grew up on an old barge anchored somewhere near Hammersmith and whose ideas of life and love were founded mainly on the movies. After two marital adventures she decides that life is quite unlike the movies. London's river is getting used to Mr. Herbert by now and he expects to have his way in the end, despite such interruptions from the crusade as his trip to Ceylon early in 1931.

This quixotic person is a strange mixture of attractive contradictions. There is always some common sense back of his nonsense. He writes without humor when he expresses his political views or when he champions the man in the street in various newspapers. He baffles classification by proclaiming himself a crusted Tory, just as he is not afraid to admit an admiration for Kipling.

A. P. HERBERT

His hobbies are talking in an alleged Irish brogue and singing Händel's *Largo* in a reedy falsetto. He is recognized as one of the best after-dinner speakers in London. His recreations, he says, are sailing, lawn tennis, the piano, and skittles. He is president of the Black Lion Skittles Club.

Besides the production of a war book, essays, librettos, and novels, Mr. Herbert has extended his versatility to several books of poems and two collections of parodies on English legal methods. The poems include *Tinker, Tailor* (1923), a book of humorously solemn rhymes for children in which the advantages of various vocations are whimsically noted, and *Laughing Ann* (1926). In 1930 he published a book called *Wisdom for the Wise*, which included *Tinker, Tailor* and *The Wherefore and the Why*. His legal satires are *Misleading Cases in Common Law* and *More Misleading Cases* (1930).

Other works by A. P. Herbert include: *Old Flame* (1925), *Plain Jane* (1927), *She-Shanties* (1927), *Topsy, M. P.* (1929), and *Ballads for Broadbrows* (1930). He sometimes writes under the pseudonym of Albert Haddock. He is the co-author of *Double Demon and Other One Act Plays* (1924) and *La Vie Parisienne*, a comic opera adaptation (1929).

Joseph Hergesheimer

JOSEPH HERGESHEIMER'S original intention was to be a painter. He therefore brings a feeling for color, a delight in shapes and texture, the more luxurious the better, and a passion for elegance to his writing, which has contributed largely to his success as a novelist.

He was born February 15, 1880, in Philadelphia, of a Pennsylvania Dutch family. A shy, bookish boy subject to frequent illnesses, he was educated for a short time in a Quaker school in his native city, and at the age of seventeen entered the Philadelphia Academy of Fine Arts. When he was twenty-one he came into a small inheritance which took him to Venice and Florence where he lived and presumably painted until his funds were exhausted. He suffered a nervous breakdown, and after months of sickness and anxiety he was sufficiently recovered to return to the United States. Realizing that he would never be a great artist, he abandoned painting and turned to literature.

Hergesheimer and Miss Dorothy Hemphill, of West Chester, Pennsylvania, were married in 1907. Years of struggle followed, and his first manuscript to be accepted was *Cavolo Repeana*, a stuffed cabbage recipe published in *Good Housekeeping* over Dorothy's signature. Shortly thereafter three articles appeared in the June, September, and November 1913 issues of *The Forum*.

The Lay Anthony, a novel (1914) proved that he had not been mistaken in his belief in his ability, and his popularity has steadily increased with the subsequent publication at regular intervals of a number of books.

Mr. and Mrs. Hergesheimer are known as Dorothy and Joe to everyone in West Chester, Pennsylvania, where they have lived since their marriage. The novelist is described as a character he himself might have written about. He is a lover of beauty and luxury above all things, and takes a sensuous delight in fine ornaments, rare silks, beautiful clothes and accessories. He is fastidious, witty, debonair and courtly. He is a sportsman, frequently visits the golf links, is interested in horse-racing, fishing, and plays a good game of poker. He entertains quietly but sumptuously, and H. L. Mencken, George Jean Nathan, Alfred A. Knopf, and James Branch Cabell are frequent visitors. His dislike for crowds is so strong that he seldom goes to the theater.

Physically, Joseph Hergesheimer is compact, powerful, massive. He is of more than average height, with closely-cropped, wiry hair that is invariably unkempt, full lips, sparkling eyes at once keen and humorous; his horned-rimmed glasses give him the appearance of a somewhat impudent, studious schoolboy.

The Hergesheimer home is an old Pennsylvania Dutch house built of boulder stones on a hill just outside of West Chester. The town thought the author mad when he purchased The Dower House, and was scandalously thrilled by his extravagance in remodeling and renovating the building, spending thousands of dollars for draperies, antique furniture, porcelain, and glass.

On working days Mr. Hergesheimer goes to his office in the business section of West Chester, at nine o'clock in the morning. All his writing is done in student's composition books with a stub pen; his secretary copies the manuscripts

JOSEPH HERGESHEIMER

from these, in triple space for revision. He keeps his notes and correspondence in an orderly fashion, filed in steel cabinets. On his return home in the evening he dresses meticulously, and eats in style like a country gentleman.

The world of romanticism and elegance and charm Hergesheimer has created for himself is reflected in all his books. He has made a passionate study of the manners and modes of life of the evolving American civilization, and American traditions form the basis of all his writing.

Hergesheimer's best known books are: *Three Black Pennys* (1917); *Java Head* (1919); *San Cristóbal de la Habana* (1920); *The Bright Shawl* (1922); *Cytherea* (1922); *Balisand* (1924); *Tampico* (1926); *Quiet Cities* (1928); *Swords and Roses* (1929); *The Party Dress* (1930); and *The Limestone Tree* (1931).

He is said to be at work on a life of Richard Brinsley Sheridan.

Du Bose Heyward

Du Bose Heyward

DU BOSE HEYWARD was born in Charleston, South Carolina, on August 31, 1885, the son of an aristocratic family whose forbears were signers of the Declaration of Independence. When he was two years old, his father died in an accident. The family, consisting of the mother, grandmother, Du Bose, and a young sister, was left in difficult financial straits. At nine years of age, Du Bose, as the only man of the household, was helping to support it by selling newspapers. At fourteen he left the Charleston public schools and went to work in a hardware store. He was always a delicate child, and at the end of two years of heavy work he became ill. His education really began during this period of illness, when he was unable to work for several years and spent all his time in reading at home.

On his recovery, he worked at the wharves in Charleston as a checker in a cotton warehouse, observing closely and learning to understand the Negroes of the waterfront. At twenty-one, in partnership with a friend, he went into the insurance business in Charleston. Nine years later, when the business was an established success, Heyward, finding himself exhausted in body and spirit, sought refuge in the North Carolina mountains, among the "People of the Hills." Here he began to paint and write poems. There was also a season of convalescence spent in the far West.

During the World War Mr. Heyward did organizing work among the Negroes of his section; in his spare time he wrote short stories. Shortly after the Armistice he met Hervey Allen, who has described his friend as bringing with him "an unusual sense of ease and virile-sensitiveness." (Heyward is thin and tall, with intense deep brown eyes.) The result of their association was an agreement to collaborate on a book of poems dealing with the legends and landscapes of Charleston. This book, *Carolina Chansons*, was published in 1922. Both Mr. Allen and Mr. Heyward were largely instrumental in the organization of the Poetry Society of South Carolina at this time. The activities of the society made poetry a living interest in the South.

In the summer of 1922 Mr. Heyward went north to the MacDowell Colony for artists at Peterborough, New Hampshire, in order to continue with his writing. There he met Dorothy Hartzell Kuhns of Canton, Ohio, a student in Professor Baker's 47 Workshop course in the drama at Harvard. In the following year they were married, just after Miss Kuhns had received the 1923 Harvard prize for her play, *Nancy Ann*. Heyward published *Skylines and Horizons,* a volume of poems, in 1924.

Heyward was persuaded by his wife to dispose entirely of the insurance business in Charleston, and together they went to live in a make-shift cottage in the Great Smokies, the mountain country where he had begun to write. Here he wrote his third book and first novel *Porgy,* based on Heyward's memory of a crippled Negro of old Catfish Row, a Negro tenement along the Charleston waterfront. Published serially in the *Bookman* and then in book form (1925), *Porgy* won instant recognition. It has been called "the first novel written about the character of an American Negro which was at once true to life and a work of art."

Mr. and Mrs. Heyward worked together on the dramatization of *Porgy*. It was produced in 1927 by the Theatre Guild—one of the Guild's most successful productions in New York and on tour—and was later brilliantly performed in London.

After a summer in Cornwall in the cottage where Hugh Walpole had written for thirteen years, the Heywards returned to North Carolina, where they built a new home, "Dawn Hill," at Hendersonville. Their daughter, Jenifer Du Bose Heyward, was born in New York in February 1930, on the very day when the proofs of Mrs. Heyward's first novel, *Three-A-Day,* reached the apartment for immediate correction.

Since *Porgy,* Du Bose Heyward has written *Angel* (1926), a novel of the North Carolina mountaineers; *Mamba's Daughters* (1929), the story of a Negress born in Catfish Row; *The Half Pint Flask* (1929), a tale of superstition; *Brass Ankle,* a play.

Samuel Hoffenstein

SAMUEL HOFFENSTEIN, humorous poet and parodist, is by nature gloomy and pessimistic. His conversation has been described as "often of sardonic raillery, barbed with the most astonishing word combinations." He speaks frequently in "tones of strained bitterness that make for him a sort of vocal sanctuary against the world."

Born in 1890, Hoffenstein was educated in the public schools in Wilkes-Barre and at Lafayette College. When he was graduated from Lafayette he returned to Wilkes-Barre where he served for a time as principal of the North Main Street School and later as a member of the Wilkes-Barre *Times-Leader* city staff. His first book of poems, *Life Sings A Song,* was published in 1916. When he became known as a poet more than ten years later this book was a much sought-after rarity.

Hoffenstein was co-author of *The Broadway Anthology of 1917.* In 1922 he became associated with the New York *Sun* and covered theatres for several seasons as "The Playgoer." As a press agent he made a reputation in theatrical New York as the wit who succeeded in creating the fantastic legend of Al

SAMUEL HOFFENSTEIN

Woods, Broadway manager. He wrote poems and gave them away to columnists. A number of his lyrics appeared in Richard Le Gallienne's *Anthology of American Verse* (1925) and in Franklin P. Adams' *The Conning Tower Book*.

One morning there appeared in Percy Hammond's column in the New York *Herald-Tribune* a burlesque signed by Hoffenstein of Burton Rascoe's "Daybook" of literary comment. It pleased Rascoe, who offered him a column in his book section. Hoffenstein conducted the column for two years under the caption, "The Belfry."

Rascoe relates that it took the utmost pressure from Hoffenstein's friends and his publisher to persuade him to collect his verses and publish them in book form. In 1928, however, he published *Poems In Praise of Practically Nothing*, containing mostly the amusing verses that had appeared in his column. The book is a sophisticated commentary on the life, foibles, and manners of our day. It speedily became a best-seller in the poetry class. In 1930 he published another book of verse, *Year In You're Out*.

Hoffenstein's special enthusiasms are Yeats, Heine, Dostoievsky, and Beethoven, besides Edna St. Vincent Millay and Dorothy Parker in America. His books are: *Life Sings A Song* (1916), *Poems In Praise of Practically Nothing* (1928), and *Year In You're Out* (1930).

A. E. Housman

ALFRED EDWARD HOUSMAN, poet and classical scholar, was born in Shropshire, March 26, 1859, the elder brother of Laurence Housman, a well known author and artist. A. E. Housman received his preparatory education at Bromsgrove School and then went to St. John's College, Oxford University, where he employed all his energies in the study of the classics.

After receiving his M. A. in 1882, Housman entered the British Patent Office as a Higher Division Clerk. He remained in the Civil Service for ten years, and in 1892 became Professor of Latin at University College, London. In 1911 he went from there to Cambridge

E. O. Hoppé

A. E. HOUSMAN

University as Professor of Latin, where he has been ever since. He is an Honorary Fellow of St. John's College, Oxford, and a Fellow of Trinity College, Cambridge.

Mr. Housman has been referred to as "a typical Cambridge don, prim in his manner, silent and rather shy, conventional in dress and manner, learned, accurate, and well-informed." This portrait is one-sided, and another commentator calls him "the belligerent don" for the forcefulness of his opinions on any subject connected with classical scholarship. An accurate and arrogant critic, he will wage active warfare against any colleague whose work appears to him careless and slip-shod. Altho reticent in larger company, he is a genial companion with his intimate friends.

Housman is not a dry-as-dust scholar who lapses occasionally into poetry, but rather distinctly a scholar, an editor, and a poet. He has published numerous articles in classical journals, principally *The Journal of Philology, The Classical Review* and *The Classical Quarterly*. His greatest scholarly work is his editing of Manilius, the first part of which was published in 1903, the second in 1912, the third in 1916, the fourth in 1920, the fifth and last in 1931.

More than thirty years were spent in editing this poem of some forty-two hundred lines, and every extant manuscript was considered in the effort to arrive at an accurate text. Intimate knowledge of the entire range of Latin and Greek literature is shown in Housman's notes. In addition to this Housman acquired an immense amount of astrological knowledge in order to understand the exposition of the bewildering details of that pseudo-science with which the Latin poet is chiefly concerned. He has also edited Juvenal (1905) and Lucan (1926).

As a poet Housman is known best for *A Shropshire Lad* (1896). Many of the sixty-three poems in this volume are melancholy in tone, all are lightly and delicately lyrical and polished. His theme repeats itself again and again: lovers are not faithful, all beauty is frail; the "rose-lipped maidens" and "lightfoot lads" are all destined to die; young soldiers are called to battle and will die futilely.

Forty-one *Last Poems* were published in 1922, twenty-six years after *A Shropshire Lad,*—a continuation of his poignant nostalgia for the passing of things. On the publication of *Last Poems* Mr. Housman said, "It is not likely that I shall ever be impelled to write much more."

Sidney Howard

SIDNEY COE HOWARD, playwright, was born in Oakland, California, June 26, 1891. He attended the University of California and developed a vigorous and keen talent for reporting. He received his A. B. in 1915. The next year he went to Harvard where he studied drama under Professor George Pierce Baker in the "47 Workshop." He went to France while the war was still in its early stages and drove an ambulance on the Western front and in the Balkans. After the United States entered the war he became a captain in the Aviation Service.

The year 1919 found Howard on the editorial staff of *Life.* His first two plays, *The Labor Spy* and *Swords,* were published in 1921. In 1922 he was back on *Life* as literary editor and he married

Nickolas Muray
SIDNEY HOWARD

Clare Eames, one of the best known actresses of the American stage, on June 1. They had one daughter, Clare Jenness Eames. *Swords* was produced in 1922, with Miss Eames in the leading part. Altho the play failed, Robert Edmond Jones did a setting for it which was regarded as one of the most distinguished designs at the International Theatre Exhibition in Amsterdam.

Howard was special investigator and feature writer for *Hearst's International Magazine* in 1923, the year he published *Casanova,* adapted from the Spanish of de Azertis. His play, *They Knew What They Wanted,* was produced by the Theatre Guild in November, 1924. It ran a year in New York and was awarded the Pulitzer Prize, adding considerably to the reputation of Pauline Lord, the principal actress. *Bewitched* (1924), written in collaboration with Edward Sheldon, and *Lucky Sam McCarver* (1925) fell short of the success of *They Knew What They Wanted.*

In the season of 1926-1927 the Theatre Guild produced two of Howard's plays in their repertory, both with success. They were: *Ned McCobb's Daughter,* a realistic study of New England life and character, and *The Silver Cord,* a drama of the mother complex.

Half Gods, a play in nine scenes, was published in the spring of 1930. It presents the new woman in her struggle for freedom, ending with the old solution: return to the man she loves and to their children. Sidney Howard always writes for the actor, it is said, even when to do so means compromise with the fundamental material of the play. He has a knack for developing the elements in his plays which make for success on the stage.

Clare Eames died in the fall of 1930. On January 10, 1931, Mr. Howard married Miss Leopoldine Blaine Damrosch, daughter of Walter Damrosch, the symphony conductor.

Howard's translations and adaptations include: *S. S. Tenacity* (1922), from the French of Charles Vildrac; *Sancho Panza* (1923), from the Hungarian of Melchoir Lengyl; *Michel Auclair* (1924), from the French of Charles Vildrac; *The Last Night of Don Juan* (1925), from the French of Edmond Rostand; and *Morals* (1925), from the German of Ludwig Thoma. He wrote *Salvation* (1927), with Charles MacArthur, and *Yellow Jack* (1928). He is the author of *Three Flights Up* (1924), a group of four stories.

Stephen Hudson

STEPHEN HUDSON is the pseudonym of an aristocratic Englishman whose real name is Sydney Schiff. In private life he is a connoisseur and patron of the arts. He has befriended and aided some of the most noted artists and musicians in Europe. His novels are fundamentally autobiographical.

To his American publisher Hudson writes: "Stephen Hudson is a pseudonym deliberately adopted for its unobtrusiveness. A name is like a label on a bottle; it may or may not correspond to or be a guarantee of its contents. My paradoxical idiosyncracy is that I take the public into my confidence and tell them all about myself in my books while reserving my personal privacy. If any reader wants to know anything more about me than my books tell him, I beg him to believe that there is, and will be, in them as much of my life as it is possible for me to mould into the form of literature."

Until he was fifty years old, Hudson was regarded as a failure by most of his relatives. The conditions of his early life prevented any serious creative efforts. He was too disturbed mentally, physically, and emotionally to be capable of calm composition. It was only after he reached full maturity that his latent talent gradually emerged and came to fruition. Thus, his works are based on "emotion remembered in tranquility."

Deliberately Hudson set himself to learn his chosen trade. He taught himself to write and each new book marked an advance in his literary development. His first book, a collection of character essays, was published in 1916. It was called *War Time Silhouettes.* One of the characters, the financier Reiss, was developed later in Hudson's novels as Frederick Kurt.

After three years of intensive study in spite of the war, Hudson wrote his first novel, *Richard Kurt* (1919). It is the story of a miserably unhappy man, living in complete luxury, who is unhappy even in the distractions he seeks as relief from his boredom with wife and family. This novel proved to be a prelude. It was followed by six other novels dealing primarily with the Kurt family, and all

Caricature by Max Beerbohm
STEPHEN HUDSON

of them centering for the most part around Richard Kurt.

Elinor Colhouse (1921) tells of the trapping of Richard into marriage by Elinor, the pivot around whom the story revolves. The narration is indirect.

The influence of Marcel Proust is visible in *Prince Hempseed* (1923), which is dedicated to him. It is the story of Richard Kurt's infancy and childhood, told in the first person singular.

Tony (1924) is told in the second person. The "you" of the story is Richard Kurt and the narrator is his brother Tony, an unscrupulous, selfish man-of-the world whose recital is a summary of their respective careers.

Myrtle (1925) differs from the others in that it does not keep to one point of view. It presents a character obliquely by showing it thru the eyes of nine dissimilar individuals. It reveals the childhood, youth, and early womanhood of Myrtle as told by her nurse, her governess, her favorite sister, and six admirers.

In *Richard, Myrtle and I* (1926) the "I" is a lesser part of Richard himself. It is a shadowy third, Richard's artistic super-self. The "I" is contemptuous of Richard and gracious toward Myrtle. Myrtle acts as arbiter between the two factions, interprets them one to the other, until peace is restored to the compound personality.

A True Story (1930) is a synthesis of several of the preceding novels. It is a psychological study of a man from childhood to maturity, dealing particularly with his relations with three women. *A True Story* is make up from *Prince Hempseed, Elinor Colhouse, Richard Kurt,* and the last section of *Myrtle,* arranged in chronological sequence.

Hudson was a good friend of Proust. He once wrote Proust that much as he loved his books he would rather see him and hear him talk than read them. Hudson was one of Katherine Mansfield's closest friends, and many of her published letters are addressed to him and his wife.

The list of Hudson's works is: *War Time Silhouettes* (1916), *Richard Kurt* (1919), *Elinor Colhouse* (1921), *Prince Hempseed* (1923), *Tony* (1924), *Myrtle* (1925), *Richard, Myrtle and I* (1926), and *A True Story* (1930).

Langston Hughes

JAMES LANGSTON HUGHES, Negro poet, has had an adventurous career. He was born February 1, 1902, in Joplin, Missouri, where his father was a lawyer. His grandparents on his mother's side were free Negroes before the Emancipation and were actively engaged in smuggling slaves North. A granduncle, John M. Langston, was congressman from Virginia during the reconstruction. His maternal grandmother was honored by President Roosevelt as the last surviving widow of John Brown's raid at Harper's Ferry.

Hughes spent his childhood, until the age of fourteen, in Lawrence, Kansas. He recalls how, as a small boy, he visited Mexico where his father had mountain property near the city of Toluca. He was there during an earthquake and he says, "I retain to this day the memory of thousands of kneeling figures crying and praying as the earth trembled."

The boy attended Central High School in Cleveland, Ohio, and was graduated in 1920. He wrote poems for the high school magazine as well as others about factories, workers, and poverty, which he says were "inspired perhaps by my reading of Max Eastman, Floyd Dell, Claude McKay in *The Liberator,* and the poems of Carl Sandburg."

After he finished high school Hughes spent a year in Mexico teaching English in a business academy and working on his father's ranch. He witnessed one of the lesser revolutions and saw three bandits hung. He spent his spare time riding, seeing bull fights, and climbing volcanoes.

He returned to the States in 1921 and entered Columbia University but left after one year to go to sea. His wanderings lasted three years. First he worked as a cabin boy from New York to the West Coast of Africa. He says he "saw the desert at Dakar, drank palm wine on the Gold Coast, bought a monkey up the Niger, and fell into the Congo." After six months he returned to New York with the monkey and six parrots, but soon set out again. He made several voyages across the wintry sea, spent Christmas 1923 in Rotterdam, and Easter found him in Paris, starving and in search of work.

He relates: "I became a doorman in a night club in the Rue Fontaine at nothing a night, tips, and one meal. As this was a European night club, little frequented by Americans, the tips amounted to practically nothing, so I sought another job as second cook at the famous Grand Duc where Florence, now of New York and Paris, was the ranking attraction. Here there was a salary, champagne, and plenty of food. I stayed in Paris until after the Olympic Games in 1924 when I departed for Italy."

After "long delightful days on the Italian lakes" and a week in Venice he was penniless once more and tried to get back to Paris. But his passport had been stolen in Milan and he was forced to become one of the many international beach combers in Genoa. "After weeks of nothing more encouraging than black bread and figs, I found a job as ordinary seaman on a boat sailing for New York. For six weeks I painted bulk heads and scrubbed decks while the tramp schooner made a circle of the western Mediterranean, touching many little islands, Sicily and Spain, and then proceeded leisurely across to New York."

"I went to Washington that winter and worked for some months in the dining room of the Wardman Park Hotel. One day Vachel Lindsay came there as a guest and I gave him three of my poems to read as he sat at the table. That evening, greatly to my surprise, Mr. Lindsay read these poems to his audience in the little theatre of the hotel, and the next day I found myself more or less a public curiosity in the dining room—a colored busboy who wrote poetry."

Hughes was awarded first prize in poetry in a contest conducted for Negro writers by the magazine *Opportunity*. That was in 1925. The next year he attended Lincoln University, a Negro school in Pennsylvania, where he received the Witter Bynner undergraduate poetry prize of $150 for his poem, *A House in Taos*. His first book, *The Weary Blues*, was published in 1926. His other volumes are: *Fine Clothes to the Jew* (1927) and *Not Without Laughter* (1930), a novel of Negro life, for which

LANGSTON HUGHES

he received the Harmon Award in Negro Literature.

His poems have been translated into German, French, Yiddish, Spanish, Russian, and Czechoslovakian. Many of his poems have been set to music. He contributes both verse and prose to magazines. He is a member of the editorial board of *Fire*, Negro art quarterly.

Richard Hughes

RICHARD HUGHES, English writer, was born in 1900. He was educated at Charterhouse and Oriel College, Oxford. Quietly conventional in his undergraduate days he possessed the reputation for having done many and various things beyond the experience of most of his fellows. It is said that he had taken to the road as a tramp, begged on the streets, and been a pavement artist, all by way of diversion in vacation. One summer he led an expedition composed of school friends and a woman thru Central Europe, attempting intrigue in monarchistic interests.

When he was an undergraduate of twenty-one, Hughes wrote a one-act play, *The Sisters' Tragedy* (1922) which was sponsored by John Masefield for a London production. It received bad reviews

RICHARD HUGHES

and ran a fortnight. On the last night Bernard Shaw saw the play and wrote a column of enthusiastic praise for it. While still at Oxford, Richard Hughes published his first book, a slim collection of poems called *Gipsy Night* (1922). It was one of the earliest productions of the Golden Cockerel Press. He wrote a three-act play, *A Comedy of Good and Evil* (1924), which was produced at the Abbey Theatre in Dublin and the Birmingham Repertory Theatre.

Hughes published his collected plays in 1924 under the title, *The Sisters' Tragedy and Other Plays.* Besides the title play, the volume included *A Comedy of Good and Evil, The Man Born to be Hanged,* and *Danger.* His second volume of verse, *Confessio Juvenis,* appeared in 1926. It contained mostly a selection of the best in *Gipsy Night.* Meanwhile, Hughes turned to short-story writing and his first book of collected stories, *A Moment of Time,* was published in 1926. There exists a rare edition of *Confessio Juvenis* consisting of six copies. A gentleman had them printed for some boys and girls he knew with the word "seduced" replaced by "bewitched."

The young author suffered from a serious breakdown for a time and was forbidden to write. He revisited America, spent three months on a farm in Virginia, roamed the hills of Connecticut, motored thru Eastern Canada, and lived in Dalmatia. During this period he changed in appearance from the rather rugged Hughes of Oxford days.

He resumed work with his first novel, *The Innocent Voyage,* published in America in 1929. It appeared later in England as *A High Wind in Jamaica* (1929). The American edition took over the English title in 1930. It is the story of a family of children bound for England from Jamaica who were captured by a pirate ship, and spent six months aboard the schooner with the pirates.

The story is based upon an actual incident, related to Hughes by an old lady who had been one of the children. After the book was published Hughes learned that Ford Madox Ford and Joseph Conrad had utilized the same actual happening in *Romance* (1901).

Richard Hughes is described by Burton Rascoe as "a tall youth with a reddish Van Dyke and reddish mustache, which is pointed at the ends and turned up. The top of his head is almost bald. He has assurance and ease and an air of polite curiosity; and at the same time he is somewhat diffident except with children. Children 'take to' him at once and talk to him as tho he were one of them. He is kind, gentle, and modest." Hughes, who is a bachelor, often entertains the children of his friends. "I wouldn't have a parent in the house," he says. The children come and stay by themselves and help with the household chores.

Hughes lives alone in a seventeenth-century stone cottage on the side of a mountain near the village of Llanfrothenpenrhyndeudraeth, Wales, but passes a few months of every year in London. He is a contributor to London and American literary journals and is co-founder of the Portmadoc Players. He was the first author of wireless plays in the world.

Rupert Hughes

RUPERT HUGHES was born on January 31, 1872, in Lancaster, Mo. His parents moved shortly to Keokuk, Iowa, on the Mississippi River, "in whose waters," he says, "I spent a large part of my boyhood." His ancestors on both sides came to America early in the seventeenth century, settling in Virginia and North Carolina. His father was a lawyer who played a strenuous part in railroad development in the Mid-West. His brother is Felix Hughes, singer.

Rupert Hughes early showed an inquiring mind. When his mother asked him what he wanted for a present he always said: "Bring me a biography of somebody." His playmates nicknamed him "History." He received his A.B. degree from Adelbert College (Western Reserve University) in 1892 and his A.M. in 1894. He took an A.M. at Yale in 1899 and came dangerously near taking a Ph.D. But he gave up his teaching ambitions for "creative work."

"On leaving Yale," he relates, "I spent a few months as a reporter on a New York daily paper and learned a good deal about the city. . . My first published works were sonnets and essays and musical and art criticism. I spent years in offices as an assistant editor of weekly and monthly magazines . . . *Godey's, Current Literature* and the *Criterion* . . . I have composed a good deal of music, edited a musical cyclopedia, written on American composers. . ." The last work mentioned, *American Composers* (1900), is a standard account of the development of music in this country up to the date of publication. Hughes is an excellent musician.

"My first theatrical production was a terrific failure, lasting one night in New York," he recalls. "I was twenty-two at the time."

In 1900 Hughes went to London as chief assistant editor of *The Historians' History of the World*, published in twenty-five volumes. He worked there for a year making constant researches in the British Museum and going frequently to Paris to study in the Bibliothèque Nationale. Back in America, he made special researches in the New York libraries, the Boston Public Library, and the Library of Congress. He worked on the book for four years and saw it thru the press. He wrote the estimate of Washington's character which appears in the history.

Hughes was a captain in the Mexican border service in 1916. He was assistant to the adjutant general in New York in 1917. He was made captain of the

infantry on January 7, 1918, major on September 4, 1918, and was honorably discharged on January 15, 1919. An impairment of hearing kept him from serving overseas during the World War. He belonged, as he says, to the swivel-chair army. Hughes became a major in the Reserve Corps on April 3, 1919. He was decorated, with the Polish Order of Polonia Restituta in 1923. His marriage to Elizabeth Patterson Dial took place December 31, 1924. Hughes lives in Los Angeles.

At a private banquet of the Sons of the Revolution in Washington in January 1926, Hughes made an extemporaneous speech in which he insisted on the greatness of Washington stripped of fable. He repeated verifiable facts about Washington's habits and activities. There were no reporters to take a stenographic record of the speech, but an editor published a garbled report—and then the fun began. The story went all over the world. Hughes was attacked and defended for many weeks. Preachers delivered sermons against him. Senators denounced him.

The result was his biography of Washington. Three volumes have been published: *George Washington, I, The Hu-*

RUPERT HUGHES

man Being and the Hero, 1732-1762
(1926), *George Washington, II,* The
Rebel and the Patriot, 1762-1777 (1927),
and *George Washington, III,* The Savior
of the States, 1777-1781 (1930). The
original plan was to complete the biography in two volumes, but the extent
of hitherto unpublished material forced
Hughes to plan two more. The fourth
volume will be devoted to Washington
the President and his last years at Mount
Vernon. Hughes went directly to the
original sources in the Library of Congress and in the Huntington Library in
California. His biography treats Washington's early life much more fully than
previous biographers. The first book
takes Washington only up to his twenty-
ninth year.

Altho Hughes' best work is as a biographer, he has devoted most of his time
to writing popular novels. These include: *What Will People Say?* (1914),
The Cup of Fury (1919), *Souls for Sale*
(1922). *No One Man* (1931) is his
twenty-fifth novel.

He has written a number of plays
for the stage and written and directed
numerous motion pictures. He is the
composer of *A Riley Album, Cain,* and
other songs.

Fannie Hurst

FANNIE HURST was born on October 19, 1889, in Hamilton, Ohio. "I
usually pass the honor on to St. Louis,"
she says, "since I was taken to Hamilton
for the exclusive purpose of being born
there in an old grandparental homestead,
and returned to St. Louis while still in
the beety, underdone infantile stage."
She spent the first twenty years of her
life in St. Louis. Her parents were
fairly well-to-do.

The fact that she was an only child
gave her long periods for reading. From
the time she was old enough to hold a
volume on her knee, her reading was
uncensored and unrestricted. At nine,
she read *Thomas à Becket;* at eleven,
Coleridge's *Christabel;* at thirteen, Dickens, Thackeray, Ouida, and the Mere-
diths. She corresponded with James
Whitcomb Riley and wrote unanswered
letters to Booth Tarkington. She col-

FANNIE HURST

lected a scrap book of verse labeled,
"Keats and Others."

At fourteen ambitious Miss Hurst submitted a masque in blank verse to the
Saturday Evening Post. She attracted
attention in high school by her showy
precocity. At one time she was nearly
expelled when it was discovered that she
was writing themes for her class-mates
in return for mathematics problems. She
manifested an excess of vitality and
engaged in athletics and dramatics, besides contributing to the *High School
News.* In spare moments she wrote
verse and fiction which she promptly
mailed out to publishers.

By the time she entered Washington
University in St. Louis, Miss Hurst had
accumulated quite a large collection of
magazine rejection slips. She wrote for
the *University Student Life.* Her striking personality brought her one or two
assignments from St. Louis newspapers.
At the university she was a good student
and participated in dramatics and outdoor sports. It was her custom to write
late at night in her suite in the women's
dormitory. A college friend relates:
"We used to speculate as to the meaning
of the midnight oil that burned in her
tower room until three and four and
sometimes five o'clock in the morning.
She never referred to these late hours,

or if teased, made light of them and would appear among us in the university dining-room next morning as fresh as if she had enjoyed a normal allotment of sleep."

Marion Reedy, editor of *Reedy's Mirror* in St. Louis, published a vignette he received from this unknown author. During their acquaintance of the next few years he was her patient adviser.

An unhappy year followed graduation from Washington University in 1909. Fannie Hurst was impatient to try her mettle but her parents kept her home. They pointed to her years of futile attempts at getting manuscripts published and her twenty-one rejection slips from the *Saturday Evening Post*. She attempted newspaper work again and produced a one-act play. Finally she broke away with graduate work at Columbia University as an excuse. Her course in Anglo-Saxon met three days a week. The rest of the time she walked around New York City or wrote in her little room near the university. She recalls: "For a stretch of twenty-six months, without even meeting an editor, writer, or publisher, absolutely ignorant of the game and an entire stranger in New York, I wrote, peddled, rewrote, repeddled, without so much as one acceptance or word of encouragement. . . I wrote all day from loneliness, and all evening for the same reason." She had the experience of not hearing "the sound of a human voice addressed directly to you for days." The twenty-one rejection slips from the *Saturday Evening Post* swelled to thirty-six.

One time Miss Hurst's parents cut off her allowance in an effort to get her to come home, but her mother quickly repented and sent a check. To gain experience the girl worked as a waitress, nursemaid, salesgirl, and sweatshop worker. She crossed the Atlantic in steerage. She lived for a few weeks in a room over an Armenian tobacconist's shop on the waterfront. She played in a Broadway show.

In her second year in New York Miss Hurst met her first editor—Robert H. Davis of *Munsey's*. He told her she could write. Success then followed swiftly, and her first book, a collection of stories called *Just Around the Corner,*

was published in 1914. In 1915 she married Jacques S. Danielson of New York, a pianist, but the marriage was not announced until five years later.

Miss Hurst published four volumes of short stories before she attempted a novel. Besides *Just Around the Corner,* they were: *Every Soul Hath Its Song* (1915), *Gas Light Sonatas* (1916), and *Humoresque* (1918). Her first novel was *Star Dust* (1921). Her second, *Lummox* (1923), established her reputation. In 1924 Miss Hurst visited Russia. The novels that followed were: *Appassionata* (1925); *Mannequin* (1926), awarded a $50,000 prize by a moving picture corporation; *A President Is Born* (1928); *Five and Ten* (1929); and *Back Street* (1931). The last is the story of a woman who loved greatly enough to live in the "back street" of a man's life.

Miss Hurst now lives in an apartment of medieval and ascetic atmosphere on West Sixty-seventh Street in New York City, where her library tables are stacked with books on science, classic history, and exploration. She is known as a charming hostess. Opulently handsome, she wears incomparable furs, lace, brocade, and glowing colors.

A. S. M. Hutchinson

ARTHUR STUART MENTETH HUTCHINSON was born in Gorakpur, India in 1879. He belonged to one of those English families whose sons naturally go into the Army, and as naturally go out to India, and it was taken for granted by his father (the late Lt.-Gen. H. D. Hutchinson, C. S. I.) from the moment his young son opened his eyes, that he would follow in the family tradition. But, owing to defective eyesight, Hutchinson was barred from the Army, so they made a medical student of him with a view to his joining the medical services of the Indian Army.

He was no more interested in medicine, however, than Keats was in pills and plasters, and it was during his two years at St. Thomas's Hospital that he first took to writing. Early in 1903 he made up his mind to give up medicine and concentrate all his powers in an

A. S. M. HUTCHINSON

in 1908 *Once Aboard the Lugger*— was finished, and published.

In 1912 he was appointed editor-in-chief of the *Daily Graphic*. His life was so full that he had little time for reading and less for writing. He used to read *Paradise Lost* in the train on his way to his office. But in his spare time Hutchinson managed to write *The Happy Warrior* (1912). And his own characterization of himself is fully borne out—"too vilely conscientious"—when it appears that after a last critical examination of the manuscript, he was convinced that the book must be rewritten. To do this with his daily labor on the *Graphic* was an appalling task, but "setting his teeth and groaning horribly," he began the revision, writing as always, with a new nib, on a square piece of paper, in neat diminutive characters. Denying himself to everybody, he finished the book in September 1912. *The Clean Heart* followed two years later in September 1914.

> "Lo, the poor author, who mid war's alarms,
> Hawks in the market his unwanted charms.
> Credit him thus much—that he can but write
> Since, being short-sighted, poor wretch he cannot fight,"

assault upon Fleet Street. Only two poems had been accepted at that time, and these by a monthly magazine, which, he says, "printed them and never smiled again—going smash almost immediately."

There were two objects kept steadily in view by Mr. Hutchinson. One was the determination to get on the regular staff of a magazine; the other was to establish himself as a novelist. As a means of achieving the first, he wrote to Mr. Arthur C. Pearson, and two interviews resulted in his going to *Pearson's Magazine* as a member of the staff. Soon after this he began planning the early form of his novel, *Once Aboard the Lugger*—. As months and years went by, however, he realized that if the novel was ever to be finished, he must have more time to himself.

So once more he took the plunge —resigned from *Pearson's* and began to devote himself to free-lance writing and his novel. Almost simultaneously, however, he was asked to come in as a night editorial writer on the *London Daily Graphic,* and to write a humorous column for the *Evening Standard* every day. He accepted both offers, and tho this meant morning and night work in a newspaper office, it left the rest of the day free for the novel. In 1907 he was made night editor of *The Daily Graphic;*

Hutchinson wrote on the fly-leaf of a friend's copy of *The Clean Heart*. For, like his own Mark Sabre, he made desperate efforts to enlist in the Army, but only gained admission in time to take part in the last stages of the conflict. As he confessed in the days following his demobilization, while in France, he often filled the silent vigils of the trenches by imagining and developing the characters which were to appear in his tremendously popular *If Winter Comes* (1921). *This Freedom* (1922); *The Eighth Wonder and Other Stories* (1923); *One Increasing Purpose* (1925), and *The Uncertain Trumpet* (1929), followed.

In 1926 Hutchinson married Una Rosamond Bristow-Gapper, a granddaughter of General Bristow. The story goes that Mrs. Hutchinson first corresponded with her husband as a reader of his books, and that the character revealed in her handwriting so impressed him that he finally arranged and brought about a meeting. And, in the romantic tradition of his own masters of the English novel, they fell in love and married, and will no doubt live happily ever after in their pleasant Sussex home.

The Book of Simon (1930) is a humorously detached account of the growth and development of their small son.

Aldous Huxley

ALDOUS HUXLEY

ALDOUS LEONARD HUXLEY was born July 26, 1894, the third son of Leonard Huxley (eldest son and biographer of the renowned scientist, Thomas Huxley) and Julia Arnold (niece of Matthew Arnold and sister of Mrs. Humphry Ward).

"I was educated," he writes, "at Eton, which I left at seventeen owing to an affliction of the eyes which left me practically blind for two or three years, an event which prevented me from becoming a complete public-school English gentleman. Providence is sometimes kind even when it seems to be harsh. My temporary blindness also preserved me from becoming a doctor, for which I am also grateful. For seeing that I nearly died of overwork as a journalist, I should infallibly have killed myself in the much more strenuous profession of medicine. On the other hand, I very much regret the scientific training which my blindness made me miss. It is ludicrous to live in the twentieth century equipped with an elegant literary training eminently suitable to the seventeenth. As soon as I could see well enough to read thru a magnifying glass, I went to Oxford, where I took my degree in English literature. Two years of my time at Oxford were years of the war. During the remainder of the war I cut down trees, worked in a government office— as long as my sight would stand the strain—and taught at school.

"In 1919 I joined the editorial staff of the *Athenaeum* under J. Middleton Murry. I married (1919, Maria Nys). I did a huge quantity of journalism, including dramatic, musical, and artistic criticism, articles on house decoration and architecture, reviews of novels, and bibliographical notes. The experience, which I should not care to repeat, taught me self-confidence. It taught me that however little one may know about a subject, one can always write an article about it, fully assured that half an hour's preliminary study will make one know ten times as much as almost anyone's readers. . ."

Most of Mr. Huxley's novels have been written in Italy. He visits London and Paris only occasionally, preferring sunlight to literary company. His recreations are reading and traveling. He adds: "I rarely take a complete holiday, as I find that my health begins to break down as soon as I stop working. Holidays are healthful only to those who dislike their work; I happen to find mine tolerably agreeable."

Huxley is tall and thin and walks with a visible stoop. Samuel Putnam once wrote, rather impressionistically, of his "legs twice as long as Lytton Strachey's. . . A willow that swayed and bent, not ungracefully, in the middle. No lassitude, however: nothing like Dunsany, whom I recall with a long white hand to his long white face. Those legs, I was soon to discover, were built for perpetual and conversational motion.

Top it all with the face of an extremely sensitive, intelligent and alive schoolboy and the handgrip of a midwestern farmer, and you'll have the author of *Crome Yellow, Antic Hay,* and *Barren Leaves.*"

Huxley has been extraordinarily prolific as a writer. After having contributed to *Oxford Poetry,* 1916, of which he was one of the editors, and to *Wheels,* an anthology of "queer, wayward poetry," he published his first book, *The Burning Wheel* (1916), a volume of poems. *The Defeat of Youth* (1918) and *Leda* (1920) were also collections of his verse, as was *Jonah* (1917), a privately printed unbound volume of poems in French and English.

His first prose volume was *Limbo* (1920), consisting of seven experimental prose narratives. Altho Huxley was attending to his editorial duties on Condé Nast's London *House and Garden* at this time, he managed to publish in quick succession *Crome Yellow* (1921), his first novel ("in the manner of Peacock," he said); *Mortal Coils* (1922), another brilliant experimental collection like *Limbo*; *On the Margin* (1923), a collection of essays, most of which had appeared in the London *Athenaeum* as *Marginalia* by "Autolycus," *Antic Hay* (1923), his second novel, "dramatizing with relentless logic the necessary implications, in terms of life, of the skepticism of Thomas Huxley—skepticism battening at the vitals of animal faith." His next books were *Little Mexican and Other Stories* (1924), which was published in the United States as *Young Archimedes and Other Sketches; Those Barren Leaves* (a novel, 1925); *Along the Road* (essays, 1925); *Two or Three Graces* (short stories, 1926); *Jesting Pilate* (essays, 1926); *Proper Studies* (essays, 1927); *Point Counter Point* (a novel, 1928); *Arabia Infelix* (poems, limited edition, 1929); *Do What You Will* (essays, 1929); *Holy Face and Other Essays* (limited edition, 1929); *Brief Candles* (essays, 1930); *Music at Night* (essays, 1931).

Point Counter Point, a novel on the grand scale, and a unique experiment in craftsmanship, is perhaps Mr. Huxley's most important work to date. A dramatization of *Point Counter Point,* entitled *This Way to Paradise,* by Campbell Dixon, was produced in London in 1930 and published with an introduction by Huxley. One of the greatest recent influences on Mr. Huxley has been the late D. H. Lawrence, who has been identified by many as the prototype of Mark Rampion in *Point Counter Point.* Mr. Huxley is now at work editing Lawrence's letters and preparing, it is said, a biography of him.

Wallace Irwin

WALLACE IRWIN was born on March 15, 1876, in Oneida, N. Y. His maternal grandfather was Charles Chauncey Greene, a descendent of the founder of Rhode Island.

He relates: "In 1880, when I was four years old and my brother, Will Irwin, six, our parents went to Leadville, Colorado, where my father had ambitions to follow silver mining. Leadville was then a primitive camp of the Bret Harte type.

"I was about fifteen when my parents moved to Denver, my father having tried mining, lumber, and cattle without success. Up to then my education had been very sketchy (my mother encouraged me in a taste for reading, but I had gone to school very little). When I entered the Denver public schools I was put in the third grade, but by the combined efforts of my mother and myself I was admitted to high school the following year." He won a medal for oratory in high school, trained for the event by his brother Will.

After graduating from high school in 1895 he spent a year in Cripple Creek as assayer in a cyanide mill for the reduction of low-grade ore, and entered Stanford University in 1896. "I took a literary prize in my freshman year and wrote the class play in my sophomore year," he recalls. "Subsequently I held the editorship of my class annual and of the literary magazine. In my junior year

WALLACE IRWIN

I was expelled the day after being elected editor of the university magazine. . . I walked up to San Francisco that night, slept in a haystack and went to work on a newspaper for experience at nothing a' week.

"After a month of almost literal starvation I made my first dollar writing topical verse at five cents a line for an obscure weekly paper. I gained a local reputation for light verse. I did my first reporting for the *Report,* Scripps-Blade paper which went bankrupt in two months, not thru paying extravagant salaries. I went on the San Francisco *Examiner,* first as a writer of rhymed headlines, then as Chinatown reporter (1900)."

In 1901 Irwin married Grace Luce of San Diego, California. The following year he became editor of the *Overland Monthly,* and during that time he wrote the *Love Sonnets of a Hoodlum* (1902), "a cycle of slang-sonnets which were intended as a literary joke." Soon afterward he published *The Rubaiyat of Omar Khayyam Jr.* (1902). He was burlesque writer for the Republic Theatre, San Francisco, in 1903.

Irwin went to New York and sold his first verse to *Life.* In 1904 and 1905 he was engaged on the *Globe,* writing a topical rhyme a day. At the same time his verses appeared in *Life* and other magazines. His first prose was for the *Satur-*

day Evening Post a series of burlesques (called *Shame of the Colleges*) on Steffins' *Shame of the Cities.* He became a staff member of *Collier's,* for which he wrote a series or rhymed lampoons on public characters in 1906 and 1907. A pseudonym that he has used is "Ginger."

About 1907 the British and Canadian press had been scathing on the subject of California's brutal treatment of the Japanese. In the midst of the dispute an anti-Japanese riot broke out in British Columbia and several Japanese were killed. Wallace Irwin wrote a *Letter of a Japanese Schoolboy* pretending to be a Japanese enjoying a brickbat wound in a Vancouver hospital and "asking to know" about where international friendship came in. Irwin says, "The letter was so popular that *Collier's* was deluged with mail, asking for more. For six months I appeared almost every week in *Collier's* signing myself Hashimura Togo. (*Letters of a Japanese Shoolboy,* 1909). Almost everybody thought the stuff was being written by a Jap. . . After a year in *Collier's* Hashimura Togo went into syndicate for two or three years. Up to 1917 he was a monthly feature in *Good Housekeeping.* He also had been serialized in *Life* for nearly a year."

Irwin's first attempt at fiction was a short story manuscript he had brought to New York with him and hawked around for years. "Finally," he says, "in a strangely altered shape, it was published in the *Cosmopolitan.*" His next fiction piece was a Christmas story called *A Transplanted Ghost.* Then he wrote several theatrical stories from his experience together with Richard Harding Davis in producing a comic opera.

His wife died in 1914, and in 1915 he married Laetitia McDonald of Louisville, Kentucky. He has two children, Donald McDonald Irwin, and Wallace Irwin, Jr. He spends his summers in "The Strongbox" at East Setauket, Long Island. The house is a Colonial relic, built in 1702 by one of the pioneers of Long Island.

Irwin's novel, *Seed of the Sun* (1921), tells the story of the Japanese farmer and the American farmer from both angles. Subsequent novels include: *Lew Tyler's Wives* (1923), *The Golden Bed* (1924), *Mated* (1926), *Lew Tyler and the Ladies* (1928), *The Days of Her Life* (1930).

Will James

WILLIAM RODERICK JAMES, cowboy author and artist, was born June 6, 1892, in a covered wagon which had halted for the night on a wind-swept hill in Montana. His father, of Scotch-Irish descent, was a cattle herder who was en route from his native Texas to Alberta, Canada. His mother, also Scotch-Irish with a little Spanish blood, died when Will was about a year old. The death of his father when he was about four left him in the care of a French-Canadian trapper, Jean Beaupré, "Bopy."

Altho the boy was much too small to mount even a pony alone, he and Bopy headed for the wilds of northeastern Canada on horseback soon after the death of the elder James. He learned the art of making camp and of cooking, and came to enjoy life in the open to such an extent that to this day he feels confined in a building.

James spent his boyhood in the far northwest, alone for weeks at a time while the old trapper was absent on fur hunting expeditions. The boy taught himself to read and write from a pile of old magazines which lay in a corner of the cabin; until he was fourteen, he says, he wrote entirely in the characters of

WILL JAMES

printing. His artist's bent early manifested itself in crude drawings on the walls and ceiling of the cabin, and he felt himself rich when Bopy brought him a large pad of paper. Not all of his time was spent indoors, for he enjoyed tramping thru the woods, and particularly riding his horse.

One day, when James was about fourteen, the trapper went to get a pail of water. Alarmed by his failure to return, the boy looked for him and found his fur cap beside a hole in the ice; for two weeks he tried to recover the body of his foster father. Entirely alone in the world, with about five hundred dollars, Bopy's available cash, James set out for Montana, where he became a "wrangler" and a "night hawk" on a Circle Diamond ranch. For twelve years he drifted thru the west as a cowboy, from Canada to Mexico, winning a reputation as an expert rider, capturing wild horses and breaking them. Several months were spent in Hollywood making wild west pictures. His ability for fancy riding was also responsible for his taking a prominent part in rodeos.

During the World War James was a member of the Mounted Scouts, U. S. A., at Camp Kearney, California, near the Mexican borderline. An injury to his side from a particularly vicious horse practically ended his riding days in 1920. That same year he married Alice Conradt, of Reno, Nevada.

The accident that terminated his active cowboy life brought into the foreground the artistic bent that had begun to reveal itself when he was a boy. Recognition was slow at first, but friends helped him to get attention from editors for his drawings, and his work began to appear in magazines. Horses had always been his chief interest, and most of his drawings were of horses in motion. He comments that he has never drawn with a model but always from memory, even tho his favorite horse, Smoky, or any number of other horses might be within his immediate range of vision. Presently he began to write sketches of cowboy life, expressed in their lingo, and it was not long before he was recognized as a writer-artist with an unusual combination of talents.

James has the appearance of a typical

cowboy, lean, lithe, and tanned. His home is at Pryor, Montana, where he has an eight-thousand acre ranch.

Will James now has several books to his credit, all illustrated by himself: *Cowboys, North and South* (1924); *The Drifting Cowboy* (1925); *Cow Country* (1927); *Smoky* (1926), which was awarded the John Newbery Medal in 1927; *Sand* (1929); *Lone Cowboy: My Life Story* (1930); *Sun Up* (1931), stories of the cow-camps.

Storm Jameson

STORM JAMESON

MARGARET STORM JAMESON in private life is Mrs. Guy Chapman. She was born in 1897 in Whitby, Yorkshire, one of the oldest and most picturesque coast towns in England. She has a passion for Whitby and still lives there. There, as a small vigorous child, she romped with her brothers. She was educated at private schools in Whitby and then went to Leeds University where she took honors in English language and literature. She was awarded a research scholarship and went to London to work at the British Museum on modern European drama. Her Master's thesis, entitled *Modern Drama in Europe*, was published in 1920.

Whitby, when she returned, could not contain her ambition or give her the means for the life she wanted. So she went to London in response to the advertisement of a large publicity company and she became an expert copy-writer. Later a journalistic opportunity lured her and she conducted a bygone weekly magazine. Her other occupations have been dramatic critic, publisher, and novelist.

Her initial effort in fiction-writing was *The Pot Boils* (1919), which she regarded years later as a bad book. Then followed *Happy Highways* (1920) and *The Clash* (1922), which showed improvement but attracted little attention. With *The Pitiful Wife* (1923) Miss Jameson came into notice. This book dropped the smartness and audacity of her first style. Its success gave her the confidence she needed.

Miss Jameson brought her experience in the advertising world into *Three King-doms* (1926). The theme of the novel is the modern problem of a woman's marriage and her career. The author comments: "Marriage is a one hundred per cent job. So is a career. Either the marriage or the career is bound to suffer when a woman tries to combine both. . . I think that it is quite possible for a woman to have a career and to run a husband, so to speak; but I don't think that she can have a career, run a husband, and bring up her children properly—as I have tried to point out in my *Three Kingdoms*. A woman can rule over any two of these kingdoms with a reasonable amount of success, but not over the three."

The Lovely Ship (1927), *The Voyage Home* (1930), and *A Richer Dust* (1931) compose a trilogy of novels dealing with the life of an English Victorian woman, Mary Hervey, in business and in love.

Miss Jameson wrote *The Decline of Merry England* (1930), to prove her contention that with the rise of the industrial middle class to power in the Puritan Rebellion the ease, spaciousness, and gusto of English life were lost. It is a hearty picture of Elizabethan England, with special emphasis on some of its great figures. She is the translator of

Day and Night Stories by Guy de Maupassant in *Collected Novels and Stories,* edited by Ernest Boyd.

Miss Jameson is a good horsewoman and loves to ride a bicycle. "I can drive a car—or smash it," she says. She is an excellent cook and enjoys walking and dancing. For recreation she reads books about ships and ship-building. In her home at Whitby are many models and pictures of ships, some of them owned by her family in the days when Whitby was a mart for "frigate-built ships that traded to India and China." Her hobby is collecting old furniture. She has one son.

Her books are: *The Pot Boils* (1919); *Modern Drama in Europe* (1920); *Happy Highways* (1920); *The Clash* (1922); *The Pitiful Wife* (1923); *Lady Susan and Life: An Indiscretion* (1924), a book of dialogues; *Three Kingdoms* (1926); *The Lovely Ship* (1927); *Farewell to Youth* (1928); *The Georgian Novel and Mr. Robinson* (1929), an essay; *The Voyage Home* (1930); *The Decline of Merry England* (1930); *A Richer Dust* (1931).

Robinson Jeffers

BORN in Pittsburgh on January 10, 1887, John Robinson Jeffers began to write poetry under the able tutelage of his father, the late William Hamilton Jeffers, L.L.D., a man of wide scholarship in languages, especially Latin, Greek, Hebrew, and Arabic. The elder Jeffers was fifty-two when Robinson was born. He had married a girl twenty-three years his junior, Annie Robinson Tuttle, who had been left an orphan and was brought up by a wealthy Pittsburgh family. Robinson has one brother, Hamilton Jeffers, born seven years after him, who is engaged in astronomical work at the Lick Observatory. Their ancestry was "all pre-revolutionary American, except paternal grandfather from North Ireland."

When he was five years old, Jeffers visited France, Italy, and Switzerland with his parents. Of the trip he says he remembers three things: "a pocketful of snails loosed on the walls of a kindergarten in Zürich, paintings of Keats and Shelley hanging side by side somewhere in London, and Arthur's Seat, the hill about Edinburgh." The trip was repeated the following year. Then he spent several years at his father's country home near Pittsburgh where he became familiar with the classics under paternal guidance.

Jeffers lived in Europe between the ages of twelve and fifteen, attending school at Vevey, Lausanne, Geneva, Zürich, and Leipzig. During the summers of those years he took walking trips with his father in the Swiss Alps. At fourteen he won a prize offered by the *Youth's Companion* for poetry. When the family returned to America he entered the University of Western Pennsylvania but they moved within a year to Pasadena, California. He graduated from Occidental College, Los Angeles, at the age of eighteen and subsequently spent "desultory years" at the Universities of Zürich and Southern California and the Medical School in Los Angeles "with faint interest." He says he wasn't "deeply interested in anything but poetry." He was a mile runner in college and afterwards was accustomed to swim miles in the sea at Hermosa Beach.

Jeffers married Una Call Kuster of Los Angeles in 1913. They were going to England in the fall of 1914 when he

ROBINSON JEFFERS

came into a legacy from an uncle, which left him independent. Free to devote his time to literature, he turned to the village of Carmel, California: "When the stagecoach topped the hill from Onterey, and we looked down thru pines and sea-fogs on Carmel Bay, it was evident that we had come without knowing it to our inevitable place."

They built their house of ocean-worn boulders—grey Santa Lucia granite—on a low bluff a hundred feet from the foam-line of the Pacific. It is a copy of an old Tudor barn in Surrey which Mrs. Jeffers liked. The whole top floor is taken up by one big attic with four beds hidden in nooks and the poet's desk at one end. Their twin boys were born in 1916. Jeffers built, practically unaided, a thirty-foot tower of the same ocean boulders brought from the shore below. The ground floor belongs to the twins, Garth and Donnan; the second floor is given to Mrs. Jeffers, and on the third floor is Mr. Jeffers' studio, a tiny cell containing only a table and a chair.

During the seven years he spent on the tower, Jeffers worked every afternoon as stone-mason and devoted his mornings to the books which brought him fame: *Tamar* (1924), *Roan Stallion* (1925) *The Women at Point Sur* (1927), *Cawdor* (1928), and *Dear Judas* (1929). He earned the title of the poet of tragic terror. George Sterling wrote: "I know of no other poet who cares less for the plaudits of the many, or even for fame in his own day and after death, than Robinson Jeffers." He is a slow worker and rewrites but little. He has an abnormally low pulse—forty in the morning and sixty in the afternoon.

Jeffers says his amusements are "stone-masonry, tree-planting, swimming, pipe-smoking, drives and walks in the coast range, reverent admiration of hawks, herons and pelicans." His discarded amusements are "long-distance running, wrestling, alcoholism, canoeing." His idiosyncracies are "almost perfect inability to write a letter or kill an animal, love of monotony and wet weather."

The poet is a good six feet tall without his shoes, slender, but powerfully limbed, and about a hundred and seventy pounds in weight. He is between a brunette and a blond, bronzed by the sun, since he seldom wears a hat, and has stern, searching blue-grey eyes. He wears puttees, and his soft shirt is invariably open at the throat.

Altho Jeffers is not shy, he is disinclined to sociability. He has a limited number of friends, but he does not seek their companionship, nor does he care to make new acquaintances. He is reserved and self-sufficient. He no longer likes travel, for he hates contacts with tourists. He is patient and never becomes angry.

Jeffers does not believe in individual immortality and is utterly irreligious as far as the conventional dogmas are concerned. He accepts the fact of the tragedy of life, but thinks existence worth the cost. He does not believe in punishment or any attempts to influence either the individual or society. He knows French, German, Latin, and Greek thoroly. His library is up-to-date. He thinks music is "just noise," altho his wife is a devotee of Irish folk-songs and has a small organ installed in the home.

Robinson Jeffers' books are: *Flagons and Apples* (1912), *Californians* (1916), *Tamar* (1924), *Roan Stallion* (1925), *The Women at Point Sur* (1927), *Cawdor* (1928), and *Dear Judas* (1929).

James Weldon Johnson

JAMES WELDON JOHNSON was born in Jacksonville, Florida, June 17, 1871. After attending the public schools of Jacksonville, he went to Atlanta University where he received his A.B. in 1894. He was principal of the Negro high school in Jacksonville for several years and then was admitted to the Florida bar in 1897. He practiced law in Jacksonville.

His brother is J. Rosamond Johnson, singer and arranger of Negro spirituals. The two of them wrote an operetta together for their own amusement, James Weldon doing the lyrics and libretto and Rosamond the music. It proved so good that they went to New York City in 1901 to sell it. They rented a back room on West Fifty-Third Street which boasted one piano and one iron bedstead. George Lederer, Lillian Russell, May Irwin, and

JAMES WELDON JOHNSON

magazines including *Century, Harper's, The American Mercury,* and *Crisis.*

Johnson received the degree of Litt.D. from Talladega College, Alabama, in 1917 and from Howard University in 1923. He was awarded the Spingarn Medal in 1925. He is secretary of the National Association for the Advancement of Colored People; a director of the American Fund for Public Service; member of the Ethical Society; member of the Academy of Political Science, and a trustee of Atlanta University. He is an authority on American jazz.

Johnson is the author of *God's Trombones* (1927), a book of seven Negro sermons in verse. The author comments: "The old-time Negro preacher is rapidly passing, and I have here tried sincerely to fix something of him." He does not claim to have originated the sermons; he has set down the essence of what he has heard. The book has modernistic drawings by Aaron Douglas.

New York is Johnson's home, where he is a member of the Civic Club. His books are: *The Autobiography of an Ex-Colored Man* (1912), *Fifty Years and Other Poems* (1917), *Self-Determining Haiti* (1920), *The Book of American Negro Poetry* (1921), *The Book of American Negro Spirituals* (1925), *Second Book of Spirituals* (1926), *God's Trombones* (1927), *Native African Races and Culture* (1927), and *Black Manhattan* (1930). He has written words for a number of songs.

Oscar Hammerstein at separate times climbed the three flights of rickety stairs to hear the comic-opera. The brothers did not succeed in selling that particular collaborative effort, but contacts they had made led to a connection with Klaw and Erlanger for whom they wrote light opera for several years.

Johnson received his A.M. degree from Atlanta University in 1904 and he did graduate study at Columbia for three years. In 1906 he was appointed United States Consul to Venezuela, and from 1909 to 1912 he was Consul at Corinto, Nicaragua. During the latter service he witnessed the revolution which overthrew Zelaya, and the abortive revolution against Diaz. He married Grace Nail of New York City on February 3, 1910.

His first book, *The Autobiography of an Ex-Colored Man*, was published annonymously in 1912 and it reappeared under his name in 1927. It is a novel, not strictly autobiographical, in which a white-skinned Negro deserts his race because of the injustice and bitterness of anti-Negro feeling. Johnson edited a book of Negro poetry and two volumes of Negro spirituals. He wrote the English version of the libretto to the grand opera, *Boyescas*, produced at the Metropolitan Opera House, New York, in 1915. He has contributed to many

Owen Johnson

OWEN McMAHON JOHNSON was born in New York City on August 27, 1878. His father is Robert Underwood Johnson, poet, one-time editor of the *Century Magazine,* and Ambassador to Italy in 1920 and 1921. The elder Johnson published his memoirs in 1923, *Remembered Yesterdays.* At the age of six Owen wrote a story for which he received one dollar from the *St. Nicholas Magazine.* When he was twelve, with the son of Richard Watson Gilder, he got out a paper bearing the honest caption, "Published as often as we can get it out." He has always been a stickler for truth.

At Lawrenceville School, in New Jersey, he founded *The Literary Magazine,* the school paper. He demanded of his contributors, "Interpret, don't invent," the rule by which he charted his own career. At Yale University, in 1889, he was elected chairman of the *Yale Literary Magazine,* the oldest college magazine in America. He began his first novel, *Arrows of the Almighty,* in his senior year, and published it a few months after graduation in 1901.

Johnson married Mary Galt Stockly of Lakewood, N.J., in 1901. He went to Paris where he wrote *In the Name of Liberty* (1905). Back in America, he rambled about dingy downtown New York where he visited the old Jefferson Market Police Court, studied New York's shyster law offices, and pictured their infamy in *Max Fargus* (1906). It was Owen Johnson who persuaded Nazimova to learn English and remain in this country. She appeared in his play *The Comet* (1908), which ran for two years in New York. His first wife died in 1910.

The author began his studies of college life with the publication of *The Humming Bird* (1910), a jolly account of the doings of various boys at Lawrenceville. It was followed by *The Varmint* (1910) and *The Tennessee Shad* (1911). The Prodigious Hickey, Doc MacNooder, Dink Stover, Hungry Smeed, and the Gutter Pup became traditional characters in college circles. It was the fashion for motorists to stop at Lawrenceville to visit the Jogger Shop where Hungry Smeed established the "great pancake record."

Stover at Yale (1911) resulted in a complete overhauling of the Yale secret society system. Many of the characters in Owen Johnson's novels are recognizable altho he disguises their identity. In *The Sixty-first Second* (1912) he portrays several prominent figures in the art and literary worlds. He began to write about women with The *Salamander* (1913) in which he pictures a curiosity— Dodo, the first flapper,—five years ahead of her time. The *locale* of *Making Money* (1914) is old Westover Court, near Longacre Square.

The late Willard Metcalfe, the painter, is the prototype for the character of

OWEN JOHNSON

Dangerfield in *The Woman Gives* (1915).

When the World War came Johnson dropped his fiction and wrote *The Spirit of France* (1915). He went to Paris where he engaged in extensive investigation work for the French Government. Johnson was awarded the cross of a Chevalier of the Legion of Honor in 1919. *The Wasted Generation* (1921) was written in Paris during the war.

Sacrifice (1929) presents the problems of the divorced woman and her readjustment. His purpose in the problem novels, he declares, is to present a true record of life, "concealing nothing, excusing nothing, without attempting to reconcile the irreconcilable."

In 1926 Mr. Johnson married for the fifth time. When his house at Stockbridge, Massachusetts, burned down in 1929 the Johnsons returned to New York to live. He is a member of the National Institute of Arts. He has written numerous short stories and magazine articles.

Other books by Owen Johnson include: *A Comedy for Wives* (1911), a play; *Murder in Any Degree* (1913); *Virtuous Wives* (1917); *Skippy Bedelle*

(1923), a reversion to the Lawrenceville stories; *Blue Blood* (1923); and *Children of Divorce* (1927).

Mary Johnston

IT is said that Mary Johnston rises at four o'clock, climbs a mountain, and writes until nine, that she dislikes publicity, and that she spends far more time preparing material for her books than in actually writing them down—a fact which is not surprising in view of the careful historical backgrounds of her novels. A small woman, with a clearcut oval face, her hair still dark and crisp, Miss Johnston is fond of tramping with her stout walking stick in the Virginia country round "Three Hills," her place near Warm Springs. She was born on November 21, 1870, at Buchanan, Botetourt County, Virginia, the daughter of Major John William Johnston, Confederate veteran, lawyer, and ex-member of the Virginia Legislature. She was a frail girl, and being taught at home, was given free access to her father's library which, like the libraries of southern gentlemen of the time, was undoubtedly full of histories (particularly those relating to Virginia), oratory (from Pericles to Patrick Henry), philosophy, and poetry.

MARY JOHNSTON

The family moved to Birmingham, Alabama, and Miss Johnston after three months of school came home again at sixteen on account of ill health. Her mother died soon after, and Miss Johnston undertook the management of her father's household and of the younger members of the family. She wrote various short stories at this time, but burned them on first rejection. A few years later, then in her twenties, she began *Prisoners of Hope* (1898), written in New York, the story goes, in a quiet corner of Central Park. It was successful and was followed in 1900 by *To Have and To Hold,* a record-making best seller at that time. After the death of her father, Miss Johnston moved back to Richmond and lived there in "Linden Row" on Franklin Street, in a square brick house with a deep pillared porch framed in wisteria vines, with magnolia trees and crepe myrtle in the yard. Then followed a period of travel abroad in search of health and finally a return to Virginia where Miss Johnston built the comfortable country house with big rooms, high ceilings and broad windows looking out over the surrounding garden —"Three Hills."

Her reputation as a writer of historical novels in this country was firmly established with *The Long Roll* (1911) and *Cease Firing* (1912). Among the books that followed were *Silver Cross* (1922), *1492* (1922), *Croatan*, (1923), *The Slave Ship* (1924), *The Great Valley* (1926), *Michael Fourth* (1926), and *The Exile* (1927). With *Silver Cross* a new tendency was observable in Miss Johnston's books which put her work in a class apart from her earlier novels of straight historical romance. "The waves of transcendentalism are fast closing over Miss Johnston's head, as they closed over Herman Melville's," a young reviewer wrote sadly.

Matthew Josephson

MATTHEW JOSEPHSON was born in Brooklyn, New York, in 1899. He was graduated from Columbia where he was a member of a group that included Lewis Mumford and Edmund Wilson. After leaving college he went to Europe and edited the magazine *Broom* in Rome and later in Paris. He was an intimate member of the group of *Surréalistes* that included Aragon, Soupault, Breton, and others. He returned to New York and tried to continue *Broom* but he had to raise so much money for it here that it ceased to be amusing.

A Wall Street brokerage firm persuaded him to become something of a financier. He succeeded in making money and enjoyed it until a bear market gave him a nervous breakdown. He abandoned Wall Street for literature again and has resisted all invitations to return.

Mr. Josephson has contributed to *Poetry, Broom, Secession, The Little Review, transition, The New Republic, The Saturday Review, Books,* and *The Outlook.* He has had a volume of poems published, *Galimathias.* His first important book, however, was *Zola and His Time* (1928). Early in 1930 his *Portrait of the Artist as American* appeared. Here he presents the dilemma of the American artist who is faced with the choice of struggling against the growth of American industrial civilization or becoming an expatriate, a "man without a country," like Henry James, Whistler, Ambrose Bierce, who are some of the artists whose disillusion and defeat Josephson reveals.

When Mr. Josephson had completed the manuscript for *Portrait of the Artist as American* and had turned it in to his publishers, he planned to go abroad to finish his research for his next book, a biography of a Frenchman which will have the scope and the detail of his *Zola.* Unfortunately the night before his boat was to sail Mr. Josephson's house was burned to the ground and he himself was badly burned trying to rescue some of his manuscripts. After recuperating in the south he spent the summer of 1930 on his farm in Connecticut continuing the work on his next book.

Considering Mr. Josephson's strong belief in the dilemma of the American artist, it may be asked why he himself lives in America. His answer to this is: "I could go away to some part of Europe and manage to get along on a small income, but I must live here to see the

MATTHEW JOSEPHSON

battle fought out and to see the nature of the transformation that will take place here; to see whether mechanism will enjoy the ultimate triumph over ideas."

James Joyce

JAMES JOYCE, who has probably been responsible for more dismay among censors and more controversy among critics than any other living writer, was born in Dublin on February 2, 1882, the son of John Joyce and Mary Murray. He was one of a large and not too prosperous family of brothers and sisters. His father was reputed to have the best amateur tenor voice in Ireland.

At the age of nine Joyce is supposed to have written a pamphlet on Parnell which was distributed in Dublin. After attending the Jesuit institution, Clongowes Wood College, and Belvedere College, Joyce received his degree from the Royal University in Dublin. At school he was characteristically independent and solitary, being the only student to refuse his signature to the letter of protest against Yeats' play, *Countess Cathleen.* He wrote an essay on Ibsen, one of the gods of his youth, for the *Fortnightly*

Review when he was seventeen. He wanted so much to understand Ibsen that he learned Norwegian in order to read him in the original. Today he feels that people can make the same effort to read him. Dante, Aristotle, St. Thomas Aquinas, the Elizabethans, and Ibsen, were his constant studies. At nineteen he published (together with another student) a little pamphlet entitled *The Day of the Rabblement* in which he belittled the idea of a National Theatre in Ireland and suggested that the production of European masterpieces would be a better investment. Padraic Colum describes the Joyce of those days:

"Joyce, when I knew him first, was a student in the old Royal University (since organized as the National University). He was very noticeable among the crowd of students that frequented the National Library or sauntered along the streets between Nelson's Pillar and Stephen's Green. He was tall and slender then, with a Dantesque face and steely blue eyes. His costume as I see him in my mind's eye now included a peaked cap and tennis shoes more or less white. He used to swing along the street carrying an ashplant in his hand for a cane. (That ashplant is celebrated in *Ulysses;* Stephen Dedalus carries it with him all thru the day and fre-

JAMES JOYCE

quently addresses it.) Altho he had a beautiful voice for singing and repeating poetry, he spoke harshly in conversation, using many of the unprintable words that he has got printed in *Ulysses.*"

Joyce's arrogance in his youth is illustrated by his remark to Yeats at their first meeting: "We have met too late; you are too old to be influenced by me." His intelligence was so keen and cold that A.E. once said to him, "I'm afraid you have not enough chaos in you to make a world." (No critic seemed tempted to make the same remark after the publication of *Ulysses.*)

After graduation from the Royal University, Joyce determined to leave Ireland. "When the soul of a man is born in this country," says Stephen Dedalus in *A Portrait of the Artist as a Young Man,* "there are nets flung at it to hold it back from flight. You talk to me of nationality, language, religion. I shall try to fly by those nets." Joyce went to Paris, where he stayed for about a year (1903-04), studying medicine at the University of Paris. The penniless student would walk thru the streets of the French capital, repeating to himself the lyrics he had written. He met Synge and read *Riders to the Sea* in manuscript. Abandoning the idea of becoming a physician, he began to train his tenor voice for the concert stage. Those who have heard him sing are convinced that if he had not ultimately chosen literature, he would have distinguished himself as a singer.

Joyce was called back to Dublin in 1904 on the death of his mother. There he wrote the stories which make up *Dubliners* and started work on his first novel, *A Portrait of the Artist as a Young Man,* which he did not complete until ten years later. *Chamber Music* (1907) was his first published volume, a collection of delicate lyrics, Elizabethan in tone and grace. Composers have set these lyrics to music over and over again.

In 1904 he married Nora, daughter of Thomas Barnacle and Ann Healy, of Galway, "a sleek blond beauty." The young couple left Ireland for the Continent. In Trieste, where they settled, Joyce taught English at the Berlitz school, and later at the Commercial Academy. Italian he knew well . . . and seventeen other ancient and modern tongues, including Greek, Sanscrit, Arabic, and all the major languages of Europe. He even contributed some articles in Italian on Irish politics to *Il Piccolo della Sera*. At this time, according to an Italian acquaintance, he was "tall, thin, smooth-shaven (a member of the giraffe family, he used to say)."

About 1912 Joyce is said to have returned to Dublin, where for a short time he conducted (unsuccessfully) a motion-picture theatre, the "Volta." He was soon back in Trieste, remaining until 1914, the year of the publication in London of *Dubliners*, his book of short stories, and of the completion of the writing of *Portrait of the Artist*. *Dubliners* had been written about ten years before, a contract for its publication had been signed in 1906 and another in 1909, but Joyce's refusal to accede to the demands of the publishers for deletions and alterations in the manuscript had delayed its appearance.

War was declared and Joyce became a free prisoner in Trieste—a British citizen living in Austrian territory. He was forced to give up his job at the Commercial Academy. The Joyces packed up and moved to Zürich. There he found friends among the other Irish exiles and helped to found a company of "Irish Players," which gave the first performance of his play, *Exiles*. *A Portrait of the Artist* appeared serially in Ezra Pound's *The Egoist* in London from February 1914 to September 1915 and was published in book form in 1916. This 'first novel' is almost entirely autobiographical, and in its pages Stephen Dedalus, the protagonist, expounds many of the esthetic theories on which *Ulysses* (written in Trieste-Zürich-Paris, 1914-21) is based. In its intensely subjective, cadenced prose, it exposes the body and soul of Stephen Dedalus (James Joyce) from his boyhood thru the painful years of adolescence until his twenty-first year (1903) when he left Dublin for Paris, crying "Welcome, O life!" In Zürich Joyce began to suffer from a serious ocular illness. Much of *Ulysses* appeared serially in *The Little Review*, New York, (March 1918-August 1920) before its publication was stopped by the courts. In 1919 the Joyces returned for a while to

Trieste, where they lived with Joyce's brother, Stan. Soon they were bound for Paris, where they have remained.

Finally, in 1922, Joyce's monumental work, *Ulysses*, was published in Paris. Its sale is forbidden in Great Britain and the United States, and hundreds of copies have been burned by the authorities. Undoubtedly the most influential work of the twentieth century, *Ulysses* records a single day, June 16, 1904, (*Bloomsday* has been proposed as a holiday by some advocates of a reformed calendar) in the life of Stephen Dedalus and of Leopold Bloom, middle-aged, sensual, kind-hearted advertisement-canvasser of Jewish descent. Bloom symbolizes the modern Ulysses and the whole work is a vast series of correspondences with the Homeric epic. Stephen corresponds to Telemachus. The scene is Dublin and scores of Dubliners, famous and infamous (many of them identified by name), walk thru the pages of the book.

James Joyce's *Work in Progress*, of which portions have appeared in print (largely in *transition*, Paris), has been called "the most curious and intricate book the world has seen." It is based on the Italian Vico's theory of the "cycle of history," so that all history, all time and space, are telescoped and seen as the present. The characters have multiple personalities. The language itself is a "new language," most of the spellings being transformed to suggest new meanings from any number of other words in several languages.

The writing of both *Ulysses* and *Work in Progress* has suffered interruption from Joyce's recurrent attacks of blindness. He has submitted to a long series of operations in an effort to save his sight. Recently, when Joyce has been able to write at all, he has had to work on large sheets of white paper with a red pencil. He reads his copy with a magnifying glass, and dresses completely in white to intensify the contrast between the written word and other objects. Joyce himself does not believe that he will ever finish *Work in Progress*.

The Joyces live in a comfortable Paris apartment. The son is studying to be a singer, and the daughter to be a dancer. Margaret Anderson, in *My Thirty Years'*

War, speaks of Joyce's gentle bearing, kindliness, the deprecating humor of his smile, his quality of personal aristocracy. He gives "the impression of having less escape from suffering about irremediable things than anyone I have ever known. It was an impression borne out by nothing that he said so much as by the turn of his head, the droop of his wrist, the quiet tension of his face, his quick half-smile." He talks little, stopping short in the middle of a witty or pungent phrase to say: "But I am being unkind." Joyce's little beard conceals a scar inflicted by a mad dog when he was five years old. To this day he allows no dogs near him, but is devoted to cats. He wears large "flashy" rings, smokes a curious pipe, and still carries an ash walking stick. Music is his chief diversion. Mrs. Joyce, a charming woman with the gift of Irish mockery, who is reputed to tease and tyrannize him, considers her husband to be a great man in spite of "his necessity to write those books no one can understand."

The works of James Joyce: *Chamber Music*, verses (1907); *Dubliners*, short stories (1914); *A Portrait of the Artist as a Young Man*, novel (1916); *Exiles*, play (1918); *Ulysses* (1922); *Pomes Penyeach*, verses (1927); and these fragments from *Work in Progress*— *Anna Livia Plurabelle, Tales Told by Shem and Shaun, Haveth Childers Everywhere*.

GEORGE S. KAUFMAN

George S. Kaufman

GEORGE S. KAUFMAN was born in Pittsburgh on November 16, 1889. He was educated in the public schools. Before he became a newspaper man his occupations included stenographer for the Pittsburgh Coal Company, surveyor for the city of Pittsburgh, and traveling salesman for a concern that made shoe laces and hat bands.

"It was Franklin P. Adams (F.P.A.) who took me away from shoes," he relates. "He and Bob Davis are responsible. I contributed to *Always in Good Humor* for a couple of years and then Frank said that if I wanted to go to the *Washington Times* and try for a column there was an opening. That was in 1912

and they paid me $20 a week, and later raised it to $25. The column was called 'This and That' and most of the time was run seven days a week.

"My real business, tho, was playing stud poker at the National Press Club. That was what hardened my character. When I had been on the *Times* about a year I started toward the composing room one day and, as I opened the door quickly, I met Frank Munsey, the publisher, coming with equal speed from the opposite direction. It gave him an awful bump and he apparently went away and said 'Who was that?' Three days later I was canned.

"I came back to New York and, to get me out of the way, Frank Adams landed me a job as reporter on the *Tribune*. After he left the *Evening Mail* I did that column for about six months. They tried to give me various hints but I didn't take any of them, so they sold the paper with, I think, a special clause in the contract that stated that I was not included in the sale. I was on the town again, so they took me back on the *Tribune*, where I began dramatic work, which I have been doing ever since. That was the fall of 1915.

"Somewhere along in there, I took the course in playwriting given by Clayton

Hamilton and Hatcher Hughes up at Columbia." From the *Tribune* Kaufman went to the dramatic staff of the *New York Times*. In 1917 he married Beatrice Bakrow. They have one daughter.

Kaufman began writing plays in 1918 when he was co-author of *Someone in the House*. Since then he has written numerous Broadway successes, most of them in collaboration. His plays include: *Jacques Duval* (1920); *Dulcy* (1921); *To the Ladies* (1922); *Merton of the Movies* (1922); *Helen of Troy, New York* (1923), musical; *The Deep Tangled Wildwood* (1923); *Beggar on Horseback* (1924); *Be Yourself* (1924), musical; *Minick* (1924); *The Cocoanuts* (1925), musical; *The Butter and Egg Man* (1925); *The Good Fellow* (1926); *Strike Up the Band* (1927), musical; *The Royal Family* (1927); *Animal Crackers* (1928), musical; *June Moon* (1929); *The Channel Road* (1929); *Once in a Lifetime* (1930). He has collaborated frequently with Marc Connelly and twice with Edna Ferber—in *Minick* and *The Royal Family*.

Kaufman acted in his play, *Once In A Lifetime*, which played in New York during the season of 1930-31. It is a satire on Hollywood and the "talkies," written in collaboration with Moss Hart.

Sheila Kaye-Smith

A S Hardy was the writer of rural Wessex, so is Sheila Kaye-Smith the novelist of Sussex fields and farms. She has always lived in Sussex. Her father was Edward Kaye-Smith, member of the Royal College of Surgeons and Licentiate of the Royal College of Physicians. St. Leonards-on-Sea, near Hastings, was their home.

Miss Kaye-Smith published her first book when she was twenty: *The Tramping Methodist* (1908). It began a series of novels which portray Sussex of past and present. Hugh Walpole says: "She deals in timeless things, the soil, trees, rivers, corn, food and drink. She has timeless themes, birth, death, love, jealousy, patience, maternity, friendship. . . She is the creator of a little world."

Her point of view is masculine. A critic said he would not be surprised if a reader were to think Sheila Kaye-Smith the pen-name of a man because of the "virility, the cognizance of oath and beer, of rotating crop, sweating horses, account book, vote and snickersnee" in the writing.

The book that brought Miss Kaye-Smith to the notice of the critics was *Sussex Gorse* (1916), the story of the fierce and passionate love of a man for the savage common of gorse and furze known as Boarzell. He sacrifices everything in life for its possession. His words are the typical slow Sussex speech: "I've won—and it's bin worth while. I've wanted a thing, and I've got it surelye—and I äunt too old to enjoy it nuther." This passion for the land is a part of most of Miss Kaye-Smith's novels. Her rustics frequently use the expression "justabout", and they call women "praeper," ladies "valiant," and troubles "tedious."

With *Tamarisk Town* (1919) Miss Kaye-Smith greatly widened her circle of readers. She did not join the literary groups in London, however, but stayed in the land that was so much a part of her life, living with her family at St. Leonards.

In October 1924 she married the Reverend Theodore Penrose Fry, a clergyman in the St. Leonards-on-Sea

SHEILA KAYE-SMITH

parish. He is an M.A. and a captain of the Fifth Durham Light Infantry. His father was Sir John Fry, Second Baronet. Reverend Fry had been ordained in the Anglican diocese of Chichester. From St. Leonards-on-Sea he went to St. James, Norland, and finally served at St. Stephen's, Kensington, London. When he went to London Miss Kaye-Smith bought an ancient oast-house in Sussex so she could remain close to the land she loved.

In October 1929 she and her husband were converted to Catholicism. They were received into the Church by the English Jesuit, Rev. C. C. Martindale, at the Farm Street Church, London.

Miss Kaye-Smith appears small in stature, but is not really so. She is very thin, with a grace made all of quiescence. Her eyes are grey and retracted a little "as if always in pain because man is not so beautiful as the earth that bore him."

She is the author of two slender books of poetry: *Willow's Forge and Other Poems* (1914) and *Saints in Sussex* (1923). The range of the poems is wide and not a few are religious, even ecclesiastical, in subject. The mystical element is strong.

Miss Kaye-Smith's novels include. *The Tramping Methodist* (1908), *Starbrace* (1909), *Spell-land* (1910), *Isle of Thorns* (1913), *Three Against the World* (1914), *Sussex Gorse* (1916), *The Challenge to Sirius* (1917), *Little England* (1918), *Tamarisk Town* (1919), *Green Apple Harvest* (1920), *Joanna Godden* (1921), *The End of the House of Alard* (1923), *The George and the Crown* (1925), *Joanna Godden Married* (1926), *Iron and Smoke* (1928), *The Village Doctor* (1929), *Shepherds in Sackloth* (1930), *Mirror of the Months* (1931), *Susan Spray* (1931).

Eric Kelly

ERIC PHILBROOK KELLY was born in Amesbury, Massachusetts, on March 16, 1884. He attended grade school and high school in Colorado and New York. He received his A.B. from Dartmouth College in 1906 and began a career of journalism. He started as a

ERIC KELLY

reporter on the *Times* in Westfield, Massachusetts, where he was employed by the *Union* until 1911. The *Hunterdon Gazette* of High Bridge, N. J., claimed his services in 1912. He worked on the *Boston Herald* from 1914 to 1918.

Kelly left in 1918 for France where he did relief work among the Polish legions. He accompanied these men to Poland where he traveled and studied for three years. In 1921 he returned to the United States and became instructor in English and Slavic literature at Dartmouth. He spent his summers from 1922 to 1924 on the *Boston Transcript*.

On July 2, 1924, Kelly married Katharine Collins Merrill of Cumberland Center, Maine. In the same year he published a booklet, *The Medieval College*. He journeyed to Poland in 1925 where he was a lecturer and student at the University of Krakow in 1925-26 at the invitation of the Kosciuszko Foundation. During this period the plot for a book took shape. Kelly returned to his teaching at Dartmouth.

The Trumpeter of Krakow was published in 1928, Kelly's first full-sized book. It was awarded the John Newbery medal for the most distinguished contribution to American literature for children in 1928. The scene of the story is laid in Krakow where, as far back as man can remember, a trumpet signal has been blown every hour from the lofty parish church of St. Mary the Virgin. Making his hero a trumpeter on St. Mary's tower in about 1462, Kelly interweaves the hero's personal fortunes with the most momentous issues in Poland's politics of the time.

Because of his friendship with the people of Krakow and particularly with the mayor, Kelly was sent one of the ancient trumpets that had been used for centuries by trumpeters of the city. This trumpet has traveled over the United States and been played before countless American and Polish children.

Kelly is a member of the editorial board of the Dartmouth *Alumni Magazine* and was its managing editor in 1928-29. He became professor of journalism at Dartmouth in October, 1929. He is a member of the Modern Language Association of America, S.A.R., and Sigma Nu. He has received the Polish Gold Cross of Merit. He is a contributor to children's magazines.

A second book, *The Blacksmith of Vilno*, was published by Kelly in 1930. It is a tale of Poland in 1832, when the land was kept in constant turmoil by the Russians. The story centers round the lost crown of Poland, which the patriots hid and re-hid whenever the Russians were suspected to be on the trail of its hiding place. The book is for older boys and girls.

Kelly's published works are: *The Medieval College* (1924), *The Trumpeter of Krakow* (1928), and *The Blacksmith of Vilno* (1930).

Margaret Kennedy

BORN in London in 1896, Margaret Kennedy's world consisted of a large house and the "uncharted immensities" of Kensington Gardens nearby until she was ten. Then her family moved to Kent; later to Cornwall. Her first literary work was a play, "relentlessly moral," she says, "tho a trifle Communist," *The Rich Man, the Poor Man, and the Bicycle*. This was performed frequently by her small cousins and some neighbors' children, to whom it had to be taught orally as its author had not learned to read or write. She used to dictate stories, plays, and poems to any one who would write them for her until her laziness in learning to do this herself caused everyone to refuse to act as her secretary. She therefore found that there was more to authorship than she had counted on, and decided to go on the stage. After having to take exercises in carriage, deportment, and enunciation she concluded that it would be simpler and more comfortable to have no career at all.

She did learn to read and write, naturally, and was trained in the other customary elementary subjects. When she was fifteen she withdrew her savings from the bank and wrote her first novel, *Laura*. She burned it soon after, and wrote four more novels and three plays all of which she promptly destroyed. During this period she was attending Cheltenham school, where she lived in a universe of books and romantic dreams much more than in the actual world about her. She then studied in Somerville College, Oxford University, taking

MARGARET KENNEDY

a degree in history. Miss Kennedy is also an accomplished musician, and was a member of Sir Hugh Allen's famous Oxford Bach Choir which undertook "anything from Palestrina to a first performance of Gustav Holst from manuscript copies."

Shortly after receiving her degree she was commissioned to write a textbook on modern European history, the last of a series. This work, entitled *A Century of Revolution* (1922) took her two years and she attributes her future success in learning the technicalities of handling words to the careful arrangement and, condensation of the material required in its writing. When it was published she was already at work on *The Ladies of Lyndon*, which, when it appeared in 1923, did not receive much attention. *The Constant Nymph* was published in 1924, and was received enthusiastically in both England and America. The story had first occurred to her the preceding spring on her first visit to the Tyrol, when she had seen a place high on a mountain where she wanted to build a house. From this idea she created the Sanger family, a large, unruly group who lived there until the death of the father, a great musician, when conventional people came and took them away from their mountain home.

In 1925 Miss Kennedy married David Davies, a young English barrister who was formerly secretary to Lord Asquith, and they settled in a charming old house with high paneled walls, round the corner from Kensington Gardens. A liking of high places determined their moving with their small daughter to the only place in London where it is possible to live on top of a hill, Campden Hill Square.

Miss Kennedy paces rapidly back and forth in her study when working out intricate details in her writing, and frequently recites passages of dialog as it is being composed, because to her the ear is a better censor than the eye. Her greatest diversions are music, travel, and dancing.

Besides *The Ladies of Lyndon* (1923) and *The Constant Nymph* (1924), which she and Basil Dean dramatized in 1926, Miss Kennedy is the author of the following publications: *A Long Week-end* (1927); *Red Sky at Morning* (1927); *Come With Me* (1928, with Basil Dean), a play; and *The Fool of the Family* (1930), a continuation of the story of the Sanger family.

Rockwell Kent

ROCKWELL KENT has been called the only truly American artist among his contemporaries because he is American in birth, in training, in point of view, in execution, and in his success. His fame does not rest on painting alone, for his more recent activities in the field of book illustration would be alone sufficient to give him an outstanding place of honor. In addition he is the author of three books of adventure.

He was born in Tarrytown Heights, N. Y., in 1882. It is said that when he first showed unusual ability as a painter his parents were alarmed, because they could not afford an artist in the family. He was graduated from Horace Mann High School, New York City, and entered Columbia University's School of Architecture, where he was a brilliant student. During his fourth year there he decided to become a painter on visiting an exhibition at the Pennsylvania Academy. He studied with William N. Chase, Kenneth Hayes Miller, Robert Henri, and Abbot H. Thayer. At his first exhibition, at the National Academy of Design in 1905, two of his three pictures were sold. Three years later, at the age of twenty-six, he held another exhibition, and one of his paintings was purchased by the Metropolitan Museum, the first time so youthful an American had been honored.

Honors, however, did not bring riches, and Kent, with a wife and children to support, was obliged to turn to other means to earn a living. He taught school, dug wells, built boats, labored on a farm, worked as a carpenter, and tried his luck as a lobsterman. He wandered thru Maine, Massachusetts, Minnesota, and Newfoundland before his fortunes changed. The pictures he painted in Newfoundland brought him sufficient notice so that when he wanted to go to Alaska in 1917 he was able to incorporate himself for $5,000 by selling shares of Rockwell Kent Common. He took his youngest son to Alaska where they lived in solitude for a year in a house Kent built. Within a year after the publication of *Wilderness* (1920), in which his experiences in Alaska are recounted, he was able to buy back all the outstanding stock.

Kent returned from Alaska with a bundle of paintings that were immediately purchased by collectors. His work since then has been acquired by the Carnegie Institute of Pittsburgh, the San Francisco Museum, the Henry Frick estate, Adolph Lewissohn, Mrs. Harry Payne Whitney, and other noted individuals and institutions.

Rockwell Kent is as famous for his adventuring as for his art. *Voyaging*, published in 1924, was the result of a journey to Terra Del Fuego. He has always believed in following the path of strongest resistance. He prefers cold countries to the tropics, mountains to luxuriant valleys, seas to inland places, and he has often declared that the stark beauty of a sheer line appeals to him more than a landscape of rich growth.

His latest adventure was a trip to Greenland in the course of which he and two companions were shipwrecked. In June 1929 the party set sail in a 33-foot vessel, a stoutly built craft with the keel made of one solid oak beam. They left Labrador and crossed the Atlantic in ten days, a trip which is said to have been accomplished last by Bjornson in 1000 A.D., and only twice before attempted. Like their predecessors of centuries before, the Kent party met with disaster, but not until the Atlantic had been crossed and the destination was only fifteen miles away.

This trip is recorded in *N by E* (1930). The sloop was named by the owner, Arthur Allen, rather than by Kent who thought the name sinister—"Direction."

ROCKWELL KENT

Mr. Kent and his wife plan to leave for Upernavik in Greenland in the spring of 1931. He will engage in research for a book on the life of Eric the Red and the Norse discovery of North America. Mrs. Kent will return to their home near Ausable Forks in the Adirondack Mountains in upper New York state in September, but Mr. Kent plans to remain a year, using the place as a base for travel to other points, in the summer by boat, in the winter by dog-sled or walking across ice to the mainland.

Aside from his own books Mr. Kent has illustrated Voltaire's *Candide* (1928), Chaucer's *Canterbury Tales* (1929), Melville's *Moby Dick* (1930), and several other books. A recent job in oils is the largest mural decoration in the world, over six thousand feet of canvas, for a small theater, the Cape Cinema, at Dennis, Cape Cod.

Kent is of average height, muscular, with a smooth bald head and intense grey eyes. As one would expect of a man whose life is so spectacularly adventurous, he seems to thrive on opposition and is frequently engaged in quarrels with steamship companies, railroad lines, and other organizations. He was married first in 1909 and again in 1926, and has six children.

Rudyard Kipling

RUDYARD KIPLING, journalist, poet, writer of fiction, traveler, country gentleman, recluse, and imperialistic Anglo-Indian, was born in Bombay December 30, 1865. His maternal grandfather was a Methodist minister, Reverend George B. Macdonald, who had four daughters. The oldest, Georgiana, married the then impecunious young painter Sir Edward Burne-Jones. The second, Agnes, married an equally poor young artist who later became president of the Royal Academy and a baronet, Edward Poynter. The youngest daughter married a wealthy iron-master, Alfred Baldwin; their son is Stanley Baldwin, former Prime Minister of England.

The third daughter of this unusual group, Alice, met John Lockwood Kipling at a picnic near the village of Rudyard, for which their son was named. Kipling *pére* was then a young modeler and designer of terra cotta in the Burslem Potteries. He soon entered an art school in Kensington, and a short time later married Miss Macdonald and went to India as director of the Bombay Art School.

RUDYARD KIPLING

Until Rudyard Kipling was six he spent most of his time with *ayahs*, learned the native language and native stories and habits. He was sent to England to be educated but, owing to poor health, lived for five years in care of the wife of a retired naval officer in Portsmouth and did not go to school until he was eleven. He was then placed in the United Service College, Westward Ho!, in north Devon, a famous public school intended chiefly for the sons of Anglo-Indian civil and military officers. *Stalky & Co.* (1899) recounts many of his school-day experiences. During his last two years in school the young Kipling was editor of the *U. S. C. Chronicle*. On his graduation at the age of seventeen he was given the choice of going to college or returning to India; he chose the latter.

John Lockwood Kipling had moved from Bombay to Lahore where he was Director of the Lahore Museum, and it was to this city that Rudyard Kipling went. There, at the age of seventeen he became assistant editor of the *Civil and Military Gazette*. He had reached maturity, had an important position, had entrée into the highest social and political circles of the city, and altho he lived with his parents, had his own servants and apartment, his dog-cart, his friends, his club, and an interesting and attractive independent life. As a filler for columns he frequently wrote verses which became so popular that he was urged to publish them in book form. These appeared in Lahore in 1886 under the title *Departmental Ditties,* and in England in 1897.

After serving on the *Civil and Military Gazette* four years he went to the Allahabad *Pioneer* and traveled from the Himalayas to the ocean, living with the army on the frontier and covering special assignments for his paper. In 1890 he left India for England, by way of China, Japan, and the United States. He tried to find an American publisher, but failed. *Departmental Ditties* had won him a modest amount of fame in England, and altho he did not have immediate success, his stories soon became popular.

Kipling and Miss Caroline Balestier, an American girl, the sister of Wolcott

Balestier, with whom Kipling collaborated on *The Naulahka* (1891-92), were married in 1892, and settled in her native city, Brattleboro, Vermont. Two of their children were born there, and many of his famous books including the Jungle Books were written there before the family left on a trip to Africa in 1897. They then settled in a quiet little Sussex village, Rottingham-near-the-Sea. Altho Kipling never returned to America to live, he has revisited this country a number of times. So great was the impression he made that at least half a dozen states have named towns for him.

Kipling now lives in semi-seclusion at Bateman's, near the village of Burwash in Sussex. His only son was killed in the World War. Kipling, a rather slight man, clad most frequently in Norfolk jacket and knickerbockers, is fond of brisk walks. Altho in his sixty-sixth year, he is said to be almost boyishly youthful with springy step, quick nervous gestures, and animated voice.

Many honors and degrees have been conferred on this "poet of British Imperialism." He was awarded the Nobel Prize for Literature in 1907 and the Gold Medal of the Royal Society of Literature in 1926. The universities which have honored him include McGill in 1899; Durham and Oxford, 1907; Cambridge, 1908; Edinburgh, 1920; Paris and Strasbourg, 1921. He was Rector of the University of St. Andrews from 1922 to 1925. The first editions of his works are now valued higher than almost any other of his contemporaries; even the printer's proof of an issue of the school paper he edited at Westward Ho! brought $1,150 a few years ago.

Among the best known of Kiplings books are the following: *Plain Tales from the Hills* (Calcutta, 1888; London, 1890); *The Light that Failed* (Calcutta, 1890; London, 1891); *Barrack Room Ballads* (1892); *The Jungle Book* (1894); *The Second Jungle Book* (1895); *Captains Courageous* (1897); *Kim* (1901); *Puck of Pook's Hill* (1906); *The Eyes of Asia* (1918); *The Years Between* (1919); *Collected Verse: 1885-1918* (1919); *The Irish Guards in the Great War* (in two volumes, 1924); *A Book of Words* (1928).

Manuel Komroff

IN spite of the Russian sound of Manuel Komroff's name, he was born in New York City on September 7, 1890. He went to Yale, but left in 1912 without bothering to take a degree. He had studied engineering, but he soon switched to music and made his first money writing scores for some of the old Kalem pictures. Then he took a job as art critic for the *New York Call* and studied painting at the Independent School.

The excitement of the outbreak of the Russian Revolution about this time proved too much for his powers of resistance, and he went to Petrograd and got a job on the *Russian Daily News*. He soon found himself editor of the sheet, most of the others on the staff finding it more healthful to escape from the country as best they could. When the Bolshevists came into power, the paper died and Komroff, out of a job, made his way across Siberia to Vladivostok, arriving there just before the railroad was cut off.

He managed somehow to get to Japan

MANUEL KOMROFF

and for many months wandered in a more or less informal manner about the islands of the Japanese archipelago, living with the natives. From Japan he went to Shanghai and got a job on the *China Press,* where he worked for several months before going back to America.

He admits quite frankly that the years following his return were hard ones. He wrote editorials for the *Daily Garment News,* as many as three a day. Then for a year he went to at least twenty movies every week as a critic for *Wid's,* now known as *The Film Daily.* And all this time on the side he was writing short stories that had nothing to do with women's wear or movies.

Finally he joined the staff of Boni & Liveright, published a volume of short stories, *The Grace of Lambs,* wrote introductions for several volumes of the *Modern Library* and prepared *The Travels of Marco Polo* for publication in 1926. The same year he went to Rome and spent many months working in the library of the Vatican preparing a second book on Marco Polo.

His first novel, *The Juggler's Kiss* (1927), brought him high critical praise among a discriminating but limited circle of readers.

In 1928 Mr. Komroff left publishing work to devote all his time to the rewriting of *Coronet,* which established him as a popular witer. *Coronet* is a panoramic romance, extending from 1600 to 1919, its theme being the decay of aristocracy, symbolized by a jeweled coronet which passes from one generation to another of the Burin family. It had been conceived originally as a short story six years before, but grew to a two-volume novel.

Komroff's next novel, *Two Thieves,* is the story of the pair who were crucified on either hand of Jesus at Calvary. Before he started to write the book he read fifty-eight volumes and filled 723 pages with notes about Palestine.

Mr. Komroff's hair is red and his mustache is red and irregular, long at the sides, imparting to his face a look quite foreign and distinguished. His eyes are penetrating and inquisitive. He is above average height, slightly stooped in an attitude of constant attentiveness.

He is unaffected and there is a complete lack of pretense about him. He neither looks nor acts like a literary man.

Altho the editor of many important books, Mr. Komroff makes frequent mistakes in spelling. His slang is pungent and has the savour of New York streets. He says "ain't" and "boloney," which for some strange reason he spells "bolognny." His written sentences are straight, keen-edged, and polished. His signature looks like the marks one makes when telephoning.

Manuel Komroff is the author of: *The Grace of Lambs* (1925), *The Juggler's Kiss* (1927), *The Voice of Fire* (Paris 1927), *Coronet* (1929), and *Two Thieves* (1931).

Alfred Kreymborg

ALFRED KREYMBORG was born in New York City on December 10, 1883. He has known two things all of his life—music and chess; the first was shared by the entire family—mother, father, older brother, aunts and uncles; the second had its beginning when he was no more than six or seven when he used to stand on a box in his father's store and watch his father and one friend or another move chessmen across the board.

Troubadour (1925), Mr. Kreymborg's autobiography, tells of his childhood in New York's East Side. He was graduated from grammar school at the age of fourteen, won a chess championship among his classmates, and entered Morris High School. Between the time he was seventeen and twenty-five he supported himself largely by chess, playing anyone at so much a game at any hour of the day or night, teaching, playing in tournaments, of which he won many, barely losing to Chajes, then the Western champion. Chess had come to be too much of a drain on his physical and mental energies, and he discontinued it for nearly twenty years. He returned to the chess world recently, and may be seen again at the Manhattan Chess Club, where his name is entered as a life-member, with this self-imposed proviso, that he will be expelled immediately if he is "ever caught starting anything remotely resembling a serious game."

After two years in high school Mr. Kreymborg worked at several clerical jobs as much as his chess activities would allow. He then went to Aeolian Hall where he sold music, met Harold Bauer, Josef Hofmann, and other famous musicians. This further stimulated his love for music, in spite of the jazz and popular music he had to sell a great deal of the time. The influence of a young poet who was a co-worker at Aeolian Hall was largely responsible for his turning to music and literature.

A series of experiments, varying in the success of their outcome, followed. He has been editor of a number of magazines, including *The Glebe,* which he founded in 1914, and *Others,* neither of which is now in existence.

Never in the least aggressive, he met— at chess, thru friends,—practically every American poet of any note. Many were opposed to his ideals, many shook their heads disdainfully or sadly over the experiments he attempted and the hopes he had for poetry to be known, and to be created on every "Main Street" of America. With this in mind he made one trip across the continent, staying for some time in Chicago where he became friends with Vachel Lindsay, Carl Sandburg, Harriet Monroe, and others of the Chicago school of poets, and going on leisurely to the west coast.

This trip to the west coast was followed by a trip abroad in 1921 in the interest of an international magazine which was being founded of American parentage in Italy, to be devoted to all the arts. This magazine, *Broom,* was the most successful of all the magazines Mr. Kreymborg founded or helped to found, and was received most enthusiastically on the Continent, in England and the United States.

Mr. Kreymborg's belief in experimental art is demonstrated by his own writing as well as in the magazines he has sponsored. His Poem-Mimes, as they were first called, or Puppet Plays, as they are now known, were first presented in the Provincetown Theater on Mac-Dougal Street in Greenwich Village,

ALFRED KREYMBORG

and later by numerous Little Theatres and dramatic clubs all over the United States.

The same interest in the unrecognized led him, with Paul Rosenfeld, Lewis Mumford, and Van Wyck Brooks to initiate the *American Caravan,* editions of which have appeared in 1927, 1928, 1929, and 1931. This is a miscellany of the new American literature.

Mr. Kreymborg's publications include *Mushrooms* (poems, 1916); *Plays for Merry Andrews* (1920); *Less Lonely* (poems, 1923); *Lima Beans* (1925; in *Provincetown Plays,* Second Series, 1917); *Funnybone Alley* (sketches in verse, 1927); *Manhattan Men* (1929); *Our Singing Strength,* an outline of American poetry, 1620-1930 (1929); (edited) *Lyric America,* an anthology of American poetry, 1620-1930 (1930).

Mr. and Mrs. Kreymborg live in New York City. He is a popular lecturer and also, with the assistance of his wife, frequently gives some of his puppet plays before schools and clubs. He is a quiet man, slight of build, fond of good talk and a pipe. One of his outstanding characteristics is the generosity he has shown toward younger or little known writers. Late in 1930 the Kreymborgs visited England, where Mr. Kreymborg lectured on modern poetry at Oxford.

Joseph Wood Krutch

JOSEPH WOOD KRUTCH, critic and essayist, was born in Knoxville, Tennessee, November 25, 1893. He received his secondary schooling in that city, and entered the University of Tennessee in 1911 with the intention of studying engineering. On reading Shaw's *Man and Superman* his attention turned from mathematics and engineering to literature, his chief interest in it being primarily analytical and critical. He received his A. B. in 1915.

Mr. Krutch got his A. M. from Columbia University in 1916. He was a classmate of Mark Van Doren who also received an A. M. that year, and a close friendship developed between the two.

During the war he was a member of the Psychological Corps of the United States Army. Directly after (1919-1920), he spent the year traveling abroad on a Columbia University fellowship. He received a Ph. D. from Columbia in 1923 and was married the same year to Mlle. Marcelle Leguia of Hendeye, France.

From 1920 to 1923 he was assistant professor of English at the Polytechnic Institute of Brooklyn. His editorial work began in 1924 when he joined the staff of *The Nation* as dramatic critic

JOSEPH WOOD KRUTCH

and associate editor, which position he still holds. He was a special lecturer with the rank of Professor at Vassar College in 1924-25, and since 1925 he has been associate professor in the School of Journalism of Columbia University.

With Zona Gale, Glenn Frank, and Carl Van Doren, Mr. Krutch helped found the Literary Guild of America in 1926, and has remained on the Editorial Board since that time. He received a Guggenheim Memorial Fellowship in 1930 and went abroad for six months to work on an extended essay on esthetics. His permanent hime is in New York City.

Mr. Krutch is of more than medium height, very slender, with fair complexion and light sandy hair. Altho scholarly, reserved, and dignified, he is not aloof, but rather an engaging conversationalist and speaker.

As would be expected, Mr. Krutch's works are largely critical. His first publication in book form was *Comedy and Conscience After the Restoration* (1924) for Columbia University's series, Studies in English and Comparative Literature. He contributed an essay, "Modern Love and Modern Fiction," to *Our Changing Morality* (1925), a symposium edited by Freda Kirchwey. *Edgar Allan Poe: A Study in Genius* (1926) is regarded as one of the most thoro analyses of this author. Mr. Krutch prefaced and edited William Congreve's *Comedies* (1927). His best known work is *The Modern Temper* (1929), a comprehensive "statement of the modern intellectual who has weighed and rejected the moral, esthetic, and other values of his predecessors and who finds only in the pursuit of knowledge that which makes life worth living."

Five Masters: A Study in the Mutations of the Novel (1930) followed. With the desire to determine why certain writers are great, whether it is the result of contemporary conditions, because the author caught the particular tempo of the time, or whether he would have been great regardless of his time, he studied and interpreted the lives, personalities, and works of Boccaccio, Cervantes, Richardson, Stendhal, and Proust.

Oliver La Farge

OLIVER HAZARD PERRY LA FARGE—that name means an extraordinary heredity. Its bearer's ancestors include Benjamin Franklin and Commodore Perry. His grandfather was John La Farge, the great American painter whom Henry Adams called the world's greatest artist in stained glass since the cathedral of Chartres was built. His father is Christopher Grant La Farge, an architect of distinction. On his mother's side are the Lockwoods, New England sea captains, and the Bayards, who can boast five United States senators, a secretary of state, and the first full Ambassador to the Court of St. James.

He was born on December 19, 1901, in New York City. Most of his life has been spent in New England at Saunderstown, Rhode Island, not far from Perry's birthplace, Kingstown. As a small boy he was fascinated by the Indians. He called himself "Indian Man." This name became corrupted into an affectionate nickname by which he is still known among his intimates. He attended St. Bernard's School and Groton School in Massachusetts.

Oliver La Farge's mother was a friend and counsellor of President Roosevelt. To her house came such notables as Henry Adams, Owen Wister, John Jay Chapman, and William Allen White.

At Harvard La Farge's literary bent was marked. He was Class Poet for 1924; president of the *Advocate*, literary magazine; and an editor of the *Lampoon*, comic publication. He made three archaeological expeditions to the Indian country of Arizona and Utah for Harvard, and contributed a series of Indian stories to the *Advocate*. He received his A.B. in 1924. Tulane University, New Orleans, sent La Farge on two expeditions to Guatemala and Mexico in 1925 and 1927. A record of the first expedition is found in *Tribes and Temples* (1927), by La Farge and Blom. When he was in New Orleans between expeditions, La Farge sent to *The Dial* an Indian tale, *North Is Black,* which was published in January 1927. Edward J. O'Brien included the story in his *Best American Short Stories* for that year.

OLIVER LA FARGE

Subsequently he was connected with the Peabody museum expedition to Arizona. He published his scientific findings as well as an occasional short story. As an archaeologist, La Farge won the confidence of the Indians and learned their customs. He witnessed their religious ceremonies and his observations provided the key to historic Indian rites and practices. He is one of the few men who can "talk to the Indians and get anything out of them."

In his first novel, *Laughing Boy* (1929), La Farge tells a Navajo love story which grew out of his intimacy with the Indians. It is the record of the life and ideals of a young Navajo, Laughing Boy, and his mate, Slim Girl. It was awarded the Pulitzer prize for 1929.

La Farge married Wanden E. Mathews of New York City on September 28, 1929. Shortly after receiving news of the Pulitzer award in 1930, he left New York for Santa Fe and the Grand Canyon where he rode five or six hundred miles on horseback thru the Indian country before his return to the East and his literary and scientific work. He says his second novel will be laid in Central America, a setting vastly different from the American Southwest. He believes it unwise for a writer to stamp himself as a "type" by repeating the characters, theme, or background of his first success. His favorite living authors are Arnold Zweig and Julia Peterkin.

La Farge's face is bronzed so that he looks like an Indian. He is described by a friend as having "dark skin, dark eye-brows and hair, and a complexion shading from Indian red to ivory. He has a long jaw, walks like an Indian, and has the low swinging gorilla-like arms which often go with great strength. Indians have actually mistaken him for one of them."

La Farge has a deep feeling for the sea. He is at home in "anything from a Rhode Island dory to a skiff, which he skulls from the stern with one oar, Channel Island fashion." The desert has no greater hold on him than Rhode Island and the sea.

His books are: *Tribes and Temples* (1927) and *Laughing Boy* (1929). *North Is Black* appears in *A Modern Galaxy* (1930), a collection of short stories edited by Dale Warren.

Selma Lagerlöf

I N the province of Värmland, Sweden, on November 20, 1858, Selma Lagerlöf was born into a large family of brothers and sisters. She sprang from Swedish gentlefolk of the landowner class. Her father was a retired army officer and her mother was descended from a long line of distinguished clergymen. Their home was Mårbacka Manor, in Sunne.

The child was never strong enough to run wild over the farm with the others, so she sat at home in a deep chimney corner reading or listening to "stories about all the great and wonderful things which had happened in the world." She was allowed to browse in the ample family library and both parents helped in her reading.

In *The Story of a Story* (in her collection of short stories, *The Girl from the Marsh Croft*, 1908), Selma Lagerlöf tells about her own childhood, in the third person: "At the start it was not the girl's intention to write about the stories and legends surrounding her. . . When she tried to write, she chose material from her books. . . She went about at home on the quiet farm, filling every scrap of paper she could lay her hands on with verse and prose, with plays and romances." She was allowed to read Tegnér, Runeberg, and Andersen thru twice each winter.

At the age of nine the girl spent the winter with her uncle in Stockholm, where the old housekeeper would often take her to the theatre. After she returned home, she played theatre with her brothers and sisters on school holidays. She relates, in the present tense: "We have no prompt book, only my memory to guide us. It is I who, with the help of quilts and blankets, make the stage scenery and it is I who make up the actors." The family was the audience. In their favorite piece she played the dual rôle of heroine and of an old man with long white hair, using her generous yellow curls for the effect.

"From that day," she continues, "I long to write great plays and not to sit on a school-bench and waste my time in composition and arithmetic. . . At fifteen I have read all the poets in the house and have written my first verse."

Miss Lagerlöf went again to Stockholm at the age of twenty-two, and in 1882, after a year at Sjoberg's Lyceum for Girls, she entered the Royal Women's Superior Training College to prepare for teaching. She remained there three years. One day it suddenly dawned

SELMA LAGERLÖF

upon her that her own Värmland was rich in material for books and she determined to write a story of Värmland's Cavaliers.

Her studies completed, she went to Landskrona in the province of Skane to teach in the Grammar School for Girls. She wrote sonnets for Swedish magazines and told endless folk tales to her pupils after school. One Christmas holiday, back in Värmland, she planned the first chapter of her story while riding in a sleigh thru a blinding snowstorm. She wrote it in verse, then did it in the repressed realistic prose style which was the fashion in Sweden. Later she discarded that style for her natural romantic manner, full of exclamations and interrogations.

In 1890 Miss Lagerlöf won a prize offered by the magazine *Idun* with the first five chapters of *Gösta Berling*. The completed novel was published in 1894, when she was thirty-six. It is a wild, romantic book into which she gathered with youthful extravagance folk tales and legends of Värmland. Following the publication of her second book, *Invisible Links* (1894), King Oscar of Sweden and his son, Prince Eugen, extended financial aid to Miss Lagerlöf. She gave up teaching in 1895 and made a trip to Italy which resulted in *The Miracles of Antichrist* (1897). A trip to the Orient brought forth *Jerusalem* (1901). At the request of the Swedish school authorities for a school reader she produced two volumes of *The Adventures of Nils* (1906-07).

Miss Lagerlöf was created Doctor *honoris causa* at the Linnaeus Jubilee of the Upsala University in 1907. She received the Nobel Prize for literature in 1909, being the first woman to receive the award, and was made a member of the exclusive Swedish Academy in 1914.

A young woman journalist, Verlma Swanston Howard, interviewed the inaccessible Miss Lagerlöf one day. They grew to be fast friends and with her English version of *Jerusalem*, Mrs. Howard became Miss Lagerlöf's chief English translator. *Anna Svärd* (1928) was her tenth translation.

Miss Lagerlöf spends her summers at Mårbacka Manor, the place of her birth and the Liljecrona's Lovdalla of her sto-

ries. In winter she lives at Falun, Delarne, where *Jerusalem* was written. At Mårbacka she cultivates 140 acres of land and looks after fifty-three tenants. She has modernized the old manor but it still retains its old dignity and simplicity. It is a friendly house with wide verandas, white colonial pillars, fine old trees, and rose gardens.

From beneath a crown of white hair, Miss Lagerlöf's eyes look at and thru one, kindly yet penetratingly. Mrs. Howard gives an impression of her: "A woman of medium height, with a fine, fair face, splendid head superbly set on neck and shoulders. . . Her sense of humor was keen. There was a twinkle in her eye, a twist about the mouth, a certain sly humor that preceded her speech, while her chuckle was inimitable."

Some of Miss Lagerlöf's novels, with their dates of publication in Sweden (indicated by italics) and the United States, are: *Gösta Berling* (*1894,* 1899); *The Miracles of Antichrist* (*1897,* 1899); *Jerusalem* (*1901,* 1915); *The Emperor of Portugallia* (*1914,* 1916); *Bannlyst* (*1918; The Outcast,* 1922); *Mårbacka* (*1922,* 1924), the story of her home and tradition; *Charlotte Löwensköld* (*1925,* 1927); *The General's Ring* (*1925,* 1928), *Anna Svärd* (*1928,* 1931); *Queens of Kungähalla* (translated 1930); *A Child's Memoirs* (*1930*), a continuation of *Mårbacka*. *The Ring of the Löwens, *published here in 1931, contains three closely linked novels: *Charlotte Löwensköld, The General's Ring,* and *Anna Svärd.*

Her volumes of short stories include: *Invisible Links* (*1894,* 1899); *From a Swedish Homestead* (*1899,* 1901); *The Adventures of Nils* (*1906-07,* 1907-11); *The Girl from the Marsh Croft* (*1908,* 1910); and *Men and Trolls* (*1916*), in two volumes.

Ring Lardner

RINGGOLD WILMER LARDNER, humorist and satirist, was born March 6, 1885, in Niles, a town in the southwestern corner of Michigan, a few miles from Lake Michigan. He attended public schools there, being graduated from the high school in 1901. His mother

RING LARDNER

wanted him to be a minister, his father an engineer. Altho having no particular ambition or aptitude in either of these directions, he attended the Armour Institute of Technology in Chicago for two years.

Mr. Lardner went to South Bend, Indiana, as a reporter on the *Times* in 1905. He returned to Chicago in 1907 and for the next three years was successively sporting writer for the Chicago *Inter-Ocean,* the *Examiner,* and the *Tribune.* He was editor of *Sporting News* in St. Louis in 1910 and 1911, and between that time and 1919 when he became connected with the Bell syndicate he contributed to the sporting columns of the *Boston American,* the *Chicago American,* and other newspapers.

Mr. Lardner and Miss Ellis Abbott, of Goshen, Indiana, were married in 1911. For the last several years they and their four sons have lived in Great Neck, Long Island, where they have a considerable estate. They keep an apartment in New York also, where Mr. Lardner does some of his writing.

"A perfect example of the traditional conception of the humorist," is the description given of Mr. Lardner, who is ordinarily solemn almost to sullenness, his face long, his eyes brooding and deep set—"hypnotic," they have been called, his eyebrows thick and sharply rising. He is at least six feet tall, broad, big-boned, and lean.

He considers it a great misfortune to have the reputation of being a humorist because casual friends and strangers react to his most serious statements as tho these were hilariously funny.

Mr. Lardner says that for seven years he went to two hundred baseball games a year, including training camps and exhibition games. While on the *Chicago Tribune* he wrote the first of his *You Know Me, Al* stories (collected 1916); this sporting series introduced the racy baseball vernacular now so well known that it has been referred to as "Lardner's Ringlish." He soon had a large popular following, but it was not for years that critics took him seriously and a second audience developed, those who read him for the sardonic humor and cutting satire which is superficially obscured by the broader, comic humor. *How to Write Short Stories* (1924), a collection of his "yarns," with a preface of burlesque instructions for beginners, and a series of humorous notes connecting the tales, was largely responsible for the growth of this second group of readers.

Altho primarily a short story writer, Mr. Lardner prefers to work on songs and plays. When sports writer he wrote songs for a quartet of White Sox baseball players which he formed; these songs are said to have been sung "feelingly" at various world series games. He and George S. Kaufman, the playwright, collaborated on *June Moon,* a comedy produced with great success in New York in 1929-1930. Mr. Lardner's cynical humor is particularly noticeable in this work.

He is author of a number of books, among which are: *Bib Ballads* (verse, 1915); *Guillible's Travels* (1917); *Treat 'Em Rough* (1918); *The Big Town* (1921); *Round Up* (selected stories previously published in magazines and in his other volumes, 1929); *June Moon* (1930).

Rosamond Lehmann

ROSAMOND LEHMANN, youthful English novelist, inherits her literary talents from both her parents. Her mother, who was Alice Marie Davis before her marriage, comes of the same family as Owen Davis, the American playwright. Her father, the late Rudolph Chambers Lehmann, was at one time on the editorial staff of *Punch* and was better known as one of the greatest oarsmen England ever produced. He had several books to his credit.

In private life Miss Lehmann is the wife of Wogan Phillips, painter, who is the son of Sir Laurence Phillips, the shipping magnate, and a nephew of Lord Kylsant and Lord St. Davids. Mr. Phillips recently held an exhibition of his paintings in London. Miss Lehmann's first husband was Leslie Runciman.

Miss Lehmann began writing verse for her own amusement at the age of six and still maintains that she prefers this medium of expression to prose, altho she has not yet seen fit to submit any of her verses for public approval. She is an inveterate reader, and altho she feels that in her actual writing she has not been influenced in her style, if she could be influenced by anybody it would be Walter De la Mare of whom she is an ardent admirer.

Dusty Answer, published in 1927, was an extraordinarily successful first novel. It is the story of an English girl, an only child whose playmates are the children next door. The story follows the group from childhood to early maturity. The girl's several loves are thwarted by disillusionment or death so that to all her eager questionings life gives a "dusty answer." The phrase is from Meredith.

In *A Note in Music* (1930) Miss Lehmann wrote again of people whose lives are streaked with eagerness and disillusion. This time they are older. As a reviewer puts it, "they ask less and they have learned to wall away despair. Their rebelliousness has lost much of its thrust. . . They listen, this time, with still faces, to the inevitable dusty answering of life." The characters are middle-class English people. To Grace Fairfax, married, childless and approaching middle-age, the beauty and youth of

ROSAMOND LEHMANN

Hugh Miller is like a bright note in music, bringing out a wistful nostalgia for past love, and at the same time desire to carry on in the future.

Miss Lehmann's novels are: *Dusty Answer* (1927) and *A Note in Music* (1930).

Henri René Lenormand

HENRI RENÉ LENORMAND, French dramatist, was born in Paris on May 3, 1882. His father is René Lenormand, a prominent writer and musician who is famed for his translations of *L'Anthologie de l'Amour Asiatique* and of poems from the Chinese, Persian, and Polynesian. In his childhood Lenormand became familiar with Oriental music, and to his father he owes the exotic touch which plays an important part in his work and gives it an African and Oriental trend. He was educated at the Lycée Janson de Sailly, and later obtained a degree at the Sorbonne.

Lenormand made his literary *début* with a modest book of prose-poems called *Paysages d'Ame*. Dealing with such themes as desire, illness, and anguish, they were written as he traveled across Scotland, England, and parts of the Continent. Some time later he shocked the audience at the Grand Guignol in Paris with a two-scene thriller entitled (in translation) *The White Folly*. Then he proceeded with longer plays.

As an apprentice in the theatre, Lenormand came under the spell of Ibsen. He caught the tone of defiance, the challenge of accepted standards. Later, puzzled by the human mind, he accepted the teachings of Freud. Thereafter, he has devoted himself to the abnormal, with instinct at war with conscience as the common *motif*. He takes symbols of the unconscious and puts them in dramatic form, creating men and women who act out little dramas with their own fateful natures.

The young playwright's first three-act drama, *Les Possédés,* was produced in 1909 at the Théâtre des Arts in Paris, under the direction of Robert d'Humières. In 1911 he married the actress, Marie Kalff, who has played in many of his dramas. *Poussière,* another three-act play, was staged by Firmin Gémier in 1914 at the Théâtre Antoine. Then he

turned to a new form and most of his subsequent plays have been written in a series of what he calls *tableaux* rather than acts—brief glimpses of people at chosen moments in their careers. Usually the series of episodes depicts a moral descent, a process of gradual disintegration.

Practically unknown until after the World War, Lenormand became one of the foremost dramatists in France within a few years' time. He met public favor for the first time in Geneva, Switzerland, where the actor-manager Georges Pitoëff produced successively *Le Temps est un Songe* and *Les Ratés*. These plays were acclaimed when they were brought to Paris on the stage of the Théâtre des Arts, *Le Temps est un Songe* in December 1919, and *Les Ratés* in May 1920. Since that time Lenormand's work has been widely played— Paris, London, Vienna, Berlin, Amsterdam, Geneva, Warsaw, New York. *Les Ratés (The Failures)* was produced by the Theatre Guild of New York in 1923.

In December 1920 Gémier founded the Comédie Montaigne and summoned Gaston Baty to stage Lenormand's play, *Le Simoun*. It was Baty's first big work and, with Gémier in the cast, it was highly successful, running for more than one hundred consecutive performances. It has been frequently revived in Paris, tho suppressed (because its theme touches on incest), in London, Copenhagen, and Algiers.

The author relates that a passage in Neitzsche, which he had read as a child, inspired this play. "It is this idea of the variation of human instincts according to climate," he says, "that sent me Southward (to Africa) where I met nearly all the secondary characters of *Simoun*: the honest tester of weights and measures; the Arab servant with the thundering voice; the prostitutes, like beautiful poisonous insects.

"I then had a desire to create a drama which should enrich French life with an exotic atmosphere like that of the novels of Loti, Conrad, and Kipling. What came of these idle fancies? Two plays, begun too soon, miscarried, begun anew,

HENRI RENÉ LENORMAND

retouched, and which still seem to me to be far from perfection: *A l'Ombre du Mal* and *Le Simoun.*"

Other plays by Lenormand that have been produced are: *Le Mangeur des Rêves* (1922); *La Dent Rouge* (1922); *L'Homme et ses Fantômes* (1924); *A L'Ombre du Mal* (1924); *Le Lâche* (1925); *L'Amour Magicien* (1926); *Mixture* (1926), which ran for a hundred performances; *L'Innocente* (1928), a one act play; *Une Vie Secrète* (1928).

Always harshly dealt with by many critics and literary groups, Lenormand has brought his unique drama to the fore aided by the enthusiasm of others among the critics, and the producers Gémier, Pitoëff, and Baty. Gémier regards him as "the dramatist who has made the strongest impression upon our theatre."

He is a member of the Coopérative du Théâtre des Arts and of the reading committee for La Chimère. When a group of sixty writers founded the Théâtre des Jeunes Auteurs, he was unanimously elected president. His home is in Paris.

Lenormand's plays require unusual staging. Baty produced the thirteen tableaux of *Le Simoun* by using one permanent frame, pierced at the back by two openings, vaguely indicating the African landscape. He used yellow and blue curtains to divide intermediate scenes. The stage was lit from the back of the auditorium. When Pitoëff staged *Mangeur des Rêves*, he draped the stage in black velvet, crossed by bands of another color and material. These strips and figures were modified, during the nine scenes, according to the place and time and mood involved, as a "symbolic commentary" on the text.

Les Trois Chambres, produced at the Théâtre Edouard VII in Paris in February 1931, shows three rooms at once on the stage. They are the adjoining hotel bedrooms of a writer, his wife, and his mistress.

The translations of plays by Henri René Lenormand include: *Failures* and *Time is a Dream* (1923); *Three Plays* (1928), containing *The Dream Doctor*, *Man and His Phantoms*, and *The Coward*.

Jonathan Leonard

THE publication of Jonathan Leonard's first book, *Back to Stay*, has an unusual history. This book was written in 1920 and 1921; *The Meddlers* three years later. Mr. Leonard, being unsuccessful in finding a publisher for either book, decided to become printer-book binder-publisher himself. He bought a hand press, the necessary type, and a book sewing frame and plow and with no experience and no aid except the information given in printers' and bookbinders' manuals, printed and bound nearly a hundred copies of *Back to Stay*.

Mr. Alfred Kreymborg, who has proved himself consistently a friend of the little-known writer, was at Cape Cod Bay at that time and became acquainted with Mr. Leonard. He was enthusiastic over *Back To Stay* and *The Meddlers*, which he read in manuscript. Part I of *The Meddlers*, "Carolus Elston," appeared in the second *American Caravan* in the fall of 1929.

A representative of a New York publishing house became interested in Mr. Leonard at the same time and his com-

JONATHAN LEONARD

pany published *Back To Stay* and *The Meddlers* in 1929. A third novel, *Sympathetic to Bare Feet,* appeared in 1931.

Mr. Leonard has had a quiet, yet diversified life. Born in Sandwich, Massachusetts, on Cape Cod Bay, in 1875, he attended Harvard University, as did his father and grandfather, and received both a Bachelor's and a Master's degree there. His interest was divided between Romance languages and painting. He studied both in Paris for a few months, and continued to study them at Columbia University, after his return, for a year.

Mr. Leonard taught for several years, at the Newark Academy, the Milton Academy near Boston, and the Evans School in Arizona. He returned to Sandwich where, by arrangement with the Dean of Harvard, he tutored boys in his own home. During the years he taught near Boston he continued his art courses, attending the Boston School of Fine Arts. He was also an officer during the world war.

The interests of all the members of the Leonard family are artistic. Mr. Leonard has largely substituted writing for painting, but there are paintings in his home done by him within the last few years. Mrs. Leonard is well known as an artist. She is the originator of the popular Cape Cod map, and also designed the jackets of her husband's books. Her secondary interest is the theater, particularly the marionette and puppet stage and plays. A son, Jonathan Norton Leonard, who lives with Mr. and Mrs. Leonard in Sandwich, is author of *Loki; The Life of Charles Proteus Steinmetz,* which was published in 1929. A daughter, Mary, was very active in dramatics while in Radcliffe College, and is in Boston at the present time continuing her study of the theatre, with the intention of directing.

Mr. Leonard is a fine-featured man of medium height, mild in manner, with grey hair and luminous eyes.

William Ellery Leonard

WILLIAM ELLERY LEONARD was born in Plainfield, N. J., on January 25, 1876, the son of Rev. William James Leonard. When he was a

WILLIAM ELLERY LEONARD

child of two and one half years he was waiting for his father at the Plainfield railroad station one day, when he was stricken with an unearthly terror by the onrushing locomotive. It was going to kill him, he thought. It was God. The terror of the vision never left him.

In 1898 Leonard received his A.B. degree from Boston University where he was an instructor in Latin for a year. In 1899 he was principal of the high school at Plainville, Massachusetts, and received his A. M. from Harvard. During the next three years he was a fellow in philology and literature at Boston University and a student at the University of Göttingen and the University of Bonn. He served a fellowship at Columbia in 1902-03 and received his Ph.D. there in 1904. While he was editor of *Lippincott's English Dictionary* (1904-06), he published his first book, *Byron and Byronism in America* (1905).

Leonard went to the University of Wisconsin in 1906 as instructor in English. His first book of poems, *Sonnets and Poems,* was published that year. He became an assistant professor in 1909. He married Charlotte Freeman on June 23, 1909, and she died May 6, 1911. In 1914 Leonard took his second wife, Charlotte Charlton. He was visiting professor at New York University during the school year of 1916-17, and was made an associate professor at Wisconsin in 1921 and a full professor in 1926. He became known for his philology course in which he maintains a high standard of scholarship.

Meanwhile several books of poems were published and Leonard's outstanding poetical work, *Two Lives,* a sonnet sequence based on his tragic first marriage, was privately printed in 1923 and offered to the public in 1925. His autobiography, *The Locomotive God,* appeared in 1927. The childhood terror of the locomotive which still haunts his soul prompted the title.

Leonard delights in walking along the sloping shores of Lake Mendota in Madison, but poor health will not permit him to venture more than half a mile from his home on Murray Street. Many nights he wanders down Murray Street to the railroad tracks to watch the locomotives switching by. He wants to impress his subconscious mind that the engines are harmless; to discipline the Locomotive-God—the symbol of horror which is implanted within him.

On his walks he wears a brown corduroy Norfolk jacket, closefitting breeches, tan stockings to his knees, and a jaunty brown hat. Usually he carries a hickory cane in one hand, a cigarette in the other. He looks every inch the poet. His eyes are luminous. A friend mentions his physical traits: "Whitening hair, tawny and long; large nose and mouth, both none-the-less acutely sensitive for their pronounced masculinity; an incisive glance, betokening mental alertness and physical vigor, never meant to be artificially impressive or embarrassing. An 'artist's' necktie, usually purple, loosely knotted in a bow; not an affectation, but a natural tie for Mr. Leonard."

Leonard is a member of the Modern Language Association of America; the National Institute of Arts and Letters; the Wisconsin Academy of Letters, Arts and Sciences; the Wisconsin Archaeological Society, and Beta Theta Pi. He belongs to the University Club in Madison.

His volumes of poetry include: *Sonnets and Poems* (1906); *The Vaunt of Man* (1912); *Poems, 1914-16* (1916); *The Lynching Bee* (1920); *Two Lives* (1925); *A Son of Earth* (1928), his collected verse; *This Midland City* (1930). Among his translations are: *Fragments of Empedocles* (1908), *Lucretius* (1916), and *Beowulf* (1923). He is the author in prose of *The Poet of Galilee* (1909) and *The Locomotive God* (1927), among other books. He has written several cycles of songs and paraphrases on the fables of Aesop. He is a contributor to magazines, technical journals, and newspapers.

D. B. Wyndham Lewis

DOMINIC BEVAN WYNDHAM LEWIS, best known in this country for his lives of Villon and Louis XI, is not to be confused with the artist and author, Percy Wyndham Lewis. They are not related in any way, and except for their names they are entirely dissimilar in appearance and in the character of their works. This Wyndham Lewis is known in England as "Beachcomber"; his column "By the Way," in the London *Daily Express,* resembles the journalistic departments of Heywood Broun and Christopher Morley in this country.

The writer gives this informal sketch of himself: "Born 1894 of a family reasonably old but lately decayed, rooted in the counties of Carmerther and Pembroke (Wales). One distinguished member about the end of the XIII century—one Rhys ap Lewis, counsellor of Llewellyn ap Griffith, the last ruling Prince of Wales (slain 1282). Since then the clan has declined into obscure small squires and clergymen, unknown to fame. I passed my earliest years in the library of a country rectory, and am probably one of the few men in the world who has ever read the sermons of Jewell and the *Ecclesiastical Polity* of Hooker at a tender age: and damned awful they were, and are. Educated thenceforth at reasonable expense, I was intended to read for the law and would have proceeded to do so at the University of Oxford, had not the Great War broken out to my greater relief. Joined the Army on September 1, 1914, as a

D. B. WYNDHAM LEWIS

private soldier in an infantry regiment, and by the time of the Armistice I had risen, without influence, social or political, to the rank of second-lieutenant. Went to France early in 1915, went into trenches, disliked them, kept on disliking them, disliked them more and more and then got shell shock (twice). This has influenced my outlook to some degree. In 1916 was sent to the Macedonian front, when I had malaria about eight times seriously, filling in the intervals with boredom and malaria. Early in 1918 invalided, by way of Malta, to England and just as I was getting out for the French front once more Armistice broke out. Demobilized late in 1918.

"In 1919 I thought of journalism, for some reason and joined the staff of the *London Daily Express* as a colyumist, conducting the "By the Way" column under the pseudonym of "Beachcomber." After four years of this I left the *Daily Express* and have since written a weekly article of an alleged light nature for the London *Daily Mail,* which I still do. I have also recently finished a play which may or may not see the London stage shortly."

He is, according to himself, "impulsive, lazy, easily imposed upon (except by the Grave and Good), temperamental, distinctly Celt, full of strong loves and hates and generally unpleasant."

Mr. Lewis lives in St. Germain, near the house once occupied by Madame De Maintenon, and he knows Paris with a thoroness possible only after years of residence there.

Among his publications in this country are: *François Villon* (1928); *King Spider,* some aspects of Louis XI of France and his companions (1929); *On Straw and other Conceits* (1929). He has also translated Barbey d'Aurevilly's *Anatomy of Dandyism* (1929) and edited an anthology of bad verse, *The Stuffed Owl* (1930), in collaboration with Charles Lee.

Sinclair Lewis

THE first American to win the Nobel Prize for Literature, Sinclair Lewis, was born February 7, 1885, in Sauk Center, Minnesota, 110 miles northwest of the twin cities of St. Paul and Minneapolis. His father, who had been born near New Haven, Connecticut, was the doctor in this prairie village of twenty-five hundred persons, and frequently he was driven on his rounds by his young son, who occasionally assisted in emergency cases. Lewis's maternal grandfather was also a physician, who had come from Canada during the Civil War to fight for the Union and had later settled in Minnesota. Lewis has a surgeon brother and a doctor uncle.

The boyhood of the now-famous novelist was typically middle-western. He was a thin, nervous, red-headed boy, distinguished in no way except for an intense interest in reading, his study of Greek with an Episcopalian minister, and a desire to study French. He was no athlete and near the bottom of his class in his grades. His decision to go east to school rather than to attend the University of Minnesota further branded him as queer.

At Yale where he went in 1903 he became known as "Red," an epithet that still sticks to him, both because of the color of his hair and because of his radical ideas. He was distinctly a nonconformist, uninterested in fraternities and the usual extra-curricular activities,—a raw lank boy tolerated somewhat affectionately as a freak. In his senior year he edited the *Yale Literary Magazine.* He received his A. B. in 1907.

For a while Lewis was a disciple of Upton Sinclair, and joined his socialist and Utopian colony, Helicon Hall, in New Jersey. He was the janitor; the community cooks were an M. A. and a lawyer; Emma Goldman and other prominent persons were there at the time.

Lewis began to make a meager living by writing verse and jokes for *Life* and *Puck*. He unexpectedly got a job as assistant editor of the now defunct *Transatlantic Tales*, which he held until he decided to go to Panama to work on the canal. He took steerage passage there, was unsuccessful in finding work, returned to the United States, and subsequently went to Waterloo, Iowa, then to San Francisco, where he reported on the *Bulletin*. He was next editor of the *Volta Review*, a magazine for the deaf, before joining William Rose Benét, another Yale alumnus, at Carmel, California. The two young men lived together in a portable bungalo, on a borrowed hundred dollars, for six months. During those months both wrote a great deal, but the only thing Lewis was able to sell was a single joke to *Judge*.

In 1910 Mr. Lewis went east again, and took an editorial job with Stokes. Two years later he became assistant editor of *Adventure*, then editor of the *Publisher's Newspaper Syndicate*, and finally editor and advertising manager of the George H. Doran Company. He left there in 1916, to devote all his time to his own writing.

Miss Grace Livingston Hegger, of New York City, and Lewis were married in 1914. They lived in Long Island and while commuting to his New York office the ambitious young author wrote most of *Our Mr. Wrenn* (1914) and *The Trail of the Hawk* (1915). Neither book was given a particularly favorable reception, but Lewis had begun publishing short stories as well. After he had begun to free lance the Lewises wandered all over the United States. A son, Wells, was born in 1917. During this time *The Job* (1917), *The Innocents* (1917), and *Free Air* (1919) were written.

Main Street (1920) was the first book to bring Lewis's name before the entire American public. It had been conceived in 1905 while he was a student at Yale. A sensational success, the book was at-

SINCLAIR LEWIS

tacked bitterly as being an unfair picture of small-town American life, and it was also defended as showing the characteristic vices of a democratic people. *Babbitt* (1922), written in England and Italy, also aroused antagonism and respect. *Arrowsmith* (1925) was planned in Hartford, Connecticut, where the Lewises had settled on their return to America. The author went to New York to do the painstaking research work necessary for a book dealing with medical school days and the life of a scientist, and met Dr. Paul de Kruif, who had just left the Rockefeller Institute for Medical Research. Together they traveled thru the Virgin Islands, the Barbados, Trinidad, Venezuela, to London, discussing the scientific details of Dr. Arrowsmith's career which Dr. de Kruif was able to supply. The book was finished in a cottage on the edge of the Forest of Fontainebleau, the same *petit château* in which George Moore had lived while writing one of his books. Lewis refused the Pulitzer prize of $1000 in 1926 for *Arrowsmith* as a protest against the restrictive terms of the award.

Mantrap followed in 1926. *Elmer Gantry* (1927), a satire on religious charlatanry, created a violent disturbance. Just as many cities had taken a perverted pleasure in claiming to be "Main Street," a number of ministers reviled Mr. Lewis for having drawn the Reverend Elmer Gantry from themselves.

Mr. Lewis's other books are *The Man Who Knew Coolidge* (1928), and *Dodsworth* (1929), the first a satire on political conditions, and the second on Americans abroad. Lewis lived in England while writing *Dodsworth* and toured the country in a motor "caravan." He says that he will never write another novel in a European setting. He is the author also of *Hobohemia* (1919), a play which was produced in New York.

Mr. and Mrs. Lewis were divorced in 1925. In 1928 he was married to Miss Dorothy Thompson, newspaper correspondent and author of *The New Russia* (1928). They have a farm near South Pomfret, Vermont. Their son, Michael, was born in 1930.

Lewis is one of the most popular American writers in European countries, and practically all his books have been translated into several languages. In accepting the Nobel Prize at Stockholm from the Swedish Academy in 1930, Lewis lived up to his reputation as a non-conformist and firebrand by his vehement speech in which he attacked the professors and men of letters who would subject American literature to conventional standards of taste and morals.

"Mr. Lewis possesses the most astounding energy of any writer I have ever come into contact with," writes Burton Rascoe. "He is thin, angular, and wiry. His head sometimes nods and his hands have tremors from highly strung nerves. He can play, dance and talk all night, deliver two lectures the next day, and play again the next night." At parties he frequently exercises an admirable talent for mimicry. Impetuous and fearless, he never runs from any sort of argument. After a recent public quarrel with another novelist, Lewis remarked: "I'm just a country hick living on a farm, and every time I leave it I get into trouble."

Wyndham Lewis

ALTHO an Englishman, Percy Wyndham Lewis was born in the United States, in Maine, in 1886. He was brought up in England and trained as a painter. When barely fifteen he entered the Slade School, the famous art school of London University, and before his next birthday had obtained a prize usually awarded to much older students. A year and a half later he left and became a wandering student on the Continent, painting, writing, and reading. He copied Franz Hals in Haarlem, Goya in Madrid; he wandered about Brittany and Spanish Galicia, his earliest writings being about the scenes and people in those places.

For a time he sat under Bergson, who was then lecturing at the Collège de France in Paris, and took a philosophy course at the University of Berlin. For some months too he painted in Munich under a Turkish master.

On his return to England in 1911 he had some of his stories accepted by Ford Hueffer (now Ford Madox Ford) for the *English Review*. While he was still undecided whether to be a painter or a writer, he met Roger Fry and was persuaded to enter the latter's Omega Workshops, a communal artistic enterprise based on William Morris's ideas, and for some time devoted all his energy to painting. The result was the organization in January 1914 of the sensational Cubist Room exhibition, which Ezra Pound hailed as the birth of a new school: Vorticism. Mr. Lewis was the leader and spokesman for the Vorticists.

Mr. Lewis proved himself a splendid propagandist for this new school of painters. His arresting appearance may have had something to do with his success as publicist for the Vorticists. Montgomery Belgion speaks of his "ample body stowed into a black jacket and nondescript trousers, and his head almost entirely concealed inside a black sombrero . . . not to mention the huge black horn-rimmed spectacles and the great black pipe screening what little of his face was not hidden by the hat."

His most widely advertised stunt was the decoration of the walls of the upstairs room in the Eiffel Tower Restaurant in London with a series of Vorticist frescoes, which not only made good "copy" for the newspapers but incidentally made the fortune of the restaurant.

In June 1914 Lewis launched, in cooperation with Ezra Pound, the explosive review, *Blast,* another outcome of his propagandist activities, with provocative illustrations by various Vorticists. After the second and final number of *Blast*—the "War Number"—Lewis enlisted in the Royal Artillery, gained a commission, and saw considerable active service. He found time, however, to finish his first novel *Tarr,* on which he had meditated for eight years. It appeared serially in the review, *The Egoist,* during 1916 and 1917, and at the end of that year it was published in book form, receiving an unusual critical reception. When he returned to civilian life he found the conditions for art very bad. Abandoning the Vorticists, he dashed off a violent appeal, *The Caliph's Design: Architects, where is your Vortex?*—started another review, *The Tyro,* which he had almost at once to abandon—and then disappeared into retirement. The following years were spent in study and foreign travel.

Nothing more was heard of Wyndham Lewis until 1925, when he published *The Art of Being Ruled,* a long essay which revealed him as a social philosopher. This was followed by *The Lion and the Fox; A Study of the Role of Hero in the Plays of Shakespeare* (1926) and by *Time and Western Man* (1927). It became evident that Mr. Lewis had been driven by what he construed to be the attitude of contemporary society towards the artist to study and write about the fundamental philosophic assumptions of that society. In *Time and Western Man* he bitterly assailed the Time-and-Flux idea.

In February 1927 appeared the first number of a review perhaps even more remarkable than *Blast.* This was *The Enemy,* a one-man magazine, wherein his vigorous assaults against current philosophic doctrines and his vitriolic denunciations of contemporary writers have first appeared. In 1928 was published the first section of *The Childermass,* which Mr. Lewis terms a sort of

WYNDHAM LEWIS

prose epic. Childermass-day is the festival of the Holy Innocents massacred by Herod. In Mr. Lewis's book the Holy Innocents are the souls that on the other side of death assemble in great concentration camps to suffer judgment before being admitted to heaven. *Wild Body* (1928) was a book of short stories, followed by *Paleface; The Philosophy of the Melting-Pot* (1929), *The Diabolical Principal* (1930), and *Apes of God* (1930), said to be a satire on the Sitwells.

Ludwig Lewisohn

"**J**EWS of unmixed blood and descent who had evidently lived for generations in the North and North East of Germany" gave heritage to Ludwig Lewisohn, who was born on May 30, 1882, in Berlin. His father and mother were first cousins. He was an only child but had a large circle of aunts and cousins. A dreamy lad, Ludwig shrank from his playmates, not thru timidity but because they interrupted his imaginings. In his autobiography, *Up Stream* (1922), he recalls how he read Grimm and Andersen and other fairy tale writers "until my eyes ached and my forehead was fevered." He was not a

LUDWIG LEWISOHN

delicate child, however, but "sturdy and broad-chested."

At the age of six Lewisohn was sent to a "gymnasium" where he received instruction in "reading, writing, arithmetic, singing, gymnastics, and 'religion.'" He was "hopelessly stupid at figures" and liked best the class in "religion." His parents might easily have had him excused from that course, but they were liberal. As Lewisohn recalls, "All the members of my family seemed to feel that they were Germans first and Jews afterwards."

Lewisohn's father suffered a breakdown following financial ruin and the family emigrated to America when Ludwig was eight years old. They settled in a small village in South Carolina where he had an uncle. Since there were no public schools in the village his mother tutored him in English. He began to write verse in German at the age of ten.

When his father failed in storekeeping the family moved to Charleston where he entered high school at the age of eleven. One day a teacher pointed to him and said, "That is the only boy who has an ear for verse." From that moment he realized that he was destined for a literary career and he determined to become a professor of literature. He gave up speaking German at home and read English classics, especially Dickens and Macaulay. "At the age of fifteen," he recalls, "I was an American, a Southerner and a Christian." He attended the Methodist church. A Charleston newspaper printed his verses as well as his articles and book reviews.

Lewisohn was graduated from high school at the age of fifteen and he entered the College of Charleston where he received his A.B. and his A.M. degrees in 1901. He had been heretofore subject to little discrimination because of his race, but he received a blow when his college crowd formed a Greek letter fraternity and left him out. He spent two years at Columbia where he took an A.M. in 1903 and received another blow when he failed to get a teaching job because he was a Jew.

The youth served on the editorial staff of Doubleday, Page & Company in 1904 and 1905. When Joel Chandler Harris founded *Uncle Remus' Magazine* he bought one of Lewisohn's stories. Lewisohn married Mary Arnold Crocker in 1906 and spent the next five years writing for magazines, living frugally in New York City. He trained himself, meanwhile, to be a novelist on Flaubert, James, Conrad, and George Moore. Theodore Dreiser liked the manuscript of his first novel, *The Broken Snare* (1908), and helped him secure a publisher for it.

In 1910-11 Lewisohn was an instructor in German at the University of Wisconsin, and he was an assistant professor of German language and literature at the Ohio State University from 1911 to 1919. In 1914 the College of Charleston granted him a Litt.D. degree. In 1919 he joined the staff of *The Nation* as dramatic editor and from 1920 to 1924 he was an associate editor. His novel *Don Juan,* based on his marital experience, was written in New York in the summer heat of 1923. Lewisohn relates that he postponed work on it until the last moment and, after repeated urgings from his publisher, wrote it in twenty-nine days. He spent the years 1924 and 1925 traveling in Europe and the Near East studying the Jewish problem.

He had identified himself unmistakably with his native race.

Lewisohn found in Europe the leisure he wanted for his writing. The year 1927 found him in Paris where he sat down one day and wrote, without erasure or correction, the first thousand words of a novel. The second day he wrote a thousand words, and the same on the third day. He says in *Mid-Channel* (1929), a continuation of *Up Stream,* that he "put the story down as it flowed . . . unpremeditated from my pen. . . At the end of four months and a half I had written without pause or hesitation the one hundred thousand words that constitute *The Case of Mr. Crump* (1927).

He established his residence in Paris, where his apartment is filled with specimens of ancient Hebrew and Jewish craft—china, pewter, and illuminated documents. He taught himself Hebrew and Yiddish, and delved deeply into the Babylonian Talmud. He became a "one hundred per cent Zionist."

"In spite of his pronounced Jewish cast of features," writes Sisley Huddleston, "Lewisohn, with his high forehead, his clean-cut face, his long hair brushed back, bears a striking resemblance to the current portraits of Goethe."

Lewisohn's novels include: *The Broken Snare* (1908), *Don Juan* (1923), *Roman Summer* (1927), *The Case of Mr. Crump* (1927), *The Island Within* (1928), *Stephen Escott* (1930), and *The Last Days of Shylock* (1931). Among his critical essays and studies are: *The Modern Drama* (1915), *The Spirit of Modern German Literature* (1916), *The Poets of Modern France* (1918), *The Drama and the Stage* (1922), *The Creative Life* (1924), *Israel* (1925), and *Cities and Men* (1927). He wrote a play, *Adam* (1929).

Joseph C. Lincoln

JOSEPH C. LINCOLN, who writes about sea folk, was born on Cape Cod, in the town of Brewster, Massachusetts, February 13, 1870. His father was a seaman and all his ancestors had been seamen. When he was a year old his father died of a fever in Charleston,

JOSEPH C. LINCOLN

South Carolina, and his mother took Joe to Boston. In summer, however, the boy got back to the Cape for fishing and swimming. He knew the fishermen and the lightkeepers. Altho he was an outdoor boy, he showed an artistic turn and built himself a miniature theatre. He went to school at Brewster and Chelsea, Massachusetts.

College was out of the question. The youth was to become a business man, so he and his mother moved to Brooklyn and he got a job in a broker's office. He hated the work. He wanted to draw, so under the guidance of Henry Sandham he settled in Boston where, with a partner, he went into commercial art work. To make the pictures sell better he often wrote verses or jokes to go with them. The verses sold better than the pictures. In 1896 he became associate editor of the *League of American Wheelmen Bulletin.* He wrote verse for publication and in 1897 he married Florence E. Sargent of Chelsea. They have one son, Joseph Freeman, who collaborated with his father in the writing of a novel, *Blair's Attic* (1929).

In 1899 Lincoln went to New York to try to make a living as a writer. His poems were mostly in the Cape Cod vernacular. He sold his first short story, a Cape Cod narrative, to the *Saturday*

Evening Post. His first book was *Cape Cod Ballads* (1902). He was busy writing short stories, but Saturday nights he worked on a novel, *Cap'n Eri,* which was published in 1904. It is the story of three old sea captains who, despairing of their joint efforts at housekeeping, advertise for a wife. Since *Cap'n Eri,* Lincoln's novels have appeared with annual regularity, or even more frequently.

A friendship with Sewell Ford led Lincoln to become a resident of Hackensack, New Jersey, where he built a Colonial house. There he attends the Unitarian Church and was at one time a member of the Board of Education. Golf is his principal diversion at Hackensack. Every summer he takes his family to Cape Cod where their home stands on a terrace at Chatham. There he fishes, swims, sails, and talks with the people who compose the characters in his books.

Each day from nine in the morning until noon Lincoln spends in his workshop, frequently a place known only to himself, and writes with a soft, stubby pencil on large sheets of yellow paper, or plans his stories. He does not approve of quick composition. "In my case, doing work that is satisfactory to me in any degree means that I must fairly sweat it out."

In 1912 Lincoln and his family lived for a while in England and traveled on the Continent. He travels round the United States a good deal, delivering lectures on "Cape Cod Folks" or giving readings from his books. He belongs to the Players Club of New York.

Lincoln is a red-cheeked, rotund, comfortable man, with bright eyes and a friendly smile. He has a great fund of stories, mostly about sea characters. When he talks he clips his words a little and sometimes says "hev" and "hed," and there is a touch of the Down East nasal twang in his talk.

He reads all sorts of books and has no favorite author. He reads a story for the story's sake and he likes or dislikes the characters "in the old-fashioned way." He does not care for the modern "problem novel." He says "there's enough sorrow in this world without finding it in books." His own stories

are always cheerful and inevitably end happily.

Mr. Lincoln's many novels include: *Cap'n Eri* (904), *Mr. Pratt* (1906), *Our Village* (1909), *The Postmaster* (1912), *Shavings* (1918), *Rugged Water* (1924), *The Aristocratic Miss Brewster* (1927), *Silas Bradford's Boy* (1928), and *Blowing Clear* (1930).

Vachel Lindsay

NICHOLAS VACHEL LINDSAY was born in Springfield, Illinois, on November 10, 1879. His home for many years was next door to the executive mansion of the State of Illinois and from the window where he did youthful writing he saw governors come and go. He graduated from the Springfield High School in 1897 and attended Hiram College for three years.

He wanted to be an artist. "I came up to Chicago," he relates, "and got a job in Marshall Field's wholesale department and registered for the night school at the Art Institute, but I had to work overtime every night but two during the first term, so I didn't get much out of that winter, I was determined to get an art education tho, and I did. For three years I was a student at the Art Institute, and while I was there I wrote some poetry. But I didn't think of myself as a poet."

Then Lindsay went to New York with a portfolio under his arm and high hopes in his heart. There he studied at the New York Art School under Chase and Henri in 1904 and 1905. "I tried to get the magazines to let me draw pictures for them," he continues, "but none of them would. I tried to get a job as a newspaper reporter. Finally I got so desperate I was willing to do anything, but I couldn't even shovel coal. I was beaten, but I couldn't go home beaten. You can't, you know. So I made up my mind I'd be a tramp and a beggar. I expected to have as hard a time that way as I had had in New York and I'll never forget the emancipation that filled my soul when the second man I ever asked gave me supper and a bed for the night for the single asking. From that day I was free.

"I made two trips thru the east that way, reciting some of my verses now and then, and leaving copies of the only poem I had printed. When I knew what I could do I decided to collect the verses which the magazines had refused and start on a long tramp thru the west, with them as my only currency. That little leaflet was the one called *Rhymes to be Traded for Bread.*"

He lectured for the West Side Y.M.C. A. of New York City in the winters from 1905 to 1908. In the spring of 1906 he tramped thru the southern states distributing *The Tree of Laughing Bells.* He lectured for the Springfield Y.M.C.A. in the winter of 1908-09 and was a lecturer for the Anti-Saloon League thruout central Illinois in 1909-10. In the summer of 1912 he walked from Illinois to New Mexico distributing rhymes and speaking in behalf of "The Gospel of Beauty."

General William Booth Enters Into Heaven (1913) was Lindsay's first book. Then he recorded *Adventures While Preaching the Gospel of Beauty* (1914). In 1914 he published his second volume of verse, *The Congo and Other Poems,* which has been described as "an infectious blend of rhyme, religion and ragtime." The novelty of syncopated sound in poetry caught people's fancy and his innovation succeeded at once.

The Congo as well as later poems reflected Lindsay's contacts with the Southern Negroes. Some of his verse is deliberate adaptation of Negro pulpit oratory and some of it imitates the exotic rhymes and figures of the Negro religious folk-songs.

Lindsay usually writes about things that are noisy, colorful, vigorous, exciting, romantic, animated—the McKinley-Bryan election, a wild Negro jamboree, the breaking-in of a colt, the entry of a Salvation Army general into Heaven, buffaloes stampeding, a tribal dance in Central Africa, or the noise of trains and automobiles on the Santa Fe Trail. The sounds in the syllables and rhythms of his verse describe the themes.

His poems are definitely written to be read aloud, to be crooned, chanted, declaimed, or even, on occasion, to be sung to some popular tune. Lindsay adeptly chants his own works and is in constant demand for public lectures and readings.

VACHEL LINDSAY

He has read his poems before the English departments of many schools and universities in the United States.

When he recited his poetry in England some years ago a hearer wrote: "He has an admirable equipment in a voice ranging easily from a harsh outcry to a fluty sweetness. He is a young man with gleaming eyes in a mobile actor's face. He tells you first in easy conversational style how he came to write the poem, and then, throwing his head far back and shutting tight his eyes, he becomes the sensitive instrument thru which his emotions blow into music."

In 1925 Lindsay married Elizabeth Connor of Spokane, Washington. They have a daughter and a son. They now live in Springfield, in his "hereditary castle"—the home of his parents. He is a member of numerous clubs and organizations.

His books of poems include: *General Booth Enters Into Heaven* (1913), *The Congo* (1914) *The Chinese Nightingale* (1917), *The Daniel Jazz* (1920), *The Golden Whales of California* (1920), *Collected Poems* (1923), *Going-to-the-Sun* (1923), *Going-to-the-Stars* (1926), *The Candle in the Cabin* (1926), *Johnny*

Appleseed (1928), *Every Soul is a Circus* (1929), and *Selected Poems* (1931). Among his prose works are: *Adventures While Preaching the Gospel of Beauty* (1914), *The Art of the Moving Picture* (1915), *A Handy Guide for Beggars* (1916), *The Golden Book of Springfield* (1920), and *The Litany of Washington Street* (1929). Many of his books are illustrated by his own drawings.

Walter Lippmann

"**L**IBERTY," Walter Lippmann says, "is not so much permission as it is the construction of a system of information independent of opinion." This is a theory with which he set forth while yet in his youth and which later developed into an outstanding trait of his character.

Walter Lippmann was born on September 23, 1889. After attending the private schools of New York City, he entered Harvard in 1906, where he devoted most of his time to the study of

WALTER LIPPMANN

philosophy and psychology. In 1912 he became secretary to Reverend George R. Lunn, Mayor of the City of Schenectady. The influence of this period and of his study of Freud is revealed in his book, *A Preface to Politics* (1913), which he published at the early age of twenty-three. He married Faye Albertson in 1917.

Mr. Lippmann became associate editor of *The New Republic,* but this career was interrupted by the War. He went to Washington in 1917 as assistant to Newton M. Baker, Secretary of War and as secretary to the organization directed by E. M. House assisted in preparing data for the Peace Conference. In 1919 he returned to resume his work at the *New Republic.* It was then that he published *The Political Scene,* shortly followed by *Liberty and the News.* The latter booklet was called forth by his opposition to the injustice of the American press in distorting news concerning Russia.

His liberalism, however, does not merge into radicalism. He does not believe in the clear-sightedness or strength of the crowd. The crowd is ignorant and he does not assume that there is a cure for it. But "I assume merely that in spite of the public's ignorance it can throw its weight on the side of reason and I try to show how it can defeat reasonable men," he says.

In 1921 he joined the editorial staff of the *New York World.* It was at this time, tho the demands of his position were strenuous, that he began working on his best known book, *A Preface to Morals* (1929). Here he sets forth his belief that what is required for successful conduct in this modern society of ours is objectivity and loyalty to reality rather than to persons and desires. He contends, also, that both intuition and scientific knowledge go to prove that virtue is the means to happiness.

Mr. Lippmann became editor of the *New York World* in 1929, a position that he held until the demise of this famous newspaper in February 1931. After a trip abroad, he will join the editorial staff of the *New York Herald Tribune* in the fall of 1931.

Hugh Lofting

HUGH LOFTING'S separation from his own youngsters during the World War led him to become a creator of illustrated stories for children. He was born in Maidenhead, Berkshire, England, on January 14, 1886. He is as much Irish as he is English. His early childhood was spent at home with his parents and brothers and sisters. To these latter he liked to tell stories. As a treat, his mother used to take him to visit a pet shop in London where he gazed longingly at the puppies. He went away to a Jesuit school in Derbyshire when he was eight and from that time he was at home only on occasions.

If, as a boy, he determined on any career for his future, it was not that of author-artist. Journeys to unexplored lands and quixotic travels held the greatest lure for him. He came to America and attended the Massachusetts Institute of Technology in 1904-05 and then returned to England to complete his technical training at the London Polytechnic in 1906-07. After a short career as an architect he became a civil engineer and visited Canada, Africa, and the West Indies in the exercise of his profession.

In 1912 Mr. Lofting gave up engineering to devote his time to writing and settled in New York. On February 22, 1912, he married Flora Small of New York City. The first story he wrote was about culverts and a bridge. Then he started writing short stories for grown-ups, which were published in magazines. It did not occur to him to make his own illustrations. Purely technical plans for architectural and engineering work were the only drawings he had made.

Mr. Lofting enlisted in the British Army in 1916 and served in Flanders and France in 1917-18. He was wounded in June 1917. His account of how he came to create the character of Doctor Dolittle follows: "My children at home wanted letters from me—and they wanted them with illustrations rather than without. There seemed very little of interest to write to youngsters from the Front; the news was either too horrible or too dull. And it was all censored. One thing, however, that kept forcing itself more and more on my attention was the very

HUGH LOFTING

considerable part the animals were playing in the World War and that as time went on they, too, seemed to become Fatalists. . .

"If we made the animals take the same chances we did ourselves, why did we not give them similar attention when wounded? But obviously to develop a horse-surgery as good as that of our Casualty Clearing Stations would necessitate a knowledge of horse language.

"That was the beginning of the idea: an eccentric country physician with a bent for natural history and a great love of pets, who finally decides to give up his human practice for the more difficult, more sincere and, for him, more attractive therapy of the animal kingdom. . . This was a new plot for my narrative letter for the children. It delighted them. . ."

After the war, in 1919, Mrs. Lofting persuaded the children, Elizabeth and Colin, to release their beloved letters long enough for her husband to show them to a publisher who immediately accepted them. When *The Story of Doctor Dolittle* was published in 1920, Mr. Lofting was showered with letters from children asking for more about the Doctor and suggesting things they would like to have him do. The result was a series of books, appearing yearly, with illustrations by the author.

Mr. Lofting was awarded the John

Newbery Medal for "the most distinguished contribution to American literature for children" in 1922 for his second volume, *The Voyages of Doctor Dolittle* (1922). His books that followed were: *The Story of Mrs. Tubbs* (1923), *Doctor Dolittle's Postoffice* (1923), *Doctor Dolittle's Circus* (1924), *Porridge Poetry* (1924), *Doctor Dolittle's Zoo* (1925), *Doctor Dolittle's Caravan* (1926), *Doctor Dolittle's Garden* (1927), *Doctor Dolittle in the Moon* (1928), *Noisy Nora* (1929), *Gub-Gub's Book* (1931).

Mr. Lofting retains a youthful appearance. May Lamberton Becker says: "His hair is bright, and tho he cuts it close, it is so thick and wavy that there seems a lot of it. His color is sunbrown and he has outdoor eyes of keen grey-blue."

Since the war, the Loftings have lived in New England. He has been eagerly sought after as a lecturer and his illustrated talks to children are popular. He lives in the country where he keeps four dogs. One of the dogs is "Swizzle," a fox terrier, that he and his children picked out in the London pet shop of his boyhood days. Mr. Lofting belongs to the Players and Dutch Treat Clubs of New York. His wife died in March 1927.

John L. Lowes

PROFESSOR JOHN LIVINGSTON LOWES, one of the greatest of living scholars of English literature, is most characteristically seen hurrying up the broad steps of the Widener Library in the Harvard Yard, a briefcase stuffed with papers in one hand and a heavy green bag of books in the other. He is a small man, weighing about 100 pounds. In his sixty-third year his neat mustache and his sleek black straight hair show no inclination to turn grey. With his slight wiry body, his pointed face, his springing step, his quick and tireless activity, he resembles nothing so much as a bantam cock in the fierceness of his energy. His voice, coming from so slight a frame, is surprisingly deep and resonant. With his pupils he is friendly and informal, genuinely interested in the young men's progress and problems. He is a chronic

smoker and has the rather absent-minded habit of stuffing his lighted pipe into his pocket before class, so that more than once, in the midst of a lecture, a peculiar smell, as of something burning, has worried his audience—followed shortly by an outpouring of smoke from the clothes of the professor.

The precision of his mind is such that it is not at all surprising that he should have begun his academic career as a teacher of mathematics. The range of his detailed knowledge in English literature is remarkable: he has conducted courses in Anglo-Saxon, Chaucer, the pre-Elizabethan period, Milton, the Romantic Movement of the early nineteenth century, the Victorian poets, and the modern novel. He is also an authority on Shakespeare, modern poetry, semantics, philology, and Coleridge. Coleridge is his great love, and to the study of his works he has devoted many years of his life. In his research for *The Road to Xanadu,* a book that puts to shame the performance of any mere detective with its minute unraveling of the threads of the poet's subconsciousness, Professor Lowes actually read (word for word) in the course of some nine crowded years, all the books that Coleridge had read or might have read during the whole period of his poetic maturity. It will be recalled that Coleridge said of himself, "I have

JOHN L. LOWES

read almost everything." Working principally from the careful (if sometimes enigmatic) records and notes that Coleridge kept, Professor Lowes heroically assimilated the same gallimaufry of odd printed matter, meanwhile attending to his numerous classes, acting as Dean of the Graduate School of Arts and Sciences at Harvard (1924-25), delivering guest lectures on occasion, contributing to American and foreign philological and literary journals, carrying on his extensive private reading, and leading an active social life. Together with the universal lore of the student and lover of books, queer unexpected bits and rags of knowledge, obscure and fantastic, are tucked into the corners of his mind; reminding one of Coleridge's own tantalizing memories of "alligators and albatrosses and auroras and Antichthones; with biscuit-worms, bubbles of ice, bassoons, and breezes; with candles, and Cain, and the Corpo Santo; Dioclesian, king of Syria, and the daemons of the elements; earthquakes, and the Euphrates," and so on, down to the "swoons, and spectres, and slimy seas; wefts, and water-snakes, and the Wandering Jew." His speech is savory of literary allusion—a characteristic, too, of his written style.

Professor Lowes' critical sympathies are with the Romanticists, altho the classic literatures are at the foundations of his learning. Faculty meetings at Harvard are said to be enlivened by frequent exchanges of wit between Lowes the Romanticist and Irving Babbitt the Humanist and Classicist. It is reported that at one meeting, when Professor Babbitt was particularly severe with all things labeled Romantic, Professor Lowes drew upon the Scriptures to reply, "In my Father's house are many mansions." Whereupon the Humanist retorted, "Yes, but they are on different floors."

John Livingston Lowes was born in Decatur, Indiana, on December 20, 1867. He received his A.B. degree from Washington and Jefferson College, Pennsylvania, in 1888 and taught mathematics there until he received his A.M. in 1891. He studied abroad in 1894-95 at the Universities of Leipzig and Berlin, returning to the United States to become professor of English at Hanover College,

Indiana. He was married to Mary Cornett of Madison, Indiana, on June 23, 1897. They have one son, John Wilber.

In 1902 he left Hanover College to study at Harvard, where he received his second A.M. in 1903, and his Ph.D. two years later. He was subsequently professor of English at Swarthmore College, Pennsylvania, 1905-09; and at Washington University, St. Louis, 1909-18. In 1918 he was appointed professor of English at Harvard University, where he has remained. As the first incumbent of the visiting professorship established by George Eastman, he lectured at Oxford University in 1930-31.

The books of Professor Lowes are: *Convention and Revolt in Poetry* (1919), in which, relating the old poetry with the new, he designates the continuous actions and reactions in English poetry,—convention giving way to revolt, which itself hardens into convention; *The Road to Xanadu* (1927), his exhaustive study of the genesis of Coleridge's two great poems, *The Rime of the Ancient Mariner* and *Kubla Khan;* and *Of Reading Books* (1929), an essay.

He is the editor, with George Lyman Kittredge, of synonyms in the *New International Dictionary;* and he has edited Shakespeare's *All's Well That Ends Well* (1912) and *Hamlet* (1914). In 1928 he edited the *Selected Poems* of his late friend Amy Lowell.

E. V. Lucas

EDWARD VERRAL LUCAS describes himself modestly in *Who's Who* as "writer, and chairman of Methuen & Co., publishers; a member of the Royal Commission on Historical Monuments (England) since 1928." A list of more than fifty publications follows; then: "Address: 36 Essex Street, W. C. Clubs: Athenaeum, Buck's, Burlington Fine Arts, Garrick, Orleans."

He was born in 1868 at Brighton, and was educated at University College, in London. He entered journalism, and was for a time on a Sussex newspaper. He then went to London on *The Globe*, and began to contribute to *Punch*, finally leaving *The Globe to* become assistant editor of *Punch,* which position he held

E. V. Lucas

for years. He also became a reader for Methuen & Company, Limited. After serving on the Board as an editorial adviser for some time, he became Chairman of the company in 1925, on the death of its founder.

Mr. Lucas is a remarkably versatile writer. His literary career began in 1898 with a volume of verse, and in the forty odd years since then he has written biographies, novels, essays, anthologies, travel books. In all, including the books he has edited, his name appears on considerably more than one hundred title pages.

He is perhaps most popular as a light essayist. His volumes of collected essays include *Fireside and Sunshine* (1906); *Old Lamps for New* (1911); *Adventures and Enthusiasms* (1920); *Fronded Isle, and Other Essays* (1928); *Traveller's Luck* (1930).

His novels, whimsical and imaginative, are called "entertainments." There are over a dozen in all, among them: *Listener's Lure* (1906); *Landmarks* (1914); *The Vermillion Box* (1916); *A Rover I Would Be* (1928); *Windfall's Eve* (1929); *Down the Sky* (1930).

Mr. Lucas has written a great deal of poetry for children, and has compiled several anthologies; a few titles from this group are: *A Book of Verse for Children* (his first published book, 1898); *Forgotten Tales of Long Ago* (1906); *Runaways and Castaways* (1908); and *The Cat Book* (1927).

An indefatigable traveler, a student and lover of art, Mr. Lucas is familiar with all the art galleries of note in England, on the Continent, and in America. He has written much art criticism for periodicals. Many of his travel books are unconventional and charming guide books, others deal more specifically with art criticism. *The Open Road* (1899); *Highways and Byways in Sussex* (1904); and *Introducing London* (1925), bear witness to his fondness for walking expeditions. Among his books on art and travel are *A Wanderer in Paris* (1909); *A Wanderer in Florence* (1911); *A Wanderer in Venice* (1914); *Vermeer of Delft* (1922); *A Wanderer Among Pictures* (1924); *A Wanderer in Rome* (1926); and *Vermeer the Magical* (1929).

Early in his career, when he was on *The Globe*, he conducted a humorous column, "By the Way." This led to his collaboration with Mr. C. L. Graves, author of *The Life of Hubert Parry* and a member of the staff of *Punch*. Several volumes came from these collaborators: *Wisdom While You Wait, Hustled History*, etc.

Mr. Lucas is said to know everybody. He is a cricket enthusiast. He is an entertaining conversationalist and has an inexhaustible supply of information about persons and events in literary circles, altho he frequents that world less than others, and is said to be partial to the company of actors, prize-fighters, non-writers of all vocations. His closest personal friends among authors in America are Christopher Morley and Don Marquis.

As to his physical characteristics, he is youngish in appearance, rather tall, rather heavy without being over-weight, and very light on his feet. His dark hair is shot with grey, his nose prominent, his complexion ruddy. He is considered "mysterious," for, while having a wide range of friends and acquaintances and being one of the best known men of letters in England, very few people can feel that they know him in the least.

Emil Ludwig

EMIL LUDWIG was born in Breslau on January 25, 1881. His father was Hermann Cohn of Breslau University, a celebrated ophthalmologist, and his grandfather was a leading iron and steel man in Upper Silesia. His father gave him the name of Emil Ludwig at birth because he wished to spare him the difficulty of bearing a Jewish name in a country where feeling against Jews runs high. Emil Ludwig himself has always emphasized his Jewish ancestry. His father's scientific work in behalf of public health caused the young man to take up the study of social welfare; but even the acquisition of a Doctorate of Jurisprudence could not kill his enthusiasm for literature.

At fifteen Ludwig became interested in playwriting, and between the ages of twenty and thirty he wrote twelve plays, all in verse, six of which have been staged. Until he was twenty-five, he "engaged in legal and mercantile pursuits." In his late twenties he married Elga Wolff, a South African of German-English extraction. They have two boys. "Until I was thirty I had never written a word of prose," he recalls. But in 1911, in the course of his first attempt to dramatize the life of Bismarck, he "hit upon a new form of portrayal" in Bismarck's letters. He took the Iron Chancellor's prose style as his model, and dropped the poetry. Shortly before the World War—in the spring of 1914—Herr Ludwig went to London as the correspondent for a daily paper. "Up to that time, my thirty-fourth year," he comments, "I had never seen an editorial room from the inside. I had never sent a news item over the wire. I had never even contributed a single 'stick' to a daily paper."

During the war he continued his journalistic activities in the chief political centers of lands allied to Germany. "I learned more than I achieved!" he remarks. "Three novels, and a number of travel pictures are all I have to show for it. Being the son and pupil of democratically inclined intellectuals, before the war I never lent my pen to the service of the princes, during the war I never used it against any of the peoples, and since

EMIL LUDWIG

the war I have always devoted it to the cause of the republic—while reserving to myself the right of championing always and everywhere the doings of men of mark."

After four years of newspaper work he gave it up to write books with the remark: "Journalism enabled me to see the world, to meet men and to understand the under-current of politics." His novel, *Diana,* made its appearance in 1918. Its sequel was *Quiet Sea* (1919). When the two were published in America they appeared in one volume, *Diana* (1929).

Herr Ludwig turned to biography and wrote *Goethe* (1920), a dramatic study. He published eleven books between 1918 and 1928, mostly biographical. They were all published in America between 1927 and 1929. The volume to give him world-wide fame was *Napoleon* (1924), published in America in 1927, and it led to an immediate demand for translations of his other books. His *Bismarck: the Story of a Fighter* (1926) is a full-length portrait of "a victorious and errant warrior," the history of a spirit that was a blend of pride, courage, and hatred.

July '14 (translated 1929) is an exposition on the origins of the World War. *Three Titans* (translated 1930), contains sketches of Michelangelo, Rembrandt, and Beethoven, emphasizing their resemblances. The author shows that the art of all three has technical as well as emotional similarity. *Schliemann* (1931) is the life of the great German archaeologist who discovered the site of ancient Troy. These titles indicate the range of Ludwig's studies.

Ludwig, as a biographer, states: "It has been my main endeavor to depict noteworthy personalities and remarkable destinies in biographical analyses. What chiefly interests me is the interaction between genius and character. In this connection the English were the first to realize that the "all-too-human" should be emphasized rather than ignored by the biographer. That is the principle which has guided me in my pen portraits of Goethe, Napoleon, and a number of other men of action and men of thought.

"My pet aversion is the historical novel, which falsifies history to meet the requirements of romantic fiction, and falsifies romance by trying to force it into the framework of history. My ideal is to produce a work which shall be strictly accordant with the available documentary evidence, but shall none the less bear the imprint of an imaginative re-creation. This comes easily to an artist who understands the determinisms that preside over human destinies great and small; and has learned that the Almighty is a better craftsman than any human author."

When Herr Ludwig is not in Paris or Vienna, or traveling with his family in Egypt, Greece, Italy, or Spain, he is living on Lake Maggiore in Switzerland. He and his wife visited America for the first time in 1928 when he made an extensive lecture tour of the country. His biography of Lincoln appeared in the following year.

Ludwig's books, with the dates of publication in Germany (indicated by italics) and the United States, are: *Diana* (*1918*, 1929) ; *Quiet Sea* (*1919*, 1929) ; *Goethe* (*1920*, 1928) ; *On Mediterranean Shores* (*1923*, 1929), travel sketches; *Genius and Character* (*1923*, 1927), portraits of twenty historical figures; *Napoleon* (*1924*, 1927) ; *William Hohenzollern* (*1925*, 1927) ; *Bismark* (*1926*, 1927) ; *Bismarck Triology* (*1927*, 1927) three plays founded on Bismarck's memoirs; *Art and Destiny* (*1927*, 1929), *The Son*

of Man (*1928*, 1928), Jesus as a human rather than a supernatural figure; *Lincoln* (*1929*, 1929) ; *July '14* (translated 1929) ; *Three Titans* (translated 1930) ; *Schliemann* (translated 1931).

Rose Macaulay

THE daughter of G. C. Macaulay, late lecturer in English literature at Cambridge, Rose Macaulay was brought up in Italy, by the sea. She recalls how, as a child, she "did a lot of bathing, paddling and canoeing, climbing with my brothers and sisters (we are a large cheerful family). I went in largely for roof-climbing and other mischievous activities. I was—and am—very fond of hockey, tennis, and boating."

She began to write before she could hold a pen properly. "I remember," she says, "how my sister and I started to write a novel, sitting under the table, when I was three. I did the talking while she worked the pencil. It's a natural impulse with children, like drawing." She composed stories and poetry as a child.

Miss Macaulay was sent to school at Oxford and later to college there. She published her first novel while still in her teens. "It was a pretty poor novel, as I

ROSE MACAULAY

remember," she comments, "but it was published." It was called *The Valley Captives* (1911).

Today Miss Macaulay is called a "feminist, a big-hearted spinster, a gentle cynic, an indulgent recorder of human weakness and folly." She is regarded as high brow by flappers and low brow by intellectuals.

When in London she resides in Princess Gardens, a restricted section set like an island in the city. Trees are grown here and a country atmosphere is preserved. Here she inhabits a small "flat," alone with her typewriter. She is the center of a literary circle in London. Her country home is at Beaconsfield. She is reticent about herself, not caring for publicity. Miss Macaulay is unmarried.

She claims to have no favorite authors. Her tastes are catholic. She finds good and bad in everybody. She believes, however, that "Anatole France always has a peculiar charm—tho he is out of fashion just now." She dislikes Thomas Hardy and Henry James. Among her contemporaries, she admires Virginia Woolf.

"I'm afraid I'm not efficient at all," remarks Miss Macaulay. "I simply can't get thru my work. There seems to be so much to do, besides writing books. Answering letters, for instance. . . But it won't do not to answer them." She believes that "love is the greatest adventure in people's lives. But it's not the only one. . . I don't think love—the relation between the sexes—is overdone."

Publishers, reviewers, readers have stamped Miss Macaulay's work as "satirical." Her reputation as a "satirical novelist" began with *Potterism* (1920), a newspaper novel. Reviewers remarked on her "cleverness and wit" and "her coolness, her confidence, her determination to say just exactly what she intends to say whether the reader will or no."

In spite of the fact that *Mystery at Geneva* (1922) was prefaced by a short notice that the author had intended a straightforward story without a meaning, it was generally accepted as a satirical sketch of the League of Nations. And most people regarded *Orphan Island* (1924) as an attack on Queen Victoria and all she represented.

Miss Macaulay's novels include: *What Not* (1919), *Potterism* (1920), *Dangerous Ages* (1921), *Mystery at Geneva* (1922), *Told by an Idiot* (1923), *Orphan Island* (1924), *Crewe Train* (1926), *Keeping up Appearances* (1928), and *Staying With Relations* (1930).

She is the author of two books of verse: *The Two Blind Countries* (1914) and *Three Days* (1919). She has published a book of essays, *A Casual Commentary* (1926). She has done occasional journalistic work.

Her books are not autobiographical, according to Miss Macaulay: "I suppose every writer uses his own experience to some extent in writing, but I have never put myself into a book, or used any important experiences. As for hobbies, I am not sure what a hobby is. I don't keep rabbits or collect stamps in these days."

William McFee

WILLIAM McFEE'S father was an English sea captain, as was his grandfather. His mother, a Canadian, accompanied Captain McFee on his voyages. The three masted square-rigger, *Erin's Isle,* of which his father was designer, builder, owner, and master, was the place of William McFee's birth on June 15, 1881. The ship was homeward bound from a voyage to India.

Upon their return to England, the family settled in New Southgate, a suburb of North London. William was educated at several schools and finally at Bury St. Edmunds, Suffolk. From 1897 until 1900 he was an apprentice in McMuirland's Engineering Shops at Aldersgate.

After a period on a water-works pumping job at Tring, McFee went into the London office of a firm of Yorkshire engineers. During these days he was deep in Socialism and Kipling; he even lectured on Kipling. He spent his evenings at the Northampton Institute and his Saturday afternoons in the reading room of the British Museum. Arthur Elder, the artist, persuaded him to take up residence near him in Chelsea. But Elder soon moved to the United States.

McFee was twenty-four and the sea was calling. So in 1906 he took a berth

WILLIAM McFEE

as junior engineer on one of his uncle's ships, the *Rotherfield*, and sailed for Genoa. He rose to the position of chief engineer with the Woodfield Steamship Company.

His first book was *Letters of an Ocean Tramp*, published in 1908. In that same year he began a novel, *Casuals of the Sea*, and completed it in 1911. He left ship and joined his friend Elder in North Carolina. There, while the manuscript of *Casuals of the Sea* made unsuccessful trips to one publisher after another, McFee worked on another novel, *Aliens,* and kept the pot boiling by writing advertisements and booklets.

Finally, in 1913, he joined the American Merchant Marine and was sent to New Orleans as a member of the port engineering staff. He was aboard the *S.S. Cartago* of the Great White Fleet when the World War broke out, and, in October 1914, he returned to England to enlist but was refused by the army. Determined to get into the war, he secured an appointment as engineer officer on a British transport, and later as sub-lieutenant in the British Navy. During most of the war he served in the Mediterranean. There he wrote a series of articles for *Land and Water*, a London magazine.

Meanwhile, *Aliens* was published in London in 1914, and *Casuals of the Sea* made its appearance in 1916. During his service in the Mediterranean McFee rewrote *Aliens* and it was published in the United States in 1918 in its revised form.

After the war McFee returned to his home with the Elders in the United States. In 1920 he married Pauline Khondroff, who came half way across the world to join him. He did not remain ashore long, however, for he went with the United Fruit Company as chief engineer. For two years he commuted back and forth between New York and the Spanish Main with full mechanical responsibility of a passenger liner that also carries the most temperamental of fruits. While combating such problems as keeping bananas at an even temperature of fifty-four degrees, whether in tropical or below-zero weather, McFee wrote *Captain Macedoine's Daughter* (1920), *Harbours of Memory* (1921), and *Command* (1922). *Harbours of Memory* is a collection of essays, most of which had been published in magazines in America.

For each voyage he gathered a new collection of reading.. A letter on one trip referred to Sallust, Florus Paterculus, Livy, Gibbon, Shakespeare, Horace, Balzac, Tolstoy, Whitman, Goethe, and Emerson.

Literature finally forced McFee ashore for good in 1922 and he became a resident of Westport, Connecticut. There, aside from the recreation of motoring, his chief pleasure is writing letters to the papers on public questions that interest him. One of his pet aversions is the preoccupation of some young authors with sex in their novels. He revisits the sea occasionally "to keep in contact with reality."

English to the core (not Scottish), William McFee is a big man, blond of complexion and hair, with a pair of vivid blue eyes. His dry wit, always on tap, is the delight of his friends. He is an enthusiastic observer of American life and absorbs the works of Harry Leon Wilson, Ring Lardner, H. C. Witwer, and the cartoons of Clare Briggs. He knows more about the American Constitution than most native citizens.

His living room is filled with mementoes of the sea, including a model of the ship on which he was born. He is an efficient correspondent. He is a lover of children and animals, and enjoys tramping over the Connecticut hills.

His works are: *Letters from an Ocean Tramp* (1908), *Aliens* (1914, 1918), *Casuals of the Sea* (1916), *A Port Said Miscellany* (1918), *Captain Macedoine's Daughter* (1920), *A Six Hour Shift* (1920), *Harbours of Memory* (1921), *An Engineer's Notebook* (1921), *Command* (1922), *The Gates of the Caribbean* (1922), *Studies in Patriotism* (1922), *Race* (1924), *Swallowing the Anchor* (1925), *Sunlight in New Granada* (1925), *Pilgrims of Adversity* (1928), *The Life of Sir Martin Frobisher* (1928), *Sailors of Fortune* (1929), and *North of Suez* (1930).

ARTHUR MACHEN

Arthur Machen

HE is a heavily-built man, with a large, genial, yet brooding, clean-shaven face. His appearance is well described by John Gunther, who says: "He reminded me of David Lloyd George, the Sphinx, a Benda mask, George Washington, Pan, W. J. Bryan, and his own Lucian in *The Hill of Dreams*. There is grotesquery in his face, and also beauty. Snow white hair, long and thick, cut horizontally in a heavy bob. Clouded blue eyes, very tired. Beautifully kept, waxlike hands. Red, glazed cheeks, which ball up and jell when he laughs." Picture him slouching across a rain-spattered street in London, wearing a long cape tossed carelessly over his shoulders and reaching nearly to his ankles, with a hat perched atop his snowy bob, "like a bird riding a wave."

Arthur Machen was born in 1863, the only child of a Welch clergyman. He says: "I shall always esteem it as the greatest piece of fortune that has fallen to me, that I was born in that noble, fallen Caerleon-on-Usk, in the heart of Gwent." He was an impressionable boy and his imagination was stirred by the wonder of the Celtic Usk, "grey and silvery and luminous, winding mystic esses, and the dense forest bending down

to it, and the grey stone bridge crossing it."

"With unlimited leisure for mooning and loafing and roaming and wandering from lane to lane, from wood to wood," the child found out all the wisdom he wanted for one lifetime before he was eighteen. Solitude was one of the chief elements of his childhood and he had the "run of a thoroly ill-selected library." De Quincey's *Confessions of an English Opium Eater* made a deep impression on his mind, and he read all of Scott with zest. At the age of seventeen, after he left school, he published a poem called *Eleusinia* (1881). He possesses the only copy of it.

When he was eighteen Mr. Machen went to Paddington where he wrote poetry and worked for one pound a week for a firm of publishers, "a peg of no particular shape in a perfectly round hole, feeling very miserable indeed." He finally succeeded in getting employment teaching small children at twenty-five shillings a week. He lived in a tiny garret, "ten feet by five," near Notting Hill Gate, and ate for his midday meal a large captain's biscuit and a glass of beer. At twenty, he says he was "tramping, loafing, strolling along interminable streets and roads lying to the northwest and west of London, a shabby, sorry figure; and always alone." In his room he wrote *The Anatomy of Tobacco*, "a grave burlesque."

After eighteen months he returned to Gwent, destitute, and translated three or four French texts of the *Heptameron.* Meanwhile, his book was published and his literary career had begun. After several more books appeared, he began his first major work, *The Hill of Dreams,* in 1895. His purpose was to write "a picaresque romance of the soul." The writing of the book, he says, was pure torture, and it was many years before it was published (1907).

This book began a long romance which Mr. Machen continued in every book he wrote after it; his work was a series of variations on the same theme. And all his writing was painful to him. He says the only book he conceived in pleasure was *Hieroglyphics* (1902).

At thirty-nine he became an actor and was a member, for a time, of the Benson Shakespearean Repertoire Company. When he was about fifty, Mr. Machen took up journalism and was for many years one of the star writers on the *Evening News.* During his varied life he has inherited a small fortune and spent it in travel. He speaks of being a beggar at sixty. His autobiography is contained in *Far-off Things* (1922), and *Things Near and Far* (1923).

The only things Mr. Machen has written that have sold well are two World War tales, *The Bowmen* and *The Angel of Mons*, published together with other legends of the war in 1915. Altho the stories are entirely imaginary, many persons have stoutly maintained that they actually witnessed the phenomena which are so plausibly related.

In 1925 Mr. Machen said: "I shall write no more. I am sixty-two and very tired. My literary career, if you want to call it a literary career, is over, over for good and all. I am done. It has been a long day—almost forty-five years long."

Mr. Machen, despite his native seriousness, is a keen wit and can laugh at himself in retrospection. His conversation is as picturesque as his appearance. He speaks in a deep sonorous voice, and his sentences are fluent, rhythmic, salty with wit, and highly intoned. He is a good companion, yet keeps many of his thoughts to himself.

His novels include: *The Chronicle of Clemendy* (1888), *The Great God Pan and The Inmost Light* (1894), *The Three Imposters* (1895), *Hieroglyphics* (1902), *The House of Souls* (1906), *The Hill of Dreams* (1907), *The Great Return* (1915), and *The Terror* (1917).

Among his volumes of short stories are: *The Bowmen, and Other Legends of the War* (1915) and *The Shining Pyramid* (1924). His books of essays include: *Strange Roads* (1923), *The London Adventure* (1924), *Dreads and Drolls* (1926), and *Notes and Queries* (1926).

Claude McKay

CLAUDE McKAY was born in 1889 in the hills on the island of Jamaica, British West Indies. He says he had no early education except what instruction he received from his brother. In his teens he went to live in the city of Kingston, where he enlisted in the service of the constabulary.

He began to write verses in the native dialect and became a sort of poet laureate of the colony. His songs and poems in the soft folk speech of the Jamaican

CLAUDE McKAY

Negro were popular. His first immature volume of poetry, *Songs of Jamaica,* was published at Kingston in 1912. In the same year *Constabulary Ballads* was brought out in London. These two volumes brought him the award of the medal of the Institute of Arts and Sciences. He was the first Negro to receive the award.

Young McKay received a sum of money which enabled him to come to the United States in 1912 to study. He entered the Tuskegee Institute, where he planned to fit himself to go back home and help his people, but the routine and discipline were not to his liking and he left after a few months. He entered the Kansas State College where he spent two years and learned from the agricultural routine that he did not want to be a farmer or teach farming. So he took the balance of his scholarship fund and made his way to New York.

There, in 1914, he became the proprietor of a restaurant on West 53d Street, but in a few months his business venture failed and all his money was lost. Then he tried to earn his living with varying success in the kitchens of summer hotels and boarding houses in New England, and in Pullman dining cars. Meanwhile he turned to poetry again, and in 1917 two sonnets appeared in *The Seven Arts* under the name of Eli Edwards. The poems attracted a good deal of attention and the editors themselves were curious to know who the writer was. McKay's work began to appear in other magazines. Some of his more belligerent verse attracted the attention of a few literary radicals and in 1920 he became associated with *The Liberator.* He was soon made associate editor.

Spring in New Hampshire, a book of poems, was published in London in 1920, and *Harlem Shadows,* another poetic volume, made its appearance in New York in 1922. Late in 1922 McKay traveled to Russia and then he established his residence in France. He became identified with what has been called the "Negro literary renaissance."

McKay began writing novels, and *Home to Harlem* appeared in 1928. It is the story of a roving Negro longshoreman who turns "home to Harlem" where he meets a girl, loses her, and then finds her again in the recesses of Harlem night life. *Banjo* (1929), subtitled "A Story Without a Plot," depicts the life on the swarming waterfront of Marseilles, where McKay was living. *Banjo* is less a story than a series of realistic pictures of the riff-raff of the world thrown up in the slum areas along the docks.

Claude McKay's works are: *Songs of Jamaica* (1912), *Constabulary Ballads* (1912), *Spring in New Hampshire* (1920), *Harlem Shadows* (1922), *Home to Harlem* (1928), and *Banjo* (1929).

Percy Mackaye

PERCY MACKAYE, dramatist and poet, was born in New York City on March 16, 1875, the son of Steele Mackaye, the Shakespearean actor who invented the "spectatorium," a forerunner of the motion-picture. At fifteen, Percy dramatized his family in a series of dialogues which he called *Half Hour Happenings in the Teeles Family,* Teeles being a transcription of Steele.

PERCY MACKAYE

Young Mackaye took his A.B. degree at Harvard in 1897. The next year, on October 8, he married Marion Homer Morse of Cambridge, Massachusetts. They traveled in Europe from 1898 to 1900, residing successively at Rome, Brunnen (Switzerland), Leipzig, and London. He studied at the University of Leipzig in 1899-1900. From 1900 to 1904 he taught at a private school in New York City.

Meanwhile, encouraged by his father, Mackaye had served his apprenticeship in the theatre. In 1906 his play, *Jeanne d'Arc,* was produced by Sothern and Marlowe in New York and London. From 1906 to 1913 Mackaye lectured on the theatre at Harvard, Yale, Columbia and other universities. In 1908 his play,

The Scarecrow, was produced. He delivered the Harvard Phi Beta Kappa poem in 1908, and has delivered other commemorative poems on Abraham Lincoln, Edison, Browning, and Shakespeare. In 1914 he received an honorary A.M. degree from Dartmouth. He was appointed to the first American fellowship in poetry and drama at Miami University in 1920.

In 1921 Mackaye and his wife explored the Kentucky mountains. Traveling sometimes on foot and sometimes on mule back, they found a primitive people whose speech bore resemblance to the idiom of Shakespeare. The lavish use of the hyphen which our modern speech has discarded gave the mountaineers' dialect picturesque vitality. "I felt that I had to capture this inimitable idiom before the radio and civilization changed it," explained Mackaye. *This Fine Pretty World,* a drama of the hills, was produced in New York in 1923.

Products of subsequent visits to the Kentucky mountains are: *Tall Tales of the Kentucky Mountains* (1926), stories of a Kentucky Baron Münchausen; *Kentucky Mountain Fantasies* (1928), folk-plays on the seeping of civilization into this region; *Gobbler of God* (1928), a narrative poem of mountain legend; and *Weathergoose-Woo!* (1929), tales of witchcraft and magic of the Southern Appalachians.

Mackaye received an honorary Litt.D. from Miami University in 1924, and he held a special seminar in poetry at Rollins College, Florida, in 1929. He was elected, in the same year, advisory editor of *Folk-Say,* national magazine of American folklore. His home is at Cornish, New Hampshire. He has three children.

Percy Mackaye is a bashful affectionate man behind the horn-rimmed gravity of the thin face crowned by a heavy mop of hair.

He is the author of some four operas, fifteen or more plays, and as many pageants. His *Caliban,* a community masque, was produced in the stadium of the College of the City of New York by a cast that included Isadora Duncan, Edith Wynne Mathison, and John Drew. Among his other masques are: *Sanctuary* (1913), a bird masque; *St. Louis* (1914), a civic masque with 7,500 actors;

The Evergreen Tree (1917), a Christmas masque; and *Roll Call* (1918), a masque of the Red Cross. Several books of verse are included in his list of publications.

Compton Mackenzie

L ITERARY and dramatic talent was abundant in the family which gave birth to Compton Mackenzie on January 17, 1883. The child's father was the well-known actor Edward Compton, author of several plays and founder of the Compton Comedy Company. His aunt was "Leah" Bateman, famous Lady Macbeth, and his uncle, C. G. Compton, was a novelist. Among his more distant relations was John Addington Symonds, and the novelist and playwright George Paston (Mrs. E. M. Symonds). His sister is Fay Compton, distinguished actress. His given name was Edward Montague Compton, but he assumed the original family name of his ancestors who were a branch of the Mackenzie clan of Scatwell.

Born in West Hartlepool, Compton Mackenzie spent his childhood at Kensington. At the age of a year and ten months he could read nursery rhymes at sight. He saw words and phrases in colors. He had a copy of *Don Quixote,* the cover of which to this day is bent over where he fell asleep on it reading in bed. He was always reading. And his eagerness for books was stimulated by warnings that he was reading too much and that books on certain shelves were not to be touched. At the age of six he had read practically every book in his father's library. He enjoyed Scott, Dickens, and Thackeray.

The boy Mackenzie attended a big public school in London. He recalls his introduction to a new world of literature when he visited a tutor at school to borrow some scholastic work and he saw beside it on the shelf a slim green volume, Oscar Wilde's *Intentions.* He put back the scholastic work and took away *Intentions* instead. He says: "A curious, exotic, strange world was opened up, as forbidden fruit."

Mackenzie continued his education at St. Paul's School and at Magdalen College, Oxford. At Magdalen he edited *The Oxford Point of View,* which he helped to found. He became business manager of the Oxford Union Dramatic Society, and distinguished himself as an actor. He received his A. B., second class in Modern History, in 1904.

In 1905 Mr. Mackenzie married Faith Stone, youngest daughter of Rev. E. D. Stone, one time master at Eaton College. They withdrew to the wilds of Cornwall, where he wrote industriously for several years. He published a book of verse in 1907 entitled *Poems,* and a play of his, *The Gentleman in Grey,* was produced at the Lyceum Theatre, Edinburgh, but did not stay long. It took him longer to get his first novel published than to write it. After seven publishers had rejected the manuscript of *The Passionate Elopement,* he sent it to Martin Secker, who was setting up in business, and when Secker published it, early in 1911, it sold so well that within three weeks it had to be reprinted. It ran thru four editions by the end of the year.

About the time this novel was published, Mr. Mackenzie came up to London and settled in Westminster where he wrote lyrics and reviews for Pélissier (Fay Compton's first husband), whose "Follies" were at their height. He wrote his second novel, *Carnival* (1912), and collected a second volume of poems, *Kensington Rhymes* (1912).

Mr. Mackenzie crossed the Atlantic to superintend the dramatic production of *Carnival* in New York, and then went to the Gulf of Naples where he settled in a villa on the Isle of Capri. Here he found an ideal retreat for his writing. He finished *Sinister Street,* which appeared in two volumes (1913 and 1914). *Guy and Pauline* was published in 1915.

Meanwhile the World War had broken out and Mackenzie went on the Dardanelles Expedition as a lieutenant in the Royal Marines. Later he became a captain. He was invalided out in 1915 and became successively Military Control Officer at Athens in 1916 and Director of an Intelligence Department at Syria in 1917. He was made a Chevalier of the Legion of Honor and received other war recognitions, including O.B.E.

Mr. Mackenzie acquired the small Isle of Jethou in the Channel group and now

COMPTON MACKENZIE

divides his year between that remote and rocky islet and his villa at Capri. His favorite island recreation is listening to the gramaphone. Jethou is about fifty acres in extent, and Mr. Mackenzie owns it all to himself. There are no shops or taxes there, but his house has all modern improvements, a library of 10,000 books, and as many phonograph records. There are wild rabbits and pheasants, with the right to shoot them; and wild waterfowl in the winter. The occupant of Jethou, who holds a lease on the island from King George, has some almost feudal privileges, such as flying his own flag. Mr. Mackenzie recently acquired a second (and wilder) island off the coast of Scotland, and therefore, in 1931, offered to rent Jethou.

Mackenzie's *Fairy Gold* (1926) describes life in the Channel Islands, and *Vestal Fire* (1927) is a picture of Capri. Mackenzie's connections with the stage are mirrored in *Rogues and Vagabonds* (1927), which details the joys and trials of a strolling actor's life. Three novels which record the writer's experiences with the Intelligence Service are: *Extremes Meet* (1928), *The Three Couriers* (1929), and *Gallipoli Memories* (1930).

Other works by Mr. Mackenzie include: *Extraordinary Women* (1928), *The Adventures of Two Chairs* (1929), *April Fools* (1930), *The Enchanted Blanket* (1930), *Told* (1930), *Athenian Memories* (1931).

Mr. Mackenzie is editor of *The Gramaphone,* and founded a weekly called *Vox,* with the intention of criticizing very candidly the London radio programs.

Archibald MacLeish

ARCHIBALD MacLEISH, the American poet, gives the following biographical sketch of himself:

"Born May 7, 1892, in a wooden château overlooking, from a clay bluff and a grove of oak trees, the waters of Lake Michigan. Father a Scot, a Glasgow man, born a Presbyterian, ultimately a Baptist, always a devout Protestant: one of the early settlers of Chicago: fifty-four when I was born: a merchant: a cold, tall, rigorous man of very beautiful speech. Mother a Connecticut woman, daughter of a Congregational minister, herself a graduate of Vassar and a teacher there: her family a sea-faring family from the Connecticut Coast about Norwich: very passionate people with

ARCHIBALD MACLEISH

many mad among them: a very strong family resemblance from one generation to the next—small dark eyes and high cheek bones and similar voices: she was my father's third wife: intelligent and energetic and tireless and virtuous.

"Four of us grew up—one to be killed flying with the British over Belgium. Public schools. Lake beach. Oak thickets. Went to a fashionable Connecticut preparatory school for four years and hated it. Went to Yale. Regular undergraduate life—football team—swimming team—Chairman of the Literary Magazine—Phi Beta Kappa —Senior Societies: began writing but learned little about it and had little life of my own. Went to Harvard Law School to avoid going to work: led my class the last year: worked terribly hard because of the competition but could never believe in the law. Married Ada Hitchcock who is a singer. This while I was in the Law School. Son born early in 1917. War: went abroad in a hospital unit so as to do the right thing but not be hurt. In France got shifted to the Field Artillery out of shame: few weeks at the front north of Meaux in July 1918: sent home to take battery in new regiment of 155 G.P.F.'s: ended up a captain of F. A. at Camp Mead with no distinction but fact that my brother, Kenneth, had been a grand flier and had been killed.

"Taught for a year at Harvard to avoid (again) going to work. Wrote a little all the time but it wasn't any good. One book of undergraduate verses, *Tower of Ivory* (1917), published while I was in France. Practiced law for three years in the office of Charles F. Choate Jr. in Boston—trying cases mostly—and did pretty well, but couldn't write. Only one desire—to write the poems I wanted to write and not the poems I was writing. Winter of 1923 decided to go to France anyway on what we had. Date the beginning of my life from that year. Went in the Fall of 1923 with two children. Lived in the Boulevard St. Michel and at Saint Cloud and later in the rue du Bac. One summer in Normandy. After that on the Mediterranean—cruising a great deal. Went one Spring for five months to Persia going down through the central cities to Bushire and

west along the Persian Gulf to Moha-
mara and back thru Shiraz and Ispahan
to Teheran. All this time reading—
mostly French poetry and chiefly
Laforgue, Rimbaud, Leon Paul Fargue,
St. J. Pierre, Valéry. Also Eliot and
Pound. Began writing in 1923. Published *The Happy Marriage* (1924), *The
Pot of Earth* (1925), *Nobodaddy* (1925),
Streets in the Moon (1926). Came home
in 1928 and live on a farm. Have since
published *The Hamlet of A. MacLeish*
(1928) and *New Found Land* (1930).
Travelled in the *monte* in Mexico alone
for some time in the early spring of
1929 going over the route of Cortez
from San Juan de Ulua to Tenochtitlan.
Do hack work in New York when I have
to."

Burton Rascoe describes MacLeish as
"a clear-eyed, deferential young man,
with an extremely Nordic head, quiet
manners, and an ungovernable passion
for discussing esthetics—esthetics in the
round, in the general, in the specific, in
the concrete—any way so long as it is
esthetics."

Maurice Maeterlinck

MAURICE MAETERLINCK, Bel-
gian poet and dramatist, was born
at Ghent on August 29, 1862. He came
of an old Flemish family, and had the
medieval mystics in his blood. He took
the regular course at the Jesuit College
of Sainte-Barbe in Ghent, and this early
religious impression made him a life-
long student of religion. After graduation in 1885 he took up the study of law
at the University of Ghent, but his heart
was in literature.

When he was twenty-four, in 1886,
Maeterlinck went to Paris where he became acquainted with Villiers de l'Isle
Adam and leaders of the symbolist school
of French poetry. He was an interested
listener when the youthful enthusiasts
gathered in Montmartre cafes and read
their manuscript verse. When his father
died he returned to Belgium, where he
spent his winters in Ghent and summers
on an estate at Oostacker.

His literary ambitions spurred by the
months in Paris, Maeterlinck commenced to write. His first publication

MAURICE MAETERLINCK

was a prose sketch, *The Massacre of the
Innocents.* Then came a thin book of
vaguely melancholy poems, *Serres Chau-
des* (Hot-Houses), published in 1889.
That same year he produced *La Princesse Maleine,* a tragedy in five acts.

Pelléas et Mélisande, a play based on
the tragedy of Paolo and Francesca,
appeared in 1892. Claude Debussy
worked for ten years setting it to music
and the opera was first performed at the
Opéra Comique in Paris. Maeterlinck
broke his friendship with Debussy when
Mary Garden was chosen to sing Mélisande rather than his wife, Georgette
Leblanc.

Monna Vanna, produced in 1902, established Maeterlinck as a practical playwright. He bought an old Norman
Abbey near Rouen (the Abbey of Saint
Wandrille), where he wrote *L'Oiseau
Bleu* (1909), the play which carried his
name to all parts of the world. When
it was ready for the stage he sent it to
Stanislavsky, director of the Moscow
Art Theatre, who produced it in the Russian language in 1908. It was performed
at the Moscow theatre more than three
hundred times. When produced in London in December 1909, *The Blue Bird*
ran for more than three hundred performances. It opened in New York in
October 1910. Its fantasy charmed both

young and old. Stanislavsky said to his players: "Let *The Blue Bird* in our theatre thrill the grandchildren and arouse serious thoughts and deep feelings in their grandparents."

The enormous cost of production of *The Betrothal* (1918) was a hindrance to its financial success. Maeterlinck wrote a war play dealing with the German occupation of Belgium, *The Burgomaster of Stilemonde* (1918). It was produced in New York in the spring of 1919 (*A Burgomaster of Belgium*). It was sponsored in London by Sir J. Martin Harvey.

In 1920 Maeterlinck visited America and made a lecture tour on which he had difficulty in making himself understood because of his meager English. He tried reading to his audience from a manuscript prepared with the English words spelled phonetically in their French vocal equivalents, but the result was described as "not a happy one." He thinks most Americans are hypocrites.

He now lives apart from the world in the French Riviera. He resides with his wife, Renée Dahon, at Médan, in the mountains behind Nice. His villa, *Les Abeilles,* is surrounded with a luxurious garden. There he is a pleasant host— except to American reporters. One time a lady reporter whom he had refused to see sent word that she had lost all her money playing roulette in Nice and that if he would not grant an interview for her magazine, there was nothing left to do but commit suicide. He gave in. Her first question was: "You must tell me, master, why you divorced your first wife, Georgette Leblanc!" He promptly escorted her to the door with the words, "Go ahead and commit suicide, madame!"

Maeterlinck considers his career finished and he admits, laughingly, that his hours are counted. He says he intends to spend the time he has left in eating, sleeping, drinking, and living well. Material joys are dear to him; he retains the appetite of a healthy man. He hates the noise and crowds of the city. He loves to walk where he can gaze at the trees and the calm horizon. His recreations have been bee-keeping, canoeing, skating, bicycling, and motoring.

Maeterlinck is described by Frank Harris as "a broad Fleming of about five feet nine in height, inclined to be stout; silver hair lends distinction to the large round head and boyish fresh complexion; blue-grey eyes, now thoughtful, now merry, and an unaffected off-hand manner. The features are not cut, left rather 'in the rough,' as sculptors say, even the heavy jaw and chin are drowned in fat; the forehead bulges and the eyes lose color in the light and seem hard; still, an interesting and attractive personality."

Maeterlinck experiments with dreams, recording and cataloging them. He says: "I have had myself waked out of a sound sleep in the middle of the night in order to be able to reproduce my dream exactly. I have satisfied myself that dreams are fragments of our future. . . Science has made a good many dreams come true." He found in the stars belief that there is no death.

Other plays by Maeterlinck include: *L'Intruse* (1890), *Les Aveugles* (1890), *Soeur Beatrice* (1901), *Mary Magdalene* (1909), *The Miracle of St. Anthony* (1919), *The Cloud That Lifted* (1923), and *The Power of the Dead* (1923).

His essays include: *Wisdom and Destiny* (1898), *The Life of the Bee* (1901), *The Buried Temple* (1902). *The Double Garden* (1904), *Life and Flowers* (1907), *Death* (1912), *The Life of Space* (1927), *Magic of the Stars* (1930), *Life of the Ant* (1930). Among his lyrics is *Douze Chansons* (1896). He showed his interest in Shakespeare in his essay on King Lear and in his translation of *Macbeth* (1910). Most of his works have been translated into English by A. Teixeira de Mattos, Bernard Miall, and F. M. Atkinson.

Heinrich Mann

HEINRICH MANN is the elder brother of Thomas Mann, winner of the Nobel Prize for Literature for 1929. He was born in Lübeck in 1871. His father was a great merchant and owner of a trade company that was over a hundred years old, and was also a Senator of the free city of Lübeck. His mother had come to Germany as a child from Brazil. Her mother, in turn, was a Brazilian of Portuguese origin. Both the brothers Mann have felt a kinship with Latin culture and, like other German writers, have spent a large part of their lives in Italy.

At the age of eighteen Heinrich Mann left his native city, studied in Berlin and wrote his first novel in 1894, *In A Family.* From 1895 to 1898 he lived in Rome and received lasting impressions of the life of the people in Italy, which he used in his curious novel, *The Small City,* much later.

The first novel, however, which was born of his already ripening knowledge, was the cross-section of Berlin life, called *Im Schlaraffenland,* published in America under the title, *In The Land of Cockaigne.* Then followed the romantic trilogy, *The Goddess, or The Three Romances of the Duchess D'Assy.* In this he tried to picture a whole world as the eyes of a young man perceived it.

Over a long period Heinrich Mann divided the subjects of his novels between German and foreign material. It was after 1922 that he devoted himself entirely to the portrayal of life in Germany before the war. The novels, *The Patrioteer,* 1924; *The Poor,* 1917; and *The Chief,* 1925, all served to build up a vast picture of the "empire"; and the novel, *Mother Mary,* which is one of the last, is a picture of post-war life in Germany.

Heinrich Mann has written various plays, among them *Madame Legros,* which has been widely played.

In December 1927, as a result of efforts to bring about a *rapprochement* between German and French thinkers, Heinrich Mann was invited to lecture at the University of Paris, and chose as his subject, "Towards an Intellectual Locarno."

Heinrich Mann is married to the daughter of a business man from Prague, and lives in Munich. He has one daughter. He has friends in Vienna, Berlin and Paris. Liberal in his sympathies and internationally minded, Heinrich Mann is a citizen of Europe first of all.

His novel, *The Royal Woman,* published here in 1930, appeared in Ger-

HEINRICH MANN

many under the title *Eugénie, Oder Die Bürgerzeit.* This title is explained by the fact that the story, in which the characters are an upper class bourgeois family, parallels the career of the Empress Eugénie. In it an interesting experiment in narrative is made: two stories are told at once—the actual story and, by implication, the story of the Empress Eugénie—fusing into one at the points of crisis.

The Little Town (1931) delves into the world of ballet and masquerade.

Thomas Mann

THOMAS MANN, winner of the Nobel Prize for Literature for 1929, had an interesting origin. His mother was the daughter of a German planter in Brazil and his Creole wife, the off-spring of a Portugese-Indian union. Her maiden name was Bruhn-da-Silva. From her Mann has inherited the romantic streak in his mind; from his father, a senator of the Hanseatic free city of Lübeck and member of an old patrician merchant family, he inherited the well-known German trait, intellectual balance.

In his address to the Swedish Acad-

THOMAS MANN

emy in Stockholm on accepting the Nobel Prize, Mann referred to Tonio Kröger, whose name gives the title to one of the author's best known stories: "I made the South represent the essence of all mad spiritual adventure and the cold passion of artistic creation; the North, on the other hand, epitomized cordiality and homely warmth, deep, tranquil sentiment and sincere humanity." Mann really characterized himself in this blend of the opposing natures of north and south.

Mann was born on June 6, 1875, in Lübeck. As a boy he liked music, and animals, and gods and legends of Greek antiquity. (The trace remains in *Herr und Hund,* and *Rede und Antwort*). At school, altho he is said to have been a dull pupil, he wrote the bulk of a youthful publication ambitiously called "A Journal of Art, Literature, and Philosophy." When Mann was fifteen years old his father died. Four years later Mann and his mother moved to Munich. There he worked in a fire-insurance office for a short time and, as nearly every artist who has had to earn his living in the business world, hated doing it. After travel for some months in Italy, he returned to Munich to work on the staff of the literary review *Simplicissimus.*

The first of his works to bear his own name was *Zweimaliger Abscheid,*

published in 1893. The following year he published *Geffalen,* a short story. *Buddenbrooks,* one of the first great novels to make the hero a family group, rather than an individual, was published in 1901, when Mann was twenty-six. This long work, which made the young author famous, is largely autobiographical; it traces four generations of a Lübeck family of a sound bourgeois stock thru its years of wealth and affluence and the succeeding years of decline until, as the symbol if its extinction, an artist emerges from its midst in the last generation.

Fiorenza, a play, was published in 1906, but there is no record of its ever having been produced. *Der Tod in Venedig* (Death in Venice), of classic form and melancholy beauty, the most distinguished of Mann's novelettes, appeared in 1912. During the bitter war period he wrote, as if compelled to turn his mind from the chaos about him, the slight book *Herr und Hund* (1918) about a man and his dog.

Already, however, he had conceived *Der Zauberberg* (The Magic Mountain), which since its publication in 1924, after ten years of labor, has been accepted not only as the peak of Mann's mature achievement, but also as one of the great books of the modern world. *The Magic Mountain* is essentially a treatise on contemporary society, and all the issues and philosophic ideas of the twentieth century western world enter into it. The locale of most of the book is a sanatorium for consumptives at Davos-Platz in the Swiss Alps, whither Hans Castorp, a young marine engineer, comes to visit his tubercular cousin, and stays to become tubercular himself. The world is seen thru the diseased minds of the patients; the book ends with society plunged into the maelstrom of the World War. It is this book which undoubtedly assured the award of the Nobel Prize to him, altho, in the words of the committee, the prize "is never awarded on the basis of a single work, but to a mind concerned with the gigantic problem of humanity."

In an interesting autobiographical chapter, translated as *Sketch of My Life,* Mann writes of the Nobel award: "It lay, I suppose, upon my path in life—

this I say without presumption, with tranquil if not uninterested insight into the character of my destiny, of my 'rôle' on this earth, which has now been gilded with the equivocal brilliance of success; and which I regard entirely in a human spirit, without any great mental excitement."

Mann is deeply concerned with the problem of international relations. He has contributed numerous essays on political, social, and literary subjects to various magazines. For a time he wrote the German letter for the American *Dial*. He has made a particular study of Goethe and Tolstoy.

Thomas Mann married Katja Pringsheim in 1905. At the present time he lives quietly with his wife and three sons and three daughters in a suburb of Munich. Of his appearance Ludwig Lewisohn has written: "He might easily be mistaken for a North German or American man of business, of a quiet and refined type, with his narrow, dark head with hair conventionally parted to the left, clipped but not too close-clipped black mustache. . . A supremely kind and earnest man, utterly untempted to make either kindness or earnestness or stylistic stringency the 'notes' of his personality." Bruno Frank assures us that behind this quiet unobtrusiveness is a dark and tremendous consciousness of evil, a terrible knowledge of the abysses of the spirit.

Mario und der Zauberer (1930), his first publication after the Nobel Prize award, is a short novel relating the tragic consequence of the visit of a crippled magician to an Italian seaside town.

Mann is at work now on a long mythological novel to be called *Jaakob und seine Söhne* (Jacob and His Sons). In order that he might portray more vividly the destiny of the people of Israel, he has traveled thru Palestine and Egypt. Many years have already gone into its writing. Mann has said that he nerves himself for a new piece of work by telling himself that this time it will be a matter of no importance, easy to do and to be completed quickly.

These books by Thomas Mann have been published in the United States: *Royal Highness* (1916); *Bashan and I* (1923); *Buddenbrooks* (1924); *Death*
in *Venice and Other Stories* (1925); *The Magic Mountain* (1927); *Three Essays* (1929); *Children and Fools* (1929); *Man and His Dog* (1930); *Mario and the Magician* (1931).

Jacques Maritain

JACQUES MARITAIN, French philosopher, was born in Paris on November 18, 1882. He was educated in an atmosphere of liberal Protestantism. In his student days at the Sorbonne in Paris he was dissatisfied with the skepticism of the academic philosophy, and the materialism of contemporary science. The philosophy of Henri Bergson appeared as a salvation. It restored his confidence in metaphysics.

But Bergsonism was not finally satisfactory to him as a seeker after the Absolute. He found the Absolute not in a philosophy but in a religion. So he chose finally the philosophy of St. Thomas because he discovered in it the hidden harmony of faith and reason. He was received into the Catholic Church in 1906, just after he had completed his studies at the Sorbonne with a degree in philosophy.

Maritain spent the next two years at the University of Heidelberg, where he

JACQUES MARITAIN

studied biology under Hans Driesch. On his return to France in 1908, he settled at Versailles under the direction of the Dominican, Père Clerissac, and pursued a study of the *Summa Theologica*. His practical work began in 1913 when he delivered a course of lectures at the Institut Catholique in Paris on the Bergsonian philosophy. The next year he became a professor there and he also taught philosophy at the Collège Stanislas and at the Petit Seminaire at Versailles. He still lectures at the Institut Catholique. Maritan became recognized as the leader of the neo-Thomist movement and of the Catholic intellectual revival in general.

In 1917 he was asked by the bishops in charge of the Institut Catholique to write for them a Course of Philosophy. So he produced his first book, *La Philosophic Bergsonicnne* (1918). Then he began a comprehensive philosophical series called *Eléments de Philosophie*, of which the first book was *Introduction Generale* (1920). The second part, *Petite Logique*, appeared in 1924.

Maritain urges in his books and magazine articles the necessity for a return to a strict Thomistic philosophical mind. The school of thought which he represents was still sufficiently in a minority in 1922 for Maritain to label himself "Antimoderne." In his book, *Antimoderne* (1922), he analyses the revolt and puts forward the reason for, and the necessary conditions of, a Thomistic revival.

Two books which followed serve as a prelude to the exposition of the principles on which he would wish to see arise a "Renaissance Thomiste." He levels destructive criticism against the philosophies that have arisen since the time of Descartes in *Réflexions sur l'intelligence et sur sa vie propre* (1923) and his *Trois Reformateurs—Luther, Descartes, Rousseau* (1925).

His *Art et Scholastique* first appeared in 1920. It deals with the Nature of Art as expressed in the teachings of the schoolmen who, without treating this subject as such, nevertheless, while discussing other matters, enumerated certain principles which can be formulated into a definite theory of esthetic. It was republished in a greatly enlarged edition in 1927.

Maritain stresses in his *Réponse à Jean Cocteau* (1926) that his is no personal school of thought, however personal it may be in expression. He has been a frequent contributor to: *Les Lettres, Revue des Jeunes, Revue Universelle, Revue Thomiste*, and *Revue de Philosophie*.

Other books by Maritain are: *Théonas* (1921), and *Primauté du Spirituel* (1927). He has won a large audience in America with these translations: *Prayer and Intelligence* (1928); *Three Reformers* (1929); *Primacy of the Mind* (1930); *Introduction to Philosophy* (1930); *Art and Scholasticism* (1930); *The Things That Are Not Caesar's* (1931), an essay on the relations of church and state; *The Angelical Doctor* (1931), the life and thought of St. Thomas Aquinas.

Don Marquis

CONTRARY to the impression one gains thru familiarity with his writings—that he is a hail-fellow-well-met sort of being, exuding mirth—Don Marquis is a shy, reticent man, possessed of much personal magnetism and a quiet geniality. It is thru his characters, archy the cockroach; the Old Soak; Captain Peter Fitzurse; Aunt Prudence Heckleberry; mehitabel, the amorous cat, that he seeks expression. He makes them intensely real and human, at once provocative of laughter and pity.

Donald Robert Perry Marquis was born in Walnut, Illinois, July 29, 1878. His initial effort was published in his home paper, the *Walnut Gazette*, but the pecuniary returns were not so great as to attract him to the profession of literature.

School teaching, clerking, baling hay, and preparatory school filled the next two years, after which he left for Washington to study the graphic arts at the Corcoran Art School. However, eighteen months devoted to charcoal drawings of inanimate objects were enough to convince the aspiring young man that art was not his calling, and he secured a position in the Census Office. In his spare moments, he reported for the *Washington Times*.

At this time, in his desire for self-expression, Don went on the road with a stock company producing *East Lynne* and *The Hidden Road*, but the company was shortly beset with difficulties and broke up, throwing him back into the anonymity of a newspaper office again.

Several years later, he took a position as an editorial writer on the *Atlanta Journal*, where he made the acquaintance of Joel Chandler Harris. The two men rapidly became warm friends and Marquis later was assistant editor of Harris's *Uncle Remus Magazine*. It was during his association with Mr. Harris that Marquis collected the impressions and material for *Carter* (1921), a study of Negro life.

In 1909 he married an Atlanta girl, Reina Melcher. She died in 1923.

In 1912 he was to be found in New York on the *Sun*, where he created "The Sun Dial." Later he conducted "The Lantern" for some time in the *Herald Tribune*.

Christopher Morley describes Marquis as "burly, grey-haired, fond of corn cob pipes and sausages, and looking like a careful blend of Falstaff and Napoleon the third."

Marquis has won his greatest popularity as a columnist and as a writer of humorous stories and verses. These include: *The Old Soak* (1921), "a kind of goldinged autobiography of what me and Old King Booze done before he went into the grave and took one of my feet with him"; *Noah an' Jonah an' Cap'n John Smith* (1921), verses; *archy and mehitabel* (1927), the adventures of archy, the literary cockroach, and his friend mehitabel, the cat, whose motto is "toujours gai"; *Love Sonnets of a Cave Man* (1928), which includes new verses and some of the best of the early humorous ones.

Among his more serious works are: *Poems and Portraits* (1922); *The Dark Hours* (1924), a drama on the betrayal, trial, and crucifixion of Jesus; *Out of the Sea* (1927), a modern dramatic version of the legend of Tristan and Iseult.

DON MARQUIS

Since Mr. Marquis has been free-lancing he has written *A Variety of People* (1929), short stories; and *Off the Arm* (1930), a novel of Paris, Hollywood, and New York.

John Masefield

ON the death of Robert Bridges early in 1930 there was speculation as to who would be his successor as Poet Laureate of England. The appointment of John Masefield to be "Poet Laureate in ordinary to His Majesty," by King George, met with general approbation and understanding. Aside from the quality of his verse, with the Labor Party in power there were political justifications for selecting a "poet of democracy," the champion of "the man with too weighty a burden." Thus on May 9, 1930, John Masefield became the twenty-second official lyric spokesman of the British nation, bearing the title that was given first to Chaucer, and later to Edmund Spenser, Ben Jonson, John Dryden, Robert Southey, William Wordsworth, Alfred Tennyson, and other illustrious poets.

Masefield was born in Ledbury, Herefordshire, on June 1, 1874, the son of a

JOHN MASEFIELD

lawyer. Both his mother and father died when he was still a young boy, and with the other Masefield children he went to the home of an aunt in Ledbury. He lived here until the age of fourteen, attending the local school; adventure of any sort appealed to him more than study, and he tramped the woods in search of excitement and novel experiences.

In an endeavor to curb his reckless spirit and rather wild nature he was indentured to a merchant ship when he was fourteen. He remained in service for nearly three years, visiting all parts of the globe. Tired of this life, he left the ship while in port in New York in April 1895, and, with his capital amounting to five dollars and a small chest of clothes, found himself a room at 53 Greenwich Avenue, in the section known as Greenwich Village. His experiences here have become legendary—how he worked at any odd job he could get, in a bakery, in a livery stable, along the waterfront, and in the saloon of Luke O'Connor's Columbian Hotel on Sixth Avenue near the Jefferson Market jail.

Chance took him from his Greenwich Avenue garret to Yonkers, where for two years he worked in a carpet factory, rising to "mistake finder" at $8.50 a week.

He was considered a queer boy, reticent and incalculable. He became acquainted with Mr. William Palmer East's bookshop, which is still in existence, and a period of intense reading began. Chaucer came first, followed by Keats, Shelley, Spenser, and Sir Philip Sidney. He started to write poetry, and some friends in Yonkers have original copies given to them at that time. He read *Paradise Lost* daily for months, memorizing a great deal of it. For prose he read De Quincey, Hazlitt, Dickens, Kipling, Stevenson, and Sir Thomas Browne.

Masefield left for England in 1897, becoming friendly with Synge in London. There he began to write the verses which appeared in his first volume, *Salt Water Ballads* (1902). This volume opens with "A Consecration" in which he announces himself as champion of "the dust and the scum of the earth." His world famous "Cargoes" and "Sea-Fever" are included in this book.

A summer spent in Devonshire with William Butler Yeats was helpful to him, and he was soon publishing verse and plays which brought him recognition and praise. A second volume of poems, *Ballads,* appeared in 1903. *Captain Margaret* (1908) was his first novel.

In spite of the bulk of his other work in fiction, drama, and essays, it is as a poet that Mr. Masefield ranks highest. *Ballads and Poems* (1910), his third volume of poetry, was followed by two which occasioned intense excitement and agitated discussion; *The Everlasting Mercy* (1911), which tells the story of Saul Kane, drunkard and poacher, his spiritual revolt and final conversion; and The *Widow in Bye Street* (1912), in which the Widow Gurney loses her reason after the death of her son Jimmy, hanged for murder. Masefield's *Collected Poems* appeared in 1923. The *Wanderer of Liverpool* (1930), the biography of an old sailing ship, told in prose and verse, was his first book after he received the Poet Laureateship.

Masefield and Constance de la Cherois-Crommelin were married in 1903. They have one son and one daughter, Judith, who has illustrated some of her father's books. Their home is at Boar's Hill, near Oxford and near the homes of Gilbert Murray and of the late Poet Laureate, Robert Bridges. John Masefield is commonly described as "shy and frightened-looking." His early struggles and poverty have left their mark on his frail body. His prominent blue eyes have a surprised, inquisitive look.

Robert Graves, who rented a cottage on Boar's hill from Mr. Masefield about 1920, speaks of his landlord as "a nervous, generous person, very sensitive to criticism, who seemed to have suffered greatly in the war, when an orderly in a Red Cross unit... He wrote in a hut in his garden surrounded by tall gorse-bushes and only appeared at meal-times. In the evening he used to read his day's work over to Mrs. Masefield and they would correct it together... Mrs. Masefield protected Jan. She was from the North of Ireland, a careful manager, and put a necessary brake on Jan's generosity and sociability."

Masefield's war experience consisted of service with the Red Cross in France and on the Gallipoli peninsula. The story of the bitter Dardanelles campaign is to be found in *Gallipoli* (1916). The best of his novels of adventure are *Sard Harker* (1924) and *Odtaa* (1926).

Altho his early life was difficult and he has witnessed bloodshed, Masefield believes in the essential nobility of man. "Tragedy at its best," he writes, "is a vision of the heart of life. The heart of life can only be laid bare in the agony and exultation of dreadful acts. The vision of agony or spiritual contest pushed beyond the limits of the dying personality is exalting and cleansing. It is only by such vision that a multitude can be brought to the passionate knowledge of things exulting and eternal."

Edgar Lee Masters

EDGAR LEE MASTERS was born at Garnett, Kansas, August 23, 1869. Thru his mother's people he is descended from Israel Putnam of Revolutionary fame. The father of the poet became a lawyer and was for eight years prosecuting attorney at Petersburg, Illinois, moving in 1880 to Lewistown, Illinois, a county seat five miles from the Spoon River, where he became one of the most notable lawyers of the state, and an influential factor in state and national politics. It is said of him that he knew more apt stories and used them to greater effect in his addresses to juries and on the stump than any man of his time and place. The poet's mother was born in Burke, Vermont, the daughter of Rev. Deming S. Dexter, a well known clergyman of Vermont.

The poet spent his early boyhood in Petersburg, going to his grandfather's farm to ride horses and roam the beautiful fields and woods of that country; and tramping about New Salem where he often went fishing with the boys of the town, as he himself has described his boyhood in *Mitch Miller*.

In Lewistown Masters entered the high school, from which he was graduated at seventeen. The boy then did newspaper work on the local weekly and began to contribute stories to the *Waverly Magazine* of Boston and the *Saturday Evening Call* of Peoria; as well as poems to the Chicago newspapers. At the same time he had learned the printer's trade, and was studying law under the supervision of his father.

At twenty-one, after four years of miscellaneous reading in which he devoted his time principally to meta-

EDGAR LEE MASTERS

physics and poetry and the study of
Latin, he entered Knox College, Gales-
burg, but his formal education ended a
year later. Returning to Lewistown, he
finished his law studies, being licensed
to practice in 1891. For a year he was
in partnership with his father in Lewistown; then he went to Chicago where
he soon opened a law office and until
the year 1920 devoted his days to the
care of an increasing and important
professional practice.

His first book, published in Chicago
in 1898, was *A Book of Verses,* consisting of about sixty poems culled from
the hundreds he had written before coming to Chicago. Most of them had been
published in newspapers and magazines.
Among the books that followed were a
drama, a collection of political essays,
and two anonymous series of *Songs and
Sonnets* (1910 and 1912). These publications attracted small audiences and
little praise.

A copy of *The Greek Anthology,*
pressed upon him by his friend William
Marion Reedy, was really the making
of Masters as a poet. It gave him the
idea for his *Spoon River Anthology*
(1915), in which some two hundred men
and women "sleeping on the hill" of a
small town in the mid-West shamelessly
confess their souls in a series of first-
person epitaphs. The epitaphs ran serially in *Reedy's Mirror,* St. Louis, from
week to week during 1914 before their
publication in book form. *Spoon River
Anthology* passed into edition after edition. It was published in England and
translated into German, Swedish,
French, and Spanish. Masters has published many books of verse since that
time, but none of them has achieved the
great success of his cynical and probing
book of epitaphs. The poetry collections
immediately following the "Anthology"
were *Songs and Satires* (1916), *The
Great Valley* (1917), *Toward the Gulf*
(1918), *Starved Rock* (1919), *Domesday Book* (1920), *The Open Sea* (1921).

Encouraged by a luncheon conversation with the sister of Theodore Roosevelt, during which they discussed the immortal fascination of Tom Sawyer and
Huck Finn, Mr. Masters turned for the
time from poetry and published *Mitch*
Miller in the fall of 1920 within a month
of his *Domesday Book.* He followed this
boy's story with *Children of the Market
Place* (1922), an historical novel with
Stephen A. Douglas for the central character; *Skeeters Kirby* (1923); and *The
Nuptial Flight* (1923). *Mirage* (1924)
is a continuation of *Skeeters Kirby,* and
with *Mitch Miller* forms a trilogy. Next
came the *New Spoon River* (1924),
depicting the change that has come over
the country with the modern megalopoli-
tan influences.

Among Masters' later books of verse
are *The Fate of the Jury* (1929), a continuation of *Domesday Book;* and
Lichee Nuts (1930), "Chinese" philosophical observations.

His *Lincoln, the Man* (1931) is a
biography written in gall, a bitter attack
against the "Great Emancipator," who,
according to Masters, was hypocritical,
vindictive, cold, and slow-witted.

Mr. Masters is now engaged, as he has
been for several years, on the production of *Atlantis,* which will be a long
poem, with America, its discovery,
growth, and development for a theme.
Mr. Masters spends much of his time
in and about New York, and in traveling
over America, which he never tires of
studying. He found the law incompatible with literature, and allowed it to
desert him in 1920, after a trip to Egypt.
His literary material has been developed
out of vast reading, and an almost incomparable contact with people. He says
of himself that he has written nothing
that was not true to life as he has seen
and lived it. He loves out-door life,
swimming, and walking, and whatever
conduces to that vitality out of which
alone the fulness of life can be enjoyed.

Mr. Masters is described by one interviewer as "ever so much like Thackeray,
with his round face and halo of hair";
by another as "broad shouldered and of
athletic build, having the earmarks of
his legal profession and none of the
mannerisms ascribed to poets." One of
his friends gives as his leading qualities
his unfeigned simplicity, unvarnished
frankness, a Gargantuan sense of fun,
and an unusual reverence for everything
genuine.

W. Somerset Maugham

W. SOMERSET MAUGHAM

WILLIAM SOMERSET MAUG-HAM was educated to be a doctor, made his fortune as a dramatist, and will probably be remembered as a novelist. He was born in 1874 in Paris, where his father, Robert Ormond Maugham, was a counselor at the English Embassy. A fairly prominent solicitor, his father was responsible for the foundation of the Incorporated Society of Solicitors in England.

Maugham spent his early childhood in Paris. Between the ages of ten and thirteen he lived in England for the first time as a student in King's School at Canterbury. Subsequently he studied in Germany at the University of Heidelberg. He is reported also to have studied painting in Paris.

It was his family's wish that he should become a doctor, so he returned to England and spent several years at St. Thomas's Hospital in London, graduating with the degrees of M.R.C.S. and L.R.C.P., but he has never practised.

His days at St. Thomas's were responsible, however, for his first novel, *Liza of Lambeth* (1897). The hospital is on the edge of Lambeth, a slum district which many Londoners consider worse than the famous Limehouse section. To the young medical student the cases that came to his attention were more interesting pathologically and psychologically than medically. *Liza of Lambeth,* dealing with the life he witnessed in Lambeth, was a failure; it was still the Victorian era, and those who read the book were shocked, saying that its author had gone out of his way to libel slum conditions.

The Making of a Saint (1898) *Orientations* (1899), and *The Hero* (1901), which followed did not arouse much attention. Mr. Maugham's early ambition was to write for the stage and in 1902 his first play—in one act—was produced at Berlin in German, *Schiffbrüchig.* That year another novel, *Mrs. Craddock,* appeared, with much greater success than any of the preceding. *A Man of Honor,* a play, followed in 1903; and *The Merry-go-round,* a novel, in 1904. *Lady Frederick* (1907) was his next play, his first real success. England had become conscious of the ability of this young writer and was particularly willing to give audience to his plays.

In 1915 Maugham published his *magnum opus, Of Human Bondage,* which is fundamentally, despite certain discrepancies of detail—for example, the club foot of the hero, Philip Carey—the story of the first thirty years of his life, including the whole period of his medical training. Altho the critical reception of the novel was not enthusiastic in either Great Britain or the United States at first, *Of Human Bondage* is generally recognized today as "a modern classic."

The Moon and Sixpence (1919) had immediate success. Always an inveterate traveler but never an aimless wanderer, the author had gone to Tahiti, seeking to discover the secret of the spell of the South Seas over the white man. The novel is based on the life of the artist, Paul Gauguin and while in Tahiti Mr. Maugham lived in the artist's cottage. The book was suppressed on that island because of the too accurate portraiture of Lavina, the famous landlady of the Tiare Hotel and uncrowned queen of Tahiti.

Out of Maugham's travels in the East have come many of his books, including

The Trembling of a Leaf (1921), a collection of short stories which contains "Rain," (originally called "Miss Thompson") later dramatized with such sensational success; *On a Chinese Screen* (1922), sketches of natives and Europeans; *East of Suez* (1922), the tragic drama of an idealistic English boy in the toils of Chinese marriage; *The Painted Veil* (1925), a novel; *The Gentleman in the Parlor* (1930), the record of a journey from Rangoon to Haiphong.

None of Maugham's plays approaches *Of Human Bondage* in stature, but no dramatist since Oscar Wilde has had such successes in the London theatre. He has given to the stage his wit, his shameless cynicism, and his masterly craftsmanship, if nothing else. *The Circle* (1921), *Our Betters* (1923), *The Constant Wife* (1927), and *The Letter* (1927) are among the best of his twenty-five or more plays.

During the World War, Maugham served in the Secret Service. *Ashenden or The British Agent* (1928) is based on his experiences of that time.

Maugham's novel, *Cakes and Ale or The Skeleton in the Cupboard* (1930), became a subject of public controversy on publication when critics accused Maugham of having maliciously portrayed therein two famous English authors, one recently dead and the other still living—Thomas Hardy and Hugh Walpole.

Mr. Maugham married Miss Syrie Barnardo, an authority on interior decoration, daughter of the late Dr. Barnardo. They have one child, a girl. Villa Mauresque, their home at Cap Ferrat, is one of the showplaces of the French Riviera, at once tropical and British, with its luxuriant gardens and terraces, and its marble swimming pool surrounded by cypresses and olive trees, five hundred feet above the Mediterranean.

Maugham is a serious man, "with the restless eye, the rather weatherbeaten youthfulness of a world roamer." He is deliberately reticent—"a man who makes his exquisite manners a shield between himself and the world." Burton Rascoe describes him in detail as "of medium height, heavy set, with a large head curving like a tilted question mark from the top of his high, slightly serrated forehead. His skin is a yellowish olive; his nose is long, straight, high-bridged, and his nostrils curve upward. His mouth is wide, thin-lipped, severe in line, and he has a protruding cleft chin which he mostly thrusts out with his head back. His hair is dark."

He writes from copious notes. No incident of his frequent journeyings from country to country is too trivial for him to record in his notebooks, along with the plots for stories and scenarios for plays, which accumulate so rapidly that it is not unusual for him to have his work planned ten years in advance. He has no fancy esthetics. "I look upon readableness as the highest merit that a novel can have," he writes. He believes in simple writing, in a balanced form: "A novel should have an inner harmony and there is no reason why the reader should be deprived of the delight which he may obtain from a beautiful proportion." He admires Swift and has a great love for the paintings of El Greco.

François Mauriac

FRANÇOIS MAURIAC was born in Bordeaux in 1885. His parents came from La Lande. He spent his youth in Bordeaux and later went up to Paris to study. Born in the Catholic faith, he felt, as he approached maturity, that he was a prisoner of that sect because he knew he could never escape from it . . . "and so I remember with what ardor I set about, at the age of sixteen, proving to myself the truth of a religion to which I knew myself bound for all eternity."

Like André Lafon, who was his literary idol, he was a poet before he became a novelist. He began by writing poetic criticisms for the *Revue du Temps Present* in 1910. Then he published two volumes of verse, *Les Mains Jointes* (1910) and *L'Adieu à l'Adolescence* (1911), both in the vein of Lafon. Fourteen years later he published another book of poems, *Orages* (1925). But he had meanwhile given up poetry for novels.

Mauriac's first novel, *L'Enfant Chargé de Chaînes,* appeared in 1913. It is the story of a young Frenchman, tortured from childhood by the devils of the flesh, who, after seeking satisfaction vainly in several liaisons, enters a Jesuit cloister to purge himself of his torments, and thereafter marries his cousin to keep himself in that happily innocuous state. *La Robe Prétexte* (1914) is another story of youth, showing the influence of Lafon and his *Elève Gilles.* In it Mauriac recalls his own youthful experiences in Bordeaux and Paris.

In his early novels, Mauriac definitely stamped himself as a writer of Southwest France, laying his stories in and around Bordeaux and La Lande. Also, he identified himself with the little group of writers which banded shortly before the war—Ernest Psichari, Emile Baumann, Robert Vallery-Radot, and André Lafon. The Catholic ascetic ideal is the motivating factor in all his work, altho only his first novels are concerned with strictly religious subjects.

During the World War Mauriac turned soldier and when the conflict was ended he returned to his writing with *La Chair et le Sang* (1920). In the same year he published a defense of his religious faith in *Petits Essais de Psychologie Religieuse.* Then followed *Préséances* (1921), a satire on the snobbishness of the rich wine merchants of Bordeaux. Mauriac says: "I have always contrasted Bordeaux with the Provençe in order to expose its nakedness, and nevertheless I love it. . ."

Mauriac came to public notice with the appearance of the *Cahiers Verts,* which took the place of the pre-war *Cahiers de la Quinzaine.* The first work to appear in the *Cahiers Verts,* called *Le Baiser au Lépreux* (1922), definitely established the author's reputation. A gloomy and terrible novel, it is a serious evangelistic document, directed against the system of intellectual rejection represented in the philosophy of Nietzsche. The protagonists are partners in an ill-assorted marriage. *Le Fleuve de Feu* (1923) deals with another aspect of unhappy marriage.

FRANÇOIS MAURIAC

Mauriac summed up all he had to say in *Genitrix* (1923), a stark and terrible story in which an aged widow loves her fifty-year-old son with a love so passionate and tyrannic that she separates him from his wife and lets her die. *La Vie et la Mort d'un Poète* (1924) is a memoir of André Lafon. In it Mauriac exposes his literary ideas. *Le Desert de l'Amour* (1925) returns to the snobbish wine merchant bourgeoisie of Bordeaux.

In 1926 Mauriac was awarded the annual French *Prix de Roman* of five thousand francs. The French Academy, delaying recognition according to its custom, gave the prize for two of his early novels, *La Robe Prétexte,* and *L'Enfant Chargé de Chaînes.*

His later works include: *Bordeaux* (1926), *Le Jeune Homme* (1926), *La Province* (1926), *Thérèse Desqueyroux* (1927), *Destins* (1928), *Le Vie de Jean Racine* (1928), *Le Roman* (1928), *La Nuit du Bourreau de Soi-même* (1929), *Trois Récits* (1929), and *Dieu et Mammon* (1929).

Mauriac has a horror of earthly love. His unique conception of love is of something terrible, disturbing, and destructive. In human matings he sees only the incessant yearning for a union more perfect than can ever be consummated on earth.

Translations of Mauriac's works published in America are: *Thérèse* (1928), *Destinies* (1929), *The Desert of Love* (1929), and *The Family* (1930). The last volume includes *The Kiss to the Leper* and *Genetrix*.

André Maurois

IN 1885, in Elbeuf, a small city in the department of Seine-Inférieure, was born André Maurois, French novelist and biographer. His name at birth was Emile Herzog.

At the neighboring lycée at Rouen the youthful Maurois distinguished himself chiefly by a mastery of the English language. His studies, however, were cut short when his family required him to return to the textile mills at Elbeuf, of which they were the owners. But life as an industrial manager in a provincial city did not at all suit Maurois; like the hero of his novel, *Bernard Quesnay,* in which there is much of his own life, his eyes were upon the literary circles of Paris. Then, suddenly, the World War. It was a turning point for many lives; but for M. Maurois, as the event proved, it was a turning point of happy augury,

ANDRÉ MAUROIS

since as a soldier he had time to write, at last. English speaking officers were scarce and valuable and he was detailed as a liaison officer to the Ninth Scottish Division, and thence after two years, to British GHQ. From the experiences and observations of these years came his first three books: *Les Silences du Colonel Bramble* (1918), *Le Général Bramble,* and *Les Discours du Docteur O'Grady* (1920).

When Maurois, who knew nothing of the mechanics of the publishing trade, had finished his first book, he showed it to a fellow officer, who took it from him and arranged for its publication with a prominent French publisher. The publisher did not have much confidence in a novel about the English, but the book has gone into well over a hundred editions.

The success of these volumes persuaded Maurois to withdraw gradually from the business world, altho for a long period he was forced to divide his time equally between literature and business, three days a week to each. His first venture in the field of biography was an experimental novel entitled *Ni Ange ni Bête* (1919), based upon the life of Shelley. Upon its publication it proved a failure, but Maurois, determined to discover the reason for this literary rebuff, sat down to rewrite the work entirely, casting it the second time in the form of a biography. The success of *Ariel: The Life of Shelley* is literary history. It became a best seller in two languages and three countries and established a reputation for M. Maurois among modern biographers. It appeared in France in 1923 and was translated a year later.

Maurois' most important works since *Ariel* have also been biographies of Englishmen: *The Life of Disraeli* (1927) and *Byron* (1930).

He believes that the new biography should differ radically from the old, which was chiefly commemorative and didactic. For one thing, he abandons the apparatus of notes, eulogies, acknowledgments, sources, bibliographies, etc. His aim is "to build a work of art," with as much symmetry and form as the novel. The biographer "must not invent anything, but his art is to forget. If he has at his disposal 200 letters and a long diary, he must know how to extract the few sentences that will convey a genuine impression." Maurois admits that "at heart, the novel appeals to me much more than biography. It is terribly difficult to invest real life with any kind of unity and beauty. It resists such treatment. . . . Life is complicated. It is not simple enough."

His novels include the autobiographical *Bernard Quesnay* (1926, translated 1927); *Climats* (1928, translated 1929 as *Atmosphere of Love*); and *The Weigher of Souls* (translated 1931).

M. Maurois was married in 1912 to Janine de Szymkiewicz; his second wife (1926) is Simone de Caillavet. He has two sons and a daughter from his first marriage, and a daughter from his second.

M. Maurois lives in Paris with his wife and his children. He is in as great demand as a lecturer in English as he is in French. On his visit to America in the fall of 1927, he lectured at Princeton, Yale, and other Eastern Universities, and his *Aspects of Biography* (1929) is based upon a series delivered at Cambridge University, England. In the fall of 1930 he lectured at Princeton as the first incumbent of the Meredith Howland Pyne Lectureship in French Literature.

It is said that he gathered material at Princeton for a life of Woodrow Wilson.

In appearance, writes Sisley Huddleston, Maurois is "a well-groomed man with sleek silvery hair brushed from the middle round a high forehead, heavy-lidded bright eyes in a hatchet-shaped sensitive face, nose and lips which reveal his race, a short-trimmed mustache. . ."

At Princeton he was seen as "the keen and sensitive type of Frenchman, a man whose appearance and every gesture exhibit a nervous, driving vitality leashed by a sympathetic understanding and yet scholarly mind. In repose he is likely to slump back in his chair, his body relaxed and only his fingers, tightly interlaced, betraying the tightly coiled energy he will display a moment later when he bends forward and sits on the very edge of the chair to speak. Then his gestures are quick and his phrases direct, unequivocal and penetrating as his own writing."

Maurois' miscellaneous publications in translation include: *Mape, the World of Illusion* (1926); *An Essay on Dickens* (1927); *Aspects of Biography* (1929); *Next Chapter, War against the Moon* (1929); *Voyage to the Island of the Articoles* (1929); *Conversation* (1930); *The Country of Thirty-Six Thousand Wishes* (1930).

W. B. Maxwell

WILLIAM BABINGTON MAXWELL was born in 1866 into a literary atmosphere. His mother was M. E. Braddon (Miss Braddon), a popular English novelist, who wrote stories of a sensational nature. His father was John Maxwell, the publisher, whose business developed into that of the London firm of Hurst and Blackett.

Maxwell had no youthful ambitions to write, however. He wanted to paint. His parents sent him to ordinary school until he was fourteen. Then he was allowed to please himself as to what further education he would have. He went to art school in London. A few years of study convinced him that he could never be a painter, so he relin-

W. B. MAXWELL

quished the brush and retired to country life, his ambitions crushed.

For a number of years Maxwell was without occupation—"at a loose end," as the English say. He spent his time hunting a good deal with the New Forest hounds, when living at his mother's beautiful country house, Annesley Bank, near Lundhurst; traveling on the Continent; and, as he puts it, "comfortably idling and perhaps learning my future trade or profession, which you will, of novelist the while."

In the long years that followed his disappointment as a painter, Maxwell's mother appeared undisturbed and offered him help. He says: "Most of the knowledge I possess of how to write and, indeed, the fact that I commenced to write at all, I owe to my mother. She was never too busy, or too immersed in her work to discuss my literary ambitions, or work of my own. She did not always know the way any story of mine was going, for I wished neither for it to be an imitation of hers nor in any way to trade upon her own great and world-wide reputation."

Maxwell began to write when his mother's novels were still in vogue, altho her popularity was waning. Avoiding her pattern, he struck out in an independent line, concerning himself more with the mysteries of human psychology than with sensational happenings. When he was thirty-five he published his first book, *The Countess of Maybury* (1901), a series of satirical, light comedy dialogs. Two years later came a collection of short stories, *Fabulous Fancies* (1903).

He credits a London publisher named Grant Richards with getting him actually started in his career. "Had I not chanced to meet Richards," he says, "I should probably never seriously have attempted to become a novelist." Richards commissioned him to write "an arresting and soul-stirring novel of modern life," and he agreed to publish it. The venture proved successful and *The Ragged Messenger* (1904) made an impression on London, despite the fact that it was a tragic story.

Novels appeared practically every year after that, except for the period of the World War. *The Devil's Garden* (1913) was banned from circulating libraries in England, with the result that its sale was greatly enhanced on both sides of the Atlantic. The American film version of the story starred Lionel Barrymore. Altho he was nearly fifty when the war began, Maxwell served thruout as sub-altern and later as captain in the Royal Fusiliers.

Maxwell's view of the novelist's function has always been "that he should show life as it is, and the minds of men and women as they are; and that there should be no limits to his freedom of choice of subject and method of dealing with it except the ordinary canons of good taste that govern the age in which he is writing. Obviously the present age is one in which great license of speech is allowed. In ordinary society young and old talk of anything and everything. . . . Why then, it may well be asked, should the novelist be squeamish or mealy-mouthed?"

Of his mother he says: "I am nothing beside her. It was she who was the instinctive writer." He takes his art seriously. He says: "The events which makes up a plot only interest me as showing the states and phases of mind which result from them, and those I try to do objectively. In *The Day's Journey* (1923) he states that there is no human creature so dull, so commonplace, but that if we understand his tenderness, his anxieties, his wistful hopes, we should not find him interesting. Maxwell looks at the world with great kindliness.

A shy man of past sixty, the expression on his face remains tragic and defeated. But his eyes are not dull. Grant Overton describes him: "His mouth is pitiful and compassionate and kind; it broods upon the things that the eyes have seen, those eyes with their deep glance, as often as not turned upward, as if fixed upon the things that lie in the mind behind them, projected somewhere ahead and up. It is a face without hope but with any amount of mercy; a heavy face that has the effect of increasing the appearance of shyness." Yet for all its tragedy, the face is not a mask. It is alive.

Maxwell is Chairman of the National Book Council in England. His wife is the youngest daughter of the late Charles William Moore of the Bengal Civil

Service. They have one son and one daughter. Their home is in London. Maxwell is a member of the Carlton, Garrick, and Beefstead Clubs.

Among his novels are: *The Guarded Flame* (1906), *Mrs. Thompson* (1911), *The Devil's Garden* (1913), *The Mirror and the Lamp* (1918), *Spinster of This Parish* (1922), *The Day's Journey* (1923), *Elaine at the Gates* (1924), *Gabrielle* (1926), *We Forget Because We Must* (1928), *Himself and Mr. Raikes* (1929), *To What Green Altar?* (1930), *The Concave Mirror* (1931).

Julius Meier-Graefe

TRAVELER, artist, critic, and writer, Julius Meier-Graefe was born in Resitza, near Berlin, on June 10, 1867. His father was General-Director Meier-Graefe. His grandfather on his father's side was a professor of philology. Julius Meier-Graefe was educated at the Universities of Berlin, Munich, Lüttich, and Zürich. In 1895 he was married.

Herr Meier-Graefe's chief literary contributions have been toward an understanding of modern art and toward a revaluation of the rôle of the past in civilization. His magazine articles appear frequently in America in the *International Studio*. His interpretations of modern artists are widely recognized.

This German critic is a tireless traveler. Two of his recent books reflect these travels. The purpose of the author's *Spanish Journey* (1927) was to pay his homage to Velasquez. Once in the Prado, to his own astonishment he found himself transferring his allegiance from Velasquez to El Greco. The story of this critical about-face, together with colorful incidents of his stay in Spain, is confided with pleasant humor in this travel diary.

Pyramid and Temple (1930) is an informal and philosophical travel-diary describing his leisurely journey thru Egypt, Palestine, and Greece. The greater portion of the book is devoted to Egypt, her monuments and sculpture, and her civilization past and present. *Pyramid and Temple* was Meier-Graefe's fortieth work.

JULIUS MEIER-GRAEFE

In his treatment of ancient civilizations he has been iconoclastic, but has given rich new life to them. He believes that Egyptian sculpture and architecture are superior to the Greek; that the Byzantine civilization was powerful and vital. He was one of the few to appraise the Tutankhamen discoveries as representing a decadent period in art.

Herr Meier-Graefe, now in his sixties, is an example of what sheer vital intellectual interest in life can do to preserve health and vigor. He endures the discomforts of travel, the vigils of study, and the labors of writing with an apparently inexhaustible energy When not traveling, he has lived of late years in Dresden and Berlin.

In his early works Herr Meier-Graefe wrote appraisals of Prince Lichtenarm, Edward Munch, Felix Vallotton, and Manet. Later works concern Corot, Courbet, Cheramy, Cézanne Van Gogh, Renoir, Delacroix, and Degas. Two of his books are on modern impressionism.

English translations of Herr Meier-Graefe's books include: *Vincent Van Gogh*, a biographical study (1922); *Degas* (1923); *Cézanne* (1927); *The Spanish Journey* (1927); *Dostoevsky*, the man and his work (1928); and *Pyramid and Temple* (1930). His chief translator is J. Hobroyd Reece.

Cornelia Meigs

WITH the common perversity of authors who are prone to write about Manhattan Island in Paris, and of the interior of Africa in a Park Avenue penthouse, Cornelia Meigs' most widely known book, *The Trade Wind* (a story of a boy's adventures at sea during the pre-Revolutionary period) was written in the inland reaches of Iowa. It is only fair to state, however, that it was based upon previous study in Salem, Mass. This was the story which won the Little Brown & Company $2,000 prize, offered in 1927 for the most suitable children's book submitted for publication. Miss Meigs' interest in the sea is a perfectly legitimate example of atavism: she is the great-granddaughter of Commodore John Rodgers, of the *Constitution*.

Cornelia Lynde Meigs was born at Rock Island, Illinois, on December 6, 1884. She used to spend the summers on her grandfather's farm in Vermont, but was educated in the Public Schools of Keokuk, Iowa, where her father is United States Civil Engineer in charge of River Improvement. Miss Meigs was graduated from Bryn Mawr in 1908, and taught English for some years after that in Davenport, Iowa, beginning at this time to write, and to try out her stories on the children of the school. She pub-lished several stories under the pseudonym of "Adair Aldon."

She has a "very large collection" of nephews and nieces, who, she says, "read my stories the moment they are written and help me much with their comments." She was herself one of six sisters, and writing of *The Trade Wind* and of her nostalgic interest in the sea (in Iowa), she says: "While my sisters made up games having to do with Robin Hood and Little John, with emigrants crossing the prairies, I was playing long games of my own that had to do with ships. The stories which I heard about my great-grandfather and his children all turned my thoughts to seafaring. I was nine years old before I first saw the sea and I have, since then, spent as much of my time near it as circumstances would possibly allow. I keep my papers and manuscripts in John Rodgers' little green sea chest that went with him to the wars and back again, and whenever I take up my pen to begin a new piece of work, the spirit of the old Commodore seems to whisper in my ear, 'Let it be about ships.'"

Miss Meigs has been described as a woman of spiritual reserve and seriousness, with an uncommon refinement of intellect and sentiment, "a mental fastidiousness that rejects inevitably the phrase or sentiment that has a tinge of commonness."

Her books are: *Kingdom of the Winding Road* (1915); *Master Simon's Garden* (1916); *The Steadfast Princess* (Drama League prize play, 1916); *The Pool of Stars* (1919); *The Windy Hill* (1921); *Helga and the White Peacock* (play, 1922); *The New Moon* (1924); *Rain on the Roof* (1925); *Trade Wind* (1927); *As the Crow Flies* (1927); *The Wonderful Locomotive* (1928); *Clearing Weather* (1928); *The Crooked Apple Tree* (1929).

CORNELIA MEIGS

H. L. Mencken

HENRY LOUIS MENCKEN has been denounced more copiously and violently than any American of the present age. His attacks upon Babbitts, professors, patriots, and politicians have met with excessively hearty response, and he has been accused of a long list of high crimes and misdemeanors ranging from slandering Abraham Lincoln to ruining the English language in America, and from taking money from the late Kaiser to working as a spy for the Bolsheviki. In 1928 Mencken succeeded in making his enemies earn royalties for him by publishing *Menckeniana, a Schimpflexicon,* in which he collected the diatribes against himself and his opinions in 'a dictionary of abuse.' His sympathizers look upon him as a champion of honest thought in America; his foes regard him as a public menace.

Mencken was born in Baltimore, Md., on September 12, 1880. His German grandfather came to Baltimore in 1848 and founded a tobacco factory which was continued by his father, a hardheaded, autocratic business man, who planned to educate his oldest son, Henry, for the tobacco business. But Henry had intentions of his own about his career. He read *Huckleberry Finn* when he was six, began "seriously" to write at twelve, and turned to poetic and musical composition at fifteen. He was educated at private schools and at the Baltimore Polytechnic, where he adopted Huxley as his god. When he was graduated in 1896 he was determined to become a journalist.

His father died and young Mencken, the new head of the family, became a reporter on the *Baltimore Morning Herald.* By 1903 he was city editor. He published his first book, *Ventures into Verse,* in 1903. In 1905 he was made editor of the *Evening Herald* and his *George Bernard Shaw—His Plays* appeared in the same year. He joined the staff of the *Baltimore Sun* in 1906 and was transferred to the *Evening Sun* in 1910. Meanwhile he became literary critic for *Smart Set* in 1908, and in 1914 he was made a co-editor of the magazine with George Jean Nathan.

The years 1916 and 1917 Mr. Mencken spent as correspondent for the German army. In 1917 his *In Defense of Women* appeared. He returned to the *Baltimore Evening Sun* in 1918 and published *The American Language* (1918). He began his famous series of *Prejudices* the following year, subsequent volumes appearing in 1920, 1922, 1924, 1926, and 1927.

H. L. MENCKEN

A contributing editor of the *Nation* since 1921, Mr. Mencken has also been a contributor to many other magazines, including the *Atlantic Monthly, Century, Yale Review, New Republic, London Nation,* and *Neue Rundschau.* He was a correspondent at the famous Scopes trial and has reported many national conventions.

In 1924 he founded, with Nathan, the *American Mercury,* a magazine of which he is now sole editor. In its pages have appeared his caustic comments on American life and his scathing denunciations of shams and hypocricies. He has been known variously as the "Blond Beast of Baltimore," the "Ogre of Hollins Street," and the "Boogey-man of the Booboisie." *Notes on Democracy* was published in 1926. It is a short summing up of Mencken's political and philosophical creed. *Treatise on the Gods* (1930) discusses the history of religion in its various forms, and the present-day attitude toward Christianity. His own position on the subject is one of amiable skepticism.

Mr. Mencken is a rather short, stocky figure of a man, plump-cheeked and boyish, with innocent blue eyes and an infectious laugh. He is an inveterate playboy and loves practical jokes. In

the midst of his voluminous work he finds
time for such pranks as sending to his
intimate friends Yom Kippur greetings
or the printed pamphlets of some sect
announcing the second coming of the
Messiah.

He loathes the theatre, and has seldom
been inside one since he forswore
dramatic criticism by inserting a full
page advertisement in a Baltimore paper
to the effect that he was thru with the
theatre and would have the law on the
next manager who sent him tickets. He
also hates, or affects to hate, putting on
dress clothes. He believes in getting the
most joy possible out of life, as long as
one does not interfere with the happiness
of others in so doing.

A bachelor and a satirist of the institution of marriage, Mr. Mencken ventured into matrimony himself in August
1930 when he married Sara Haardt, a
contributor to the *American Mercury*.
Mr. Mencken was just shy of fifty when
he took the vows. His wife published a
novel in 1931, *The Making of a Lady*.
He continues to live in Baltimore, where
most of his writing and editorial work is
done. He visits New York for a few
days each month in connection with his
duties on the *American Mercury*.

His long list of books includes criticism, philosophy, plays, and verse. His
books, other than those mentioned,
include: *The Philosophy of Friedrich
Nietzsche* (1908); *The Artist*, a play
(1912); *A Book of Burlesques* (1916):
A Book of Prefaces (1917); *Selected
Prejudices* (1927); and *James Branch
Cabell* (1927).

Mr. Mencken is part author of: *Men
vs. the Man* (1910); *Europe After 8:15*
(1914); *The American Credo* (1920);
and *Heliogabalus*, a play (1920). He is
the editor of *The Players' Ibsen* (1909)
and *The Free Lance Books* (1919).

Leonard Merrick

LEONARD MERRICK'S life might
well have furnished the plot for one
of his novels. He was born on February
21, 1864, at Belsize Park, on the outskirts of Hampstead, his name at birth
being Leonard Miller. Altho brought up
in luxury with an education at private

LEONARD MERRICK

schools and Brighton College, he was
thrust suddenly into poverty. He went
with his parents to South Africa when
he was eighteen and, entering the South
African Civil Service, became a clerk in
the Magistrate's Court on the Diamond
Fields.

After suffering great hardships there,
he made his way with difficulty back to
England when he was twenty. He had
been born "stage-struck" and his one
ambition was to achieve fame as an
actor, so he obtained an introduction to
Augustus Harris, who gave him an
engagement to act in a touring company
that was traveling the country with one
of the sensational Drury Lane melodramas. He proved himself a capable
player and he legally adopted his stage
name, Merrick. But after two years
with the company his enthusiasm for the
actor's life cooled and he retired from
the profession for good.

At twenty-three young Merrick started
writing and his first book appeared when
he was twenty-four. Unsuccessful at
earning his living by writing, he voyaged

to New York. There, in the small bed-room of a boarding house, while he searched for a theatrical job, he wrote *Violet Moses,* his second novel. But he didn't get the job and, still penniless, he returned to England with his manuscript. *Violet Moses* was rejected by one publishing firm but accepted by a second. His third novel, *The Man Who Was Good* (1892), was rejected by the firm which had published *Violet Moses,* but promptly accepted by the firm which had refused its predecessor.

Mr. Merrick published some half dozen novels before he started to write short stories, which, he confesses, are his preference. "A novel takes an eternity to write"—he is a slow writer—but "one can attempt all sorts of experiments in form with the short story, and one never need pad by so much as a syllable." He cannot write a short story until he "gets hold of an idea"; sometimes he must wait two months between stories. He has found it difficult "to keep body and soul together by his pen."

In 1894 Merrick married Hope Butler-Wilkins of Northampton. While he was in his thirties he lived for some time in Paris. At intervals in the following years he left the retirement of his English home to visit Paris where he found ideas and stimulation such as London did not offer. He confesses he does not love London. It is the most comfortable of cities, he admits, but he finds it un-inspiring and he can work better and more easily when he is almost anywhere away from it—especially in Paris.

Mr. Merrick's wife died in 1917, leaving one daughter. Her novel, *Mary-girl,* was published posthumously in 1920. In 1918 Mr. Merrick's novels and stories were reissued in a collected edition with introductions by some of the most famous literary men of the day, including Barrie, Pinero, Wells, Howells, and Chesterton. Until the appearance of the collected edition Mr. Merrick had been writing for thirty years without receiving much recognition. Even since that time many critics have expressed the opinion that he does not enjoy the popularity that his gift as a story-teller deserves.

Merrick is described by Frank Harris as "a small, handsome man, slight but wiry and healthy, with melancholy, dark brooding eyes, long straight nose, and large black mustache." His ancestry is Jewish.

He is a personality of a gracious and retiring nature, and he is seldom seen in literary circles. He has no skill in self-advertisement. His comment is: "Of course I have been disappointed when my books were freely praised by the critics and did not meet with the large circulations I had hoped for them, and sometimes, when I have thought about it, I have had a suspicion that perhaps I wrote too much of artists. . ." And he adds that if readers are to be told of the artist, "they don't want to be saddened by a tale of his failure."

He has experienced much of the life he has depicted in his books. *The Position of Peggy Harper* (1911) was written from his stage experiences. His plays include: *The Free Pardon* (with F. C. Philips), *When the Lamps are Lighted, My Innocent Boy, The Elixir of Youth,* and *A Woman in the Case* (with George R. Sims).

One of Mr. Merrick's best known novels is *Conrad in Quest of His Youth* (1903), a subtle and sophisticated story of Conrad's endeavor to resurrect his past loves and his discovery of a new one. In contrast to the unhappy themes of his early stories is the gay and lively tone of *The Little Dog Laughed,* a collection of short stories published in 1930. Among previous volumes of short stories are: *This Stage of Fools* (1896), *Whispers About Women* (1906), *The Man Who Understood Women* (1908), *While Paris Laughed* (1918), *A Chair on the Boulevard* (1919), *To Tell You the Truth* (1922), *The Call from the Past and Other Stories* (1924), and *Four Stories* (1927).

Mr. Merrick's novels include, besides those mentioned: *Cynthia* (1896), *One Man's View* (1897), *The Actor-Manager* (1898), *The Worldlings* (1900), *When Love Flies Out o' the Window* (1902), *The Quaint Companions* (1903), and *The House of Lynch* (1907).

Edna St. Vincent Millay

EDNA ST. VINCENT MILLAY was born to her poetic name on February 22, 1892, in Rockland, Maine. She spent her grammar and high school days in Rockland and in Camden, Maine. While she was still a little tomboy she published verses in *St. Nicholas* and won numerous awards. At the graduation exercises in Camden High School her essay, written in verse, won the prize.

In the interval between graduation and entrance to Barnard College, Columbia University, Miss Millay studied music and literature. She was encouraged by her mother, who recognized her poetic gift. A woman who visited the simple Millay household one day became interested in the girl's poetry and supplied funds for her to go to college. After a brief period at Barnard, Miss Millay went to Vassar where she won the cup awarded in the Intercollegiate Poetry Contest.

At the age of nineteen, while still a schoolgirl, Miss Millay expressed her love for nature in her first long poem, *Renascence* (1912), which won for her nation-wide fame and admiration. It was the outstanding feature of *The Lyric Year* (1912), an anthology edited

EDNA ST. VINCENT MILLAY

by Frederick Pinney Earle and Mitchell Kennerley. She received her A.B. degree in 1917 and wrote the words and music for the three exercises at graduation time. In the same year she published her first slim black volume, *Renascence and Other Poems* (1917).

Miss Millay went to New York and supported herself at first by writing short stories under various pseudonyms. She lived in a lodging house on Twelfth Street in Greenwich Village. Llewelyn Powys, in his *Verdict of Bridlegoose,* describes his impression of her at that time: "She was dainty with a daintiness that can only be compared with the daintiness of Queen Anne's lace. . . I came to appreciate the rash quality of her nature, heedless and lovely. . . She might disguise herself in all the pretty frippery that she could buy at Wanamaker's, she might be photographed for *Vanity Fair* every day of the week, and yet below her laces and ribbons there will always remain a barefoot poet, doomed yet redeemed, under the shadow of Eternity." She knew poverty, but she had many friends.

A Few Figs from Thistles, her second book of verse, appeared in 1920. *Second April* followed in 1921. Miss Millay joined the Provincetown Players in the capacity of playwright and actress. Alfred Kreymborg recalls that she used to appear at rehearsals, "when she appeared at all, an hour or two in arrears," but that her complete "understanding of the pantomimic demands of the part" compensated for her irregularity.

Miss Millay experimented with poetic drama and she published three plays, all in 1921: *Two Slatterns and a King; The Lamp and the Bell,* a five-act drama written in Paris and performed in the Vassar open air theatre at the June 1921 commencement; and *Aria da Capo,* a one-act satire on war which was presented by the Provincetown Players and translated into French for production in Paris.

She was awarded the Pulitzer Prize for poetry in 1923 with *The Harp-Weaver.* Part Four of the book contains twenty-two sonnets which are considered representative of Miss Millay's best work. Her sonnets, of all her writings, have received the highest praise: it is the form in which she prefers to write.

In 1923 she married Eugen Jan Boissevain, an importer, and moved to a farm in the Berkshires where she has spent much of her time since. She makes occasional pilgrimages to New York City and Italy. On her first visit to Rome she expressed a desire to leave the city as soon as possible. "The ghosts of the emperors have chilled my bones," she said. And fled to Vienna.

In spite of ill health, Miss Millay devoted the summer of 1926 to the completion, according to contract, of the libretto for *The King's Henchman* (1927), an opera composed by Deems Taylor. It was produced at the Metropolitan Opera House in New York City early in 1927.

Miss Millay lectures frequently and is well known as a reader of her own poems. Llewelyn Powys described her four years after their first meeting: "She possessed the same fragile appearance, the same brittle, shell-like, pearl-like appearance that had always set me marvelling. And her lovely leprechaun eyes, yellow-green in color, had the same strange light in them that I had observed at first, like the light of baffled mistrust in the eyes of an infinitely desirable mermaiden who finds a crowd of alien creatures looking down at her. . ." She has thick coppery gold hair, which was red in her childhood. She talks clearly, with marked precision and poise. Robinson Jeffers, to her mind, is the greatest American poet.

On her infrequent visits to New York, Miss Millay buys the latest gowns and frocks and shoes and hats before retiring to her country home, where she and her husband dine formally every evening. During the day she writes or putters about her garden in a tweed dress and sweater. She works hard at her poetry, but only when in the mood for it. Cheap notebooks ("Composition, 10 Cents") are scattered over the rambling farmhouse, including one that is always kept by her bed with a supply of sharp pencils. She sometimes finds it difficult to decipher her scrawl when the time comes to transcribe the verses.

In March 1931 she told an interviewer that her next book would be called "Epitaph for the Race of Man." The title springs from her cognizance of the "horrible and cruel things men do to each other."

The works by Edna St. Vincent Millay include: *Renascence* (1917); *A Few Figs from Thistles* (1920); *Second April* (1921); *Aria da Capo* (1921); *The Lamp and the Bell* (1921); *Two Slatterns and a King* (1921); *The Harp-Weaver* (1923); *Distressing Dialogues* (1924), a collection of smart and amusing sketches published under the pseudonym "Nancy Boyd"; *The King's Henchman* (1927); *The Buck in the Snow* (1928); *Selected Poems for Young People* (1929); *Fatal Interview* (1931), a volume of 52 love sonnets.

Renascence was translated into Spanish and appeared in Pan-American papers. It is said Miss Millay is the only American poet besides Poe to be translated into Spanish.

Sarah Gertrude Millin

IT is natural that Sarah Gertrude Millin's books should all deal with South Africa for she was born there and has lived there all her life. Her parents were Isaiah and Olga Liebson. A Jewess, she was never discouraged as a child from knowing human beings of all kinds and colors—from the shameful to the acclaimed. Thus she gained an understanding of all classes of people.

In school she had the highest scholarship of any girl in South Africa, and her friends predicted a brilliant university career. Ingratiating letters reached her from various colleges. But she turned her back on academic fame and followed her own secret path to literary success. When she was nineteen she published her first short story and ten years later her first novel appeared—*Dark River* (1920). Since then she has written a novel a year and become noted as the portrayer of life in South Africa.

God's Stepchildren (1924) are the half-castes of South Africa—the Bastaards. The tale covers four generations, starting with the poor English missionary who settles in a miserable Hottentot village and, in his loneliness, marries a

SARAH GERTRUDE MILLIN

native girl. He dies in squalor and wretchedness but he has started a new generation marked with a color-streak. The fortunes of the daughter, the granddaughter, and the great-grandson make up the story.

Mrs. Millin's husband is Philip Millin, King's Counsel, a member of the Johannesburg bar. Her home in Johannesburg stands amid a conflagration of marigolds which she planted herself. There are few servant troubles in her household, for she has a cook and a Zulu houseboy. The cook, a Cape colored woman, is one of "God's Stepchildren." They keep control of the house in the quiet morning hours while Mrs. Millin is writing.

She entertains her quests in an informal atmosphere around a table served by the "Stepchild." Other guests arrive before dinner is over, perhaps, and join the circle at the "walnuts and wine" stage. When it draws quite late the bridge tables are brought out and Mrs. Millin plays cards—not dreamily, with one mental eye on her next chapter—but at lightening speed and with deadly accuracy.

Her husband, a successful barrister, is far from the meek partner of a successful woman; he has a personality as firmly developed as his wife's. He has a way of kneeling down in front of the bookcase at the homes of his friends and becoming lost to the world. He does not glare if his own guests kneel before the Millin books, which line nearly every wall of the house and are now threatening to invade the kitchen. Mrs. Millin and her husband are fond of visiting second-hand book shops and sometimes they come home with as many as thirty volumes.

Mrs. Millin has written for the *London Mercury, London Adelphi, Nineteenth Century, Nash's Magazine,* and *Cosmopolitan.* She has visited Europe three times and America once.

Among her books are: *The Dark River* (1920), *Middle Class* (1921), *Adam's Rest* (1922), *The Jordans* (1923), *God's Stepchildren* (1924), *Mary Glenn* (1925), *The South Africans* (1926), *An Artist in the Family* (1927), *The Coming of the Lord* (1928), and *The Fiddler* (1929).

A. A. Milne

"I WAS born in London, on January 18th, 1882, but nobody believes it. At the age of eleven I went to Westminster School with a scholarship and for a year worked very hard, but at twelve I began to feel that I knew enough and thereafter took life more easily. Perhaps the most important thing that happened there was that I began to write verses, parodies, and the like for the school paper. One evening when another boy and I were looking at a copy of a Cambridge undergraduate paper, *The Granta* which had come to the school, he said solemnly: 'You ought to edit that some day.' So I said, equally solemnly: 'I will.' This sounds like the story of the model boy who became a millionaire; I apologize for it, but it really did happen. I went to Cambridge, in spite of the fact that everybody meant me to go to Oxford, and edited *The Granta.*

"I left Cambridge in 1903 with a very moderate degree and a feeling in the family that I had belied the brilliant promise of my youth, and that it was about time I got to work and did something. Schoolmastering and the Indian civil service were two of the professions suggested. The first was not very exciting; the second meant more examinations to pass; so I said that I was going to London to write. I had enough money left over from my Cambridge allowance to keep me for a year, and by the end of the year I saw myself the most popular writer in London—editor of *The Times, Punch,* and *The Spectator,* member of all the important literary clubs and intimate friend of Meredith and Hardy. My family was not so optimistic. They saw me at the end of the year deciding to be a schoolmaster. However, they gave me their blessing; and I went to London, took expensive rooms and settled down to write. . .

"By the end of the year I had spent my money and I had earned by writing—twenty pounds. So I moved to two cheap and dirty rooms in a policeman's house in Chelsea and went on writing. The second year I made about one hundred and twenty pounds and lived on it. In the third year I was making two hundred pounds, for several papers were now getting used to me, but in February 1906 a surprising thing happened. The editor of *Punch* retired, the assistant editor became editor, and I was offered the assistant editorship. I accepted and was assistant editor until the end of 1914."

That is Alan Alexander Milne's own account of his life up to the time he began to publish books. He collected his *Punch* essays in three volumes: *The Day's Play* (1910), *The Holiday Round* (1912), and *Once a Week* (1914). They appeared, together with *The Sunny Side* (1921), in a single volume, *Those Were the Days* (1929). He was married in 1913 to Dorothy de Selincourt.

During the World War he served with the Royal Warwickshire Regiment on the Western Front. Before going to France he was sent to a training camp at Totland Bay in the Isle of Wight. There he found leisure moments to write *Once on a Time* (1917), a fairy story for grown-ups, which was acted by a group of soldiers and their wives in a small auditoriuom near the camp. Mr. Milne and his wife both played in it. Then he tried his hand for the first time as a dramatist and wrote *Wurzel-Flummery* (1917), a satirical comedy.

Mr. Milne suffered a breakdown, spent a while in a hospital, and then was sent

A. A. MILNE AND CHRISTOPHER ROBIN

to act as signaling instructor at a fort on Portsdown Hill. There, after each long day of teaching, he would go home to the cottage where he and his wife were living, and dictate to her, until he had produced three plays in succession: *Belinda, The Boy Comes Home,* and *The Lucky One.* These appeared, with *Wurzel-Flummery* and *The Red Feathers* in his collective volume, *First Plays* (1917).

When Mr. Milne was demobilized, his old post on *Punch* was waiting for him but he decided to devote all his time to his own writing. He turned out three books of essays. His play, *Mr. Pim Passes By* appeared in 1919, and it was included in his volume of *Second Plays* (1921). In 1923 Mr. Milne published his third collective volume, *Three Plays,* containing *The Dover Road, The Truth About Blayds,* and *The Great Broxopp.*

About this time Mr. Milne's small son, Christopher Robin, began to inspire his father's writing. He calls himself "Moon" and has nicknamed his father "Blue." The author wrote several books about his son's favorites who include Pooh, Piglet, and Eyore: *When We Were Very Young* (1924), *Winnie-the-Pooh* (1926), *Now We Are Six* (1927), and *The House at Pooh Corner* (1928). Then he dedicated three more books to his son: *The Christopher Robin Story Book* (1929), *The Christopher Robin Reader* (1929), and *The Christopher Robin Birthday Book* (1931). The illustrations for these books were done by E. H. Shepard. Several of Mr. Milne's verses have been set to music by Harold Fraser-Simson.

Mr. Milne is tall and sunburned and has blue eyes and a wide sudden smile. His figure is trim and his face is alert and clean-shaven. He is restlessly alive and gives you the impression of being an outdoor man. Golf is his one recreation. He says his work comes easy to him. He lives in a red house in a green square in Chelsea. He has tried all kinds of writing.

Plays published by Mr. Milne following his third collective volume in 1923 include: *Success* (1923), *To Have the Honour* (1924), *Ariadne* (1925), *The Ivory Door* (1927), and *Michael and Mary* (1930). Among his other works are the following novels: *Mr. Pim* (1921), *The Red House Mystery* (1921).

Ferenc Molnar

ALL of Molnar's work reflects his iridescent personality. "With his full moon face, and that smooth, round monocle which glistens under his eyebrow like some lunar lake, the Hungarian dramatist seems an overgrown boy masquerading. Like a boy, he makes no effort to act otherwise than he feels. His moods have become a legend," writes William Leon Smyser.

The Hungarian dramatist whose life is so intimately associated with his native city of Budapest invests even the following brief account of his early years with his own particular quality of ironic humor:

"I was born on January 12, 1878. This was followed by a five-year hiatus. Then, in quick succession, I attended various schools for sixteen years. Most of this time was spent at a parochial school and the last of it at the Royal College of Sciences whence, because of crowded space conditions, I withdrew to the Central Café in order to complete my legal

FERENC MOLNAR

training. I devoted an entire year to the study of criminal law and statistics, for I was ambitious to become an authority in those fields. In fact I wrote a disquisition on the the two subjects which, in 1896, was published in the *Pesti Hirlap*. My first fictional stories and verses appeared in a humorous magazine called *Urambátyám*. Likewise in 1896, I suddenly swooped down upon the editorial sanctum of the *Pesti Hirlap* to announce my intentions of becoming a journalist. But the managing editor happened to be away hunting; and I waited for his return. Thus, it was only fourteen years later that I landed the job. Meanwhile I attached myself to the *Budapesti Naplo* and the *Pesti Naplo*. During this period, in spare moments, I perpetrated short stories, novels and even, indeed, plays.

"My first dramatic effort was a weird, spectacular play called *A Kék Barlang* (The Blue Cave), which was successfully produced, in the early nineties, on a flimsy stage built (at a cost of eight whole guldens) within the basement home of a friend. I did the settings, too, while my chum contributed paper puppets of his own making. The première of this play, staged with the aid of all sorts of blue bottles filched from the surgery of my father, a physician, ended in a riot. In consequence of which, my next play had to languish for a decade thereafter, until the Comedy Theatre of Budapest saw fit to present it. This protracted pause may have left its baneful impress upon all my later dramatic efforts."

As reporter for the *Budapesti Naplo,* young Molnar hunted up "human interest" stories in the slums, associating with the denizens of the Budapest underworld and learning their argot. This contact was of service to him later in writing one of his finest plays, *Liliom.* His short novel, *A Derelict Boat* (1901), attracted little attention. His first adult play was based upon a series of sketches called *Joszi,* originally published as *Humoresques* in 1902 and made into a play in 1904. His literary reputation was not established, however, until the Hungarian production in 1907 of *The Devil,* which also made him known in America.

Molnar found no conflict between journalism and the drama. Even after his success as a playwright was established, he continued to write his gay and witty feuilletons, which correspond to the work of the American columnist. In fact, he still writes them, altho he is no longer attached to any one paper, and frequently finds the material for his plays in his own random observations, short stories, and causeries, which appear in the leading periodicals of half a dozen countries.

Liliom was produced in 1909, when the author was thirty-one. Among the plays that followed were *The Guardsman* and *The Phantom Rival,* both of which were later produced in this country.

During the World War, Molnar was correspondent for his paper on the German-Austrian front. His daily column of war news was of such commanding interest that it had the unique distinction of being published as well in two of the leading enemy papers, the *London Morning Post* and the *New York Times.* These bulletins were later published in book form under the title, *A War Correspondent's Diary.*

Molnar found time, even in the first stress of the war, to write a long novel *Andor,* and *Fashions for Men,* a play. When he was assigned to military headquarters a little later, he turned to the

drama again, writing *The White Cloud,* his only war play, in which part of the action, as in *Liliom,* takes place in heaven. His last play to be written during the war was *Carnival.*

After the war he wrote *The Swan,* which won him the French Cross of the Legion of Honor. It was brilliantly produced here later with Eva LeGallienne in the leading role. In all, fifteen plays by Molnar had reached the American stage by 1931, including recently *The Play's the Thing, Olympia,* and *One, Two, Three.* Among the plays not yet produced in this country are *Still Life, Riviera, The Fairy,* and some shorter pieces.

Molnar is said to reverse the usual routine of existence, rising at sunset and retiring with the dawn. When in Budapest he is most likely to be found at one or another of his favorite cafés,—either the Otthon Club or the Café New York, or perhaps the café on the third floor of the artists' club, "where he will sit for hours drinking a variety of plum whisky known as slivovitz and either talking with some friend or noting down impressions on the back of envelopes." The café is his preliminary workshop.

When his loose notes begin to take shape, Molnar disappears into the seclusion of his suite at the Imperial, where he closes his blinds and lights the lamp in order to preserve the illusion of midnight. Here he drinks black coffee while writing feverishly. In a few days he emerges, again the complete man about town.

Madame Molnar is the celebrated beauty Lili Darvas, one of the outstanding figures of the Hungarian stage.

A collection of Molnar's *Plays*— twenty in all—was published in this country in 1929, with a foreword by David Belasco. Many of Molnar's plays have also been published individually in translation. Among his other books translated into English are: *Husbands and Lovers* (1924), nineteen dialogs; *Prisoners* (1925), a novel; *Eva and The Derelict Boat* (1926), two novelettes; and *Paul Street Boys* (1927), a story of two rival schoolboy gangs in Budapest.

Harriet Monroe

HARRIET MONROE was born in 1860 in Chicago, daughter of Henry Stanton Monroe, one of the city's leading lawyers, and Martha Mitchell Monroe. Her father, whose ancestry was Highland Scotch and Puritan Yankee (one branch springing from John Alden and Priscilla), had come to the young city from New York state after a college course and admission to the bar; and her mother had been brought there in childhood from Akron, Ohio.

Her childhood was passed in the outskirts of the growing city, studying at the public grammar school and playing much out-of-doors with her father's dogs and horses. When she was seventeen a severe illness induced her parents to send her to a southern school, and after two years she was graduated from the famous old Academy of the Visitation at Georgetown, D. C., altho she has never been a Roman Catholic.

Some local success as a poet and writer of prose led to an invitation from the Committee on Ceremonies of the World's Columbian Exposition to write an ode to be read at the Dedication of Buildings ceremony on the four-hundredth anniversary of the Discovery of America. *The Columbian Ode* was

HARRIET MONROE

her response to this request, and on the great day the poem was partly read and partly sung before an audience of one hundred and twenty thousand persons in the vast empty hall which was afterwards filled with manufactures and liberal arts. It was one of the magnificent festivals of the world; all nations and all the states of the Union were represented with delegations and troops, famous orators spoke as the buildings were formally dedicated. And before this splendid assemblage the young poet, called to the front of the platform, received from the Vice-president of the United States a laurel wreath presented by the women of Chicago.

After this spectacular literary debut, Miss Monroe had rather hard sledding as a poet, supporting herself for twenty years with journalism, lectures, etc. Her first book, *Valeria and Other Poems,* was published in 1893. Her second, a memoir of her brilliant brother-in-law, *John Wellborn Root: Architect,* was issued in 1896; in 1904 appeared her book of five modern plays in verse, *The Passing Show.*

In 1911, after a trip around the world to visit her sister at the American Legation in Peking, Miss Monroe decided that something must be done to break down the stone wall of public apathy which then made the lot of American poets desperate in the extreme. She resolved to start a poets' organ, a magazine which should welcome their experiments. In June 1911, her novelist-friend, Mr. H. C. Chatfield-Taylor, strongly commended the project, and advised her to get a hundred persons to give fifty dollars annually for five years, himself to head this list of sponsors of a neglected art. When this guarantee was secured, Miss Monroe corresponded with poets in America and England, and in October 1912 appeared the first number of *Poetry: A Magazine of Verse.*

"At that time," she has said, "no poet, with the possible exception of James Whitcomb Riley, could earn his bread and salt thru his art. Manifestly the poets needed an organ of their own to plead their cause with a neglectful world."

Artistically the little magazine was an extraordinary success from the first. The early numbers introduced to the public many poets afterwards famous, such as Vachel Lindsay, Carl Sandburg, Joyce Kilmer, the insurgent group of "imagists," Rabindranath Tagore (in English), etc; and it gave their first American appearance to Robert Frost, Rupert Brooke, and many others.

Poetry, which was the first organ of the art, and always hospitable to experiments, has easily maintained its lead, presenting hundreds of poets, both conservative and radical, while other magazines in its field have begun and vanished. To appear in *Poetry* is the ambition of countless young poets and the reward of the best of them.

Miss Monroe's later volumes, in addition to the three above mentioned, are: *You And I* (poems), 1914; *The Difference And Other Poems*, 1923; and *Poets And Their Art* (essays), 1926. Her anthology of twentieth-century verse, *The New Poetry,* was first issued in 1917, and the enlarged edition in 1923.

"I know," says Miss Monroe, "that I have given over twenty years of my life to editorship, but it has been the most interesting job I have ever had. There have been times when the future has looked black for the magazine, but we have always managed to pull thru."

Miss Monroe's associates speak of her as "a frail little person," tolerant, quiet, generous, but firm, who still opens the daily mail, the great load of manuscripts of poetry, with unflagging enthusiasm.

George Moore

GEORGE MOORE was born in 1852 at Moore Hall, County Mayo, Ireland. His father was a member of Parliament. Sir Thomas More, of whom certain portraits remain among the family treasures, is said to be one of his ancestors. George was a shy boy and had an inveterate distrust of himself. As a youth he rode his father's race horses, read Shelley, went to school a little, and studied art. His parents regarded him as an atrocious child and expected his life to be a failure.

GEORGE MOORE

At the age of twenty he decided he could educate himself better in a French café than at Oxford or Cambridge, so he shipped to Paris, taking with him an English valet. He conformed to conventions for eight months, and then the valet returned to England, leaving him free to live the life of the Latin Quarter. He joined a group of artists and writers which included Manet, Degas, Pisarro, Renoir, Sisley, and Monet. He became an especial friend of Manet, who painted his portrait.

He wrote a comedy called *Worldliness* and went to London where his attempts to get it produced were fruitless. Returning to Paris, he devoted himself to painting until he knew he could not succeed at it and then definitely laid aside the brush for poetry. As a poet he came under the influence of Gautier, Baudelaire, Mallarmé, Verlaine, Balzac, and Zola. "Zola was the beginning of me," he says. During the last two of his ten years in Paris he wrote verse and occasional articles and found himself thinking more easily and swiftly in French than in English. He found verse, English or French, easier than writing prose. Two books of poems were published, *Flowers of Passion* (1878) and *Pagan Poems* (1881). Then he discovered that poetry was not his occupation.

Mr. Moore left Paris in 1882, "suddenly, without warning anyone." He says if he had stayed two years longer he would never have been able to identify his thoughts with the English language. He went to London, an intensely French-looking Irishman, took ragged rooms in a Strand lodging house where he lived on two pounds a week, and turned to journalism for his immediate livelihood. His mind had taken permanent shape in the French language and he found that he couldn't express himself in English prose. But he didn't give up as he had given up poetry and painting when he had found he couldn't express himself in those mediums. He had a story to tell. So he set about the laborious task of learning prose composition.

His first book in prose was *A Modern Lover* (1883), a novel. He says it was the work of a young man who in a moment of inspiration hit upon an excellent anecdote and, being without skill, devised an uncouth text out of memories of Balzac, Zola, and Goncourt. Of *A Mummer's Wife* (1885) he says, "The book isn't written at all; you can't call a collection of sentences, or half-sentences, prose, any more than you can call the inhabitants of a hospital an effective regiment." But he had the avowed intention of liberating English fiction from its Victorian shackles and he took his place immediately as a rebel.

He was described at that time as a youth of thirty-three with long yellow hair (often standing on end), sloping shoulders, female hands, and an engaging vivacity of mind.

While he worked at his prose, he studied the contemporary English writers. Steps in his development were *A Drama in Muslin* (1886) and *Confessions of a Young Man* (1888). Then came the three great novels of his prime: *Esther Waters* (1894), *Evelyn Innes* (1898), and *Sister Teresa* (1901). He brought to the novel a new honesty, a clarity of vision, a severe simplicity. He had meanwhile written numerous bits of artistic criticism, which were collected into volumes published in 1891 and 1893.

Detestation for the Boer War caused Moore to return in 1901 to Ireland, where he remained until 1910, producing only three books. When he went back to London, he established his present residence in Ebury Street and set to work on the reminiscences of *Hail and Farewell,* which filled three volumes.

In order to prepare himself for the task of recreating the story of Jesus, he visited Palestine and then published *The Brook Kerith* (1916). In this work and *Heloise and Abelard* (1921) he believes that he attained the peak of his artistry.

Wilde once remarked that Moore had to write prose for seven years before he found that there was such a thing as grammar and another seven years before he found that a paragraph was architectural. Even after more than forty years of diligence he still has trouble with grammar and spelling. He says: "It's incredible the trouble I have to take in order to produce even the passable sentence which other men write unthinkingly." To indicate how crude his early prose was and how much it improved he calls attention to a comparison of the opening chapter of *Esther Waters* in the original edition with the opening chapter of the revised edition in 1920. Moore is always revising his old books.

Today George Moore's face is lined, his hair is white, and his mouth drops, but he still has the look of a small boy. As he sits in his study, his small-boned, fleshly body is sunken into perfect immobility in his low chair, but his head and eyes are never still. He loves to talk of poetry. He is no longer tempted to write poetry save in an occasional French exercise. He is not a great reader, but remembers what he reads and is loyal to his early intellectual loves and prejudices. He reads aloud slowly, clearly, with something of a child's straightforward manner. An acquaintance says the first thing that struck him about the author was the sound of his voice—the most distinctly masculine voice he ever heard. Moore surrenders the whole of his attention to the interest of the moment, whether it be conversation, writing, or food. He is a spare eater.

Among his novels, besides those mentioned, are: *Ulick and Soracha* (1926) and *Aphrodite in Aulis* (1930). Moore rewrote his first novel, *A Modern Lover,* and called it *Lewis Seymour and Some Women* (1917).

Among his autobiographical books are: *Confessions of a Young Man* (1888), *Memoirs of My Dead Life* (1905), *Ave* (1911), *Salve* (1912), *Vale* (1914), *Avowals* (1919), and *Conversations in Ebury Street* (1924). *Ave, Salve,* and *Vale* form a trilogy, *Hail and Farewell.*

Moore has written several plays and numerous short stories. His critical studies include: *Impressions and Opinions* (1891), *Modern Painting* (1893), and *Reminiscences of the Impressionist Painters* (1906).

Marianne Moore

MARIANNE MOORE

MARIANNE MOORE was born in St. Louis, Missouri, in 1887. She was graduated from Bryn Mawr College in 1909, taught stenography for three and a half years, and from 1919 until May 1925 was an assistant in the Hudson Park Branch of The New York Public Library. She was a member of the editorial staff of *The Dial* from May 1925 until *The Dial* was discontinued in July 1929. About 1915, she began contributing to an English journal, *The Egoist,* and in 1920, poems of hers were collected by her friends, H. D. and Mr. and Mrs. Robert McAlmon, and published under the title, *Poems,* by the Egoist Press—without, however, the knowledge and supervision of the author. In 1924, a book of poems by her with the title, *Observations,* was published in America. She received the *Dial* Award for 1924. Her work includes criticism and essays.

Some have been led to assert that her verse is no more than highly sophisticated prose comment; Miss Moore believes, however, that the substance of an author's work is likely to be homogeneous, the verse sharing the preoccupations of the prose, and the prose, certain properties of the verse. Poems by Miss Moore have been included in the principal contemporary anthologies.

Of what she would regard as influences upon her work, Miss Moore says, "Impetus to produce as good work as I could, has come, I think, first, from reading; from reading authors whose material and method afforded me keen enjoyment; Chaucer, Spenser, Sir Philip Sydney, Sir Francis Bacon, Sir Thomas Browne, Defoe, Bunyan, Dr. Johnson, Edmund Burke, Leigh Hunt, Anthony Trollope, Thomas Hardy, Henry James, W. B. Yeats, W. H. Hudson, Professor George Saintsbury. I have been entertained and instructed by advertisements and book reviews in *Punch, The Spectator, The English Review, The Dial,* by H. T. Parker's music criticism in The Boston Evening Transcript, Henry McBride's page on art in *The Sun;* by Gordon Craig's publications. And I have learned, I feel, from trade journals and technical books that were a pleasure to me and that seemed, from their obligation to exposit accurately, effective as writing; John McGraw's *How to Play Baseball,* Christy Mathewson's *Pitching in a Pinch,* Harold Baynes's manual on dogs, articles in the *Journal of Natural History,* for in my work I have been influenced also by fondness for outdoor life, tennis and sailing in particular— the latter, vicariously in the person of my brother more than in my own right. Tho the work of gifted persons I have mentioned has had an automatic attraction for me, I admit that in anything I have written, I have never achieved what satisfied me. In writing, it is my one principle that nothing is too much trouble. I may add that it has been of interest to me now and again to record, as accurately as I could, the phraseology of concentrated and thoughtful persons (educated or uneducated) with whom I have been associated. Notes appended to my book, *Observations,* show that reading, and the conversation of my friends have been the inspiration of that work."

"An astonishing person with Titian hair, a brilliant complexion and a mellifluous flow of polysyllables which held every man in awe," is Alfred Kreymborg's description, in *Troubadour,* of Marianne Moore, who "talked as she wrote and wrote as she talked, and the consummate ease of the performance either way reminded one of the rapids of an intelligent stream."

Paul Morand

PAUL MORAND, a cosmopolitan and yet thoroly French writer, was born in Russia of French parents, on March 13, 1888. "On my father's side," he says, "we are Russian Frenchmen since 1848. My grandfather was manager of

PAUL MORAND

the Imperial bronze foundry in St. Petersburg. There my father was born. Do you know any Russian Frenchmen? Curious people, moved more deeply by everything French, delicate and meticulous, with, however, treasures of indulgence for the follies of the Russians. When my father established himself in Paris, he frequented chiefly English people and those with English sympathies."

In Paris Morand *père,* a writer himself, having collaborated with Marcel Schwob, was Conservateur of the Dépôt des Marbres, where the State stores the blocks of marble it has purchased for the use of sculptors who obtain official commissions. Paul Morand, "a silent barelegged boy," used to play among the marbles. Morand père later became director of the Ecole Nationale des Arts Décoratifs.

On the advice of Lord Alfred Douglas, Morand was sent to England alone at the age of thirteen. He attended an English public school and Magdalen College, Oxford University. He was interested principally in diplomatic history and international law, and spent months in the British Museum.

On his return to Paris, M. Morand entered L'École des Sciences politiques, receiving a diploma in political science and a degree in law. Between the time of his entry into the diplomatic service and 1925 he was ambassadorial secretary at Rome, special attaché to the French Ministry of Foreign Affairs at Madrid, attaché at London, and finally a *chef de section au service des oeuvres françaises a l'étranger,* attending to the distribution of French literature in foreign countries.

When asked once by an interviewer how he happened to begin writing, his reply was: "I really did not want to become anything in particular. I felt no call to be an author but I did not know how to spend my evenings . . . During the War I occupied a diplomatic post in London and there I wrote *Tendres Stocks* (English translation, *Green Shoots,* 1924), a book of observations on the English woman. I then laid by my pen for three years."

Ouvert la Nuit (tr., *Open All Night,* 1923) and *Fermé la Nuit* (tr., *Closed All Night,* 1925) followed, and in 1923

Morand was given the Renaissance Prize in France in recognition of the originality of his writing. Thus, he says, he found himself a novelist without having intended to be one. In 1925 he left the diplomatic service to travel more extensively and to write. He has had the greatest success in both fields. He had been everywhere, he says, except to Polynesia and South America, but he plans to go there. To travel is "not only a pleasure to people of our time but a duty . . . America is the workshop, England the garden, France the kitchen, Germany the music chamber, the North Pole the ice box of this dwelling. Let us investigate every corner so that we may know what we have inhabited."

All of his books give evidence of his familiarity with many countries and people. He does not judge what he sees, the night clubs in cities all over the world, peculiar contacts, situations and behavior, but merely records dispassionately. Not all of his works have been translated into English; *Lampes à Arc,* an early book of poems, has not, nor has *L'Europe Galante* (1925), one of his most discussed books. *Black Magic* (1929), eight stories of Negro life in various settings, in the United States, the West Indies, etc., is one of his most popular books in America. *New York* (1930) was written in America and describes the metropolis, to quote the author, "in the Marco Polo manner but without ornaments and anecdotes, simply a kind of interesting guidebook, but a complete and accurate one." *World Champions* (1931) is an American novel, dealing with the fortunes of four friends, graduates of Columbia University.

When this cosmopolite can be found at home it is in a new apartment house at the foot of Eiffel Tower, in Paris. He is at once eager and contemplative, with a talent for asking questions in a distinct but soft voice, and with brown flashing eyes that seem to see everything significant that is going on. M. Morand is tall, slender, very dark; his carefully parted hair is smooth and black; only his hands, which are thin and sensitive, betray occasional nervousness. He represents, it has been said, "the modern French literary man of the world." Morand is married to the Princesse Soutzo.

Paul Elmer More

PAUL ELMER MORE, critic, editor, author, and teacher, was born in St. Louis, Missouri, on December 12, 1864. He is not the only distinguished member of his family, for his name in *Who's Who* is flanked by those of three brothers: E. Anson More, author; Brookes More, poet; and Louis Trenchard More, professor of physics and dean of the graduate school at the University of Cincinnati.

He received an A. B. from Washington University in St. Louis in 1887, and an A. M. in 1892. The following year he was granted an A. M. at Harvard, where he taught Sanscrit in 1894-95. From 1895 to 1897 he was an associate professor of Sanscrit at Bryn Mawr College. In 1900 he published his *Life of Benjamin Franklin* and in the same year he married Henrietta Beck of St. Louis. They have two daughters.

Mr. More became literary editor of the *Independent* in 1901, and in 1903 he joined the staff of the *New York Evening Post* in the same capacity. The

PAUL ELMER MORE

first of the *Shelburne Essays* appeared in 1904. In 1909 he took over the editorship of the *Nation,* which position he retained until 1914. "As critic," observed the late Stuart B. Sherman, who was one of his contributors, "he wrote for immortality with one hand what, as editor of the *Nation,* he ruthlessly abridged with the other. . . As an editor he taught his reviewers to fear nothing but deviations from the truth and the insidious vices of puffery and log-rolling."

In his preface to *The Wits,* Mr. More relates how he composed these essays during the strenuous years of editorial work in New York when he begrudged a Sunday dinner because it broke up his one precious day of "scholarly leisure." He intimates that the unifying spirit of this book was a hope that it would "vex somebody." It did.

When he resigned as editor of the *Nation,* he withdrew from New York to Princeton, New Jersey, as Sherman says, "in order that his children might grow up among the English-speaking peoples. . . " He disliked the strenuous life of the metropolis, and admits that he is happier in Princeton where "there are more days in the week." He lectures on Plato in the Department of Classics at Princeton University and since 1914 has enjoyed plenty of "scholarly leisure."

Besides adding to the *Shelburne Essays,* which have now reached the proportions of eleven volumes, containing one hundred and twelve essays, Mr. More has published since he took a chair at Princeton: *Platonism* (1917), *The Religion of Plato* (1921), *Hellenistic Philosophies* (1923), *The Christ of the New Testament* (1924), *Christ the Word* (1927), *The Demon of the Absolute* (1928). His scholarly translations include: *The Judgment of Socrates, Prometheus Bound, A Century of Indian Epigrams.*

He has been associated for some years with his friend, Professor Irving Babbitt of Harvard, in a crusade on behalf of Humanism against the Naturalism which is dominant in art and literature, and, to some extent, in ethics and politics. "The direction of his spiritual pilgrimage," writes Philip S. Richards,

"may be determined from the fact that he started with an almost negative philosophy, tempered by a firm belief in the moral law and a reverence (which he has never quite shaken off) for the mystics and sages of India; while he has ended as a fervent advocate of the theology of the great Greek fathers. Socrates, Plato, and Athanasius are to him the three greatest names in the history of thought. . . Dr. More holds, not only that apart from Christianity there is no hope for religion in the modern world, but also that in Christianity alone the Greek tradition, initiated by Socrates and Plato, found its proper fulfilment and consummation."

Stuart Sherman estimates the man: "If W. D. Howells was the dean of our fiction, Mr. More is the bishop of our criticism. His classical and Oriental scholarship, his reverence for tradition, his reasoned conservatism, his manner, a little austere at first contact, and his style, pure and severely decorous, all become the office. . .

"One may visualize him in these later years, since his retirement from editorial duties, as sitting in external and internal placidity under a pallid bust of Pallas in a commodious library, learnedly annotating in fine small hand an interleaved edition of Plato, or poring with a reading glass over the Greek folio of Origen, or perhaps quite lost to the world in the wilderness of Leo XIII's Aquinas. . .

"Mr. More enjoys a Saturday evening with a tale of Anna Katharine Green; or will good-naturedly meet the Princeton pundits and Bluestockings at a rubber of bridge, bringing to the solution of its problems the logical rigor of Duns Scotus and the transcendental insight of Plotinus." He has a motto carved in tall Greek letters across the wide face of his mantel shelf, of which the gist is: "Man's affairs are really of small consequence, but one must act as if they were, and this is a burden."

"P.E.M.," as his friends know him, is of average height, slender, and brisk and energetic in his walk. One of his recreations is reading detective stories, and it is said he has a standing order with one of the Princeton stores for a copy of every book of this sort that appears. At the insistence of his publishers, he is now considering writing an essay on the mystery tale to be included in the second volume of the new series of *Shelburne Essays*. He is a confirmed Tory.

Christopher Morley

CHRISTOPHER DARLINGTON MORLEY was born at Haverford, Pennsylvania, on May 5, 1890. His parents, altho they have lived in this country for many years, are English by birth. His father, Dr. Frank Morley, the distinguished mathematician, is a graduate of Cambridge University who came to Haverford College in 1887 as professor of mathematics. His mother is a gifted musician and poet, whose father was at one time associated with the famous London publishing house of Chapman and Hall. One of Christopher's brothers, F. V. Morley, is now a director of that enterprising English publishing house, Faber and Faber.

On the lovely and quiet campus of Haverford College, Christopher Morley lived until he was ten years old. In 1900 Professor Morley moved to Baltimore to take the chair of pure mathematics at Johns Hopkins, which he still occupies. Six years later Christopher was back in Haverford as a freshman at the college, where he was graduated in 1910. The files of the student magazine, *The Haverfordian*, show some entertaining products of his pen in both prose and verse. In 1910 he was awarded the Rhodes scholarship, representing Maryland, and spent his next three years at New College, Oxford. There he wrote and published his first book, *The Eighth Sin* (1912), a collection of verses. (The eighth and ninth sins are the prices it fetches in present-day auction sales.) The long delight of those Oxford days has endeared England to Morley forever.

In 1913 he returned to America and embarked modestly on a publishing career with Doubleday, Page & Company. Mr. F. N. Doubleday recalls that "he had one point especially I remember, and that was that when he had an enthusiasm for a book and an author he would never

CHRISTOPHER MORLEY

let you forget it. I give him credit for his early discovery of the merits of Mr. William McFee's work." During Morley's sojourn of nearly four years at Garden City, he married Miss Helen Booth Fairchild, a New York girl whom he had met in England, and he wrote his first novel, *Parnassus on Wheels* (1917), in which he introduced the idea of the wagon bookshop.

For the next few years Morley was associated with the *Ladies Home Journal* and the *Philadelphia Evening Ledger*. In 1920 he initiated his playful but responsible column, "The Bowling Green," in the *New York Evening Post*. Altho it terminated in 1924, Morley carries on the tradition with its namesake running currently in the *Saturday Review of Literature*.

After *Songs for a Little House* (1917), a sheaf of lyrics, and *Shandygaff*, a book of essays, came *The Haunted Bookshop* (1919), which revives Roger Mifflin, the quaint little bald-headed bookseller of *Parnassus on Wheels*. By 1931 Mr. Morley had written close to forty books and edited half as many again. He believes that he crossed over the line that separates the journalist, essayist, and versifier from the imaginative artist in 1921 with a short story called

Referred to the Author (included in *Tales from a Rolltop Desk*).

The best of Morley as a poet is in two books of his verse, *Chimneysmoke* (1921) and *Parson's Pleasure* (1923). The best of him as a writer of imaginative prose is in two novels, *Where the Blue Begins* (1922), the story of the dog Gissing's search of God, and *Thunder on the Left* (1925), which is at once a fairy tale, a tragedy, and a fantasy about the question: Are grown-ups really happy?

For the writing of *Thunder on the Left* the Morley household (which includes four little Morleys) temporarily abandoned "Green Escape," their Long Island home, and set sail for France, coming to rest eventually in an old stone house in Normandy near Mont St. Michel. From "Clos Margot" Morley wrote to his publishers, "I am living in a kind of dream, trying to get the hang of this new story, which fascinates me by the sheer impossibility of doing it right. . . I've got to show the whole thing thru a veil of moonlight, as it were" Another result of the summer in Normandy was *The Romany Stain* (1926), essays.

In 1928, in association with Gribble, Milliken, and Throckmorton, Morley engaged in a romantic theatrical venture at the Old Rialto theatre in Hoboken, "The Last Seacoast of Bohemia," across the Hudson river from New York. There have been few more hilarious audiences than those that came by ferry and tube to shout, hiss, and throw missiles at the performers of old Dion Boucicault's *After Dark* and Barras's *Black Crook*, both revived from the stage of the "gas light era." The hilarity, it is true, may have been partly caused by Hoboken's famous Beer. Other productions by Morley and company were *The Blue and the Gray* and *The Second Mate*, which was written by Morley and Felix Riesenberg. The appearance of the producers themselves in the cast was not infrequent. Early in 1930 the Hoboken adventure, like all good things, came to an end, but Morley has given us the story of its heyday in *Seacoast of Bohemia* (1929); other "sundry ejaculations" on the theme are available in *Born in a Beer Garden; or, She Troupes to Conquer* (1930), by Morley, Throckmorton, and Nash. "Literature gone Hoboken" is a phrase that has been applied to *Rudolph and Amina; or, The Black Crook* (1930), a sentimental fantasy with musical comedy outlines.

Mr. Morley is a serious man with a rich vein of sentiment. He has many enthusiasms and more friends. Loose of limb, shambling in gait, with pawkish face and the eyes of a man who has laughed a great deal, he "likes to be called Kit Morley and to be thought to resemble Shakespeare's contemporary Kit Marlowe, always has himself photographed with a pipe in his mouth, and averages two puns to a page."

The Haverford Edition of Christopher Morley's works was published in 1927. It groups his writings under the twelve following titles: *Parnassus on Wheels* and *Kathleen; The Haunted Book Shop; Essays* I, II, III; *Inward Ho!* and *Religio Journalistici; Poems; Short Stories; One-Act Plays; Where the Blue Begins;* and *Thunder on the Left.*

John Mistletoe (1931) is Morley's "personal testament."

Honoré Willsie Morrow

MRS. HONORÉ WILLSIE MORROW comes on her mother's side from a family of old New Englanders. Her mother was Lilly Bryant, her father William Dunbar McCue, and in her baptismal name is retained the memory of a French ancestral strain—Honoré is a family surname. Her father was an Ohio man, the youngest of the nine children of a Methodist circuit preacher.

After taking her A.B. at the University of Wisconsin, she went to Arizona and there she wrote her first book, *The Heart of the Desert* (1913).

After two years in the west, Mrs. Morrow came to New York, where her short stories began to appear in various magazines. Theodore Dreiser offered her a job on the *Delineator,* but she refused, and continued her free lance work, writing short stories and articles. She did a series of articles on the American Indian, another on the divorce problem, a series on Immigration and one on the Reclamation Service. Her research work on Reclamation was the starting point for *Still Jim* (1915).

In 1914, Honoré W. Morrow became editor-in-chief of the *Delineator*. In spite of that full-time job, she produced in the next five years not only *Still Jim*, but *Lydia of the Pines* (1917), *Benefits Forgot, A True Story of Abraham Lincoln* (1917), and *The Forbidden Trail* (1919).

In 1919, Mrs. Morrow resigned from her editorship and since then she has devoted herself to creative writing. Every one of her novels has been based on some large issue. In *Lydia of the Pines* it was forest conservation; in *The Forbidden Trail*, desert reclamation; in *The Enchanted Canyon* (1921) it harks back again to the Reclamation Service; in *Judith of the Godless Valley* (1922) it is the American need of the sturdy religious faith of our forefathers; in *The Exile of the Lariat* (1923) it is the problem of the relative importance of staple industries and scientific research. In *The Devonshers* (1924) a whole community is arraigned, thru an individual, for failure to live up to the ideals of its pioneer ancestors.

In 1925, with the publication of *We Must March*, her historical flair became apparent. The diary of Narcissa Whitman was the basis of this narrative of the winning of Oregon. In 1926, for the first publishing list of her husband, William Morrow, Mrs. Morrow wrote *On to Oregon! The Story of a Pioneer Boy*. This, the only book she has written especially for younger readers, was dedicated to her son, Richard.

The publication in 1925 of two short books, *Benefits Forgot* and *The Lost Speech of Abraham Lincoln* had suggested the character of Mrs. Morrow's industrious research and given promise of the Lincoln Trilogy to come: *Forever Free* (1927), *With Malice Toward None* (1928), and *The Last Full Measure* (1930). *Forever Free* presents Lincoln's first years in the White House, from the beginning of the Civil War to the moment when the President fixes his signature to the Emancipation Proclamation. *With Malice Toward None* opens with the year 1863 and closes with the return of Abraham Lincoln to Washington from City Point after the fall of Richmond. With the publication of *The Last Full Measure*, Mrs. Morrow

HONORÉ WILLSIE MORROW

brings the chronicle of Lincoln down to the moment of his assassination.

Mrs. Morrow's other publications are *The Splendor of God* (1929), a novel about Adoniram Judson, first Baptist Missionary to Burma in 1813; and three biographies: *The Father of Little Women* (1927), a study of Bronson Alcott; *Mary Todd Lincoln* (1928); and *Tiger! Tiger! The Life Story of John B. Gough* (1930).

In the winter Mrs. Morrow lives in New York, and takes a keen interest in the education of her children. In the summer, in her Connecticut home, her favorite avocation is gardening. She has great vitality and is unusually tall, with blue eyes and masses of black hair.

R. H. Mottram

AN anecdote which R. H. Mottram tells with great gusto concerns his voyage to Greece when he overheard the canon of some cathedral criticizing the age when every Tom, Dick and Harry seemed to be engaged in writing. "Why, the time is coming," Mottram heard the self-appointed critic say, "when every bank clerk will be an author." Mottram was greatly amused, for he is just that— a bank clerk who turned author.

R. H. MOTTRAM

Ralph Hale Mottram was born on October 30, 1883, over Gurney's Bank in Norwich, the bank where his father and grandfather had been clerks and where he followed them. "Banking clerks in England are traditionally servants of the family which owns the bank," he explains. "We were servants of the great Quaker banking family of Gurney." His great-grandfather kept the "King's Arms" inn in Norfolk and raised pigs.

Despite the "servitude" of his family, young Mottram had the advantages of a good education. He went to private school in Norwich and later at Lausanne, Switzerland. The home, he recalls, "was fairly full of books—the Bible in the first place, at the extreme left, then Shakespeare, Scott, Dickens and the rest." He was "strongly influenced" by Dickens.

Altho he came of an old Quaker family, Mottram went to war and served with His Majesty's Forces from 1914 to 1919. Because of his command of French he was promptly detailed as an interpreter. "I spent the war in Flanders," he relates, "partly as troop commander, partly as a sort of military diplomat." He had the job of making peace with the Flemish peasants whose farmlands the soldiers used for their not too gentle games of football.

Mottram returned from the war to his bank job in Norwich. He had always written more or less but had never published a thing. The war and the farmsteads in Flanders, however, furnished him with material for a saleable novel, *The Spanish Farm* (1924). "It's not one farm," he explains, "it's all of them. And the characters aren't individuals, but composites. The book just simply had to be written. I sat down to write it, but I didn't think of it as art."

He did his writing in the evenings and on bank holidays out at his home in the suburb Eaton. His wife, a Scotch university girl, corrected his manuscripts and proofs, after the little Mottrams were safely tucked in bed. The sale of the novel started slowly. Then it was awarded the Hawthornden prize and it became a best seller in England. The terms of the award stipulate that it must go to an author under forty years of age. Mottram was well along in his thirty-ninth year when he received it.

Two more war novels followed promptly: *Sixty-four, Ninety-four* (1925) and *The Crime at Vanderlynden's* (1926). The three were published together in 1927 to form *The Spanish Farm Trilogy*. "I have spread my message," said Mottram. "War is war, it's horrible and it's useless. . . It must not happen again."

But he had something to say on another topic and he began it with *Our Mr. Dormer* (1927). "It's the story," he explains, "of the great English commercial middle class that lives and dies in the provinces. It hasn't been adequately depicted anywhere. They plod thru life in the rut that is their tradition, doing their duty and apparently nothing else—the class to which I belong." His twenty-eight years of banking experience and his Quaker upbringing served as the background for *Our Mr. Dormer*.

Following the appearance of *Our Mr. Dormer*, Mottram left the bank to become a full-time novelist. His counter, he reflected, "had been touched by the hand of a Mottram for 148 years." He had sold the moving picture rights for *The Spanish Farm* and the serial rights to *Our Mr. Dormer*. So he retired to his suburban home, where he still does his writing at night. "During the day I roam, tend my garden, do all the things a provincial Englishman does." He makes occasional trips to London to see his publisher or deliver a lecture, and in his ardour for Norwich he leaves no doubt among folks as to where he is from.

A friend describes Mottram as about five-foot-ten, but his frame is so broad and he has such a pugnacious kind of energy, that you get the impression of bigness. He is prompt and impetuous always. He is almost bald, has a very wide and firm but not prominent chin, and eyes which are uncannily small and very piercing. His nose is huge. He makes a proud display of his strong Norfolk accent.

Mottram is constantly seeking to add to his store of knowledge. He is not bookish. Rather, he seeks knowledge from men and places. He cultivates acquaintances who can feed his mind. During the war he formed the habit of mentally classifying people. He likes to travel and hopes to visit America some day.

Altho he has become an author, Mottram doesn't play the part in the least. He doesn't move in literary circles, and he doesn't care about literary fads or modern movements. He is an ardent provincial—a dyed-in-the-wool Norfolker. "I was born there, spent all my life there, and there I hope to die."

R. H. Mottram's books include: *The Spanish Farm* (1924), *Sixty-four, Ninety-four* (1925), *The Crime at Vanderlynden's* (1926), *The Spanish Farm Trilogy* (1927), *Our Mr. Dormer* (1927), *The English Miss* (1928), *Ten Years Ago* (1929), *The Boroughmonger* (1929), *A History of Financial Speculation* (1929), *New Providence* (1930), *Poems New and Old* (1930), *Europa's Beast* (1930), *Miniature Banking Histories* (1930), and *Rich Man's Daughter* (1930). He is co-author of *Three Personal Records of the War* (1929).

Dhan Gopal Mukerji

DHAN GOPAL MUKERJI was born of Brahmin parentage—the priest caste of India—in a small village near Calcutta on July 6, 1890. As the youngest son it was often his duty when a

DHAN GOPAL MUKERJI

little lad to tend the village temple and before he was eleven years old he was taking charge of its rituals—performing marriage ceremonies and burning the dead. He had a great love and reverence for his mother, who found in the depths of her own heart an answer for each of life's perplexities. Her last request was: "Keep the doors of your mind open, so that not one of God's truths will have to go away because the door is shut."

The Mukerji home stood at the edge of the jungle and in the evening after the lights were out Dhan used to sit by the open window and gaze out at "the tremendous masses of dark trees with the emptiness gleaming around them." When he was older the holy men took him into the jungle at midnight to watch until dawn. "The animals are our brothers," the holy men told him. "They want to talk to us; we must understand them." He gained a knowledge of jungle life which, as a man, he wove into stories for children.

At the age of fourteen Dhan was initiated into the priesthood, the vocation of his family. Then for two years he made a pilgrimage thru vast India, begging his way from village to village, searching for the truth which lies beneath all things. But the priesthood did not satisfy his hunger for knowledge, so he went to the University of Calcutta and then to Japan where he studied industrial machinery and Western methods of production.

Finally he completely broke the ties of caste and country and went to America in 1910, armed with a picturesque knowledge of what he terms "Miltonic" English. His last borrowed dollar went toward his entrance fees to the University of California and while he was studying there he sought any kind of employment: dishwashing, working in the fields, carrying an old soapbox for a group of anarchists. He had the experience of going hungry. He received his Ph.B. in 1914 from Leland Stanford University, where he had gone for his senior year. The story of his early struggles in America as well as his life in India is contained in *Caste and Outcast* (1923).

Following graduation, Mukerji lectured on comparative literature at Leland Stanford and addressed men's and women's clubs thruout the country. He lectured extensively in England. In 1918 he married Ethel Ray Dugan of Norristown, Pennsylvania. He published two volumes of poetry and two plays.

By 1921 twelve years had passed since Mukerji left his native India and his heart was hungry for the sight and sound of his own country. He journeyed back to refresh his spirit in the agelong peace of India, and found an India filled with the murmur of political discontent, its beauty dimmed by the growth of Western industrialism. "How can we bring about deeper understanding between the souls of the East and West?" he asked the holy man at Benares. From the lips of the holy man came the answer: "There are no East and West to quarrel; there are only spirit seekers and matter mongers, who can be united thru compassion." Dhan Gopal Mukerji took this for his message. *My Brother's Face* (1924) is the story of his visit to modern India.

He returned to America and took up his residence at New Milford, Connecticut, where he lives with his wife and one son, Dhan Gopal II. Mukerji was awarded the John Newbery Medal for "the most distinguished children's book" of 1927. The book was *Gay-Neck* (1927). Among his other stories for children are: *Kari the Elephant* (1923),

Jungle Beasts and Men (1923), *Hari the Jungle Lad* (1924), *Ghond the Hunter* (1928), *The Chief of the Herd* (1929), and *Rama, the Hero of India* (1930). The illustrations by Boris Artzybasheff for *Gay-Neck* and *Ghond the Hunter* were selected by the Institute of Graphic Arts as among the best of their respective years.

He visited his native country again in the winter of 1929-30 and watched with dismay the turbulent conditions arising from the passive resistance of his admired Gandhi. He wrote an account of it all in *Disillusioned India* (1930). He is a staunch supporter of his race and has little in common with tourists who write disparaging accounts of conditions in India.

The Mukerji books for adults include: *The Face of Silence* (1926), *The Secret Listeners of the East* (1926), *A Son of Mother India Answers* (1928), *Devotional Passages from the Hindu Bible* (1929), and *Visit India with Me* (1929).

Lewis Mumford

LEWIS MUMFORD is one of the youngest and most influential critics of American life and literature. He was born not far from where he now lives with his wife and child in Long Island, on October 19, 1895. He received his education like other New York boys at the public schools and was graduated at the age of sixteen from the Stuyvesant High School with an elementary, technical, and scientific education.

He began writing for popular technical magazines when he was fourteen years old and at eighteen he contributed an article and a short story to the *Forum*. Troubled by ill health he pursued his education in rather a desultory fashion at City College, at Columbia University and New York University, as well as at the New School for Social Research, where he later lectured.

In 1919 he began his critical career writing reviews for the *Fortnightly Dial*, and shortly afterward became an associate editor of that magazine, alternating his duties with editorial work on a London review. During the existence of the *Freeman*, Mr. Mumford wrote many

LEWIS MUMFORD

signed and unsigned pieces for that paper.

Besides his activities as a reviewer, Lewis Mumford has appeared as lecturer at the New School for Social Research and the School of International Studies at Geneva.

In 1922, Mr. Mumford was one of the thirty Americans who contributed to the book *Civilization in the United States* and during the same year his first book, *The Story of Utopias,* was published. This was followed in 1924 by *Sticks and Stones* and in 1926 by *The Golden Day,* a work which won wide critical acclaim. *Herman Melville* (1929) was a complete biography as well as an exhaustive criticism of the great imaginative American writer. Indeed, in Mr. Mumford's method of writing biography, he uses history, literature, philosophy, psychology, and criticism for a single end: the rounded interpretation of a man's life, his work, and the society in which he lived. Mr. Mumford is also a contributor to *The New Republic, The American Mercury,* and *Scribner's.* Considered as an authority on architecture, he has contributed to the *Journal of the American Institute of Architecture.* He is also an editor of *The American Caravan.*

Mr. Mumford is now at work on his next book which will be on the Arts in America. He will develop several of the themes that first interested him during the writing of *The Golden Day,* and he will pursue his critical estimate of American life to the present day.

Mr. Mumford is tall, soft-voiced, with a dark earnest face and courteous bearing. He is interested in young writers and has encouraged many of them.

Gorham Munson

"MY father was the son of a farmer in the Catskill Mountains," writes Gorham B. Munson, American critic. "He broke away from the land, went to college and theological seminary, and entered the ministry of the Methodist Episcopal Church. I was born on May 26, 1896 at Amityville, Long Island, New York, where my father then had his church. Every few years my family moved, as is the custom in the Methodist Episcopal clergy, and I grew up in Norwalk (Connecticut), Hempstead (Long Island), and Brooklyn (New York).

"At a very early age *cacoethes scribendi* took hold of me. Even before I could write, I dictated an unfinished story to my grandmother on the maternal side, and at the age of ten I was writing imi-

GORHAM MUNSON

tations of Sir Walter Scott and historical works. My father encouraged this streak, and sympathized with my craze for reading.

"When seventeen years old, I matriculated at Wesleyan University, Middletown, Connecticut, where I had the privilege of studying literature under that courtly old gentleman, Professor Caleb T. Winchester. I also made the staff of the *Wesleyan Literary Monthly* and the board of the college year-book.

"Rejected because of defective eyesight for military service, I entered in 1917 on teaching in private schools such as the Ridgefield School for Boys in the lower Berkshires and the Riverdale Country School just outside New York city. This was a false start, and after a few years of it I escaped to Greenwich Village.

"My marriage to Elizabeth Delza took place in 1921, about a year after I had met her in a little theatre venture. She is a dancer by profession and since 1924 has been in charge of the dancing instruction at the Walden School of New York city. We spent almost a year in Europe, studying and travelling from July 1921 to May 1922. Since then I have lived in New York City and have been engaged in writing, lecturing, and editorial work.

"To take the last first, I was managing editor for several popular magazines from 1924-1928 and a member of the editorial department of Doubleday, Doran and Company from 1928 to 1930. My lecturing has consisted principally of courses on American literature given at the New School for Social Research, New York city, and of instruction in writing at the annual Writers' Conference held by Middlebury College. My professional writing began in 1919—book reviews for the fortnightly *Dial* and the *New Republic*. My first paid for articles appeared in the *Freeman* in 1920. I suppose I have contributed to about fifty periodicals and newspapers—from *Physical Culture* to the *Criterion*.

"From 1922 to 1924 I edited a small review, *Secession*, which rallied *The Dial* and the *Little Review* for being slow-paced and championed the early work of several writers now highly praised.

"My books have been as follows:-
Waldo Frank: A Study (1923), *Rob-* *ert Frost: A Study in Sensibility and Good Sense* (1927), *Destinations: A Canvass of American Literature Since 1900* (1928), *Style and Form in American Prose* (1929), and *The Dilemma of the Liberated* (1930). The first book was rather groping; the others were written from a single unified viewpoint which apparently is alien to my contemporaries. I have sometimes described this viewpoint as being post-Nietzschean or radically religious. Metaphorically, it is Black Sheep criticism and meets a Black Sheep's fate.

"I do not believe that the literary artist is the flower of creation, but conceive it possible that if enough men of various types would work for it, a new age of mankind might be inaugurated. Interest in politics I regard as futile, but economics is a fascinating subject and an economic reform must precede any restoration of politics as a worthy concern of man. My recreations are verse-writing, playing tennis, and motor-boating.

"At present I belong to no clubs and make a foozle of the secret handshake when I meet a brother in Delta Kappa Epsilon. Leisure for the acquisition of scholarship in occult tradition is my greatest wish for the future."

J. Middleton Murry

THIS is John Middleton Murry's brief account of the facts of his life and the beliefs he affirms:

"I was born in London on August 6, 1889, and educated in strict classical tradition at Christ's Hospital and Brasenose College, Oxford. In my third year at Oxford (1911) I founded, with Michael Sadleir, an advanced *revue des jeunes* called *Rhythm* (which lasted for about eighteen months, becoming *The Blue Review* for its last three numbers). Thru this I made the acquaintance of Katherine Mansfield, whose stories were the most notable feature in the magazine, and early in 1912 we married. As I was still a scholar of my college at Oxford, this marriage compelled me to retire precipitately from Oxford. I was taken on to the old pea-green incorruptible *Westminster Gazette,* where I eventually became the third literary critic, junior to Walter De La Mare and Beresford, and—after a wanderjahr in Paris, as 'literary' correspondent of the *Times*—art critic (1913-14).

"I was invalided out of the army at the very beginning of the War; and a hard time began. In 1915-16 literary men felt the pinch severely: there was no market for them. In 1916 I was paid £10 for my first book, *Fyodor Dostoevsky,* and glad to get it. At the same moment I began to write for the *Times Literary Supplement,* and have done so ever since. At the end of 1916 I was taken into the Intelligence Dept. of the War Office, and edited "The Daily Review of the Foreign Press." Immediately after the Armistice I was offered the editorship of the revived *Athenaeum,* which had a brief and, I am told, brilliant career for eighteen months. After that I retired abroad with Katherine Mansfield, who was now seriously ill, and lived on the Riviera and in Switzerland, writing weekly articles for Massingham's *Nation* and the *Times Literary Supplement.* When Massingham was turned off the *Nation* I decided to retire also. At that moment Katherine Mansfield died, in January 1923.

"Some four months later I founded *The Adelphi,* with certain convictions and views which it has pleased my critics to label "mystical." In fact, I am not in the least an anti-intellectualist. I regard myself, quite simply, as one who has made his ethical and religious values consistent with the literary values. After all, tho I have written novels and poems and even a play, I am first and foremost a literary critic. I have tried to make myself a good one, and therefore I have been compelled to justify to my own reason my invincible prefences.

"What is to others my chief crime as a critic is, in my own eyes, my chief virtue—namely, that I take literature very seriously indeed. With Keats I hold that 'the fine writer is the most genuine being in the world,' with Milton, 'that he who would not be frustrate of his hope to write well hereafter ought himself to be a true poem.' I regard the man of genius as prophetic of a condi-

J. MIDDLETON MURRY

tion of life which humanity may one day attain.

"My life of Jesus is, in my own eyes, a work of the kind that a literary critic must perform, if his judgments are to have meaning. He has to settle what are the supreme human values: and settle the question not in the abstract, but in the concrete. This I have tried to do in *Jesus, Man of Genius*: one day its necessary counterpart will be written in a life of Shakespeare."

About the time of his marriage with Katherine Mansfield, Murry was described enthusiastically by Henri Gandier, the sculptor, as "strong in body, with refined features and a magnificent head like a Greek god."

In 1924 Mr. Murry married again. Violet le Maistre, oldest daughter of Charles le Maistre, prominent English engineer, is his second wife. They have one son and one daughter. Their home is at South Acre, Yateley, Hants. Golf is the author's recreation. Murry resigned from the editorship of *The Adelphi* in 1930 to devote all his time to his writing.

Essays and studies by John Middleton Murry include: *Fyodor Dostoevsky* (1916); *The Evolution of an Intellectual* (1919); *Countries of the Mind* (1922); *Pencillings* (1923); *Discoveries* (1924);

To the Unknown God (1924) ; *Keats and Shakespeare* (1925) ; *Jesus, Man of Genius* (1927) ; *Things to Come* (1928) ; *God* (1929) ; *Studies in Keats* (1930) ; *Son of Woman,* a life of his friend D. H. Lawrence (1931).

He has published a book of *Poems* in 1921 ; a play, *Cinnamon and Angelica* (1920) ; and three novels, *Still Life* (1917), *The Things We Are* (1922), *The Voyage* (1924). He also edited the journal and the letters of Katherine Mansfield after her death.

George Jean Nathan

"WHAT interests me in life," confesses George Jean Nathan, the American dramatic critic, "is the surface of life: life's music and color, its charm and ease, its humor and its loveliness. The great problems of the world—social, political, economic and theological—do not concern me in the slightest. . . . If all the Armenians were to be killed tomorrow and if half of Russia were to starve to death the day after, it would not matter to me in the least. What concerns me alone is myself and the interests of a few close friends."

His life has been called a comedy of manners. A bachelor by choice, he has

GEORGE JEAN NATHAN

lived for the past twenty years in a theatrically luxurious, if somewhat fusty, apartment on the top floor of a venerable apartment hotel on West Forty-fourth street, New York. The apartment is noted for its "divans, cushions, shaded lights, and various elegant devices for the holding, passing around, and consumption of alcoholic liquors." He is a handsome, dapper man of medium height, with dark eyes widely set and a slightly smiling mouth. He eats well and smokes incessantly. Long ivory cigarette holders are among his favorite accessories. His wardrobe included thirty-eight overcoats at the last published inventory, ranging from "heavy Russian fur to the flimsiest homespun. . . and one with an alpine hood attachment."

George Jean Nathan was born in Fort Wayne, Indiana, on February 14, 1882, but it seems doubtful whether he will ever look more than thirty-five. He received his A.B. degree in 1904 from Cornell University, where he edited one of the college papers, and spent the following year in Italy at the University of Bologna. On his return to the United States he worked on the editorial staff of the *New York Herald* (1905-06) ; and from 1906 to 1908 he was dramatic critic and associate editor on the *Bohemian Magazine* and *Outing*. In 1908 began his famous association with the *Smart Set*, of which he was dramatic critic until 1923 and co-editor with Mencken from 1914 to 1923. *The American Mercury* was founded by Nathan and Mencken in 1924 ; Nathan was co-editor until 1925, and from 1925 to 1930 he was contributing editor. Altho he has given up active editorial connection with the *Mercury*, Nathan can hardly be said to be idling: he is dramatic editor of *Judge* (since 1922) and *The New Freeman* (since 1930), consulting editor of *Arts and Decoration* (since 1924), and editorial contributor to the *London Daily Express* and the *London Sunday Chronicle*. He is the one living American dramatic critic with an international reputation. In prestige he is the successor of Huneker, at whose feet he sat in his early newspaper days in New York, when it was a great privilege to drink Pilsener with that prodigious conversationalist at the round table sanctum in Scheffel Hall off Union Square. Nathan likes to hark back to those days.

No criticism can be crueler than Nathan's. . . when he wants to be cruel. He has no patience with bad plays. His exits from the theatre are watched with grave concern. If he gathers up his stick and high hat and strides up the aisle at the end of the first act, the producers weep; if he stays thru the second act, they become animated with hope; if he remains till the final curtain—which is Nathan's great silent compliment— there is no limit to their exuberance. That is not to imply that Nathan is himself incapable of enthusiasm. "He brings to the theatre," writes Ernest Boyd, "an endless delight and interest in all its manifestations, and he is as happy to praise the beautiful body of a Ziegfeld Follies girl as the first manuscript of a Eugene O'Neill, to applaud a W. C. Fields as a Dunsany, to do propaganda for native organizations like the Washington Square Players, the Neighborhood Playhouse, and the Provincetown Theatre, as for foreign dramatists as dissimilar as Lennox Robinson, Schnitzler, Sean O'Casey, Molnar, Shaw, and Sacha Guitry. And he will deride all these with equal gusto when pretentiousness causes them to deteriorate. . ."

Nathan denies that he is an iconoclast or cynic (except regarding marriage, politics, and bad plays). He cites his early editorship with Mencken of the *Smart Set* as proof of his constructive attitude. This magazine was the first to recognize Eugene O'Neill and F. Scott Fitzgerald. Nathan also points to his espousal of the cause of Dreiser, "the most important American author"; of Sinclair Lewis, "the most significant"; and of Willa Cather, "the best of our stylists."

Nathan's deliberately insolent attitudes and confessions might persuade us to regard him as a quite inhuman and unbearable person, "but the truth is," we are told, "he is a highly entertaining and pleasant fellow, whose very hypochondria is not distressing, even when it takes the strange form of perpetually plugging his nostrils with pink cotton over which some medicinal incantation has been pronounced, or of unceasingly inhaling a tube of menthol—these being apparently his chief winter sports."

His books, most of which deal with the theatre, include: *The Eternal Mystery* (1913); *Another Book on the Theatre* (1916); *Mr. George Jean Nathan Presents* (1917); *The Popular Theatre* (1918); *The Critic and the Drama* (1922); *The World in Falseface* (1923); *Materia Critica* (1924); *The Autobiography of an Attitude* (1925); *The New American Credo* (1927); *Land of the Pilgrim's Pride* (1927); *Art of the Night* (1928); *Monks are Monks* (1929); *Testament of a Critic* (1931).

Robert Nathan

ROBERT NATHAN was born in New York City on January 2, 1894. He was educated privately at several schools at home and abroad: the Ethical Culture School in New York; the Château de Lancy in Geneva, Switzerland; the Dutch Collegiate School in New York; Philips Exeter Academy; and Harvard. His first short stories and poems appeared in the *Harvard Monthly*.

In 1915 Nathan married Dorothy Michaels of Rochester, New York. They were divorced in 1922. A daughter, Joan Frederick, was born of the marriage.

Satirical fantasy is the outstanding characteristic of the novels and poems

ROBERT NATHAN

of Robert Nathan. His first novel, *Peter Kindred*, appeared in 1919. At that time he was working in an advertising agency, but he gave up that work to devote himself entirely to writing. He was a lecturer at the New York University School of Journalism in 1924-25.

Nathan draws very well and is a fine musician. He plays the piano and the 'cello, and he writes music and sings. A great deal of his musical feeling is found in his prose and poetry. He is also an expert swimmer and tennis player. His favorite indoor sport is fencing and he belongs to the Fencers' Club of New York.

Of all books, Nathan chooses *Don Quixote* as the best, and he likes Anatole France for "his wisdom, his biting geniality, and his style." He writes very slowly and painstakingly. Between the beginning of a manuscript and the finished book, many drafts and revisions are made. He likes best of all to write about children and animals, as his books bear witness, especially: *The Fiddler in Barly* (1926) and *The Woodcutter's House* (1927).

There is Another Heaven (1929) suggests that a Calvinistic and democratic heaven would be of necessity a pretty dull place. It is also about the plight of a converted Jew who changed his name from Levy to Lewis, turning Christian because he wished someone to love him.

Other novels by Robert Nathan are: *Autumn* (1921), *The Puppet Master* (1923), *Jonah* (1925), and *The Bishop's Wife* (1928), a characteristic fantasy in which a real angel, who comes to a bishop's house as archdeacon of the new cathedral, falls in love with the bishop's wife. Woven into the tale is a gentle satire on the worldliness of the modern church. *The Orchid* (1931) narrates a spring interlude in a strange little group of New Yorkers.

Nathan's books of poetry are: *Youth Grows Old* (1922) and *A Cedar Box* (1929). His poems combine wisdom with whimsicality and sadness. He is the composer of a sonata for the violin, and of several songs. He did the illustrations for a book of tales by Dorothy Mayer, *Tina Mina* (1930).

Nathan is a charter member of P.E.N., and he is secretary and a charter member of The Poets. He also belongs to the Authors and Town Hall Clubs of New York City, where he lives. He is of Jewish descent. During the winter of 1930-31 he lived in Paris with his second wife, Nancy Wilson, daughter of Professor Edmund B. Wilson of Columbia University.

John G. Neihardt

JOHN G. NEIHARDT was born near Sharpsburg, Illinois, on January 8, 1881. When he was five years old he became acquainted with the great western plains while living with his pioneering grandparents in northwestern Kansas. After five years of struggle in Kansas City, the widowed mother moved her family to Wayne, Nebraska, then a crude town that had not yet quite forgotten the frontier.

The boy wrote his first verses when he was twelve. His family was too poor to afford books, so he saved soap wrappers and procured as a premium a paperbound copy of Tennyson's *Idylls of the King* for his first volume. At the Nebraska Normal College in Wayne he paid his tuition for three years by ringing the class bell twice every fifty minutes of the day. His progress was rapid and he completed the scientific course at sixteen.

After a varied career as farm hand, school teacher, hobo, bookkeeper, beetweeder, and marble-polisher, the youth moved with his family to Bancroft, Nebraska, at the edge of the Omaha Indian Reservation. There he lived among the Indians from 1901 to 1907, formed an intimate acquaintance with them, and learned to see and feel as one of them. He was liked and trusted by the old-timers among the Omahas, who knew him only as "Tae Nuga Zhinga" (Little Bull Buffalo). In 1907 he published *The Lonesome Trail*. He extended his Indian acquaintance to the Crows and to the Sioux, who dubbed him "Igimou Chicakala" (Little Cat).

Neihardt married Mona Martinsen, a New York sculptress, on November 29, 1908. Experiences as a newspaper reporter followed, but his head was full of dreams that rhymed and the city desk wanted news. His discharge from that

JOHN G. NEIHARDT

job led to employment as porter in a restaurant where he scrubbed floors for a while. Soon his Indian tales began to find favor in the magazines. Poetry was the thing he cared for most, however, and the realization came to him that a great American epic could be written concerning the western advance of the white race to the Pacific slope.

To familiarize himself with the territory which was to form the background of his epic, he traveled thru the country in an open boat, descending the Missouri River from the head of navigation at Fort Benton, Montana. After becoming intimately acquainted with the whole vast country of his saga, he searched every available record of the enthralling exploits of the wandering bands of trappers and traders who explored the wilderness in search of furs from the British boundary to Mexico and from the Missouri to the Pacific. *The Song of Hugh Glass,* the first part of the epic, was published in 1915. After three and a half more years of devotion to his task came *The Song of Three Friends* (1919), which was awarded the Poetry Society prize of $500 for the best volume of verse published by an American in 1919.

In 1921 Neihardt was appointed poet laureate of Nebraska by act of the legis-

lature. In 1923 he became professor of poetry at the University of Nebraska, which had honored him with a Litt.D. degree in 1917. The third volume of his cycle, *The Song of the Indian Wars,* was published in 1925. The following year he was made literary editor of the *St. Louis Post Dispatch.*

With his wife and four children, he now lives on Lake Taneycomo in the Ozark Mountains near Branson, Missouri. He is a member of the Order of Book-fellows, Sigma Tau Delta, and an honorary member of the Companion Order of Indian Wars of the United States.

Among Neihardt's books of poems are: *The Divine Enchantment* (1900), *A Bundle of Myrrh* (1907), *Man-Song* (1909), *The River and I* (1910), *The Stranger at the Gate* (1912), *The Song of Hugh Glass* (1915), *The Quest* (1916), *The Song of Three Friends* (1919), *The Song of the Indian Wars* (1925), and *Collected Poems* (1926). His novels include: *The Dawn-Builder* (1911), *Life's Lure* (1911), and *Splendid Wayfaring* (1920). Two books of short stories are *The Lonesome Trail* and *Indian Tales and Others* (1926). *Two Mothers* (1921) is a play, and *Poetic Values* (1925) is a volume of essays.

Alfred Neumann

ALFRED NEUMANN describes himself as a typical man of 1895, that is, of that generation prematurely turned into men by the coming of the war. He was born at Lautenberg, West Prussia, October 15, 1895, but within two or three years he was in Berlin. The capital was his second home and the beautiful period of his boyhood in his parents' home was spent there. In 1913 he was vacillating between further study and the publishing business—eventually he combined them —when a happy chance took him to Munich. He began to write. He also entered the famous house of the late Georg Müller, where he wrote catalog "blurbs" for a living and poetry for himself. At the same time he attended the course of Ephraim Frisch at the University and later became an editorial assistant on the *Neue Merkur,* founded by Frisch in

ALFRED NEUMANN

1914. Both Müller and Frisch were his teachers. He lived in the atmosphere of the book and his own tentative first flights were beginning to take definite shape. Then the war broke out and his third home, together with his career, was abandoned.

After the war, he returned to literature. His first volume of poems had been published in 1917, and he followed this with a biography of Musset in 1925. After his first novel, *The Brothers* (1924), he took up the historical studies which soon led to his historical romances, a field which he has since made conspicuously his own. *The Devil* had an instantaneous and enormous success in Germany, winning the Kleist prize, Germany's most important literary award. It is the story of Oliver Necker, the barber of Ghent, and of Louis XI of France; in its enigmatic psychic melodrama these two lives indissolubly merge thru love and hate, intrigue and war, and, above all, thru a mystic affinity that triumphs even over jealousy. This historical romance was published in England and America in 1928. In England it was called *The Deuce*.

It has since been followed by *The Rebels* and its sequel, *Guerra*. In the meantime, he wrote *The Patriot*, a play

on the assassination of Czar Paul I, from which Emil Jannings made perhaps his finest American motion picture. As a stage play, *The Patriot* was produced in New York in 1928, but ran for only a few nights, despite critical approval.

The following books by Alfred Neumann are available in English translation: *The Devil* (1928); *The Patriot,* a play in three acts, adapted by Ashley Dukes (1928); *The Rebels* (1929) and its sequel *Guerra* (1930), historical novels dealing with the Carbonari revolt in Tuscany in the 1830's under the leadership of Gasto Guerra; *King Haber, and other stories* (1930), containing three long short stories: *King Haber, Schoolmaster Taussig,* and *The Patriot.*

A. Edward Newton

A TEMPERAMENTAL affinity seems to exist between A. Edward Newton and one of his favorite 18th century authors. It is not Samuel Johnson, tho Mr. Newton is one of the world authorities on the Doctor. Mr. Newton, "King of Bibliophiles," successful business man, wearer of checked suits, and an eminently "clubable man," is, rather, like an American edition of Charles Lamb. His humor has an Elian whimsicality, and at the same time a New World sprightliness—but it is particularly in his feeling for books that he reminds one of the witty and gentle Charles Lamb; he loves them with the same absorption, the same peculiarly intimate and personal affection.

When his publishers sent Mr. Newton a questionnaire asking, in the highflown latinisms of publishers' language, for "adequate bibliographical material, much of which cannot be obtained from the necessarily limited information in *Who's Who,*" Mr. Newton refused to reveal anything that could be used with discretion for publicity purposes. His schooling was had, he said, "in Public Reformatories." To the question *"Any Ancestral Notables, etc.*: he replied with irritating generality, "many Kings and Queens"; to *Married or Single?*: "Alas, yes!"; *Children*: "Too many—two"; to *Favorite Sports*: "Rocking"; *Clubs*:

"Expelled"; and, with deplorable levity, to *Army Service*: "Afraid to go."

But certain facts (less humorous, but more accurate) are available: Alfred Edward Newton was born in Philadelphia in 1863, was educated at private schools, entered the electrical business in Philadelphia, and is President of the Cutter Electrical and Manufacturing Company; he married Miss Babette Edelheim of Philadelphia in 1890. He has been honored with degrees from three universities for his work in English literature; he is one of the foremost authorities in the world on Dr. Johnson; is a member of the board of governors of the Doctor's house in Gough Square; is the author of *The Amenities of Book-Collecting and Kindred Affections* (1918), *A Magnificent Farce and other Diversions of a Book-Collector* (1921), *Dr. Johnson—A Play* (1923), *The Greatest Book in the World* (1925), *This Book-Collecting Game* (1928), and *A Tourist in Spite of Himself* (1930); is a frequent contributor to the *Atlantic Monthly*, and has been called by *The New York Times,* "the world's most popular book-collector."

Mr. Newton claims that he has discovered "How to Be Happy tho Married"—it is to be very busy with the unimportant. He invented the slogan "Buy a Book a Week." He owns the manuscript of *Far From the Madding Crowd,* the only Hardy manuscript in the possession of a private individual. He paid $62,500 for the Earl of Carysfort's copy of a first folio Shakespeare, and owns Dr. Johnson's silver teapot, a first edition of the Dictionary, and the original and unexpunged first edition of Boswell's *Life.* He has probably done more for the encouragement and instruction of American book collectors by his writings and his example than any other man alive. But tho he is spiritually and temperamentally closer to the 18th century—Johnson, Goldsmith, Lamb, and Blake are among his favourite authors—than to any other, he says, "I have little respect for a collector who is not willing to back his judgment as to the value of a modern book," and he thinks that *The Forsyte Saga* "probably will be read a hundred years hence with more interest than it is today." Mr. Newton repre-

A. EDWARD NEWTON

sents a type all too rare in America. "As life tends to become more and more distracting, let us hold on to the family of books," writes this President of an electrical manufacturing company, with a sort of civilized sanity in a gadget-mad world. "The damned telephone keeps ringing all the time, and now the radio has added its distractions. For myself, I have no desire to hear a political speech, a concert, a sermon, some cheap jokes, and a lot of 'static,' all in one evening. I prefer to live behind the times with a book."

Mr. Newton's busy and successful career has not precluded his development as a well-rounded man, urbane and cultivated, sociable and humorous. Once he remarked in reference to an admiring article written about him: "I read this paper to my cigar-store Indian, the only person in the family I could get to listen to it, and we blushed together."

In September 1930 Mr. Newton made the principal address at the annual meeting of the Johnson Society of Great Britain. Following the meeting at Lichfield, Mr. Newton went to Dorsetshire, where, on Egdon Heath, he dedicated a granite monolith to the memory of Thomas Hardy. The funds for the erection of this memorial were secured from the sale of Mr. Newton's monograph *Thomas Hardy, Novelist or Poet?* issued in 1929 in a limited edition for that purpose.

Meredith Nicholson

MEREDITH NICHOLSON was born on December 9, 1866, in Crawfordsville, Indiana, the son of poor countrytown folk. "I was undoubtedly below the average child in my ability to learn," he recalls. "Physically I was far from robust, and I was shy, sensitive, preyed upon by a multitude of fears. I was sent to the public school (in Indianapolis) at six, and for nine years my mother was constantly visiting my teachers to try to solve the problem presented by my deficiencies." After half a year of high school, completely defeated by algebra, he gave up and went to work. He was fifteen years old.

Young Nicholson began his self-conducted education by working in a drug store where the Latin inscriptions on bottles inspired him with a desire to learn foreign languages. He was employed subsequently in a printing establishment at two dollars a week, as a court reporter at the same wage, and in a law office at five dollars a week. Meanwhile he became interested in books, which included Oliver Optic, Scott, and *The Last Days of Pompeii*.

At sixteen he began to "scribble" and occasionally his offerings were printed in the local weekly journals. While he was in the law office he sent a short poem called *Grape Bloom* to a New York weekly paper which paid him three dollars for it. He relates: "I spent more than this amount buying copies of the paper, but never saw my poem in print." Then he won a prize of ten dollars offered by a Chicago newspaper for a short story, *The Tale of a Postage Stamp*.

"Nothing troubled me very much at that time except my ignorance," he says. "Whenever I was alone with pencil and paper I practiced writing—every sort of thing. My pride was aroused; what others knew I wanted to know. It was sheer good luck that threw me with men of cultivation at this formative period. They never knew how much I learned from them!" He was inspired by a long succession of heroes, including General Custer and Mark Twain. One hero he knew intimately—James Whitcomb Riley.

His mother was a well-educated woman and he says he derived from her a keen curiosity as to all things of contemporaneous human interest. The two of them would often attend public meetings together and listen to the orators. Current events and politics were discussed constantly in the home.

At nineteen Nicholson joined the staff of the Indianapolis *Sentinel* where Scott C. Bone was his city editor. He worked from noon until half past two in the morning for twelve dollars a week, a sum which "looked munificent." Night work gave him no chance to read, however, so he got a job on the *Indianapolis News*, an afternoon paper, where he remained for twelve years, passing from one positon to another. He read all the good prose he could get his hands on.

At twenty-one he had acquired more than the equivalent of a college education. He taught himself Latin, Greek, French, and Italian, and "gathered such fruit as pleased me from the tree of knowledge and didn't worry about the rest." In later years he remarked: "I can see now that I would never have been a successful student if I had gone to college; the

MEREDITH NICHOLSON

routine of a fixed curriculum would have crippled my initiative."

Nicholson knew nothing of social life until he was twenty- three or four. "I knew no girls except my sister's friends," he says. "I attended only two or three parties in my school days and didn't enjoy them particularly."

On June 16, 1896, when he was thirty, Nicholson married Eugenie Kountze. They have three children, to say nothing of three grandchildren including Meredith Nicholson III. They live in Indianapolis.

Nicholson's self-attained scholarship was rewarded when he received an honorary A.M. degree from Wabash College in 1901 and from Butler College in 1902. Wabash College conferred a Litt. D. upon him in 1907, Indiana University an LL.D. in 1928, and Butler College an LL.D. in 1929.

He proudly calls himself a "provincial American." He has taken an active interest in politics, has been a candidate for office, and served on the City Council of Indianapolis. He refused an appointment to Portugal when Woodrow Wilson offered it to him, preferring to observe and write of the political aspects of his own country. He is a staunch, old-fashioned Jeffersonian Democrat.

Nicholson's reputation was established by the mystery novel, *The House of a Thousand Candles* (1905). In his novel, *A Hoosier Chronicle* (1912), appears a good deal of autobiographical material. His other novels include: *Port of Missing Men* (1907), *Siege of the Seven Suitors* (1910), *Otherwise Phyllis* (1913), *Broken Barriers* (1922), *Hope of Happiness* (1923), *And They Lived Happily Ever After* (1925), *The Cavalier of Tennessee* (1928).

In many of his essays one finds much of his religious experiences, ethical thought, and political ideas. They include: *The Provincial American* (1913), *The Valley of Democracy* (1918), *The Man in the Street* (1921), and *Old Familiar Faces* (1929). The last is a small volume of reminiscences. His stories and essays appear frequently in magazines.

Harold Nicolson

"**Y**OU ask me to give you 'some information' about myself," says Harold Nicolson. "This is very awkward. We English are a shy race. I am all for giving you information about myself, were it not that it sounds egotistic and rather snobbish. I trust that you will use it with discretion.

"Well, I am 39 (I am really over 40, having been born in 1886, but I say 39 because it sounds better). My father was Lord Carnock, one of the founders of our entente with France, a friend of King Edward, and Ambassador in Madrid and St. Petersburg before he became head of the Foreign Office in London. My mother is a great-granddaughter of the Irish Rebel, Hamilton-Rowan, from whom, doubtless, I inherit my dislike of authority. I, being their third son, was born when my father was in charge of our legation at Teheran, Persia."

Harold Nicolson spent his first years in Persia, Hungary, Bulgaria, Morocco. He was educated at Wellington College and then at Balliol, Oxford. In 1909 he entered the Foreign Office; a year later he was appointed to the Embassy in Madrid; and in 1911 he was sent to Constantinople.

HAROLD NICOLSON

"In 1913," he says, "I married Victoria Sackville-West, only child of Lord and Lady Sackville of Knole, Kent, who has written things of greater merit than anything I have done myself."

Mr. Nicolson served on the British Delegation to the Peace Conference in 1919; he was made First Secretary of the Diplomatic Service in 1920. Another period of service with the Foreign Office brought him, as Counsellor, back to the city of his birth, Teheran, in 1925; and then to Berlin, before his resignation in 1929. Despite these pressing duties Mr. Nicolson did not neglect his writing.

"When I returned to England after that congested drama known as the Paris Peace Conference I thought I had better write a book. So I wrote *Paul Verlaine*. Then other biographies: *Tennyson, Byron, Swinburne*. In 1925, when I went back to Persia as Counsellor of Embassy and could find no books of reference in that arid country, I wrote *Some People*, which is really an autobiography on what I think is an original model. In it I have tried, under the guise of flippancy, to indicate my own development from acute diffidence to a perfectly modest and amused assurance.

"What more can I say? I live in a 14th century home among apple orchards. I play tennis very badly. I wear clothes that are a little too young for me. . . I like pictures. I hate music. . . I have never been to America but am very interested in Americans. . . I think your great merit is architecture, and Mr. Archibald MacLeish—who is a good poet. Mr. Hugh Walpole tells me you are very intelligent, especially in Boston."

Mr. Nicolson, after his retirement from the diplomatic service, accepted the literary editorship of the London *Daily Express*. His biography of Lord Carnock (1930) is a son's tribute to his father, set in a frame of historical narrative.

Harold Nicolson's publications are: *Paul Verlaine* (1921); *Sweet Waters* (1921), a novel; *Tennyson* (1923); *Byron, the Last Journey* (1924); *Swinburne* (1926); *Some People* (1927), nine semi-biographical sketches; *The Development of English Biography* (1928); *Sir Arthur Nicolson, bart., first*

Lord Carnock, a study in the old diplomacy (1930), published in the United States as *Portrait of a Diplomatist*.

Charles G. Norris

CHARLES GILMAN NORRIS was born in Chicago on April 23, 1881. From the age of ten when he undertook an elaborate historical novel which he called *In the Reign of the Grand Monarch*, his one ambition was to write. But by the time he was graduated from the University of California in 1903, Frank, eleven years his senior, had established himself as a great writer and their father, a wholesale jeweler, feeling that one genius in the family was enough, destined the younger son for his business.

The urge to write remained and in a few years Norris came East and obtained a job on the editorial staff of *Country Life* for five dollars a week. Two years of reporting dog shows in Madison Square Garden and contributing articles on "Hints for Tulip Raisers" and "Fire Risks in the Country Home" convinced him as to his father's wisdom. Returning to California, he became circulation manager of a Southern Pacific trade journal.

While in San Francisco Norris met young Kathleen Thompson, star reporter on a morning newspaper. Because he wanted to marry her and because marriage required more money than he was making, he went back to New York to join the staff of the *American Magazine* which at that time included Peter Finley Dunne, Ida Tarbell, Lincoln Steffins, and John S. Phillips. In 1909 he and Kathleen Thompson were married and both settled down to write.

The chief difficulty for Mr. Norris was to win the right to his own name. In 1911 his wife published her first novel, *Mother*, which sold over six hundred thousand copies. In addition to being "Frank Norris's brother" he had become "Kathleen Norris's husband."

His first novel, *The Amateur* (1915), was the story of a hopeful young artist who comes to New York intent on conquest. Six publishers rejected his second novel, *Salt, or the Education of Griffith Adams*. By the time it was finally accepted and published, in 1917, the United

CHARLES G. NORRIS

The Norrises live in Saratoga, California. They have one child, a son.

To a young writer who interested him, Mr. Norris wrote: "May one whose early literary aspirations were dragged in the muck, stamped in the face and kicked about generally, offer a bit of advice to another who, perhaps, is experiencing something of the same unpleasantness. I can see you are burning to write. Set fire to all your ships, sell out your business, resign from your position and— WRITE. If you have courage to do this—no matter how many other people are dependent upon you—nothing on God's green earth can stop you. The profession of writer is known to me fully. There is no flavor on its menu which I have not tasted. Only two things are necessary to succeed in it: faith and perseverance."

Kathleen Norris

KATHLEEN THOMPSON NORRIS was born in San Francisco on July 16, 1880. Her father, James Alden Thompson, tho born in Hawaii, came of a Boston family and was manager of a bank. The home life of the Thompsons —a family of eight—was an unusually happy one.

States had entered the war and Norris was in the army, a captain and then a major of infantry. *Salt* became a best-seller.

"My sole purpose in writing my books," says Mr. Norris, "is to make people think. In *Salt* I tried to give a picture of our national system of education, to show the good and ill effects of our schools and colleges. In *Brass* (1921), the novel following *Salt*, I attempted to present different phases of what we understand as marriage, to show some of the reasons why people cannot get along with one another." *Bread* (1923) presented the problems of the woman in business; *Pig Iron* (1925) was a study of the materialistic influences in American life; *Zelda Marsh* (1927) gives us the history of a woman whose heredity and environment combined to end her life in disaster; *Seed* (1930), a novel of birth control, pictures the gradual disintegration of an entire family because its women either bore their husbands more children than they could decently care for or refused to have them at all.

In addition to his novels Mr. Norris has written *The Rout of the Philistines*, a poetic drama, performed by the Bohemian Club as a "grove play" in 1925.

When Kathleen was nineteen, her mother (of whom she has written in her novel *Mother*) succumbed to pneumonia; a month later her father died. The six children—a boy of twenty was the oldest —were left practically destitute. Kathleen found employment with a hardware firm at a salary of thirty dollars a month, and at the close of the day would return home to make beds and shoulder the greater part of the domestic responsibilities. Her older brother found a job with an electrical firm, and her younger sister, Teresa, who later married William Rose Benét, worked in a private kindergarten. In this way the children subsisted for almost two years. The story of these years is to be found in the autobiographical *Noon* (1925).

In the fall of 1903 Kathleen, who had been educated privately at home when her parents were living, attempted a year's course in the English department of the

KATHLEEN NORRIS

University of California, only to be recalled when it was less than half completed, by the needs of her brothers and sisters. She took a position as a librarian and in her spare time practised writing. Her first successful effort was a story entitled *The Colonel and the Lady*, which was accepted by *The Argonaut* of San Francisco in 1904, and for which she received $15.50. After a period of settlement work, she did newspaper reporting. It is said that one editor dismissed her with the information that she could not write. She was with the *San Francisco Call* for two years.

In April 1909 Kathleen Thompson became Kathleen Norris upon her marriage to Charles Gilman Norris, the younger brother of the author of *The Pit*. The young couple crossed the continent to New York, where Charles Norris got a job with the *American Magazine* for $25 a week. Both of them were determined to write.

Mrs. Norris was the first to market her work. A newspaper (*The Telegram*) gave a prize of $50 for the week's best story to one of her contributions. Mr. Norris then disinterred a short story, *What Happened to Alanna*, that his wife had written a few years before and sent it out. The manuscript came back some twenty-eight or thirty-eight times,

but finally *The Atlantic Monthly* accepted it. Mrs. Norris received a copy of the magazine containing her story in the hospital just after the birth of a son, Frank. Success came rapidly. Mr. Norris is still his wife's agent. Grant Overton, in *The Women Who Make Our Novels,* quotes Mrs. Norris: "No written word of mine has ever been placed, edited, sold, contracted for, except thru my husband's hands. Nothing is written until it has been discussed and planned with him. I used to say that in justice his name should appear with mine on the title-page of more than one of my books. But this matter he settled once and for all by beginning to write books of his own."

A short story contest, conducted by the *Delineator,* was the indirect cause of *Mother* (1911), Kathleen Norris's first book, that made her known to thousands of Americans. This book was written first as a short story for the *Delineator* contest. When Mrs. Norris saw that it would run to nearly three times the number of words stipulated, she laid it aside and submitted another story, that failed to win the prize. Discouraged, she went back to her original story, which was eventually published in the *American Magazine.* Five different publishers immediately requested her to enlarge the story for publication in book form. More than 25 editions of the book have since appeared. It was even published serially by Edward Bok in the *Ladies' Home Journal* after the book had already enjoyed a wide circulation. Since *Mother,* Mrs. Norris has published more than thirty novels, of which the best is *Certain People of Importance* (1922), the detailed history of the Crabtree family from its dim New England origin to its later California days.

"One of my most vivid childhood memories," Stephen Vincent Benét has said, "is of Kathleen Thompson, in the white shirt-waist period, walking down a San Francisco street looking for all the world like one of the best of the Gibson girls." Another friend reports that she still looks like a Gibson girl. . . "a gracious hostess, tall, striking, carefully tailored. . . a woman with rare charm and a remarkable sense of humor. . . a racy Irish love of the ridiculous."

The fine and comfortable home of the Norrises in Saratoga, California, at the foot of the Santa Cruz mountains, is forever overflowing with guests. It belongs, in a sense, to youth. . . to the son, nephews, nieces, and cousins who pleasantly overrun the ranch.

Among the many popular books of Mrs. Norris are: *Mother* (1911), *The Story of Julia Page* (1915), *The Heart of Rachael* (1916), *Josslyn's Wife* (1918), *Certain People of Importance* (1922), *Noon* (1925), *Little Ships* (1925), *Barberry Bush* (1927), *The Foolish Virgin* (1928). Three of her novels appeared in 1930: *Passion Flower, Margaret Yorke,* and *The Lucky Lawrences,* followed by *The Love of Julia Borel* (1931). *Hands Full of Living* (1931) is a series of talks with women, suggested by Mrs. Norris's correspondence with the thousands of women who have written to her for counsel.

ALFRED NOYES

Alfred Noyes

ALFRED NOYES, poet and critic, and sometime Visiting Professor of English at Princeton University, was born at Wolverhampton in the county of Staffordshire, England, on September 16, 1880. He was educated at Exeter College, Oxford, where he did a vast amount of reading and pulled an oar with distinction on the Exeter College eight.

After leaving Oxford he went to London and very soon began writing poetry that became known. His first volume was *The Loom of Years,* published in 1902 when he was twenty-two. (The poems in this volume are now included in *Collected Poems* Vol. 1.) George Meredith praised his work, but it was *The Flower of Old Japan* (1903) and *The Forest of Wild Thyme* (1905) that established his early popularity. He published his epic poem, *Drake,* serially in *Blackwood's Magazine,* as if it were a new novel and was hailed as a very new sort of poet, particularly when he innocently admitted on his first visit to America that he earned a living by writing poetry.

Mr. Noyes' most ambitious poetic projects have been *Drake* (1908), an epic of the maritime Elizabethans in twelve books of blank verse; a companion volume, *Tales of The Mermaid Tavern* (1912), in which the great Elizabethan poets appear; and *The Torch Bearers, An Epic Trilogy of Scientific Discovery* in three parts: *The Watchers of the Sky* (1922), *The Book of Earth* (1925), and *The Last Voyage* (1930).

In 1907 Alfred Noyes married an American girl, Miss Garnett Daniels, a daughter of Col. B. G. Daniels, of the United States Army, and in 1913, already widely known in America by his poetry, he made his first visit to this country to give the series of Lowell lectures at Boston. During his visit he also lectured at various universities and colleges, including Princeton. He was given the honorary degree of Litt.D. by Yale. In the following year he was made visiting professor at Princeton, a chair he held till 1923.

During the War, Mr. Noyes, unable because of defective eyes to get into military service, worked untiringly for his country with his pen and on the lecture platform. In 1916 he was attached to the Foreign Office of the British Government; and in 1918 the value of his work was recognized by the honor of an appointment as Commander of the Order of the British Empire.

Mr. Noyes now lives in London, spending his summers usually in Devonshire. He has made a number of visits to the United States for lecture tours, the most recent being in the fall of 1928.

He is an unassuming man of serious aspect, whose robust body and vigorous manner make him appear much younger than he really is. Many persons who do not like poetry enjoy reading or declaiming his narrative verses. "The Highwayman" has long been a standard favorite, along with "Forty Singing Seamen" and "The Barrel-Organ."

As if to prove his versatility, Mr. Noyes' unpretentious light novel, *The Sun Cure,* was published in 1929. It is an amusing tale of a young English clergyman whose sun bath lasted too long to be quite respectable.

Mr. Noyes' *Collected Poems* have been published in four volumes (Vols. 1 and 2 in 1910, Vol. 3 in 1920, Vol. 4 in 1927). His other books include: plays, *Sherwood, or Robin Hood and the Three Kings* (1912), *Rada: A Belgian Christmas Eve* (1915); critical studies, *The Sea in English Poetry* (1913), *Some Aspects of Modern Poetry* (1924); short stories, *Walking Shadows* (1918); novels, *The Winepress: A Tale of War* (1913), *The Hidden Player* (1924), *The Sun Cure* (1929).

SEAN O'CASEY

Sean O'Casey

SEAN O'CASEY, Irish playwright, was born and brought up in a Dublin tenement house. He did not go to school but received his education in the streets of Dublin where he sold newspapers to earn a livelihood. For a while he worked in a big news-agency for nine shillings a week and had to be on the job at four o'clock in the morning. He did not learn to read until he was twelve years old.

Like most residents of the slums, he drifted into that occupation known as "general laborer," engaging in any work that was offered him. He has been a

dock-laborer, a hod-carrier, a stone breaker on the roads, a railway workman, and a builder's laborer.

In an effort to organize his fellow workers, O'Casey was for a time connected with the Irish Transport Workers' Union. He went with the workers thru the great strike of 1913, wearing a pair of boots frequently re-soled with cardboard. His first play (never produced) was written to interest the strikers and hold them together.

He helped organize the Irish Citizen Army, which fought in the streets of Dublin in 1916 under James Connelly. In 1919 he wrote *The Story of the Citizen Army,* his first published work. It is a slim, grey, shilling booklet about Connelly's little band.

Since that time O'Casey has written drama. He began as an amateur, writing in the hours of leisure following the day's work. A regular attendant at the Abbey Theatre in Dublin, he learned his technique by watching the plays produced there. Eight of his plays were rejected, it is said, before *The Shadow of a Gunman* was staged at the Abbey Theatre in April 1923. It made his Dublin reputation in a single night and packed the theatre for weeks with enthusiastic audiences. It was an unusual experience for the Abbey to be compelled to turn away hundreds of people every night.

O'Casey then became connected with the Abbey Theatre and his forthcoming working-class plays were awaited with unusual excitement. *Kathleen Listens In* was produced in October 1923, *Juno and the Paycock* in May 1924, and *Nannie's Night Out* in September 1924. On February 8, 1926, *The Plough and the Stars* was staged. It played to a tensely interested house the first night, but on the second night there was a hostile demonstration by a group of hysterical women who claimed to be offended by the appearance of the Irish tri-color in a public house. During the uproar William Butler Yeats is said to have rushed out without his hat and returned with a crowd of friends who applauded vigorously from the gallery and encouraged the players to proceed. The play deals with the Easter Rebellion of 1916 and takes its name from the device on the flag of Connelly's Citizen Army.

The Hawthornden prize was awarded to Sean O'Casey in 1926 for his play, *Juno and the Paycock*. This British prize, of one hundred pounds sterling, is given to the best work of imaginative literature produced during the year by a writer under forty. In that same year the play was presented in New York and London.

O'Casey's war play, *The Silver Tassie* (1928), brought about a battle between W. B. Yeats and himself and was rejected by the directors of the Abbey Theatre. It was produced in America in October 1929 at the Greenwich Village Theatre, following a run in London.

His plays are serious. He labels them tragedies but they have been played and accepted as comedies. His plays depend for their significance upon personalities rather than plots, upon character rather than story.

Padraic Colum describes O'Casey as a man with the long and powerful body, the long and powerful arms of one who has wielded the pick-axe. He has a salient nose, and a face that bears the marks of the many illnesses he has been thru. He is dreamy-eyed and shabbily dressed. An admirer of Shaw, he thinks that *Back to Methusaleh* gives a complete gospel. A Protestant who has been brought up among devoutly Catholic people, he can view the Irish people somewhat objectively. Yet he loves them all and believes in them. He has taken active part in the movement for the revival of the Irish language. In 1927 he was married to Eileen Reynolds, whose stage name is Eileen Carey.

Sean O'Casey's published plays include: *Two Plays: Juno and the Paycock; Shadow of a Gunman* (1925); *The Plough and the Stars* (1926); and *The Silver Tassie* (1928).

Peadar O'Donnell

PEADAR O'DONNELL was born in the Gaelic-speaking part of Triconaill, the ancestral home of the O'Donnells who were the last of the Irish chieftains to be overthrown by the British. The district is rocky and barren; the "farms" have been made out of patches between rocks or from reclaimed bogs. After attending St. Patrick's in Dublin, Mr. O'Donnell taught on an island, going to school each morning by boat and earning a reputation

PEADAR O'DONNELL

for reckless boatsmanship. In 1916, he went to the larger island of Arranmore to teach.

"Life in the islands," Mr. O'Donnell says, "was wonderful. We never discussed ideas much, except to take sides in such questions as fairies, ghosts, and book-learning, but we did know all about the noggin of whiskey Brian the Cooper had hid in the kettle, how Booney McGill came to get the brood stallion, and how the 'Master' was nearly drowned in Johnny Byrne's 'flat.' We were a great people with a nice friendly superior attitude towards mainland folk who had little sea sense and were a touch mountainy."

Arranmore folk went across yearly to work in Scotland at the potato diggings. Mr. O'Donnell followed them there and became intensely interested in their problems. Out of that interest he felt his way into the Labor movement, joining a union.

Then came troubled times—the days of the Black and Tans—and Mr. O'Donnell, like many others, disappeared into the hills where he became the commander of the Active Service Unit, or Flying Column, composed of "wanted" men who kept the struggle against the British forces tuned up. In May 1921 he was severely wounded and escaped capture only by the good office of a herd of deer that crossed a mountain ridge behind him and which his pursuers mistook for a movement of men, suspecting that they had been lured into a trap.

Mr. O'Donnell says he began writing quite by accident. He considers that Gaelic peasant Ireland—the remnants of the Irish of history—have not been faithfully reflected in recent Irish literature, and he promises to speak straight up out of their lives so that they, reading about themselves, will nod and say, "'tis true for him; 'tis true for him" in their Gaelic way.

In a controversy over peasant conditions Mr. O'Donnell hurled the challenge: "I know peasant Ireland around the coast as no other person in Ireland knows it."

Peadar O'Donnell's first novel, *Storm,* which begins with a storm off the coast of Donegal, attracted little attention when it was published about ten years ago.

His second novel, *Islanders,* is titled *The Way It Was With Them* in the American edition (1928). It is the story of a humble Irish family in their tiny fishing village on Ireland's coast. Liam O'Flaherty had read the manuscript in 1925 and found a publisher for it.

In 1927 O'Donnell was in jail. There the news came to him that the entire Sullivan family in Adrigoole, County Cork, had died of starvation. In a fury of rage and pity he wrote *Adrigoole* (1928), a tragic story of Irish peasantry on the treacherous bog-land.

The Knife (1931) is published in America under the title, *There Will Be Fighting.* In this novel the author scrutinizes the motives that animated the people of a border county during the time of rebellion and civil war.

"Peadar O'Donnell has published four novels dealing with different aspects of peasant life and their reaction to the national struggle," writes Mary Manning of Dublin. "He is only thirty-five, and tho years of intense fighting, forty-one days hunger strike, and ceaseless revolutionary activities have left their mark on him physically, he is terrifically alive. At the moment (March 1931) O'Donnell is free. I mean he has not been in the hands of the police for the last twelve months, but one never knows... He lives in a perfectly respectable suburban quarter of Dublin."

Peadar O'Donnell's next novel is to be the last of a series. Then he will start work on a history of Ireland from 1830, somewhat in the style of Kropotkin's *French Revolution.*

Liam O'Flaherty

LIAM O'FLAHERTY is an Irishman who has packed more excitement and adventure into his youthful existence than the average writer twice his age. He was born in 1896 in the Arran Islands, where Synge wrote his *Playboy of the Western World.* His parents were poor, but they were hardened Catholics and fierce patriots. He was educated in the Jesuit College, where he studied for the priesthood, and later at University College, Dublin, where he had secured a scholarship.

The youth was intensely religious, and when the hierarchy of Ireland urged the people to save Catholic Belgium, he joined the Irish Guards under an assumed name. It was, his brother Tom records, the greatest scandal that ever happened in the O'Flaherty family. He made up for it by writing letters home in Gaelic, describing with some glee the German advances on the Western Front. After a year he was shell-shocked and returned to Ireland, where he took part in the Irish Revolution, organizing ex-soldiers in Dublin and conducting a comic opera war of his own during which his little army requisitioned whatever it could from the municipality and seized and held a public building for a week.

When life grew too calm in Ireland, Mr. O'Flaherty traveled across half the globe, working at a dozen jobs, meeting men of every sort. He shipped to South America, chopped logs in Canada, and engaged himself in some mysterious business in Asia Minor at the time when the Turks were driving out the Greeks. He visited America where, his brother says, he was always cheerful and utterly penniless, earning his living by working in restaurants and print shops, or soapboxing for the Labor party, for he is an excellent and moving speaker whose voice has the record of reaching six blocks in quiet Dublin. While he was employed in a Hartford tire factory, he began to work out his first short stories, which he invariably threw into the waste-paper basket when they were finished.

Mr. O'Flaherty went to London and wrote his first novel, *Thy Neighbor's Wife* (1924). Other books followed in rapid succession and they have won recognition in England, France, Russia, and America. The Soviet Government has published several of his novels and one of them, *The Informer* (1925), received a prize in France. *Mr. Gilhooley* (1927), a staccato novel, has been dramatized and produced. The failure of the dramatic version did not seem to distress the author inasmuch as he received fifteen hundred pounds for the rights. *Two Years* (1930) is an autobiographical record of the period following his

LIAM O'FLAHERTY

demobilization, in which he gives an account of his extraordinary travel adventures. His home is in Dublin when he isn't at his Arran cottage or voyaging to some distant port where he indulges his eagerness for new sights and sounds.

When he writes, Mr. O'Flaherty cuts himself off from the rest of the world, but when he has finished a book he takes his vacation with the same thoroness. He loves the spendthrift gesture. He loves to take some one he likes to dinner, or drink heartily, or bet on horses. In the first few pages of *Two Years* he tells how he won five pounds by picking the right horse and thus managed to get to London. Nowadays when he visits his literary agent in London he takes all the money he can get and in a short time it is gone. Then he sets to work like a demon. He writes fast, drawing upon his wealth of experience absorbed when he wasn't thinking of what use he could make of those experiences.

O'Flaherty has been described as looking like a refined and virile gangster because there is something unfettered and lawless about his manner. He is lean, hard, healthy-visaged, and his features are clear. He bears no superfluous flesh but is slim and lithe, with pointed ears and a sharp-looking nose. He speaks a normal English, with hardly a suggestion of a brogue. He can talk for hours on dozens of subjects with no abatement of zeal. A charming mimic, he delights in rehearsing one of William Butler Yeats' Monday evening receptions for men only.

He likes Ernest Hemingway the best of all modern writers—as a man and as a writer. He is also fond of Dreiser's work. In his opinion any writing that is good "must come out of reality," and to him reality is in the present. Born a mystic, he has become a realist and now believes that "the only true mysticism comes thru reality."

Mr. O'Flaherty has published several books of short stories, including *Spring Sowing* (1926), *The Tent* (1926), *The Fairy Goose* (1927), *Red Barbara* (1928), and *The Mountain Tavern* (1929). His novels and other works include: *Thy Neighbor's Wife* (1924), *Black Soul* (1924), *The Informer* (1925), *Mr. Gilhooley* (1926), *The Life of Tim Healy* (1927), *The Assassin* (1928), *A Tourist's Guide to Ireland* (1929), *The House of Gold* (1929), *The Return of the Brute* (1929), and *Two Years* (1930).

JOHN RATHBONE OLIVER

John Rathbone Oliver

JOHN RATHBONE OLIVER was born in Albany in 1872 and spent his early life there. His father, General Robert Shaw Oliver, who was born in Boston in 1847, secured a commission in the army during the Civil War, when he was only seventeen and a freshman at Harvard. At the end of the war he remained in the army, and was captain of cavalry for a good many years, and saw a great deal of active service among the Indians in the Far West. His mother was born in Albany, New York, and was the eldest daughter of General John F. Rathbone.

The boy went to school in Albany until he was thirteen, and then was sent to St. Paul's School, Concord, New Hampshire, of which the headmaster at that time was Dr. Henry Coit. He left St. Paul's at seventeen, having passed his entrance examinations for Harvard, and was abroad for almost two years. In Germany, he studied piano diligently and at one time wished to devote his whole life to music, but, returning to America, he entered Harvard and was soon immersed in undergraduate activities. At Harvard he was a member of "The Institute of 1770," the Signet, Hasty Pudding, etc., was chief editor of the Harvard monthly, and class poet, graduating *summa cum laude*, with distinction in the classics and English.

From 1894 to 1897 he taught Latin, Greek, and English at St. Paul's School. He was graduated from the General Theological Seminary in 1900 and for the next three years was curate of St. Mark's Church, Philadelphia.

It was not until he was thirty that he began to be interested in medicine. At this time he was visiting Innsbruck, in the Austrian Tyrol, so he entered the famous university there, took the full medical course, and served as surgeon in the Austrian Army for some months.

On his return to America, toward the end of 1915, he was offered a position at the Phipps Psychiatric Clinic of Johns Hopkins Hospital, under Professor

Adolf Meyer. He was assistant resident at Phipps for some time, and later began private practice in Baltimore, where he has been practicing ever since.

In 1917, together with Judge James P. Gorter, of the Supreme Bench of Baltimore, and Judge Carroll T. Bond, of the Court of Appeals of Maryland, he founded the Medical Service or Institute of Legal Medicine, in connection with the Superior Courts of Baltimore. Ever since that time he has held the position of chief medical officer to the Supreme Bench of Baltimore. To the development of this work he has given a large part of his time during the past eight years. He is also intimately connected with Johns Hopkins University, being at present a Fellow by Courtesy. He lives in Alumni Memorial Hall, of which he is warden.

Since 1927 he has been professor of the history of medicine in the University of Maryland. He is also a member of the staff of clergymen at Mount Calvary Church, Baltimore.

Dr. Oliver's first two novels were *Fear: The Autobiography of James Edwards* (1927), and *Victim and Victor* (1928). His third book was *Foursquare: The Story of a Fourfold Life* (1929), an autobiographical volume. His third novel, *Rock and Sand,* appeared in 1930.

The substance of Dr. Oliver's books is drawn from the "fourfold" activities of his life: his experiences with criminals in the courts and prisons; his psychiatric practice; his academic life; and his religious duties.

Eugene O'Neill

EUGENE GLADSTONE O'NEILL was born in a Broadway hotel in New York City on October 6, 1888. His father was James O'Neill, a popular actor who was enormously successful thruout the country in *Monte Cristo*.

"My first seven years," says Eugene O'Neill, "were spent mainly in the larger towns all over the United States—my mother accompanying my father on his road tours in *Monte Cristo* and repertoire, altho she was never an actress..."

The next six years he attended Catholic boarding schools and in 1902 entered Betts Academy at Stamford. Following his graduation in 1906, he matriculated at Princeton, where he was suspended before the end of his first year because of some prank.

He worked for a while as secretary of a New York mail order house in which his father had an interest, but disliked the business. In 1909 he married Kathleen Jenkins of New York and the following year a son, Eugene, was born. Their marriage was of a short duration and they were formally divorced in 1912. Meanwhile, O'Neill set out in 1909 on a gold-prospecting trip to Honduras. When he returned home in 1910 he was made assistant manager of his father's company, which was playing *The White Sister,* and toured with it for three months. He was not interested in the work, however, and embarked on a sea voyage to Buenos Aires where he worked at numerous jobs, from each of which he either walked out in disgust or was discharged. He preferred to drink and hang around the waterfront making friends with sailors, stevedores, and the down-and-outs. His ambition was "to be a two-fisted Jack London 'he-man' sailor."

Other sea voyages followed and, in 1911, after his last voyage, he won at

EUGENE O'NEILL

gambling one day in New York. With the money he went on a wild spree and after several days he found himself aboard a train for New Orleans. On his arrival he learned that his father was there, playing in a vaudeville version of *Monte Cristo*. Eugene appealed to him for money but his father's only offer was a part in the company. He took it and played an unimportant rôle on tour for the remaining fifteen weeks of the season. When he returned with the family to their summer home in New London, Connecticut, he got a job on the *Telegraph* where he did reporting and contributed verse to a column for about six months.

In December 1912 his health broke down under the strain of long irregular living and indiscriminate drinking, and he was sent to a sanatorium with a touch of tuberculosis. The five months at Gaylord Farm in Wallingford, Connecticut, where he was treated during the winter of 1912-13, marked the turning point in his life. He says he began "thinking it over." For the first time he paused to reflect on his many experiences and the urge to write plays came over him.

After he was discharged as cured he spent more than a year living with some friends named Rippins whose home overlooked Long Island Sound. There he read, exercised, and wrote. "After I left the san," he says, "I kept up the sleeping outdoors for over a year and kept pretty careful watch over myself generally." To build up his health he "went swimming in the Sound every day during the winter." He read classic and modern drama, "especially Strindberg."

During this period O'Neill wrote eleven one-act plays, two long ones, and some verses. His first play was called *A Wife for a Wife*, but it was never published or produced. He sent two plays to a New York manager who refused to read them "because plays by actors' sons are never good!" O'Neill's father, who had never understood him and always thought him a bit crazy, gave him a boost by financing the publication of his first book. Issued in the American Dramatists' Series, it was called *Thirst and Other One-act Plays by Eugene G. O'Neill* (1914).

In the year 1914-15 he studied at Harvard as a member of Professor Baker's famous 47 Workshop class. After spending the next winter in Greenwich Village, New York, he went to Provincetown, Massachusetts, in the summer of 1916 and came in touch with the newly organized Provincetown Players. This group, under the leadership of George Cram Cook, was the first to produce O'Neill's plays. The initial play was *Bound East for Cardiff*, produced in a natural setting in the Wharf Theatre in the summer of 1916. This play and another one-acter, *Before Breakfast*, were published in *Provincetown Plays* (1916).

Thirst was produced at the Wharf Theatre that same summer and then the players moved to the Playwrights' Theatre in Macdougal Street, New York. The Provincetown Players helped establish O'Neill as a dramatist and his plays helped them to prosper. Ten plays by him were presented in Macdougal Street between 1917 and 1920.

In the meantime, O'Neill had received recognition from Nathan and Mencken whose *Smart Set* published three of his plays: *The Long Voyage Home* (1917), *Ile* (1918), and *The Moon of the Caribbees* (1918).

O'Neill's period of apprenticeship ended in 1920, when his full-length play, *Beyond the Horizon*, was produced by John D. Williams in the Morosco Theatre in New York. It was awarded the Pulitzer Prize for the best play of the year, and thenceforth the author's rise was rapid. He has since won the Pulitzer Prize twice again with *Anna Christie* (1922) and *Strange Interlude* (1928). The latter is a lengthy drama of nine acts, which requires about five hours for production. It usually starts in the afternoon, with an intermission for dinner after the fifth act. The play is conspicuous for its candour and for the "asides" in which the characters utter their secret thoughts in altered voice.

A selected list of O'Neill's other outstanding dramas includes: *Emperor Jones* (1921), *The Hairy Ape* (1922), *Desire Under the Elms* (1924), *Marco Millions* (1924), *The Great God Brown* (1925), *Lazarus Laughed* (1926), and *Dynamo* (1928). His position now as the foremost American dramatist is unchallenged. His plays have been produced and read in England, France, Germany,

Russia, Czechoslovakia, Japan, and the Scandinavian countries.

As his success continues, O'Neill grows more reticent and retiring. He is by nature sensitive and nervous, and he speaks haltingly except when in the company of intimate friends. He is harder to interview than the President of the United States. He is so seclusive that he will not eat in a restaurant if he can help it. He stays away from the theatre because he can "always do a better production" in his mind. "Acting, except when rarely inspired," he says, "simply gets between me and the play." He has seen only three of his own plays.

O'Neill is tall and slender and wiry, with long arms and strong hands. His body is as lithe as an athlete's. His face in repose has a certain chiseled tho not althogether cold severity, but his smile is disarmingly frank and engaging.

After his marriage to Agnes Boulton Burton in 1918, he took a place near Ridgefield, Connecticut. They had two children. Most of his summers he spent in a lonely made-over life-saving shack on the sand dunes of Cape Cod, four miles from Provincetown and civilization. One year he wrote for seven months in Bermuda. He will not have an inland house without a swimming pool. He usually spends half a day writing and the other half swimming, boating, or engaging in other kinds of exercise.

In 1928 O'Neill went to France and established a residence at Château du Plessis, Saint Antoine-du-Rocher. For a time he traveled. When he visited Shanghai incognito, a report was circulated that he lay seriously ill in a hospital there, and he left the city in high indignation. In 1929 he was divorced from his second wife and married Charlotte Monterey, an actress.

Early in 1931 O'Neill reported that the new play about which he had been so reticent was nearing completion and would soon be sent to the Theatre Guild, which planned to produce it during the 1931-32 season. The play is really three plays, a trilogy which will require three successive evenings for production. He expected to return soon to the United States and buy an estate in the South.

In one of his long, flat, cardboard-covered notebooks O'Neill has sketched the outlines of more than thirty plays to come.

Rose O'Neill

ROSE CECIL O'NEILL, author and illustrator, was born in Wilkes-Barre, Pennsylvania, in 1874, the daughter of a William Patrick O'Neill, a quaint booklover from Ireland. She was educated at the Sacred Heart Convent. It was originally intended that the girl should be an actress, but she was too sensitive for public passion. So she turned to art, and by the time she was fifteen, untaught, she was a successful illustrator.

From Omaha, Nebraska, where the family had moved, she came on to New York, where for years she was a leading illustrator for numerous magazines, including *Life*, *Harper's*, *Good House-keeping*, *Collier's*, and *Cosmopolitan*. She served on the staff of *Puck* from 1897 to 1903, contributing short stories and verses with illustrations by herself.

On June 7, 1902, Miss O'Neill married Harry Leon Wilson, the novelist. He was her second husband. She illustrated his novels, *The Spenders* (1902), and

ROSE O'NEILL

Lions of the Lord (1903). She is now separated from him.

Miss O'Neill published her first book, *The Loves of Edwy*, in 1904. She studied art in Italy and France from 1905 to 1907, and exhibited in the Paris Salon in 1906 to 1907. She was made a member of the Societé des Beaux Arts, Paris. *The Lady in the White Veil* appeared in 1909.

Her chief commercial success was the invention of the Kewpies. In addition to their frequent magazine appearances in drawings and light rhymes, she published several books about them, including: *Kewpies and Dotty Darling* (1913), *Kewpies: their book, verse, and poetry* (1913), *Kewpie Kutouts* (1914), and *Kewpies and the Runaway Baby* (1928).

Miss O'Neill attained considerable recognition as a poet in 1922 when she published her collected volume of verse, *The Master Mistress*.

For many years Miss O'Neill lived at a retreat, Bonnybrook, in the Ozark Mountains of Missouri. Later, she divided her time between a studio on Washington Square in New York City, a villa at Capri, and a home on the Saugatuck River near Westport, Connecticut. Her Capri villa was the guest house of a seventeenth century convent. It has an oleander court and a grape-vine court; inside, the ceilings are vaulted and gilded and the walls are hung with old tapestries. The stairs are of marble and the floors of mosaic taken from the villa of Tiberius. There she wrote her novels *Garda* (1929) and *The Goblin Women* (1930), which are pagan, extravagant, perplexed, quite unlike her Kewpie dolls and books.

Miss O'Neill's ample house in the wild Connecticut woodland is called "Carabas" after the marquis in *Puss in Boots*. Here, when she returns to America, she writes and entertains. On occasion she will read Francis Thompson aloud for eight or ten hours at a stretch, as long as her guests can remain awake. Her costume at "Carabas" is a flowing velvet robe, usually red, and she lets her yellow hair curl to her shoulders like a medieval page. Such costumes are not bizarre at "Carabas"; they have a certain fitness in the huge hall and the long dining room with its tables flanked by couches.

Miss O'Neill's books include: *The Loves of Edwy* (1904), *The Lady in the White Veil* (1909), *Kewpies and Dotty Darling* (1913), *Kewpies* (1913), *Kewpie Kutouts* (1914), *The Master Mistress* (1922), *Kewpies and the Runaway Baby* (1928), *Garda* (1929), and *The Goblin Woman* (1930).

Oliver Onions

THE fact that anyone should be named George Oliver Onions so amused a certain English lad's schoolfellows and caused them to taunt him so much that he finally discarded his family name and became just plain George Oliver to save himself further embarrassment. But when he turned author he adopted Oliver Onions for his *nom de plume*, pronouncing it "O-nī-ons."

From Bradford, Yorkshire, where he was born in 1873, George Oliver Onions went to London to study at the National Arts Training Schools, now the Royal College of Art, at South Kensington. He studied at South Kensington for three years and in 1897 a scholarship permitted him to go to Paris for further art study. There, at Calarossi's, he was on the editorial staff of the French student periodical, *Le Quartier Latin*.

When he returned to London his life was by no means care-free. He designed posters, made sketches at dress rehearsals, illustrated books, and performed other artistic tasks. Finally he became a war artist for a weekly publication.

Gelett Burgess, then living in London, persuaded him to write *The Compleat Bachelor* (1901), as an experiment. The story was so successful that he sent the manuscript to America where it appeared in *Harpers' Bazaar*. So at the age of twenty-eight, he turned his back on George Oliver, the artist, and became Oliver Onions, the writer. The following year, 1902, he published a book of short stories, *Tales from a Far Riding*. In 1903 his first novel, *The Odd-Job Man*, appeared.

From the time of the appearance of his first experiment, Mr. Onions has constantly experimented. It has been his aim not to turn out a staple product or settle into a groove, but to provide something new at every turn. He has written satires, crime stories, tales of the supernatural, social novels, and psychological novels.

Mr. Onions' artistic training sharpened his visual faculties as a writer and he often employed his former craft in making hasty sketches of visualized scenes before writing them down. He still does occasional drawing, he modestly admits, and has designed the jackets for some of his books, signed "G.O."

Fiercely independent, he is a born fighter. He says he has never consented to "give the public what it wants" but has always offered it what he chose to give. *Little Devil Doubt* is an attack, joyous and savage, on the methods of the "Yellow Press." It is an exposure of the policy of dragging literature and art down to the level of the illiterate. The book contains, incidentally, a good deal of autobiographical matter. Like his hero, Georgie, Mr. Onions spent some time as draughtsman in a printing office, and like him too, acted as artist for the syndicated press. *Little Devil Doubt* was followed shortly by a prolonged piece of irony, *Good Boy Seldom,* a relentless history of the progress and fall of a rogue of finance.

Mr. Onions is an enthusiast for ideas and shows himself to be thoroly acquainted with his characters and situations. His best work is in his psychological trilogy, *In Accordance with the Evidence, The Debit Account,* and *The Story of Louie* (1913). These three books were later rewritten into one long novel and published as *Whom God Has Sundered* (1926).

This writer is a craftsman with a most scrupulous conscience and a joy in mastering technical difficulties. He is not content to rely on second-hand experience. If he wants to describe a flight to Germany and back, he takes the journey himself. If chemical flesh stains constitute an item in a story he is writing, he experiments on his own skin. In his conscientiousness Mr. Onions frequently recasts his manuscripts and even his final proofs are often full of interlinear additions and corrections. He is far from a

OLIVER ONIONS

rapid worker, altho he now has more than twenty-five books to his credit.

Today Oliver Onions lives about a mile outside of Windsor, still George Oliver in private life. He is sturdily built, with broad shoulders, a square jaw, and a glint in his eye. He was a boxer at one time. His recreation now is motoring. He does not care to talk about books he has written, but will discuss with enthusiasm the one he is working on. He will wax eloquent on any scientific or technical appliance, and is alert to every modern doctrine or fresh invention. Most of all, he likes to talk about his two boys, both educated at Shrewsbury School. His wife is Berta Ruck, the novelist.

Books by Oliver Onions, besides those mentioned, include: *The Exception* (1911), *Gray Youth* (1914), *Mushroom Town* (1914), *The New Moon* (1918), *A Case in Camera* (1920), *The Tower of Oblivion* (1921), *Peace in Our Time* (1923), *Ghosts in Daylight* (1924), *The Spite of Heaven* (1925), *Cut Flowers* (1927), *The Painted Face* (1929), and *The Open Secret* (1930).

E. Phillips Oppenheim

"I'M just a yarn-spinner, I'm not what you fellows call a literary man," says E. Phillips Oppenheim with a comfortable air of repose—the exact antithesis of the *non palma sine pulva* agitation of the ambitious artist. The reporter to whom he was talking asked him what, then, he wrote for, fame? Or for money? He said slowly, "Fame—or money—I don't believe I think of either when I'm writing a book. All I want is the best story possible. Yet sometimes I feel that one of my stories, if it's well done, may be remembered after I'm gone."

Mr. Oppenheim was born in London in 1866 and educated at the Wyggeston Grammar School. At school he was fairly prominent for "literature, history, and classics," but he never went beyond the sixth form, not going up to Oxford to his father's college "owing to inability to pass the simplest mathematical examination." Entering his father's business, he wrote stories on the side until he was convinced that his ability as a "yarn spinner" justified his devoting his whole time to writing. His first short story was published when he was eighteen, and two years later his first novel appeared—*Expiation* (1887).

In 1892, he married Miss Elsie Hopkins, of Chelsea, Massachusetts. There

E. PHILLIPS OPPENHEIM

is a story, probably apocryphal, that Oppenheim met, and fell in love with Miss Hopkins when she was travelling with her father, Judge Hopkins, in England. His sentiments were reciprocated, but the magisterial parent advised the beginning author to renew his suit when his prospects were more certain. Within the year Oppenheim, with a check for a thousand pounds in his pocket—his first big earnings as an author—set sail for Boston. Arriving at Miss Hopkins' home before any of the household were awake, he camped on the doorstep until he could gain admittance. When he returned to England, it was with his bride.

They have one daughter, and live for most of the year at Cagnes on the Riviera, in the Villa Deveron. Here Oppenheim gets up late, breakfasts leisurely, and wanders into his library or out to the summer house in the course of the forenoon. Until lunch, he strides back and forth, dictating to his secretary, who takes it all down in shorthand and makes a typewritten copy.

It seems likely that his habit of giving form orally to the first broad line of a story results in that objective style and that sense of quick-moving action characteristic of all his work—qualities present in the literature of the narrative spoken, not read, from the time of the Homeric rhapsodes to the radio bedtime story tellers. When his characters get into inextricable difficulties, or the plot refuses to come clear and clean, he says, "Three dots...," leaves this particular problem, and goes on. Perhaps the next day he will go back and solve the difficulty, or wait until the revision of the first typewritten draft to find the solution for his obdurate characters or his intractable plot.

In the afternoon (he has a glass of Port after lunch) he plays golf (or, in England, shoots in season) until tea time, and after dinner has a quiet game of auction—or now, no doubt, contract bridge. E. Phillips Oppenheim is hardly the man to continue to play auction when the civilized world is engaged in discussing the merits and disadvantages of the Vanderbilt convention. For Mr. Oppenheim is one of the most civilized men alive. When he is not at Cagnes, he is generally to be found in his rooms in

Clarges Street—near the Green Park, in the very center of the lively and exciting world of Mayfair which forms the background of so many of his novels— such as a 1930 one, *The Lion and the Lamb.*

He has made several visits to America to see his wife's family and his publishers. He likes the United States. "My only fear," he said once of the 18th Amendment, "is that it may make me a drunkard." He is a gourmet, and a judge not only of good whiskey, but (a far more perilous and involved matter) of good wines as well. "I have made it my hobby for many years," he writes, "to frequent the cafés in all the cities which I visit in my travels. I make the acquaintance of the maître d'hotel whenever possible, and in my conversation with him, and by studying the types represented among the patrons, a good idea for a story inevitably suggests itself."

Up the Ladder of Gold (1931) was Oppenheim's 116th book since 1887. Of that number, 88 are novels. The remainder, with the exception of a book of travel, are volumes of short stories. His present regular output is two complete novels and two volumes of connected short stories annually. *Clowns and Criminals* (1931) is an "Oppenheim Omnibus" of over 900 pages, containing five of his books.

Martha Ostenso

OF her early life, Martha Ostenso writes:

"Where the long arm of the Hardangerfjord penetrates farthest into the rugged mountains of the coast of Norway, the Ostenso family has lived, in the township that bears its name, since the days of the Vikings. The name means Eastern Sea, and was assumed centuries ago by an adventurous forebear who dreamed of extending his holdings over the mountains, and thru the lowlands of Sweden, eastward to the shores of the Baltic. Altho his dream never came true, the family name recalls it and the family tradition of land-holding has persisted unbroken; the land that borders the lovely fjord

MARTHA OSTENSO

is still in the family's possession, handed down from eldest son to eldest son.

"My father, a younger son, was free to indulge his roving disposition. A few years after marrying my mother he decided to emigrate to America.

"My mother's parents lived high up in the mountains, remote from the softening influence of the coast towns. At their home it was, near the little village of Haukeland, that I was born. This, the first of many small towns in which I have lived, is known to me only thru hearsay, for when I was two years old we came to America.

"The story of my childhood is a tale of seven little towns in Minnesota and South Dakota. Towns of the field and prairie all, redolent of the soil from which they had sprung and eloquent of that struggle common to the farmer the world over, a struggle but transferred from the Ostenso and Haukeland of the Old World to the richer loams of the new. They should have a story written about them, those seven mean yet glorious little towns of my childhood! In one of them, on the dun prairies of South Dakota, I learned to speak English. What a lovely language I found it to be, with words in it like 'pail' and 'funeral' and ugly words, too, like 'laughter' and 'cake' and 'scratch' ! What strange sounds the new words made to me!

"Later, in another of my little towns, I learned that it was fun to make things with words. It was while living in a little town in Minnesota that I became a regular contributor to the Junior Page of the *Minneapolis Journal*, and was rewarded for my literary trial-balloons at the rate of eighty cents a column. In the public school of that little town there still hangs, perhaps, a large print of a rural scene in a resplendent frame, with a neat name-plate at the bottom of it. That also came from the *Journal*, in recognition of an essay which, in my eleven-year old opinion, placed me abreast of Emerson.

"When I was fifteen years old I bade good-by to the Seven Little Towns. My father's restless spirit drove him north to the newer country. The family settled in Manitoba.

"It was during a summer vacation from my university work that I went into the lake district of Manitoba, well toward the frontier of that northern civilization. My novel, *Wild Geese*, lay there, waiting to be put into words. Here was the raw material out of which Little Towns were made. Here was human nature stark, unattired in the convention of a smoother, softer life. A thousand stories are there, still to be written."

More formally recorded: Martha Ostenso was born in Bergen, Norway, in 1900, the daughter of Sigurd Brigt Ostenso and Lena Tungeland Ostenso. Her schooling was mostly in Minnesota and at the Brandon (Canada) Collegiate School. Afterward she attended the University of Manitoba. She began writing, as an adult in all seriousness, at Winnipeg in 1920. In 1921-22 she took a course in the technique of the novel at Columbia University, New York. Her first novel, *Wild Geese* (1925), gave her trouble and she put it aside in some discouragement. Friends in Minneapolis who had read the manuscript drew her attention to the prize contest instituted jointly by *Pictorial Review*, Dodd, Mead and Company, and Famous Players-Lasky Corporation,

urging Miss Ostenso to finish her book and enter it in the competition. This she did, winning the prize.

Before *Wild Geese* she had done secretarial work for a while with a charity organization in Brooklyn, New York. She really began as a poet, her very first book of all, a collection of her verse called *A Far Land* having appeared the year before her novel. Miss Ostenso now lives in a charming old house not far from Washington Square in New York.

Wild Geese was followed by *The Dark Dawn* (1926), *The Mad Carews* (1927), *The Young May Moon* (1929), and *The Waters Under the Earth* (1930). The last is the story of the disaster that inevitably touches the seven Welland children, whose human affections and impulses set them at odds with the tyrannous affection of their father.

Giovanni Papini

GIOVANNI PAPINI, Italian author, was born in Florence on January 9, 1881. He began his literary career in 1903 when he founded the review, *Il Leonardo*, a feature of the early-century Florentine renaissance. His collaborators in its management included Prezzolini, Borgese, Vailati, Costetti, Spadini, and Calderoni. A typically Tuscan organ, it ran from 1903 until 1907. Meanwhile, in 1906, Papini published his first volumes: *Il Tragico Quotidiano*, a collection of short stories, and *Il Crepuscolo dei Filosofi*, a book of criticism.

In 1908 *La Voce*, another review, was started with Prezzolini and, for a time, Papini as editors. It was in *Il Leonardo* and the early *Voce* that Papini evolved as a critic of works of art. His style was marked by deliberate crudities and barbarisms. The polemist and Dionysiac poet were locked in combat within him.

About 1910 Papini faced a spiritual crisis in which it seemed that thought, life, and art had failed him. His former idealism lay shattered, for the egoist had met the egoist's Nemesis, self-repletion. The first instinctive gesture, one of escape, was to create an extraneous value, a value outside of itself, and the fruit of this effort was *L'Altra Metà* (1911), in which an attempt is made to erect a philosophy of negation and contradiction. The attempt was none too successful as is apparent in *Un Uomo Finito* (1911), a poetic autobiography.

La Voce, an organ at once literary, political, and philosophic, which numbered among its contributors such men as Croce, Gentile, and Soffici, became defunct in 1913. In that same year Papini and Soffici founded a third review, *Lacerba,* which was smothered by the war in 1915. In the pages of both *La Voce* and *Lacerba,* Papini did much to provide a basis for a national culture and to diffuse a new intellectual atmosphere, by combatting old ideas and agitating for new ones. The note of hate, nevertheless, remained dominant. In *Lacerba,* Papini even attacked the personality and tradition of Jesus.

The World War seemed to act as a catharsis for Papini because he emerged from it purged of his bitterness and possessed of a growing clarity and serenity. He became editor of the review, *Vraie Italie,* in 1919. The next year he was converted to the Roman Catholic Church. His one-time caustic and skeptical attitude had entirely vanished in his *Storia di Cristo* (1921), a book which achieved immense success. He had made a grand tour of all the philosophers and philosophies only to find that they had "nothing to say," and finally settled into mysticism.

Papini, today, is a great penitent, a modern St. Augustine who has gone thru all the varieties of religious experience, and who is now sitting down to examine his own soul. It is with a certain proud humility that he identifies himself with that church father, finding in such fraternal identification a justification and a balm. Like Bousset, whose disciple he is, his tendency ever is to "interiorize theology." As a convert, Papini offers his *Saint Augustine* (1930), a study in the psychology of conversion.

Gog, which appeared in Italy at the close of 1930, is a *conte philosophique,* a collection of brief and witty satirical tales dealing with the foreign adventures of a Mr. Goggins ("Gog" for short), "one of the richest men in the United States."

GIOVANNI PAPINI

Papini's thesis in this book is anti-modernism.

Papini believes that it is thru biography that we see history. The great of the past, he says, are historic fragments in which we are to find ourselves, cadavers into which we are to put the breath of life.

Books by Papini published in America include: *Life of Christ* (1923), *Failure* (1924), *Memoirs of God* (1926), *Prayer to Christ* (1926), *Laborers in the Vineyard* (1930), *Life and Myself* (1930), and *Saint Augustine* (1930). His translations published in England include: *Twilight of the Philosopher* (1906), *The Tragic of Everyday* (1906), *Twenty and Four Minds* (1912), *A Finished Man* (1913), and *Bread and Wine* (1926).

Dorothy Parker

DOROTHY ROTHSCHILD PARKER was born in West End, New Jersey, on August 22, 1893, the daughter of J. Henry and Eliza Marston Rothschild. She attended Miss Dana's School in Morristown, New Jersey, and the Blessed Sacred Convent in New York. Her father was Jewish, her mother Scotch. She says that the only thing she

DOROTHY PARKER

learned at school was that if you spit on a pencil eraser it will erase ink.

She worked on *Vogue* in 1916-17, earning the munificent salary of $10 a week at first. F.P.A. first encouraged her by printing her verses in his column in *The Mail*.

In 1917 she was married to Edwin Pond Parker, 2nd, of Hartford, Connecticut, from whom she is now divorced. She served as dramatic critic on *Vanity Fair* from 1917 to 1920.

Mrs. Parker is opposed to prohibition, censorship, and reformers. During the Sacco-Vanzetti disturbances she was arrested in Boston for "loitering and sauntering," and paid a $5 fine.

In the spring of 1927, Mrs. Parker published a book of poetry, *Enough Rope*, which became that phenomenon of the publishing world, a best-seller in verse. The book contains light and humorously cynical verse.

Mrs. Parker prefers to be considered a satirist rather than a humorist. She usually writes in longhand, crossing out every other word in order to achieve the utmost simplicity. Ernest Hemingway is her favorite author. She tries to avoid a feminine style.

Mrs. Parker became a member of the editorial staff of *The New Yorker* in 1927, reviewing books with flippant candor as the "Constant Reader." Her second collection of verse, *Sunset Gun* (1928), for the most part, plays variations on the bitter love theme of *Enough Rope*.

Her first book of prose, *Laments for the Living* (1930), contains thirteen short stories and sketches. One of the stories is "Big Blonde," which won the O. Henry Memorial Prize. Her own favorite is "Telephone Call."

At Mrs. Parker's apartment in the Algonquin hotel a good portion of New York's smart literary set gathers daily at five. She is slightly over five feet in height, dark, and attractive, with somewhat weary eyes and a sad mouth. Her clothes come from Paris. Her favorite possession is Robinson, a dachshund. She is superstitious, pessimistic, and hates to be alone. Being extremely nearsighted, she wears glasses when writing, but has never been seen on the street with them. Flowers and a good cry are reported to be among her favorite diversions.

Anne Parrish

ANNE PARRISH was born in Colorado Springs, Colorado, on November 2, 1888. She spent her early childhood in Colorado Springs and attended the Misses Ferris' School there. When she moved to Claymont, Delaware, she continued her education at the Misses Hebb's School in nearby Wilmington.

"My father and mother were both artists," she says, "so I was brought up in a studio, more or less." Maxfield Parrish is a cousin and her brother, Dillwyn Parrish, is a painter and illustrator.

She says: "I have traveled a good deal, making a good start at the age of six months, in this country, Europe, England and Wales, the West Indies, Iceland, Norway, Sweden, and Denmark." In the summer of 1930 she cruised around the Mediterranean, and rode "camels in the desert and donkeys in the Holy Land during the really hot weather."

In 1915 Miss Parrish was married to Charles Albert Corliss, a native of Troy, New York. Her husband is a prominent corporation official. They have homes in New York and Englewood, New

Jersey, where Anne Parrish has her own garden to work in, "the thing I love best to do after writing." She is often in the company of her husband's sister, Mrs. Thomas W. Lamont, wife of the Secretary of Commerce in President Hoover's Cabinet.

With her brother, Dillwyn, she wrote and illustrated two books for children: *Knee-High to a Grasshopper* (1923), and *The Dream Coach* (1924), each doing half of the writing and half of the pictures. Brother and sister also collaborated on a group of short stories and sketches called *Lustres* (1924).

A Pocketful of Poses (1923) was her first novel. It is the story of a girl who poses from childhood until affectation and romantic untruthfulness become second nature. *Semi-Attached* (1924) concerns a girl who has observed so much unhappy marriage that she is unwilling to wed. But in Switzerland she persuades a young man to dispense with the actual ceremony and return to the United States with her, apparently married.

Miss Parrish's third novel, *The Perennial Bachelor* (1925) was awarded the $2,000 Harper prize and won her a wide circle of readers. The book spans a man's lifetime from the time he is a pampered child to the age of sixty when

ANNE PARRISH

he is still a beau who goes to young parties, unaware that everyone laughs at him.

Novels that followed are: *Tomorrow Morning* (1926), *All Kneeling* (1928), *The Methodist Faun* (1929), and *Floating Island* (1930). The last is a book for children about a house that is being transported with its occupants to the tropics when it is shipwrecked on Floating Island. It is illustrated by the author.

Isabel Paterson

ISABEL PATERSON (née Bowler) was born on Manitoulin Island, Lake Huron, Canada, of English, Irish, and American descent. "I don't seem to have room to say anything about my education, marriage, family, or accomplishments," she once wrote, "except briefly and in the order named: None; yes; large; none."

Mrs. Paterson was "about in the middle" of a large family of children, four boys and five girls. When she was quite small the family went to Utah, and then traveled from there to the Northwest in a prairie schooner. The most of her childhood was spent on a cattle ranch in Alberta, Canada. Reading and writing seemed as natural faculties as sight, she says, and she taught herself both at so early an age that she cannot remember when she could not read. The ranch in the wilderness was a lonely place, however, even tho there were many brothers and sisters with whom to play, and few books were accessible. She attended country school in a log cabin for two and a half years, from the age of eleven to thirteen, the only formal schooling she has ever had.

Mrs. Paterson was still a young girl when she left the ranch and went to Calgary, Alberta. She secured a clerical job with the Canadian Pacific Railroad, and later with a firm of American investment bankers, then went to Spokane, Washington. Her first position there was on a newspaper, and she was transferred from the business to the editorial department. Her next move was to Vancouver, British Columbia, where she was on a newspaper for about two

ISABEL PATERSON

in County Clare, Ireland. She is apt to break into a spontaneous and delightful laugh, and again she may discuss seriously any number of topics. She is essentially quiet. Some one has described her as having "a sort of Thackeray drawing-room air about her . . . a mild and scene-avoiding person, yet she can dispatch pompous and fatuous persons about their business. Among sensible persons, naturally and logically, she is the flower of courtesy, tact, good sense, wit and information, information that is so varied that she might be termed an encyclopedestrian."

She has been west a number of times, as well as having traveled abroad, and likes the scenery of the west coast of the United States better than that of the east, but she always returns to New York City, where she makes her permanent home.

years, doing for the most part dramatic criticism and editorial work.

Mrs. Paterson went to New York City from Vancouver, and found a job on the *New York American.* She wrote for the feature page, interviewing people on miscellaneous subjects, etc. Before working for the Fox Film News Reel she was for a short time on the editorial staff of the Hearst magazines.

In 1922 Mrs. Paterson joined the staff of the New York *Herald Tribune,* where she has remained, acting as staff reviewer on the daily paper and writing a number of reviews for the Sunday section *Books,* in addition to her weekly page of book chat, "Turns with a Bookworm."

Mrs. Paterson is author of five novels: *The Shadow Riders; The Magpie's Nest; Singing Season* (1924); *Fourth Queen* (1926); and *Road of the Gods* (1930).

One who reads the page "Turns with a Bookworm" without having met Mrs. Paterson gets a mistaken picture of her, that of a gay, rather flippant sort of person, dashing around from one literary tea to another with never a thought of work. Mrs. Paterson does have wit, vivacity, a comic sense, but also much common sense. She is small, with black hair and very blue eyes which she probably gets from a grandmother who lived

Julia Peterkin

JULIA PETERKIN (née Mood), Pulitzer Prize winner for 1928 with a novel dealing with the South Carolina Gullah Negro, *Scarlet Sister Mary,* was born in Laurens County, South Carolina, on October 31, 1880. Her father, Julius Andrew Peterkin, was a doctor. Her mother died soon after her birth and she and her older brother and two older sisters were raised by their grandmother.

Mrs. Peterkin says that she was not a studious or precocious child. She was spurred to study because of her adoration for an older sister, in whose class in school she wanted to be. She was successful in fulfilling this desire, and was graduated from Converse College, Spartansburg, at the age of sixteen. The following year she received her A.M. from this college. In order to show her independence, she registered in a teachers' agency much against the wishes of her family, and was given a country school at Fort Mott that fall. Even tho the school was small and she had only seven pupils, it was a difficult job for a seventeen-year old teacher. Abandoning a project is not one of Mrs. Peterkin's characteristics, however, and she remained there for two years. At the end of that time she married William George Peterkin, a cotton planter.

Since 1903 Mrs. Peterkin has been mistress of Lang Syne Plantation, near Fort Mott. There are hundreds of Negroes on the plantation and few whites. The nearest doctor or lawyer is ten miles distant, and it has been her lot a countless number of times to be "judge, jury, doctor, and family adviser." Her twenty-five year old son is now manager of the plantation, and Mrs. Peterkin likes to be thought of by the Negroes as merely "Cap'ns wife or young Cap'ns mother."

Isolated to a certain extent as she is, Mrs. Peterkin has had a number of hobbies, and believes every country woman needs at least one. "During the years I have lived at Lang Syne Plantation," she writes, "the score or more hobbies I have had have added tremendously to the pleasure of my days. Growing roses, raising Llewellyn setters, fancy pigeons, white Holland turkeys, have been great fun. I have gotten thrills out of embroidering beautiful linens, out of watching the sunshine glitter on the burnished feathers of my pet game cocks. I have planted unusual fruits and vegetables just for the sake of seing how many I could get to grow in this climate; not because any of these things were important, but because I enjoyed doing them. I have never hesitated to discard a hobby as soon as it failed to interest me."

Thus, when she was about forty, she turned to music with the decision to learn as many Beethoven sonatas as she could. She found a music teacher in Columbia, forty-odd miles from the plantation, and twice weekly made the trip for her lesson. She joined a music club, and found that her hobby had become work because her pride would not allow her not to play well and take part in programs.

About that time, the foreman of Lang Syne Plantation died in a tragic manner. He had been six feet four, and was stricken with a disease so terrible that it was necessary to amputate his legs at the hips. His dying request was identical with the words of April at the end of Mrs. Peterkin's *Black April*: "Bury me in a man-size box—You

JULIA PETERKIN

un'erstan'?—A man-size-box-I-been-six-feet-fo—."

When she told this simple but brutal story to her music teacher his comment was, "You ought to write that story. You tell stories better than you play." And Mrs. Peterkin, who had never thought she could write even a good letter, turned to recording a variety of the incidents in the lives of the Gullah Negroes around her. She loves the Negro and understands him. She appreciates the simplicity of the minds of her dark-skinned friends, without sentimentalizing over them.

Green Thursday, a collection of sketches, (1924), was written without the knowledge of even her husband or son. Some of the sketches appeared first in the Richmond *Reviewer*, and attracted the attention of H. L. Mencken and other critics. Her other books are: *Black April* (1927) and *Scarlet Sister Mary* (1928), dramatized in 1930-31 with Ethel Barrymore in the leading rôle. A fourth book is in preparation. She has also contributed to the *American Mercury* and other periodicals.

Carl Sandburg once told Mrs. Peterkin that she is the only writer he knows who is not a literary person. Her writing is one part—a major part now—of a full life. She is a housekeeper, a mother, she has her plantation, and in the country there is much frolicking, much entertaining. She rides, hunts, fishes, and swims.

Mrs. Peterkin is striking in appearance, a tall straight woman with red hair and grey-green eyes. Her expression is calm, her voice beautiful and low with a characteristic South Carolinian accent, her manner poised and charming.

Eden Phillpotts

EDEN PHILLPOTTS recently said, "I saw somewhere that I have one hundred and fifty items in the British Museum Catalog. It is shocking if true, but I can't help it."

Mr. Phillpotts was born November 4, 1862, at Mount Abu, in the Rajputana province of India, where his father, the late Capt. Henry Phillpotts, was Resident Political Agent. Sent back to England in early boyhood, he attended school in Plymouth for a few years.

The magic of Dartmoor, "the huge monotony, that stretched formless, vague, vast, toward boundaries unseen," first laid hold of his spirit when, at the age of fourteen, he tramped the thirteen miles from Plymouth to Princeton. ("How well I recall giving my first order to a waiter at the inn: 'Ham and eggs!'")

EDEN PHILLPOTTS

At seventeen Eden Phillpotts left school and went to London, full of young dreams and hope, in order to study for the stage; but finding that his ability did not justify perseverance he soon grimly gave up the idea of becoming a famous actor. For ten years, from 1880 to 1890, he worked as a clerk in the Sun Fire Insurance Office in London.

In this unhappy decade of his life, young Eden learned his lesson of poverty and struggle—the long days in the counting-room followed by the lonely evenings of writing, revising, and tearing up of manuscripts which mark the first steps of the writer's career.

He did editorial work on *Black and White* and, later, on the *Idler*. From the very beginning he wrote of Devonshire, where his parents came from, and, more specifically, of Dartmoor, that "uplifts itself in the middle of Devonshire in South-west England .. at once the subsistence and ruin of the men that toil on its vast curving flanks." The moorfolk wondered at the young man, recently of London, who used to roam over the wildest places, halting at noon at some lonely inn, where he would sit quietly in a corner, listening to the racy talk of farmers and peasants over their tankards.

His first books were *Lying Prophets* (1896) and *Children of the Mist* (1898). Phillpott's novels are sometimes said to derive from Hardy's, but the truth is that he wrote his earliest Dartmoor novels before he had even heard of Hardy. In 1927-28 Phillpott's Dartmoor novels were published in a new collective edition of twenty volumes.

The Dartmoor novelist and playwright is described as a systematic hard worker by a writer in the London *Bookman* who says:

"It has been said that a work reveals, to some extent, the personality of its author. I believe that view to be true. Applying it to Eden Phillpotts in relation to his work, there is no question about its truth. You cannot be for long in his company without discovering that the comedy in his novels clearly reflects the inherent humor of the man himself. This came home to me when I first met him in the heart of his beloved Dartmoor.

"How does a regional novelist like Phillpotts set to work? I asked him that question. 'I go to a place,' he said, 'with an empty mind, and let my story come out of the place to me. I never have any idea what story a place is going to tell me till I get there; but I have never failed to find a new scene tell me a new story. The story gradually develops, and I live with it thru a varying period—generally about six months. Then it reaches a stage when the people have become alive to me and clamor to me to begin writing about them.'

"During my visit I came to know him as a hard worker. Each division of the day was planned out. This method he acquired when in business before taking to literature, and the habit has remained. As a rule the morning was given over to creative writing. In the afternoon he would revise or correct proofs until tea time, which afforded a brief respite. Fine weather, of course, would lure him out of doors and vary the routine, but complete relaxation did not come till evening, when tobacco and talk held sway."

Mr. Phillpotts' first wife, whom he married in 1892, died in 1928, leaving a son and a daughter. He took a second wife in 1929.

Mr. Phillpotts has lived, of late, in Torquay, a charming little town built on seven hills overlooking the English Channel, and in Exeter. His two pet enthusiasms are his cat, "a most masterful creature," and his shrubs and flowers. On the latter subject he is quite an authority and he spends much of his leisure cultivating his garden, in which plants and flowers grow in a great profusion of varieties, many of them having been sent to him by admirers in other countries.

Mr. Phillpotts recently received the freedom of Torquay—a unique honor for an English novelist and one that is usually reserved for royalty itself and visiting magnates.

Phillpotts' Dartmoor novels include: *Sons of the Morning* (1900); *Widecombe Fair* (1913); *Children of Men* (1923); *The Jury* (1927). He has also written many historical novels: *Evander* (1919) is laid in Greece; *The Lavender Dragon* (1923) is medieval; *The Treasures of Typhon* (1924), Roman. Among

his volumes of short stories are: *Up Hill, Down Dale* (1925); *It Happened Like That* (1927); *The Torch* (1929). *Yellow Sands* (1926), written with his daughter Adelaide, is his most successful play. His volumes of poems include: *A Dish of Apples* (1921); *One Hundred Sonnets* (1929).

Boris Pilnyak

BORIS PILNYAK, Russian novelist, whose real name is Boris Andreyevich Vogau, is descended, on his father's side, from the German colonists of the Volga, who came to Russia in the sixties of the eighteenth century. On his mother's side, Pilnyak is of Russian descent. His mother was the daughter of a Volga merchant. His father is still actively practicing veterinary surgery.

Pilnyak was born on October 12, 1894, in the city of Mozhaisk, Moscow province. His childhood and youth were spent in the town of Kolomna, near Moscow, which is the scene of his novel, *Mashiny i Volki*. He was graduated from a Realschule in Nijni Novgorod in 1913, and he began to write in 1915 as a university student in Kolomna. His early literary work was confined to a

BORIS PILNYAK

few short stories, chiefly imitations of Bunin, which were printed in Kolomna.

The Revolution of 1917 brought Pilnyak out as a writer. Because of extreme near-sightedness he could not take part in military activity, so he became a feature writer (feuilletonist) on a provincial newspaper. During the first year of the war he suffered his share of starvation and misery along with his countrymen, wandering from town to town in quest of food, and living in constant anticipation of death.

In the summer of 1918 Pilnyak began to write about the suffering he had seen in the Revolution, publishing his short stories in various periodicals. He collected them in his first volume, *Bylyo* (1920), which passed unnoticed. Meanwhile he resumed his higher education at the Moscow Commercial Institute where he was graduated with a major in economics in 1920. At Moscow he helped organize a small literary group devoted to a study of the Russian modernists, which brought him some recognition and encouragement.

Pilnyak became acquainted with Maxim Gorky and lived with him in Petrograd in 1920, while he started work on his novel, *Goly God* (*The Naked Year*). With the publication of his second group of short stories, *Ivan da Marya* (1922), he was hailed as the literary sensation of the hour and rose to recognition as the foremost interpreter of the spirit of the Revolutionary society.

Goly God was completed at Kolomna and London in 1923-24. The novel, regarded as Pilnyak's masterpiece, is a description of the famine year of 1918-19. The scene is a small provincial city, Ordynin, which takes its name from the principal family of the place. "There we see," writes William A. Drake, "mixed in a frantic medley and united alone by their common suffering, all the elements of the new Russia—the Ordynins, decayed and divided, going their several ways to destruction; the peasants, 'still living in the Stone Age,' their eyes turned in indolent adoration toward the past and utterly dazed and helpless before the sudden shifting of immediate events; the Bolshevist commissars, the 'Leather Jackets,' brusque, active, and arrogantly confident of the future. We see them all as Fate has molded them, in their fundamental separateness, the superstition of the peasants contrasting the materialism of their new masters, anarchy contrasting communism, and the two finding a common basis only in death, starvation, drunkenness, and sexual excess."

The novel has no plot, no unity of time or place, and almost no coherence. It deals with the peasants, the workers, and the bourgeoisie. The theme is the contrast of these classes in the flux of the new order.

The sequel to *Goly God* is the novel *Mashiny i Volki*. It presents a similar segment of the same society, at a further point in its development in the new order. The story centers about the erection of a factory in the town of Kolomna by a Bolshevist commissariat. Both these novels of the Revolution are violent and full of abrupt transitions. The author views the change from peasant retrogression to Bolshevist progress as a struggle between the wolves and the machines. His own sympathy is with the peasants rather than the workers. He is not a Communist. Altho he supported the Revolution launched by Lenin, he is at heart an anarchist.

"He has borrowed," says Drake, "the dialectical virtuosity of his style from Aleksei Remisov; its typographical idiosyncrasies and its pseudo-philosophical accent from Andrey Viely. His skepticism derives from Chekhov, and his treatment of sex from Rozanov and Aleksei Tolstoy. His debt to Ivan Bunin is likewise great."

Pilnyak is a large, big-chested, pink-faced, clean-shaven man with blond hair, blue eyes, and a ready, disarming smile. He does not speak English. When he came to the United States in March 1931 for a three months' visit, he revealed that he is one of the richest persons in Russia and estimated that his income in 1930 was about twenty times that of Joseph Stalin, the Communist dictator, who receives slightly over one hundred dollars a month. In the Russia of the Revolution, he explains, the successful writers and artists have, as a class, the highest incomes, because nearly all common wages are fixed by the government.

Since the government set out to teach everyone to read, he says that a novel which sells only twenty thousand copies in Russia is not regarded as a success. *Goly God* had a sale of five hundred thousand copies. It has been translated into eight tongues. The writer has traveled widely thru the USSR, has been in England, Germany, Greece, Turkey, Palestine, The Pamir, on the borders of Afghanistan, in Mongolia, China, Japan, and on Spitsbergen.

A part of *The Volga Flows into the Caspian Sea,* which appeared under the title of *Mahogany,* was denounced by Soviet critics as a libelous thrust against the Soviet Union, and cost Pilnyak the presidency of the All-Russian Union of Authors. In 1930 he wrote *The Red Trees,* which was severely criticized in the Russian press, and which another Russian author described as "a cry of despair against the Soviets."

Boris Pilnyak is recognized today as a power in Soviet literature whose influence has affected numerous of his contemporaries. He is the founder of a new school.

The translations of Pilnyak's works published in America are: *Tales of the Wilderness* (1925), *The Naked Year* (1928). *The Volga Flows into the Caspian Sea* is scheduled for publication here in 1931.

LUIGI PIRANDELLO

Luigi Pirandello

LUIGI PIRANDELLO, the Italian dramatist and novelist, was born in Girgenti, Sicily, on June 28, 1867. The name is of Hellenic origin; his father owned a sulphur mine. Pirandello began to write at the age of eighteen and produced, during the next few years, five volumes of poetry. At nineteen he went to Rome to study, and he later attended the University of Bonn in Germany, where he was graduated in philosophy. Returning to Rome, he became a teacher of Italian literature at the Normal College for Women, where he remained for some thirty years.

When he was twenty-three, Pirandello was induced by another Sicilian writer, Luigi Capuana, to turn to fiction, and in the next twenty-five years he published twenty volumes of short stories and three novels, besides a collection of lectures on *Humor.* His celebrated novel, *Il fu Mattia Pascal* (1904), sold only two thousand copies in eighteen years. Then, when the author's genius on the stage called attention to the merits of the novel, it sold more than a hundred thousand copies in two years. It is the story of a man who shams death in order to begin life anew in a different atmosphere and under another name, but in vain.

In 1912, when he was forty-five, Pirandello was persuaded by the playwright, Nina Martoglio, to dramatize one of his short stories, *La Morsa,* into a one-act piece. His first three-act play, *Se non Così,* was produced at Milan in 1913, and he was launched in the drama.

During the World War Pirandello wrote in isolation. It was partly to provide himself with some intense mental absorption, to offset the horrors and anxieties of war (his only son was fighting on the Italo-Austrian front) that the one-time writer of short stories turned his attention to the stage. He lived a secluded life in a sunny apartment on the outskirts of Rome, leaving only to teach his classes at the girls' lyceum. He rarely accepted invitations; he allowed nothing to distract him from the solitude of his study.

Pirandello's early plays were dialect dramas and comedies written in the Sicilian dialect of Girgenti and played in that idiom by the Sicilian actor, Angelo Musco. From this manner he passed to light comedy in the Shavian manner, then to the "grotesques" and the man-marionette plays, and finally to his fully-matured psychological dramas. *Six Characters in Search of an Author,* produced in Rome in 1921, made Pirandello a dramatist of importance. The play nearly caused a riot the first night. Thereafter the author was the subject of much argument, receiving both high praise and strong abuse. *Six Characters in Search of an Author* (*Sei personaggi in cerca d'autore*) takes place on an unset stage, where a company is assembling to rehearse a play. Six persons enter the scene, announcing themselves as the uncompleted and unutilized creations of an author's imagination, seeking to act out the drama which is inherent in them but has never been articulated. The drama contains the complete life history of all six characters. Outside of Italy the play was first produced in London, and subsequently in America, Ireland, Argentina, Portugal, Spain, Holland, Russia, Poland, France, Norway, Czechoslovakia, and Hungary. It is considered Pirandello's masterpiece. The New York production opened in December 1922; there was a revival April 1931.

Pirandello's other most celebrated work is *Enrico IV* (1922), a satirical comedy concerning a nobleman who goes mad as the result of an accident and imagines himself a king. When he regains his reason and discovers that the world has left him so far behind he cannot possibly fit himself into it again, he decides to feign insanity. The play was produced in New York in January 1924 under the title *The Living Mask.*

His success as a playwright caused Pirandello to come forth from his retirement and to give up teaching at last in 1921. In 1925 he founded his own theatre in Rome and began to take his company on summer tours thru Europe, especially in England, France, and Germany.

The hermit-like professor became an active, husting playwright—an elegant, fashionably-dressed gentleman who rushes about Europe, writing comedies in hotels and *wagon-lits*. He sometimes goes by airplane to attend *premières* of his plays in France or Germany. His plays have been translated into some fifteen languages. He always keeps a suitcase packed because he says he never knows when the desire for travel will seize him.

When J. J. Shubert visited Pirandello in Paris in the summer of 1930 to buy the rights for *As You Desire Me* and *Tonight We Improvise,* he found the author in his hotel room, clad in bright red and blue pajamas, seated at a portable typewriter. He was working on a new play, *I Giganti della Montagna,* which translates roughly into *The Mountain Giants.*

As You Desire Me opened in New York in January 1931 with Judith Anderson heading the cast, following the play's successful production all over Europe. It is based on the famous Brunelli-Canella "mixed identity" affair, which was the talk of Italy for five years.

Pirandello announced his intention of visiting America in 1931. "In America everybody's young," he believes. "In Europe it's difficult to find youth." He says that he does not intend to make money in New York. "No, the only reason I want to visit America again is to free myself of the chains so grandiosely known as our traditions. They hamper advance like a strait-jacket... Europe is senile; full of animated corpses. They still live in the glories of two centuries ago. America is eager to see new things in the theatre. If my plays fail there I can at least have the assurance that they got a hearing without any preconceived prejudice."

Members of his companies regard Pirandello as a fine actor. At rehearsals he demonstrates the parts. Even when he writes he feels the passion for acting. One day some masons who were at work on a building outside his study window saw a bald-headed man with close-cropped grey beard jump up from his writing table and prance about, gesticulating and declaiming. They reported to the porter of Pirandello's flat their suspicions that they had seen a lunatic. Pirandello loves to sit unrecognized at performances of his plays and laugh when people next to him confess to being mystified by the drama.

In 1924 when he was lecturing in Barcelona, Pirandello explained his drama in these words: "People say that my drama is obscure and they call it cerebral drama. The new drama possesses a distinct character from the old; whereas the latter had as its basis passion, the former is an expression of the intellect. One of the novelties that I have given to modern drama consists in converting the intellect into passion."

The writer sums up his attitude: "I see, as it were, a labyrinth where our soul wanders thru countless conflicting paths without ever finding its way out. In this labyrinth I see a two-headed Hermes which with one face laughs and with the other weeps. It laughs with one face at the other face's weeping." Over and above the comedy, with its undercurrent of tragedy, says Walter Starkie, "we see the author snarling his contempt for human society."

The translated plays by Pirandello published in America include: *Sicilian Limes* (1921); *Three Plays*: containing *Six Characters in Search of an Author, Henry IV, Right You Are* (1922); *Each In His Own Way*, and two other plays: containing the title piece, *The Pleasure of Honesty, Naked* (1923); *One-Act Plays* (1928).

The translated novels are: *The Late Mattia Pascal* (1923); *Outcast* (1925); *Shoot!* (1927); *The Old and the Young* (1928).

Ezra Pound

OF English descent, Ezra Loomis Pound was born in Hailey, Idaho, on October 30, 1885. His ancestors were early settlers in New England and he is distantly related to Longfellow thru his mother, Isabel Weston.

At the age of fifteen he entered the University of Pennsylvania, where he

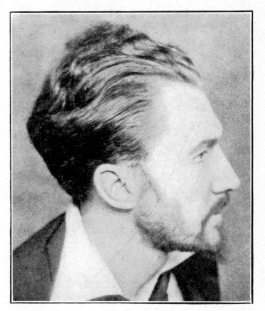

EZRA POUND

spent two years enrolled as a special student "to avoid irrelevant subjects." After two years at Hamilton College he was graduated in 1905 with a Ph.B. He returned to the University of Pennsylvania with a fellowship in romance languages, and served as an "instructor with professorial functions" from 1905 to 1907. He received an A.M. in 1906.

Pound went to Europe in 1907 in search of further material for a thesis on Lope de Vega, and he traveled in Spain, Italy, and Provence for about a year. For a time he lived in Venice, where he published his first book of poems *A Lume Spento* (1908), and then he went to England. He settled down in London and occupied himself for more than ten years with translating, lecturing on the arts, writing poetry, and contributing to the *Fortnightly Review, The Dial*, and *Poetry*.

Shortly after his arrival in London he published *Personae* (1909), and altho he was a total stranger, the volume made a definite impression on the critics. *Exultations* (1909) was printed in the autumn of the same year. Both these books of verse showed the author's familiarity with medieval literature, Provençal singers, and Troubadour ballads.

Pound wrote and lectured constantly in the interests of the "new poetry." In 1913, thru his efforts, the Imagists emerged as a group. He is said to have invented the word *imagisme.* He collected poems illustrating the Imagist point of view and edited the anthology, *Des Imagistes* (1914). In 1914 he married Dorothy Shakespear. In the same year he founded, with Wyndham Lewis, the famous propagandist organ of the Vorticists, *Blast,* which had a short but explosive existence. He served as foreign correspondent for *Poetry* from 1912 to 1919, and was London editor of *The Little Review* from 1917 to 1919.

The militant author went to Paris in 1920 and made his home there for four years. In 1922 he served *The Dial* as Paris correspondent. Margaret Anderson writes her recollection of him there: "He was living in one of those lovely garden studios in the Rue Notre Dame des Champs. He was dressed in a large velvet beret and flowing tie of the Latin Quarter artist of the 1830's. He was totally unlike any picture I had formed of him. Photographs had given no idea of his height, his robustness, his red blondness—could have given no indication of his high Rooseveltian voice, his nervousness, his self-consciousness."

Alfred Kreymborg's impression of him in Paris was: "an athletic figure in velveteens, wide-open collar . . . more Parisian than Parisians. . . There was never any doubt as to his contempt for the land of his birth. Nor for the land of his recent adoption—England. France was his country now. . . He seemed ill at ease, even in Paris, altho he had been accepted by many of the younger Parisians. By temperament . . [he] belonged to a romantic era like the trouvère days of the Middle Ages. A victim of the illusion of places, he turned on each town as the illusion wore away and betrayed the many spotted faults of a commonplace surface. He was constantly escaping somewhere in an effort to find himself."

Pound tired of France and moved to Rapallo on the Italian Riviera, where he has lived since 1924, working on his *Cantos* and contributing occasionally to magazines. In 1927 he founded *The Exile,* published by Pascal Covici in New York, London, and Paris. He edited the magazine thru four issues until it became defunct in October 1928. Pound was the recipient of the 1927 *Dial* Award of two thousand dollars for distinguished service to American letters.

A pioneer in new forms, Ezra Pound has "helped to broaden many of the paths which a score of unconsciously influenced poets tread," says Louis Untermeyer. But he is too special and too intellectual to achieve popularity for himself. He is a personality and a bundle of enthusiasms, starting movements only to discard them quickly for new ones. His most ambitious work is his yet unfinished *Cantos,* complex and fugual in structure, bewilderingly timeless in dimension.

As a propagandist he has been remarkably successful. He has championed a dozen innovators. He praised James Joyce and Tagore when they were unknown and helped them to positions of recognition. He fought for the musician Antheil, publishing a brochure on his harmonic experiments, and wrote a study of *Gaudier Brzeska* (1916) before that sculptor was heard of. He anticipated the flood of Chinese and Japanese translations when he published *Cathay* (1915).

Besides his adaptations of Chinese poetry and Japanese Noh plays as literary executor for Ernest Fenollosa, from whose notes he paraphrased *Cathay,* Pound has translated medieval Provençal poetry, Latin poetry of the Empire, and modern French poetry. As composer, he wrote the music of an opera, *Le Testament* (1919-21), which had a partial performance in Paris in 1926.

Among his books of poems, besides those mentioned, are: *Provença* (1910), *Ripostes* (1912), *Lustra* (1916), *Quia Pauper Amavi* (1919), *Poems 1918-1921* (1921), *Personae* (Collected Poems 1926), *Selected Poems* (1928), *XXX Cantos* (1930).

His prose includes: *The Spirit of Romance* (1910), *Pavannes and Divisions* (1918), *Antheil and the Treatise on Harmony* (1924), and *Imaginary Letters* (1930).

He is the translator of: *The Sonnets and Ballate of Guido Cavalcanti* (1912); *Certain Noble Plays of Japan,* from the

Fenollosa manuscript (1916); *Noh, or Accomplishment,* with Fenollosa (1917); *Twelve Dialogues of Fontenelle* (1917); *The Natural Philosophy of Love* by Remy de Gourmont (1922); *The Ta Hio* (1928); and *Cavalcanti Complete* (1930).

He has edited, among other works, *A Catholic Anthology* (1915) and *Letters of John Butler Yeats* (1917).

John Cowper Powys

JOHN COWPER POWYS is a member of a family rich in literary traditions and achievement, both past and present. His father was Rev. Charles Francis Powys, the Vicar of Shirley, descended from the ancient princes of Mid-Wales, from whom the author says he inherited "stubborn tribal emotions, earth-bound, volcanic, inarticulate, and crafty." His mother sprang from the line that included the poets William Cowper and John Donne. From her he inherited "capricious and rather morbid sensitiveness, saturated with a mania for books."

He was born on October 8, 1872, in the county of Derbyshire, England, at Shirley, a little village on the famous King's Highway between Derby and Ashbourne, where his father was clergyman. He was the eldest of eleven children. Three of his brothers have also become writers: Llewelyn Powys, T. F. Powys, and A. R. Powys. Philippa, a sister, is a poetess. The children were allowed to "run wild" in the large garden and orchards of the country vicarage.

With his brothers he went to school at Sherborne, in Dorset, and he attended Corpus Christi College at Cambridge. He attracted attention by his brilliant attainments at college and at graduation was awarded an honors degree in the Historical Tripos.

On entering public life he speedily made a name as a speaker, and attracted large audiences thruout England as staff lecturer for the Extension Societies of Oxford, Cambridge, and London Universities. Thus he initiated a career as lecturer, critic, and writer which has carried him far from the quiet English country-

JOHN COWPER POWYS

side. His popularity on the American platform has kept him here much of the time. He has lectured in forty of the forty-eight states.

Some writers he has praised are: Walter Pater, Henry James, Marcel Proust, Dorothy Richardson, Theodore Dreiser, and Edgar Lee Masters. Specific books he has recommended include: Constance Garnett's translations of Dostoievsky, Thomas Mann's *Magic Mountain,* Wyndham Lewis's *Time and Western Man,* Spengler's *Decline of the West,* Unamuno's *Tragic Sense of Life,* Keyserling's *Travel Diary,* and Doughty's *Arabia Deserta.*

Mr. Powys lives in New York and spends much time traveling round the country, but hidden away in the south of England, in Sussex near Arundel Castle, is a bit of land, a small "cottage-garden," to which he may some day return. He is tall and gaunt, an intense man, whose appearance has often been likened to Abraham Lincoln's. His wife is the former Margaret Alice Lyon of Middlecot, South Devon. They have one son.

His brother Llewelyn says: "Both I and Theodore have originality. John Cowper has genius. John's distaste for modernity is even more extreme than my own. He is a pantheist: he can draw up from nature, for whose moods he seems to be a medium. He must have the naked earth under him that he may draw up its virtues into himself; when he's on a macadam or concrete road, for example, he seems to be shut off from his great source."

John Cowper Powys's most ambitious work to date is the long novel *Wolf Solent* (1929), the story of Wolf Solent's return to the Dorset village of his ancestors, an ingrown community, malicious, perverse, rotten with vices. A mystic love of nature pervades his book.

The Meaning of Culture (1930) is, says the author, "the essence and epitome of a slowly accumulated 'message' that has been gathering shape in my mind for the last ten years."

Mr. Powys's books of criticism include: *Visions and Revisions* and *Suspended Judgments*. Among his other works are: novels, *Wood and Stone, Rodmoor,* and *Ducdame;* poetry, *Wolfsbane, Mandragora,* and *Samphire;* philosophy, *The Complex Vision, The Religion of a Skeptic,* and *In Defense of Sensuality* (1930).

Llewelyn Powys

A CONSTANT struggle for life against tuberculosis has been the lot of Llewelyn Powys since he was twenty-five years old, and he was nearly forty before he became well enough to resume the literary career he had begun as a youth.

He was born at Dorchester, Dorset, on August 13, 1884, the youngest of the literary Powys boys. He was educated at Sherborne School and Corpus Christi College, Cambridge. Following graduation he published several articles and stories, and in 1908 he visited America, lecturing in colleges under the University Extension Society.

He was of a nervous temperament, and had always been conscious of feeling unwell, but never suspected the serious nature of his malady. In November 1909 he burst a blood-vessel and it was discovered that he had that "terrible disease," tuberculosis.

During the next five years he spent several long periods in the mountains of Switzerland in an attempt to heal his lungs, interspersed with visits to the English countryside. At times he was apparently cured, then the malady broke out anew after some slight over-exertion. An inordinate lover of life, he was certain he would die young, and was constantly brooding over mortality. Every time he coughed he sickened with the sense of impending disaster. No one seemed to hold any hope for his recovery, and an old English woodcutter told him he would soon be "wearing a green coat" in the churchyard.

Finally, in 1914, at the invitation of his brother Willie, he went to British East Africa where he found the dry altitude agreeable. He worked there for five years as manager of a large stock farm, and returned home much improved in health. He stayed in England a year, lost all his money in investments in German marks, and renewed his incentive to write.

Then, in 1920, Mr. Powys went to New York where he lived with his brother John Cowper in meager quarters in Twenty-first Street. Every night he slept on the roof. The work of rebuilding his fortunes was slow, laborious, and discouraging. No room was small enough for his purse and a vignette of his African days, carefully and painfully composed, earned for him a mere three

LLEWELYN POWYS

dollars and seventy-five cents. Publishers rebuffed him and editors turned him away. One summer he went to California and took treatment for his lungs. Finally he won recognition with the publication of stories and impressions of Africa called *Ebony and Ivory* (1922).

Then followed *Thirteen Worthies* (1923), sketches of such figures as Chaucer, Marlowe, Izaak Walton, and John Bunyan. He suffered another attack of his disease as the result of a hunting expedition in the Rocky Mountains, but on his birthday in 1924 he sent a cable to his brother in England to show that he had at any rate reached forty without "wearing a green coat."

In 1924 Mr. Powys returned to his native Dorsetshire, taking with him his American bride, Alyse Gregory of Norwalk, Connecticut. There, on White Nore Cliff, "the proudest, wildest headland of all the Dorset Coast," Mr. Powys wrote *Black Laughter* (1924), *Skin for Skin* (1925), and his judgment of America, *The Verdict of Bridlegoose* (1926). His wife, who was a managing editor of *The Dial*, published a novel in 1926, *She Shall Have Music*.

In 1928 the couple traveled in Palestine, and Mr. Powys, with his great knowledge of the Old and New Testaments, wrote a story of the birth of Christianity, *The Cradle of God* (1929), and *A Pagan's Pilgrimage* (1931). In 1930 he published his first novel, *Apples Be Ripe*.

In middle life, Mr. Powys has just as strong a distaste for dying as he had in his youth. "I don't want to die," he says. "I want to live to a great old age as my father and grandfather and great-grandfather did before me." He feels that he is a reversion to a past age. "The age I love," he says, "is the age of Henry Hudson." He maintains a hostile attitude toward anything supernatural, mystical, or metaphysical, and is completely indifferent towards science and politics. He champions the pleasures of the sense. He hates radios, motor cars, paint and powder: all that perverts life.

John Cowper Powys detects in him four major literary influences, Walter Pater, Guy de Maupassant, Lytton Strachey, and most of all, Charles Lamb. His brother further believes that

Llewelyn is most entirely himself in his autobiographical works, *Confessions of Two Brothers* (1916), and *Black Laughter*. "In these he appears as the insatiable amateur, the incorrigible adventurer, the life-intoxicated world-child, for whom style and questions of style must all of them fall into a secondary position compared with a certain tough and yet timid curiosity. . ."

Llewelyn's recreation, ever since he started combatting tuberculosis, has been walking for miles at a time in the open country.

Among his books are: *Confessions of Two Brothers* (1916), *Ebony and Ivory* (1922), *Skin for Skin* (1925), *The Verdict of Bridlegoose* (1926), *Henry Hudson* (1927), *The Cradle of God* (1929), *Apples Be Ripe* (1930), *Hour on Christianity* (1930), *A Pagan's Pilgrimage* (1931).

T. F. Powys

THEODORE FRANCIS POWYS was born in 1875 at Shirley, in Derbyshire. He was educated at private schools, and for a year or two attended the Dorchester Grammar School. Before he was thirty he became a resident of the Dorset village of East Chaldon,

T. F. POWYS

which is said to be "bewitched." There he retired, hoping that in its peace and quietude he might forget the life of cities and work out a system of philosophy for himself. In 1905 he married Violet Rosalie Dodds, and in the home thus established he has done all his literary work.

Every day from eleven to one-thirty he shut himself in the house and endeavored to transfer his thoughts into words. Nearly twenty years of this life of seclusion and writing continued before Theodore Powys published any of his work. His cupboard was well filled with manuscripts, many of them printed by hand in letters half an inch high, which had made the rounds of innumerable agents and publishers.

Then, Stephen Tomlin, a young sculptor, who was a fellow-villager, sent some of Mr. Powys's manuscripts to David Garnett, author of *Lady Into Fox,* and the immediate result was the publication of *The Left Leg* (1923).

The tale which gives this book of short stories its title deals with rustic life in Southern England, as do all of the author's works, and it illustrates his determination not to conceal any portion of man's evil. It is a long short story of about ninety pages, describing the lust of an old farmer for the possession, body and soul, of every creature in the village. Thirty-three characters are portrayed, sometimes with no more than a single trait of speech or habit. The other two stories in the book are written in the same vein of uncompromising realism.

The second book that came out of Mr. Powys' cupboard was named after the poisonous shrub, *Black Bryony* (1923). It is the novel of a Salvation Army lass who, despite her uniform, steals money and seduces men. In all of Mr. Powys's books that followed there is a pervading atmosphere of monotony and gloom.

His style, which employs the simplest language, is distinctive. It would be unmistakable in a group of anonymous sentences. John Cowper Powys calls his brother Theodore "undoubtedly the most original" of the four brothers who write; "original in both subject matter and in style." He seems to isolate Hardy's Dorset locale from the rest of the earth "until it is so soaked by fairy rains and

so blighted by magic moons as to become rather a projection of one man's creative mind than a reproduction of any actual human province." He sees events remotely, "as if thru a filmy mist."

John Cowper continues: "My brother's humor, wrinkling his tragic mask, is utterly unlike any other humor that I have ever encountered. It has a directness that approaches its object with the tap of a raven's beak... It is humor that has a deep, sweet-bitter subterranean malice in it; a malice that moves close up to the thing it is handling and catches it off-guard and disarrayed; catches it, if it is alive, sneezing, gobbling, scratching, stretching, shivering with fear or with desire, prowling off on some affair 'that has no relish of salvation in't.' "

Coming of many generations of clergymen, T. F. Powys is by nature a religious man and by tradition a Christian. He says that he "believes a great deal too much in God."

T. F. Powys plants cabbages and mends his ever-breaking fence. He believes in monotony. He is happy when he does the same each day. He still writes from eleven to one-thirty. Clad in homely tweeds, he walks the same path nearly every afternoon, going past the inn to the mill on the heights above. He prefers the winter to summer. His favorite authors are Rabelais, Samuel Richardson, Montaigne, and Scott. During the War he went three times to the Dorchester Barracks, where he was treated kindly, but was politely sent home again.

J. B. Chapman describes him: "In appearance he is tall and broad-shouldered; his features are strong and clean-cut; his lofty forehead is surmounted by a shock of grizzled hair, and from beneath beetling brows his eyes peer out with the steady, questioning gaze of the seeker. There is humor, too, in that face, for tho the mouth closes like a trap, an upper lip of almost Irish length and an occasional twinkle from those searching blue eyes tend to mitigate the sternness of the other features."

John Cowper says he has "a deep-bitten, uncompromising, inveterate hostility to every form of careless strength or casual well-being."

Books by T. F. Powys include: *The Left Leg* (1923), *Black Bryony* (1923), *Mark Only* (1924), *Mr. Tasker's Gods* (1925), *Mockery Gap* (1925), *Innocent Birds* (1926), *Soliloquies of a Hermit* (1926), *Mr. Weston's Good Wine* (1928), *The Dewpond* (1928), *The House With the Echo* (1929), *Fables* (1929), *Kindness in a Corner* (1930), and *White Paternoster* (1931).

J. B. Priestley

JOHN BOYNTON PRIESTLEY was born in Bradford, Yorkshire, England, in 1894, the son of a schoolmaster; and received his early schooling in Bradford.

He served for the entire war period as man and officer in the British army in France. As a convalescent officer he amused himself with writing essays for the *Yorkshire Observer* shortly before going up to Cambridge (Trinity Hall) in 1919.

At the University he took a leading part in the journalistic and literary activities of the colleges and won a considerable outside reputation as a parodist with his little volume, *Brief Diversions*. This was followed almost at once by a book of essays, *Papers from Lilliput*. Almost immediately upon leaving Cambridge for London he became literary adviser to one of the largest publishing houses and began a series of essays in *The Challenge* which were afterwards reprinted in *I for One*, the book which first brought his work into the notice of the more important critics in England and America.

He contributed a number of critical essays to the *London Mercury* and was subsequently invited to write for many of the better known periodicals in England. His witty reviews of contemporary novels in *The Daily News* (to which he has been a constant contributor) became one of the best known features of the newspaper and soon he published his *Figures in Contemporary Literature*. His critical volumes include: *The English Comic Characters* and *George Meredith*. He has also edited an anthology, *Fools & Philosophers*, se-

J. B. PRIESTLEY

lections from the great comic passages in English literature.

Mr. Priestley's great popularity began with *The Good Companions* and continued with *Angel Pavement*, long hearty sentimental novels of English life in the old tradition. Since giving up his journalistic activities, Mr. Priestley has devoted all his time to literature. He is missed in the literary circles about Fleet Street where he was one of the most popular visitors.

Priestley's novels have frequently been likened to Dickens, but the author himself sees no resemblance: "I am not like Dickens at all. It is just a habit of critics and reviewers to pad out copy."

Mr. Priestley is a pudgy, slow-spoken, matter-of-fact individual of medium stature, whose constant companion is a briar pipe. His accent betrays his Yorkshire origin. His first wife, Patricia Tempest, died in 1925. His second wife, whom he married in 1926, is Mary Wyndham Lewis. There are five little Priestleys—all girls: Angela, Barbara, Sylvia, Mary, and Rachel, ranging in age from ten years to a few months. The London home of the Priestleys is in charge of a staff of seven, which includes nursemaids, governesses, cooks, and maids.

Mrs. Priestley avers that "Jack" is not in the least temperamental. "And if a meal's late it doesn't matter. And he doesn't swear if he loses a cuff button. He's wonderful with the children. He'd spend all his time playing with them if I didn't make him work. He improvises music for their little plays and has a beautiful time with them."

Priestley works in his study from 10 a.m. until 1 p.m., indulges in tennis or badminton until tea time, plays with the children until 6.30, and then works for an hour or two before going to bed or out for the evening. He seldom if ever corrects a manuscript. His essays are dashed off in almost no time.

In the center of the ceiling in the Priestley drawing room is a postage stamp that the family prizes highly. It is Sir James Barrie's reward for "The Peter Pan Gavotte" as played on the piano by Priestley *père* and danced by the little Priestleys. Mrs. Priestley explains that it is not unprecedented for Sir James to toss a penny with a postage stamp to the ceiling of a room where he has been entertained. If the stamp sticks to the ceiling, Sir James permits his host to keep it. Priestley's closest friend is Hugh Walpole, with whom he collaborated on a humorous romance, *Farthing Hall* (1929).

His novels are: *Adam in Moonshine* (1927), *The Good Companions* (1929), and *Angel Pavement* (1930). Among his essays: *Brief Diversions* (1922), *Papers from Lilliput* (1923), *Talking* (1926), *Open House* (1927), and *Apes and Angels* (1928). His critical studies include: *Figures in Modern Literature* (1924), *The English Comic Characters* (1924), *Fools and Philosophers* (1925), *George Meredith* (1926), *Peacock* (1927), *The English Novel* (1927), *English Humour* (1928).

Mr. Priestley visited New York early in 1931, found it a "nightmare city," and left hurriedly for a short lecture tour in the Mid-West. Tahiti was the destination of Mr. and Mrs. Priestley. His next novel will be laid partly in America, with an American as one of the three principal characters. Scenes and action will stretch across the continent from New York to San Francisco, thence to Tahiti, in the same path that the Priestleys took.

Arthur Quiller-Couch

SIR ARTHUR QUILLER-COUCH was born in Cornwall on November 21, 1863, the eldest son of Thomas Quiller-Couch and the grandson of Jonathan Couch, of Polperro, the ichthyologist. He was educated at Newton Abbot College; Clifton College; and Trinity College, Oxford. Today he is one of the most famous men of letters in England, known everywhere as "Q."

One day at Oxford he purchased a penholder for three halfpence in a shop facing the schools, and went to write an examination. "I did none too well with it," he recalls. "On hearing the result in my rooms, I took up the penholder and addressed it saying: 'Very well, my lad. Now you and I shall have, sooner or later, to make good'—and with that innocent accomplice every page of my books has been written." The first volume with which the pen was disciplined was called *Dead Man's Rock* (1887). Since that day the author has written more than fifty books of short stories, novels, poems, essays, and even fairy tales.

After lecturing at Oxford on the classics in 1886-87, the youth removed

ARTHUR QUILLER-COUCH

to London where he became connected with *The Speaker* at its commencement. He signed his articles "Q." In 1891 he left London for his native country, where he has since resided. He retained his connections with *The Speaker* until 1899. The first book to be published after he returned to Cornwall was *I Saw Three Ships* (1892). From the windows of his residence, The Haven, at Fowey, Cornwall, he could watch the ships going in and out of Plymouth harbor. He can still watch the ships in the harbor. In 1897 he was commissioned to finish Robert Louis Stevenson's novel, *St. Ives.*

Sir Arthur Quiller-Couch was knighted in 1910. In 1912 he became professor of English Literature at Cambridge, a position which he still holds. His learned honors are numerous: M. A. Oxford, M. A. Cambridge, and Litt.D. Bristol. He is a Fellow of the Royal Society of Literature, a Fellow of Jesus College, Cambridge, and an Honorary Fellow of Trinity College, Oxford. He was a member of the Academic Committee under King Edward VII.

"Q" is tall, slight, blond, and athletic-looking. Ships are his love. He is a great yachtsman and is a member of the Royal Fowey Yacht Club. In spite of his tan breeziness and his Yo, Heave Ho air, he speaks like a scholar. Yet he does not take his learning too seriously. C. L. Hind says: "He is of the Stevenson school—gay, original, with flashes of insight, wearing his learning lightly and bending it to bright use in the give and take of the day's work." His wife, whom he married in 1889, is Louisa Amelia Hicks of Fowey. They have one daughter.

His last novel was *Foe-Farrel,* published in 1918. Since then he has devoted most of his time to criticism and editing. Some of his other novels are: *Fort Amity* (1904), *Poison Island* (1907), and *Lady Good-For-Nothing* (1910).

Essays and studies by "Q" include: *On the Art of Writing* (1916), *Studies in Literature* (1918, 1922, 1929), and *On the Art of Reading* (1920).

"Q" is the editor of the *Oxford Book of Verse* and the *Oxford Book of Prose.*

Lizette Woodworth Reese

LIZETTE WOODWORTH REESE was born on January 9, 1856, in the small village of Waverly, Baltimore County, Maryland. She had two sisters, one a twin. Her mother, a German, loved gardens and daffodils, and was "as sure of God as she was of the sun." Mrs. Reese seldom read herself but the children often read to her. Lizette's father was a silent man "with the tense and stern characteristics of his Welsh ancestry." He had been a soldier in the Confederate Army.

After receiving an education chiefly in private schools, Miss Reese became a teacher at St. John's Parish School in her village, at the age of seventeen. She says she was "raw, eager, dreamy, fond of young people, and had the gift of authority." There were fifteen pupils. An old building on the York Road, which she passed every day on the way to the school, inspired her first poem, *The Deserted House.* She spent weeks writing it. Then she took it to the editor of the *Southern Magazine* who published it in June 1874. She received no remuneration, but the thought of success was ample payment for the girl of eighteen.

Miss Reese found composition a diffi-

LIZETTE WOODWORTH REESE

cult task. She thought quickly and the picture in her mind was clear, but expression was slow in coming. She found it hard to make words as vital as her thoughts.

In 1876, when she was twenty, Miss Reese was transferred to an English-German school in Baltimore, where she taught half the day in German and half in English. The next year she became teacher of English literature in a high school for Negroes, where she spent four happy years. Then, in 1901, she took a position in the Western High School of Baltimore where she remained for twenty years.

Meanwhile she kept on writing. She tried stories for Sunday School papers, essays for school journals, and reams of poems. The latter she mailed to weekly papers and countless magazines "as far north as Cambridge in Massachusetts, and as far west as Chicago and St. Louis." Thirty-three of these she collected in *A Branch of May,* published in the spring of 1887. To her surprise she received laudatory reviews on her initial volume. "I used to run with the notices to mother," she relates, "and read them aloud to her, and her cool acceptance of them did much to keep me from growing heady."

She sent a copy of the book to Edmund Clarence Stedman who responded with a friendly letter, and a warm acquaintance grew between the two. At his home she met many literary people of the day.

In 1891 Miss Reese published her second volume, *A Handful of Lavender,* which included the poems in *A Branch of May.* Then followed *A Quiet Road* (1896). After a long silence, which she explains by remarking that she had nothing to say, she published *A Wayside Lute* (1909). It contained *Tears,* her best-known poem, which had been published in *Scribner's Magazine* in 1899. The check for *Tears* arrived the day her father died. Another silence of more than ten years and then she published *Spicewood* (1920) and *Wild Cherry* (1923).

Miss Reese resigned her position at the Western High School in 1921, after forty-five years of continuous teaching. On May 15, 1923, the school unveiled a bronze tablet inscribed with her poem, *Tears,* one of the most famous sonnets written by an American. She says: "Whenever I think of this tribute, of this tablet made fast in a place familiar to so many young people, it warms the very cockles of my heart."

Her *Selected Poems* were published in 1926. A year later came a new book of verse, *Little Henrietta,* occasioned by a recollection of the shock she experienced as a child when her small cousin died at the age of six. It embodies scenes from her youth. "From the very beginning of my writing verse," she remarks, "the critics have insisted upon the English setting; but the setting is pure Maryland, nothing more. Parts of Maryland are very English in look."

Commencing her work in a period when old-fashioned elegance and sentiment were in vogue, Miss Reese anticipated the next generation and wrote verses shorn of verbal tricks and false postures.

In 1929, when she was nearly seventy-five, she published her reminiscences in *A Victorian Village.* The next year she brought out a new volume of poems, *White April* (1930).

The books of poetry by Miss Reese are: *A Branch of May* (1887), *A Handful of Lavender* (1891), *A Quiet Road* (1896), *A Wayside Lute* (1909), *Spicewood* (1920), *Wild Cherry* (1923), *Selected Poems* (1926), *Little Henrietta* (1927), *White April* (1930).

Erich Maria Remarque

A SLIM, fair-haired young man with melancholy blue eyes, whose skill at evading reporters is surpassed only by his ability in driving his great black Lancia at terrific speed thru any sort of traffic—this is one description of Erich Maria Remarque, author of one of the most spectacularly successful books ever published. *Im Westen Nichts Neues* appeared in Germany in January 1929; since then it has been translated into twenty-nine languages, sold approximately 4,000,000 copies thruout the world, and been converted into a sensationally popular moving picture.

Remarque was born in Onasbrück,

Westphalia, of a family of French emigrés who settled in the Rhineland during the French Revolution. He is an orthodox Roman Catholic. He is not a French Jew; he is not sixty-five years old, nor is he twenty-five. (It appears that he was really born in 1897.) His real name is not Paul Kramer. He is not the effete son of a family of great wealth. He is not the author of a book setting forth the art of mixing cocktails; nor did he write a novel on experiences in brothels. Such reports have actually been sent out about him from German military circles hostile to *All Quiet on the Western Front,* his publishers say.

Remarque left school at eighteen, went into the army and straight to the Western Front. During the war his mother died, his friends were killed. In 1918 he was alone amidst a desolation of unutterable waste, of vitiated purpose, of achievement betrayed.

The bankrupt years and months brought him little peace. He became a teacher in a country school not far from his own home. The quietness of the life gave him no rest; the contrast between the external serenity and his own inner chaos was too great. He took up a nomadic life, he peddled things from door to door, he joined a gypsy troupe. He became at one time, conscious or not of the bitter and gigantic irony of the gesture, organist in a mad house.

He became, in succession, manager of a small business, motor car dealer, draughtsman, and dramatic critic. But he was subject to recurring black moods of depression. In the conscious effort to throw off this burden by giving expression to it, he wrote *All Quiet on the Western Front*—starkly, in fullness of his necessity, presenting one soldier's view of the war, the fate of a generation and true comradeship.

The manuscript was rejected by several publishers. Finally accepted, it began to attract attention when it was brought out first as a magazine serial, but not until it appeared on the bookstalls did the house of Ullstein realize that it had published the most popular book of the century.

"Fame and fortune have not spoiled him," reports his German literary agent,

ERICH MARIA REMARQUE

Herr Otto Klement. "His only real extravagance—aside from his divorce—has been the purchase of the Lancia motorcar. He's turned over his home to his wife and he lives in a little out of the way hotel, where no one can find him. He doesn't want to meet people. It's impossible to get him on the telephone. My home is one of the few homes he visits, and he often spends an afternoon here without saying a word—sitting at the piano most of the time. For he's quite a good musician. He's the shyest man I've ever met, yet one of the most simple and understanding."

Remarque's second novel—translated as *The Road Back* (1931)—deals with the post-war problems of the returned soldier. "That generation," says Remarque, "was confronted upon its return home by a maelstrom of an uprooted world thru which it was to find its way back into everyday life, into professional and other duties and into many—often incomprehensible—problems of peace... I have been working on the book for a year and my greatest difficulty has been coping with the abundance of material."

After the date of publication of his second book had been announced by twenty-one publishers thruout the world, Remarque became dissatisfied with the closing chapters and fled to Switzerland, where he made his final revisions early in 1931.

Agnes Repplier

THE essayist Agnes Repplier was born of French parentage in Philadelphia on April first, 1858. She was terrified by such tasks as learning the alphabet or arithmetic, and did not learn to read until she was ten years old. Her mother read aloud to her, and she learned poetry "literally by the yard." She developed a rare memory. At seven she recited a poem for company with such fervor that her audience was moved to rapturous applause.

When she finally learned to read, little Miss Repplier skipped almost at once from picture books to Hayward's translation of *Faust*. She began to write almost at the same time. Her formal education was received from French nuns at the Sacred Heart Convent of Torresdale, Pennsylvania, where she was

AGNES REPPLIER

taught to speak French. The story of her school life is told in *Our Convent Days* (1905).

Miss Repplier's literary career began when, as she says, "I had to earn my liv ing, and writing was the only thing could do." She wrote short stories sold some of them to *The Cath World*. When she visited New York she called on the editor who stunned her with the remark that her stories were "little more than blurred and badly dige transcripts of other people's books.' didn't think she would ever make a su writer, and suggested that she try her hand at essays.

"He told me to go home and write an essay on Ruskin, and send it in," sh relates. "I did, and it was accepted, ar I've written essays ever since, only tur ing to fiction when I wanted to say something that could not be put into the other form."

Her first volume was *Books and Men* (1888), in which she discourses on such subjects as "The Decay of Sentiment," "The Benefits of Superstition," and "Some Aspects of Pessimism." The discussion of these serious subjects is lightened by flashes of wit, a quick scholarship, and a keen intelligence. All her essays are distinguished by a happy combination of pleasant informality with strict regard for form. They are never loose-jointed, yet are always free from stiffness.

Of more than medium height, Miss Repplier is erect and alert, and gives an impression of elastic and well-tempered strength. Her eyes are at once keen and friendly. A fine head, crowned with vigorous grey hair, thrusts slightly forward as she talks, and her voice is vivid and incisive. Her face is interested and mobile. She speaks freely of other people's books, but reluctantly about her own. Her favorite essayists are Andrew Lang and Augustine Birrell. Lang she loves for his scholarship, warm with a sense of affection "that only a Greek scholar can have," and for his sad heart and his gay temper. "He hated cheerfulness," she says, "and so do I. Yet he was always gay."

Miss Repplier's youthful political sympathies were Democratic, but in the high tide of Democratic enthusiasm when

Bryan's silver tongue was sweeping the country, she turned Republican. Altho government problems interest her to an unusual degree, she has taken no part in ~ropaganda, not even in the fight for 'frage. Rather than devote herself to ~ses, or support certain groups, she ~fers to "walk by herself." She watches the current of contemporary life and comments on it without favor.

Miss Repplier holds a strong devotion France, and she has spent many y vacations there. Ill health re- ~ly has prevented her from going abroad, and she has spent her vacations in Quebec. Altho for many years a popular lecturer, she never liked lectur- ~g and has now given it up. She loves usic, not because of its content, but cause it stimulates her imagination.

She still lives in the city of her birth, in a brick house with white marble steps and a brass door knob. Her front room is walled with books, and on her hearth usually purrs "the fireside sphinx." She firmly established pussy in American lit- erature with a book by that title in 1901, and further celebrated her in an an- thology of verse and prose, *The Cat* (1912). But she does not always have a cat. "They leave, and then they come ♦back, at will."

Miss Repplier has been honored with the degree of Litt.D. by the University of Pennsylvania (1902), Yale (1925), and Columbia (1927). She was awarded the Laetare medal by the University of Notre Dame in 1911. Altho not a "joiner" she belongs to the Acorn, Col- lege, and Cosmopolitan Clubs. She was one of the first four women honored by the National Institute of Arts and Letters.

Her essays include: *Books and Men* (1888), *Points of View* (1891), *Essays in Miniature* (1882), *Essays in Idleness* (1893), *In the Dozy Hours* (1894), *Varia* (1897), *The Fireside Sphinx* (1901), *Compromises* (1904), *A Happy Half-Century* (1908), *Americans and Others* (1912), *Counter-Currents* (1916), *Points of Friction* (1920), and *Under Dispute* (1924).

She is the author of three biographical works: *J. William White, M.D.* (1919), an eminent Philadelphia surgeon; *Père Marquette* (1929), the French Jesuit

missionary who with Joliet first explored the headwaters of the Mississippi; *Mère Marie of the Ursulines* (1931), the seventeenth century French saint who, after a brief married life, entered the Ursuline order and was sent to Quebec to establish a convent.

Elmer Rice

ELMER L. RICE was born as Elmer Reizenstein in New York City on September 28, 1892. He changed his name after years of trying to make people understand it over the telephone. He attended high school in New York and was graduated *cum laude* from the New York Law School in 1912, after studying nights while he worked as office boy and finally as managing clerk of a downtown law office. The follow- ing year he was admitted to the bar, then suddenly gave up law and announced, to the horror of his family, that he was going to write a play.

Young Rice blasted theatrical tradi- tion when, as an unknown, he had his first play accepted thru the naïve pro- cedure of mailing it to a producer. *On Trial,* which was the first play to employ

ELMER RICE

the technique of the movie "cutback," was a Broadway success in 1914.

For several years after the production of *On Trial,* Rice was associated with the Morningside Players and other amateur organizations. He served as dramatic director for the University Settlement, New York, and was chairman of the Inter-Settlement Dramatic Society. His plays produced during this period, some written in collaboration, include: *Iron Cross* (1917), *Home of the Free* (1917), *For the Defense* (1919), *Wake Up Jonathan* (1921).

In 1923 came one of Rice's best-known successes, *The Adding Machine,* which has been acted in England and several countries on the Continent, as well as by the Theatre Guild of New York. The play is an example of dramatic "expressionism." It is the tragedy of a poor clerk who has passed a life of deadly monotony doing nothing but add figures, only to be supplanted after years of service by a more efficient adding machine. In his desperation and sense of outrage, he murders his employer.

In 1924 Elmer Rice wrote, with Dorothy Parker, *Close Harmony,* which successfully toured the road under the title of *The Lady Next Door.* With Philip Barry, he wrote *Cock Robin,* a mystery play produced in 1927.

In spite of the author's previous successes, *Street Scene* was rejected by nearly every theatrical manager in New York. It was finally sponsored by a veteran producer whose judgment of public taste was no longer regarded as infallible, and whose own son declined to share half the profits. After an unpretentious opening, *Street Scene* ran more than a year in New York and was awarded the Pulitzer Prize as the outstanding drama of 1929.

It is said that Rice originally called this play *Landscape with Figures,* and thereafter changed it to *Street Scene.* A tragedy of the New York tenements, it has one setting—a brown stone front—and the story is concerned with the lives of those who live therein. The plot centers round an Irish woman whose drunken husband returns home unexpectedly, her daughter who is wooed by a Jewish lad downstairs, and the neighbors who cluck and smirk over the scandal.

Two other plays by Rice produced in 1929 were *See Naples and Die* and *Subway.* The former, a farce, is said to have been written by the author for his own pleasure at a time when he was recovering from an illness and when *Street Scene* was going begging for a producer.

Elmer Rice's first novel, *A Voyage to Purilia,* published in the spring of 1930, is a satire on the motion pictures. His wife, whom he married in 1915, was Hazel Levy of New York City. They have two children.

The published works of Elmer Rice are: *Morningside Plays* (1917), *On Trial* (1919), *The Adding Machine* (1923), *Street Scene* (1929), *Subway* (1929), *Cock Robin* (1929), *See Naples and Die* (1930), *A Voyage to Purilia* (1930).

Henry Handel Richardson

HENRIETTA RICHARDSON was born at Melbourne, Australia, the eldest daughter of Lindesay Richardson, an English doctor. Her parents were ambitious for her, but showed greater interest in her unusual musical talent than in the stories and verse that she wrote as a child. She spent the latter years of her girlhood at the Presbyterian Ladies' College, one of the best schools in Melbourne. There she was a good student and was graduated creditably, altho she often questioned the many restrictions. A cantata of her own composition was performed at commencement.

At eighteen Miss Richardson was sent to the Conservatorium of Leipzig where she studied piano for nearly four years. But when she measured herself beside the brilliant foreigners, she felt she could never equal them professionally, so she abandoned music.

The desire to write had always stayed with her, and she determined on literature for a career. With an income which permitted her to travel round the Continent, she learned several languages, read omnivorously, and observed human beings. Not a facile writer, she studied form and style. Then she went to England and settled in Harrow, where she began her first novel, *Maurice Guest*. After a delay of more than five years owing to illness and other circumstances, during which time some writing was done on the Riviera, the book was published in 1908.

Miss Richardson feared she would be judged too tolerantly if her sex were known. So she twisted her name into a masculine form by changing the Henrietta to Henry and assuming Handel for its musical association. The ruse succeeded. The sex of the writer of *Maurice Guest* was never questioned. Only a man, readers thought, could have depicted the passion that bound Maurice to Louise Dufrayer in defiance to the call of his intellectual and artistic needs. Critics were enthusiastic, but the book sold poorly.

The second volume by Henry Handel Richardson, written in a lighter vein, was *The Getting of Wisdom* (1910), a gay satire on boarding school life in Melbourne. The blunders and embarrassments of a raw country girl and the trifles of dress and girlish etiquette were recorded as only a woman could record them. It was evident that the Presbyterian Ladies' College of Melbourne was the model, and Miss Richardson was recognized as the author.

She returned to her native land in 1912 to gather material for a long story of Australian life that had been running thru her mind. She read about the gold rush days in Ballarat, and visited all the places she had chosen to use in the trilogy. She talked with early colonists. She ransacked Victoria for government documents, out-of-print pamphlets, and files of small town newspapers. She spent weeks in libraries and old bookstores looking at faded prints.

Returning to England, she settled in her present home, a large house looking south and east over Primrose Hill Park and Regent's Park to the hills beyond London. Here she began her saga of Australian life, just before the World War. All her books have taken years to write. *The Fortunes of Richard Mahony* (reprinted in 1930 as *Australia Felix*) took three years and was published in 1917, almost unnoticed. Illness and

HENRY HANDEL RICHARDSON

other obstacles delayed the second volume, *The Way Home,* until 1925. The public was still indifferent.

Miss Richardson took a little less than three years to write *Ultima Thule,* the closing volume of the trilogy. Published in January 1929, it won an immediate audience and went into three editions in a few weeks. The American edition, published in the fall, was a success. With the triumph of *Ultima Thule,* Miss Richardson came into her own after twenty years of perseverance. An unattractive picture on the whole, the book was resented in Australia much as *Main Street* was resented in America. Nevertheless the author was presented with a gold medal by the Australian Literature Society for the best novel written by an Australian in 1929.

In her trilogy, Miss Richardson depicts thirty years in the lifetime of a generation beginning in the 'fifties, centering about an Irish doctor who goes to Australia, marries, and rises to an established position in Melbourne. But he is dissatisfied and twice uproots himself and his family to "chase rainbows." Still unhappy, he returns to Melbourne where the defects of his character prove his ruin, and his mind declines. Thru it all, his wife's love holds firm, even during his imbecility that leads to death.

Henry Handel Richardson is tall, with fine black hair waving naturally about a serious face. Her eyes, humorously penetrating, are a little weary, as one might expect from a person who has written relentlessly of tragedy. A woman of arresting personality, she does not seek publicity and seldom goes out at night lest it should tire her for work the following day. She does not even belong to a club.

Altho a philosopher who likes quiet life, Miss Richardson is not a recluse. She loves swimming and tennis like a good Australian. She has a summer cottage in Dorset, and drives her own car. Golf she is reserving for old age. She is the wife of a London University professor.

The books by Henry Handel Richardson are: *Maurice Guest* (1908), *The Getting of Wisdom* (1910), *The Fortunes of Richard Mahony* (1917), *The Way Home* (1925), and *Ultima Thule* (1929). *Maurice Guest* was reprinted in 1922 with an introduction by Hugh Walpole who, along with John Masefield, Carl Van Vechten, and Ernest Newman, fostered the book to a sort of subterranean popularity. A new edition was issued in 1930 containing the author's revisions.

Lola Ridge

LOLA RIDGE is an American poet who was born in Dublin, Ireland, and spent her girlhood in Australia and New Zealand. When she was a baby her mother took her to Sydney, where she studied art at the Académie Julienne under Julian Rossi Ashton. Altho her ambition was to be a painter, she spent some of her time writing poetry.

In 1907 she came to the United States with the manuscript for a book of verse, but deciding the poems were unsatisfactory, she destroyed them. Having given up painting, she supported herself for three years by writing fiction for popular magazines. She stopped this work, she says, "because I found I would have to do so if I wished to survive as an artist."

Then for several years she earned her living by various means—organizing educational movements, writing advertisements, doing illustrations, posing as artist's model, and working in a factory. She was one of the editors of *Others*, a magazine founded by Alfred Kreymborg, and took it over when he gave up active management of it. When it became apparent the struggling publication could not survive, she resigned. Kreymborg recalls that "she kept the movement going by giving a party nearly every time she sold a poem or an article, tho editors sent her sums hardly ample enough to be converted into the refreshments gracing her dark room on Fifteenth Street." He calls her "the frailest of humans physically and the poorest financially."

In 1918 her long poem entitled *The Ghetto* was published in the *New Republic*. It is a poem of the city—its brutalities and its beauties. Totally unknown as a poet, Miss Ridge was hailed as the "discovery" of the year. The same year she published a book of verse with *The Ghetto* for its title poem. After that she destroyed no more of her work. Her next books of verse were *Sun-Up* (1920) and *Red Flag* (1924).

Miss Ridge went to Boston at the time of the execution of Sacco and Vanzetti. On September 1, 1927, back in New York after two consecutive sleepless nights, she began to write what is now *Firehead* (1929), altho she did not know it. She put down the first lyric of the narrative before she realized what she was about—a lyric without plan, written out of intense emotion. Some time during that week she saw the whole thing except for the last section. She was ill then—as she has been much of the time. She was confined to her bed in bare quarters on the top floor of a drab brownstone house on West Fourteenth Street, where she had struggled for years against illness and poverty. The bulk of the poem was not written until she was invited to spend the summer at the artist's colony, Yaddo, in Saratoga Springs, New York, where she says she writes better than anywhere else.

Unmentioned, even by implication, Sacco and Vanzetti served to inspire a poem about Jesus Christ. *Firehead* relates the events of the day of the Crucifixion. The poem is divided into nine parts, eight of them presenting a specific character associated with the event of the Crucifixion: Christ, John, Judas, the two Marys, Peter, the Merchant of Babylon, Thaddeus the Unborn, and the Bondman. Part nine describes the Resurrection.

Altho sympathy for the oppressed was the motivating force of *Firehead*, Miss Ridge did not write it as propaganda. She wrote it for herself. "Let anything that burns you come out whether it be propaganda or not," she believes. "I write about something that I feel intensely. How can you help writing about something you feel intensely?"

Miss Ridge does not care what interpretation is put on the poetry she produces. "We're entirely too afraid of what people will say," she comments. "There is entirely too much consciousness of group opinion." She is not concerned with thoughts of sales or success. "All I want to do is to be allowed to write," she says simply. She believes now that much of the work she destroyed when she first came to New York could have sold easily; she has concluded it was not so bad as she thought at the time. Today she feels better fitted to write than ever before. She says she sees things more clearly and more deeply.

She believes American poetry is full of promise. "We have major poets in America today," she says. "Our poetry is much richer than the English. How can anyone doubt our wealth when we have both Robinson Jeffers and Edwin Arlington Robinson?" It is her opinion that poetry is not necessarily the property of youth. "The emotions spend themselves in youth, but if the mind keeps on growing the emotions are revivified." Altho she is not concerned with the methods of other poets, she buys their books when she can, and, when she cannot, she borrows them. She does not believe in poetry groups. Since poets are distinctly individualities, she says, poetic groups inevitably break up.

Harry Salpeter summarizes his impression of her: "Blood-drained, ravaged

LOLA RIDGE

by illness, she is like a bright, untarnished double-edged sword in her courage and her integrity." He adds that she is "more spirit than body" and "selfless almost beyond reason." When Llewelyn Powys met her he was "impressed by the beauty of her face, like the impassive death-mask of a saint."

The books of poetry by Lola Ridge are: *The Ghetto* (1918), *Sun-Up* (1920), *Red Flag* (1924), and *Firehead* (1929).

Mary Roberts Rinehart

MARY ROBERTS was born in Pittsburgh in 1876. Her father ran a sewing machine store, but his real interest lay in inventions which never brought him returns. She attended the Pittsburgh public schools and was editor of the high school paper, while her other activities included playing the piano in chapel and running a debate society. At fifteen she wrote three short stories for a local newspaper and received a dollar apiece for them.

When she was seventeen Mary Roberts began a nurse's training against the wishes of her family. She attended the Pittsburgh Training School for Nurses,

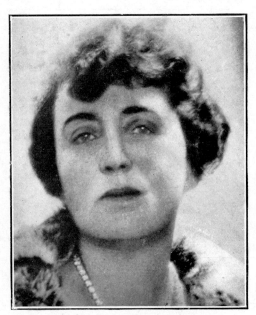

MARY ROBERTS RINEHART

where she met Dr. Stanley Marshall
Rinehart, a surgeon. In the last year
of her training her father killed himself.
Four days after graduation, when she
was nineteen, she married Dr. Rinehart.
They settled in Sewickley, a suburb of
Pittsburgh, where they lived for about
twenty years.

Three sons were born to Mrs. Rinehart before she was twenty-five, and
their care took all of her time. She had
to suppress the desire to write. Her own
health was poor. Once she sent an article
on "Home Nursing in Typhoid Fever"
to the Ladies' Home Journal and it was
returned. Finally she contracted diph-
theria from one of her children and
while she was convalescing she wrote
two poems which were accepted by a
magazine and brought her twenty-two
dollars. Encouraged, she "wrote reams"
of poetry and now and then it was accepted. When she had recovered she
wrote a book of poems for children and
went to New York to hunt a publisher,
but gave up after six refusals.

At the age of twenty-seven, in 1903,
Mrs. Rinehart began to write stories in
earnest when she and her husband lost
all their money in a stock market panic.
They were twelve thousand dollars in
debt. An incident her husband related

one day furnished the basis for a story
which she sent to Munsey's Magazine
and for which she received thirty-two
dollars. Then she began to write fast,
and at the end of a year she had sold
forty-five stories and earned more than
eighteen hundred dollars.

She did her writing in odd moments
of the day when the children were away
or in the evenings when they were asleep.
She wrote on a card table, and for a
while with two fingers on a typewriter.
Today she writes by hand, using an un-
filled fountain pen which she dips.

Mrs. Rinehart says if she had been
well she probably would not have written much, but her poor health afforded
her time for authorship. While waiting
for one of her frequent operations, she
penned her first long story, The Man in
Lower Ten, which ran serially. Her next
serial was The Circular Staircase, which
was accepted by a publisher—her first
book. It was published in 1908, and The
Man in Lower Ten followed in 1909.
The publisher was enthusiastic over her
work and accepted more stories. The
family debt was cleared.

Mystery stories come easily to Mrs.
Rinehart. Her device for keeping up the
interest is to have the initial crime
merely the forerunner of others to follow, and she has been credited with
developing a new technique in the detective novel.

She had ambitions to be a playwright
and in 1908 she submitted a one-act play
to David Belasco who liked it and asked
her to rewrite it in three acts. Double
Life was produced at the Bijou Theatre
in New York in 1907. Belasco was always amused by the fact that she made
her own summer dresses. In collaboration with Avery Hopwood she wrote
Seven Days (1909) from her story,
When a Man Marries (1909); Spanish
Love (1920); and The Bat (1920),
based on The Circular Staircase. The
Bat started the vogue for mystery plays.

Other plays by Mrs. Rinehart include
(with dates of production): The
Avenger (1908), Cheer Up (1913),
Tish (1919), Bab (1920), and The
Breaking Point (1923).

For fourteen years Mrs. Rinehart
nursed her mother, who had become an
invalid. Altho the editors' demands on

her time have been great and the earning of fifty thousand dollars a year is no trick at all, she has always tried to place the demands of her home first. She has refused the editorship of a large woman's magazine, and doubled and trebled her income while actually lessening her output.

She and her family spent a year in Vienna and London while Dr. Rinehart studied diseases of the heart and lungs, and she rested and wrote. When they returned, he established a tuberculosis dispensary which became one of the largest in the country.

In 1915 *The Saturday Evening Post* sent Mrs. Rinehart abroad as war correspondent. She went clear to the front and became friendly with Marshal Foch. The War drew Dr. Rinehart to Washington for the supervision of health in military training camps, and he has remained in the Government Health Service since. He and Mrs. Rinehart now live in Washington, where she is a distinguished hostess in the society of the capitol. She frequently spends her summers in Wyoming. In 1925 she was given a Litt. D. degree by George Washington University. Two of her sons are partners in the firm that now publishes her books.

Among the many novels by Mrs. Rinehart are: *The Circular Staircase* (1908), *The Amazing Adventures of Letitia Carberry* (1911), *K* (1915), *The Amazing Interlude* (1918), *A Poor Wise Man* (1920), *The Breaking Point* (1922), *The Red Lamp* (1925), *Lost Ecstasy* (1927), *Two Flights Up* (1928), *This Strange Adventure* (1929), and *The Door* (1930). Her autobiography, *My Story*, was published in 1931.

Elizabeth Madox Roberts

ELIZABETH MADOX ROBERTS was born in 1885 at Perryville, near Springfield, Kentucky, in the "Pigeon River country" where she now makes her permanent home. Her roots are deep in the local soil, all of her forebears having been Kentuckians since 1803. Some of them came from Virginia over Boone's Trace in the 1770's

ELIZABETH MADOX ROBERTS

with just such a pioneer band as she describes in *The Great Meadow* (1930).

Before her career as a writer began, she lived for some time in the Colorado Rockies. From 1917 to 1921 she studied at the University of Chicago, taking a Ph.B. degree, and writing poetry which won her the Fiske Prize and later appeared in book form as *Under the Tree* (1922).

"Against the background of a western university, its outlay of large imitated architecture, republican cloisters and Gothic laboratories," writes Glenway Wescott, a fellow student, "there was the young southern woman, alone absolutely original, unimpressed by the setting of evils and plagiaries, meek and insinuatingly affirmative, untouched by but kindly toward all our half-grown basenesses."

After graduation Miss Roberts came to New York. Wescott, who was commencing his own distinguished career as a novelist, recalls her then, "during the helpless interval between the coming of age and the maturing of the first important work, down one of those wild New York streets, scarcely occidental in mood, where the workers go half naked and Negro boys throw balls to pallid boys and girls," seated in her small dark room "with her yellow-crowned head bowed almost between her knees as are figures in certain Blake drawings; now signalling from the window with a towel when she had need of human attendance, now like royalty in a convent drawing apart in an arrogant and pious self-communion . . . thinking, thinking, remembering, biding her time, uttering extensive dreamy theories and troubling witticisms, with an occasional incorrectness of folk-songs in her speech."

Later still, when her work was well known, altho her personality remained a riddle, she lived in "a decorous sky-scraper suite," writing often for more than twelve hours at a sitting; "then, in a blue-feathered hat, a floating kerchief, ventured forth with a brother or devotee into the common city, finding it as delicately bizarre as if she had invented it also."

Her first novel, *The Time of Man* (1926), represents several years of work. It was received with enthusiasm in England as well as America, and has since been published in German, Swedish, and Dano-Norwegian editions. It is the story of the Chessers, a family of poor whites from the Kentucky hills, who with the restless urge of pioneers keep moving on from place to place. The narrative centers about the daughter, Ellen Chesser, who vaguely yearns for beauty and something better than the troubled life of the Chessers. She marries a luckless young farmhand. They are just about to settle down finally on a farm of their own when the hostility of their neighbors sends them forth again with their children on their wanderings, a "far piece" this time.

After finishing *The Time of Man*, Miss Roberts lived for a time in California, where she worked on *My Heart and My Flesh,* her second novel (1927). *Jingling in the Wind,* a fantasy, appeared the following year, but is not to be regarded as a successor to *My Heart and*

My Flesh in the Roberts chronology, as she began it earlier and carried its writing along with her other two books, turning from one to the other for diversion.

The Great Meadow (1930) followed after an interval of two years. It was the first novel Miss Roberts ever contemplated writing, the idea having been at work in her mind for more than fifteen years.

In her own account of the writing of *The Great Meadow* Miss Roberts tells of early memories of her grandmother who dressed in the same fashion as her mother and grandmother before her and who had the lore of the family ever at the tip of her tongue. "Her speech was archaic and fluent and her memory keen, but her tales were never adorned with fancies." *The Great Meadow* is, thus, really the story of Miss Roberts' own forebears who followed the trail she describes in the novel; and the characters are made up of figures from her grandmother's memory.

"I thought it would be an excellent labor if one might gather all these threads, these elements, into one strand, if one might draw these strains into one person and bring this person over the Trace and thru the Gateway in one symbolic journey."

An illustrated and enlarged edition of her poetry, *Under the Tree,* was published in 1930.

Edwin Arlington Robinson

TO the tiny village, Head Tide, Maine, belongs the honor of being the birth-place of Edwin Arlington Robinson. Here on December 22, 1869, he was born, but the next year the family moved to Gardiner, immortalized as Tillbury Town in so many of his poems.

In 1891 he entered Harvard University where he remained for two years. Then the long illness of his father compelled him to return to Gardiner, where he continued to write poetry, most of which was thrown away.

In 1896, with entire faith in his poetry's worth, he issued a privately printed booklet bound in blue paper and entitled *The Torrent and the Night Before*. On the fly leaf appeared the notice: "This book is dedicated to any man, woman or critic who will cut the edges of it. I have done the top." In reply to a review in *The Bookman* for February 1897 that observed, "The world is not beautiful to him, but a prison house," Robinson wrote, "The world is not a 'prison house,' but a kind of spiritual kindergarten where millions of bewildered infants are trying to spell 'God' with the wrong blocks." This dilemma and this pity are the core of his poetry.

Shortly after the publication of *Children of the Night* in 1897, Robinson came to New York, strong in his determination to devote his life to his poetry. In 1900 he lived for a time in Yonkers "on an ignominious little street, atilt like a house roof all of cobbles, opposite a factory. It was the meanest little house in the mean street." Next we find him in New York City "in a sordid stall on the fifth floor of a dreary house on West Twenty-third Street." The family property by this time having vanished, for subsistence he necessarily held a number of odd jobs, among them inspector on the subway that was then being built, but he always continued to write.

In 1905 Theodore Roosevelt, then President of the United States, wrote an enthusiastic review of Robinson's poetry for the *Outlook* which brought the poet a wider audience. Desiring to help Robinson, the President offered him a consulship in Mexico, but the poet declined, saying that he preferred to remain in New York. He accepted a position in the Customs House and for several years he held this, finally relinquishing it to devote his whole time to writing.

It was in 1911 that Robinson spent his first summer at the MacDowell Colony at Peterboro, New Hampshire, where much of his work of the following years has been written. He spends his winters in Boston and New York and his summers at the colony. Robinson holds the unique distinction of having been three times awarded the Pulitzer prize for poetry: in 1922 for his *Col-*lected Poems*, in 1925 for *The Man Who Died Twice*, in 1927 for *Tristram*.

He has been described as follows: "A tall slender man. A high forehead with dark thinning hair. Quiet, contemplative eyes which peer thru spectacles. A short, dark mustache (English fashion) barely concealing a thin, secretive mouth. A gravity of demeanor that often breaks into a smile which trembles curiously about the mouth. He dresses quietly, generally in dark clothes, and always carries a cane. When he walks he stoops slightly, the droop of the scholar who is an inveterate reader. He wears a soft hat. He never talks about his own poetry. He never criticizes other people's poetry. He wouldn't read in public for a million dollars...."

"I don't know whether I am a great poet or not," he once remarked to a friend. "Time alone can tell about that. But I do know that I have never consciously injured any one. And that at least is something."

A kindly fatalist and agnostic, he has thought and written much of men who have failed, the sort of men he knew in the days of his poverty. The prototype of Captain Craig, for example, is an Alfred H. Louis, "a sort of literary Trader Horn," whom he met in New

Doris Ulmann
EDWIN ARLINGTON ROBINSON

York about 1896. "The failures are so much more interesting," he says. "There is a world of tragedy in the individual's futile struggles against a fate too powerful for him."

Robinson's two favorite books are Shakespeare and the Bible. He is also very fond of Dickens, Thomas Hardy, *Don Quixote*, and *Moby Dick*. Hardy's *Dynasts* he considers the greatest long poem of the nineteenth century. For recreation, he is an omnivorous reader of detective and mystery stories, with a special fondness for Sherlock Holmes, Bulldog Drummond, and the books of E. Phillips Oppenheim. He is an enthusiastic admirer of the operas of Gilbert and Sullivan.

These are the poetic works of Edward Arlington Robinson: *The Torrent and the Night Before* (1896), *The Children of the Night* (1897), *Captain Craig* (1902), *The Town Down the River* (1910), *The Man Against the Sky* (1916), *Merlin* (1917), *The Three Taverns* (1920), *Lancelot* (1920), *Avon's Harvest* (1921), *Collected Poems* (1921, 1924, 1927), *Roman Bartholow* (1923), *The Man Who Died Twice* (1924), *Dionysus in Doubt* (1925), *Tristram* (1927), *Sonnets, 1889-1927* (1928), *Cavender's House* (1929), *Modred, A Fragment* (1929), *The Glory of the Nightingales* (1930). He has also published two plays: *Van Zorn* (1914) and *The Porcupine* (1915). Two editions of Robinson's *Selected Poems* were published in 1931; one is edited by a French admirer, Professor Charles Cestre, author of *An Introduction to Edwin Arlington Robinson* (1930); the other is edited by Professor Bliss Perry of Harvard.

Romain Rolland

ROMAIN ROLLAND was born on January 29, 1866, at Clamecy, France, in the district of Nièvre. On his father's side he came of a family of notaries, and his mother's family were magistrates, and lawyers. He received his early education in the schools of Clamecy, being destined by his parents for the Polytechnic School; but, inspired by the lessons in music he had received

ROMAIN ROLLAND

from his mother, he determined to devote himself to that art.

At twenty Rolland entered the École Normale Supérieure in Paris. Here he became acquainted with the works of Wagner and Tolstoy, the two men, he says, with Shakespeare, who have had the greatest formative influence upon him. He is wholly in sympathy with Wagner's theories of music and with Tolstoy's ethical ideals.

After three years of study, in 1889, he went to Rome where he enrolled in the École Française de Rome. There he wrote a play, *Orsino*, based on Shakespeare's methods. He returned to the École Normale in 1891 to continue his studies and the following year he married. A little later he was sent to Italy on an official mission, and while there he collected the material for his thesis, *Histoire de l'Opera en Europe avant Lulli et Scarlatti* (1895). He received the degree of Doctor of Letters.

In 1895 Rolland became professor of the history of art at the École Normale Supérieure. Two years later he joined the faculty of the Sorbonne, where he introduced the study of the history of music in 1903.

From 1898 to 1902 was the heroic period of Rolland's life. In 1898 the

Théâtre de l'Oeuvre produced *Alert,* a play in three acts, and thenceforth "the life of Romain Rolland mingles so profoundly with his work that the former has no other aim, no other reason for being." He determined to write a dramatic commentary on the French Revolution—a sort of epic comprising a decade of drama. The result was the cycle of seven plays: *Pâques Fleuries, Le 14 Juillet, Les Loups, Le Triomphe de la Raison, Danton, Le Jeu de L'Amour et de la Mort,* and *Les Léonides.* These plays, tho complete in themselves, are (taken as a whole) successive acts in the *Cycle de la Revolution* (1909).

Rolland's most famous work is the romance of *Jean-Christophe* (1904-12), the life-story of a musician of genius. It appeared in ten volumes, divided into three series: *Jean-Christophe, Jean-Christophe à Paris,* and *La Fin du Voyage.* He conceived the whole work while he was in Rome, ten years before the first volume, *L'Aube* (1904), appeared. Beethoven is the substantial prototype of Jean-Christophe.

"I was isolated, stifling like so many others in France in a world of moral enmity," he relates in describing the genesis of the work. "I wished to breathe, I wished to react against an unhealthy civilization, against opinion corrupted by a false minority. I wished to say to this minority: 'You lie! you do not represent France.' For this I needed a hero with clear vision and a pure heart, whose soul was unsullied enough to give him the right to speak, and whose voice was strong enough to make itself heard. I built this hero patiently. Before deciding to write the first line of my book I carried it within me for years; Christophe did not start on his journey until I had seen his road to the end. . ."

Rolland was in Switzerland when the World War broke out and he became unpopular in his native country because of a series of articles published in the *Journal de Genève* during September and October 1914. The articles were collected in book form under the title *Au Dessus de la Mêlée,* which reached nine editions in 1915. Rolland's popularity,

meanwhile, increased in other lands because of his political views. He was awarded the Nobel Prize for Literature in 1915.

He has served as music critic on one important review and he was founder of another. As playwright, it is the dream of his life to establish a People's Theatre, which shall express their aims, their ideals and their wrongs, and set forth their obligations and their opportunities. He has written a book on the subject, entitled *Le Théâtre du Peuple* (1901). His other critical and historical works include: *François Millet* (1902), *Beethoven* (1903), *Michel-Ange* (1906), and *Mahatma Gandhi* (1924).

"My state of mind," Rolland writes to a friend, "is always that of a musician, not of a painter. At first I conceive like a nebulous musical impression the whole of a work, then the principal motives, and, above all, the rhythm, not so much of isolated phrases as the sequence of the volumes in relation to the whole, the chapters in the volumes, and the paragraphs in the chapters." He now lives in a villa at Villeneuve, Switzerland, on Lake Geneva.

In Paris, where Roman Rolland is a frequent visitor, he may occasionally be seen in the company of "advanced" artists and politicians: a tall thin man, who has never lost his professional air, wearing an old-fashioned frock coat.

His works of fiction, besides *Jean-Christophe,* include: *Colas Breugnon* (1918), *Clerambault* (1919), and a trilogy entitled *L'Ame Enchantée* which contains *Annette et Sylvie* (1922), *L'Été* (1924), and *Mère et Fils* (1927).

Nearly all of Romain Rolland's writings have been published in America. Among them are: *Jean-Christophe* in three volumes (1910-13), *Michelangelo* (1915), *Handel* (1916), *The People's Theatre* (1918), *Colas Breugnon* (1919), *Clerambault* (1921), *Pierre and Luce* (1922), *Gandhi* (1924), the three volumes of *The Soul Enchanted* (1925-27), *Beethoven the Creator* (1929), *Prophets of a New India* (1930), *Goethe and Beethoven* (1931).

Ole Rölvaag

IN a lonely fisherman's hamlet on the rocky shores of Helgeland, Norway, Ole Edvart Rölvaag was born on April 22, 1876. For generations his people had followed the sea, and it was intended that he should do the same. When he told his mother one day, as a small boy, that he wanted to be a poet, she only laughed.

His youthful imagination was developed by reading classic and romantic literature and his first book was *The Last of the Mohicans*. One time he walked fourteen miles to a neighboring village to borrow a copy of *Ivanhoe*. He was sent to school for a few weeks each year. When he was ten years old he started to write a novel, taking care to hide the manuscript from the older brother who shared his room. One day the brother demanded to know what Ole was hiding and in the struggle that followed the manuscript was torn to shreds.

At fourteen Ole was withdrawn from school by his father because he was "not worth educating." He took his place in the fisheries and became an expert sailor. But he felt he did not have a chance to express his real self; he had a longing for something he couldn't define. After six years as a fisherman he forsook the

calling of his ancestors and went to America, turning his back on an offer of a fine new fishing boat and a successful career. He did not know what lay beyond the horizon but he wanted to find out.

In South Dakota, at the age of twenty, Rölvaag went to work as a laborer on the farm of an uncle. He picked up a smattering of English and saved a little money. When he was twenty-three he went to the Augustana College at Canton, South Dakota. "The moment I came in touch with books and study it was as if a heavy curtain had been lifted," he relates. "I found out that I loved study passionately." After three years there he entered St. Olaf College at Northfield, Minnesota, where he spent four years. Two summers he traveled as a salesman in the country, working the first half of every week and reading in small town libraries the rest of the time. In his studies he found, to his joy, the satisfaction of the vague longing of his childhood. When he was a senior he wrote a novel which was never published, but he still keeps the manuscript.

After he received his A. B. with honors in 1905, Rölvaag borrowed money and studied a year at the University of Oslo, in Norway. He joined the faculty of St. Olaf College in 1906 and has been teaching there since. He was married on July 9, 1908, to Jennie Marie Berdahl, of Garretson, South Dakota. They have had four children, two of whom are deceased. In the year of his marriage Rölvaag became a naturalized citizen. He received his A. M. degree in 1910.

Rölvaag's first published work was *Ordforklaring* (1909). Other novels followed regularly, all written in the Norwegian language because the author finds quicker and fuller expression in his native tongue.

After he had written four novels, dashed off in odd moments during summer vacations, Rölvaag read one day that an eminent Norwegian novelist was planning to visit the Northwest to gather material for a novel of pioneering. He was infuriated. Here was the novel that he had lived so vividly himself but had never found time to write. Now someone proposed to steal his thunder thru superficial "study." The more he thought

OLE RÖLVAAG

of the thing the more he "saw red." So he obtained a leave of absence and wrote (in Norwegian), first in a cabin among northern Minnesota pines, then on the prairies of South Dakota, then in London, and finally in Norway, *Giants in the Earth* (1927). The book marked him uniquely a Norwegian-American writer, "European in art and atmosphere," and distinctly American in scene and viewpoint. A chance meeting with Lincoln Colcord led Rölvaag to write an English version of the novel. Colcord polished the translation and wrote a biographical preface. Translated novels that have followed are *Peder Victorious* (1929) and *Pure Gold* (1930). The latter was inspired by a news item about a man who was digging a basement for a new dwelling when he unearthed two crocks containing gold worth about six thousand dollars. It seemed to Rölvaag "beyond all measure insane that people could find pleasure in saving up good money for no better purpose than digging it down into cold ground." So he wove a story round the imaginary owner of the crocks.

Rölvaag, as head of the Norwegian Department at St. Olaf College, teaches eight hours a week. He does much reading in two languages and writes every day. He keeps an eye out for students of talent whom he can help personally. He has served as president and secretary of the Norwegian-American Historical Association and is a member of the Minnesota Educational Association and the Society for the Advancement of Scandinavian Study.

The author-teacher bears in his smooth face the mark of serious determination, not without a trace of humor. The thin hair that fringes his bald head is blond. He has the appearance of a thoro American and speaks with scarcely any accent. Two writers who he believes will live long after their contemporaries are forgotten are Julia Peterkin and Glenway Westcott. "The unforgiveable sin," he says, "is to write about life untruthfully."

Rölvaag's early works include: *Ordforklaring* (1909), *Amerika-Breve* (1912), *Paa Glemte Veie* (1914), *Deklamationsboken* (1918), *To Tullinger* (1920), *Laengselens Baat* (1921), *Ombring Faedrearven*, essays (1922), *I De*

Dage (1924), *Riket Grundlaegges* (1925), and *Norsk Laesebok, I, II, III,* (1919-25).

Bertrand Russell

BERTRAND ARTHUR WILLIAM RUSSELL was born at Trelleck on May 18, 1872, the second son of Viscount Amberley. An earldom was created in 1861 for his grandfather, Lord John Russell, Liberal Prime Minister and a follower of John Stuart Mill. Bertrand Russell fell heir to that title in March 1931 upon the death of his brother, the second Earl Russell.

Left an orphan at the age of three, Bertrand Russell was brought up by his grandmother at Pembroke Lodge in Richmond Park. Taught by governesses and tutors, he acquired a perfect knowledge of French and German, and laid the foundation for a lucid prose style. At Trinity College, Cambridge, he obtained a First Class in Mathematics and Moral Sciences.

When he left Cambridge in 1894 Russell was attached to the British Embassy in Paris for several months. In December 1894 he married Alys Pearsall Smith. They spent some months in Berlin where

BERTRAND RUSSELL

he studied social democracy, and then settled in a small cottage near Haslemere where Russell devoted himself to philosophy. In 1896 he published *German Social Democracy.*

At the Mathematical Congress in Paris in 1900 Russell became interested in the Italian mathematician Peano, and after a study of his works wrote *The Principles of Mathematics* (1903), his first important book. With Dr. A. N. Whitehead, he developed the mathematical logic of Peano and Frere, and jointly they wrote *Principia Mathematica* (1910).

In 1910 Russell was appointed lecturer at Trinity College, Cambridge, where he had been made a fellow after graduation. He made frequent trips to the Continent, and occasionally abandoned philosophy for politics. When the World War broke out he took an active part in the No Conscription Fellowship and was fined one hundred pounds for issuing a pamphlet on conscientious objection. His library was seized in payment of the fine, and altho it was sold to a friend, several valuable volumes were lost. Trinity College canceled his lectureship. When he was offered a post at Harvard, where he intended to give a lecture course, the military authorities prevented his departure from England. In 1918 he was sentenced to six months' imprisonment for his pacifist views expressed in an article in the *Tribunal.* He wrote his *Introduction to Mathematical Philosophy* (1919) in prison.

When he was released a group of Russell's friends arranged for him to give some lectures in London which resulted in his writing *Analysis of the Mind* (1921). He made a brief visit to Russia to study conditions and wrote *The Practice and Theory of Bolshevism* (1920). In the fall of 1920 Russell went to China to lecture on philosophy at Peking University. The following spring he fell ill with pneumonia and was on the point of death for three weeks. Some Japanese newspapers announced his decease and the Chinese offered to bury him by the Western Lake.

Russell returned to England following his recovery and in September 1921, after his wife had obtained a divorce, he married Dora Winifred Black, author

of *The Right to be Happy* (1927). For six years they spent their winters in Chelsea and summers near Lands End. He supported himself by lecturing, journalism, and writing books.

In 1922 and 1923 Russell stood as the Labour candidate for Parliament in Chelsea and his wife was a candidate in 1924.

In 1927 Russell and his wife started a famous nursery school, which has been a success in every way, except financially. The heavy drain on his income has forced him to write voluminously and make several lecture trips in America to cover the deficit. Russell's conception of freedom in the nursery school has shocked the English; some of Russell's own friends deplore the time he has spent in the school as a comrade of children. But the youngsters who have had the privilege of sitting in his study, in the tower room of a large country house in Sussex, talking about history with one of the wisest men in England, will probably be as regretful as Lord Russell himself that 1931 is to be the last year of the school.

Russell, on becoming a peer of the realm and a noble lord in 1931, announced that he would take his seat in the House of Lords, where he hopes to speak not on partisan measures but on social questions, such as divorce.

Burton Rascoe describes him as "a thin, wiry man, a little below medium height, with a hatchet face, furrowed cheeks, a Scot's complexion, and a heavy shock of white hair. He looks a little like Henry Ford. He has a quizzical smile and an alert look of intense curiosity. He has a fund of anecdotes and tells them well." Amiable and human, he can enjoy a gay party and have a playful time. He is fond of adding "malicious footnotes" to his manuscripts.

Russell planned to publish *The Meaning of Science* in the fall of 1931. Speaking early in 1931 of the book, he said: "The scientific society in its pure form is incompatible with the pursuit of truth, with love, with art, with every ideal that men have hitherto cherished. If such a society is ever created, it will therefore probably perish thru the fact that the individuals composing it will find life unbearable. . ."

The varied works of Bertrand Russell, besides those mentioned, include: *The Problems of Philosophy* (1911), *Principles of Social Reconstruction* (1917), *Mysticism and Logic* (1918), *Roads to Freedom* (1918), *The A.B.C. of Atoms* (1923), *The Prospectus of Industrial Civilization* (1923), *The A.B.C. of Relativity* (1925), *On Education* (1926), *The Analysis of Matter* (1927), *Philosophy* (1927—*An Outline of Philosophy* in English edition), *Sceptical Essays* (1928), *Marriage and Morals* (1929), *The Conquest of Happiness* (1930).

"Æ"

George William Russell
("Æ")

GEORGE WILLIAM RUSSELL used the signature "Æon" in the theosophical papers which first brought him before the reading public. But the printer could decipher only the first two letters—Æ—. Characteristically, Russell accepted this accident as an augur, and wrote from that time on under the shortest pseudonym in Irish literature. This man with the strange pen name is perhaps the outstanding personality in Ireland today. He is a poet, philosopher, painter, essayist, editor, politician, and economist.

"Æ" was born in Lurgan, County Armagh, on the 10th of April, 1867. He was a boy "who saw," as they say in Ireland. In the ancient Gaelic myths he found friends to accompany him in his solitary walks over the lovely hills near his home. He was a mystic even before he was a poet; yet he has always retained the blunt practical side of the Irish character. He came to Dublin at an early age. It was not until he was sixteen and a student at the Dublin School of Art that his real education began. There he met W. B. Yeats and formed those ties of young manhood which were to result in the formation of a group of mystics and poets from which sprang the Irish Literary Renaissance. At seventeen he was working in a draper's shop.

While Russell was seeing his early pamphlets and verses thru the press, Sir Horace Plunkett was forming the Irish Agricultural Organization Society to spread the teaching of cooperation thruout Ireland. In 1897 "Æ" became an organizer for the society and traveled the roads of Ireland on a bicycle, founding poultry and creamery societies, exposing the tricks of money lenders, and helping to convert the Irish farmer to the gospel of cooperation which was to prove so rich in tangible gain to the rural population. At first Russell was a bit given to abstractions in his talks to the people. After one of these early speeches, a parish priest, with the broadest of brogues, brought him down to earth by rising and addressing the somewhat bewildered farmers in this manner: "What the speaker has been tryin' to tell ye is that if ye buy a bonniv (a little pig) at the fair in Lochvay for ten shillin's and take him home and feed him a bit and sell him again for twenty shillin's in the fair at Balmashal ye'll make ten shillin's on it." After some years as an organizer, "Æ" became assistant secretary to the Irish Agricultural Organization Society, and in 1905 he was appointed editor of its official organ, *The Irish Homestead*—parent of *The Irish Statesman*.

In his writings for this paper "Æ" the economist and "Æ" the poet found complete expression. Cream separators and poetry, at his hands, met in a juxtaposition which was strangely lacking in incongruity. During all these years he wrote verse from the sheer drive of inspiration. The art of painting came to him without instruction, as if it were indeed the gift of those fairies in whom he stoutly believes. The fame of his wisdom and goodness spread thruout Ireland. He came to be the center of the brilliant intellectual life of Dublin, drawing men to him by his gentleness.

In this man practical experience, common sense and the visions and hopes of a mystic have always been linked. Playing an active part in the founding of the Irish Theatre, molding the style of George Moore, writing and seeing thru the press various books of mysticism and poetry, editing his influential newspaper —these were some of "Æ's" interests outside of his work as an economist.

When the *Irish Statesman,* which he began to edit in 1923, was forced to suspend publication in 1930, his friends gave him a check equivalent to $4000 in token of their sorrow over its passing and of their high personal regard for him.

His Sunday nights are notable social events in Dublin. In his simple little house in Rathgar avenue, crowded with paintings and figurines and innumerable books, he lowers his big hulk of a body upon a crippled sofa, and with eyes half closed, lids almost veiling them, intones poetry in a chant like one of the ancient Irish bards. He must have escaped from the age of heroes and giants into the welter of this prosaic century, surmises a friend, who describes him as "a gross man physically, above six feet in height, weighing 200 pounds or more, inclined to obesity. His face is almost alarmingly red. His hair and grizzled beard and mustache are sandy grey, with mustache and beard liberally stained with tobacco, for he is an inveterate smoker. But one forgets his physical attributes when the man begins to talk. . . George Russell could talk a singing bird out of a tree or a frightened mouse out of its hole."

"Æ's" volumes of poetry include *Collected Poems* (1913, American edition 1926), *Voices of the Stones* (1925), *Midsummer Eve* (1928), and *Vale* (1931); among his essays and mystical studies are *Imaginations and Reveries* (1915), *The Candle of Vision* (1919),

and *The Interpreters* (1922); a play, *Deirdre,* was published in 1907; his economic and political studies include *Cooperation and Nationality* (1912) and *The National Being* (1917).

Rafael Sabatini

RAFAEL SABATINI was born in 1875 in Jesi, a diminutive city of the Italian Marches, remarkably suitable for the childhood of a historical romancer, with its medieval walls, ancient cathedral, and crumbling palaces. His mother was an Englishwoman and his father the Maestro-Cavaliere Vincenzo Sabatini.

He was sent to school first in Switzerland, and from there went to the Lycée of Oporto, Portugal. "I learned English," he says, "when I was a child in Italy. My mother was English and I spoke English as a child. Besides we traveled a good deal and spent a lot of time in England. When I was a very young man I came to England to go into business, but I began writing instead. I was interested in nothing much but history as a child. I have always considered English my language and have never thought of writing in any other language."

Mr. Sabatini began writing just at the time when the demand for the historical romance was beginning to wane. His first novel, *The Tavern Knight,* was published in 1904. Continuing to write novels of the past, he built up a small but very enthusiastic following in England and in many of the English colonies. His great success came with the publication of *Scaramouche* in the United States in 1921 after it had been rejected by six publishers. This was his nineteenth volume. Edition after edition was printed. *Captain Blood* was another great success in the following year. One reason for the sudden popularity of these two books was that the reading public was ready for them. During the War popular attention was too firmly fixed on the actual fighting in France to be interested in gayer, more cavalier encounters. A number of Sabatini's novels—published in England and

RAFAEL SABATINI

imported here—had fallen on stony ground during this period.

For some years Mr. Sabatini has been a British subject; London is his home. His passion for outdoor sports, however, leads him to salmon fishing in the Cumberland Derwent and skiing in the Alps. In wartime he served in the Intelligence Department of the War Office, where his extensive knowledge of languages made him extraordinarily valuable.

He married, in 1905, an English-woman, Ruth Goad. They were divorced in 1931.

Mr. Sabatini works very systematically. Usually he begins work at 9.30 and continues until 1 o'clock. The rest of the day he walks and goes to games and does about what any one else might do, except that he keeps on thinking about his novel . . . and perhaps, also, about his salmon fishing. (He is very proud of his skill at that sport.) Altho he travels considerably he does not like to visit beforehand the scenes of his novels, lest the modern background blur the older one that his mind has constructed. Not being fond of "the literary life," he knows few writers and novelists, and never has time to read novels.

He is a big man, tall, well built, with reddish hair, flashing hazel eyes, and the features of a Cesare. He is likeable, approachable, and without affectation.

Late in 1930, when his novel *The King's Minion* had just been published and his play about Cesare Borgia—*The Tyrant*—was going into rehearsal for production in New York, Mr. Sabatini came on a visit to the United States.

V. Sackville-West

VICTORIA MARY SACKVILLE-WEST is an English noblewoman who is almost equally well known as poet, novelist, the wife of the Hon. Harold Nicolson, and the daughter of the third Baron Sackville of Knole Park.

Knole Castle, where she was born in March 1892, has been celebrated in history, poetry, and fiction. It is the setting for Virginia Woolf's novel, *Orlando*, which has been generally recognized as a portrait of Miss Sackville-West, blended with her illustrious ancestors. The castle is the subject of one of Miss Sackville-West's own books and it serves as the background for another. The magnificent park, with its seven acres of buildings, was a gift of Queen Elizabeth to her Lord Treasurer, Thomas Sackville, from whom V. Sackville-West descends.

Knole Castle is said to contain three hundred and sixty-five rooms, one for every day in the year; fifty-two staircases, one for every week; and seven courts, one for each day in the week. The walls are of grey stone, in many places ten and twelve feet thick, and most of the rooms are rather small and low. The windows are rich with armorial glass. Many of the floors are made of black oak trees sawed in half and laid with the rounded side down. The paneled walls are hung with countless pictures which include Van Dykes, Gainsboroughs, and the Sackville portraits of ten generations.

In this mysterious fifteenth century house "Vita" Sackville-West was educated. As Hugh Walpole puts it, whereas most English authors come from the middle classes, she "grew up, without thinking it in the least odd, among the Edwardian aristocracy of England. A duke was as little interesting to her as a police officer is to Edgar Wallace." Yet she had a desire to be independent, a determination to distinguish herself without the aid of her favorable circum-

V. SACKVILLE-WEST

stances. Nor was she in a hurry about this business. She spent years in writing and stored the manuscripts away in drawers.

In the year 1913 she married the Hon. Harold Nicolson, journalist and diplomat. He is the author of biographies of Verlaine, Tennyson, Swinburne, Byron, and his own father, Lord Carnock.

V. Sackville-West and her husband have traveled in Persia, Hungary, Bulgaria, and Morocco. They live, with their two sons, Benedict and Nigel, in a fourteenth century home among the apple orchards at Long Barn, Weald, Sevenoaks. They are closely identified with the celebrated Bloomsbury group which includes such names as Lytton Strachey, John Maynard Keynes, Virginia Woolf, and E. M. Forster. Mrs. Woolf is Mrs. Nicolson's best friend among writers; they meet constantly and understand each other perfectly.

Miss Sackville-West made her literary appearance as a poet with *Poems of West and East* (1917). The book failed to attract attention, and she turned to prose, publishing four novels and two volumes of short stories between 1919 and 1924. Of these, *The Heir* (1922) received the greatest commendation.

Her novel, *Challenge,* was suppressed in England and published in America in 1923.

In 1926 she established her reputation as a poet when she published *The Land,* which was awarded the Hawthornden Prize in 1927. It is a long tribute to the English countryside and the English peasant, done without sentiment or melodrama. Interspersed with lyrics, it has no narrative. It is full of technical information and contains a complete farmer's year.

The Edwardians (1930) is a novel portraying a phase of the "smug and healthy snobbishness of the British race." The setting for the book is the pompous, over-stuffed era of Edward VII, with Chevron (Knole Castle) for the immediate background. The author explains that "no character in this book is wholly imaginary." The leading actor is the young Duke Sebastian, handsome, charming, and sulky, master of one of England's greatest estates (Chevron).

The book concerns itself with the young duke's half-conscious struggle to tear his roots from an ancient soil in which the dead seem more alive than the living. Yet dabble as he will in casual love affairs with a mature married beauty, the caretaker's daughter, a doctor's wife, and an artist's model, he realizes that the only thing he can be is what he is, a slave to nobility. The incidental characters range from King Edward down to the housemaids in the servants' hall. There are those who see in Duke Sebastian a study of the present Prince of Wales, with his disinclination to marry and settle down to the routine of royalty.

Hugh Walpole has described the authoress as a woman with every sort of talent, very handsome, and possessing a beautiful voice. He says the famous house of Knole in Kent for a background gives her personality a sort of legendary color. "She has done everything in her life . . . simply because she thought it would be a delightful thing to do."

Novels by V. Sackville-West include: *Heritage* (1919), *The Dragon in Shallow Waters* (1922), *Challenge* (1923), *Gray Wethers* (1923), *Seducers in*

Ecuador (1924), *The Edwardians*
(1930). Her books of poems are:
Poems of West and East (1917), *Orchard and Vineyard* (1921), *The Land*
(1926), *King's Daughter* (1930). *The
Heir* (1922) is a volume of short stories.
Knole and the Sackvilles (1922) is a historical study of the family house, and
Passenger to Teheran (1926) is a travel
book.

George Saintsbury

GEORGE EDWARD BATEMAN
SAINTSBURY has lived thru two
widely different periods of English literature, the Victorian and the modern. To
both eras he has lent an unbiased mind
as critic and historian of literature, and
has formed opinions that are wholly
"home-grown." Born at Southampton
on October 23, 1845, he was educated
at King's College School in London and
at Merton College, Oxford, where he
received a B. A. in 1868.

After a brief time as assistant master
of the Manchester Grammar School, he
went to Guernsey where he spent six
years as senior classical master of Elizabeth College. From 1874 to 1876 he was
headmaster of the Elgin Educational
Institute.

Mr. Saintsbury began his literary
career in 1875 as critic for the *Academy,*
and for ten years was actively engaged
in journalism as reviewer for the *Manchester Guardian* and the *Saturday Review.* In an editorial fifty years after he
started to write, the *Guardian* recalled
that at thirty Mr. Saintsbury seemed to
have read every book in the world and
to have heard every idea; "and one can
be sure that he composed his first paragraph for print with the same appalling
sophistication, the same energetic contempt for highfalutin novelty, that has
distinguished him from all other British
critics during two generations."

He was professor of rhetoric and English literature at Edinburgh University
from 1895 to 1915. His scholarship has
been rewarded with many honors: Hon.
LL.D. Aberdeen, 1898; Hon. D.Litt.
Durham, 1906; President of the English
Association, 1909; Hon. Fellow of Oxford, 1909; Fellow of the British Acad-

emy, 1911; Hon. D.Litt. Oxford, 1912,
and Hon. LL.D. Edinburgh, 1919.

"I have never yet given a second-hand
opinion of any thing, or book, or person," wrote Mr. Saintsbury in the preface to his essay, *Notes on a Cellar Book*
(1920).
Another ex-
planation of
his freshness
is contained in
a remark from
one of his
books: "I have
never tried to
be in the fash-
ion for the sake
of being in it,
and seldom, I
think, to be out
of it merely for
the sake of be-
ing out of it.

GEORGE SAINTSBURY

Logic and his-
tory have been
the only external guides I have accepted
in temporal things, except where pure
taste has reigned alone—as for things
not temporal one need not speak here."

Mr. Saintsbury is an expert connoisseur of wines. Speaking of the wines
he has experienced, he says in *Notes on
a Cellar Book*: "When they were good
they pleased my sense, cheered my
spirits, improved my moral and intellectual powers, besides enabling me to
confer the same benefits on other people."

Threats of prohibition in England
have been his particular torment, added
to the torment of being a Tory. He takes
every opportunity to speak on the matter. In a footnote in *Notes on a Cellar
Book* he relates: "One of the most agreeable incidents of my life in connection
with port is quite recent. Soon after I
had published something about wine in
the *Athenaeum,* and since America
'went dry,' two students of that mis-
guided country wrote to me saying that
they had found it impossible to refrain,
after reading the article, from sallying
forth, purchasing some so-called port
wine (I hope it was not very bad), and
drinking my health in it. It would be
difficult for a teacher to have a more
gratifying testimonial to the efficacy of
his teaching..."

On his eightieth birthday, the London Times saluted Mr. Saintsbury with the remark that he must still be a young man because he had always written like one. He has never changed. The character of his work is the same as it was at thirty and he retains his youthful strength. What is rare, he has the respect of his young contemporaries, altho he is now past eighty-five. He is a member of the Athenaeum Club.

Mr. Saintsbury's thin white hair and white flowing beard give him much the appearance of a patriarch who has stepped from the pages of the Old Testament. He wears old-fashioned small-framed glasses.

He drew upon his catholicity of taste and wide range of interests to produce three unique books of "Scraps" containing little necrologies, as well as comments on politics, education, grasshoppers, and the order of drinks. He writes about sausages or the principles of literary criticism with equal facility and charm.

Among his many books are: *A Short History of French Literature* (1882), *A Short History of English Literature* (1898), *Minor Caroline Poets* (1905, 1906, 1921), *A History of English Prosody* (1906, 1908, 1910), *The History of English Criticism* (1911), *A History of the French Novel* (1917, 1919), *Notes on a Cellar Book* (1920), *A Scrap Book* (1922), *A Second Scrap Book* (1923), *Collected Essays and Papers* (1924), and *A Last Scrap Book* (1924).

Felix Salten

HIS father was a failure, he was bullied by his schoolmates, he was forced to live on charity. These circumstances caused Felix Salten to assert himself and turn life into account. He was born in Ofenpest, Austria, on September 6, 1869. His father, once a successful but visionary executive, had failed in his daring exploitation of a coal mine and settled into dejection. Cowed by the sense of defeat, he took his wife and seven children to Wahring, a suburb of Vienna. The boy went to school at the Vienna gymnasium.

FELIX SALTEN

Felix was small and weak for his age, and conscious of the family misfortune. A neighborhood bully cuffed and tormented him constantly. Then, one day, "something snapped" in him and he turned on the older boy and beat him unmercifully. From that day he has been conscious of his power.

The money earned by his elder brothers and sisters was not sufficient to support the family and Felix went into the city once a month where he received a "dole" of about ten dollars at his cousin's insurance office. Finally he balked at the idea of accepting charity and demanded a job. His unfriendly cousin was obliged to give him one. Oppressed by the miserable affairs of his family, the lad began to express himself secretly by writing stories. Soon he discovered that these manuscripts could bring him some financial return and by the time he was eighteen he had sold several short stories. He quit his job.

For several years Salten earned just a bare living with his writing. Then he became contributor to the magazine called *The Beautiful Blue Danube* whose writers include Schnitzler, Hermann Bahr, Beer-Hoffman, and Hugo von Hofmannsthal. His association with these established men of Austrian letters,

College, "for like the voice of Tennyson, it is an unforgetable part of his poems."

Harry Hansen continues: "Altho Carl uses no gestures and rarely alters his attitude, his face is a sensitized mirror of his moods. When he aims a thrust at some inhuman practice that has aroused his indignation his lower jaw sticks out, his lip seems to curl and he drawls out his words as if taking careful aim; when he reads the *Rootabaga* stories he is as a big boy among children; his eyes are wreathed with happy wrinkes and he chuckles with inward mirth at his own lines."

Of the way he writes, Sandburg says: "Poems are the result of moods. I don't approach a subject in the same mood every day. Maybe some days I am in the mood for the prairie, the skies, the trees. On other days I can feel the noise, the jumble, and the confusion of the city. There are days when I could not have written or even tolerated the idea of *Smoke and Steel*."

One afternoon Sandburg conceived thirty-eight definitions of poetry, which were first published in the *Atlantic Monthly* for March 1923. Some of his definitions are: "Poetry is a sliver of the moon lost in the belly of a golden frog... Poetry is a phantom script telling how rainbows are made and why they go away... Poetry is the achievement of the synthesis of hyacinths and biscuits."

Among Carl Sandburg's books of poems are: *Chicago Poems* (1916); *Corn Huskers* (1918); *Smoke and Steel* (1920); *Slabs of the Sunburnt West* (1922); *Selected Poems*, edited by Rebecca West (1926); *The American Songbag*, a compilation of ballads (1927); *Good Morning, America* (1928); *Early Moon*, a selection of his poems for children with some new lyrics (1930).

Sandburg's tales for children in prose are: *Rootabaga Stories* (1922); *Rootabaga Pigeons* (1923); *The Rootabaga Country* (1929), selections from his two previous Rootabaga books; *Potato Face* (1930).

His works of biography are: *Abraham Lincoln, the Prairie Years* (1926); *Steichen the Photographer*, the story of his wife's brother (1929).

George Santayana

GEORGE SANTAYANA, poet and philosopher, was born in Madrid on December 16, 1863, of Spanish parents, Augustin Ruiz de Santayana and Josefina Borrás. At the age of nine he came to the United States and was educated at Harvard. After receiving his A.B. in 1886, he studied for two years in Berlin and then returned to Harvard to teach philosophy in 1889. During his more than twenty years there, he advanced from instructor to professor and became one of the most noted teachers in the history of the university and one of the most appreciated minds in America.

His first literary work was in verse, *Sonnets and Poems* (1894). The prose which followed received far more attention than this slender book. His first essay in philosophy was *The Sense of Beauty* (1896). Santayana spent 1896-97 as an "advanced student" at King's College, Cambridge, and he was the Hyde Lecturer at the Sorbonne in Paris in 1905-06.

Santayana's most ambitious work, on which he labored for seven years, was *The Life of Reason*, published in five volumes while he was in Paris: *Reason in Common Sense* (1905), *Reason in Society* (1905), *Reason in Religion*

GEORGE SANTAYANA

(1905), *Reason in Art* (1905), and *Reason in Science* (1906). Apart from the value of these volumes as philosophic speculation, they are packed with wise thoughts, subtle fancies, and penetrative criticism of life. In a preface to a new edition of the work twenty years later, Santayana says: "There is hardly a page that would not need to be rewritten" to express his present opinion faithfully; yet there has been, he says, "no change in my deliberate doctrine, only some changes of mental habit."

He abandoned his post at Harvard in 1912 to devote himself to literature. In 1914 he went to Europe, where he has since wandered from country to country, adding to his philosophical works and producing an occasional poem. Most of the time he has lived in England and France.

Santayana was at Oxford when the World War was declared in August 1914 and he remained there thruout the struggle, making excursions over the country-side. He got to know the land and the people intimately. He regarded England, even in wartime, as "pre-eminently the home of decent happiness and a quiet pleasure in being oneself." The result of his stay was *Soliloquies in England* (1922), containing a subtle interpretation of the English and their country, from skylarks to college dons. He finds the English people, notwithstanding their stupidities and irrational habits, the nearest parallel to the ancient Greek temperament which is his ideal.

Scepticism and Animal Faith (1923), labeled an "Introduction to a System of Philosophy," is the first volume of a new system to supplement and modify the old, not to supersede it. This was followed by *Dialogues in Limbo* (1925), *Platonism and the Spiritual Life* (1927), *The Realm of Essence* (1928), *The Realm of Matter* (1930), and *The Genteel Tradition at Bay* (1931). In the last book the author defines humanism and appraises its significance.

Santayana prefers his later prose as an expression of his philosophy rather than his early verse. Yet he says: "What I felt when I composed those verses could not have been rendered in any other form. Their sincerity is absolute."

In 1923, having achieved fame as a philosopher, Santayana prefaced his collected *Poems* almost apologetically after revising them: "Of impassioned tenderness or Dionysiac frenzy I have nothing, nor even of that magic and pregnancy of phrase—really the creation of a fresh idiom—which marks the high lights of poetry. Even if my temperament had been naturally warmer, the fact that the English language (and I can write no other with assurance) was not my mother-tongue would of itself preclude any inspired use of it on my part; its roots do not quite reach to my center. I never drank in in childhood the homely cadences and ditties which in pure spontaneous poetry set the essential key." His other poetic works include: *Lucifer* (1898) and *The Hermit of Carmel* (1901). His sonnets are regarded as his best work in verse.

"In natural philosophy I am a decided materialist—apparently the only one living," he states. "I believe there is nothing immortal. . . No doubt the spirit and energy of the world is acting in us, as the sea is what rises in every little wave; but it passes thru us; and cry out as we may, it will move on. Our privilege is to have perceived it as it moved."

Despite his materialism and scepticism, Santayana discusses the problems of religion with sympathy and tolerance: "Religion is human experience interpreted by human imagination. . . Matters of religion should never be matters of controversy. . . We seek rather to honor the piety and understand the poetry embodied in these fables."

He follows the ethics of Aristotle: "In Aristotle the conception of human nature is perfectly sound: everything ideal has a natural basis, and everything natural an ideal fulfilment. His ethics, when thoroly digested and weighed, will seem perfectly final."

Among other philosophical essays and studies by George Santayana are: *Interpretations of Poetry and Religion* (1900); *Three Philosophical Poets, Lucretius, Dante, and Goethe* (1910); *Winds of Doctrine* (1913); *Egotism in German Philosophy* (1916); *Philosophical Opinion in America* (1918); *Character and Opinion in the United States* (1920).

Siegfried Sassoon

SIEGFRIED SASSOON, the English soldier-poet who has raised his voice against war, was born on September 8, 1886. His father was a well-to-do country gentleman of Persian Jewish ancestry and his mother was an English woman, sister of the sculptor Hamo Thornycroft. He was educated at Marlborough Grammar School and Clare College, Cambridge.

An out-of-door youth, he excelled in field sports, tennis, and fox-hunting. Yet he devoted much of his time to the study of poetry. Shelley, Masefield, and Hardy were his favorites, and he admittedly adopted the Masefield manner. Between 1911 and 1916 he issued, anonymously, seven small privately printed volumes of verse. Some of the titles were: *Twelve Sonnets, Melodies, An Ode for Music, Hyacinth,* and *Apollo in Doelyrium.* He is fond of music.

When the World War broke out, Sassoon enlisted (August 3, 1914) and went to the front. The war changed him; he went gaily but became embittered by the sight of misery and bloodshed. He served four and a half years and won the Military Cross for valor in rescuing the wounded.

Up to this time Sassoon's published work, as described by his friend Robert Graves, had consisted of "a few privately-printed pastoral pieces of eighteen-ninetyish flavor and a satire on Masefield ('The Old Huntsman') which, about half-way thru, had forgotten to be a satire and was rather good Masefield." Now he began to write poems exposing the ruthlessness of war—its horrors and brutalities. While he was at the front, these violent and bitter verses began to attract attention in the *Cambridge Magazine,* one of the few pacifist journals published in England during the war. With the publication of his volume, *The Old Huntsman* (1917), which began with the Masefield satire and concluded with a series of indignant war poems, Sassoon became one of the leading younger poets of England. He sent a copy "for a joke" to Sir Douglas Haig, commander of the British forces.

In the spring of 1917 Sassoon was in heavy fighting in the Hindenburg

SIEGFRIED SASSOON

Line. With a bombing party of six men he attempted to capture some trenches. Altho shot thru the throat, he continued bombing until he collapsed. He was sent back to England, "beastly weak and in a rotten state of nerves." In the military hospital he resolved that the war must end and that he must do all in his power to prevent its going on.

In July 1917 "Second-Lieutenant S. L. Sassoon, Military Cross, recommended for D.S.O., Third Battalion Royal Welch Fusiliers," acting "in wilful defiance of military authority," refused to serve further in the army. In a statement made to his commanding officer which he caused to be published in certain pacifistic newspapers in England, Sassoon declared: "I am making this statement... because I believe that the war is being deliberately prolonged by those who have the power to end it. I am a soldier, convinced that I am acting on behalf of soldiers. . . I have seen and endured the sufferings of the troops, and I can no longer be a party to prolong these sufferings for ends which I believe to be evil and unjust. . ."

In further private protest Sassoon threw his Military Cross into the sea. He expected and wanted to be court-martialed, but the War Office, instead of pressing the matter as a disciplinary case, had him examined by a medical board, which declared him temporarily insane and sent him to a convalescent home for neurasthenics. On his "recovery," he was sent to Palestine. After a short period of service in the Holy Land, he returned to the French front and was wounded again, shot thru the head. At the end of the war he was a captain.

After the armistice, he took a prominent part in the General Election, supporting Philip Snowden on a pacifist platform. His three wound stripes and the mauve and white ribbon of his military cross saved him from the hostility of threatening civilian crowds.

Sassoon published *Counter-Attack* (1918), *Collected War Poems* (1919), and *Picture Show* (1920). There was scarcely a phrase that did not protest the glorification of war.

Sasson was a journalist in London for a time, but he continued to write poetry. In 1920 he visited America, where he gave lectures and readings from his poems, stressing the criminality of war. Charles Lewis Hind records an impression of him as lecturer: "He is shy on the platform; he does not know how to stand properly; he mixes up his points; and when he reads his poems, he reads to himself, not to the man at the top of the gallery. Yet he 'puts it over' because he is sincere... because he laughs at himself. So his audience is tense for half the time, and for the other half is rippling with laughter. A lady sitting next to me during one of his lectures on war poetry whispered: 'I shall never again say that Englishmen have not a sense of humor.'"

Recreations was privately printed at Christmas 1923 for Sassoon's friends. The publication of *Lingual Exercises for Advanced Vocabularians* in 1925 was even more limited. Most of the verses in these two volumes appear in *Satirical Poems* (1926).

Sassoon's first "novel," *Memoirs of a Fox-Hunting Man,* published anonymously in England in 1928, was awarded the two most coveted English literary prizes: the Hawthornden Prize and the James Tait Black Memorial Prize in 1929. Both this and his second prose work, *Memoirs of an Infantry Officer,* are autobiographical.

Sassoon is not enthusiastic about the older contemporary British poets. He has one great admiration—Thomas Hardy. His favorites among the younger poets include Rupert Brooke, Julian Grenfell, and Charles Sawley. His appreciation of the ironists and satirists includes Richard Aldington, Herbert Read, J. C. Squire, and Osbert Sitwell.

Sassoon is young in appearance, with an angular face and a full head of black hair. He is tall and alert.

The books of poetry by Siegfried Sassoon include: *The Old Huntsman* (1917), *Counter-Attack* (1918), *Collected War Poems* (1919), *Picture Show* (1920), *Satirical Poems* (1926), *The Heart's Journey* (1928). His works of prose are: *Memoirs of a Fox-Hunting Man* (1928), *Memoirs of an Infantry Officer* (1930).

Lyle Saxon

LYLE SAXON and Louisiana are closely associated. He was born September 4, 1891. Growing up in Louisiana, he began his career there, and at the present time is recognized as an authority on the history and background of the state.

Mr. Saxon sketches his life and his work briefly: ten years on the New Orleans *Times-Picayune;* at the present time at work on a novel.

When he lived in New Orleans, Mr. Saxon bought a house on Royal Street and furnished it to satisfy his discriminating taste. The house was three stories high, with wrought iron balconies and a charming patio—a house typical of the French Quarter when the French Quarter was New Orleans, the period described in his *Fabulous New Orleans.*

At the present time he divides his time between an apartment on Christopher Street, New York City, and a cabin on Melrose Plantation, Louisiana. This Cane River cabin is of course not like his Royal Street house, but it also is unmistakeably Louisianian in its romantic setting. Its remoteness (the nearest town is Natchitoches, several miles

LYLE SAXON

away) makes it an ideal place for writing, and it is there that he has done most of his work.

Lyle Saxon is over six feet tall, a big genial man whom *The New Orleanean* further characterizes as "a bon vivant, a bibliophile, a raconteur, a conversationalist, an artist with a jigger of absinthe, a lazy man, and a writer without an enemy."

Mr. Saxon was working on *Father Mississippi* at the time of the May 1927 flood, and was sent to that area immediately to cover the story for *Century Magazine.* He spent practically all of his time the three months he was in the flood district in the actual work of rescuing and caring for refugees. The experiences he had and the material he collected appeared later in three articles in *Century* which were incorporated in his book *Father Mississippi.*

Altho Mr. Saxon's literary reputation has been achieved as an historian, he is frank in saying that his primary interest is in fiction. His short stories have appeared in the *Century, Dial, New Republic,* and various other magazines. He has been included in both the O. Henry and the O'Brien *Best Short Stories* collections, as well as in the first *American*

Caravan. "The Centaur Plays Croquet," which appeared in the *Caravan,* is striking for its fantasy, and is entirely different in mood from that for which he has become known. "Cane River," "Lizie Balize," and other of his short stories have recently been translated into German.

Mr. Saxon's belief that a person should know his own territory, and his knowledge of the traditions, the folk-lore and the history of Louisiana are clearly shown in *Father Mississippi* (1927), *Fabulous New Orleans* (1928), *Old Louisiana* (1929), and *La Fitte The Pirate* (1930).

Isidor Schneider

ISIDOR SCHNEIDER was born in Horodenko, Poland (then Austria-Hungary), August 25, 1896. He came to the United States when he was six, and grew up on the East Side, New York City.

An interest in drawing which he has sustained and developed evidenced itself when he was quite young. His medium then was chalk and colored crayon, and his subject invariably the same, portraits of either Washington or Lincoln, drawn on the sidewalk. His range of subjects is wider now, and he works with pencil and water color.

Mr. Schneider attended public school and New York City College, which he left in his senior year both for financial reasons and because his personal views on the World War and ideas on international citizenship had brought him into conflict with certain faculty members. Since 1918 he has been in the publishing business in various connections.

He is a heavy clear-eyed man, calm in temper, deliberate in speech, a pipe smoker, a lover of geography.

Mr. Schneider, his wife, and baby daughter live in Queens, Long Island. The small daughter is named for the woman who is in his estimation the greatest woman poet in American literature—Emily Dickinson.

Mr. Schneider's work is quite evenly divided between poetry, prose fiction and criticism. Two books, *Dr. Transit,* a novel (1925) and *The Temptation of Anthony and Other Poems* (1928) have been published. Only his initials (I.S.) were used on the title-page of *Dr. Transit.*

Mr. Schneider has contributed to *The Dial, The Little Review, Poetry, Forum, Saturday Review of Literature, transition* (1930), published under the auspices appeared in the First (1927), Third (1929), and Fourth (1931) *American Caravan. Coolidge: or the Future of History,* a humorous satire, is included in the "symposium to end symposiums," *Whither, Whither or After Sex What?* (1930).

In addition to a second novel on which he is now working, his poetry, and his critical writing, Mr. Schneider is making a study of Chinese literature and civilization and is becoming recognized as an authority on all questions concerned with China. His review of Professor Holcombe's *The Chinese Revolution* (1930), published under the auspices of Harvard University and Radcliffe College, is being translated and used as a preface to the Chinese edition of Professor Holcombe's work.

Mr. Schneider believes there is an overemphasis in contemporary prose

ISIDOR SCHNEIDER

writing on simplicity. While there is nothing worse, he believes, than poor fine writing, good fine writing by its accentuation of significant detail and careful use of similes and metaphors clarifies and simplifies material. A good deal of supposed simple writing makes for obscurity by its colorlessness. He looks forward to a new interest in style and a wide new use of rhetoric.

Arthur Schnitzler

DR. ARTHUR SCHNITZLER, Austrian novelist and playwright, was born in Vienna on May 15, 1862, of a medical family. His grandfather was a doctor, his father was Professor Johann Schnitzler, a famous laryngologist, and it was inevitable that young Arthur should adopt a medical career. Upon graduation from the university he worked in his father's clinic for many years. For a time he traveled thru Germany and England studying medical conditions and lecturing. He became known as a brilliant physician and an outstanding specialist in laryngology. At one time he wrote a learned paper on *Nervous Diseases of the Voice.*

Suddenly, without explanation, Dr. Schnitzler gave up his successful career when he was about thirty, and secluded himself from his family to write *Das Märchen,* his first play. It was produced in Vienna but was withdrawn as being immoral. In America it was played by Nazimova under the title of *The Tale.* His first work to be published was *Anatol* (1893), a series of love episodes in the adventurous career of a rich young Viennese. Altho Schnitzler has written many plays, *Anatol* never loses its popularity in Europe, and it is presented nearly every season in Vienna. There have been two productions of *Anatol* in New York, the last in 1931 with Joseph Schildkraut in the leading role. *Das Märchen* was published in 1894.

Schnitzler's first real success was *Liebelei,* played in the Burg-theatre Vienna in the fall of 1895. The American version of this play was called *Flirtation.* The author's dramas often deal with the same subject—the lover and a mistress or two. "My critics sometimes say that I am always concerned with the virtue of women," he says. "I suppose that is true, since I find that most of the passionately dramatic things of life—especially its tragedies—are concerned with the virtue—or lack of it—of women." His main interest has always been the psychological element in the lives of his characters. *Reigen* (1900) is a series of dialogues relating Viennese amours in such detail that it could not be performed until 1920.

Schnitzler lives in a luxurious villa on Sternwarterstrasse which overlooks the city of Vienna. Here he spends the greater part of every year, writing in his garden or in his study. When he buries himself in work, his family often does not see him for days. His food is served in the study and no one is permitted to disturb him.

He is a painful worker and takes months to write a long story or a play. He revises every page dozens of times and when the work is completed he puts it away for six months or a year. After that, it undergoes further revision.

Herr Schnitzler works on several books at once—sometimes as many as four or five. "I like to write a play and a novel at the same time," he says. "By that I mean when I am tired of writing one I turn to the other and find it refreshing. The styles of writing the two are so very different. I find fiction is more confining and I feel the dead weight of it after I have been writing steadily for some time; whereas playwriting is always exciting. . ." He never knows which of his books will be finished first; often they reach completion about the same time, as was the case with *Fraülein Else, Traumnovel,* and *Frau de Richters.* Sometimes he writes standing up before an old-fashioned slant desk; more often he dictates to his secretary.

The author confines his reading to biographies and history; he doesn't read novels any more. Besides German literature, he reads in French, English, and Italian. Of American writers he is fond of Frank Harris and Eugene O'Neill. He prefers travel to other pastimes and feels that it has taught him more than books. He has traversed all of Europe

ARTHUR SCHNITZLER

and the Orient. When he is on vacations he becomes impatient for his work, being happiest when he is writing.

He has never visited America. He is afraid of the critics, the receptions, the interviews, and the dinners. He would like to "go to America, perhaps, as a private man and make a journey thru the country for pleasure—not to lecture."

Schnitzler loves the open country and used to cycle thru miles of countryside. Nowadays he takes long walks, always keenly observant of the things about him. He makes jottings in a notebook wherever he goes and uses the material in his books. He keeps an elaborate filing system.

He is rather short and slightly hunched. Altho he wears his clothes badly, his bearing is majestic. He is nearing seventy, but his skin is clear and his eyes are bright and alert. A well-shaped beard covers his chin and a thick mustache curves under an aquiline nose. He is reticent about meeting strangers, yet his manner is gracious and friendly.

Translations of Schnitzler's plays include: *Anatol* (1911); *Liebelei* (1914); *Comedies of Words* (1917); *Intermezzo, Countess Mizzie,* and *The Lonely Way* (1926); *Professor Bernhardi* (1928). Among the translations of his novels and other stories are: *Viennese*

Idylls (1913), *Bertha Garlan* (1918), *The Shepherd's Pipe and Other Stories* (1922), *Road to the Open* (1923), *Dr. Graesler* (1923), *Fraülein Else* (1925), *Beatrice* (1926), *None But the Brave* (1926), *Rhapsody* (1927), and *Daybreak* (1928). The last six titles were collected into a single volume, *Six Viennese Novelettes,* in 1931. *Flight into Darkness,* the psychological study of a disordered mind, is scheduled for publication here in 1931. The Theatre Guild expects to produce Schnitzler's play, *The Lonely Way,* in 1931-32.

Evelyn Scott

EVELYN SCOTT was born in Clarkesville, Tennessee, in 1893, and spent her early years in New Orleans. Even as a child she wrote, and at fourteen had some short stories published under a pseudonym. She was the youngest student ever admitted to Tulane University. At twenty she fled from the United States and spent the next three

EVELYN SCOTT

years, practically as an exile, in Brazil with Cyril Kay Scott. The story of this adventurous and tragic period of her life is told in *Escapade* (1923), a remarkably frank and vivid autobiographical work.

After her return to America she published *Precipitations* (1920), a volume of verse; and a play, *Love,* produced in New York. This was followed by two novels, *The Narrow House* (1921), and *Narcissus* (1922), which gave her a definite place in contemporary letters, altho the morbidity of her theme prevented her from gaining the recognition of the wider public. *Escapade* (1923) was her next book.

In 1925 she published *The Golden Door* and, in 1927, two books entitled *Migrations* and *Ideals.*

She has written two children's books: *In the Endless Sands* (1925), in collaboration with Cyril Kay Scott, her first husband; and *Witch Perkins* (1929).

Her book, *The Wave* (1929), is a story of the Civil War, showing its realities in the lives of those who felt its impact. It has little in common with the conventional historical novel. **Mrs.** Scott, a Southerner herself, spent more than two years in collecting the material for *The Wave.* "War itself," she says, "is the only Hero of the book." She gives the following explanation of her title: "Whatever the philosophy of an actor in a war, he must constantly be convinced of his feebleness when attempting to move in an emotional direction contrary to that of the mass. This propulsion of the individual by a power that is not accountable to reason is very obviously like the action of a wave."

In the spring of 1930 Mrs. Scott had two books published. One was a volume of poetry, entitled *The Winter Alone,* and the other was a story of adventure laid in Portugal. The title is *Blue Rum,* and the identity of the author was concealed under the pseudonym "E. Souza."

Mrs. Scott is of unusual appearance. Her eyes have the color and sparkle of blue lightning. They are large and round and of a disturbing intensity. Her brown hair is cut like a boy's and is usually half way round her face before she remembers to push it back. Her mouth is wide and mobile; in sombre moments it droops at the corners and imparts a doleful seriousness quite at variance with the blue eyes and the shaggy hair, but at other times it spreads out in a friendly, unpretentious, boyish smile.

Life for Evelyn Scott has been a series of startling experiences in many places, and since leaving New Orleans at the age of twenty she has lived in Brazil, Bermuda, France, England, Portugal, Spain, Algeria, and Canada, returning in between times to New York. She has a son who was born in Brazil.

Mrs. Scott was recently married to John Metcalfe, the English writer. Most of 1930 was spent in Santa Fe, New Mexico. In Santa Fe and in Devon, England, Mrs. Scott has been working on a sequel to *The Wave*.

The books of Evelyn Scott are: *Precipitations* (1920), poems; *The Narrow House* (1921), a novel; *Narcissus* (1922), a novel; *Escapade* (1923), an autobiography; *The Golden Door* (1925), a novel; *In the Endless Sands* (1925), with Cyril Kay Scott, a Christmas story for boys and girls; *Migrations* (1927), a novel, "an arabesque in histories"; *Ideals* (1927), short stories, "a book of Farce and Comedy"; *The Wave* (1929), a novel; *Witch Perkins* (1929), a story of the Kentucky hills for children; *The Winter Alone* (1930), poems; *Blue Rum* (1930), a novel of adventure published under the pseudonym "E. Souza."

Anne Douglas Sedgwick

ANNE DOUGLAS SEDGWICK was born in Englewood, New Jersey, on March 28, 1873, the daughter of George Stanley and Mary (Douglas) Sedgwick. She was educated by a governess at home. This is what she recalls of her early American years:

"I see a starry scintillating sky on a snowy night, a Christmas tree, and the orchards and gardens where I and my sisters played in summer—but nothing distinctive or typical. Much clearer are the pictures of a visit to Southern Ohio—to my mother's family—during the life in England,—so very different are they

ANNE DOUGLAS SEDGWICK

from the pictures of the Middle West that I find in modern American novels. Sobriety, sweetness, tradition are the things that best fit my memories of my grandfather's and grandmother's home: an Emersonian flavour, a love of books and nature."

At the age of nine she went to live in England, where she still makes her home, and the most definite impressions of her childhood are of the London that she evokes in the first chapter of *Tante*— "the London of Gilbert and Sullivan operas, Langtry, buns, hansom cabs, and fogs; walks with a governess in Rotten Row, and frequent visits to the National Gallery and the Old South Kensington Museum."

At eighteen she went to Paris, where she studied painting ("never working very hard, I fear, and with no special talent") for five years. She did, nevertheless, exhibit a portrait of her sister in the Champs de Mars Salon.

She turned to writing quite by accident. She was in the habit of telling long continued stories to her sisters. One of these stories, which she set down in writing, was shown by her father to a publisher, who accepted it. It was called *The Dull Miss Archinard* ("a very feeble little affair that I trust no one will ever wish to re-read") and it was published in 1898. Then her career as a novelist started in earnest, altho it was not until the publication of *Tante,* her ninth novel, in 1911 that she became well known.

In 1908 she married Basil de Sélincourt, an Englishman in spite of the French name. During the war she gave her entire time and energy to a hospital in France that had been organized by friends of hers. "My mind," she says, "is still very full of France and I have always read a great deal of French and think as easily in French as in English (altho my accent and often my genders leave much to be desired!) so that the contrasts and clashes between English and French life are still uppermost in my mind." Mr. and Mrs. de Sélincourt both consider France the most beautiful country in the world and frequently return to it.

Their home is in Kingham, Oxfordshire, the heart of the Cotswold. Esther Forbes gives us a glimpse of the novelist in this lovely setting: "The half-light closed around the hedge and arbor of the English garden; the orchard beyond us sharpened into a purple silhouette against the sunset. She sat serene and upright by the tea-table like a Dresden goddess. The coil of prematurely white hair, the purple eyes, the pink and white smoothness of her moulded features, lent her a statuesque quality which was sweetly dispelled by her smile and by the gentle irony of her conversation."

Mrs. de Sélincourt writes in the mornings, as a rule, for two or three hours at a large table looking out at the garden. She confesses that she often wastes long moments in watching the birds when she should be working. Birds and dogs are especially dear to her. She greatly enjoys singing in the village Choral Society, of which her husband is conductor. "We are sixty members and often give orchestral concerts with an Oxford orchestra to help us. We have given Brahms' Requiem and Hayden's Creation and Bach's Christmas Oratorio, among other things, and to sing in this great splendor of sound is one of my delights, tho I have no voice to speak of."

Tolstoy's *War and Peace* is her favorite novel. Her own books start with people, imaginary always, yet often to be traced to past memories. "The background rises to fit them," she explains, "and the situation to express them." She writes and rewrites three or four times. She prefers not to formulate any rules in regard to novel-writing. "Life—more abundant life—is all that one can ask of a novel and it is because in Tolstoy the sense of life's depth and abundance is given so matchlessly that I care for him so much."

The publications of Anne Douglas Sedgwick include: novels, *Franklin Winslow Kane* (1910), *Tante* (1911), *The Encounter* (1914), *The Third Window* (1920), *Adrienne Toner* (1922), *The Little French Girl* (1924), *The Old Countess* (1927), *Dark Hester* (1929), *Philippa* (1930); short stories, *The Nest* (1913), *Autumn Crocuses* (1920, American title: *Christmas Roses*); and *A Childhood in Brittany Eighty Years Ago* (1919), a picture of old-world life in France.

Mrs. de Sélincourt visited the United States for the first time in twenty years in the autumn of 1930 when her novel *Philippa* was published.

Gilbert Seldes

GILBERT VIVIAN SELDES' talents are so varied and his dislike of publicity so strong ("I am not picturesque and dislike stunting one's private life to attract attention to one's public work," he writes) that it is difficult to keep up with all his activities. He is the only man who has ever contributed steadily and simultaneously to both *The Dial* and the *Saturday Evening Post.* He was editor of the former ("*there* was an editor for you," was Sherwood Anderson's comment) and at one time successfully filled the positions on *The Philadelphia Public Ledger* of music critic, military expert, war correspondent, and editorial writer on international affairs.

Mr. Seldes was born in Alliance, New Jersey, on January 3, 1893, and educated at Central High School, Philadelphia, and at Harvard, A.B., 1914. He was on the staff of the *Harvard Monthly,* and was a very active member of the Harvard Dramatic Club: his play, "The

Orange Comedy," saw its first production in 1926 by the club.

During the War, he was twice at the British Front as a newspaper correspondent. After the United States entered the War, Mr. Seldes served in the American Army—in Southern camps. Here, in accordance with the tradition of Southern hospitality, he was once given his breakfast in bed, brought to him (still a private) by a corporal—one of the rare experiences of life! From 1914 to 1916 he was on the staff of *The Philadelphia Evening Ledger* as foreign correspondent; was political correspondent in Washington for *L'Echo de Paris* in 1918; associate editor of *Collier's*, 1919; associate and managing editor, and dramatic critic of *The Dial*, 1920-23; and contributing editor to the *New Republic*.

In 1924 he married Miss Alice Wadhams Hall of New York City, in Paris. They have two children, Timothy and Marian, and live in New York. In 1929 Mr. Seldes became dramatic critic for *The New York Evening Graphic,* a tabloid newspaper.

One of the underlying convictions of his critical theory is that the critic should react violently, in one way or another, to the particular artistic stimulus which he is judging. "Criticism," he thinks, "ought to be angry instead of being merely smart." He is opposed to both the gushing girl and the superficial, smarty, and detached schools of criticism —and he thinks dramatic critics should be made to buy tickets out of an allowance fund provided for them, and not be given seats by managers, a custom which, he thinks, puts the critic at a psychological disadvantage.

Mr. Seldes himself has fared very well with the critics lately—and in accordance with his formula. His adaptation of the *Lysistrata* of Aristophanes, produced in the spring of 1930 in Philadelphia and New York, achieved that rare thing, both *succès d'estime,* and box office success. This revival of a comedy based on the existing political situation in Athens in the fifth century B.C. played to capacity houses in New York for months. In the controversy about the pronunciation of the title, he takes the

GILBERT SELDES

side (in spite of his Harvard background) which favors stressing *tra* and not *sis,* as is shown by these lines of his printed in the *New York World* under the caption, "We Fear the Translator Bringing Accents":

Speaking of Greek, you have forgot a Lot if you don't say "Lysistrata."

On the heels of the *Lysistrata* production appeared Mr. Seldes' book, *The Future of Drinking.* It is a sagacious and witty examination of the art of drinking in America, past, present, and future under the regime of Prohibition, and is the latest addition to a list of literary productions of extraordinary range and diversity: *The United States in the War* (1917); *The Seven Lively Arts* (1924); *The Wise-Crackers,* a play, produced in 1925; *The Orange Comedy,* produced in 1926; *The Stammering Century* (1928); *The Wings of the Eagle* (1929), a novel; *An Hour With the Movies and the Talkies* (1929); *Lysistrata* (1930); and *The Future of Drinking* (1930). Under the pseudonym of "Foster Johns" he has published two mystery novels: *The Victory Murders* (1927) and *The Square Emerald* (1928).

George Bernard Shaw

GEORGE BERNARD SHAW, Irish dramatist and critic, was born in Dublin on July 26, 1856, of a family of English origin. He inherited a love of music. "I come of a Protestant family of true-blue garrison snobs," he says, "but before I was ten years of age I got into an atmosphere of freedom of thought, of anarchic revolt against conventional assumptions of all kinds... I was forbidden nothing and spared nothing... My mother, brought up with merciless strictness... had such a horror of her own training that she left her children without any training at all... My humorous father, a sort of mute inglorious Charles Lamb... disgusted my mother by his joyless furtive drinking and his poverty and his general failure..."

Shaw's education began, he says, when he left school and went to work in the office of a Dublin land agent. "I am an educated man because I escaped from school at fourteen, and before that was only a day-boy who never wasted the free half of my life in learning lessons or reading schoolbooks." He says his culture is largely musical. Shelley, Wagner, Beethoven, Ibsen, and Nietzsche influenced him strongly. He has always been interested in science. "I even claim to have made certain little contributions to the theory of Creative Evolution... Socialism sent me to economics, which I worked at for four years until I mastered it completely... I do not read any foreign language easily without the dictionary except French." Shaw made his first appearance in print in 1875 when he wrote a letter to *Public Opinion* declaring himself an atheist after hearing Moody and Sankey preach.

At the age of twenty (1876) Shaw went to London and was employed for a while by the Edison Telephone Company. Between 1879 and 1883 he wrote all his novels, which include: *The Irrational Knot, Cashel Byron's Profession, An Unsocial Socialist,* and *Love Among the Artists. Immaturity,* the first novel he wrote, did not appear in print until 1930, when a collected edition of his works was issued.

In 1884 Shaw joined the Fabian Society and added to its fame by editing the *Fabian Essays* (1889) and publishing various other works on Fabianism. He displayed a capacity for arousing attention. During his first nine years in London his literary earnings amounted to six pounds, and he lived in poverty.

In 1885, thru William Archer, Shaw got work reviewing for the *Pall Mall Gazette.* Then he served as music critic for the *Star* from 1888 to 1890, signing his articles "Corno di Bassetto"; and for the *World* from 1890 to 1894. From 1895 to 1898 he was critic of drama for the *Saturday Review.* Managers used to complain because he often went to the theatre in ordinary dress; others objected because he laughed in the wrong place. The articles signed G.B.S. were popular because they were invariably amusing. He collected them in two volumes called *Dramatic Opinions and Essays* (1907).

At the close of his ten years as critic, Shaw wrote: "For ten years past, with an unprecedented pertinacity I have been dinning into the public head that I am an extraordinarily witty, brilliant, and clever man. That is now part of the public opinion of England; and no power on earth will ever change it. I may dodder and dote. I may pot-boil

GEORGE BERNARD SHAW

and platitudinize; I may become the butt and chopping-block of all the bright, original spirits of the rising generation; but my reputation shall not suffer; it is built up fast and solid, like Shakespeare's, on an impregnable basis of dogmatic reiteration."

Meanwhile, Shaw turned to playwriting as the most adequate means for broadcasting his opinions, and because there was more money on the stage than in the bookstalls. His first play, *Widowers' Houses*, was produced in 1892 at the Royalty. He published *Plays: Pleasant and Unpleasant* (1898), in two volumes, containing seven of his best-known dramas. The pleasant plays are: *Arms and the Man, Candida, The Man of Destiny*, and *You Never Can Tell*. The unpleasant are: *Widowers' Houses, The Philanderer*, and *Mrs. Warren's Profession*. In 1898 he married Charlotte Frances Payne-Townshend.

At about the turn of the century, Vedrenne and Granville-Barker started producing Shaw's dramas at the Court Theatre. To the surprise of every one, the plays were popular. People patronized them partly out of curiosity, partly out of fashion. Shaw became a cult by actually treading on people's toes. He held the most unpopular opinions he could find, and professed not the slightest respect for customary conventions. Some of the professions and practices he has held up to ridicule are: doctors, marriage, vaccination, military men, snobbery, politicians, and modesty.

Many people believe Shaw's plays are better read than acted because of their elaborate introductions, stage directions, and descriptions of characters. His plays have sold as well as novels. They were more popular in America than in England, and were introduced with great success in Germany by Siegfried Trebitsch.

Shaw was awarded the Nobel Prize for Literature in 1925, but gave the seven thousand pounds to the Anglo-Swedish Foundation. *The Apple Cart* (1929) was written specially for the first annual Malvern Festival in 1929, which was instituted as a tribute to the genius of Shaw. *The Apple Cart* and *Getting Married* were produced in America by the Theatre Guild in 1930 and 1931 respectively. Shaw's collected works were published in a uniform edition in 1930. He still lives in London.

G.B.S. once explained: "My method, you will notice, is to take utmost trouble to find the right thing to say, and then say it with the utmost levity. And all the time the real joke is that I am in earnest."

Shaw is a vegetarian. He does not drink or smoke. He has never been physically strong and is easily exhausted by work. Frank Harris relates "that his work often exhausted him so that he was fain to go into a dark room and lie flat on his back on the bare floor, every muscle relaxed, for hours, just to rest." Shaw records in *Who's Who* that his recreation is "anything except sport."

Harris describes Shaw at forty: "very tall, over six feet in height and thin to angularity; a long bony face ... rufous fair hair and long, untrimmed reddish beard (now white); grey-blue English eyes with straight eyebrows tending a little upwards from the nose and thus adding a touch of Mephistophelian sarcasm to the alert, keen expression. He was dressed carelessly in tweeds with a Jaeger flannel shirt and negligent tie; contempt of frills written all over him... His entrance into the room, his abrupt movements—as jerky as the ever-changing mind—his perfect unconstraint —all showed an able man, very conscious of his ability, very direct, very sincere, sharply decisive."

C. L. Hind recalls him as a lecturer in his prime: "I can see him now walking rapidly about the platform, the tall, lanky, springing figure, the mustardy-grey suit he always wore, the wide, heavy, health-boots ... eyes that can be amused, alert, penetrating, but never angry. He always looked the same... walking furiously in the street, or coming to a public dinner where he had been announced to speak, ridiculously late, slipping in with the sweets so as to avoid the odor, to him horrible, of the joint course... He has a ready smile."

In Frank Harris's second series of *Contemporary Portraits* appears a sketch entitled: "Shaw's Portrait by Shaw, or How Frank Ought to Have Done It."

Some of the things Shaw tells about himself are: "He has the art of getting on intimate terms quickly . . . all Shaw's friends agree that he is laughably vain. . . Shaw is an incorrigible and continuous actor, using his skill as deliberately in his social life as in his professional work. . . He addresses a letter high up in the left hand corner of an envelope . . . leaving room for the postman's thumb. . . He justifies his refusal to use apostrophes and inverted commas in printing his books on the ground that they spoil the appearance of the page. . . He is interested in phonetics and systems of shorthand. . . He likes machines as a child likes toys, and once nearly bought a cash register without having the slightest use for it. . . When in London (he) swims in the bathing pool of the Royal Automobile Club every morning before breakfast, winter and summer. . . Every really busy man, he declares, should go to bed for eighteen months when he is forty, to recuperate. . . Shaw is not really a social man. He never goes anywhere unless he has business there. He pays no calls. . . There is a cutting edge to Shaw that everybody dreads. He has in an extreme degree the mercurial mind that recognizes the inevitable instantly and faces it and adapts itself to it accordingly. . . Once, at Westminster Bridge underground station, Shaw slipped at the top of the stairs, and shot down the whole flight on his back, to the horror of the bystanders. But when he rose without the least surprise and walked on as if that were his usual way of negotiating a flight of steps, they burst into an irresistible shriek of laughter. . . He is fond of saying that what bereaved people need is a little comic relief, and that it probably explains why funerals are so farcical. . . Shaw, therefore, with all his engaging manner and social adroitness, appears as one who does not care what he says, who is callous in some of the most moving situations in life, and whose line can never be foreseen, no matter what the subject is."

Among the plays published by George Bernard Shaw since his first volume are: *Three Plays for Puritans* (1900), containing *The Devil's Disciple, Caesar and Cleopatra, Captain Brassbound's Conversion; Man and Superman* (1903); *Major Barbara* (1905); *The Doctor's Dilemma* (1906); *Getting Married* (1908); *Pygmalion* (1912); *Back to Methusaleh* (1921); *Saint Joan* (1923); *The Apple Cart* (1929).

His essays include: *The Quintessence of Ibsenism* (1891), *The Sanity of Art* (1895), *The Intelligent Woman's Guide to Socialism and Capitalism* (1928).

M. P. Shiel

MATTHEW PHIPPS SHIEL was born in the West Indies on July 21, 1865. His father was an Irish ship owner who attained some celebrity as a local Methodist preacher.

Mr. Shiel's interest in and respect for science is not merely fortuitous, but can be traced directly to his education at London University, where he received the A.B. degree, and at St. Barts Hospital, where he studied medicine. He had prepared for his higher education at Harrison College in Barbadoes.

M. P. SHIEL

Nor was it altogether chance that Shiel did not complete his medical course. The first operation he attended was for strabismus on the eyeball, and this so instilled him with a dislike for surgery that he abandoned the medical profession altogether. Soon after this, idly gazing at the sky one afternoon, he was impelled to write *Prince Zaleski*. However, this was by no means the first literary effort of the young author. At the age of thirteen he had published a weekly paper, issuing seven copies of each number written by hand—a year before this he had completed the manuscript of a novel and by the time he was fifteen was the author of a serial that was published in a newspaper.

Shiel's early work attracted the attention of men of letters like Stevenson, Wilde, Arthur Machen, Dowson, and Pierre Louÿs, but his popular reputation was established when he wrote *The Yellow Danger*. It was so successful that the author was immediately besieged by many periodicals with exceedingly tempting offers—"easy labor," he comments, "by which one makes two or three thousand pounds a year; but then, to make real books of the serials one must needs rewrite, and that is trying."

Among the better known of Mr. Shiel's novels during the period that immediately followed this are *The Lord of the Sea*, *The Isle of Lies*, and *Unto the Third Generation* (1903). From the outbreak of the War, however, Mr. Shiel abandoned literature for a while, but returned to it when he published *Children of the Wind* (1924), followed by *How the Old Woman Got Home* (1927) and *Here Comes the Lady* (1928).

Mr. Shiel's devotion to science is apparent in practically every one of his works, and he still continues to experiment, for his own pleasure, in chemistry and physics. These, with mountain climbing and mathematics, now constitute his hobbies. He writes of himself:

"No longer a boy, I have found out how to live in high health and never have a pain or anything like that. Yet I don't get many ultra-violet rays, liking the stars better than our sun, living mostly at night, sleeping by day—except when travelling, for I am often in France, Italy, Spain: mostly I have lived between London and Paris. As to my books, I have no little fun writing them; I don't take very long, but am long beginning, making sure that all that work will be of some novelty and interest to somebody. I have written over twenty books, and only two of them to get money: the others I was inspired to write."

Mr. Shiel now resides in Sussex, England. He took a second wife fifteen years after his first wife died. Among his other books are: *The Purple Cloud*, *Cold Steel*, *The Last Miracle*, *Dr. Krasinski's Secret* (1929), and *The Black Box* (1930).

May Sinclair

MAY SINCLAIR was born at Rockferry in Cheshire, and was one of six children, the other five being boys. She was educated partly at home, partly at Cheltenham College. Among her schoolfellows was another child, destined in after life to become a writer—Mrs. Allen Harker—but the two novelists did not draw together in friendship until after schooldays were at an end. Her family was Scotch, with members of the clergy predominating. She was always very advanced and independent, one of those keen-minded girls with very little tolerance for sham and the placid dullness which passes for convention. Miss Beale, the founder and head of Cheltenham College, which was already one of the most famous educational institutions in England, took a great fancy to her and encouraged her in her writing.

Returning home Miss Sinclair began to produce verse, and by the time she was twenty had already written a little sheaf of poems. In those days Mr. Gladstone was a force scattering postcards of well-meant but badly-expressed encouragement ("he was sensible of the merits they contained") to beginners, and the usual postcard, with the addition of a few reviews, was perhaps the sum total of what happened to the two modest books of verse which she published in 1887 and 1890. These were succeeded some time afterward by an article on metaphysics which she had been commissioned to write for an

MAY SINCLAIR   *Olive Ismay*

American journal. Thus Miss Sinclair's first publications in England were verse, and in America prose.

A friend having suggested that she had it in her to write novels, she tried her prentice hand on *Audrey Craven* (1896), of which she now thinks very little. This was published on the half-profits system, and brought little grist to the mill. It was followed by *Mr. and Mrs. Nevill Tyson,* and *Two Sides of a Question,* and with the publication of each of these, Miss Sinclair's standing improved, until recognition came in both hemispheres with the publication of *The Divine Fire* (1904). This book, her first really successful one, was received even more favorably in America than in England.

Miss Sinclair now lives in St. John's Wood, London. For some years, whenever London seemed too full of a clamant vitality for her to work in peace, she fled to a little village in Yorkshire; but, as so doing meant spending nearly a whole day in the train, the northern home has been exchanged for one in Gloucestershire—in the Cotswold Hills.

Miss Sinclair had a great deal of first-hand experience in the War. In 1914 she went to the front with a field ambulance corps which was driven from one Belgian city to another before the ad-vancing Germans. Her *Journal of Impressions in Belgium* (1915) gives an interesting account of her experiences, many of which were thrilling.

She also worked with Mr. Hoover in Belgium and was very active in war work in England. She is a feminist and has been connected with the most progressive movements of the day.

Miss Sinclair is well versed in philosophy, in the Greek classics and Elizabethan literature. She has said: "I can think best in the country, and work best in town—the former, strange as it may seem, offers too many distractions. I work hard at all my novels, especially with regard to style. Each character has to be thought out, to be alive and present to me, before I can begin. I sketch out the whole book carefully, and each chapter separately, before writing a line. Therefore, as the whole is before me more or less, it doesn't matter where I begin a novel. I frequently begin in the middle. I write sometimes rapidly, sometimes at a snail's pace. I have no regular methods of work, no theories of art, no test of it except excellence of style and construction, and truth to life —the latter the supreme test."

Miss Sinclair has made several visits to America. After meeting her, James Walter Smith wrote in the *Boston Transcript*: "I shall not quickly forget the impression Miss Sinclair made upon me. I think of her as a small and demure being in black sitting with her hands crossed in her lap. If I had not known her as one of the most brilliant writers of the day, I should have thought her the prim mistress of some young ladies' finishing school. Her manner was as quiet as her dress. Her power—indefinable, all-observant, analytic—is to be found in her eyes; what those eyes miss isn't worth hiding or trying to hide."

Miss Sinclair's works include: novels, *The Divine Fire* (1904), *The Three Sisters* (1914), *Mary Olivier* (1919), *Mr. Waddington of Wyck* (1921), *Anne Severn and the Fieldings* (1922), *The Life and Death of Harriet Frean* (1922), *The History of Anthony Waring* (1927); short stories, *Uncanny Stories* (1923), *Tales Told by Simpson* (1930); biography, *The Three Brontës* (1912); philosophy, *The New Idealism* (1922).

Upton Sinclair

A FIGHTER with his pen, Upton Sinclair comes of fighting men. He was born in Baltimore on September 20, 1878. His immediate ancestors were in the early United States Navy; before that in the British Navy. The Civil War swept away what fortune they possessed and the novelist was born in the sterile atmosphere of a Southern family with leisure class traditions but no money.

Sinclair began to write hack fiction at fifteen and earned his way thru the College of the City of New York. At seventeen he set out to learn the violin and he practiced ten hours a day for two years. In his last year of college he got a leave of absence for several months, stayed at home, and read omnivorously. He says the three men who had the most to do with shaping his thought were Jesus, Hamlet, and Shelley. He received his A. B. in 1897.

"When I got to be twenty (1898), and had marriage in view," he relates, "a desire to write serious things overwhelmed me." He gave up the writing of dime-novels and in 1900 married Meta H. Fuller. They had one son. "From twenty to twenty-six I nearly starved. All my novels of that time—*King Midas* (1901), *Prince Hagen* (1903), *Arthur Stirling* (1903), *Manassas* (1904), and *A Captain of Industry* (1906)—brought me less than one thousand dollars altogether. I lived alone on four dollars and fifty cents a week in New York and I lived in the country with my family for thirty dollars a month." Four years of this time he did graduate work at Columbia.

Since he gave up hack writing Sinclair has "written exclusively in the cause of human welfare," nearly all his work being part of the class war. "What brought me to Socialism," he says, "was more Christianity than anything else." Many who favor his Socialistic views cannot stomach his Puritanism.

"When I wrote what really interested me, I never stopped day or night for weeks at a time. I mean that I had the thing I was writing in my mind every moment—I think even while I was asleep. I developed a really extraordinary memory for words; I never put pen

UPTON SINCLAIR

to paper till I had whole pages all by heart in my mind. I would walk up and down thinking it over and over, and it would stay in my mind—whole scenes."

In 1906 Sinclair took part in the government investigation of Chicago stockyards. Moved by the bloodiness and torture of the industry, he wrote *The Jungle* (1906), an attack on the meat lords. The book swept the country. Someone remarked that it gave the nation a stomach-ache. His story resulted in at least a temporary righting of the evils he had pointed out.

Book after book followed, each laying open one of the fester spots of capitalistic society. Many of the books sold well. Sinclair came to be called a "Millionaire Socialist," and he was accused of turning his "love of justice into high-power limousines." In 1917 he defended himself in an article in *Pearson's Magazine*, denying that he ever kept his money or that he ever owned an automobile. "I made thirty thousand dollars out of one book (*The Jungle*)," he wrote, "and proceeded at once to invest it in a Socialist colony (the Helicon Home Colony at Englewood, New Jersey), so organized that I had no possibility of making profit out of it; it burned down, and I lost nearly everything, and started again. The next time I was on my feet, I launched, here in California, a Socialist dramatic enterprise, again without possibility of profit; and when I had got out of debt from that, I went in a third time, trying to get justice, or a tiny modicum of it, for the slaves of the Colorado coal mines." He says he has refused many handsome offers of money in order to devote his energies solely to his Socialist books and propaganda articles.

In 1911 Sinclair was divorced from his first wife and in 1913 he married Mary Craig Kimbrough, daughter of Judge Kimbrough of Greenwood, Mississippi. She is the author of sonnets which have appeared in various magazines and have been collected and published by her husband. The Sinclair home is in Pasadena, California, where the author publishes some of his own writings. Mr. and Mrs. Sinclair have conducted some rather startling experiments in mental telepathy. Their conclusions appear in *Mental Radio*.

Upton Sinclair is a slight, well-built man of average height, with a boyish face and manner. He preaches the importance of care of the body and for years contributed a monthly article to *Physical Culture* on dietetics. On the tennis court he is the picture of confident grace, and one of his requirements for a secretary is that he should be able to play a rattling match at least once a day.

The author has run for various political offices on the Socialist ticket. He was a candidate for Congress from New Jersey in 1906. Since his removal to California he has been Socialist candidate for Congress (1920), the Senate (1922), and for governor of California (1926). He is the founder of the Intercollegiate Socialist Society and the American Civil Liberties Union of California.

Among Sinclair's books since *The Jungle* are: *The Metropolis* (1908), *Samuel the Seeker* (1910), *Love's Pilgrimage*, autobiographical (1911), *Damaged Goods* (1913), *King Coal* (1917), *Jimmie Higgins* (1919), *They Call Me Carpenter* (1922), *The Goslings* (1924), *Oil!* (1927), *Boston* (1928), *Mountain City* (1930), *Mental Radio* (1930), *Roman Holiday* (1931).

His plays include: *Plays of Protest* (1912), *Hell* (1923), *Singing Jailbirds* (1924), *The Pot Boiler* (1924), and *Bill Porter* (1925).

Sinclair's works have been published in thirty-four countries. Russia led the long list of translations in 1930 with one hundred and ninety-four, Germany had thirty-six, Japan thirty.

Edith Sitwell

EDITH SITWELL is descended from a long line of English ancestry—the Lords of Midhope and Barnaby who intermarried with the Hallamshire family, and more remotely from the tall, blue-eyed Norman chiefs who came into the North of England in the 11th century. Her father, Sir George Sitwell, was the fourth baronet of his line, and the family estate at Renishaw Park has been in the possession of her forefathers for more than 600 years. She was born in 1887.

Of the "Three Sitwells," Edith and her brothers, Osbert and Sacheverell, all of whom are gifted poets and prose writers, Edith is perhaps the greatest artist. Arnold Bennett, writing of her in 1923, says, "To my mind Edith Sitwell is the most accomplished technician in verse (unless it be Robert Bridges) now writing. Her skill dazzles me, who once attempted rhyme." She is over six feet tall, blond, with a long sharp-featured face and straight fair hair and grey eyes. As children she and her two brothers were a favorite subject for portrait groups, among the famous artists who have painted them being Sargent and Max Beerbohm. The Sargent portrait was painted when Edith was eleven, Osbert six, and Sacheverell a little over a year old.

Her earliest memories are of Renishaw, a great rambling fan-shaped edifice surrounded by meadows, valleys, and rugged moors. On this estate, heavy with reminiscences of Feudal England, Edith and her two brothers spent their early youth, with no reminders of an encroaching industrial age except perhaps the miners who passed by twice a day from the slag heaps on a neighboring hillside, leaving or returning to their grimy collieries. The Sitwells divided their time between this family estate and Scarborough on the sea-coast, where the family also owned a house, and the sea front of Scarborough probably inspired many of Miss Sitwell's earlier poems. When they were older they were taken by their parents to Florence and to wander thru Italy and Spain for a part of the year.

Edith's early reading consisted of the staple children's books—the fairy tales of Grimm and Hans Andersen chiefly—and at the age of 14 she knew no poets but Shakespeare and Shelley. She had never heard of Keats until she ran across a volume of his poems in a German bookshop some years later. At 17 she made the acquaintance of Swinburne's works and afterwards the exciting discovery of the French poets, of whom Baudelaire is perhaps her favorite.

The first poem she ever wrote was "Serenade" composed during a "bout of measles" at the age of 24, and subsequently her first published work "Drowned Suns" appeared in the *London Mirror.*

Desire for leadership seems to be one of her dominant characteristics—the result of an unusual inheritance and a naturally brilliant mind, and in 1916, as the leader of a group of younger English poets she established *Wheels,* an annual anthology of verse. This lasted for five years but in 1921 was discontinued. During its existence Edith and her two brothers were the most constant and important contributors. In 1923 she conducted another poetic experiment with her much-discussed public recital in Aeolean Hall in London. When the audience was assembled they found, instead of the customary lecture table, that they were confronted with a strange curtain painted by Frank Dobson and representing three primitive archways. In the center arch was a huge female painted with closed eyes and open mouth, through which came the voice of Miss Sitwell reading aloud the poems of the group to the rhythms of a musical accompaniment. The recital, which was considered very effective, was designed to carry out her theory that in poetry the emphasis must be placed principally

EDITH SITWELL

upon the musical cadences, and that as an art it should be dissociated from the individual's personality just as music is. Edith Sitwell is herself an ardent student of music and an accomplished pianist.

She is an extreme individualist, so much so that she has often been accused of striking an attitude, but her acute sense of humor—despite her statement that she "in early youth took an intense dislike to simplicity, morris-dancing, a sense of humor, and every kind of sport except reviewer-baiting, and has continued these distastes ever since"—and her delight in joyous nonsense touched with satire, often evident in her poetry, all serve to deny such an accusation. She directs her natural exuberance and energy, a family trait, toward the ends of art, making it her *raison d'être.*

Among her publications are *The Mother and Other Poems* (1915); *Clowns' Houses* (1918); *Bucolic Comedies* (1923); *The Sleeping Beauty* (1924); *Elegy on Dead Fashion* (1926); *Rustic Elegies* (1927); *Gold Coast Customs* (1929); *Alexander Pope* (1930), a biography and zealous appreciation of Pope's work; *Collected Poems* (1930).

Osbert Sitwell

OSBERT SITWELL, English poet and playwright, was the second born of the three distinguished Sitwells. He says: "I was born in December 1892 and the first thing I remember is political commotion in the house, for my father stood for Parliament seven times and was elected five." As the oldest son, he is the heir to the Sitwell title and will be fifth baronet.

Of Renishaw Park, the country estate of his family which was built in 1625, his memories are of its Jacobean center holding together the great wings, its meandering canal, and its gardens and park. There he and his brother and sister soaked in the legendry of their Norman ancestry; of Catherine Swynneford who was believed to have been the sister of Chaucer's wife Phillippa; of John of Gaunt, Catherine's husband; of lovely Lady Elizabeth Coyningham, imperious mistress of George IV; of Lord Albert Coyningham (the first Baron Londesborough) whose first wife, a famous beauty who died young, was the sister of Lady Chesterfield; and of the Lady Bradford admired by Disraeli.

Osbert was sent to Eton. "I hated it passionately and still do," is his remark. He intimates that he gained his real education during the holidays from Eton when he returned to the family estate with its tradition, books, and tapestries, and roamed the grounds with his brother and sister.

When he finished school he "was made to go to an army crammer's and finally to enter the army at the age of eighteen." He served in the Grenadier Guards from 1913 to 1919, taking part in the World War.

He is "deeply interested in any manifestation of sport." In 1913 he founded the Renishaw Park Golf Club, and in 1914 the Whiston Golf Club. He recalls that he played against the Yorkshire Cricket eleven, left-handed, when he was seven years old. He remarks that he was put down for the Marylebone Cricket Club on the day of his birth by W. G. Grace, but has now abandoned all other athletic interests in order to urge the adoption of new sports such as: Pelota, Kif-Kif, and the Pengo (especially the latter). He says he spent the winter of 1927-28 in the Sahara studying the Pengo. In 1924 he founded the Rememba Bomba League, whatever that may be, and reconstituted it in November 1927.

Mr. Sitwell admits that he likes to travel and that he has recently been to Turkey, Greece, Morocco, Spain, Italy, Austria, Germany, Hungary, and France, Cyprus, Rhodes, and Asia Minor. He says he is always inclined to buy a house in each place he visits but fortunately seldom has money enough to do so. Altho Renishaw is still his home, he has a house in London which is the gathering place for left wing artists of all sorts.

He is most fond, he says, "of talking and thinking: that is to say, talking first and thinking afterwards." He likes pictures and sculpture (to look at not to make). And he is very fond of overhearing casual conversations in hotels, of swimming, and of good food and drink. His recreations, he remarks, are "regretting the Bourbons, repartée, and tu quoque." His face is rather Neronian and his back stooped.

One of his pranks was to sit on the housetop across from the residence of a hostess whose invitation he had refused, and thru a high-powered megaphone

OSBERT SITWELL

announce the guests as they arrived, giving them such names as Mussolini, the Prince of Wales, Sinclair Lewis, and Mary Pickford. His brother Sacheverell is devoted to him and calls him the most brilliant conversationalist since Wilde.

Among his works are: *Twentieth Century Harlequinade* (1916), *Argonaut and Juggernaut* (1919), *Who Killed Cock Robin?* (1921), *Triple Fugue, and Other Stories* (1924), *Before the Bombardment* (1926), *England Reclaimed* (1927), *All at Sea* (1927), *The Man Who Lost Himself* (1929), *Dumb Animal and Other Stories* (1930). In collaboration he has written *The People's Album of London Statues* (1928) with Nina Hamnett, and *Sober Truth* (1930) with Margaret Barton. *The Collected Satires and Poems of Osbert Sitwell* appeared in 1931.

Dumb Animal was withdrawn from publication in England after the story, "Happy Endings," had been judged libelous.

Sacheverell, born in 1900, is the youngest of the Sitwell trio. He attended Oxford for a while but is mainly self-educated. Like his brother, he has traveled extensively and is devoted to games. He has an intense interest in the arts. "A certain indefinite quality about his features" reminded one interviewer of "a sad doll that has been left out in the rain." Known chiefly as a lyric poet, his principal work is *Doctor Donne and Gargantua* (1930), an unfinished narrative poem of which six cantos have been published, representing the spiritual and the physical worlds in conflict. He has published several other volumes of poetry. His prose works include: *Southern Baroque Art* (1924), *German Baroque Art* (1927), *The Gothick North,* in three volumes (1929-30).

Constance Lindsay Skinner

CONSTANCE LINDSAY SKINNER knows whereof she speaks when she deals with the Canadian Northwest. She was born in northern British Columbia five hundred miles from a railroad at the Hudson's Bay trading post where her father was factor. Her child-

CONSTANCE LINDSAY SKINNER

hood was spent among fur traders, Indians, and mounted policemen. She received her early education in a private school in Vancouver and under tutors.

Her father's family, descending from that Cyriac Skinner to whom Milton addressed two sonnets, included Charles Reade; her mother's included Lady Anne Lindsay, who wrote "Auld Robin Gray," and David Lindsay, poet and historian, the friend of John Knox.

Altho her background is Canadian she has long been known in the United States as a historian, having contributed two volumes—*Pioneers of the Old Southwest* and *Adventurers in Oregon* —to "The Chronicles of America" series in 1919.

At eleven, Miss Skinner was the author of a still unpublished novel. At fourteen she wrote and produced a three-act operetta, and at sixteen she was a special writer for several Canadian newspapers. Two years later she became a full fledged reporter on the *San Francisco Examiner,* chronicling everything from fire, murder, and sudden death to symphony concerts. Later she wrote for the *Chicago American.*

Her first novel, *Builder of Men* (1913), was published only in Germany.

Miss Skinner has covered a wide field in her writing. Her poetry has won prizes from the London *Bookman* and the magazine *Poetry* and has been translated into Russian, Spanish, French, and German. She is the author of several books for children, moving picture dramas, novels, plays, and many short stories and magazine articles.

And with it all she has found time to be a member of the Executive Committee of the Poetry Society of America, a Fellow of the Royal Geographical Society of Great Britain, and a Fellow of the American Geographical Society.

Among Miss Skinner's recent publications are *Roselle of the North* (1927), *Ranch of the Golden Flowers* (1928), *Andy Breaks Trail* (1928), and *Red Man's Luck* (1930)—all books for young readers; *The Search Relentless* (1925), and *Red Willows* (1929)—novels; and *Songs of the Coast Dwellers* (1930), a book of Indian poems.

Oswald Spengler

OSWALD SPENGLER, German philosopher, was born at Blankenburg-am-Harz on May 29, 1880. He studied mathematics, philosophy, history, and art in Munich and Berlin. His doctor's thesis, on Heraclitus, was his sole publication before the work that instantly made him famous.

In 1912 Spengler, then an obscure teacher, formulated the central thesis of *Der Untergang des Abendlandes (The Decline of the West)* and he completed

OSWALD SPENGLER

the first volume before the World War broke out in 1914. Then, in the dark months that followed he revised the manuscript by candlelight in the cramped, sunless, and almost heatless back room of a tenement house in the west side of Munich. He could not afford a private reference library. When he lived thus dingily, he cared for his own needs and ate usually in restaurants frequented by laborers. His antidote for all ills was strong Chinese tea, consumed in large quantities.

The author's difficulties continued when he tried in vain to find a German publisher to undertake the enterprise in the precarious wartime conditions. Finally his work was brought out in Vienna in the summer of 1918. Not until the third edition in 1919 was it taken over by a German publisher.

The book was notably successful from the start. In 1921 Spengler let it go out of print and he rewrote it, using the specific facts of the war as illustration of his theses. The book was a prophecy in the sense that its interpretation of history was uniquely ratified and fulfilled at the moment when the Western nations, under the delusion that they were waging war against each other, began waging suicide. Spengler sees history as a living organism. His great work attempts to prove, by analogies from the past, that our Western culture must pass thru the inevitable stages of all growth: youth, maturity, old age, and death. Youth and maturity lie behind us, he says. The death of our civilization is at hand.

With the appearance of the revised German edition in 1923, *Der Untergang des Abendlandes* became a world affair. *The Decline of the West,* translated by Charles Francis Atkinson, was published in America as follows: first volume, *Form and Actuality* (1926); second volume, *Perspectives of World History* (1928). It has gone thru several editions.

The volume of foreign comment on *The Decline of the West* has been huge. In France Spengler's interpreters number Henri Lichtenberger of the University of Paris and Paul Ernest Laurent Fauconnet of the Sorbonne. Italy became the scene of a spectacular literary duel between Giuseppe Rensi, defender of Spengler, and Benedetto Croce, opponent. In Russia the Soviet gave the book enthusiastic sanction on the basis of the first volume, but suffered a change of heart when the second convicted it of having acted against its own interest. It is believed in Germany that a Russian edition was destroyed on the eve of publication; and it is certain that the Soviet has forbidden the use of Spengler's ideas as a basis of university lectures. Berdyayev has, nevertheless, used Spengler's philosophy of history as the core of nearly all his recent work. Among other translations are Japanese and Spanish.

Spengler has a mania for light, air, and untrammeled vistas. Immediately following his success he acquired a long suite of enormous rooms along the facade of an apartment house on the Windenmayerstrasse in Munich, overlooking the "green Isar." Here he has space to stride back and forth in a way which apparently frees his thoughts as nothing else does.

His walls are decorated with Indian, Persian, and Turkish weapons he has collected, as well as Italian, French, and German paintings of value. He gets pleasure out of gathering objects of art only when he ferrets them out himself in obscure places. His library, now expanded to several thousand volumes, is distributed thruout every room of the house. He said once: "There are two more works that I have to write. When they are done, I am going to throw my library into the Isar."

Spengler loves museums and art galleries; he appreciates music from classic to modern and chooses to play eighteenth century compositions himself; he likes the theatre and delights especially in the comedies of Shakespeare and Molière. His passion among countries is Italy and he visits it whenever he can. His peculiar abhorrence is professional photographers, altho he is perfectly willing to have snapshots taken informally by his friends. When he was finally enticed into a studio in Munich, the dozen exposures revealed a great variety of expressions—some of them seeming hardly to belong to the same person—corresponding to his intellectual many-sidedness reflected in *The Decline of the West*. He understands finance, machinery, economics, politics, engineering, and institutions generally.

The author is heavily and solidly built, his smooth face is usually austere, and his high head is completely bald. His physical vigor is immense and he takes frequent walking trips in the Brocken, in the Harz Mountains (where live his sisters and his friend the poet Droem), and in Switzerland. He climbs for hours without tiring, is practically immune from the effects of heat and cold, always wears the lightest of clothing, and hikes just the same in defiance of the fever and atrocious headaches of which he is an occasional victim. He almost never consults a physician.

Besides mountaineering, Spengler's favorite diversion is conversation with peasants, whose lore he collects and repeats with the jovial gusto of a combined poet and man of the world. His own Harz country abounds in peasant and small-town types, poetic, witty, obstinate, superstitious, full of practical jokes, and equally full of ghost stories. Spengler is without personal political ambition and, as an occasional public speaker, without artifice or deliberate oratory.

Other works by Oswald Spengler, chiefly concerned with contemporary political problems are: *Preussentum und Sozialismus* (1920), *Pessimismus* (1921), *Politische Pflichten der deutschen Jugend* (1924), *Neubau des deutschen Reiches* (1924).

Wilbur Daniel Steele

"THERE is so little of 'human interest' about me. I seem to be pretty much the common or garden variety of person, anxious about the wellbeing of my family (wife and two boys), always losing everything, and having difficulty with my income tax returns. My main desire is to have the moon.

"There are, of course, data. Born in Greensboro, North Carolina, (O. Henry's birth-place, which has nothing to do with the question) in 1886, I went to kindergarten in Berlin and finished my formal

WILBUR DANIEL STEELE

education in Denver, graduating from the University of Denver (where my father is a professor of Biblical literature) in 1907. All my forebears having being connected with the ministry of the Gospel in the Methodist Episcopal faith, I was from my earliest youth reared to be a painter; accordingly, having worked in summer- and night-classes in a Denver art school while in college, I came East in 1907 to pursue my studies in the Museum School in Boston. The most important thing I got there was a wife (Margaret Thurston), whom I married some time later (1913). In 1908-09 I was in Paris, at the Académie Julian, and in Florence and Venice, etching.

"It was during that winter that I began to write stories, playing hookey from the Académie to do it—and they were pretty awful stuff. The following summer I drifted to Provincetown, Massachusetts, and have been there, with longer or shorter hiatuses, ever since. The hiatuses, the more important ones, have taken me to The West Indies (1916-1917), to the coasts of Ireland, England and France, as naval correspondent (1918), to Bermuda (1919-20), and to North Africa, France, and England, (1920-21-22)."

In this modest sketch of himself, Mr. Steele neglects to mention the fact that he has been four times a winner of O. Henry Memorial Prizes. He was awarded second prize in 1919 for the story, *For They Know Not What They Do;* received a special award in 1921 for maintaining the highest level of merit for three years among American short story writers; tied with Julian Street in 1925 for first honor with the story, *The Man Who Saw Through Heaven;* and took first prize in 1926 with *Bubbles.* In addition, he won the fourth *Harper Magazine* short story contest.

A middle-aged man with grey eyes and brown, stubborn hair, Mr. Steele has a general "wind-blown" appearance —even in his clothes. His clothes fit, but he does not seem to take them seriously, just as he does not take himself seriously. Altho many of his stories are grim, he is neither grim nor melancholy himself. And he is not self-centred.

Unlike many authors who are given to spasms of creation followed by periods of rest, Mr. Steele is at his desk nearly every day in the year. Sometimes he will sit for days, "getting a story." Then he sets it down, carefully, methodically, almost painfully. He usually works four or five hours a day, with an average output of less than six hundred words a day. "This is written in long-hand, in ink," relates Frank B. Elser, "in a script that would put many etchers to shame. To read it one needs a magnifying glass. At the close of each day's work he transcribes this hand-written draft on the typewriter and tucks the installment away until the story shall have been completed. He then revises and condenses the typewritten script. Finally ... he recopies it himself and takes it to the postoffice like the veriest of tyros."

Altho born in North Carolina and reared in Denver, Mr. Steele has turned for much of his material to the New England Coast and the sea which he came to know when he was grown. The first story to bring him recognition was about Cape Cod, *A White Horse Winter,* published in the *Atlantic* in 1912. His home for many years was on the island of Nantucket, Massachusetts. About 1930 he moved to Charleston, South Carolina.

Short stories by Wilbur Daniel Steele appear in such magazines as the *Pictorial Review, Harper's, Scribner's,* and *Atlantic.* His collected volumes include: *Land's End* (1918), *The Shame Dance*

(1923), *Urkey Island* (1926), *The Man Who Saw Through Heaven* (1927), *Tower of Sand* (1929).

Among his novels are: *Storm* (1914), *Isles of the Blest* (1924), *Taboo* (1925), *Meat* (1928). His plays include: *The Giants' Stair* (1924), *The Terrible Woman* (1925).

Gertrude Stein

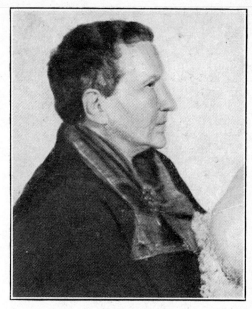

GERTRUDE STEIN

GERTRUDE STEIN was born in 1872 in Allegheny, Pennsylvania. When she was a year old her family went to Europe and lived three years in Vienna and one year in Paris. When the girl was five her family returned to the United States and settled in San Francisco.

"I was brought up ... in Oakland and San Francisco," she relates. "As a child I was an omnivorous reader, going thru whole libraries, reading everything. I attended Radcliffe College at Cambridge. Just like everybody else, I wanted to write, but nobody encouraged me very much. I think the first person to take an interest in my writing was Vaughn Moody... I was tremendously impressed with George Eliot and Louisa M. Alcott."

Miss Stein was graduated in 1897 from Radcliffe, where she was a favorite pupil, in psychology, of William James. Then she attended Johns Hopkins Medical School and specialized in brain anatomy. But her literary ambitions caused her to abandon scientific research, and she went to London where she spent a year studying Elizabethan prose. She settled in Paris in 1903.

Her first book was a trio of character sketches of women, *Three Lives* (1909). "I found money to publish it myself," she says. "No publisher would look at it. But that did not discourage me; I was not the first author who paid his own admission."

Among her earliest friends in Paris was Picasso, the artist, whose work was long ridiculed before it became celebrated. "Nobody had ever heard of either of us," she says, "and we worked harmoniously together, each on his own. I started to write portraits of every-body who came to the house—Picasso, Matisse, Carl Van Vechten, all who wrote or composed or painted. I called this collection *Geography and Plays* (1922)."

Miss Stein spent two years writing *The Making of Americans* (1926) and she finished it in 1908. Then, for nearly twenty years it waited for a publisher. "Nobody wanted to publish the book," she explains, "and I had no money to do so myself; finally a friend, young and enthusiastic, pushed it thru." This huge novel, four and one half inches thick, records the wanderings and mental development of three generations of her own family.

Gertrude Stein has been recognized as a leader of the extremists in literary expression. Her method is akin to that of the ultra-modern "stream of consciousness" school, but even less restrained. She chooses her words for their sound rather than their sense. She has always been "tremendously interested in the volume and rhythm of words."

Jean Cocteau writes: "I can sense her rhythm even in translation; she possesses the *métier poétique.* Her *Portrait of Picasso* is like a bas-relief; I seem to run my fingers over it, as tho it were a piece of plastic art. Hers was the first writing which struck me as being a new thing in the English language."

The writings of Miss Stein are unintelligible to many persons. Her defense for her peculiar form of literary expression is: "I take things in and they come out that way, independent of conscious process." But she adds: "All this foolishness about my writing being mystic or impressionistic is so stupid. Just a lot of rot. I write as pure, straight, grammatical English as anyone, more accurate grammatically than most. There isn't a single one of my sentences that a school child couldn't diagram. They're perfectly simple and direct. Every word I write has the same passionate exactness of meaning that it is supposed to have. Everything I write means exactly what it says."

There is much speculation as to whether Gertrude Stein's work is childish babble or the product of genius. Sherwood Anderson believes that she "may be, just *may* be, the greatest wordslinger of our generation." Her apartment is full of manuscripts which have never been published.

"Lack of popular success in America is the last of my worries," is her own comment. "I am working for what will endure, not for a public. Once you have a public you are never free. No one who is ever to be really great succeeds until he is past forty, be he inventor, painter, writer, or financial genius. The early setbacks aid the eventual greatness. Quick success is killing."

Gertrude Stein has lived in the same apartment in the rue de Fleurus in Montparnasse for more than twenty-five years. The entrance is on a quiet court. The living-room, tastefully hung with Picassos, Braques, Juan Gris, and Cézannes, reflects her acumen in buying modern painters before they become masters. Some of the portraits are of herself. The great, high-ceilinged room is full of odd chairs, bibelots, candlesticks, lamps, with a great couch in the centre and a wood fire at the far end. There, Miss Stein is noted for her hospitality and her comfortable talk.

Eleanor Wakefield describes the author: "The first impression of Gertrude Stein brings a sense of solid genuineness, cordiality and good, homely humor. Nothing of the mystic or the freak— just one of the 'home folks.' She is short and heavy. Her face is sunbrowned and ruddy. Her brown eyes look straight at one. Close-cropped, iron grey hair forms a short bang across her forehead. She brushes it forward with her hand occasionally as she talks." She laughs often.

Margaret Anderson speaks of her as "a healthy, robust, amusing woman who dresses in brilliant flowered chintz, heavy men's shoes, drives a battered Ford to her farm and likes to sit about swapping talk with the garage man before she composes addresses to the students of Oxford." Her clothes are a part of her reputation. She has been known to attend Drury Lane performances in London "adorned in a short corduroy skirt, a white silk shirt, sandals, and a tiny hat perched up on her monumental head."

When Gertrude Stein visited Muriel Draper in London she "would sit in Buddhistic calm until some topic of conversation arose which stimulated her interests. And then she would talk for hours, a steady flow of ideas in an almost boring logical sequence, some of them profound and others merely a form of brilliant dialectic. Her point once gained or, in any case, her opponent once retired, she would sink back into calm and absorb intuitively what no longer aroused her intellectually."

"I live in Paris for the calm and peace that is so necessary to my work," Miss Stein explains. "French people never interfere. They are pleasant and cordial, without being intrusive. I like that. I know my neighbors. I talk to the *concierge* about new traffic regulations or to my friends about our dogs or automobiles. But we never bother each other. I haven't any patience with these half-baked esthetes who sit around the Dome or the Rotonde and talk about the 'higher life.' When Picasso and I visit each other we don't talk about anything but ordinary things."

Despite her long residence in Paris, Miss Stein considers herself the "most utterly Americanized" person in the world. The mention of the word "expatriate" drives her into a rage. During the World War she was a staunch American supporter. She drove her little old Ford down the lines, distributing supplies to the doughboys and visiting hospitals. She was decorated by the French Government with the Reconnaissance Française.

Among the books by Gertrude Stein are: *Three Lives,* short stories (1909); *Tender Buttons,* poetry (1914); *Geography and Plays,* plays (1922); *The Making of Americans,* novel (1926); *Composition as Explanation* (1926), and *Useful Knowledge* (1928), essays. A collected edition of her works, beginning with *Lucy Church Amiably,* a novel, was announced for publication in Paris in 1931.

James Stephens

LITTLE is known about the origin of James Stephens, Irish poet and story teller. He was born in Dublin in February 1882. A street gamin, he spent his boyhood and youth in abject poverty. He educated himself and learned stenography. George Russell (Æ) "discovered" him working as a typist in a lawyer's office in Dublin and encouraged him in his imaginative writing.

At that time Stephens had written a number of poems and stories which he had failed to get printed. Many of the stories which were afterwards highly praised had come back from the editors. His first publications were the "Jottings of a Philosopher" which appeared in a Dublin paper. His first book was a collection of verse entitled *Insurrection* (1909). The "Jottings of a Philosopher" were elaborated into *The Crock of Gold* (1912), which was written with indelible pencil in stenographer's notebooks. This book of prose fiction brought him his first widespread recognition and it was awarded the Polignac Prize as being the best book of its year.

Stephens set about making a series of books from the old bardic tales of Ireland. The first two of these are: *Deirdre* (1923) and *In the Land of Youth* (1924). *Deirdre* was awarded the Talltean Gold Medal. The author's ambition,

JAMES STEPHENS

he declares, is to give Ireland something that will correspond to the Arabian Nights, "a new mythology to take the place of the threadbare mythology of Greece and Rome." To this end he has been enthusiastically absorbing literature and studying the Irish language. He believes that Ireland's one hope of retaining her independence and her glory lives in keeping alive the Gaelic tongue. He is an ardent Nationalist and has worked hard for the establishment of the Irish Free State.

Of his books he laughingly says: "If I were giving prizes to myself I should certainly hand at least six gold medals, each as big as a tub, to *The Demi-Gods* (1914), and I should give twenty-six bigger and brighter and better medals to the *Irish Fairy Tales* (1920). *Deirdre* and *In the Land of Youth* are too recent for me to say much about them, but I will agree with anyone that a medal twice as big as a door would not half. . . However, you will gather that I approve of my own books; they are my favorite reading while I am writing them."

John Cowper Powys says: "The humor of James Stephens is not merely playful and roguish; it is sardonic. What is so fascinating about James Stephens' work is that he uses the quaint, original, dialect expressions derived from the Irish peasantry to pour forth a certain drastic, but not altogether disillusioned philosophy of his own."

James Stephens has made several visits to America. When he came to this country in 1925 Burton Rascoe set down his impression of the elfin Irishman: "a bent little figure, not more than four feet ten inches in height, with a long head and a face like a faun's. . . His brown eyes shifted about nervously with a timorous and appealing look, like those of a small animal that has been caught up and caressed. His hands were deep in his pockets and this, together with his military heels, gave him a pitched-forward appearance, as tho he were thrown out of balance. . . His mouth was loose and open with excitement, and around the corners was a mischievous smile. . . His nose was short and pugged; his brow high and receding. His upper eyelids were contracted into sharp lines forming triangles. His skin was dark and his hair black and wiry. His age was indeterminable; he might be anywhere between thirty and sixty. . . He was utterly without self conscious pose, solemnity, inhibitions, suppressions, or affectations. Never have I seen a man who impressed me as being so easy, free and natural, so untamed by society, so untouched by convention, so spontaneous, pagan and joyous . . . there was something innocent and child-like about the free play of his mind and spirit."

Stephens speaks in a delicious Irish brogue and a musical voice, and accompanies his anecdotes with comical mimetics. When he recites poetry, he swings from side to side with the rhythm. His memory is filled with poems, stories, and epigrams, and he is always willing to talk. He can recite by the hour without notes. When he lectures he has nothing of the professional platform manner about him.

He is an authority on Gaelic art and is assistant curator of the Dublin National Gallery. He spends much of his time in Paris, where he finds freedom for his creative work. The Café Lilas, on the crest of Montparnasse, is his favorite haunt. He says it is the one spot in the Latin Quarter quiet enough for work and conversation.

His two closest friends are "Æ" and Stephen McKenna. Before he sailed for one of his visits to America, Stephens says he and McKenna spent three days together "and we had a grand conversation. We began at eight o'clock in the morning and continued until two the next morning. Then we would begin at eight again in the morning and continue again until two o'clock. And at the end of those three days we hadn't even scratched the surface of the things we wanted to talk about." He and McKenna sing Irish songs to the accompaniment of a concertina between conversations.

Books of poetry by Stephens include: *Insurrections* (1909), *The Hill of Vision* (1912), *Songs from the Clay* (1915), *The Rocky Road to Dublin* (1915), *The Adventures of Seumas Beg* (1915), *Green Branches* (1916), *Reincarnations* (1918), *A Poetry Recital* (1925), *Collected Poems* (1926), *Outcast* (1929), and *Theme and Variations* (1930).

His prose fiction includes: *The Crock of Gold* (1912), *The Charwoman's Daughter* (1912), *The Demi-Gods* (1914), *Deirdre* (1923), and *In the Land of Youth* (1924). His books of short stories are: *Here Are Ladies* (1913) and *Etched in Moonlight* (1928). *On Prose and Verse* (1928) contains two essays. He has written a one act comedy, *Julia Elizabeth* (1929). *Irish Fairy Tales* (1920) is a book for children.

G. B. Stern

GLADYS BRONWYN STERN HOLDSWORTH is her legal name, altho her readers know her as plain G. B. Stern, and her friends call her "Peter," after the heroine of her novel, *Twos and Threes* (1916). An English Jewess, she was born in London on June 17, 1890. When she was seven she wrote a play, mostly because the billiard room in the Stern home made a good stage. Altho she was fond of writing as a child, she had her heart set on a dramatic career. She was educated at Notting Hill High School, but left school at sixteen and traveled in Germany and Switzerland. For two years she attended the Royal Academy of Dramatic Art.

As she puts it, her "early struggles were comparatively few." At seventeen, when her first poem was accepted by the first editor to whom she sent it, she decided on a literary life. She wrote her first novel, *Pantomime,* in her twentieth year, and published it three years later (1914).

In 1919 Geoffrey Lisle Holdsworth, a prominent English journalist, read *Twos and Threes* while he lay wounded in a hospital. He objected so strongly to the hero that he wrote to the young author, complaining bitterly that she had been unfair in the characterization of the man in the book. She defended herself with spirit, and in her reply, asked the writer to come and see her. He came, and three months later they were married.

Miss Stern wrote a trilogy on Jewish life: *Children of No Man's Land* (1919), *Tents of Israel* (1924), and *A Deputy was King* (1926). In the American editions the first two were titled *Debatable Ground* and *The Matriarch.* In *Mosaic* (1930) is interwoven the story of the Paris branch of the prolific Jewish family of the trilogy. *The Matriarch* established her reputation in America. It was dramatized and produced in London and New York. Subsequent dramas by Miss Stern produced in London are: *Debonair,* 1930, and *The Man Who Pays the Piper,* 1931.

Miss Stern's life is closely linked with her books. It has been remarked that the books influence her life after they are written. One cannot visit her lofty villa at Diano Marina, Italy, without being constantly reminded of her novels. In this house, perched among the olive trees on a hill that is approached only by mule-track, G. B. Stern writes. No matter who are her guests—whether Rebecca West, Noel Coward, Clemence Dane, Louis Golding, or Humbert Wolfe—she retires to her room each morning after breakfast where she writes and dictates to her secretary.

She comes down to dinner wearing the Chinese coat described in *A Deputy Was King.* The barking of her ubiquitous dogs has been heard in *The Dark Gentleman* (1927). Her three smart Italian

G. B. STERN

maids immediately remind the visitor of those in *A Deputy Was King.* She and her friends wear the shorts, blouse, and sandals in which her heroine, Loveday, is costumed in *Debonair* (1928). Each night she disappears up a ladder to retire to a bunk-bed, just as Theo does in *Thunderstorm* (1925).

Sewell Stokes writes: "While her many readers are laughing at the wit she has brought to bear on some character in her books, the original of that character—be it a stout and trivial woman, or a tall cynical man—is surely dying, stabbed to the heart by her pen. . . . One might easily imagine her a mail-coated woman whose body is proof against the arrows of humanity's weaknesses. Yet no falser impression than this one could exist. For her cynicism is the defence of a rank sentimentalist. It is easy, I should think, to make G. B. Stern weep real tears. What an asset she would be to film producers!"

She lists her recreations as "talking, swimming, motoring, and a profound interest in wine and wolf-dogs."

Publications by G. B. Stern, besides those mentioned, include: *See-Saw* (1914), *Grand Chain* (1917), *A Marrying Man* (1918), *Larry Munro* (1920), *The Room* (1922), *The Back Seat*

(1923), *Bouquet* (1927), *Petruchio* (1929). *Larry Munro* was titled *The China Shop* (1926) in the American edition.

Besides her novels, Miss Stern has done free-lance journalism and reviewing, and has published numerous short stories. The latter have been collected periodically into: *Smoke Rings* (1923), *Jack A'Manory* (1927), and *The Slower Judas* (1929).

Grace Zaring Stone

G RACE ZARING STONE was born in New York City on January 9, 1896. She is the great-granddaughter of the Socialistic reformer, Robert Dale Owen, who was a member of Congress and Ambassador to Naples, and as a firm believer in spiritualism, wrote *Footprints on the Boundary of Another World* (1859).

She was educated in a convent in New York and in Paris, but at fifteen decided that she had had enough of school. Music was her serious study and was to be her career. She studied dancing, too, at the Duncan School in Paris. While still a young girl she went alone to Australia where she stayed with an aunt

GRACE ZARING STONE

for a year. She returned by way of New Guinea, the East Indies, and Malaya.

Grace Zaring Stone resumed her studies in France until the outbreak of the World War. She worked for six months in the British Red Cross and then her health demanded that she take a rest.

She is the wife of Lieutenant Commander Ellis S. Stone of the United States Navy. Since their marriage she has lived two years in the West Indies, a year and a half in Europe while her husband served with the European Squadron, and two years in China, where her husband was stationed during the civil war and revolution.

Her first book was *Letters to a Djinn* (1922), a comic travelogue novel in the form of letters.

Mrs. Stone published *The Heaven and Earth of Doña Elena* in 1929. It is the story of the Mother Superior in a Spanish convent who fights an inevitable love.

For her third novel, *The Bitter Tea of General Yen* (1930), she drew upon her experiences during the harrowing years in China. After eight months in Shanghai where there was continual fighting, Mrs. Stone had persuaded her husband, who commanded the flagship of the Yangtse river patrol, to take her to Hangchow for a rest and a change. The capital city mentioned in the book is in reality Hangchow, and at the time the Stones went there the province was ruled by just such an intelligent, unscrupulous, and benevolent gentleman as "General Yen." In *The Bitter Tea of General Yen,* the author introduces a cultivated New England girl who goes to China to marry a medical missionary, and suddenly finds herself in this setting. The book was published in England under the title, *Bitter Tea.*

Mrs. Stone is a tall slender woman, a witty conversationalist, vivacious and reckless in spirit, with dark brown curly hair and bright hazel eyes.

The Stones now live in Washington, D.C., with their young daughter, Eleanor. The books by Grace Zaring Stone are: *Letters to a Djinn* (1922), *The Heaven and Earth of Doña Elena* (1929), *The Bitter Tea of General Yen* (1930).

Lytton Strachey

LYTTON STRACHEY has been credited with establishing a fresh standard for biography in the English language. He is a master of irony who does not hesitate to make his characters seem human, sometimes "all too human."

Giles Lytton Strachey, coming of an intellectual and literary family, was born on March 1, 1880. He was the son of a British general, Sir Richard Strachey, the Indian administrator. His mother, the late Lady Jane Strachey, was herself an author and considered one of the brilliant women of her generation in England. St. Loe Strachey, late editor of the London *Spectator,* was his cousin. Of his five sisters and three brothers, three appear in *Who's Who*: J. P. Strachey (sister), principal of Newnham College, Cambridge; Philippa Strachey, secretary of the London Society for Women's Service; and Colonel Richard John Strachey.

Mr. Strachey was educated at Trinity College, Cambridge, where he wrote poems. After graduation he became an occasional contributor to the monthly and quarterly reviews. His first book was *Landmarks in French Literature* (1912), written for the Home University Library. With it he became a leading critic of French literature.

At first no publisher seemed to care about accepting his biographical work, *Eminent Victorians.* When it did appear in 1918, it was unexpectedly successful. The author produced vivid and caustic portraits of Cardinal Manning, Florence Nightingale, Dr. Arnold, and General Gordon. He removed the whitewash from these heroic figures and made them real.

In the preface to *Eminent Victorians* Mr. Strachey speaks his mind on the quality of English biography: "The art of biography seems to have fallen on evil times in England. . . With us, the most delicate and humane of all the branches of the art of writing has been relegated to the journeymen of letters; we do not reflect that it is perhaps as difficult to write a good life as to live one. Those two fat volumes, with which it is our custom to commemorate the dead—who does not know them, with their ill-

LYTTON STRACHEY

digested masses of material, their slipshod style, their tone of tedious panegyric, their lamentable lack of selection, of detachment, of design?"

He states his idea of the functions of the biographer: "To preserve, for instance, a becoming brevity—a brevity which excludes everything that is redundant and nothing that is significant—that, surely, is the first duty of the biographer. The second, no less surely, is to maintain his own freedom of spirit. It is not his business to be complimentary, it is his business to lay bare the facts of the case, as he understands them. That is what I have aimed at in this book—to lay bare the facts of some cases, as I understand them, dispassionately, impartially, and without ulterior intentions."

Queen Victoria (1921), which he took three years to write, established Mr. Strachey as a biographer of eminence. None of his historical facts were new but he presented them in a new way. He made the famous queen a real woman. Readers were drawn to the book by its glimpse of royalty at close range. In it the career of the queen falls into five periods—the Melbourne period, her married years, the years of seclusion and unpopularity which followed the death of the Prince Consort, her emergence under the influence of Disraeli, and finally her apotheosis in old age as the mother of her people and the symbol of their imperial greatness.

Then followed *Books and Character* (1922) and *Pope* (1926). In *Elizabeth and Essex* (1928), the author turned back to the golden age of England. The great queen, most accomplished woman of her age, at fifty-three admits to intimacy the handsome and ambitious Essex, then a youth of twenty. With less irony than in his previous biographies, Mr. Strachey pictures the two as figures of romance in this tragic history.

Mr. Strachey is a member of that brilliant group of intelligentsia living in the vicinity of Gordon Square, London, which includes J. M. Keynes, the economist; Clive Bell, the art critic; Vanessa Bell, the artist; Virginia Woolf, the novelist; and Leonard Woolf, the editor and publisher.

There is a scholarly and aristocratic quality about Mr. Strachey which everything about him bears out, from his tall thin figure and narrow face to his tapering fingers. In appearance he personifies the idea of the cloistered thinker. To the passer-by in the street he might appear merely as a tall, thin man with a great red beard. But on closer scrutiny the pallor of study grows visible and the large spectacles no longer conceal the brooding and the vision in his big eyes.

He works with intensity. "I have to bury myself in the country when I want to work," he remarks. "It isn't so much the noises of London that prevent concentration, but the constant social calls on one's time—the exits and the entrances."

Mr. Strachey's mind has been called romantic. Yet he has found his influences in the English eighteenth century and the great French masters whose style is sharp and clear have impinged on his strong modernity.

André Maurois says of the biographer that he "is no hero-worshipper. On the contrary, he is a hero-wrecker, an idolbreaker"; also that he is "a very deep psychologist." But he adds if this new type of biography were "written for the pleasure of destroying heroes, it would be a rather despicable art."

Essays and studies by Lytton Strachey are: *Landmarks in French Literature* (1912), *Books and Characters* (1922), and *Pope* (1926). His works of biography are: *Eminent Victorians* (1918), *Queen Victoria* (1921), and *Elizabeth and Essex* (1928).

T. S. Stribling

THOMAS SIGISMUND STRIBLING, the novelist, was born at Clifton, Tennessee, on March 4, 1881, the day Garfield was inaugurated. Most of his childhood summers were spen' in northern Alabama with a maiden aunt. Stribling still remembers walking thru cotton about twice as high as his head, reaching up after bolls about twice as big as his fist and pulling out the frosty down, section by section.

After graduation from the public schools of Clifton, Stribling went to the Normal School in Florence, Alabama, to train to become a teacher. But he proved a failure as a disciplinarian, being in his own words "just as curious to see what the kids were going to do next as they were." He resigned after his first term and took his LL.B. degree at the University of Alabama in 1904. His first literary enterprise was on the *Taylor-Trotwood Magazine* in Nashville: he

T. S. STRIBLING

was a sort of office boy. And his first literary products were "moral adventure stories for the Sunday school magazine." In these stories he showed how diligence and virtue were always rewarded, and how a boy who never smoked cigarettes would undoubtedly get to be a great banker or financier, and would lend money to the boy who did smoke cigarettes, and would foreclose on the cigarette smoker's farm eventually.

Stribling's first novel, *Birthright* (1921), was the story of a southern mulatto with a Harvard degree. *Fombombo* (1922) and *Red Sand* (1923) were novels of adventure laid in Venezuela. In *Teeftallow* (1926) and *Bright Metal* (1928) he wrote again of the Tennessee hill country, returning to the Venezuelan background, with which he is familiar, in *Strange Moon* (1929). *Clues of the Caribbees* (1929), short stories about Professor Poggioli, philosopher and psychologist, who takes a sabbatical year loafing and solving crimes among the islands of the Caribbean, was followed by *Backwater* (1930), a novel of the Arkansas country. Stribling is co-author of the play, *Rope,* a dramatization of Teeftallow, which was produced in New York in 1928.

In 1931 Stribling published *The Forge,* the first of three novels which he plans as a southern cycle. "It is so long," he writes, "that children should be started reading it early in order to complete it by the time they reach old age."

The Forge, set in the old South, concerns itself with the fortunes of an Alabama family during the Civil War period. The lives of these middle-class Vaidens are traced against an historical background which gives an added depth and significance to the details of the family life.

Mr. Stribling lives and works at his home in the Tennessee hills, close to the life which he is depicting in his cycle. He is a bachelor, lean, tanned, scholarly, diligent.

Ruth Suckow

R UTH SUCKOW is a small-town product. She was born in Hawarden, Iowa, on August 6, 1892, the daughter of a Congregational minister

RUTH SUCKOW

who moved from parish to parish. Before her majority she had acquired a thoro knowledge of the life of her region, from the smallest rural village to the city of Des Moines.

She was one of those scribbling children. When other girls were primping before the mirror, she was in her corner writing endlessly. She was educated at Grinnell College, at a dramatic school in Boston, and at the University of Denver, where she received her A.B. in 1917.

For a while Miss Suckow taught school at the University of Denver, but while she was in Colorado she met a woman who was an apiarist and who taught her to keep bees—and sell honey. Armed with this knowledge, she decided to run her own apiary in the summers and devote her winters to writing. For six years she was owner and manager of The Orchard Apiary at Earlville, Iowa, and conducted her business at a profit.

As a writer, Miss Suckow had one advantage at the start—she did not need to depend upon her writing for a living; she did not have to think of pleasing editors. Her early stories were bought by H. L. Mencken, who printed them in *Smart Set,* of which he was then editor. He announced his discovery to the literary world in no uncertain terms, and after that she progressed rapidly toward recognition.

Soon her stories were being accepted by several magazines and she gave up her bee farm to devote all her time to writing. Her first book was a novel, *Country People* (1924), which chronicles three generations of a sturdy German-American family thru the hardships of pioneer life in Iowa.

The Odyssey of a Nice Girl (1925), her second novel, is the record of a girl's life up to marriage. In 1926 Miss Suckow collected some of her short stories in *Iowa Interiors*. *The Bonney Family* (1928) covers twenty years in the life of a minister and his family in a small Iowa town. *Cora* (1929) presents the painful Americanization of an immigrant German family and follows the fortunes of a daughter. In *The Kramer Girls* (1930), the author sets forth the lives of three sisters who have a feeling of affection and tenderness for each other.

Along with her novel writing, Ruth Suckow has continued to produce short stories, a large number of which have appeared in the H. L. Mencken's *American Mercury*. In March 1929 she was married to Ferner Nuhn of Cedar Falls, Iowa. Her home now is in New York City, where she finds the best atmosphere in which to write.

The list of her novels is: *Country People* (1924), *The Odyssey of a Nice Girl* (1925), *The Bonney Family* (1928), *Cora* (1929), and *The Kramer Girls* (1930). She has also published a book of short stories, *Iowa Interiors* (1926).

Frank Swinnerton

BORN at Wood Green, a suburb of London, on August 12, 1884, Frank Arthur Swinnerton suffered a severe illness at the age of eight which forced him out of school, and left him in such delicate health that recurring breakdowns have been frequent since. His formal education was negligible. He read continually, however, and at fourteen, when he became a clerk in a London office, he was better educated than most youths of his age.

At eighteen, when he was working for the publishing house of J. M. Dent & Company, he finished writing a novel. This book, as well as the next two, the young author destroyed. Then, having joined the publishing firm of Chatto & Windus, he published *The Merry Heart* (1909). Word of its acceptance came to him on his twenty-fourth birthday. Thereafter followed *The Young Idea* (1910) and *The Casement* (1911). Arnold Bennett became interested in Swinnerton when he read the manuscript of *The Casement*.

The book that won general attention for Swinnerton was *George Gissing* (1912), a critical study. His study of *R. L. Stevenson* (1914) caused a stir among Stevensonians in England and America. Bennett says: "It is a destructive work. It is very bland and impartial, and not bereft of laudatory passages, but since its appearance Stevenson's reputation has not been the same."

During the World War Swinnerton was rejected by the army and subsequently was laid low by a long and serious illness which proved nearly fatal. During convalescence he wrote *The Chaste Wife* (1916). His outstanding work, *Nocturne* (1917), was produced in a period of domestic stress, illness,

FRANK SWINNERTON

anxiety, and loneliness. He wrote it hurriedly, in six weeks, spending some of that time aboard Arnold Bennett's yacht, which served as a setting for one of the scenes. *Nocturne* moved H. G. Wells to extraordinary enthusiasm. *September* (1919) was written in four months.

Meanwhile, Swinnerton continued his association with Chatto & Windus, usually working at the office from Tuesday morning to Thursday night of each week. The rest of his time he spent at home, writing fiction and carrying on other journalistic activities which included a monthly London Letter and critical papers. In spite of the difficulties under which he carried on this volume of work, Swinnerton protests that he is one of the laziest fellows in the world, and would rather lean out of the upstairs window and watch a cricket match on the common nearby than put pen to paper.

After nineteen years with Chatto & Windus, Swinnerton resigned recently, and gave up some of his journalistic work, to devote himself exclusively to writing. While he was still with the publishing firm, Arnold Bennett commended him as a literary adviser: "He tells authors what they ought to do and ought not to do. He is marvelously and terribly particular and fussy about the format of the books issued by the firm. Questions as to fonts of type, width of margins, disposition of title-pages, tint and texture of bindings really do interest him. And misprints—especially when he has read the proofs himself—give him neuralgia and even worse afflictions."

Swinnerton evidences deep satisfaction in his sixteenth century stone cottage in Surrey, with its flower-gardens in front, orchards on either side, and vegetable-gardens and a stretch of greensward in back. He is an enthusiastic gardener. The house is simply furnished with modern conveniences that do not destroy its mellowness. A path behind the house leads to a neat and orderly studio where Swinnerton produces his immaculate manuscripts in a clear, beautiful, letter-press handwriting. Whenever he completes a book he sits down to a hot plum pudding, no matter how warm the weather.

"His somewhat reddish, pointed beard," says Grant Overton, "the twinkle in his eyes, have caused it to be said that Swinnerton is French in appearance—with the instant addition that no one could be more English. But I question the 'English.' He is exceptionally easy to get acquainted with, which is not exactly a traditional English trait. His sense of humor is one capable of, and practising, frivolity; and the standard Englishman avoids being frivolous from a feeling of impropriety, or perhaps insecurity, and for reasons of dignity."

Bennett describes him as a young man of "medium height, medium looks, medium clothes, somewhat reddish hair, and lively eyes. If I had seen him in a motorbus I should never have said, 'A remarkable chap.'"

Swinnerton is known as a surpassingly good raconteur and an excellent mimic. Floyd Dell, who was one of the first Americans to recognize Swinnerton as a writer, says: "Swinnerton tells stories delightfully. These stories chiefly concern his literary friends; he makes one know them, their foibles and their gestures and their very intonations of voice, in these anecdotes. He has his enthusiasms and his prejudices, and he makes the most of them. His genial satire and good humored malice are a great part of his conversational charm." He has an infectious laugh.

In 1924 Swinnerton married Mary Dorothy Bennett. His first wife was Helen Dircks, a poet, whose slim volume, *Passenger*, was prefaced by himself.

The first book by Frank Swinnerton to be published in America was *The Happy Family* (1912). *The Merry Heart*, his first novel, did not appear in this country until 1929, and his second, *The Young Idea*, until 1930. Some of the other novels by him are: *On the Staircase* (1914), *Shops and Houses* (1918), *Coquette* (1921), *The Three Lovers* (1922), *Young Felix* (1923), *The Elder Sister* (1925), *Summer Storm* (1926), *A Brood of Ducklings* (1928), *Sketch of a Sinner* (1929). He says he was happiest when he wrote his first novel and *Young Felix*. A book of essays is entitled *Tokefield Papers* (1927).

Arthur Symons

BORN in Wales on February 28, 1865, of Cornish parents, Arthur Symons is known as the English jack of all literary trades—poet, critic, dramatist, biographer, translator, editor. He was educated privately, spending much of his time in France and Italy.

Symons began his literary career as the editor, in 1884-86, of four of Quaritch's *Shakespeare Quarto Facsimiles*. In 1886 he published his first book, *An Introduction to the Study of Browning*. His editorial work continued in 1888-89 with seven plays of the "Henry Irving" Shakespeare.

At an early age he was attracted to the French Symbolists and he became a leader of the cult in England. He published *The Symbolist Movement in Literature* in 1899, and spent his evenings, says Yeats, "at the Alhambra and the Empire, watching the ballet ... investigating the problem of symbolism in gesture." His own verse and prose were influenced, in both subject matter and style, by a close study of the French

ARTHUR SYMONS

writers, especially Baudelaire and Verlaine. Symons' early works were mainly in verse. *Days and Nights* (1889), a series of dramatic monologes, was his first book of poems. Then followed *Silhouettes* (1892), *London Nights* (1895), and *Poems* (1901).

Meanwhile, Symons became a member of the staff of the *Athenaeum* in 1891, and of the *Saturday Review* in 1894. In 1901 he married Rhoda Bowser. Frank Harris pictures Symons at twenty-six as a young man "some five feet nine or so in height, straight and slight, with rosy cheeks, thick, light-brown hair and good, bold features. When he uncovered, the breadth of forehead struck one; but ... the chief impression was one of health—delicate health."

Harris remarks about his outspokenness and enthusiasm. "What are we," Symons would say, "but seekers after love? That is our quest from the cradle to the grave. Love is our Divinity, Love our Holy Grail." Long a Casanova enthusiast, Symons discovered the two missing chapters of the last volume of his Life, and unearthed the letters of Henriette, who loved Casanova for more than fifty years.

Symons suffered for some time from recurrent spells of amnesia. In September 1908, when he was in Bologna, Italy, his nerves were nearly at a breaking point. "It was noticed by the people who kept the hotel," he says, "and by the woman who was with me that I was in a state of intense exasperation." After a violent scene at the hotel in which he refused to go back to England, he made his way to the town of Ferrara.

After a sleepless night in a hotel there, he wandered feverishly into the countryside, as if to escape something. Frightened by a terrible inner tension, he ran blindly, falling into ditches; he slept in haystacks. After a few days he was picked up by the Italian police and thrown into a black dungeon in Ferrara as a madman. Beaten and starved by the jailers, he was rescued from cruel treatment by the Italian ambassador, and put in a quiet sanitarium near Bologna where he grew better.

In November 1908 Symons was taken to England where he spent a year and a half of misery and horror in an asylum.

Despite the suspicion of insanity that was fastened upon him, he improved and wrote much that was later published. He was aware of all that happened during his unhappy confinement and was able to see it objectively. There was only a brief time, he says, when he lost his power to reason coherently.

In his *Confessions* (1930), Symons speaks of the unnecessary torture to which he was subjected in the name of medical treatment: "as far as my knowledge extends, no man, such as I am, a poet, a writer of prose, a dramatist, a traveler, who has lived with the certainty of being always free, has been so cruelly and so unjustly confined in a prison whose name I shall never mention—where I should never have been sent—the scars and stigmata of which, the scars of persecution and the stabs that my flesh has received, will remain, part and parcel of this suffering self of mine until the last wind extinguishes the last flickering candle."

In the spring of 1909 Symons fell ill with pneumonia, which the doctors said would kill him or restore his reason, if he survived. He gradually recovered, mentally and physically, aided by the generosity of John Quinn, millionaire American art and book collector. He pays glowing tribute to Quinn in his *Confessions*.

Symons' temporary madness was a part of his life of literary suggestion and imitation. He sees in himself certain traits which he discovered in the poets and authors he admired. He tells of choosing a hotel in Bologna where Byron had stayed, and how he relived Byron's life; of selecting another hotel which was "such as those Baudelaire was too often obliged to frequent." Like the men he admired he became mad. But all genius is abnormal, he argues.

He writes of the experience twenty years afterward, calmly and clearly but with bitterness—as one would describe a nightmare after waking. He paints himself as the typical neurasthenic artist. "I have always been highly strung," he says, "over-nervous, over-excitable, over-sensitive, and the least jar on my nerves always upsets me. I hate total darkness as much as men who are on the point of being hanged hate hell." He says that he was born "not only a Fiend hid in a Cloud but a serpent of sorts."

Harris says: "The terrible experience is written in his haggard mask, in the straggling grey hairs and the withdrawn eyes . . . high, bony forehead, the sharp ridge of Roman nose, the fleshless cheeks; the triangular wedge of thin face shocks one like the stringy turkey neck and the dreadful, claw-like fingers of the outstretched hand. A terrible face—ravaged like a battlefield; the eyes dark pools, mysterious, enigmatic; the lid hangs across the left eyeball like a broken curtain."

Following his recovery, Symons continued writing, doing mostly prose studies. He has been referred to as an "elderly dandy, still using the same fashions, the same postures, and the same intonations" that were popular in the nineties. He established his residence at Island Cottage, Wittersham, where his pastimes are hearing and playing music, and seeing dancing.

Among the books by Arthur Symons are: *The Symbolist Movement in Literature* (1899), *Studies in Prose and Verse* (1904), *Spiritual Adventures* (1905), *Studies in Seven Arts* (1906), *The Romantic Movement in English Poetry* (1909), *Colour Studies in Paris* (1918), *Charles Baudelaire* (1921), *Dramatis Personae* (1926), *A Study of Thomas Hardy* (1927), *Studies in Strange Souls* (1929), *Confessions* (1930), *From Toulouse-Lautrec to Rodin* (1930), *Translation of the Adventures of Giuseppe Pignata* (1930).

Genevieve Taggard

GENEVIEVE TAGGARD was born November 28, 1894, in Waitsburg, Washington, where her maternal grandfather had gone with his twelve children after the Civil War in search of mild winters and free land. When she was two years old her parents carried the search for mild winters a step further by going to Hawaii. The Taggards labored at Kalili, near Honolulu, building a large school and a very small mission.

GENEVIEVE TAGGARD

"By the time my parents arrived in Hawaii," says Miss Taggard, "the early missionaries had all the land, and nothing was left but the spiritual values, of which there was an inexhaustible supply. By the time we left eighteen years later, we were poorer than when we went down."

The Taggard children preferred Hawaii to Washington. "Twice we went back to Waitsburg for the tonic of a winter after the climate had bleached us sallow. Everything seemed ugly except the snow, and that was incredible at the age of eleven. The farm children ostracized us because we had lived with the heathen. It was even worse the second time when I was writing poetry and inclined to rebellion—at the age of fifteen. The Main Street loathing hit us all very hard, and we went back to our Kanakas unanimous for the other life."

In 1914 Miss Taggard left Hawaii for good to enter the University of California. In 1920 she crossed the contin-

ent and came to New York City, where she was the founder and one of the editors of *The Measure, A Journal of Verse,* and contributed to *The Masses.* Two years later she published her first book of poems, *For Eager Lovers.*

In 1929, after returning from a year's residence in southern France, Miss Taggard became instructor of English at Mt. Holyoke College.

"I've rolled like a marble," she comments, "from one little pocket on the map to another—Waitsburg, Washington, to Honolulu, Hawaii, to Berkeley, California, to New York City, to Hartford, Connecticut, to San Francisco, to New Preston, Connecticut, to New York City, to Antibes, France, to South Hadley, Massachusetts." But she knows her country and sees it more clearly for having observed it in the beginning from the outside, at arm's length, in her island seclusion. She is at home almost anywhere. Her poetry has taken root as firmly in the soil of New England as in Hawaiian earth. "In New England it was as if I had never stirred from the farmpatch of Connecticut. I know farm folks, I think, because all the Taggards and Arnolds were farmers, until my father and mother broke away. I know New Englanders, I think. Western Americans have a secret the East has never guessed. And the Hawaiians know how to smile; the Chinese, how to be indifferent; the Japanese, how to stand pain and play games. I could even live on Main Street now and not mind it."

It is interesting to observe that Miss Taggard's poetry, in its progress, has followed her from ocean to ocean across the continent. If her earlier work breathes the weather of the Pacific, it is true that her recent poems, with their metaphysical leanings, are washed in the more astringent waters of the Atlantic.

Miss Taggard is a moderately-sized person who gives the impression of being of noble proportions. "The chief beauty of her face," remarks a friend, "is its plasticity and the long thin mobile mouth; her coloring is of the medium brown variety, but warm."

In 1931 Miss Taggard was awarded a Guggenheim Memorial Foundation Fellowship for creative work abroad.

Her books of poems are: *For Eager Lovers* (1922), *Hawaiian Hilltop* (1924), *Words for the Chisel* (1926), *Travelling Standing Still* (1928). In 1930 she published *The Life and Mind of Emily Dickinson,* a poet's biography of her favorite poet. Miss Taggard has compiled and edited *May Days* (1925), an anthology of verse from *The Masses* and *The Liberator,* and also edited *Circumference, Varieties of Metaphysical Verse, John Donne to the Present* (1930). She contributes poetry and criticism to many periodicals.

Rabindranath Tagore

S IR RABINDRANATH TAGORE, Indian poet, humanist, patriot, educationalist, and artist, was born in Calcutta on May 6, 1861, the seventh and youngest son of Maharshi Debendranath Tagore, a scholarly, high-minded, and deeply religious Bengali. His grandfather was Prince Dwarkanath Tagore. He was educated privately, and from his earliest years was so sensitive to beauty and music that at the age of eight he began to write verse. When he was still quite young his father took him on a trip which lasted for some months to Armitsar and the Himalayas. His life was changed when he returned to Calcutta, and for the first time he was admitted into the society of his mother and his young sisters-in-law who were brought as brides to the family dwelling.

As children he and his brothers learned English painstakingly and reluctantly, and when he was seventeen he accompanied his second brother to England with the intention of studying law and going back to India as a barrister, which idea he soon abandoned. On his return to his native country he began to contribute verses to the *Bharati,* a journal edited by his oldest brother. In his *Reminiscences,* written when he was about fifty but dealing mostly with his young manhood (English translation 1917), he says that when he reviews his life he thinks that from the age of fifteen or sixteen to twenty-two or twenty-three it was one of utter intellectual disorderliness. Nevertheless, he had "attained a place

RABINDRANATH TAGORE

as the youngest of the literary men of the time; and some of his contemporaries chose to call him by the name of 'the Bengal Shelley.' "

When he was twenty-four he went to the country to take charge of his father's estates, and he wrote many of his poems, songs, and plays there. He and his brothers wrote, sang, and acted, with the desire to discuss and test everything. Tagore's religious credo was being evolved at this time; that truth is all-comprehensive, that there is no such thing as absolute isolation in existence. He summarizes his views in *Sadhana* (English translation 1914), a small book based on the teaching of the Upanishad and drawing from the sacred texts the authority for his own message, originally given as discourses to his students at Bolpur. In it he says that the price of the attainment of the freedom of consciousness is "to give one's self away."

His political views are parts of his ethical creed, and it has been his desire that the Nationalist movement in India should consider social reforms before political freedom. Altho a strong patriot with faith in and love for his fellow countrymen, he believes in universal friendship, and is convinced that the East and the West, instead of being irreconcilable, should be complementary.

In 1901 Tagore founded the famous school, Santiniketan, at Bolpur, Bengal, ninety miles from Calcutta. This was done with a two-fold purpose, as an advancement over the conventional methods of instrucion, and to further international fellowship. When he was thirteen he had run away from school in revolt against the traditional methods which were employed and which his school is attempting to correct.

In addition to the school, now called Visva Bhrati and practically an international college, there is an institute of rural reconstruction, whose object is to help the villages become "self-respectful, acquainted with the cultural traditions of their own country, and competent to make efficient use of modern resources in improvement of their physical, intellectual and economic conditions."

Tagore was awarded the Nobel Prize for Literature in 1913, and gave the entire amount, about $40,000, to his school. He also gives practically the whole of the income from his Bengali works. Quakers in England and America and a few individuals have given small donations, but for the most part Tagore himself supports the school.

He was knighted in 1915 and in 1919 resigned his knighthood as a protest against the methods adopted for the repression of disturbances in the Punjab. He later allowed his title to be used.

Tagore has traveled thru practically all of the Orient and Occident many times. His latest visit to the United States was in 1930 after he had been on an extended trip thru Russia, France and Germany. Art exhibitions of his paintings were held in the various countries. In 1927 or 1928 he turned to painting and drawing in colored inks as a new means of expression. There is no connection between his work as a poet and as an artist. He says: "When I start to write a poem I have a vision before my eyes, a mental representation. My verses attempt to communicate images seen or created. But when I draw I do not know what I am going to make. I take my pen and begin to draw and suddenly I see a head or a flower or a cloud."

Tagore was married in 1885, and has one son and one daughter. His daughter is married to Nagendra Gangulee, noted Professor of Agriculture and Rural Economics at the University of Calcutta.

Tagore is slight and frail, with white hair and long flowing beard and moustache, and very dark eyes. The robes of dark blue or black which he always wears emphasize his patriarchal appearance. His movements are slow and quiet, and his voice, tho thin, musical.

The following is a partial list of his translated works: *Gitanjali* (1913); *The Crescent Moon* (1913); *One Hundred Poems of Kabir* (1914); *Lectures on Personality* (1917); *Red Oleanders* (1925); *Fireflies* (1928); and *The Religion of Man* (1931), in which the author tells of his boyhood and the slow evolutions of his idea of God.

Booth Tarkington

NEWTON BOOTH TARKINGTON was born in Indianapolis, Indiana, on July 29, 1869. His father, a lawyer and Civil War soldier, lived to the age of ninety (died 1922). For a time in his childhood, the boy was affected by nervous disorders resembling St. Vitus attacks. But in his teens he improved and had a spirit of deviltry which he kept to middle age.

Tarkington was schooled at Phillips Exeter Academy, Purdue University, and finally Princeton, where he was a popular student and took active part in social life. He sang, drew, composed music, wrote, and occasionally acted in class plays. After graduation he returned to Indianapolis.

"I never wanted to be a writer," he says. "It was my ambition to be an illustrator. In 1895 I had a pen drawing accepted by *Life* and then I thought my start had come. But the same magazine rejected thirty-one subsequent drawings and I kept on writing and quit drawing."

For eight years he wrote constantly and earned exactly twenty-two dollars and fifty cents. Finally a magazine editor accepted one of his stories, *Cherry*, but it was shelved as a mistake in judgment and unearthed only after the publication of *Monsieur Beaucaire* in *McClure's Magazine* brought him recognition. His first book, however, was *The Gentleman from Indiana* (1899). *Monsieur Beaucaire* appeared in book form in 1900 and proved to be a popular romance. It was later produced on the stage and the screen. *Cherry* was published in book form in 1903.

"I had no real success," the author remarks, "until I struck Indiana subjects." But James Whitcomb Riley, whom he had known since he was eleven, did not approve of Tarkington's early books and wrote in his copy of *Monsieur Beaucaire*: "This is like Goldsmith." Tarkington had great respect for his elder's opinion and he recalls how pleased he was when Riley approved of *Penrod*. His first works were frankly imitative, patterned after eighteenth century authors, particularly the French school.

Tarkington was married in 1902 to Laurel Louisa Fletcher of Indianapolis. He served in the Indiana Legislature in 1902-03. "When I left Princeton I was a Socialist," he says, meaning he was a humanitarian with a passion for justice. In the legislature he was an insurgent Republican. "I used to introduce practically all the labor bills," he recalls. One time he drew up a bill that would put those afflicted with blindness under the care of the state and teach them to make brooms. When the Broom Makers' Union defeated his measure with the complaint that the competition would ruin their trade, he says he abandoned his idealism and became a conservative for life—in his writing as well.

The author began publishing his humorous stories of adolescence with *Penrod* (1914), and continued them with *Penrod and Sam* (1916) and *Seventeen* (1916). His tales of the modern industrial city include *The Turmoil* (1915), *The Magnificent Ambersons* (1918), *The Midlander* (1924), and *The Plutocrat* (1927). *The Magnificent Ambersons* and *The Midlander* were combined as *Growth* (1927).

Booth Tarkington has twice been awarded the Pulitzer Prize for literature: in 1919 with *The Magnificent Ambersons*, and in 1922 with *Alice Adams*. The latter is generally considered his most finished novel.

Altho he has written many successful

BOOTH TARKINGTON

plays, Tarkington does not consider playwriting his "real trade." His earlier dramas were done in collaboration, most of them with Harry Leon Wilson.

About 1917 Tarkington began to lose his eyesight, and he resorted to glasses of all sorts in an attempt to preserve his vision. But in August 1930 he became totally blind. After undergoing several operations on his eyes in January 1931, he regained partial sight. "At present the picture is a smudge," he says, "but I can distinguish color and form, and my doctors say that my vision will return."

For many years Tarkington has spent his winters in an old red brick house in Indianapolis, and his summers at Kennebunkport, Maine, in a home that is commonly referred to as "the house that Penrod built." The living room at Kennebunkport is two stories high, with tall windows on one side and a full-length balcony on the other. The author's study houses a collection of ship models.

It has been Tarkington's custom to write mornings and, when in Maine, spend the afternoons in a motorboat. In the evenings he frequently used to go to the movies (while he still had his vision)—mainly for the sake of the walk. The worse the picture, the more restful he seemed to find it. Other evenings he would play double-decked solitaire and then read until about one.

Vague ideas and suggestions for plot formed quantities of pencilled notes, which no one but the author could decipher. As long as his eyes held out, he wrote every day, including Sunday. His average output was about fourteen hundred words a day, in addition to revision of the previous day's work. He wrote at a drawing board, always in longhand. When the story was finished it would undergo further revision and then be typed. After that it was seldom touched.

Tarkington never reads his own books after he has returned the proof sheets. "I cannot open a new book of mine without pain," he says. "I am always sure there is something I should have said better than it appears."

He does not read novels, particularly the modern ones. He loves biography, preferably French. Four of his favorite authors are: Cherbuliez, Daudet, Balzac, and Dumas. Of the English he prefers Meredith, James, Hardy, Wells, and Bennett. He believes that Mark Twain, Henry James, and William Dean Howells have had the greatest influence upon modern literature.

Tarkington dislikes sex plays, or sex stories of any kind. He says the sex play "is Parisian in all its inferences, but the French do that sort of thing with far more finesse and artistry. Ours is too turgid, suggestive, obvious." He has always carefully edited his own works for suggestiveness.

He is without affectation. He is known as a good host, and a sympathetic listener. His second wife, whom he married in 1912, is Susannah Robinson of Dayton, Ohio. He has received several honorary degrees: A.M. Princeton, 1899; Litt.D. Princeton, 1918; Litt.D. De Pauw, 1923; Litt.D. Columbia, 1924.

Among the other novels by Booth Tarkington are: *The Two Vanrevels* (1903), *In the Arena* (1905), *The Conquest of Canaan* (1905), *The Beautiful Lady* (1905), *His Own People* (1907), *The Guest of Quesnay* (1908), *Beasley's Christmas Party* (1909), *Beauty and the Jacobin* (1911), *The Flirt* (1913), *Ramsey Milholland* (1919), *Gentle Julia* (1922), *The World Moves* (1928), *Young Mrs. Greeley* (1929), *Mirthful Haven* (1930).

Allen Tate

JOHN ORLEY ALLEN TATE was born on November 19, 1899, in Fairfax County, Virginia. He was brought up in Kentucky and Tennessee, receiving his early education in public and private schools in Louisville, Nashville, and Washington, D. C. Thereafter he attended Georgetown University, the University of Virginia, and Vanderbilt University where he was graduated in 1922. He tells Kentuckians he is a Tennesseean, and he tells Tennesseeans he is a Kentuckian.

After engaging for a time in freelance literary criticism, Tate became one of the founders of *The Fugitive,* a journal of poetry published at Nashville. The magazine grew out of the literary and philosophical discussions of a group of seven friends—Donald Davidson, James Marshall Frank, Sidney Mitron-Hirsch, Stanley Johnson, John Crowe Ransom, Alec B. Stevenson, and Allen Tate—who issued their first cooperative number in April 1922. The authors used pen-names.

ALLEN TATE

The foreword explained with some youthful insolence: "Official exception having been taken by the sovereign people to the mint julep, a literary phase known rather euphemistically as Southern Literature has expired, like any other stream whose source is stopped up. The demise was not untimely: among other advantages, *The Fugitive* is enabled to come to birth in Nashville, Tenn., under a star not entirely unsympathetic. *The Fugitive* flees from nothing faster than from the high-caste Brahmins of the Old South. Without raising the question of whether the blood in the veins of its editors runs red, they at any rate are not advertising it as blue; indeed, as to pedigree, they cheerfully invite the most unfavorable inference from the circumstances of their anonymity."

Among the poets who later joined the "Fugitives" were Robert Penn Warren, Merrill Moore, and Laura Riding. In December 1925 the magazine ceased publication. An anthology of verse from this group, entitled *Fugitives*, was published in 1928. Altho the "Fugitives" never defined what they fled from or issued a group manifesto, they tended to foster original expression, mature and intricate verse. They were together long enough to achieve a definite significance in the development of contemporary American poetry.

As poet and literary critic, Tate has contributed verse and essays on philosophical and literary subjects to journals in America, England, and France.

Tate published his first book of verse, entitled *Mr. Pope and Other Poems*, in 1928. Among the poems contained in the volume are: "Death of Little Boys" and "Ode to the Confederate Dead." His poetic method, he acknowledges, consists in playing the rôle of hawk, "gradually circling round the subject, threatening it and filling it with suspense, and finally accomplishing its demise without ever quite using the ultimate violence upon it."

Tate is the author of two biographies: *Stonewall Jackson, the Good Soldier* (1928); and *Jefferson Davis, His Rise and Fall* (1929).

In 1928 Tate went abroad to spend two years in France on a Guggenheim Fellowship. Since his return to America in 1930, he has devoted himself to the writing of a biography of Robert E. Lee to be added to the series that contains *Stonewall Jackson* and *Jefferson Davis*.

He has settled at Clarksville, Tennessee, in an old house which stands on a bluff dropping a sheer two hundred feet to the Cumberland River. The house, he says, was built one hundred years ago.

Tate is mild, blond, and youthful in appearance. The mildness, however, is somewhat deceptive. He has strong and definite convictions in matters literary and political; and he expresses these convictions with an incisive and sometimes demolishing wit.

The books by Allen Tate are: *Mr. Pope and Other Poems* (1928), *Stonewall Jackson* (1928), *Jefferson Davis* (1929).

Sara Teasdale

SARA TEASDALE was born in St. Louis, Missouri, on August 8, 1884, of an old American family. Her ancestors on both sides fought in the Revolution, and one ancestor, Major Simon Willard, was founder of Concord, Massachusetts.

The youngest of several children, and not strong, Sara Teasdale grew up as a shy, imaginative child. Once when asked when she first really enjoyed poetry she answered, "My mother, like everybody else's mother, has incredible tales of my reciting every jingle in 'Mother Goose' at an infinitesimal age. But for the poetry that everyone would agree is worthy of being called so, Christina Rossetti's 'Christmas Carol' was probably the first that I loved."

Her early education was received at home. Later she attended a private school for girls in St. Louis. Her first attempts in verse included translations from Heine and other German poets.

In 1903 she was graduated. She continued her writing and with several of her friends undertook the publication of a monthly magazine called *The Potter's Wheel*. This unique publication was limited to one copy each month, in manuscript, with original illustrations in photograph, black and white, and color.

SARA TEASDALE

Friends of the contributors showed much interest in the magazine, which continued for several years.

Thru all this time Miss Teasdale had been a systematic reader and one of her special treasures is a fat note-book in which, as a very little girl, she began to enter the titles of all the books she read.

She traveled widely in the United States and has spent several winters in California and the Southwest. Her first journey to Europe came in 1905. For some time she remained in southern Europe and the Near East, visiting Greece, Egypt, and the Holy Land. During this period she was writing verse and upon her return in 1907 she had her first recognition from the noted William Marion Reedy, who published her blank verse monolog, "Guenevere," in *Reedy's Mirror.* This same year her *Sonnets to Duse and Other Poems* was published.

By this time Sara Teasdale had entrée to the leading magazines and her poems were welcomed by *Harper's, Scribner's, The Century,* and others. With *Helen of Troy and Other Poems* (1911), a volume of love songs, the author entered

the element in which she has excelled.

The summer of 1912 the poet spent in Italy and Switzerland where she wrote *Rivers to the Sea* (1915). Every few years has found Miss Teasdale traveling in some new land. On December 19, 1914, she married Ernst B. Filsinger of St. Louis, from whom she was divorced in 1929.

A collection of Miss Teasdale's lyrics, *Love Songs* (1917), was awarded the Columbia University-Poetry Society of America prize for the best book of poems of the year. She received another prize from the Poetry Society of America in 1918. *Love Songs* went thru five printings in 1918. In 1917 she edited a collection of one hundred love lyrics written by American women, entitled *The Answering Voice.* The second edition in 1918 contained fifty additional poems.

Flame and Shadow (1920) contains the poem "Let It Be Forgotten," which many people consider her finest lyric. *Rainbow Gold* (1922) is an anthology of poems for boys and girls. In the summer of 1923 Miss Teasdale visited England. In 1924 she went to France where she wrote the "Pictures of Autumn" included in her next volume, *Dark of the Moon* (1926).

Many of Sara Teasdale's lyrics have been set to music, and her poems have been translated into several foreign tongues. In 1926 a book of her verse was translated into the Japanese by M. Mijutani, a poet of that race. Other Japanese translations have been made by the poets Yaso Saijiyou and Rikuso Watanabe.

In 1930 Miss Teasdale brought out, for young people, a selection of her verses, old and new, called *Stars Tonight.*

Books of poetry by Sara Teasdale include: *Sonnets to Duse* (1907); *Helen of Troy* (1911); *Rivers to the Sea* (1915); *Love Songs* (1917); *Flame and Shadow* (1920); *Dark of the Moon* (1926).

Frank Thiess

FRANK THIESS, German novelist, was born in 1890, in Livland, a district more Russian than German. As a youth he always considered himself a

Russian. He served his literary apprenticeship in four years of journalistic activity, broken only by a brief period of soldiering on the Eastern Front.

At thirty, determined to be an author, he prayed that he might live to the age of eighty so that he might accomplish the work he planned to do—a program for which even fifty years seemed none too long a period. Frail in constitution since boyhood, he then began systematically to subject himself to a rigorous *régime* of gymnastics with such good results that photographs of Frank Thiess soon began to embellish the pages of sporting as well as literary periodicals. For a time he was known better as an athlete than as a writer.

With a sound body, he felt ready to undertake his self-imposed fifty years' task. The transition from journalist to man of letters was no easy one. At the time he began to produce his mature work, expressionism was the current German literary vogue, and the intelligibility of his books found few admirers. So unfashionable was his work that the German publishers viewed his first offerings with unanimous disdain. He finally resorted to the expedient of presenting them in the guise of Italian translations in order to get them published at all. After his work became successful, Thiess says "the same publishers who returned my manuscripts unread ran after me like hungry chickens."

Some of his numerous short stories are being adopted as texts in German schools. Besides his early novels he has written *Frauenraub* (*Interlude*), a novel dealing with the concepts of sin and renunciation growing out of an illicit love affair. This psychological study is one of Thiess's major productions and has been his most successful novel in English.

For several years Thiess has been engaged in a serious project which has interested him since he first began to write. It is a tetralogy of modern youth; a series of books representing the havoc and changes wrought by the World War in the generation with which he has grown up; a composite picture of contemporary German society. Three of the four books have already appeared, in both German and English. In their logi-

FRANK THIESS

cal sequence they present successively the childhood, adolescence, youth, and maturity of the twentieth century generation.

The first of the four segments to be written was *Der Leibhaftige* (*The Devil's Shadow*), showing the semi-symbolical protagonist in his young manhood. In the second novel of the series, *Das Tor zur Welt* (*The Gateway to Life*), he is described at adolescence. The story of childhood, the third to appear, is *Abschied vom Paradies* (*Farewell to Paradise*). The concluding volume, entitled *Die Feuersäule* (*The Pillar of Fire*), is still unfinished.

Thiess has drawn, to some extent, from his own experiences in these four books. For example, his own boyhood school, Aschersleben, serves as the model for Annenstadt in *Das Tor zur Welt*. For the rest, he has relied upon his sensitive imagination, his powers of observation, his mystic sense, and his human sympathy. The total result is a vivid and terrible picture of a world destroyed and rebuilt—Germany in the period when she was left dazed, exhausted, and uncomprehending by the tragic blow of defeat after so many hopes and sacrifices.

The translations of novels by Frank

Thiess published in America are: *The Gateway to Life* (1927), *The Devil's Shadow* (1928), *Interlude* (1929), *Farewell to Paradise* (1929).

Sylvia Thompson

"**Y**OU wouldn't read half a novel, would you?" Sylvia Thompson asked Ellery Sedgwick, editor of the *Atlantic Monthly*, when she saw him in 1926.

Perhaps Mr. Sedgwick was touched by this suggestion of a charming credulity. He said, at all events, that he *would* read half a novel, and did, coming back on the boat. And in spite of the incompatibility of deck chairs and manuscripts, he was so impressed by the book that he immediately sent for the rest of it. And so *The Hounds of Spring* was published in 1926.

From his acquaintance with Sylvia Thompson, as well as from the book, Mr. Sedgwick says she is "a genuine composite of the youth who have grown up since the War."

She began *The Hounds of Spring*

SYLVIA THOMPSON

when she was at Somerville College, Oxford, in order, according to her own story, "to escape eating oranges and playing the phonograph"—quite literally, literature of escape!

Miss Thompson was born in Scotland in 1902, her home was in Lyndehurst, England, and she went to school at Cheltenham. Here, at the age of sixteen, she wrote her first novel, *Rough Crossing* (1921), which was followed by *A Lady in Green Gloves* (1924).

In July 1926, she married the man who shared with H. G. Wells in the dedication of *The Hounds of Spring*, Theodore Dunham Luling, an American artist who was studying at the Slade School in London and at Oxford. They have two children. She says her ambition is to have six children, innumerable friends, and no ugly furniture. She is fair, with delicate coloring and a classic profile.

Mrs. Luling is convinced that a broad, normal life, full of human contacts, is more likely to make a good novelist than "all the wastes of Bloomsbury, and all the chatter of Chelsea." Since her marriage, she has published *The Battle of the Horizons* (1928), *Chariot Wheels* (1929), *Portrait by Caroline* (1931).

Miss Thompson comments on her sixth novel: "*Portrait by Caroline* deals with young people of my own age as I know and as far as I understand them. It deals with a situation which twenty years ago could only have led to scandal or tragedy, but which today seems to find its place in the inconsequent and yet attractively rhythmic pattern of modern life." The story centers about the conventional triangle, in which a woman who seeks a new thrill in life deliberately falls in love with an old school friend of her husband's.

The novels by Sylvia Thompson are: *Rough Crossing* (1921); *A Lady in Green Gloves* (1924); *The Hounds of Spring* (1926); *The Battle of the Horizons* (1928); *Chariot Wheels* (1929); *Portrait by Caroline* (1931), which is titled *Winter Comedy* in England.

In 1931 Sylvia Thompson journeyed to a favorite haven of English authors, Majorca, the Spanish island in the Mediterranean, to work on a new book.

H. M. Tomlinson

THE East End of London, with its docks for ocean-going vessels, was the scene of Henry Major Tomlinson's birth in 1873. He was brought up among the wharves and "learned all about ships" when he was very young. Altho he "always wrote" he had no intention of becoming an author. The elder Tomlinson was a lover of music and taught his son an appreciation of Beethoven, Händel, and Mozart. He led the family in reading of the Bible every evening. Young Tomlinson learned the importance of Darwin and Huxley from him.

At the age of twelve Tomlinson began to earn his living and he spent his youth "making out bills of lading for the *Cutty Sark* and all those now 'legendary' clipper ships." He had an intense dislike for the exacting routine. As a complete change, he gave all the time he could "to the Guildhall Library, the British Museum and such odd pursuits as bug hunting (as mockers call it) and attempts at geological surveying." He used to browse among the shelves of the employees' library of the East and West India Company where he went to exchange books for his father.

"I was familiar with all Emerson's work before I was twenty," he says, "and I was not much older before I became acquainted with a greater teacher in Thoreau, whose *Walden* I carried constantly in my pocket. . . Whitman came much later, and was a wholly different influence. *Moby Dick* is in a class by itself." He considers Melville one of America's "most significant portents since the Declaration of Independence."

Tomlinson had been scribbling since he was a child "and judiciously burning it all, at intervals." But during his employ as shipping clerk, the London *Morning Leader* accepted some of the writing he did "on the side."

He relates: "When most energetic men are safely married and well on the road to fortune, I was only married and considering that I'd had enough of shipping. I had grown to hate commerce." He was thirty-one. One day he "had a row with the boss" and his job was ended. So the editor of the *Morning Leader* gave him full-time work.

H. M. TOMLINSON

When the tramp steamer which his brother-in-law captained made a wild voyage from London 2,000 miles up the Amazon River, he went along. He returned in about a year and his first book, *The Sea and the Jungle* (1912), was a story of that trip. He was on the staff of the *Daily News* when the World War broke out and was at the time "in Belfast waiting for civil war." He was a war correspondent in Belgium and France from August 1914, and official correspondent at General Headquarters of the British Armies in France, from 1915 to 1917. He says the war provided "no inspiration, only horror."

From 1917 to 1923 Tomlinson served as literary editor of the *Nation and Athenaeum* under Massingham, the Liberal editor. His second book, *Old Junk*, appeared in 1919. He left the *Nation* when Massingham did and then spent nine months in East India travelling for *Harper's*. The result was *Tidemarks* (1924). He says he learned in the East "that there are no longer any continents or hemispheres. The earth is one damn ball."

Gallions Reach (1927), returns to the scene of his youth, in the heart of the Royal Albert Docks in London. His comment is: "Every novel is autobiographical; it can't help it." *Gallions Reach* was awarded the Femina-Vie Heureuse Prize.

Among authors, Tomlinson likes Hardy, Dickens, the Brontës, Meredith, Chekhov, Mark Twain, and Sinclair Lewis. He does not care for Balzac. "There is no difference," he believes, "between prose and poetry—only between prose and verse." That is the clue to his own work. "I work so slowly," he says, "and therefore have so little time when I do read I prefer to read what I already know."

Tomlinson is concerned with thoughts rather than events. "That is because I think the mind is all that matters," he explains. "The world is what we think it is. If we can change our thoughts we can change the world. And that is our hope."

He has been described by an interviewer as "sandy, grizzled, baldish." He believes that he didn't design any of his books but that "they came merely with an unexpected change of wind." He remarks: "I never expected to write, you know. It's all so accidental—it just happened in spite of me."

H. M. Tomlinson's fiction writings include *Gallions Reach* (1927), *Illusion 1915* (1930), and *All Our Yesterdays* (1930), a story of the World War and its background. Among his other works are: *The Sea and the Jungle* (1912), *Old Junk* (1919), *London River* (1921), *Waiting for Daylight* (1922) *Tidemarks* (1924), *Under the Red Ensign* (1926), *Gifts of Fortune* (1926), *Between the Lines* (1930), and *Out of Soundings* (1931) which is illustrated by his son, H. Charles Tomlinson.

Henry Chester Tracy

HENRY CHESTER TRACY was born at Athens, Pennsylvania, on August 26, 1876. His parents were pioneers and built their own home in the woods. At the age of two he was taken to Marsovan, Turkey, where he spent his childhood. His father, Charles Chapin Tracy, taught in a seminary there which later became a college of which the elder Tracy was president as well as architect. The organization enjoyed conspicuous success until it passed into the hands of the Turks in 1914.

Meanwhile, when he was twelve years old, Tracy started back to the United States, traveling with his parents in Switzerland, Greece, Italy, England, and Scotland. Back in Pennsylvania, he attended private school for a year and then went to Oberlin, Ohio, where he studied at the Academy and later the College. His parents returned to Turkey.

Following his graduation from Oberlin College in 1902, Tracy taught there for two years and then went West. During his three years of adventure he was principal of a high school in Vernal, Utah, and homesteaded there; cut trails in Glacier Park for the Great Northern Railway; kept bees in Idaho. In November 1906 he married Miriam Lee of New York City.

In 1909 Tracy went to Berkeley, California, as an assistant in zoology at the University of California. After receiving an A.M. there in 1910, he moved to Hollywood where he was a biologist in the Hollywood High School and Junior College for thirteen years.

Tracy gave up teaching in 1923 to

GEOFFREY NORMAN

HENRY CHESTER TRACY

devote himself to writing and research. His first book was *An Island in Time* (1924), which reflects the serenity of the old Armenian culture he knew as a boy. In it the son of a rich Armenian merchant recounts the events of his life. *The Shadow Eros* (1927) is an allegorical tale.

The writer turned to the essay form with *Towards the Open* (1927), in which he sets down his reaction to the formalism of present-day education. " 'The Open' towards which we are moving," the author explains, "is a more natural and a freer life in which a man's responsibility is measured by his real relation to his social-natural environment (as shown by the allied sciences bearing on that relation), and his value is measured by his real capacity, discovered under treatment to which he is entitled as a man. This means not merely an objective towards which we move as towards some remote end, but a very present and significant attitude of mind."

Tracy taught English for a time in the William Institute of Berkeley, where he experimented with the language. After eighteen months of observation, during which he demonstrated to high school teachers how they might interest English classes in the sight and sound values of words, he determined to write something on English as a human experience. The result was *English as Experience* (1928), which Zona Gale calls "a manual of esthetic such as a normally alert reader would wish to use as a guide to active appreciation" of literary values.

American Naturists (1930) contains sketches of twenty-one leading Americans who have been eminent for spiritual, esthetic, literary, or scientific reasons. Among them are: Theodore Roosevelt, John James Audubon, John Burroughs, William Beebe, Mary Austin, Frank M. Chapman, and Walter Pritchard Eaton.

In 1930 Tracy got "in touch with education again" as a teacher at the Progressive School in Los Angeles. He lives with his wife and two sons in Los Angeles.

Zona Gale sums up her impression of the man: "In varied ways he has tasted life: he has found birds, as an emotion, and written of them. He has come to love and to know music, to paint startlingly well in water colors and oils. . . In a day when the sordid is modish, Mr. Tracy writes about beauty with imaginative delicacy and without a trace of sentimentality. He believes in beauty."

The books by Henry Chester Tracy are: *An Island in Time* (1924), *Towards the Open* (1927), *The Shadow Eros* (1927), *English as Experience* (1928), *American Naturists* (1930).

Arthur Train

ARTHUR TRAIN believes in facts. When he was assistant district attorney of New York County, he knew each case that he handled thoroly—inside and out. As a novelist, he studies thoroly the subject of which he proposes to write, and—whenever possible—draws from his own store of emotions and experiences.

The son of Charles Russell Train, attorney general for Massachusetts from 1873 to 1880 and prominent member of the Massachusetts bar, Arthur Train was born in Boston on September 6, 1875. After he was graduated from Harvard in 1896 he entered the legal profession and was admitted to both the Suffolk (Massachusetts) and New York bars. He served as assistant district attorney for New York County from 1901 to 1908 and again in 1914-15. In 1910 he was appointed special deputy attorney general for the state of New York to prosecute political offenders in Queens County. He was the prosecutor, in 1914, of the banker Henry Siegel at Geneseo, New York. He was a member of the firm of Perkins and Train from 1916 to 1923.

Train's first wife, Ethel Kissam whom he married in 1897, died in 1923. They had three daughters, all of whom are married. In 1926 the writer married Mrs. Helen C. Gerard of Newport, Rhode Island. They have one son.

Train's writings date back to 1905 with the publication of *McAllister and His Double*. For thirteen years, he added to his list of literary achievements, at the same time continuing his legal career.

ARTHUR TRAIN

of *Puritan's Progress.* "This keen scent deprives our pleasures of spontaneity. We are in the main good-natured and generous. There is plenty of raucous hilarity and back-slapping, but, while we have a sense of humor, we are not really gay. And gaiety, if we but recognize it, is the most comprehensive of virtues, for it signifies faith, hope, charity and courage."

Arthur Train's books include: *McAllister and His Double* (1905); *The Prisoner at the Bar* (1906); *True Stories of Crime* (1908); *Mortmain* (1909); *Courts, Criminals, and the Camorra* (1911); *The Goldfish* (1914); *Tutt and Mr. Tutt* (1920); *By Advice of Counsel* (1921); *Tut, Tut, Mr. Tutt!* (1923); *His Children's Children* (1923); *The Needle's Eye* (1924); *Page Mr. Tutt* (1926); *When Tutt Meets Tutt* (1927); *Illusion* (1929); *Paper Profits* (1930); *The Adventures of Ephraim Tutt, Attorney and Counsellor at Law* (1930); *Puritan's Progress* (1931).

The famous character of Mr. Tutt was created just before Mr. Train decided to give up the law, and devote himself to the writing of fiction.

Arthur Train's legal background peculiarly fitted him to such authentic legal stories as the Tutt books. But when he cannot resort to his own experiences for his facts, he goes out after them. In *Illusion*, for example, the central character is a young actor with a background of the circus "big top." Before writing it, Train studied the patois and characteristics of theatrical and circus folk, the personal histories of many of them, and their code. Then he wrote the book.

Paper Profits (1930), a novel of the 1929 Wall Street disaster, was written from his own knowledge of the stock market and the people concerned with it. In the fall of 1930 his Tutt stories were collected into one volume under the title, *The Adventures of Ephraim Tutt, Attorney and Counsellor at Law. Puritan's Progress* (1931) is an informal history of American manners and customs from the time of the Puritans to the present day.

"We Puritans have a keen scent for the fumes of Hell," declares the author

Miguel de Unamuno

MIGUEL DE UNAMUNO Y JUGO, Spanish man of letters, was born in Bilbao on September 29, 1864. He received his education in Madrid, where he gained a degree in philosophy and letters. In 1892 he became professor of Greek language and literature at Salamanca University, and in 1900 was made rector of the university.

"He was certainly the symbol of that university town," says Dr. Walter Starkie, who visited Unamuno in Salamanca. "In the evening we would go to the Plaza Mayor for coffee, and his table was surrounded by myriads of sightseers who had come from all parts of Europe to pay court to the 'mystic.' When surrounded by friends and admirers he would become jovial and fire off one paradox after another. He delighted in pulling the beards of solemn old professors and adopting with them the Socratic method of pretending to be ignorant. He would also discuss the plots of his novels in the intervals of making, with extraordinary agility, queer little paper birds.

"In Salamanca he was in his element for it was a small town steeped in Castilian tradition. In the mornings I have seen him walk ten miles without feeling the slightest touch of weariness. In appearance he resembles an oak tree, with an owl's head. Everything suggested strength, the strength and steadfastness of the Basque, a rugged simplicity not devoid of a certain crudeness. In his dress he shunned adornment; his coat was buttoned right up to the neck. His actions were brusque, and one felt that he was the personification of the hardy mountaineer, peaceful in his home-life, fond of the country and its simple pleasures. . .

"In his study there were no dimmed lights or mysterious corners—all was sunny, and from the broad balcony we could see in the distance the graceful tower of the Monterey, which might be a symbol of Salamanca's beauty. Unamuno has always been a voracious reader: books in every language were strewn about his room, and he seemed to be equally at home in the literature of England as in that of South America. In the evening he would walk slowly along the banks of the river Tormes, where once Lazarillo the Knave used to scamper."

Unamuno took part in a campaign against government corruption and abuses. He was so outspoken in his newspaper articles and his speeches that he was removed from the rectorship of the university where he had taught and written for thirty years. Primo de Rivera's *coup d'état* of 1923, which established a military dictatorship, aroused him to such vehement denunciation that in February 1924 he was exiled to one of the Canary Islands. The government, after being strongly criticized for the sentence, granted amnesty in July 1924, but he refused to return to Spain. He went to Paris to live—in the country which gave him a helping hand in his exile.

Valéry Larbaud, André Gide, Paul Souday, the Comtesse de Noailles, and other intellectuals welcomed him to Paris. Jean Cassou, writing in the *Mercure de France*, proclaimed him a modern Don Quixote who cries out in the wilderness. "Such is the agony of Miguel de Unamuno," he said, "a wrestler, wrestling with himself, with his people and against his people; a man of war, hostile, fratricide, tribune without a party, solitary exile, preaching in the desert, provocative, vain, pessimistic, paradoxical, torn to bits between life and death, invincible and yet always vanquished." In the cafés of Montparnasse he was surrounded by admirers, as he was in Salamanca.

The year 1928 found Unamuno back in his beloved native Basque country, settled in the little town of Hendaye on the borderland between France and Spain. From both countries people throng to see him, and altho past sixty-five, he pursues his literary work indefatigably. The inhabitants of the town all touch their hats to him and call him "Master." He can be found almost any day, seated in the town's leading café. "I cannot live without discussions or contradictions," he says, "and when nobody outside discusses with me or contradicts me, I invent someone within myself who does it."

Del Sentimiento Tragico de la Vida (1913) is generally regarded as the author's masterpiece. The translation, *The Tragic Sense of Life*, introduced him to American readers in 1921. A long mono-

MIGUEL DE UNAMUNO

log on death, the book exalts the human capacity for suffering in an age plunged in materialism, and preaches ceaselessly the gospel of the Middle Ages and Don Quixote. The latter figure has been raised by the author to a mystical plane and has become a new Don Quixote who rides out to overthrow the goddess of reason. In his *Vida de Don Quijote y Sancho* (1914), Unanumo sets forth his belief that all life is a pilgrimage to the tomb of Don Quixote.

In *L'Agonie du Christianisme*, Unamuno continues his sermon against modern materialism, exclaiming against those unhappy modern European countries where people think only of life: "Unhappy countries indeed, those wherein men do not continually think of death!" The central idea of this book is that man is not born with a soul, but has to make himself one before he dies. The writer sums up the essence of Christianity in the poem, *El Cristo de Velasquez* (1920), a long series of mystic meditations.

Unamuno's novels are philosophic in quality, with a minimum amount of physical detail and with maximum devotion to the interaction of passions and ideas. There is irony and even humor in Unamuno's writings, but no frivolity. He says: "The glory of Spain is principally due to the fact that it cannot be either frivolous or jovial." He is full of passionate egotism and loves to talk about his own work. He has a horror of pedants.

Only a few of Miguel de Unamuno's numerous works have been published in America. They include: *The Tragic Sense of Life* (1921), *Essays and Soliloquies* (1925), *The Life of Don Quixote and Sancho* (1927), *The Agony of Christianity* (1928), *Mist* (1928), *Three Exemplary Novels and a Prologue* (1930). *The Agony of Christianity* (1928) was translated into English from the French version by Jean Cassou, because the book had not been published in Spain.

Sigrid Undset

SIGRID UNDSET, the Norwegian novelist who won the Nobel Prize for Literature in 1928, was born on May 20,

1882, in Kallundborg, Denmark. Her father was Ingvald Undset, a prominent Norwegian archaeologist and author of *The Beginning of the Iron Era* and *From Akershus to Acropolis*. His research work took him all over Europe, and in his absence his wife, a Dane, remained with her parents in Kallundborg.

When a child, Sigrid Undset was taken to Oslo (then Christiania) where her father taught in the University and she went to private day school. She recalls in a series of articles in the Norwegian newspaper, *Aftenposten*, that her childhood home was in a dull and dusty street. She spent her summer holidays in the country, or with her mother's family. She liked to stay at Kallundborg where she listened for hours to an aunt who told strange fairy tales. From early childhood she loved stories, and when she was old enough she became a diligent reader.

As the eldest of three girls, Fröken Undset took the place of a son in the household at an early age and assisted her father in his research work. Her

SIGRID UNDSET

knowledge of the medieval ages dates back to the time when, as her father's assistant, she pored over old books of scientific and popular works of history, archaeology, and religion, and developed a profound taste for sagas and ancient traditions of the Viking period.

Sigrid Undset's father died when she was eleven. Following graduation from the Christiania Commercial College at sixteen, she was thrown upon her own resources and got a job in the office of a lawyer who had been her father's friend. For ten years she supported herself by doing secretarial work, while she dreamed of a literary career. She spent her evenings and holidays writing.

Her first novel, *Fru Marta Oulie,* the story of an unhappy marriage, was written in secret. The first inkling her employer had that she had been writing came when he arrived at his office one morning in 1907 to find her book on his desk. *Fru Marta Oulie,* written in diary form, was received with mild approval. Her second book, a bitter one, was published in 1908 with the ironical title *Den Lykkelige Alder* (The Happy Age). She made her first attempt at recreating the past in *Viga Ljot* and *Vigdis* (1909), a saga from the Viking time. A small collection of poems appeared in 1910.

Fröken Undset achieved her first popular success with the publication of *Jenny* (1911). The novel created a sensation, and went thru many editions. A study in feminine psychology, it follows the same general plot as her other novels of modern life, which are realistic descriptions of middle-class homes and families in Oslo, such as her own. Her heroines are usually young girls who grow up in unromantic atmosphere, have to work at dull routine to help support the family, find little expression for their love of beauty or learning, meet young men who fall below the ideal of their dreams, suffer disillusion in marriage, and are enveloped in tragedy.

Her volumes of novelettes and stories published between 1912 and 1917 treat the same class of people as her novels. *Poor Souls* (1912) contains her most famous short story, "Simonsen," the tale of a good-for-nothing, lazy old fellow who is nevertheless gentle and bright.

The novel *Spring* (1914) surprised her readers by ending happily. Shortly after her success with *Jenny,* Sigrid Undset married the well-known Norwegian painter, Anders Avarstad.

After ten years of writing realistic fiction about contemporary life, Fröken Undset rewrote, in Norwegian, Malory's *Morte d'Arthur.* This seemed to bring back all her passion for the medieval scene, and in the next ten years she devoted herself entirely to narratives of the Middle Ages. She was the first writer to apply the technique of the modern psychological and realistic novel to a vanished epoch.

Following considerable research into the history, religious and social conditions, life, work, and manners of the Norwegian people in the fourteenth century, she wrote a medieval trilogy, *Kristin Lavransdatter* (Kristin, the daughter of Lavrans): *Kransen* (1920), *Husfrue* (1921), and *Korset* (1922). It is the story of Kristin from birth to death. The Norwegian edition of these three bulky, rather expensive volumes, sold about one hundred and twenty thousand copies. Then came Swedish, Finnish, Dutch, American, English, and German editions.

Kristin Lavransdatter has been called a glorification of the Catholic Church of medieval times. The chapter relating Kristin's pilgrimage to the shrine of St. Olav, in the choir of the Nidaros Cathedral, gives a vivid impression of what Catholic faith meant to people of the fourteenth century. Sigrid Undset's admiration for the majesty and beauty of that church is unbounded. She was received into the Catholic Church in 1924 at the Chapel of Hammer.

Her next historical novel was a tetralogy, *Olaf Audunssön I Hestviken,* published between 1925 and 1930. It is the story of Olaf Audunssön and Ingunn, his wife, trying to live together in spite of the black cloud caused by the fact that Olaf murdered her former lover. The plots of *Kristin Lavransdatter* and *Olaf Audunssön* are linked by a curious similarity. In the first novel a splendid woman asserts her right to love a weak and essentially unworthy man. In the latter, the situation is much the same with the sexes reversed. Upon the completion of the four books of *Olaf Audunssön,* the author turned back to the modern novel for her next works. *Gymnadenia* (1930) was followed by a two-volume sequel, *Den Braendende Busk* (1931).

Since 1925, when her marriage was amicably annulled, Sigrid Undset has lived with her four children at Lillehammer, a small Norwegian artistic resort on a lake some distance from the capital. Their house dates back to the year 1000, and it has been restored and furnished with genuine old Norse pieces. The only modern things in it are a piano and the plumbing. Fröken Undset has a remarkable collection of antique laces from the convents of Belgium and France. She wears the national costume of the Viking matron of the Middle Ages, and puts on modern clothes only for trips to the city. Her house is near the medieval ruins of the Hammer Cathedral, famous as a tourist shrine, which she helped reconstruct.

Sigrid Undset is the third woman to receive the Nobel prize for literature. "I have not the time to receive you," she told reporters following the award in 1928. "I am studying Scholastic Philosophy." She undertook a study of St. Thomas when such a thing was unheard of in her country. She performed another independent act when she expressed her "old fashioned" ideas about woman's place in the home in *From a Woman's Point of View* (1919), a collection of articles.

The translations of Sigrid Undset's works published in America include *Jenny* (1921) and the two historical novels. The trilogy of *Kristin Lavransdatter* appeared as follows: *The Bridal Wreath* (1923), *The Mistress of Husaby* (1925), and *The Cross* (1927). The three appeared in one volume in 1929. The tetralogy of *Olaf Audunssön,* under the title of *The Master of Hestviken,* was published as follows: *The Axe* (1928), *The Snake Pit* (1929), *In the Wilderness* (1929), and *The Son Avenger* (1930).

Louis Untermeyer

LOUIS UNTERMEYER, American poet and anthologist, has written the following objective account of himself:

Louis Untermeyer was born October 1, 1885, in New York City, where he lived, except for brief intervals, until 1923. His schooling was fitful and erratic; he liked to boast that he was the least educated writer in America. He attended the De Witt Clinton High School, but his failure to comprehend the essentials of geometry prevented him from graduating, and the halls of colleges were unknown to him until he became an occasional lecturer.

In youth his one ambition was to be a composer. At sixteen he appeared as a semi-professional pianist; at seventeen he entered his father's jewelry manufacturing establishment. For almost twenty years he commuted to Newark, New Jersey, being advanced from designer to factory manager and vice-president. In 1923 he retired and, after two years of study abroad, returned to America to devote himself entirely to literature. . . .

His work is divided into four kinds: his poetry, his parodies, his translations, and his critical prose. His initial volume

LOUIS UNTERMEYER

of verse, *First Love* (1911), was a sequence of some seventy lyrics in which the influence of Heine and Housman were not only obvious but crippling. . . .

It was with *Challenger* (1914), reissued in a slightly revised edition in 1920, that the author first spoke in his own idiom. . . *Challenger* was succeeded by *These Times* (1917). . . *The New Adam* (1920) is . . . "a frank expression of the modern poet's conception of love. . ."

Roast Leviathan (1923) was considered by many the ripest and most varied of his volumes, especially by the English critics. . . Ungratefully enough, the author himself deprecates the transatlantic encomiums, preferring *Burning Bush* (1928) to any of his volumes. Physically the smallest of his books, it is poetically the fullest; the key is quieter, but the tone is surer. . . The same year saw the publication of *Moses* (1928), miscalled a novel. Actually the work is a cross between an historical reconstruction and a phantasia. . .

New Songs for New Voices (1928), in collaboration with David and Clara Mannes, is a collection of modern poems set for the first time to modern music, in which the editor made his public *début* as a not too serious composer. *Blue Rhine—Black Forest* (1930) is a day- and guide-book, where humor, unknown legends, and explicit directions wind themselves thru western Germany.

Four volumes of his critical satires appeared: *The Younger Quire* (1911), a tiny burlesque of an anthology (*The Younger Choir*) issued anonymously, of which only one hundred copies were printed; "*—And Other Poets*" (1917); *Including Horace* (1919), paraphrases of the Latin bard as various classic and modern poets might have rendered him; and *Heavens* (1922) in which the poet after gently mocking his contemporaries, bade farewell to the field of parody. The four were combined, with several new satires, in *Collected Parodies* (1926), which the author, with great self-restraint, refrained from calling "Parodies Lost."

As translator, he has published several volumes, of which the best known are *Poems of Heinrich Heine* (1917, revised edition 1923) and *The Fat of the Cat* (1925), freely paraphrased from the Swiss stories of Gottfried Keller.

A book of essays, *The New Era in American Poetry* (1919), was amplified and made into a more balanced and comprehensive set of twenty subdivided chapters under the title *American Poetry Since 1900* (1923). The two critical anthologies, *Modern American Poetry* and *Modern British Poetry,* have been revised and enlarged several times since their original publication in 1919 and 1920 and are used as textbooks in the universities.

A collection of modern poems for young people was published in two editions: *This Singing World* (1923) and *This Singing World for Younger Children* (1926). *Yesterday and Today* (1927), a "comparative anthology," contrasted the poetry of the present with that of the immediate past. These volumes were adopted in high schools and junior colleges, as was *The Forms of Poetry* (1926), a "pocket-dictionary of verse."

Besides admitting himself the author of these too many volumes, Untermeyer was also one of the editors of *The Seven Arts* and *Paper Books,* itinerant lecturer at various universities, a fairly regular contributor to *The Saturday Review of Literature.* In 1928, he achieved his lifelong desire, acquiring a farm, a trout-stream and half a mountain of sugar-maples in the Adirondacks.

———

Since writing the above sketch of himself, which appeared in the fourth revised version of *Modern American Poetry* (1930), Untermeyer has completed a new verse anthology, *Early American Poetry,* intended as a companion volume to *Modern American Poetry.* The book will appear in the fall of 1931.

Untermeyer's wife, whom he married in 1907, is Jean Starr Untermeyer. She is the author of several books of poetry, including *Growing Pains* (1918), *Dreams Out of Darkness* (1921), *Steep Ascent* (1927). Their home is "Stony Water," Elizabethtown, Adirondack Mountains.

Paul Valéry

PAUL VALÉRY, French poet and philosopher, was born in 1871 in the small provincial town of Cette on the Mediterranean, at the foot of Mont St. Clair. As a child he used to sit on the quays of the port or wander beside the canals, dreaming of becoming a sailor. As a young man, however, he planned to be an engineer. It was by accident, he says, that he became a poet.

When he was eighteen, Valéry left the provincial university of Montpellier to take his twelve months of military training, but returned to the school during the year for the gala celebration of the university's six hundredth anniversary. In a moment when his habitual restraint was lifted, while he was taking part in the fun-making at a café, he met the youthful poet, Pierre Louÿs, who was two years his senior. When Valéry expressed some of his ideas to his new friend, Louÿs told him he ought to write. Louÿs encouraged his protégé by sending him poem after poem and daring him to do something better. When he started a literary review, *La Conque*, in 1889, he published some of the youth's offerings.

After he received his university degree, Valéry went to Paris at the age of twenty. His passive response to the urgings of Louÿs now turned into eagerness: "Not since the Renaissance has one seen so great a thirst for knowledge and understanding, so large a number of experiments, so disinterested a desire to raise the level of accomplishment." In his room on the rue Gay-Lussac he set up a blackboard where he worked out geometrical problems and wrote occasional poems. He produced his verses with great pains, concentrating on every word, every syllable, every sound. He used the method for which he is now famous—searching out exhaustively his thoughts before daring to express them on paper, and then torturing them into complete expression.

Valéry fell under the influence of the Symbolists and became a member of the literary group that gathered about Mallarmé. He says: "We were brought up on music, and our literary heads dreamed only of deriving from language almost

PAUL VALÉRY

the same effects which purely sonorous periods produced upon our nervous system." But he felt that there were certain harmonies of the mind which he must discover. The first result of his departure from Symbolism was in his book, *Introduction à la Méthode de Leonardo da Vinci* (1895). In Leonardo he saw his ideal: a genius who was "a complete system in himself." *La Soirée avec Monsieur Teste* embodies the philosophic conceptions which the great painter had awakened in him.

Following the death of his first great friends in Paris, Valéry lived in partial retirement for twenty years, publishing only one poem. Interminably he wrote, studied, and meditated. He sought a fundamental attitude underlying all operations of the mind, and tried to develop his own mind as an instrument of precision. All his values became transformed.

When, at the insistence of André Gide and Louÿs, he began to write for publication again, literature no longer existed for him as an end of itself but as a form of mental exercise to be valued because it was difficult. His primary object was a defense of the conscious mind. He reappeared in print with *La Jeune Parque* (1917), a collection of philosophical poems. Then followed rapidly: *Odes* (1920), *L'Album de Vers Anciens* (1920), *Charmes* (1922), *Fragments du*

Narcisse (1922), *Poésies* (1923), and *Variété* (1924). The last is a group of philosophical essays, among them "La Crise de l'Esprit," a study of the post-war European mind. The book had a large circulation; a translation, by Malcolm Cowley, was published here in 1927—*Variety*.

In 1921 Valéry was voted the fore-most poet in France by his contemporaries in a referendum conducted by the review, *La Connaissance*. The choice caused some sensation, for he was un-known to the large public and remained so, in great part, until his election to the French Academy in 1925. He was given the place left by the death of Anatole France.

Ever since he came to Paris as a youth, Valéry has continued his active interest in economics and mathematics, two studies which interest him as much as poetry. He has applied the economic principle of supply and demand to the marketing of his books, making most of his writings inaccessible. He has had only two popular editions; the rest have been limited to a thousand copies or less. By this method he aims to dictate what company his works shall keep. He is admittedly an intellectual snob. His editions, consequently, are among the costliest in Europe, and his poetry is profitable to him. As for his essays, they are written only on commission from magazine editors, usually with the subject assigned.

Valéry is a business man rather than a bohemian. He is aware of modern science and modern method, and both writes and analyzes his poetry according to these standards. He does not appreciate romance. He gets no thrill from adventure. He will allow no poetic ecstasy to betray his better judgment. Nothing can shake his calmness.

He looks more like a scientist than a poet. William Leon Smyser describes him thus: "Somehow Valéry has escaped the usual earmarks of poetry. His long, sallow face, hollow cheeks and broad jaw are those of an energetic personality, not given to dreaming. The eyes are lively and the mustache bristles. The solid, practical frame has been built for activity... Valéry's eyes are dark and shadowed, but their glance pierces. His lips are sensitive, but they are usually set in a firm line." His hair is grey. When he speaks his voice warms and expands but there is nothing of poetic frenzy about it. He speaks analytically.

His whole interest, like that of a scientist, lies in methods, problems, puzzles, and techniques. His excuse for interest in any social, scientific, or literary phenomena is in the solution of a problem. "The completed work of art," he says, "I consider as without interest. The only thing that arouses my curiosity is its actual creation." He is interested in poetry only as an experiment, as an opportunity to master an idea.

When he has developed an idea in his mind, Valéry takes off his coat and pounds it out on the typewriter. Then he re-types it several times, until he has expressed every nuance of the idea, and the essay or poem has become unintelligible to the average person. Because he works over a theme in this manner until few readers can understand him, he has been accused of writing "sound poetry" that conveys no meaning. He does not argue the matter; he can see little value in disputes. To him, the only occupation worth effort is creation.

Social life appeals to Valéry only when it offers some unusual opportunity, such as when he explained the work of the French physicist Perrin at a dinner celebrating the Nobel award; or when, on becoming a member of the French Academy, he followed the custom of delivering an address about his predecessor, but created a scandal by insidiously neglecting to refer to his subject, Anatole France, by name.

"Poets have lived their best days," Valéry says. "Soon, when every one has his airplane attached beneath his window and can fly in a few hours to Timbuktu, or to the Norwegian fjords, what will be the use of poems and novels? We will need them no longer. Literature, which is the most artificial form of art, must disappear, for modern taste demands distractions that give a sharper impression, something more vivid, something more animated."

Valéry's political dream is a Europe brought into harmony by intellectuals: "Public opinion is at bottom built by the few. Without intervening or directing, the intellectuals could create opinion, if only they would study and interpret events dispassionately and report."

Carl Van Doren

CARL VAN DOREN, editor, author, critic, was born in Hope, Illinois, on September 10, 1885, the son of a country doctor and the oldest of five boys. When he was quite small, the family moved to a farm near the village, and the boy attended country school until the age of fifteen.

After leaving the district school he went to Urbana, where he completed the high school course in three years. His interest then was centered in football, which he played enthusiastically, but he read poetry secretly. He was valedictorian of his high school class, and entered the University of Illinois with a four-year scholarship. He played on the freshman football team, but suddenly lost interest in it and in athletics in general and turned his attention to reading and study.

During his college course Mr. Van Doren won preliminary, final, and special honors. In his junior and senior years he edited the literary monthly, *The Illi-*

CARL VAN DOREN

nois Magazine, and was class poet and president of the honorary senior society. He received his A. B. in 1907, and remained at the University of Illinois for a year as a graduate student and as Assistant in Rhetoric. During the year he spent a good deal of his time selecting books for the library of the Department of English, which had received a large appropriation.

Mr. Van Doren was at Columbia University in 1908-1909 with a scholarship, and the following year with a University Fellowship. He then went to Europe with Stuart P. Sherman, whom he had known at the University of Illinois. They were together for three months, and Mr. Van Doren stayed abroad for several months after Sherman's return to America. He was at work on a biography of Peacock undertaken for his dissertation, which was published under the title, *The Life of Thomas Love Peacock* (1911). He received his Ph. D. in 1911.

Mr. Van Doren was offered an appointment in the English Department at Columbia, and taught there as an instructor from 1911 to 1914, and as assistant professor from 1914 to 1916. He then became headmaster of The Brearley School in New York City, remaining there until 1919 when he resigned with the intention of doing free lance writing. He became literary editor of *The Nation* at the invitation of the editor, Oswald Garrison Villard, and acted in this capacity until 1922. He is still a contributing editor of this magazine. From 1922 until 1925 he was literary editor of *The Century Magazine.* Resigning from this position, he determined to confine his work to his own writing, which he did for a year and a half.

In 1926 Zona Gale, Joseph Wood Krutch, Glenn Frank, and Carl Van Doren founded the Literary Guild of America, with Mr. Van Doren as editor in-chief. This work approaches more nearly his ideals in acquainting a large number of people with well selected literature. He retained a partial connection with Columbia, as lecturer in American literature, from 1916 to 1930.

Most of his publications have been critical in nature. He was managing editor of *The Cambridge History of American Literature* (1917-21). His own books include: *The American Novel* (1921); *Contemporary American Novelists* (1922); *Many Minds* (1924); *James Branch Cabell* (1925); *American and British Literature Since 1890* (with Mark Van Doren, 1925); *Swift*, a biographical study with an interpretation of the man's character and temperament, 1930). He has also written short stories in *Other Provinces* (1925), and a novel, *The Ninth Wave* (1926).

Mr. Van Doren and Miss Irita Bradford were married in 1912, and have three children. Mrs. Van Doren is literary editor of *Books*, the literary section of the Sunday *New York Herald Tribune*.

Mr. Van Doren has a penthouse apartment in New York City. From the windows of his spacious office in the Literary Guild offices, a view of a great deal of the western side of Manhattan can be obtained.

Mr. Van Doren is over six feet tall and rather large framed. He gives an appearance of ruggedness, which is carried out by his statement that in his twenty-two years in New York he has not been confined to his house by illness for one whole day. His voice is full and pleasant, his expression firm but sympathetic. Dark brown eyes contrast vividly with his short-clipped, steel-grey hair.

MARK VAN DOREN

Mark Van Doren

MARK VAN DOREN, younger brother of Carl Van Doren and himself an author and poet of distinction, was born on a farm near the village of Hope, Illinois, on June 13, 1894. He lived there for six years before moving to Urbana where he remained until his twenty-first year. He received his A. B. from the University of Illinois, in Urana, in 1914, and was elected to the honorary scholistic society, Phi Beta Kappa. The following year he took graduate work in English literature, and received an A. M. in 1915.

Mr. Van Doren went to Columbia University directly after leaving the University of Illinois, but his studies there were interrupted by the World War. He served for two years in the Infantry. On his return to Columbia in 1918 he was given a William Byard Cutting Fellowship and he and Joseph Wood Krutch, a classmate and close friend who received the same traveling fellowship, went abroad for a year. They traveled thru England and France, spending most of the time in London and Paris

Mr. Van Doren received his Ph. D. from Columbia in 1920, and began to teach in the English Department immediately. He is an Assistant Professor at Columbia, and also gives lectures at the New School for Social Research. In 1924 he succeeded his brother as literary editor of *The Nation*, remaining on the staff until 1928.

Henry David Thoreau—A Critical Study (1916) was Mr. Van Doren's first published book. It was followed by *John Dryden* (1920). Since then he has been interested mainly in poetry, and has published four volumes of poetry: *Spring Thunder, and Other Poems* (1924); *7 p.m., and Other Poems* (1926); *Now the Sky, and Other Poems* (1928); and *Jonathan Gentry*, Mr. Van Doren's first long narrative poem (1931). A collection of short poems will be published in the fall of 1931 under the title, *The Perilous Path*.

Mr. Van Doren has edited a number of works, for the most part early Americana such as *Correspondence of Aaron Burr and His Daughter Theodosia* (1929). His most impressive *Anthology of World Poetry* (1929) is "an honest attempt to select the best of the available English translations from some fifteen ancient and modern languages and arrange them in chronological sequence from the Thirty-fifth Century B. C. to the Twentieth Century A. D. Over four hundred poets are represented by more than thirteen hundred poems."

He is joint-author with Carl Van Doren of *American and British Literature since 1890* (1925).

Mr. Van Doren and Miss Dorothy Graffe were married in 1922. They have two sons, Charles Lincoln and John. Mrs. Van Doren is author of three novels, has edited several books, and has been associate editor of *The Nation* since 1926.

The Van Dorens have an attractive duplex apartment in New York City, where they live during the winter, and a farm near Cornwall, in the mountains of northwestern Connecticut, where the summer months are spent. Mr. Van Doren is of medium height, with dark hair, strikingly dark eyes, a full mouth and an attractive smile. He is an interesting conversationalist, with the ability to draw out his companion more than the latter realizes. His personality, sense of humor, and the saneness of his ideas make his college classes and lecture courses popular.

Hendrik Willem Van Loon

HENDRIK WILLEM VAN LOON was born on January 14, 1882, in Rotterdam, Holland, just around the corner from the birthplace of Erasmus. "I was the son of a rich father," he relates, "who lived in a realm a million miles away from that of his child and never made the slightest effort to construct a bridge across that chasm... And so I escaped entirely into the past and re-evaluated all the adventures of my own existence into terms of a bygone era. Even today I know the seventeenth century better than the twentieth..."

When he was eleven years old he saved his pennies until he could buy "twenty blue copy-books" and then started to write a history of the world.

HENDRIK WILLEM VAN LOON

He recalls that he passed a statue of Erasmus every day on his way to school and that people said Erasmus turned a page of the book in his hand every hour. "I used to stand in front of the monument for hours, but never saw him turn a page." That incident started him off as a doubter and a seeker after truth.

Van Loon came to the United States at twenty-one and was graduated from Cornell University in 1905. After a year at Harvard he married Eliza Bowditch of Boston and went to Russia as Associated Press correspondent during the Revolution of 1906. Then he spent four years at the University of Munich where he received a Ph.D. in 1911. Back in America, he was three years a lecturer on history and art in various universities. He confesses that he learned the tricks of lecturing by frequent attendance at vaudeville theatres when he first came back to hunt employment.

In 1913 Van Loon published *The Fall of the Dutch Empire,* which was followed by *The Rise of the Dutch Kingdom* (1915) and *The Golden Book of Dutch Navigators* (1916). He established himself as an historian of his native country. Meanwhile, in 1914, he was sent by the Associated Press to Belgium at the outbreak of the World

War. After lecturing on modern European history at Cornell in 1915-16, he continued his activities as correspondent in England, France, Italy, Switzerland, Holland, Norway, Sweden, and Denmark until 1918. During those years he crossed the ocean eight times and once, when returning from this country to Holland on a Dutch ship, the vessel struck an English mine laid for German boats and was blown up. Van Loon was severely injured and two operations nearly cost him his life. He still feels the effect of the experience upon his nervous system.

After the war Van Loon returned to America and lived in poverty while he made unsuccessful attempts at writing advertisements. "I had three books behind me," he says, "but nobody read them, and so the royalties would not even buy beans." The Harvard Club in New York City extended him credit on meals while he prepared *Ancient Man* (1920), intended as the first section of a twelve-volume history of the world. In 1920 he married Helen Criswell. *Ancient Man* put him on his feet financially, but he gave up the idea of a series and condensed the rest of his history into one volume, *The Story of Mankind* (1921). The first three chapters of the book had been written five years before on Department of Modern History stationery at Cornell. The author relates that when he peddled the manuscript in New York, every publisher shook his head and said, "Yes, this is a very pretty idea but it won't sell." It went thru thirty American editions and was translated into more than a dozen tongues.

The Newbery Medal was awarded to Van Loon in 1922 for *The Story of Mankind*. He came into international prominence. With the royalties from the book he bought a home in Westport, Connecticut, built in Dutch style.

In 1922-23 Van Loon organized the history department at Antioch College, Ohio, and the next year he was associate editor of the *Baltimore Sun*, as conductor of a column of comment on current topics. *The Story of the Bible* (1923), treating the subject as a continuous historical narrative, was written principally at Cambridge, near the spot where Erasmus pursued his Biblical studies. The book was criticized by the church because Van Loon omitted the story of the Resurrection, in which he does not believe.

He says he cannot understand why his next book, *The Story of Wilbur the Hat* (1925), which he called a "spiritual philosophy for children," failed to impress the public. "But few people knew what it was all about. Our liberals in America are interested only in political and economic liberalism, not in cultural liberalism. I work for an intelligent, humanistic point of view. I seek to indicate that Man is more important than anything else in the world—more important than religion, or painting, or literature. I have tried to show that Man is the centre of the universe. In America we have materially solved everything and spiritually solved nothing." *Tolerance* (1925) is a history of intolerance thru the ages.

R.v.R. (1930) is a fictionized biography of the famous Dutch painter, Rembrandt van Rijn, "who lies in a pauper's grave somewhere in Amsterdam." The book takes the form of an imaginary diary of a contemporary of Rembrandt. Van Loon says: "It took me twenty years to gather the material I needed... The book had to be lived and the good Lord saw to it that I could live it. I revived an imaginary great-great-great-grandfather because I needed him to say all I had to say... Two whole years he spent dictating this fable to me... in the high-ceilinged old room of my house in Veere, that house called 'de Houttuyn' or 'Woodyard' in which my ancestors had lived..."

"Hendrik Willem Van Loon," writes David Karsner, "stands fully six feet, weighs perhaps two hundred and twenty-five pounds, has a smooth, round, almost cherubic face that carries not a wrinkle in its pleasant, jovial contour and dresses in the latest pattern of fashion—a scarlet cravat, monocle and all. He presents a picture of a playboy, a handsome physical specimen who has taken life as he found it and not made too much fuss over the setbacks he has suffered and the privations he has known...

"His manner is sympathetic, warm and genial... There is a merry twinkle in his light brown eyes and they are always laughing, not at life but with it... When he is particularly 'worked up' over a knotty point concerning the antecedents of primitive man, or a question of theology that has survived thousands of years despite the efforts of logic and reason to unhorse it, he turns to his violin and bow just as some men pick up golf clubs. . ."

Van Loon speaks and writes in ten languages as well as their dialects. When he eats in a restaurant he draws pictures on the tablecloth to illustrate his conversation, and he signs the check with a sketch of an elephant or a mouse, according to the size of the meal—usually an elephant. "I have lived with history all my life," he says, "and I have found it neither a dead nor a respectable subject. . . I have found all of it more romantic than fiction."

Among the other books written by Van Loon are: *A Short History of Discovery* (1918), *America* (1927), *The Life and Times of Pieter Stuyvesant* (1928), *Man, the Miracle Maker* (1928).

Van Loon plans to publish a geography in the style of *The Story of Mankind* in the fall of 1931.

Carl Van Vechten

CARL VAN VECHTEN was born in Cedar Rapids, Iowa, on June 17, 1880. He received his Ph.B. from the University of Chicago in 1903, and in 1906 became assistant music critic on the *New York Times* under Richard Aldrich. This position he held until 1913, with the exception of 1908-09 when he was Paris correspondent for the paper. During his period as critic he conducted two departments in the *New Music Review* and contributed musical biographies to the revised edition of the *Century Dictionary* (1911). He edited the *Programme Notes* for the Symphony Society of New York in 1910-11. He was dramatic critic for the *New York Press* in 1913-14.

Van Vechten's early books were naturally critical. He began with the publication of *Music After the Great War* in 1915. Among the critical works that followed are: *Interpreters and Interpretations* (1917), *The Music of Spain*

CARL VAN VECHTEN

(1918), and *In the Garret* (1920). All of this work that he has cared to preserve is now included in the two books, *Red* (1925) and *Excavations* (1926). His reading audience was necessarily a small one.

Contained in *Red* is the essay, "Valedictory," in which the author expresses his intention of retiring from criticism. His point is that critics should retire at the age of forty, because after that age prejudices are formed which preclude the possibility of welcoming novelties. One's intellectual arteries harden, so to speak. He says that, after twenty years of theatre and concert criticism, "music, the drama, singers, and actors began to have precious little new to say to me, and I began to have precious little new to say about them." So he ceased to write about them.

After his self-critical gesture, Van Vechten discovered that a critic is not too old at forty to become a novelist. When he wrote *Peter Whiffle* (1922), a novel, neither he nor his publishers hoped for a sale of more than two thousand copies. But it appeared on the best-seller lists, where all his succeeding books have been. He challenges the ancient gibe that a writer does not turn to criticism until he has failed as a creative artist, and says that if more novelists had been critics we should not have so many bad novels.

The Blind Bow-Boy (1923) and *Firecrackers* (1925) are both novels of the artistic and society sets in New York, and *The Tattooed Countess* (1924) goes back to the small town Iowa of his childhood. *Nigger Heaven* (1926) is the result of his long interest in Negro life in America, especially in New York, and it has been his most widely read book. *Spider Boy* (1928) is a satirical extravaganza on Hollywood and its cinematic civilization. *Parties* (1930) is a novel of certain of New York's contemporary younger generation, wealthy, bored with life and each other, and perpetually in need of artificial stimulation.

Carl Van Vechten's personal tastes are as extraordinary as his books. Whereas most writing men do not even trouble to acquire a decent library, he collects not only first and rare editions, but bindings, holographs, autographs, manuscripts, pamphlets, newspaper clippings, postcards, paintings, and even book jackets. Unlike most collectors, he reads the books on his shelves. He is also a great connoisseur and collector of cats.

Moreover, Van Vechten is always collecting authors of whom no one else seems ever to have heard and he is usually hot in pursuit of some new literary discovery. Some of the writers whose work he has been instrumental in bringing before the public eye are: M. P. Shiel, Edgar Saltus, Henry B. Fuller, Marmaduke Pickthall, Ronald Firbank, Arthur Machen, Haldane MacFall, and Baron Corvo. He took his full share in the rediscovery of Herman Melville. The original papers which first announced these enthusiasms are now included in *Excavations*. They all grew out of his critical work, literary and musical, with which he made his own entrance into the literary world.

Van Vechten's one major superstition is concerned with the signing of his contracts and a celebrated person has been found to witness his signature of each: Fania Marinoff for *Peter Whiffle*, Hugh Walpole for *The Blind Bow-Boy*, Sinclair Lewis for *Red*, Theodore Dreiser for *The Tattooed Countess*, James Weldon Johnson for *Nigger Heaven*, Charlie Chaplin for *Spider Boy*, and Texas Guinan for *Parties*. Fania Marinoff, a Russian actress, is his wife.

Llewelyn Powys, in *The Verdict of Bridlegoose*, describes the novelist (somewhat acidulously) at a literary gathering: "Carl Van Vechten sat silent on a hard chair, his clever head drooping slightly to the left. Indeed, I have never been in the company of this famous wit when he did not appear to me to be drooping like an aging madonna-lily that has lost its pollen and has been left standing in a vase which the parlormaid has forgotten to refill with fresh water."

Among the other critical essays by Carl Van Vechten are: *Music and Bad Manners* (1916), *The Merry-Go-Round* (1918). He is the author of a book on cats, *The Tiger in the House* (1920), and the editor of another, *Lords of the Housetops* (1921). He is the composer of *Five Old English Ditties* (1904). His home is in New York City.

Hugh Walpole

HUGH SEYMOUR WALPOLE, English novelist, was born at Auckland, New Zealand, in 1884. His father was the Right Reverend George Henry Somerset Walpole, D.D., sent from England in 1882 as incumbent of St. Mary's Pro-Cathedral in Auckland. When his son was five years old, Dr. Walpole removed to New York where he taught for seven years in the General Theological Seminary, and Hugh was sent to Cornwall, England. In 1896, when the boy was twelve, his family returned to England and settled in the Cathedral town of Durham where his father was principal of Bede College. The elder Walpole was Bishop of Edinburgh from 1910 until his death in 1929.

Walpole was educated at King's College, Canterbury, and at Emmanuel College, Cambridge. At the age of twenty, when he was an undergraduate at Cambridge, he wrote two novels. He destroyed one, and the other waited five years for a publisher. When he left the university, Walpole tried preaching for a while and then schoolmastering in a

HUGH WALPOLE

copies, but with no greater net monetary profit to the author than the first one." It attracted attention, however, and thereafter novels followed yearly from Walpole's pen. He won an American following and reaped comfortable profits with *Fortitude* (1913), "the story of a romantic boy and what life did to him." Since then his books have sold well on both sides of the Atlantic.

The Dark Forest (1916) and *The Secret City* (1919) grew out of Walpole's experiences in Russia during the first two years of the World War as a Red Cross orderly and a special agent for the government to promote pro-Ally sentiment in Petrograd. His heroism in rescuing a wounded man under fire was rewarded with the Georgian Medal. Walpole was twice awarded the James Tait Black Prize by the University of Edinburgh: for *The Secret City* in 1919 and *The Captives* in 1920.

Many of Walpole's novels reflect the background of his boyhood. *The Cathedral* (1922) recalls Durham. He has followed the life of an English boy from childhood to manhood in the *Jeremy* books (1919, 1923, 1927).

In 1930 Walpole told an American interviewer: "I have been working for some years now on an ambitious project —a big four-volume novel covering the past two centuries of the social history of England. The first of them, *Rogue Herries,* was published this spring (1930). It deals with about fifty years of the eighteenth century under the Georges. Then will follow a volume each on the Regency, the Victorian period, and our modern world right down to 1930. The characters? Oh, the middle and upper classes. They are, after all, the people I know best. There will be none of this primitive, 'back to the soil' stuff. I grew up in the shadow of an Anglican cathedral, and it's pretty hard to break away from the old ties." *Judith Paris,* the second book of the Walpole's tetralogy will be published in the fall of 1931.

"His broad, sturdy frame," writes Kenneth M. Gould in describing Walpole, "unostentatiously draped in a brown sack suit, breathes wholesomeness and self-reliance. He has a sculptor's head, chiseled, it almost seems, from marble.

provincial boys' school, both to his dislike. So he went to London, rented a room in Chelsea for four shillings a week, and started to break into literary circles.

One day, at a literary luncheon, Walpole impressed the editor of the *London Standard* with his knowledge of English fiction and was invited to write some book reviews for the paper. He accepted the offer but when his first batch of reviews was written he perceived they were bad, and in despair he went to the reading room of the British Museum to meditate. There he happened upon Ethel Mayne, the short story writer, who told the youth, amid his tears, that the reviews were too stilted and suggested that he rewrite them as if he were talking to somebody about the books. This he did, and the reviews were accepted. For several years he contributed to the *Standard.*

The Wooden Horse, Walpole's first novel, was published in 1909 and sold seven hundred copies. "The author's profits therefrom," comments Arnold Bennett, "were less than the cost of typewriting the novel... Mr. Walpole was quite incurable, and he kept on writing novels. *Maradick at Forty* (1910) was the next one. It sold eleven hundred

The chin juts strongly from beneath a generous mouth. The eyes, ringed with the traces of a genial humor, gleam steadfastly thru flexible shell spectacles. His great dome of a forehead, crowned with a fringe of sandy hair, bespeaks reserves of power, a blend of natural simplicity and habitual reflection."

Walpole works hard but is seldom tired; he keeps within his capacity. He avoids the temptations of over-writing and diversifies his life with lecturing. He makes frequent visits to America where he is in great demand as a lecturer. For several years he has acted as a guide in America to English literature, just as in England he points the way to the best in American literature. He has done much to interest the British public in the importance of American writers. He has been referred to as the "toastmaster of literature." He is gracious, kindly, tactful; never melancholy, dissatisfied, or unhappy. His criticisms do not bring rebukes and he is not a storm center like some of his contemporaries. He is head of the English Book Society, an organization similar to the American "book clubs."

In his 1930 visit to America Walpole remarked: "It is only three years since I was here last, but in that time I seem to feel a marked change in the American literary scene. Your novelists—at least many of the younger ones—are turning away from the post-war realism, the minute description of sordid experiences. There is an upsurge of the romantic spirit, a more delicate type of fantasy, a new emphasis on the worth of the individual. There is Willa Cather, still growing. I rate her at the top of American fiction, and I believe her best years are still ahead of her. Thornton Wilder is another I admire. Sinclair Lewis, too, has an unquenchable vitality. One can expect almost anything from him...

"In England now we are experiencing the same swing toward romanticism that begins to appear here (in America). A group of younger men like Priestley, Martin Armstrong, Gerald Bullett and others, occupy a strong position. Virginia Woolf is another true creative artist in fiction."

Walpole is a bachelor, lives in an attractive apartment in London near Piccadilly, and belongs to four clubs. In the English lake district he has a retreat where he can enjoy silence and peace with his dogs, books, and pictures. He loves comfort and the company of friends. Now a wealthy man, he collects objects of art and rare manuscripts. He is fond of travel.

The war impressed Walpole with the unimportance of physical death. He believes that spiritual life does not end with physical death. To him the purpose of life is the education of the soul.

Among the books by Hugh Walpole are: *Mr. Perrin and Mr. Traill* (1911), *The Prelude to Adventure* (1912), *The Duchess of Wrexe* (1914), *The Golden Scarecrow* (1915), *Joseph Conrad* (1916), *The Green Mirror* (1918), *The Thirteen Travellers* (1921), *The Young Enchanted* (1922), *The Old Ladies* (1924), *Portrait of a Man with Red Hair* (1925), *Harmer John* (1926), *Wintersmoon* (1928), *The Silver Thorn* (1928), *Anthony Trollope* (1928), *Farthing Hall*, with J. B. Priestley (1929); *Hans Frost* (1929); *Above the Dark Tumult* (1931).

Sylvia Townsend Warner

SYLVIA TOWNSEND WARNER, English poet and novelist, was born at Harrow on the Hill, in Middlesex, in December 1893. Her father was a schoolmaster. As a student of music she became interested in research work in the music of the fifteenth and sixteenth centuries, and spent ten years of her life, beginning when she was twenty-three, as one of four editors of a ten-volume compilation entitled *Tudor Church Music*.

In 1922, when she was twenty-nine, Miss Warner started to write poetry on the side. Three years later she published a square book of verse bound in blue cloth called *The Espalier* (1925). The volume was scarcely noticed except by a few critics. In 1926, when her prolonged learned research was completed, she turned to fiction and published *Lolly Willowes*. This novel, first acclaimed by David Garnett, author of *Lady Into Fox*, attracted wide attention and was the initial "book-of-the-month" in America.

SYLVIA TOWNSEND WARNER

A fantasy, its moral is that a maiden aunt can do many more exciting things than act as a beloved pincushion to an exhausting number of relations.

Miss Warner turned from fantasy to philosophy in *Mr. Fortune's Maggot* (1927), the story of a missionary who fails to realize the hopelessness of his quest for converts on a Pacific island, where he has a devoted and charming servant called Lueli. Her third novel, *The True Heart* (1929), describes the passionate and constant love of a poor orphan girl. *Elinor Barley,* a tale, appeared in a limited edition in 1930.

Meanwhile, in 1928, Miss Warner published her second collection of poems under the title, *Time Importuned*. A story in verse, *Opus 7* (1931), concerns a village woman who contrives the plan of selling flowers from her garden in order to buy herself gin, after the World War. The narrative pictures community life of the English village, where all is gossip, and gives, incidentally, an ironic account of the war.

A poet of rural England, Miss Warner lives, paradoxically, in an early-Victorian house in London with a tiny garden. She is a master of domestic crafts—herbs, cookery, wines. "Essentially sociable," writes Oliver Warner, "and generous to excess, she is an au-thority upon all manner of Satanic and magic arts; the blandishments of the Evil One are known to her, and the secrets of dire poisons. But she is a lover of the occult with a difference. She is a sceptic, a Pyrrhonian, as are almost all the intelligent among her contemporaries; and in place of the traditional cat, a beautiful, infinitely majestic black chow is her accomplice. Together they walk, but in broad daylight, and their haunt is Kensington Gardens."

Altho her outlook is mainly English, Miss Warner enjoys her widest vogue in America. She was guest critic on the *New York Herald Tribune* for a few weeks in March 1929. Unmarried, she is small, slender, dark, and wears heavy glasses. For several years she has been working on a biography of Theodore Francis Powys, stay-at-home member of the literary Powys family.

The books by Sylvia Townsend Warner are: *The Espalier* (1925), *Lolly Willowes* (1926), *Mr. Fortune's Maggot* (1927), *Time Importuned* (1928), *The True Heart* (1929), *Elinor Barley* (1930), *Opus 7* (1931).

Jakob Wassermann

JAKOB WASSERMANN was born of Jewish parentage on March 10, 1873, in the Bavarian industrial city of Fürth. In his autobiography, *Mein Weg als Deutscher und Jude* (1921), he tells how his father, an unsuccessful merchant, scorned the idea that his son should be a writer and left him to work out his destiny alone. The boy was restless, sensitive, ambitious, unhappy. He rebelled against the poverty that narrowed his opportunities and the anti-Semitic prejudices in Germany of that period.

As a child he was shocked by the bitterness of the Old Testament and conceived a repugnance for the book. At school (the gymnasium of Fürth) he read the New Testament and was attracted by its spirit of tenderness. He did not become a Christian, however, but merely came to love another Jew whose spirit spoke to his own more deeply than that of Moses. Then he happened upon the writings of Spinoza, who had made a like discovery and whose work was to influence his own.

"Wassermann's youth," writes William A. Drake, "was full of hardships and disappointments. In 1890 he received a tuition scholarship at Munich, but lacking funds, he was forced to pursue his studies amid harrowing privations. Then he went to Wurzburg and obtained a small commercial clerkship, at a salary just sufficient to keep body and soul together, only to lose it thru the prejudice of a fellow-worker, who procured his dismissal by a disgusting contrivance. In despair, Wassermann then presented himself to serve his time in the army. Upon his discharge, he obtained a clerkship in Freiburg, which he lost when, at his wit's end, he stole a pitiful sum to preserve himself from actual starvation."

After suffering all the degradations of hunger and rejection, Wassermann finally found a publisher for his first three works: *Melusine* (1896), *Die Schaffnerin* (1897), and *Die Juden von Zirndorf* (1897). Then, at the end of eight years of "wandering and poverty," he settled in Vienna in May 1898, where he was married, in 1901, to Julie Speyer, a writer. In her *Wassermann und Sein Werk*, his wife records: "for the first time, he found the well-marked outlines of a cultured tradition. Everything there contrasted sharply with the pettiness which he had elsewhere encountered and which he has scorned with so much vehemence ... an atmosphere of freedom and refinement, of ease and inspiration." Frau Wasserman writes novels under the name of Marta Karlweiss, and her *Viennese Lover* was published in this country in 1930. It gives a picture of post-war Vienna.

Following his marriage, Wassermann received some recognition for his *Die Geschichte der Jungen Renate Fuchs* (1901), and his reputation grew steadily with: *Der Niegeküsste Mund* (1902), *Der Moloch* (1903), *Alexander in Babylon* (1905), *Das Kunst der Erzahlung* (1905), *Die Schwestern* (1906), *Caspar Hauser* (1908), *Die Masken Erwin Reiners* (1910), *Der Goldene Spiegel* (1911), and *Faustina* (1912). His first great success, however, came

JAKOB WASSERMANN

with the publication of *Das Gänsemännchen* (1915). A few years later *Christian Wahnschaffe* (1919) brought him wealth and world-wide fame. It was the first of his books to be brought out in America, under the title of *The World's Illusion* (1920). In 1920 he began *Der Wendekreis*, planned as a ten-volume work, of which the first four were: *Der Unbekannte Gast, Oberlin's Drei Stufen, Ulrike Woytich,* and *Faber oder die Verlorenen Jahre.*

When the plaudits of success began to annoy Wassermann, he acquired a villa at Altaussee, a tiny village in the province of Steierm in the Bavarian Alps, across the lake from the peasant cottage where he lived as a boy. "I had always remembered it and hoped that some day I could own it," he says. "It was the home of Meyerbeer. There are still some of his things in it. ... I am very content here. ... I wake up in the morning and see my mountain and my lake. More beautiful than any painting. And the radio brings me good music and the world's news. And when I am thru with working I can take a walk along country roads and go into workmen's cottages. I can work for days and not hear the noise of traffic or see a lot of automobiles—and the mass confusion of the crowded cities. I could not work well there."

Wassermann's home is provided with every modern convenience and is luxuriously furnished with rare objects of art —costly furniture, exquisite marbles, tapestries, and valuable pictures. Here he writes about the miserable city life he knew in his youth, with its poverty and its suffering.

In 1930 Wassermann told an American interviewer: "My new book is *Der Etzel Roman*, 'The Etzel Romance' you would say. The first volume is already completed. Etzel is already twenty-one years old. But I have much more to do. Another volume to write..."

Wassermann spends a long time writing his books. "*The World's Illusion* required the better part of ten years," he says, "and it took three to write the one volume of *The Maurizius Case*. I write six or seven hours a day—and yet I write slowly. And I have a great deal of reading to do. The first part of *Der Etzel Roman* has much to do with medicine. So I have now been studying medicine, yes, actually studying it for four or five months.

The author feels that his characters are more real than the people around him. "Etzel has been living here in this room with me now for many years," he told his guest, "I know every move that he makes, just how he looks, just when he is sad or glad... He is my favorite, my boy..." To those who feel he makes Maurizius too unsympathetic, Wassermann replies: "I am not writing melodrama—or sympathy stuff. It is a story of a life—you know I derived it from an old legal case... Life is not always lovely or fine."

Wassermann is a small man, yet he gives the impression of greatness. His forehead is high and his bright eyes are retrospective. His manuscripts, written in a minute hand, are covered with endless corrections. There are thousands of books in his house and he deplores the fact that he cannot read them all. He likes especially English authors. Of the Americans he prefers Theodore Dreiser and Sherwood Anderson. He thinks *The American Tragedy* is the finest thing that has come out of America.

The translations of Jakob Wassermann's works published in this country include: *The World's Illusion* (1920); *The Goose Man* (1922); *Faber, or, The Lost Years* (1924); *Gold* (1924); *Oberlin's Three Stages* (1926); *Wedlock* (1926); *The Triumph of Youth* (1927); *World's Ends*, five stories (1927); *Caspar Hauser* (1928); *The Maurizius Case* (1929); *Columbus* (1930).

Evelyn Waugh

EVELYN WAUGH was born in London in October 1903, the son of Arthur Waugh, literary critic and managing director of Messrs. Chapman & Hall, well known London publishing firm. Another gifted son in this family is Alec Waugh, novelist and traveler.

Mr. Waugh received his education at a small college near London, and was Senior History Scholar at Hartford College, Oxford. He also studied painting at an art school in London, and then was an assistant school master for a year.

EVELYN WAUGH

Next we find him trying his hand at being a student of carpentry for three months, the remaining nine months being spent in a study of fashionable society. The books he has written so far are *Rossetti: A Critical Biography* (1928); *Decline and Fall* (1929), a novel; *Vile Bodies* (1930), a novel; and a book of travel published in England under the title of *Labels,* and in America as *A Bachelor Abroad* (1930). The following is set down in Mr. Waugh's own words: "Recreations: eating, drinking, drawing, and traveling. Chief aversions: love, conversation, the stage, writing, Wales."

Evelyn Waugh writes with humor, that subtle metallic kind of humor, swift and cynical, which belongs uniquely to this generation. *Decline and Fall* tells the story of Paul Pennyfeather, a theological student at Oxford, who is expelled as the result of a prank, and who engages in various rococo adventures in a smart boy's school before returning to the seminary. *Vile Bodies* is an ultra-modern satire on the ultra-modern antics of London's bright young people. Thru the mad whirl of extravagant parties runs the love story of a young writer and the daughter of a decaying aristocrat, who became engaged and disengaged at frequent intervals.

Despite his youth, Mr. Waugh has attained a reputation in the literary world which many writers of more mature years might well envy. He has already contracted to write a life of Swift for his publishers. Mr. Waugh also plans to pay a visit to America in the near future, as his elder brother did in 1930. While here he will devote himself to a study of the composite life that goes to make up New York City, and will undoubtedly record his observations.

H. G. Wells

HERBERT GEORGE WELLS, that "exuberant, amiable Cockney Englishman," was born at Bromley, Kent, a suburb of London on September 21, 1866. His father, the son of a gardener, was a professional cricketer and kept a small china shop. His mother, the daughter of an innkeeper, was a lady's maid before her marriage and became

H. G. WELLS

a housekeeper when her husband's business failed.

The youth, thrown upon his own at thirteen, largely educated himself. His early desultory schooling was sandwiched in between periods of apprenticeship to dry-goods dealers and druggists. He finally won a scholarship at the Royal College of Science at South Kensington and took a B.Sc. there with honors at the age of twenty-two. After several strenuous years of teaching and tutoring during which he wrote a biology text, his health broke down. While he was convalescing on the south coast, he began to write essays and sketches.

Wells went up to London, where Frank Harris printed one of his essays in the *Fortnightly Review* in 1891, and he embarked upon a career of educator-journalist which he still maintains is his field rather than that of literary artist. Writing came easily to him and he turned out quantities of essays, reviews, and scientific articles. In 1895 he published *Select Conversations with an Uncle,* and in the same year came the first of his scientific romances, *The Time Machine.*

Some of his early novels were banned from households and libraries, but the author grew bolder and found boldness the best of advertisements. In the books that followed, at the rate of more than two a year, Wells evolved from romanticist to sociologist and thence to evangelist. He has "lived aloud." His changing ideas are recorded in his books.

The novel *Tono-Bungay* (1909) established him. It is a sort of bird's eye view of contemporary English life. He has never lost his big public since then. Following the publication of *Tono-Bungay* he joined the Fabian Society and attempted to reorganize it, but was frozen out. Now he ridicules the group —he always belittles what he dislikes, and he dislikes anything that resists change. His intimate friends during this period of novel writing were Arnold Bennett, George Gissing, Joseph Conrad, Henry James, and Stephen Crane.

During the World War, Wells was the chief protagonist of the liberal interpretation of the war as a prelude to Utopia. Since the war he has proposed a world state (not a League of Nations), governed by an intellectual aristocracy for the benefit of the many, a scheme combining the advantages of internationalism and nationalism, communism and capitalism. He has always dealt in futures. Even his most laborious study of the past, *The Outline of History* (1920), was undertaken with an eye on tomorrow. *The Science of Life* (1929) done in collaboration with Julian Huxley and his son G. P. Wells, a research worker, is a companion volume to *The Outline of History*.

Wells is reported to have remarked in a speech made in London in 1930 that he had devoted two hundred days of hard work every year (since the war) to attacking the war system. "I have ruined a good second-class reputation as a novelist by that occupation," he said. "It has led the reviewers to describe me as a propagandist. If I wrote a poem about a skylark, they would somehow discover propaganda in it."

On another occasion Wells remarked: "I see knowledge increasing and human power increasing. I see ever-increasing possibilities before life, and I see no limits set to it all. Existence impresses me as a perpetual dawn. Our lives, as I apprehend them, swim in expectation."

He thinks that modern civilization, with all its faults, is infinitely superior to the ancient civilizations of Greece and Rome. Yet he sees in modern empires the signs of decadence which destroyed those ancient civilizations. "I believe there's a crash coming... We've got to have a complete readjustment of the political systems of Europe, together with, or rather arising from, an equally complete moral and intellectual revolution."

A. St. John Adcock characterized him: "Socialist, scientist, practical idealist, immensely interested in men and affairs, insatiably curious about all life, its origins, implications, possibilities, restlessly delving into the history and mystery of the past for truths that would light his guesses at the darker mystery of the future, it was natural for Wells to put his latest interests into each new book that he wrote, whether it was a matter-of-fact philosophical treatise or romantic or realistic fiction."

Wells has a wide vogue outside his own country and is popular in America, Russia, Germany, Scandinavia, and France.

For twenty years Wells lived at Easton Glebe, an old Georgian house in Essex, where he did his writing in a thatched workroom of white plaster. He says his life there ended with the death of his wife, Amy Catherine Robbins, in 1927. If he stayed, he would become an old man and he has no intention of falling into what he calls "the venerable pose." His two sons are launched in the world. So now he divides his life between an expensive London apartment and two villas he rents at Grasse, on the Riviera.

Most of his work is done at Grasse. One of the villas he uses as a guest house, the other as a workshop; one house is luxurious, the other strictly utilitarian. He usually works most of the day and joins his friends in the evening. The guests are met by a high-powered car and are given the key to the wine cellar until the host arrives. Altho Wells is not gregarious, his list of acquaintances is enormous. He knew Anatole France. Maxim Gorky gave him the bronze of Tolstoy which adorns his London apartment.

"H.G.," as he is known in England, is not a striking personality. In a crowd he is not an impressive figure and as a lecturer he is not a success. His voice is high and thin. C. Patrick Thompson describes him as a "robust, heavy, shortish man, with massive face, powerful neck and drum of a chest, always very neatly dressed, with carefully pressed trousers... The pale, imaginative eyes smile easily and genially under curiously tufted brows. The mouth is kindly. The nervous system is tense-strained, and its owner can be irascible, especially if some one arouses his dislike. He is not a polite conversationalist."

His favorite attitude is a hunched-up pose. "There is something, I think," says Beverley Nichols, "a little typical of H. G. Wells in the way in which he sits down. The spine is curved, the small hands are tucked away, the neck is bent. The whole posture suggests a spring at tight pressure which may at any moment uncoil itself and leap out in the most surprising directions."

Wells inherited his father's physical energy and love of sports, but he prefers games of his own invention. He used to engage guests in a sort of pseudo-tennis game in a barn behind his home in Essex. He is the author of two books on "Floor Games."

In the earlier days he would go on walking tours while he thought out the general scheme of a story. Now he can work anywhere, even on a train. He never lets an idea escape him. He will get up from bed to scribble down some thoughts. He has enough ideas in his notebooks to keep him busy for one hundred and fifty years.

Some of the numerous books by H. G. Wells are: *The Wheels of Chance* (1896); *Love and Mr. Lewisham* (1900); *Kipps* (1905); *Tono-Bungay* (1908); *Ann Veronica* (1909); *The History of Mr. Polly* (1910); *Mr. Britling Sees It Through* (1916); *The World of William Clissold* (1926); *The Way the World is Going* (1928); *The King Who Was a King*, film synopsis published as a book (1929); *The Autocracy of Mr. Parham* (1930).

Franz Werfel

FRANZ WERFEL, poet, novelist, and playwright, was born at Prague, now the capital of Czechoslovakia, on September 10, 1890, the son of a rich and cultured Jewish manufacturer. His young talent was carefully nourished by every advantage of education, environment, and travel. After a period at the Prague gymnasium, he received his advanced schooling at Prague and Leipzig where he majored in philosophy.

As a youth, Werfel frequented the active literary society of the Bohemian capital, which then included such notable figures as Max Brod, Gustave Meyrink, and the great Czech poet, Otakar Brezina, some of whose works Werfel translated into German in *Winde von Mittag bis Mitternacht*.

Werfel spent his twentieth year in further study at Hamburg, where he wrote his first volume of poems, *Der Weltfreund* (1911). It attracted considerable interest, and when his second volume, *Wir Sind*, appeared in 1913, the success of the twenty-three year old poet was immediate. These two books together with *Einander* (1915), his third poetic volume, express the idea of the community of souls in all living things and conceive tragedy as the basis of life.

FRANZ WERFEL

The writer was recognized as a new prophet of spiritual renascence. He expressed his philosophy of life in the poem in *Wir Sind* called "Ich bin ja noch ein Kind."

Meanwhile, after a year of still further study back in Prague, Werfel joined the faculty of the University of Leipzig as lecturer in 1912. He left his teaching post when the World War was declared and served on the Russian front from 1915 to 1917—bravely in spite of his repugnance of the carnage. That tragic experience, together with subsequent political troubles, affected his work deeply.

After the war Werfel settled in Vienna, where he has lived in studious retirement since 1918, devoting himself to the desperate task of teaching men to love one another and to draw close to the verities of life. He has sought the destruction of obstacles to brotherhood erected by tradition. His novels, *Nicht der Mörder, der Ermordete ist Schuldig,* and *Der Abituriententag,* deal with the revolt of youth. The last (*The Class Reunion* in translation) is the story of a Viennese judge who is confronted with a prisoner of the same name as a class mate whom he allowed to shoulder the blame for a crime of his own. Of Werfel's other novels, *Der Tod des Kleinburgers* (*The Man Who Conquered Death*) concerns a poor but valiant old gentleman whose insurance will provide for his family and save them from disgrace if he can survive his sixty-fifth year. The book was published in 1926.

Werfel's dramatic works, which express variations of his message, include: an adaptation of Euripides' *Troades* (1915); *Der Spiegelmensch,* a symbolic trilogy (1920); *Juarez und Maximilian* (1924); a biographical novel of the opera *Verdi* (1924); *Paulus unter den Juden* (1926). He has engaged in journalistic work and is the author of numerous essays. He has written a stirring article on Cabrinovich, the Serbian assassin of the Austrian Archduke, contributed to *Die Neue Rundschau* in 1923. He is known first as a poet, however.

Franz Werfel was introduced to the American public in 1925 with the publication of *Verdi*. Subsequent translations published in this country include: *The Goat Song,* a drama in five acts (1926); *Juarez and Maximilian,* a dramatic history in three phases and thirteen pictures (1926); *The Man Who Conquered Death* (1927); *The Class Reunion* (1929); *The Pure in Heart* (1931). The plays, *The Goat Song, Schweiger,* and *Juarez and Maximilian* have been produced in New York.

Glenway Wescott

GLENWAY WESCOTT was born in Kewaskum, Wisconsin, on April 11, 1901. His father is a farmer, as his forebears in America have been since the early seventeenth century. "My immediate family," he explains, "has aristocratic rather than middle-class prejudices; it does not hoard up its sons for the sake of the family fortune, but regards it as a duty to make gifts of them to 'the State' or to 'humanity' by way of the army, the church, the educational professions, and even the fine arts, in so far as the latter accomplish a 'service to humanity.'"

When he was a child, Wescott's family intended that he should become a minister of the gospel, but his personal

GLENWAY WESCOTT

ambition was to be a musician. At the age of twelve he went away from home to attend school and has returned since only for vacations. He attended the high schools at West Bend and Waukesha and, without taking a degree, the University of Chicago, where as president of the Poetry Club he was directed toward literature.

For a while Wescott wrote reviews for the magazine *Poetry*. His novel, *The Apple of the Eye*, was begun at Bryant's birthplace in Massachusetts and was finished in New York after a year's absence in England and Germany. It was published first as a serial in *The Dial* under the title, *Bad Hand;* the book edition appeared in 1924.

Since then, the youthful author has lived in France, most of the time in the Mediterranean fishing village of Villefranche, where, he explains, he can write most economically and quietly. He goes bathing in the sea for diversion and makes frequent visits to Paris. In 1926 he collected twenty of his poems in a volume called *Natives of the Rock*. The following year he published *Grandmothers*, a family portrait, which won *Harper's* 1927-28 Prize Novel Contest. It is a family album in which each chapter is a portrait and each portrait a mirror of the days of his grandfather and grandmother. It is a presentation of the young American's attitude toward the background of America, the history of America, the love of the soil and the feeling of belonging to America.

Like Sinclair Lewis, Glenway Wescott thinks the Middle West frightful but does not know how to dispense with it. He expresses his uneasy regard for his native state in the introductory essay to the volume of short stories, *Goodbye Wisconsin* (1928): "How much sweeter to come and go than to stay; that by way of judgment upon Wisconsin."

In the same essay he defines the Middle West: "A place which has no fixed boundaries, no particular history; inhabited by no one race; always exhausted by its rich output of food, men, and manufactured articles; loyal to none of its many creeds, prohibitions, fads, hypocrisies; now letting itself be governed, now ungovernable... There is no Middle West. It is a certain climate, a certain

landscape; and beyond that, a state of mind of people born where they do not like to live."

Wescott proposes in *Goodbye Wisconsin* a solution for himself thru art: "I should like to write a book about ideal people under ideal circumstances. No sort of under-nourishment, no under-education, nothing partial or frustrated, no need of variety or luxury—in short, no lack of anything which, according to its children, Wisconsin denies."

But in *The Babe's Bed* (1930) he is still wandering, unable to accept Wisconsin or break from it. It is the story of a young man who returns to his Mid-Western home where "lived a mother, a father, a young daughter, another in ill health with her husband and baby..." There is little action in the story, but a great deal of reflection on the part of the home-comer as to the future of the babe.

Glenway Wescott is youthful and slender, with a long smooth face, wistful eyes, boyish turned-up nose, and sensuous mouth. He is fond of comic-strips. Margaret Anderson recalls him when he was getting his start on the staff of *Poetry*: "Glenway had such clipped and distinguished speech that I thought he was English. No, he explained, he came from Wisconsin but he loved the English language and had trained himself to speak it beautifully." He writes, likewise, in a trained style, poetic and concise.

Here are some of the ideas Wescott has expressed: "Never live in Paris: everyone there has done some harm to everyone else... Never live in New York either: a town in which 'it is as essential to wear one's heart on one's sleeve as one's tongue in one's cheek'...

"I believe that American youngsters are equal in force, elasticity, beauty, and the other natural gifts to the Greeks. In the fourth university year, let us say; not much longer. Something happens to them; the flower turns out to be seedless...

"I believe that in the near future descriptive writing about average American destinies must inevitably be that of a reporter, an analyst, a diagnostician...

"To the young man with ambition enough to matter, premature marriage is the worst of dangers. It means earning a living by whatever is at hand; beggars of jobs cannot experiment, ought not to be far-sighted or fastidious. It means Wisconsin forever..."

The books by Glenway Wescott are: *The Apple of the Eye* (1924), *Natives of the Rock* (1926), *Grandmothers* (1927), *Goodbye Wisconsin* (1928), *The Babe's Bed* (1930).

Wescott is at work now in France on a two-volume novel.

Rebecca West

ANNOUNCEMENT of a new novel by Cecily Isabel Fairfield would create little excitement in the literary world, for few people know that it is the real name of Rebecca West, the English critic and novelist.

Cecily Isabel Fairfield was born in Ireland on Christmas, 1892, the daughter of the late Charles Fairfield of County Kerry. Her mother's father was Alexander Mackenzie, one of the first to introduce Schumann's music in England. Her mother inherited his musical talent and was educated at Dusseldorf, but her career was interrupted by the shock of her brother's death. She never fully recovered from it and was an invalid most of her life.

Cecily Fairfield's father had a romantic career an as army officer in Ireland, a prospector in Illinois and Mexico, a war correspondent in Europe, an editor in Australia, and a favorite apostle of Herbert Spencer in England. He was sixty when she was born and he died in South Africa when she was ten. He was of an English family that had settled in Ireland under Edward VI. Among his collateral ancestors were three of the wives of Henry VIII, including Anne Boleyn.

The girl was reared in Edinburgh and received her education there at George Watson's Ladies' College. At the age of seventeen she first appeared in print. When she was still seventeen she went to London in response to an acting offer and attended a dramatic academy which she "simply loathed."

She relates: "I acted for a while in repertory, and that gave me my nom-de-

REBECCA WEST

plume. I acted the part of Rebecca West in *Rosmersholm* and thought that would do as well as any other. Then I wrote an article for the *Freewoman* and that started me off (1911). I stayed on and wrote for suffrage until the editor got arrested. Then I wrote book reviews and newspaper articles." She joined the staff of *The Clarion* as political writer in 1912. Subsequently she contributed to *The Daily News*, *The New Statesman*, *The New Republic* (in America), and many other magazines and newspapers.

Miss West's first book was *Henry James* (1916). Her first novel was *The Return of the Soldier* (1918), a story of the fancies of a shell-shocked veteran. Her second novel was *The Judge* (1922), an unconventional love story. *Harriet Hume* (1929), the third novel, is a study of the psychic relationship between a girl musician and a politician. It is labeled "a London fantasy."

Miss West likes Stendhal, Turgenieff, Proust, and Lady Murasaki. The last, she explains, is a Japanese writer who "lived about a thousand years ago, but she's very modern, very psychological, like Proust." She thinks Thackeray is greater than Dickens and she "can't stand Galsworthy."

An interviewer described Miss West as a "willowy, dark-eyed, mercurial, very feminine" creature who likes to sit on the floor. She looks at one with coal-black eyes, an archly wrinkled brow, and says effective and unexpected things. Her manner is "a mixture of roguish impudence and wide-eyed wonderment." She lives in a constant turmoil, inward and out. Her world is full of dramatic situations, adventure, and romance. One never knows what she may do next, but it always proves to be different. She has an old-fashioned pianola in her home.

As a girl Miss West had a reputation for being untidy in her appearance. A friend recalls how her hair was "perpetually combed to a frenzy by her agitated fingers." Nowadays, the friend continues, "she has an altered reputation for wearing, with maddening equanimity, clothes of a design and build and tender selection that reveal how, all along, she has been their lover, tho only recently their conqueror."

Miss West, who has called the average British husband "a perfect nuisance," was married on November 1, 1930, to Henry Maxwell Andrews, a London banker. The word "obey" was omitted from her vow. The ceremony took place at Abinger, Surrey, altho her residence is in London.

Her works include: *Henry James* (1916); *The Return of the Soldier* (1918); *The Judge* (1922); *The Strange Necessity* (1928), a book of essays; *Harriet Hume* (1929); *D. H. Lawrence* (1930); and *Ending in Earnest* (1931). The last book is made up of essays which appeared in *The Bookman* during 1929 and 1930 as "Letters from Europe." *War Nurse* (1930), a novel, appeared serially under Miss West's name, but was published pseudonymously ("Corinne Andrews") in book form.

Edith Wharton

EDITH NEWBOLD JONES was born in New York City on January 24, 1862. Her mother was a Rhinelander, one grandmother was a Schermerhorn, and the other a Stevens, all well-known New York families. Her great-grandfather, Ebenezer Stevens, was a general in the Revolutionary War.

EDITH WHARTON

Her father had an independent income, and she spent much of her childhood and youth in Europe, where her family lived at one time for five years without coming home.

The girl did not attend school or college, but was educated at home by governesses and tutors. In her studies abroad she mastered French, German, and Italian, and became thoroly saturated with the civilization of Europe, past and present. From the time she was small she loved to write, and was observant of all her surroundings. She was always eager to obtain criticisms of her work. When in this country the family spent the winters in New York and the summers at Newport, in a house on the bay, half way out toward Fort Adams.

In 1885, when she was twenty-three, she married Edward Wharton, a Boston banker. They lived in New York, Newport, and Lenox, and went frequently to Europe.

Edith Wharton began her literary career four years after her marriage with the publication of a sonnet called "Happiness" in *Scribner's* for December 1889. Her first short story, "Mrs. Manstey's View," a narrative of humble city life, appeared in the same magazine for July 1891. Her stories continued to appear in

Scribner's and in 1899 she collected them under the title, *The Greater Inclination.* Her second collection was *Crucial Instances* (1901), which led to a significant friendship with Henry James, the writer who most strongly influenced her work. James, after reading the stories, remarked that he wanted to "get hold of the little lady and pump the pure essence of my wisdom and experience into her."

Mrs. Wharton's first novel was a story of eighteenth century Italy called *The Valley of Decision* (1920). It was followed by *Sanctuary* (1903), a novelette or long short story—a form borrowed from James. *The Descent of Man* (1904) was her next group of short stories. The *House of Mirth* (1905), a novel of American society, was a best-seller and it firmly established her reputation. *Ethan Frome* (1911), a novelette, is a tragedy of love and frustration among New England folk. Despite its brevity, it seems likely to stand as the author's most permanent work.

Since 1906 Mrs. Wharton has made her home in France, in summer at St. Brice, near Paris, and in winter at Hyeres, Provençe. When the World War broke out she was in Paris and she plunged at once into relief work. She opened a workroom for skilled women workers of the quarter where she lived who were thrown out of employment by the closing of the workrooms; she fed and housed six hundred Belgian refugee orphans. In recognition of her services France awarded her the cross of the Legion of Honor and Belgium made her a Chevalier of the Order of Leopold. Meanwhile, she wrote articles and stories on the war which included *Fighting France* (1915) and *The Marne* (1918). After the war she visited Africa with General Lyautey at the invitation of the French government and wrote as a result, *In Morocco* (1920).

The Age of Innocence (1920) is one of Edith Wharton's most successful novels. It employs the material she had hitherto used only for background—the social life of old New York into which she was bred. The story concerns a man whose life is held in check by the rigid conventions of the seventies, and who is obliged to go ahead with his marriage to a girl whose cousin he loves. His desire to leave his wife is quenched forever by the news that she is with child. The novel was awarded the Pulitzer Prize. It was published in France in the *Revue de Deux Mondes* as a serial, *Au Temps de l'Innocence,* from November 15, 1920, to February 1, 1921.

In 1924 Mrs. Wharton published, in separate volumes, four novelettes of *Old New York: False Dawn* (the 'forties), *The Old Maid* (the 'fifties), *The Spark* (the 'sixties), and *New Year's Day* (the 'seventies). The author was made an officer of the Legion of Honor in 1924. When she visited the United States the next year she was awarded the Gold Medal of the National Institute of Arts and Letters, the first woman to receive the award, and she was given an honorary Litt.D. degree by Yale University.

Mrs. Wharton was described some years ago as an exquisitely dressed woman with "browny hair, a finished manner, and an air . . . the kind of air that glides about European letters and art, and looks startled when anyone mentions America." In spite of her long residence abroad, Mrs. Wharton has retained an American point of view. Her culture is revealed especially in her travel books, which include *Italian Villas and Their Gardens* (1904), *Italian Backgrounds* (1905), and *A Motor-flight Through France* (1908).

Mrs. Wharton says of her literary master, Henry James: "The writing of fiction was still, when his career began, an unformulated art in English speaking countries." She defines his conception of the novel, which is likewise her own: "For him every great novel must first of all be based on a profound sense of moral values and then constructed with a classical unity and economy of means."

In her essay on *The Writing of Fiction* (1925), she restricts the rights of the critic to two questions: "What has the author tried to present and how far has he succeeded?"

Among the other books by Edith Wharton are: *The Fruit of the Tree* (1907), *The Reef* (1912), *The Custom of the Country* (1913), *Xingu and Other Stories* (1916), *Summer* (1917), *The Glimpses of the Moon* (1922), *Twilight*

Sleep (1927), *The Children* (1928), *Hudson River Bracketed* (1929), and *Certain People* (short stories, 1930).

Thornton Wilder

THORNTON NIVEN WILDER was born on April 17, 1897, in Madison, Wisconsin, where his father, Amos Parker Wilder, was editor of the *Wisconsin State Journal.* He was the second of five children, of whom the eldest, Amos Niven Wilder, is the author of *Battle-Retrospect* (1923) and *Arachne* (1928), books of poems. His mother was Isabel Niven, daughter of the Reverend Doctor Niven, pastor of the Presbyterian Church at Dobbs Ferry, New York.

In 1906, when Wilder was nine years old, his father went to China where he was American consul-general at Hong Kong for three years and at Shanghai for five years. Thornton, meanwhile, attended high school at Chefoo, China. Upon his return to America in 1914, the elder Wilder became secretary of the Yale-in-China Movement at New Haven, and from 1920 to 1929 he was associate editor of the *New Haven Journal-Courier.*

Thornton Wilder, when he came back from China, continued his education at a high school in Berkeley, California, and at the Thacher School at Ojai, California. He was a student at Oberlin College from 1915 to 1917, and served as a corporal in the Coast Artillery Corps at Narraganset Bay in 1918. He received his A.B. from Yale in 1920. "As an undergraduate at Yale," writes William Lyon Phelps, who has known Wilder since he was a boy, "he was unusually versatile, original and clever. He played and composed music, wrote much prose and verse, and stood well in the studies of the course. He was a shining light in the Elizabethan Club and in that small group known as 'The Pundits.'" For two years after graduation he studied at the American Academy in Rome.

In 1921 Wilder became a house master and teacher at the Lawrenceville School in Lawrenceville, New Jersey, where he remained seven years. He taught

THORNTON WILDER

French because it left him free to wander where he wished in the paths of English literature. He was determined to write for pleasure rather than for profit. He received an A.M. at Princeton in 1925.

From his experiences in Italy, he wrote *The Cabala* (1925), a novel about a group of sophisticates in Rome. The book enjoyed a critical success at home and in London, but its sale was small and its appeal limited. A play, *The Trumpet Shall Sound* (1926), written while the author was in college, was modestly produced for a few performances by the American Laboratory Theatre.

The Bridge of San Luis Rey appeared in 1927 and it sold thousands of copies a day at a time when the author was unknown to the world at large. A philosophical novel, it became a best-seller, and was awarded the Pulitzer Prize. William Lyon Phelps says that it "was accepted by the publishers because they thought so fine a book ought to be printed; but they had no belief in its success with the public, and they have not yet recovered from the shock." *The Bridge of San Luis Rey* gave Wilder an international reputation. He has been discussed in the press of France, Italy, Spain, as well as Great Britain and America.

The setting of the book is in Lima, Peru, two centuries ago. A monk who watches five persons plunge to their doom when a bridge of osier breaks, reconstructs the lives of these persons to determine whether their manner of existence made them deserving of death. After an exhaustive study, he finds that all five lives touched upon one another. Most of the book was written while Wilder was a member of the MacDowell Colony at Peterborough, New Hampshire, during summer vacations.

The Angel That Troubled the Waters (1928) is a collection of short, poignant dramatic moments crystallized into tiny three-minute plays. Some of these were written while Wilder was at college.

Until the spring of 1928, Wilder steadily refused to neglect his job of teaching for the invitations that showered him from New York and elsewhere. The supplications of the magazines were in vain. He declined the urgings of publishers to take quick advantage of his success. He said he would write what he planned to write and nothing more.

In 1928 Wilder gave up his teaching duties at Lawrenceville and went to Europe where he spent the greater part of a year working on his third novel. *The Woman of Andros* (1930) is based upon the theme of the *Andria,* a comedy by Terence. The woman of Andros is Chrysis, a Greek hetaira, who has established herself on the island of Brynos and gathered about her the young men of the neighborhood, charming them all by her beauty and wisdom.

Upon his return in 1929, Wilder made a lecture tour, regarding it as a stimulating experience. In 1930 he took a lecturing post at the University of Chicago, which keeps him busy only six months of the year. His creative interest has turned to the drama, and in March 1931 he sailed for France presumably to work on a play. He is unmarried.

All the works of Thornton Wilder deal "with the mystery of death and judgment, the tragedy of beauty, and pity of the ending of life's comedy." He makes no attempt to fit life into his theories; his theories grow naturally out of his experience and observation of life. If he has a favorite subject, it is the human soul. Unchanged by fame, he feels that he has much to learn and wants to study Greek and Latin.

The publications by Thornton Wilder are: *The Cabala* (1925), *The Trumpet Shall Sound* (1926), *The Bridge of San Luis Rey* (1927), *The Angel That Troubled the Waters* (1928), *The Woman of Andros* (1930).

William Carlos Williams

WILLIAM CARLOS WILLIAMS, author and physician, was born on September 17, 1883, in Rutherford, New Jersey. His mother, Raquel Helene Hobeb Williams, of French and Spanish ancestry, was born in Mayaguez, Porto Rico; and his father, William George Williams, half English and half Danish, was born in Birmingham, England. Dr. Williams has also a trace of Dutch and of Jewish blood in his veins.

Of his early education Dr. Williams says: "I ate nursery rhymes from my English grandmother's fingers. . . . My mother and father talked nothing but Spanish so that I could not or should not understand what they were saying. Thus I got to understand Spanish perfectly and received no bad habits of English speech.

WILLIAM CARLOS WILLIAMS

"I avoided everything possible in the nature of work while at grammar school . . . . Then I went to Switzerland to school where I enjoyed the asphodel which grew plentifully along the edges of the soccer field where I loved to disport myself. Was the youngest member of the school soccer team, the Château de Lancy, now the Ecole International where my boys went to school three years ago.

"I studied hard at Horace Mann High School in New York City, enjoyed taking history from Miss Butler, sister of the President of Columbia University, and English under 'Uncle Billie' Abbott. . . Ran myself sick on the track team. Was told I had heart disease. I went from high school to the University of Pennsylvania. . . ."

He received his M.D. from the University of Pennsylvania in 1906, and later took post-graduate work at the University of Leipzig. After returning to the United States he took up his residence at Rutherford, and has had an active medical practice there since that time.

Dr. Williams and Miss Florence Herman, of Rutherford, were married in 1912. They have two sons, William Eric and Paul Herman, who are in school in Switzerland.

Dr. Williams admits a leaning toward poetry in his Horace Mann High School days, but it was not until he was in college that he began to write. *Poems*, a thin five-by-four-inch book, was published quietly in 1909. *The Tempers* (London, 1913) created more interest, and Dr. Williams found that his "curiously exotic work," his deviation from the conventional in structure and idea, made him one of the leaders of the experimentalists and radicals. His other books, which have upheld his position, are: *Al Que Quiere* (1917); *Kora in Hell* (1920); *Sour Grapes* (1921); two books of essays, *The Great American Novel* (Paris, 1923) and *In the American Grain* (1925). His novel, *A Voyage to Pagany* (1928), is the story of a small town practitioner who is dissatisfied with his spiritual, cultural, and intellectual environment in the United States and goes to Europe; he encounters the continental attitude toward life in France, Italy, and

in Vienna, but returns to America with his ideals still confused.

Dr. Williams is essentially interested in things American. In awarding the *Dial* Prize for 1926 to him, in recognition of his service to letters, the editors of *The Dial* say: "This modest quality of realness which he attributes to 'contact' with the good Jersey dirt sometimes reminds one of Chekhov. Like Chekhov, he knows animals and babies as well as trees."

In answer to an inquiry his reply was: "What am I doing now? Trying to get published with no success as always. Oh yes, I'm writing a play for the Theatre Guild which they will neither read, accept, nor stage—more's the loss. It's a shame those who can write decent stuff aren't authorized to go ahead regardless of cost, audience or anything but the presentation of excellence—it might possibly be the beginning of a complement to the Marx Brothers—blessed inheritors of Chaplin's grotesquer moments, multiplied. But—tut."

Henry Williamson

HENRY WILLIAMSON was born in 1897 in a village of Bedfordshire, England—in the house where his people had lived without interruption for more than four hundred years. His grandfather had all the books of Richard Jefferies in the house, and the boy fed on them. "I was a solitary, like Jefferies," he says. He thinks that children suffer abominably—"the freaks, I mean, like myself." He had hardly emerged "from misery" when the War came. As a youth of seventeen, Williamson became a private in the British Army and served in Flanders, at the Battle of Ypres.

He returned from the war, "twenty-three and grey-haired." Upon re-reading Jefferies he had a kindling experience. "Scenes of my boyhood—the fields, the trees, the birds—came back to me poignantly. I saw where my salvation lay—in nature. It purged the war for me; it was Proserine returning from the shades. This is the theme of *The Flax of Dream*—Maddison hearing God in the voice of the woodlark, on the last day of his life."

HENRY WILLIAMSON

Following the war, Williamson spent several "wretched months" as a reporter on the *Weekly Dispatch* under Lord Northcliffe. "I made an awful journalist," he comments. He was finally discharged when he failed to get an interview with a certain nobleman on the subject, "Will Side Whiskers Return?"

"Then followed a period of deep despondency. I had nothing but my army pension of forty pounds, and one short article in the *Daily Express* on the country each week. The literary editor didn't really want the thing but he let me do it out of kindness of heart... I went occasionally to the gallery at Covent Garden and I dreamed my books there. Already I was at work on my first novels—*The Beautiful Years* (1921) and *Dandelion Days* (1922).

"For night's lodging I would sleep on a friend's couch, or on the embankment, or out in Kent on a haystack. I had five or six favorite haystacks. I was solitary and happy; the stars were my companions. I'm afraid the stars sometimes failed me; and then, to recreate the 'ancient sunlight' I used to drink. Of course I developed a suicidal trend, but I was too sane. I had no friends; I longed for love, but men and women alike found me morbid. Finally I decided to break with it all and go to Devon." The legend has it that Williamson walked the two hundred miles to his future home on Exmoor, with five pounds and Jefferies' *The Story of My Heart* in his pocket.

Here he rented a cottage which he used to "explore for owls as a boy," and settled down. "I had my pension, and managed to earn another forty pounds by writing. It was the happiest time of my life." The authors who helped him in this period were Galsworthy, Bennett T. E. Lawrence, Frank Swinnerton, Walter De La Mare, and J. C. Squire. "I love Arnold Bennett," he said a few months before Bennett died. "Over and over again he has gone out of his way to say a decent word on my behalf. A most charming personality; sensitive to his fingertips."

Williamson began his career with the publication of the first of a series of four autobiographical novels, *The Beautiful Years* (1921). The other three books of the group, which is known as *The Flax of Dream*, are: *Dandelion Days* (1922), *The Dream of Fair Women* (1924), and *The Pathway* (1928). The last is the story of a family living in an old manor house on the Devon coast in post-war days, into whose lives comes the soul of Shelley in the body of Will Maddison, a gifted, ne'er-do-well poet.

Tarka the Otter was awarded the Hawthornden Prize of one hundred pounds in 1928. *The Wet Flanders Plain* (1929) is a series of reminiscences and bitter reflections occasioned by a trip thru the battlefields, years after the war. *The Village Book* (1930) was nine years in composition, 1921-30. Some of the portions of it are mere jottings which were made on the backs of envelopes, on match boxes, or odd bits of paper. They constitute a monument to the dying strongholds of rural England. Of his *Patriot's Progress* (1930), Williamson says: "It strikes me as awfully bald and spare. It was just hack work. I was asked to illustrate the line-cuts with words, and did the job cursing the infernal labor."

In 1930 Williamson revised his *Dream of Fair Women* and left only a few lines of the original text unaltered.

"I wrote five versions of that book nine years ago," he said, "each truer than the last. Now I'm nearly a hundred years old and have just learned how not to write." His next work, he said, would be "a trilogy of novels gestating in me for nearly ten years. In *The Flax of Dream*. . . I've treated the theme of Man's aspiration in the romantic manner. The new trilogy is the story of Philip Maddison, the London cousin of William Maddison of *The Pathway*."

"Writing is just slavery," he remarks. "You have to force yourself to keep on and on and on. I often feel I can't write and never could. . . I'm a retrospective writer. Some say I'm a very sad writer. I'm always looking back to things of my own life that have gone. Friends, places, trees. . . People seem to think that because I have a reputation as a nature writer I'm interested in nothing else. . . I'm a glutton for experience." When he visited New York in 1930 Williamson found the city "vastly stimulating," and expressed boyish enthusiasm for the Empire State Building, the Automats, the game of "Murder," and the Flea Circus.

J. Fletcher Smith describes Williamson: "He is tall and slim; his head is small, and his hair (tho not the neat clipped mustache) is greying rapidly. He looks a decade older than his thirty-four years, seems temperamentally melancholy and strangely weary. He has a low, pleasant, agreeable English voice, which can say enthusiastic things, but almost always in a dry, unenthusiastic way. Something appears suppressed within him, bullied into hiding." He bears an uncanny resemblance to John Masefield. He is unassuming and has a lively sense of humor. He dislikes interviews.

The books of Henry Williamson published in America are: *Dream of Fair Women* (1924); *Sun Brothers*, nature stories (1925); *The Lone Swallows*, nature essays (1926); *The Old Stag*, stories (1927); *Tarka the Otter* (1928); *The Pathway* (1929); *The Beautiful Years* (1929); *The Wet Flanders Plain* (1929); *Ackymals*, a limited edition (1929); *Dandelion Days* (1930); *The Village Book* (1930); *Patriot's Progress*

(1930). The English edition of *Sun Brothers* is called *The Peregrine's Saga* (1923).

Edmund Wilson

EDMUND WILSON was born in Red Bank, New Jersey, May 8, 1895. He got his elementary schooling in Hill School, a well known boys' preparatory school in Pottstown, Pennsylvania. His editorial and literary tendencies were evident even at that time and he was one of the editors of the school magazine. He later edited the literary magazine at Princeton University, where he was graduated in 1916. Altho not in the same class, F. Scott Fitzgerald, John Peale Bishop, and Edmund Wilson were in Princeton at the same time and were close friends. A few years later he and Mr. Bishop were associated on *Vanity Fair*.

Mr. Wilson served in a hospital unit in France for a year and a half during the War. Since then he has lived in New York. He is married and has a seven year old daughter.

Mr. Wilson is of medium height, with reddish hair and brown eyes. He is quiet, reticent, and reputed to be shy. Among his friends he is known, aptly, as "Bunny."

EDMUND WILSON

After reporting for the *New York Sun* his first year in New York he went to *Vanity Fair* as managing editor. For the past few years he has been on the editorial staff of *The New Republic;* until the winter of 1930 his special department was the book review section.

Altho Mr. Wilson is recognized as being severe, a critic who demands precision of thought and speech, he has an undisputed reputation of being fair at all times and of belonging to the extremely small group of competent critics in America. He is always ready to help a young or an unknown writer who he thinks has genuine ability.

The bulk of Mr. Wilson's work is critical, but poetry, a novel, and a number of satirical essays and humorous sketches have also been published. He has contributed to *The Bookman, Poetry, Theatre Arts Monthly, Atlantic Monthly, The Dial, Saturday Review of Literature, New Republic,* and other magazines.

The Undertaker's Garland, by John Peale Bishop and Edmund Wilson was published in 1922. The book is a collection of fantastic descriptions of deaths and funerals in verse and prose, and satirical and grimly humorous reflections on the World War and on life.

Discordant Encounters (1927) contains plays and dialogs on cultural questions, the old and the new social forces being attacked and defended. There are imaginary arguments between Paul Rosenfeld and Matthew Josephson, Van Wyck Brooks and F. Scott Fitzgerald, and others.

A novel, *I Thought of Daisy,* was published in the fall of 1929, and a book of poems, *Poets, Farewell!,* soon after.

Axel's Castle, which was published in 1931, contains critical essays, a few of which are reprints in revised form from a series of studies that appeared in *The New Republic* in 1929 and 1930. James Joyce, T. S. Eliot, whom Mr. Wilson was one of the first to recognize, Paul Valéry, and Marcel Proust are among the authors discussed in this volume, which takes its title from the half-Wagnerian, half-romantic Gothic castle in the depths of the Black Forest occupied by the mysterious protagonist of Villier de l'Isle Adam's *Axel.* The conception of such a person in such a set-ting, according to Mr. Wilson, suggests the essential quality of the imaginative literature from 1870 to 1930.

Owen Wister

OWEN WISTER was born in Philadelphia on July 14, 1860. His father was a physician and his mother, Sarah Butler, was the daughter of Fannie Kemble, the great English actress, and Pierce Butler of Georgia and Philadelphia. He went to school in Switzerland when he was ten years old and afterward to a school in England for a short time.

As a student at St. Paul's School in Concord, New Hampshire, where he discovered that he could "make tunes and devise harmonies," the boy determined to become a composer. At Harvard he took part in campus theatrical and musical activities, and was graduated in 1882 with highest honors in music. His first published work was *The New Swiss Family Robinson* in the *Harvard Lampoon* of 1882.

Wister spent the next two years in Paris studying composition. He played his most ambitious composition, *Merlin and Vivien,* for Liszt and the famous composer wrote Fannie Kemble that he had "un talent prononcé" for music.

He returned to America near the beginning of 1884 and became a clerk in the Union Safe Deposit Vaults in New York where he "sat on a high stool computing interest." He was one of the organizers of the Tavern Club, a group of artists and writers, of which William Dean Howells was the first president.

Wister's first novel was *A Wise Man's Son,* his own story with "a bitter-sweet ending," which was "full of hard swearing, hard drinking, too much knowledge of good and evil." Howells read it, assured Wister he could write, but advised him not to show the manuscript to a publisher "because some publisher might accept it, and the clerk would regret such a book when he was older." So "no publisher has ever seen that novel." Still the youth did not take his writing seriously.

Wister left his clerking job in the

spring of 1885 and decided to go to Harvard Law School "since American respectability accepted lawyers, no matter how bad, which I was likely to be, and rejected composers, even if they were good, which I might possibly be." While he was "nibbling at Blackstone" back in Philadelphia until law school should begin in the fall, his health "very opportunely broke down." He spent the summer hunting on the ranch of some friends in Wyoming, and discovered a new point of view. "This accidental sight of the cattle-country settled my career," he writes. But not immediately.

Revived in health, Wister entered the Harvard Law School in the fall of 1885 and was graduated in 1888. He became a member of the Philadelphia bar in 1889 and practiced for two years in the Philadelphia office of Francis Rawle. But every summer he answered the call of the wilderness. "I couldn't get Wyoming out of my head."

On every Western expedition he kept a diary, he says, full of realistic details about "pack horses, camps in the mountains, camps in the sage-brush, nights in town, cards with cavalry officers, meals with cowpunchers, round-ups, scenery, the Yellowstone Park, trout fishing, hunting with Indians, shooting antelope, white tail deer, black tail deer, elk, bear, mountain sheep... I don't know why I wrote it all down so carefully, I had no purpose in doing so... In the autumn of 1891, I returned from my fifth summer in search of health and big game in Wyoming, and wrote two stories about that country and its people."

"Hank's Woman" and "How Lin McLean Went East" were published in *Harper's Magazine* in 1891. The matter was settled. Wister threw up law and became a writer. He stayed in Rawle's law office, however, where he "worked at fiction for twenty-five years, and at law nevermore." In ten years he made fifteen journeys to the West. Theodore Roosevelt, whom Wister had known at Harvard, congratulated him on his first two stories and from that time on, gave the writer steady interest and encouragement. Roosevelt read everything Wister published, sent him letters of comment, and sometimes wrote reviews. In one of his letters Roosevelt said: "I doubt if

OWEN WISTER

you have in America a more consistent admirer of your writings." He always addressed Wister as "Dan."

Wister's first volume of Western stories was *Red Men and White* (1895). It was followed by *Lin McLean* (1898). On the day the Spanish-American War was declared (April 21, 1898), Wister married Mary Channing Wister of Philadelphia, a distant cousin. His wife, from girlhood, was actively interested in helping the needy and unfortunate children of Philadelphia. When she died in 1913 the flags on Philadelphia public schools flew at half mast and fifteen years later a memorial tablet to her was unveiled in the new school building that bears her name. She left six children, three boys and three girls, all of whom are living. One daughter, Marina Wister, is the author of two volumes of poems: *Helen and Others* (1924) and *Night in the Valley* (1930).

Owen Wister's third Western volume was *Jimmy John Boss* (1900). His best-known work, *The Virginian*, appeared in 1902. He wrote in 1929 of the novel: "It had the luck to be a 'best seller' for six months, was dramatized, heartily damned by the New York critics, ran for a while in non-American Broadway, for ten years on the road, is still played in stock after twenty-seven years, and has been three times filmed, and once translated. It made money, actual money;—an agreeable experience, wholly new for its author."

With the royalties from *Lady Baltimore* (1906) Wister built a summer home in Rhode Island. *Lady Baltimore* is a novel about Charleston, South Carolina. Roosevelt, from the White House, wrote Wister a letter of fifteen typewritten pages criticizing the book. When Wister came to prepare the novel for the uniform edition of his books in 1928, he accepted a good many of Roosevelt's objections and made changes in the text.

In *Roosevelt: the Story of a Friendship* (1930), Wister constructed an intimate biography from his long friendship with Roosevelt and his personal correspondence with him.

Owen Wister is a big man with broad shoulders, grey hair and mustache. His home is in Bryn Mawr, Pennsylvania, but he spends a great deal of his time in France. He is a member of the Société des Gens de Lettres de France, and he is a fellow of the American Academy of Arts and Sciences. He received an LL.D. from the University of Pennsylvania in 1907 and L.H.D. from Williams in 1912. He was a member of the Board of Overseers of Harvard University from 1912 to 1925.

Some of the other books by Owen Wister are: *The Dragon of Wantley* (1892), *U. S. Grant* (1900), *Philosophy 4* (1903), *The Seven Ages of Washington* (1907), *The Pentecost of Calamity* (1915), *A Straight Deal* (1920), *Neighbors Henceforth* (1922), *Watch Your Thirst* (1923), *When West Was West* (1928). His works were collected into eleven volumes in 1928.

P. G. Wodehouse

PELHAM GRENVILLE WODEHOUSE, English humorist, was born at Guildford on October 15, 1881. He was educated at Dulwich College, where he spent more time writing Greek farces about his schoolmates than he did in preparation for the Classical Sixth.

For a time, in deference to anxious relatives, he tried to become a banker in London. When, after two years, his employer told him he would never make a success in commerce, he agreed with alacrity. He was earning more money with his pen in his spare time than the bank was ever likely to pay.

From then on, he struck out boldly as a writer. After a period of free-lance work he joined the staff of the *London Globe*, where he conducted the cheery "By the Way" column from 1903 to 1909. His success as a columnist opened the doors to all the leading magazines, while editors and playwrights on both sides of the Atlantic pursued him with contracts.

His first visit to America was in 1904. In 1909 he settled down here for a year to write short stories for magazines. Since then he has made more than twenty trips to America, usually spending half of each year in New York.

Back in England in 1910, Wodehouse lived for three years in the country, with twelve dogs for companions. His house was practically devoid of furniture. An elegant visitor once remarked: "I see you are just on the point of moving into this house. Where was your home before?" His tastes in clothes are simple, too. New suits are a torture to him. He was married, in 1914, to Mrs. Ethel Rowley, widow of Leonard Rowley of Dee Bank, Cheshire. They have a daughter.

Wodehouse began publishing books in 1902 and came into favor with his stories about an uncommonly sharp lad named "Psmith": *Psmith in the City* (1910), *Psmith, Journalist* (1915). Since then his numerous books have been persistent best-sellers on two continents. He has created a long line of laugh-provoking characters who bob in and out of his stories. Some of them, besides Psmith, are: Jeeves, Mr. Mulliner, the Oldest Member, Lord Tilbury, the priceless Bertie Wooster, Honoria Glossop, Hamilton Meamish, "Soapy" Molloy, Judson Coker, and Stanley Featherstonehaugh Ukridge.

"His types of men and women are few," says Louis J. McQuilland, "and he does not endow them with complexes. His hero as a rule is rather devoid of

grey matter, but sometimes he is quite
well off as regards muscle and brawn;
at others he is merely a very lovable,
silly ass with an exceedingly limited vocabulary. His heroine, however, is
always quick of understanding. She is
petite and attractive... The Wodehouse
villain is a cunning customer who over-
reaches himself and comes to final noth-
ingness... Wodehouse's old people are
eccentrics, and he specialises in uncles
who are much better-hearted than they
appear to be. He is quite at home (in
fiction) with the criminal classes—
abortive burglars, blackmailers and such
like. His small boys are precocious to
the last degree."

Wodehouse began writing musical
comedies in collaboration with Guy Bolton and the composer Jerome D. Kern.
He has written more than twenty-two
shows with Bolton. His theatrical activities include productions with George
Grossmith and Ian Hay. With the latter
he has done *A Damsel in Distress; Baa,
Baa, Black Sheep;* and *Leave it to
Psmith.* With Valeria Wyngate he
adapted *Her Cardboard Lover* from the
French. Most of his musical comedies
have been produced in America. The
best known in England are: *Kissing
Time* (1921), *The Golden Moth* (1921),
The Cabaret Girl (1922).

In June 1929 Wodehouse's partial
record was: one hundred and forty-two
short stories published in the *Strand
Magazine* during twenty years; nine
boys' stories; twenty-six novels; collaboration in about thirty musical comedies. Since then he has continued his
rapid pace. He spent some time in
Hollywood in 1930, writing dialog for
the talkies.

Wodehouse writes quickly. One time,
when he was convalescing from an attack
of the mumps, he wrote thirty short stories in a month, but none of them was
published. Nowadays, his output is never
more than seven short stories a year. He
does all his work direct on a typewriter.
A conscientious workman, he always
writes the first three hundred words of
a story a dozen times, and never lets the
story go until he has written it thru
from start to finish three times. That is
the only way, he finds, to "spot bits of

P. G. WODEHOUSE

over-writing which will creep in when
one is hammering the thing out."

He has an uncanny capacity for disappearances. "Whenever he finds himself
at a party," says Beverley Nichols,
"where the ground is a little too thick
with millionaires, or where too many
peeresses are calling to their young, or
where the wits are warbling too shrilly,
he disappears... These disappearances
are really the key to his character, which
is dominated by a loathing for display."
Altho his own conversation is colorful,
he often disappoints his hearers by not
attempting to be witty. He never talks
about himself. It is also his custom to
disappear every Saturday afternoon and
go alone to a football match. For years
no one, not even his family, knew where
he went.

"I imagine Plum (as he is called)
makes quite a lot of money," observes
Nichols. "But I am quite certain that
money to him means principally a curious and almost mythical product which
enables one to purchase golf balls and
books. After these essentials to life have
been obtained, money is something
which, when it arrives in large quantities,
must be handed to one's wife rather as
tho it were an explosive." He takes a
childish interest in his small private

banking account, which is made up of insignificant sums that come to hand, and which never seems to rise much above a hundred pounds.

"He is the type," writes McQuilland, "of the perfect uncle, with a twinkle in his eye... His hair recedes a little and he wears spectacles, but he is devoted to cricket and talks of it with zest." D. B. Wyndham Lewis says: "I should sum P. G. up as being an extraordinary sunny sort of bloke, still young in middle age, and certainly the man to go out of his way in the doing of generous things."

Some of the books by P. G. Wodehouse are: *Leave it to Psmith* (1923) *The Inimitable Jeeves* (1924), *Meet Mr. Mulliner* (1927), *Money for Nothing* (1928), *Mr. Mulliner Speaking* (1929), *Summer Lightning* (1929), *Very Good, Jeeves* (1930), *Big Money* (1931).

Humbert Wolfe

HUMBERT WOLFE, English poet, has set down the following account of himself:

Born Via Fattebenefratelli, Milan, Italy, 5th January, 1885. Brought to Bradford, Yorkshire, in the same year, and educated in that painful example of

HUMBERT WOLFE

a modern industrial town at Bradford Grammar School. At Bradford Grammar School had the great fortune, in Mr. Battersby and Mr. Barton, of being under the care of two distinguished men of letters, both in their own way poets. Left Bradford for Wadham College, Oxford, and there started writing verse, but was disturbed by metaphysics. As a result of this disturbance entered the Civil Service by examination in 1908 in the Board of Trade. Married two years later to Jessie Chalmers Graham of Edinburgh. Have one daughter.

In the years 1910 to 1914 occupied largely with discovering what pilotage was not universally compulsory, and why poetry was involuntary. Wrote a certain number of poems never published, except occasionally in the pages of the old weekly *Westminster Gazette,* and a novel called *The Count of Saldeyne* consistently refused up till 1915 by all publishers, and then put away.

During the War an ardent disciple of militarism, and an official of the Ministry of Munitions, suffering violent change of heart when it was fashionable to do so immediately after the Armistice. Recovered a part of his wandered soul about 1919 and published his first book of verse, *London Sonnets,* in that year. Complete silence reigned after this first publication, but a certain amount of reviewing work in the *Saturday Review* encouraged the continuance of literary activities, not wholly prevented by writing for the Carnegie Foundation *Labour Supply and Regulation,* and articles of the same kind in the *Encyclopaedia Brittanica.*

In 1921 a second and equally unsuccessful book of verse, *Shylock Reasons with Mr. Chesterton,* was published. This was followed in 1922 by a little book of fables in prose called *Circular Saws,* which cut no wood or ice. The next year saw the publication of *Kensington Gardens* which, in a very small way, began to attract attention. This was followed by *The Unknown Goddess* (1925) which had a success of esteem but not a general success, the first public notice attracted by this author being with a book of satires called *Lampoons* (1925). This interest was increased by *Humoresque,* published six months later, and was given something like general currency by a long satire, *News of the Devil* (1926).

But with *Requiem,* in 1927, the author emerged from comparative obscurity into comparative recognition. *Requiem* was followed in rapid succession by *Others Abide* (translations from the Greek Anthology), *Cursory Rhymes* (1927), *The Silver Cat* (1928), and *This Blind Rose* (1928). The author having now attained a position in which he is violently attacked by some of his brother poets, we may assume that he has reached the point fixed enough to suggest that he should be disestablished.

Apart from his literary activity he has been in charge of the wages work of the British Ministry of Labour, and has for seven years represented Great Britain on the Governing Body of the International Labour Office at Geneva. This has involved a certain amount of public speaking which has perhaps induced the air of rhetoric in his verse about which complaint is often made.

For the rest, he has no interests and no hobbies. He detests every form of game alike and all people who play them. His only merit is that of a hard worker, but the results of his work do not necessarily indicate that this is a merit.

He is, of course, of Jewish birth and of no political creed, except that his general view is that money and its possessors should be abolished.

Wolfe has been called the "handsomest poet in London." He is slender and his lean, smooth, hawk-like face has the look of a tragedian. He has heavy black hair and long, slender hands. During the day he is Principal Assistant Secretary to the Ministry of Labour and he writes his poems in the small hours of the morning. He is a prolific writer.

Some of Humbert Wolfe's books that have appeared since *This Blind Rose* are: *The Craft of Verse* (1928); *Dialogues and Monologues* (1929); *Notes on English Verse Satire* (1929); *Early Poems* (1930); *George Moore; The Uncelestial City* (1930), a satire in verse; *Tennyson* (1930). The volume of *Early Poems* contains *London Sonnets* (1919) and *Shylock Reasons with Mr. Chester-*

ton (1921). *Winter Miscellany* (1930), edited by Wolfe, is an anthology of prose and verse for the winter season.

Thomas Wolfe

THOMAS CLAYTON WOLFE was born in Asheville, North Carolina, in 1900. He was graduated at the age of nineteen from the University of North Carolina, where he was one of the original members of the Carolina Playmakers, working under Professor Frederick H. Koch. Three years later he received the degree of Master of Arts from Harvard University, where he studied under Professor George Pierce Baker in the 47 Workshop.

Wolfe's first bow to the book-reading public was so modest as to be hardly noticed. It was with a play, "The Return of Buck Gavin, the Tragedy of a Mountain Outlaw," which appeared in Professor Koch's collection of *Carolina Folk-Plays* (second series) in 1924. This play had been given production on

THOMAS WOLFE

The Playmakers' Stage at Chapel Hill, North Carolina, March 14 and 15, 1919. Wolfe himself played Buck Gavin, the fierce but kind-hearted murderer, dressing for the part with a great wig of black hair and a wild black beard.

Following his departure from Harvard, Wolfe traveled and studied in Europe, preparatory to becoming a member of the faculty of New York University as an instructor in the English department.

Look Homeward, Angel (1929), his first novel, took him almost three years to write. This "Story of a Buried Life" (as it is subtitled) was begun while the author was staying in England, and the news that the manuscript had been accepted reached him when he was in Vienna. The title of the book is taken from Milton's *Lycidas*. The story deals, in a rhythmic and sometimes rhetorical prose, with a stormy and original family of Southerners, the Gants. The father, a strong, lecherous, and often drunken man, and his wife, a self-centered, greedy, and shrewd real-estate investor, are portrayed as parents who thwart and stifle the lives of their children. The youngest child, Eugene, tries to break away from the ruins of his family, but tho he manages in the end to go north to Harvard, he carries with him a sense of the pain, loneliness, and futility of wasted life.

Altho no city or state is specifically mentioned in *Look Homeward, Angel,* those who know something of the author's early life have no trouble in recognizing the scene of most of the action. Some critics regard the novel, which is more than 600 pages long, as a refutation of Sinclair Lewis's *Main Street* in that it shows the wild and rich variety of life and character that may be found in a southern small town. In Lewis's first interview with reporters after receiving notification of the Nobel Prize award in 1930, the author of *Main Street* said: "If Wolfe keeps up the promise of *Look Homeward, Angel* he has a chance to be the greatest American writer of all time."

Wolfe resigned his teaching position at New York University in January 1930 to devote all his time to writing his second novel. A few months later he was awarded a Guggenheim Memorial Foundation Fellowship for creative writing, and in May 1930 went to Europe in accordance with the provision of the fellowship. He returned in March 1931 with three hundred thousand words of *October Fair,* which will be published in the fall of 1931. He occupied himself after his return with the rearrangement and revision of his manuscript. Like his first novel, this one must be cut considerably for publication.

Thomas Wolfe is youthful in appearance and is rather large and heavy. He has the expressive countenance of a visionary, with a high forehead, clear eyes, and a cleft chin. He has a friendly personality. It is said that he does most of his writing from midnight till five in the morning. Dostoievsky is his literary idol. James Joyce has also been an influence on his work.

Charles Erskine Scott Wood

IN his long lifetime, Charles Erskine Scott Wood, has followed successively three widely different careers— soldier, lawyer, poet. He was born on February 20, 1852, in Erie, Pennsylvania, the son of William Maxwell Wood, surgeon-general of the United States Navy. Following family tradition, he took up military life as a boy and, after attending Erie Academy and Baltimore City College, was graduated from West Point Military Academy in 1874.

At twenty-two Wood entered the United States Army as second lieutenant and served in the Indian campaigns of the Northwest, fraternizing with the Indians themselves, learning from their wisdom, and being accepted in their tribes. He took part in the Nez Percé campaign of 1877 and the Bannock and Piute campaign of 1878, advancing to the rank of first lieutenant.

In 1882, when he was still in the army, he published Mark Twain's ribald *1601,* as a friendly gesture. A few copies of the book were run off a hand press for private distribution.

Wood left the army to study law, and in 1883 he received the degrees of Ph.B. and LL.B. from Columbia. He was admitted to the bar the following year and settled in Portland, Oregon, where he became known as the most distinguished and picturesque attorney in the Northwest. He had two offices. In one he met corporation clients; to the other, a secret chamber, came poets, peasants, artists, hoboes, dreamers, cultists, borrowers, cranks, sinners, saints, scientists, fanatics, gentle souls, the rich, the lean. He found in law an opportunity to defend the weak against the strong, impossible in the profession of war.

This secret chamber was a treasure trove. Here he gathered rare rugs, furnishings, bronzes, marbles, paintings, and old editions. Here he met the poet, Sara Bard Field, who became his wife.

In 1901 Wood published *A Book of Tales, Being Myths of the North American Indians.* In 1904 his symbolic *A Masque of Love* appeared. In 1915 a series of satires under the general heading of *Heavenly Discourse* appeared in *The Masses.* These were continued at irregular intervals for more than ten years. They showed the influence of Mark Twain. In the same year he issued the first version of *The Poet in the Desert,* a pageant of protest in one long poem, conceived in the form of rhapsodic dialogs between a Poet, Truth, and Justice.

In 1918 a limited number of privately printed copies of *Maia* appeared. *Maia* is a sonnet sequence of the seasons with numerous interjections by the author and a few interpolations by Sara Bard Field.

Somewhere along the years, Wood became a liberal and further up the curve of life, a radical. The Utopia of anarchism intrigued him, but unlike many converts, he did not lose his sense of humor. Preachers who dogmatically take no account of environment in conditioning men's "souls," chauvinists and jingoists who would beat the plowshare and the pruning hook into swords, were the especial butt of his humor. He hates war.

In 1919 Wood retired from his law practice and turned wholly to poetry. He moved to California to live in the sunlight. His home is at Los Gatos, on a hill overlooking an ocean bay. Nearly eighty years old, Wood continues active writing and his poems are printed in current magazines. He is a veritable Lear in appearance, with his flowing

CHARLES ERSKINE SCOTT WOOD

white hair and beard. A friend has described him as "wise and mellow with many years,—one who walks the vine-draped hills of Los Gatos with the gods, looking down on tiny villages and checkered orchards, and chuckling not unkindly as he listens to the discourses of puffing little men."

C.E.S. Wood's vest pocket reminds one of a pipe organ because of the number of huge fountain pens he carries— all filled. He has the ability to write wherever he may be: on a street car, standing in queue before a ticket window, waiting for the doctor, waiting between trains, sitting in hotel lobbies. Every little odd minute of the day is scribbled over with ink.

Heavenly Discourse caused more discussion upon publication as a book in 1927 than it did in *The Masses.* The attack upon American religious social, and economic phenomena found a large audience. The sketches are regarded as good examples of rough and ready journalistic satire. One of the papers is on the Sacco-Vanzetti case. *The Poet in the Desert* was reissued in popular form in 1928.

The works by Charles Erskine Scott Wood include: *A Book of Tales* (1901); *A Masque of Love* (1904); *The*

Poet in the Desert (1915); *Maia* (1918); *Circe* (1919); *Heavenly Discourse* (1927); *Poems from the Ranges* (1929); *Too Much Government* (1931), in which the author sums up his theories of life and society.

Virginia Woolf

VIRGINIA WOOLF'S circumstances are easily summarized, but to explain briefly what she is trying to do with the novel is more difficult. So let circumstances be taken first. When she was born in London in 1882 at 13 Hyde Park Gate South (which became 22 Hyde Park Gate in 1884), she was named Adeline Virginia. The "Adeline," however, seems to have vanished without trace from her signature. Her father was Sir Leslie Stephen, the noted biographer, literary critic, and freethinker; her mother was Stephen's second wife, the lovely Julia Prinsep Duckworth, a widow with three children when Stephen married her in 1878.

In the year of Virginia's birth, James Russell Lowell, then American ambassador to England and one of her parents' closest friends, sent the Stephens some "Verses Intended to Go with a Posset Dish to My Dear Little God-Daughter." "The newly born," he prayed, would inherit "her father's wit."

> I wish her next, and 'tis the soul
> Of all I've dropped into the bowl,
> Her mother's beauty—nay, but two
> So fair at once would never do...
> I simply wish the child to be
> A sample of Heredity.

"A sample of Heredity" in the Stephen family would find it difficult to avoid distinction. Stephen's first wife was a daughter of Thackeray, and half the most scholarly families in England—Darwins, Maitlands, Symondses, Stracheys—are related to Virginia Woolf. She was the third of four children born of his second marriage: Vanessa, Julian Thoby, Adeline Virginia, and Adrian Leslie. Her older sister Vanessa is the wife of Clive Bell, the art critic.

William Rothenstein recalls the shy, silent, lovely Stephen girls "in plain black dresses with white lace collars and wrist bands, looking as tho they had walked straight out of a canvas by Watts or Burne-Jones."

It is told that Virginia and Vanessa were brought up never to speak unless they had something to say. Virginia's education was "at home" where, among other studies, she learned Greek. There were many things to learn in the crowded Stephen household and many distinguished persons to meet, for men like Meredith, Lowell, Oliver Wendell Holmes, Stevenson, Ruskin, Hardy, Gosse, Dr. A. Ward, Mark Pattison, Sir George Trevelyan, John Morley, and James Bryce were numbered among her father's friends. On Sunday afternoons, a friend recalls, "the room would be very full, and there were poets and painters and novelists there; and there was music, good music. . ." Mrs. Stephen was "the sun and centre of the lively and pleasant group," while her husband looked on, his blue eyes "radiant with delight."

The summers were spent in Cornwall, by the sea at St. Ives, in "a small but roomy house with a garden of an acre or two all up and down hill, with quaint little terraces divided by hedges of escalonia, a grape-house and kitchen-garden, and a so-called orchard beyond." In *To the Lighthouse* Virginia Woolf seems to have drawn from the memory of this Cornish home of her childhood.

Mrs. Stephen died in 1895, when Virginia was thirteen. Leslie Stephen became Sir Leslie Stephen in 1903; he died in the following year.

Virginia and Vanessa, "young ladies as remarkable for their beauty as for their intellect," lived in a small house in Bloomsbury, London. The house became the meeting place of their two brothers and their small group of friends when they left Cambridge. This was the nucleus of "The Bloomsbury Group" which has become internationally famous thru such members as Clive Bell, Leonard Woolf, E. M. Forster, Lytton Strachey, John Maynard Keynes, as well as Virginia Woolf herself.

In 1912 she married Mr. Leonard Woolf, and together at Richmond, a suburb of London, they presently set up a small hand-press and began producing with it a few books in limited editions, including her own. The Hogarth Press became so successful that it has developed into a real publishing house.

Before he married, Mr. Woolf was for a time in the Ceylon Civil Service, as a result of which he wrote a novel, *The Village in the Jungle.* On his return to England he grew interested in labor questions and began writing on cooperation in industry and on economic imperialism. He was literary editor of the London *Nation* from 1923 to 1930.

Mr. Forster and others equally authoritative consider that Mrs. Woolf is of the race of pioneers as a novelist. She seeks to convey the reality, the atmosphere, the spirit of a character by new methods. As Mr. Forster well says, she works in a storm of atoms and seconds, her highest joy is "life; London; this moment of June," and her deepest mystery "here is one room; there another." She is aware, to put it differently, of the variety of feeling that goes into one single instant and the mysterious relation which seems to link events occurring apart. Others of course have this awareness, but she thinks that it is what most concerns the novelist.

Raymond Mortimer summarizes Mrs. Woolf's work and her development as a novelist. "Her first novel, *The Voyage Out* (1915), was written, I believe, when she was only twenty-four, but it was some years before it was published in a revised form. It is fairly traditional, technically, and resembles more than anything the novels of Mr. E. M. Forster. But already essential qualities destined to branch exuberantly out of her work are here in bud—a runaway imagination and a hypertrophied sensibility to the variety and simultaneousness of human life. Her next book, *Night and Day* (1919), is a failure. But the chief point of the book is that it was a serious attempt to adapt her mind to the exigencies of the academic novel. Meanwhile, she was writing front-page articles for the dignified *Times Literary Supplement,* reading deeply, widely, passionately and learning Greek—she was never at a university. With *Monday or Tuesday* (1921) she emerged definitely with the liveliest imagination and most delicate style of her time. But these were only sketches. *Jacob's Room* (1922) was the first full-size canvas. It is the life

VIRGINIA WOOLF

of a man told by the effect he has on the persons and objects with which he comes into contact—a sort of detective story in which the particularities of the protagonist are deduced from the tracks he has left in the snow. There is no plot. *Mrs. Dalloway* (1925) is an even more gallant and successful experiment. We follow two persons, a fashionable hostess and a melancholic clerk, thru their day. Technically, this is Mrs. Woolf's most remarkable novel. But *To the Lighthouse* (1927) is probably her best. Here, for the first time, some of the characters become solid, particularly the old man, in whom one may fancy one recognizes the nobly eminent features of Sir Leslie Stephen himself. And in a transitional passage of extraordinary virtuosity, time passes. It is as if each book contained the seed of its successor—Mrs. Woolf's work is a dynasty, interrupted by one pretender. For in *Orlando* (1928) time keeps passing. We are swept from Queen Elizabeth to 1928."

Mrs. Woolf has also written *The Common Reader* (1925), a collection of essays mostly literary, which established her reputation as a critic. *A Room of One's Own* (1930) is based upon two papers she read to the Arts Society at Newnham and the Odtaa at Girton. In this book she considers the subject of women and fiction and decides that women, having a rather ignominious and subservient past, have their creative lives before them—provided they can find the two keys to freedom—fixed incomes and rooms of their own.

"From the first," writes Mr. Mortimer, "Mrs. Woolf has been in love with life. Everything excites her, beggars and duchesses, snowflakes and dolphins. . . I know only one other person whose writing and whose talk are so closely related, and that is Jean Cocteau. Neither he nor Mrs. Woolf talks like a book; but their books talk like a person. Incidentally, among the people I know, whose company is a delight, I consider these two in a class apart."

A new novel by Mrs. Woolf, *The Waves*, will be published in 1931.

Willard Huntington Wright
(S. S. Van Dine)

THE mysterious Willard Huntington Wright was born in 1888 in Charlottesville, Virginia. He was educated at St. Vincent College, California, 1903;

WILLARD HUNTINGTON WRIGHT

Pomona College, California, 1904; and Harvard University, 1906. At Harvard he was a prize student in anthropology and ethnology. In 1907 he married Katharine Belle Boynton of Seattle, Washington, and in the same year became literary editor of the *Los Angeles Times*.

During his six years with the *Times*, Wright also served as literary critic for *Town Topics*, 1910-14; dramatic critic for the same, 1912-14; and editor of *Smart Set Magazine*, 1912-14. In 1915 he became art critic for *The Forum*, the following year he was literary critic for *International Studio*, and in 1917 he served as literary editor of the *New York Evening Mail*. In 1918-19 he was music critic and art editor of the *San Francisco Bulletin*, and in 1922-23 he was art critic for *Hearst's International Magazine*.

Beginning in 1913, Wright published various books on art, literature, and music, which were regarded as scholarly works, but gave him little fame. In 1916 he published a novel, *The Man of Promise*, dealing with the failure of a man of high talent, which received little attention.

About 1925 Wright underwent a long illness. During his convalescence, by way of occupational therapy, he wrote *The Benson Murder Case*, in which he created the character of Philo Vance, a master sleuth. In order that his mystery novels should not be judged in comparison with his previous scholarly works, he adopted the pseudonym of S. S. Van Dine, taking an old family name from his maternal grandmother who was a Van Dyne.

The Benson Murder Case was published in *Scribner's Magazine* and then in book form in 1926. By the time the second of the series, *The Canary Murder Case*, appeared a year later, Van Dine had become a best-seller, Vance was a household word, and guessing the author's identity was a favorite pastime. When Van Dine wrote an article for a Chicago paper, he responded to the editor's malicious request for a photo with a caricature of himself (having been a painter) which was faithful in every detail, yet unfaithful in general impression. It had the prehensile ears, hair parted to the right, beard, mustache, and monocle. This drawing led to a comparison of the works of S. S. Van Dine with those of Willard Huntington Wright, and thus to a discovery of the author's closely-guarded identity thru certain similarities in those works.

In 1927 Wright published, under his own name, an anthology called *The Great Detective Stories*, which he prefaced with a thirty-five page essay on the types of detective fiction produced in America, England, France, Germany, Austria, and Russia since Poe and Gaboriau. Under his own name he also wrote an introduction to *Some Famous Medical Trials*. At the same time he wrote articles on detective fiction under his pen-name. Under both names he expressed some of the same ideas, in some of the same language. When this evidence was presented, together with other clues, he finally admitted his identity. When Wright's neglected novel, *The Man of Promise,* was reissued in 1929 after he became known as S. S. Van Dine, it received high praise.

Meanwhile, at the rate of one a year, Wright continued to produce Philo Vance's ingenious solutions of baffling murders. After the *Canary Murder Case* came: *The Greene Murder Case* (1928), *The Bishop Murder Case* (1929), *The Scarab Murder Case* (1930). The author allotted himself six years to produce the complete works of S. S. Van Dine. After the publication in 1931 of the sixth of the series, *The Autumn Murder Case,* he planned to bid farewell to his successful pseudonymous self and return to his old identity. He planned then to complete the writing of *Philology and the Writer* and *Modern Music.* The latter is to supplement *Modern Painting* (1915) and *Modern Literature* (1926) and, like them, will be applications of the critical theory enunciated in *The Creative Will* (1916).

Wright is the very model for Philo Vance himself. A versatile scholar, he is acquainted with languages, literatures, sciences, art, criminology, medicine. He has studied abroad. An interviewer who visited Wright in his study in the West Seventies of New York City writes: "The gentleman seated opposite us was meticulously groomed and completely at ease in his soft flannel robe. His grey Van Dyke befits his character perfectly. The expression of his eyes changes with his conversation from quiet amusement to intense interest and back to amusement in the course of a sentence. A straight nose and high forehead complete the impression of dignity and extraordinary alertness... As we talked he lighted a fresh cigarette at regular ten minute intervals, each time selecting a new holder from a right-hand drawer of the desk."

The visitor found the room perfectly conceived for the study of a master sleuth: "It is a large room, rather high, with solid book-shelves against the walls to a convenient reaching height. Above the shelves are hung modern paintings, the predominant note of which is brilliant coloring. These paintings stand out remarkably in the rather dim light of the study. On the north wall is probably the most complete library of detective fiction ever assembled; against the west wall is, perhaps, the most complete private library of Egyptology, including many papyri, in the United States; and the remaining space is given to subjects interesting to a gentleman who delves into arts and sciences."

Other books by Willard Huntington Wright include: *Songs of Youth* (1913); *Europe After 8:15,* with H. L. Mencken and G. J. Nathan (1913); *What Nietzsche Thought* (1914); *Richard Hovey and His Friends* (1914); *The Forum Exhibition of Modern American Painters* (1916); *Misinforming a Nation* (1917); *Informing a Nation* (1917); *The Great Modern French Stories* (1918); *The Future of Painting* (1923).

Wright married for the second time in October 1930. His wife is Eleanor Rulapaugh, known professionally as Claire De Lisle, a portrait painter. They are living in Los Angeles.

William Butler Yeats

WILLIAM BUTLER YEATS, Irish poet and playwright, was born at Sandymount, near Dublin, on June 13, 1865. He is named for his paternal

WILLIAM BUTLER YEATS

and thereafter he contributed occasional verse and prose to that journal and the *Irish Monthly*. At twenty-one he definitely gave up painting for literature. His first book, entitled *Mosada,* a dramatic poem, appeared in 1886. The following year he went to London and worked for some years as a journalist. Between 1888 and 1890 he compiled several volumes of folk stories and fairy tales.

The Wanderings of Oisin (1889) established Yeats as a lyricist when he was twenty-four. The poems in the volume were all written at Sligo. Since then he has published numerous books of verse, articulating his strong belief in the supernatural. His early verse is full of Hinduism and Celtism. From Blake he derived a belief in poetry as a form of magic and in 1901 he wrote an essay on magic. He has always written poetry with difficulty, rarely producing as much as nine lines a day.

The Countess Kathleen (1892) is the drama of a noblewoman who sells her soul to save her people from starvation. When the play was performed in Dublin, it was hissed and cat-called, and a pamphlet was issued inciting Catholic feeling to put a stop to the "blasphemy." The play continued its run however, and scored a victory over the objectors which paved the way for freedom of literature in Ireland. *The Land of Heart's Desire* (1894) is a one-act drama about a dreamy bride who, on May Eve, is called away by the fairies.

George Moore's first impression of Yeats was at a performance of *The Land of Heart's Desire,* "striding to and forth at the back of the dress circle, a long black cloak drooping from his shoulders, a soft black sombrero on his head, a voluminous black silk tie flowing from his collar, loose black trousers dragging untidily over his long, heavy feet..." His hair was black and his skin yellow.

"He had an artificial manner," wrote William Rothenstein, "and when he was surrounded by female admirers his sublimity came near to the ridiculous at times." In his London rooms Yeats held forth every week "on fairies and magic, the cabala, and the philosopher's stone. Sometimes, at these gatherings, Miss Florence Farr would croon to the ac-

grandfather who was rector of Tyllylish Down. His father, John Butler Yeats, was a well-known artist. Jack Butler Yeats, his brother, is a noted painter of Irish landscape and life, and one of his sisters is the founder of the Cuala Industries near Dublin.

When he was a small boy, Yeats's parents moved to London but he spent much of his childhood and youth at Sligo, where his mother's father was a merchant and ship-owner. At the age of about ten he went to London where he attended the Godolphin School in Hammersmith, but at fifteen he returned to Ireland and attended the Erasmus Smith School in Dublin.

Then, because his father wished it, he studied painting for three years, but he was restless and unproductive. He preferred to browse in libraries, reading translations, or making them, from Gaelic tales and poems. Still better, he liked to sit by the turf fires in old Connaught and listen to the folk tales of the peasantry. A dreamy, gentle youth, he had a great zest for reciting poems, even in the middle of the night.

When he was nineteen, Yeats's first poem, "The Island of Statues," was published in the *Dublin University Review* companiment of the single-stringed instrument which Yeats had invented."

Yeats identified himself with the "decadent" group of poets (including Symons, Henley, and Dowson) who gathered at the Cheshire Cheese in London. In 1894 he paid a visit to Verlaine in Paris. He became deeply concerned over the literary development of his native country. In the preface to his *Book of Irish Verse* (1895) he expressed the hope that Irish poetry would "some day be great enough to lead a world sick with theories to those sweet well-waters of primeval poetry, upon whose edge still linger the brotherhoods of wisdom, the immortal moods."

When he was about thirty-five, Yeats turned for a while to the theatre as the best medium for giving Ireland a characteristic literature of her own. About the beginning of the century, with the help of Lady Gregory and others, he founded the Abbey Theatre of Dublin, and he set about the task of supplying it with plays. Some of the plays were in verse and some in prose. They included: *Cathleen ni Houlihan* (1902), *The Hour Glass* (1903), *The King's Threshold* (1904), *Deirdre* (1907). He soon had to abandon his vision of a folk-theatre. He discovered Synge in Paris and persuaded him to return to Ireland and write plays for the Abbey Theatre. Synge did not approve of Yeats's mystic theories of the drama, but Yeats produced his plays. Later, with the plays of Sean O'Casey, the Abbey Theatre took a naturalistic turn which Yeats refused to tolerate.

Since 1900 Yeats's literary reputation has increased steadily. He is the accepted leader of the Irish movement. Lady Gregory and Synge never would have written plays if they had not met Yeats, and Yeats led George Moore to Ireland where he wrote for nine years. In 1923 he was awarded the Nobel Prize for literature, and several honorary degrees have been conferred upon him. Since 1922 he has been a senator of the Irish Free State. He still writes poetry and in 1928 published *The Tower*, which contains some of his finest work.

In *A Packet for Ezra Pound* (1929) Yeats reveals that his wife (Georgie Lees) is a medium and that the theories he sets forth in *A Vision* (1926) were communicated thru her by supernatural beings. Four days after their marriage in 1917, Mrs. Yeats surprised him by producing automatic writing, which was continued daily thereafter. From early youth Yeats has been subject to strange hallucinations and trance-like states, and he is an enthusiastic believer in her seances.

Yeats has made numerous visits to America and has been the butt of facetious remarks in the press because of his belief in fairies. Burton Rascoe describes the visitor as a "tall, stooped, very poetical (and professorial) looking man with his black hair streaked white" and wearing beribboned glasses. He has a tendency towards absent-mindedness, and recently his hearing has been impaired. At a dinner given for him in Chicago, "he so far forgot where he was as to begin chanting some verses while a brother poet was paying an eloquent and thoughtful tribute to him, and continued so audibly and monotonously that the other poet forgot the conclusion to his talk and had to sit down in great confusion... Like most poets Yeats reads his own verses badly; indeed, he mangles them by reciting them in a dreary monotone, with care only for the beat of a measure."

The poet lives with his wife and two children in an ancient tower on the outermost Irish coast. As a member of the senate, he presides at official receptions in a silk hat, inspects the plumbing of the government schools, and conscientiously sits thru all the movies it is his official duty to censor. He is much occupied with politics and society.

Yeats said once he would like to spend the rest of his life rewriting the poems that he had already written. The latest collected edition of his works in both verse and prose, containing many revisions, was published in 1926 in six volumes. Many observers are of the opinion that his poems have suffered in the process of alteration. His lyrics have admittedly arisen out of one great early passion,—for Maud Gonne, the actress.

"Yeats's solemn height and hieratic appearance," writes George Moore in *Hail and Farewell*, "authorize the literary dogmas that he pronounces every season. He is the type of the literary fop, and the most complete that has ever appeared in literature." Moore calls him "a sort of monk of literature" because he is all intellect, and his thoughts are abstracted from the world. His laugh is described as "the most melancholy thing in the world."

The works of William Butler Yeats include: poetry, *The Wanderings of Oisin* (1889), *The Wind Among the Reeds* (1899), *In the Seven Woods* (1903), *The Green Helmet* (1910), *The Wild Swans of Coole* (1919), *The Tower* (1928), *The Winding Stair* (1929); plays, *The Countess Kathleen* (1892), *The Land of Heart's Desire* (1894), *The Shadowy Waters* (1900), *Cathleen ni Houlihan* (1902), *Deirdre* (1907), *Four Plays for Dancers* (1921), *Plays in Prose and Verse* (1923); stories and sketches, *John Sherman* (1891), *The Celtic Twilight* (1893); *The Secret Rose* (1897), *Stories of Red Hanrahan* (1904); essays, *Ideas of Good and Evil* (1903), *Per Amica Silentia Lunae* (1918), *The Cutting of an Agate* (1919), *Essays* (1924); autobiography, *Reveries over Childhood and Youth* (1915) and *The Trembling of the Veil* (1922), published together as *Autobiographies* (1926).

E. H. Young

EMILY HILDA YOUNG, whose name in private life is Mrs. Daniell, was born in Northumberland in 1880. She was married in 1902 and went to live in Bristol, which provided the setting for *William*. Her husband was a solicitor in Bristol. He went into the World War, altho past the usual service age, and was killed shortly before the Armistice.

Miss Young worked as a groom in stables during the war, and in 1918 went to London. She now lives quietly in the country about half an hour from London. The greater part of the year she spends in writing, but her summers are spent in rock-climbing in Wales, Switzerland, or the Dolomites. At this sport she is an acknowledged expert, and has mapped out many new rock-climbing trails

E. H. YOUNG

hitherto inaccessible even to skilled men rock-climbers.

Unlike most literary figures today, Miss Young has little to do with professional literary life. She goes to no public dinners, knows no celebrities, and does not care for the company of "lions." She has been called "the apostle of quiet people" in the British press.

"The story of the modest little suburban housewife who happens to be sitting next to me in the railway carriage interests me more than famous people," she says. "The little housewife's accounts of her sister's matrimonial difficulties or the story of her husband's losing his place in an office, are more real to me than the affairs of the political, literary, art, or social world."

For amusement, Miss Young prefers old-time melodrama to modern plays about decadent society: "Give me good old rattling melodrama, with plenty of pistols and black-mustached villains, where you can leave your brains behind at the door, and enjoy a succession of thrills."

Miss Young's quietly grim features seem to have locked up much pain and pity with the years. Her eyes are penetrating and her mouth is set in a long, meditative curve. She is a hardy woman, one who has worked with her hands.

The novel *William* (1925) is the story of a self-made man of unusual broad-mindedness and vision. Believing in the real happiness of his favorite daughter who has run away from her husband with a lover, he battles with his furious family and relatives. This book introduced E. H. Young to American readers in 1926.

The Malletts (1927) is the novel of a woman who consistently refuses to marry her neighbor until she is past thirty, and then falls in love with him when he brings home a pretty bride. *Moor Fires* (1927) is the passionate life story of two brothers and two sisters who live with their stepmother in an old house on the edge of the moor. *The Vicar's Daughter* (1928) relates the suspicions of the members of a vicar's family that he is the parent of a country girl who comes to the household with a letter from her mother. When relations are strained to the breaking point the gigantic mistake comes out, and the good vicar never guesses what it is all about.

Miss Mole (1930) was awarded the James Tait Black Memorial Prize for fiction in 1931. It is the story of a courageous, pitiful, happy-go-lucky spinster on the wrong side of forty, who goes from post to post until she becomes housekeeper to a pompous nonconformist minister. She succeeds marvelously in this capacity until along comes a man who knows about her past.

ELLA YOUNG

Ella Young

ELLA YOUNG, Irish poet and authority on Celtic mythology, was born in 1865 in County Antrim in Northern Ireland, and spent her girlhood in the south and midlands. She was graduated from the Dublin Royal University with honors in history, jurisprudence, and political economy. For many years she made her home in Dublin, where she was a member of the brilliant group which has fostered the Celtic Renaissance in literature, including Padraic Colum, William Butler Yeats, Lady Gregory, Dr. Douglas Hyde, Fiona Macleod, and James Stephens.

Immediately after graduation Miss Young began her researches in Celtic mythology and the first fruit of her labors was the old Celtic myth of creation, which she pieced out from many fragments of folk-tradition. On becoming an authority in this field, she was asked to write on Celtic mythology for the *Celtic Year Book*.

In preparation for her task of interpreting this native culture, Miss Young sought her material first-hand by first learning to speak the Gaelic language and then living in the only regions where the old legends and sagas are still kept alive. She lived in the little thatched huts on the hillsides, she sailed in archaic Irish fishing rigs listening to the yarns of the fishermen, and she drove thru the isolated country behind primitive ox teams. She made the life of the Irish peasant her own and learned the secret of the inimitable Irish peasant spirit.

"Around the peat fires of Irish huts," writes Jane Verne Terrill, "they told her stories of pookahs, the mischievous elves who play tricks on people, of the lake horses ridden by fairy horsemen, of fairies playing at favorites and dropping pennies in the path of such as please them. Sometimes the story-teller of the clan would be there, and that would be an occasion worth recording, for he would recite in rhyme—often for so long as three evenings without break—a saga of Ireland in uncorrupted Gaelic as ancient as the English of Beowulf!"

So Miss Young collected her treasure of legend, and from it pieced the complete cycles. The result of her twenty years of research is found in her books of fairy tales and folk lore, most notably in *Wonder Smith and His Son* (1927). The material thus gathered also lends atmosphere to her volumes of verse, which include *The Weird of Finovar* and *The Rose of Heaven.*

The continuation of her exhaustive work in mythology was to have been sponsored by the University of Dublin, but, heartbroken by the deaths of nearly all her friends in the Irish Revolution, Miss Young came to America in 1926 on a temporary passport as a lecturer. She is a lecturer of note and had long been a favorite in Ireland, where she appeared before such learned societies as the Gaelic Society of Trinity College and the Irish Literary Society. She has also spoken at other European universities.

In this country she has lectured at Columbia, Vassar, Smith, Stanford, Berkeley, Northwestern, and many other schools. "If I have anything to interest an American audience," she says, "it will be because I have lived in wild places amongst a primitive people, and have heard by turf fires in little mountain cabins stories a thousand years old, and tales of fairy creatures that happen amongst such people even now—and because I have myself a heart that loves such stories and such adventures."

Miss Young remained in America nearly five years. Finally she left California in October 1930 because of the constant irritation of getting her visitor's visa renewed every six months. She went to Canada in order to re-enter under the immigration quota and become an American citizen. When she sought re-admission the American consul at Victoria, British Columbia, refused a visa on the grounds that she might "become a public charge." In reply, a number of American scholars, writers, and business men guaranteed that she would never become a public charge,

and in April 1931 she was finally admitted.

Books published by Miss Young since first coming here are: *Wonder Smith and His Son* (1927), the story of Gubbaun Saor; *Tangle-Coated Horse* (1929), a collection of episodes from the celebrated Fionn Saga; *To the Little Princess* (1930). Her next work, *The Unicorn With Silver Shoes,* which was to have been published in 1931, was delayed because the forced sojourn in Canada and her consequent disturbance of mind kept her from completing the manuscript.

The state of California, where Miss Young has done most of her writing in this country, she likens to her native Ireland. Of America as a whole she says, "It is a land pulsing with life, a many-colored splendor: its hills, like the hills of Ireland, have a spiritual quality; it is a vibrant huge majestic Sphinx that has not yet uttered the word of its wisdom."

Miss Young believes in the supernatural heroes of whom she writes. "She herself has heard the ring of the fairy bells in the ocean," says Miss Terrill; "she has seen the pookahs at their mischief; she has herself been enchanted on a fairy hill. Even here in America she has heard orchestral music in the grasses of Connecticut,—music of instruments such as we all know, and of some which have never been heard by those who cannot hear the fairies. And so she knows that the things of which she writes are as true as anything is true in a doubtful world."

The books by Ella Young include: *Celtic Wonder Tales* (1923), *Wonder Smith and His Son* (1927), *Tangle-Coated Horse* (1929), *To the Little Princess* (1930).

Francis Brett Young

FRANCIS BRETT YOUNG was born in 1884, the eldest son of R. Brett Young, an English doctor. He was brought up near Hales Owen, Worcestershire, between the Black Country and the valley called "Severn-side." When he was five he announced he was going to be a poet.

Young attended public school at Epsom College, where he edited the school magazine. Then he was sent, under protest, to Birmingham University to study medicine. He felt that his gifts were those of a writer, and he became editor of the undergraduate magazine. "Most of my reading at this time," he says, "centered on the English poets of the eighteenth century. Shenstone had opened this door for me—Shenstone, who was born and bred near my home, and whose 'Leasowes' was described by Doctor Johnson as the envy of the rich and the admiration of the skilful."

But his enthusiasm for verse did not hinder his studies and in 1906 Young qualified as a doctor. For two years thereafter he traveled in the Far East as a ship's doctor, visiting Korea, Japan, and China. Upon his return he married Jessie Hankinson of Avechurch, Worcestershire, whom he had known in his student days at Birmingham. He has a passion for music and his wife is an accomplished singer. He made researches in German *lieder* and accompanied his wife on the piano at many concerts in Birmingham and London. She was the last artist to sing Bach in the Queen's Hall in 1914. It is not generally known that Mr. Young is a composer and that he has written music for the *Songs of Robert Bridges* (1912).

Dr. Young settled at Brixham, in the south of Devon, in 1908, as a general medical practicioner and novelist. Up to this time, his writings consisted largely of poetry and essays, pronounced by the editors to be "over people's heads." His patients were nearly all fishing people, simple and hardy creatures, speaking a racy dialect. They and their life make the subject of his second published novel, *Deep Sea* (1914).

The first two books Young wrote were rejected by thirty-two publishers each. The first to appear, *Undergrowth* (1913), written in collaboration with his brother E. Brett Young, sold less than five hundred copies. He was many years "arriving" as an author. *The Dark Tower* (1914), now one of his best known works, was eclipsed by the World War. It is the story of an unsuccessful man who, as a last resort, returns to the

FRANCIS BRETT YOUNG

home he left in disgust, and there falls in love with his brother's wife.

Dr. Young was released from his practice in Brixham in 1915 and was granted a commission in the Royal Army Medical Corps. After a short training period, he went to East Africa, where he was attached as medical officer to the Second Rhodesian Regiment. With this battalion he took part in the first invasion of German East Africa. The verses scribbled in his field service notebook were published under the title of *Five Degrees South* (1917).

Taken ill with malaria, Young was invalided back to England, a sixty per cent disability according to the army medical boards, and in his own phrase, "four-tenths of a man." Yet he served for a time as registrar of the military hospital at Salisbury Plain, doing arduous office work and writing at night.

The Armistice found Young a very sick man, weakened with over-work. Forbidden to continue medical practice or to reside in the British Isles, he went to live on the island of Capri and devote his time to writing. There he bargained with the Italian author and architect, Edwin Cerio, to design him a house in exchange for English translations of some of Cerio's stories, which were published under the title of *That Capri Air*. In this house he still lives for the greater part of each year, on the terraced mountainside above Anacapri, a thousand feet above the Bay of Naples. The house is shaded by an olive grove in which Young has made a rose garden. He does his writing in a lofty cool room, and his wife sings in a long music room with an imposing grand piano at one end.

Sea Horses (1925) relates the events that take place aboard a tramp steamer which transports a woman and her child from Naples to a port in East Africa, where she is going to rejoin her worthless husband. *The Portrait of Clare* (1927) was awarded the James Tait Black Memorial Prize. It is entitled *Love is Enough* in the American edition. In two volumes, it tells a quiet leisurely story of a gentlewoman from girlhood to middle age; she is brave, sufficiently humorous, loving, yet holds her emotions in control.

Young's method of writing is to set down the narrative first in a species of verbal shorthand and expand it later into the prose of his permanent text. He is grateful now for the medical training which he regretted at the time: "There is no other education in humanity to compare with the doctor's life."

He travels widely; Egyptology is his favorite study now. He has regained his health. "No one would suggest that he was not still young," writes Arnold Glyde, "for he goes thru life with that air of gay detachment which is the especial charm of a certain type of Englishman. . . He has the spare figure of an Englishman who keeps fit, and that way your Englishman has of gazing above one's head as if he saw something interesting there. Also, he must smoke a pipe very soon after breakfast, and continue for most of the day; also, for him a chair is not a seat to be sat upon, but a thing to get astride of, to rest one foot upon and then the other, anything rather than a seat in which to rest. . ."

Francis Brett Young's novels about Africa include: *Marching on Tanga* (1918), *The Crescent Moon* (1918), *Pilgrim's Rest* (1922), *Woodsmoke* (1924). Some of his other books, most of which are "Severn-side" novels, are: *The Iron Age* (1916), *The Young*

Physician (1919), *Poems* (1919), *The Tragic Bride* (1920), *The Black Diamond* (1921), *The Red Knight* (1921), *Cold Harbour* (1924), *My Brother Jonathan* (1928), *Black Roses* (1929), *Jim Redlake* (1930). The last is called *The Redlakes* in the American edition. His plays include *Captain Swing* (1919) and *The Furnace* (1928).

Stark Young

STARK YOUNG takes his Christian name from a remote ancestor who, having saved the life of Edward III of Scotland, was advised by that king to call himself Stark because he was so brave. He was born in Como, Mississippi, on October 11, 1881.

"When I was something over fourteen," he relates, "a little pig fell in the cistern at the school I attended, and typhoid broke out and the school closed. It was a sort of seminary where young ladies boarded, but the town pupils were both girls and boys. Since there was nothing else in town except a very dubious public school, I was sent to the university, to which I was admitted on the condition that I pass the December examination, a few weeks off."

The University of Mississippi, located at Oxford, was a "quiet old place, with an enormous grove of oaks, and buildings somewhat in the Jeffersonian tradition." The faculty at that time was composed of gentlemen of the old South impoverished by the Civil War. As a student, he says, he "escaped the belief, just then beginning to be heard of, that mechanical surface and the outer powers of money are the prime things in living." After graduation in 1901 he abandoned rural serenity for Columbia University, where he took graduate work in English and received an A. M. in 1902.

Young then went to live in a hut in the mountains of North Carolina, studying Dante and Catullus, and writing poems. He stayed six months. During the next six months he taught in a military school in Mississippi and then, at the age of twenty-two, took a trip to Italy. He went to Italy every year thereafter until the World War.

Beginning in 1904, he taught English for three years at the University of Mississippi. During that time he published a book of verse, *The Blind Man at the Window* (1906) and a play in verse entitled *Guenevere* (1906). Young went, in 1907, to the University of Texas, remaining for eight years and becoming a full professor of general literature. In 1911 he published a collection of one-act plays in prose and verse. In 1915, at the invitation of Alexander Meiklejohn, he joined the faculty of Amherst College, where he served as professor of English for six years. One of those years was spent in Spain and Italy. He published three more plays in 1919.

In 1921 Young went to New York City and became a member of the editorial staff of *The New Republic,* for which he still writes articles on the theatre and its personages, as well as dramatic criticism. The first three years of his association with that magazine he was also associate editor of the *Theatre Arts Monthly,* and in 1924-25 he was dramatic critic for the *New York Times.*

Meanwhile, Young has continued his writing. He collected some of his essays on the theatre in *The Flower in Drama* (1923). One of his most praised books, *The Three Fountains,* containing sketches and studies on Italy, was published in 1924, and has been translated into Italian. In the same year the Provincetown Players produced his play, *The Saint.* In 1926 the Stage Society of London produced his *The Colonnade.* He directed Lenormand's *The Failures* for the Theatre Guild and O'Neill's *Welded* for Selwyn. His novels include: *Heaven Trees* (1926), *The Torches Flare* (1927), *River House* (1929).

The Street of the Islands (1930) is a book of short stories with southern and Latin setting. In January 1931 Young sailed for Italy to give the George Westinghouse lectures, established in 1924 to acquaint Italy with American culture and ideas. He was to speak at the Universities of Rome, Milan, Padua, Florence, Palermo, and elsewhere.

Stark Young does not regret the fact that the closing of his boyhood school cut short his preparatory training and deprived him of the "minor master-

Doris Ulmann

STARK YOUNG

pieces" of literature which children usually read. He regards *The Wreck of the Hesperus, Hiawatha, The Lady of the Lake, Evangeline,* and the other standard school texts as a "form of literary measles which it was not necessary for me to have at all."

As a result, he says today: "Thanks to the martyred pig, I associate poetry with high sound, profound feeling, thought and sensuousness, an inexhaustible vitality in rhythm such as life has, with brilliance, poignancy, surprise, and distinction. And so far nothing convinces me of any need for an early dosage with these fifth-rate pieces, more difficult really because less exciting and infinite than good poetry..."

In an essay entitled "Not in Memoriam, But in Defense" which appears in a symposium by twelve Southerners, *I'll Take My Stand* (1930), he expresses some of his opinions on the South: "Southern education has suffered from the Civil War, from the poverty due to chaos, bad methods at home and tariffs at Washington... As for the pride that people meet in Southerners, it is a kind of *amour propre,* sometimes a sort of mad self-respect and honor complex... We are an enthusiastic people and it is certain that, once having turned industrial, we shall be zealous about it."

Stark Young's quizzical face is surmounted by a high forehead. The top of his head is bald. He is unmarried, and he paints for amusement.

Some of the remaining books by Stark Young are: *Three Plays* (1919); *Sweet Times, and The Blue Policeman,* plays for children (1925); *Glamour,* essays on the theatre (1925); *The Theatre,* a summary of the arts that contribute to the art of the theatre (1927).

Arnold Zweig

ARNOLD ZWEIG was born in Gross-Glogau, Silesia, on November 10, 1887. He was educated for the teaching profession at various universities including Berlin, Munich, Rostock, Rubingen, and Heidelberg, specializing in philosophy, languages, Germanic studies, and French and English literature. He knows Shakespeare and the Elizabethans, and is thoroly at home with the English moderns such as Meredith and Hardy, who are comparatively little known to Germans. Among his translations are poems by Poe and a number of Kipling's

ARNOLD ZWEIG

Barrack Room Ballads, in which the metre and rhyme are perfectly preserved.

He published his first volume of short stories in 1910. In 1913 his play, *Ritual Murder in Hungary,* was produced with marked success by Max Reinhardt in Berlin and thruout Germany and Austria. From 1915 to the end of the World War he was a soldier in a German Labor Corps in Northern France, Serbia, and Macedonia, spending thirteen months at Verdun before he was removed to Eastern headquarters.

Following the war Zweig published a number of volumes of short stories and essays on social and political questions. His first full-length novel, *Streit um den Sergeanten Grischa,* was published in Germany in 1927. Like Feuchtwanger's *Jud Süss (Power),* the book was first conceived as a play, but the atmosphere of the Germany of 1920 was not conducive to the production of a work with its implications. So Zweig set about elaborating the theme in novel form and produced the book that brought him wide recognition as a fiction writer.

The Case of Sergeant Grischa, the English translation, was published in the United States in 1928. Based on an actual happening during the World War, the novel tells how a Russian soldier-peasant escapes from a German prison camp and wanders between the lines trying to get back to Russia. A peasant woman aids him, loves him, and helps him on his way with the uniform and passport of a dead spy. Grischa is recaptured and sentenced to death as the spy. He is able to prove his identity, but the wheels of the military machine have been set in motion and the frantic efforts of Grischa's friends are powerless to save him.

The novel is the central piece of a triptych of which the collective title in English is to be *A Trilogy of the Transition.* It will be preceded by *Education Before Verdun* and followed by *The Crowning of a King.* These further volumes in the Grischa series will be translated as soon as the German version is ready.

After its appearance as a novel, *Streit um den Sergeanten Grischa* was put into dramatic form and produced in Germany by Reinhardt in 1930.

Arnold Zweig's second work to be published in this country is *Claudia* (1930), a series of episodes which picture the growth of an understanding of life in Claudia Eggeling, a sensitive German girl of the upper classes, during the time of her courtship and the early days of her married life.

The translations of Arnold Zweig's novels published in America are: *The Case of Sergeant Grischa* (1928), *Claudia* (1930).

Stefan Zweig

HAD it not been for the World War, Stefan Zweig's career might have continued to the end to be that of the talented globe-trotter, the restless searcher after new experiences, personal and spiritual, in Asia, Africa, North Amrica, on the Continent, and the British Isles. He might have gone on writing verse, translating Verhaeren, Verlaine, and others; he might have continued his work of paying a debt to society by gathering for his own country the cultural fruits of the lands he visited. For the traveler (as Zweig himself puts it) carries a spiritual message from nation to nation, and the time that he gives to journeying is time given to others' learning.

Stefan Zweig was born of Jewish parents in Vienna in 1881. He was educated thoroly, thanks to the comfortable circumstances of his family, and he published two volumes of verse before his university career was done. Animated by curiosity for new sights and experiences —a desire to know the world and to live dangerously—he found companionship in Rome, Paris, London, Florence, Berlin, and wandered over the world for the sake of wandering.

"When the world was drunk with war" Zweig dared not openly express his will for peace in books or periodicals. In his preface to the second American edition of *Jeremiah* (1929), a drama in nine scenes, he relates: "The moral compulsion to silence was, thruout the years of the war, the most intolerable of our torments. In such periods of mental stress, art sometimes presents herself as the only helper. For my own

STEFAN ZWEIG

part, since in those days I could not say in plain terms what I felt and thought I chose the only way left open to me, that of symbolism, of historical allegory. I had to find an emblem for us, the unheard, the despised, the ridiculed; and I found it in the book of books, in the primal source of my race, in the figure of Jeremiah, sublimest among the adversaries of war, martyrized for his convictions.

"Amid the rage of battle, amid the clamor of the phrase makers, amid the volley-fires of false news, I turned my attention inwards, formed a present out of the past, translated the present back into the past. Such was the origin of this drama (*Jeremiah*).

"Since it was wholly symbolical, seemed remote from the conflicts of our time, it was allowed to pass the censorship, and appeared in its original German dress during the year 1917, in time to express the muzzled thoughts and the muted feelings of thousands. Access to the stage was, indeed, forbidden in Germany and Austria while the war lasted. But neutral Switzerland was open, and in Zürich *Jeremiah* was staged in 1917, as one of the first attempts in dramatic form to withstand the prevailing lunacy of war."

The shock of the war caused Stefan Zweig to seek new values; his world was overthrown; esteemed friends succumbed to the madness; little remained. Like so many who encountered the spectre of war in the transitional thirties, he was remade by it, and at its conclusion he was spiritually reintegrated. His past life, tho part of him, was yet behind him; a new life, heretofore undreamed of, had begun. He deserted his beloved Vienna, settled in Salsburg and proceeded to carry out a conscious literary program that has made him a conspicuous figure in Continental letters.

Zweig's works found popular as well as intellectual appeal, and in the spring of 1927 his volumes of fiction were in their fortieth, seventy-fifth, thirty-second, fiftieth, and sixtieth thousands, respectively. His works have been translated into many languages. A volume in French, with an introduction by Romain Rolland, has appeared. His complete works, with Maxim Gorky's introduction, are published in Russian.

Many of his books have appeared in America: *Conflicts* (1927) contains three psychological studies of novelette length, each based on a motive furnished by a morbid sex-urge. In *Adepts in Self-portraiture* (1928) Zweig holds up to the mirror of their own writings Casanova, Stendhal, and Tolstoy, setting down the mental and physical characteristics he sees reflected there, and thus producing a rounded self-portrait from youth to age, of each of the three figures.

Zweig's modern adaptation of Ben Jonson's famous comedy, *Volpone* (1928), was produced in Germany, all over Central Europe, and in America by the Theatre Guild in 1928. In *Three Masters* (1930) Zweig gives short interpretative sketches of the lives and works of the three men whom he considers the "supremely great novelists of the nineteenth century": Balzac, Dickens, and Dostoievsky. *Joseph Fouché* (1930) is the biography of the politician who rose to power in the time of the French revolution, became minister of police under Napoleon, and whose ability to shift sides at opportune moments amounted to genius.

Other translations of Stefan Zweig's works published in America include: *Paul Verlaine* (1913); *Emile Verhaeren* (1914); *Romain Rolland* (1921); *Jeremiah* (1922); *Passion and Pain* (1925); *Invisible Collection* (1926). His magazine articles appear in Germany and America. The chief translators of his works into English are Eden and Cedar Paul.

LIVING AUTHORS [1]

[1] Phonetic approximations to the pronunciation of certain foreign and unusual names are given in parentheses. The accented syllable is italicized.

Beresford, Lord
berries. ferd

Pe
Pe
Pe
Pi
Re

Meynell as Kennel

Porgy

Delano De
Roosevelt
Rozev

Irita VanDoren eye re

Synge as thing

see also following pages

Wild Names I Have Met

Excerpts from a booklet by

Alfred H. Holt

Instructor in English at Williams College

To ANYONE who has not had to express learned judgments as to the correct pronunciation of names connected with English and American literature, it may be surprising how many debatable ones there are. While conducting courses in literature, I have run into several hundred frequently mispronounced names — among them the following:

Aldous (Huxley): — "all′-dus." Similarly, the *al* in John Galsworthy (and in the Chicago & Alton Railway) is pronounced *all*.

Baden-Powell, Lord (founder of Boy Scouts): — long *a*, long *o*; rhymes with *Lowell*.

Balliol (College, Oxford): — long *a* as in *bay*, despite double *l*. *Magdalen* College is pronounced "maudlin."

Beresford, Lord: — pronounced "berries-ferd."

Bowdoin (College): — "bo-dn."

Bottome, Phyllis: — the *tome* rhymes with *home*, and is accented.

Brontë: — originally "Prunty"; the *e* may be long or short, but not as if the final syllable were "tay."

Broun, Heywood: — "broon."

Buchan, John (English author): — "buck-an."

Cabell, Branch: — (excerpt from personal letter) "*gabble* is the correct rhyme."

Čapek: — Professors Craigie and Shipley almost agree on "tsah-peck" as the native rendering of the playwright's name, while his publishers tell me it should be "shar-peck." Most of us will continue to call him "kay′-peck."

Cather, Willa: — rhymes with *lather*, as used in shaving.

Cleopatra — third syllable, "pay," not "pat."

Cohan, George M.: — I am informed that Broadway pronounces it like "Cohen," though it is not a modification of the latter name. The fact that his first wife was Ethel Levy proves nothing. He is an Irish-Catholic.

Don Juan: — Byron pronounced it with a good, stand-up, English *j*, and rhymed it more than once with "new one."

Don Quixote: — this has for many years been anglicized into "Quicks-oat," like a trade-name for a breakfast-food, and is hereby recommended.

Dramatis Personae: — Browning probably did not say "pair-so-nigh," but he certainly accented the first word on the first syllable and the second on the second. Memorize the following couplet, if you think it's worth memorizing:

> *Dramatis Personae*
> *Rhymes with "Oh, baloney."*

Dunsany, Lord: — (personal letter) ". . . the second syllable accented and pronounced 'say'."

108

See also next page

Ervine, St. John: — we should pronounce the Irish writer's surname as if it were "Irvin," and batter the first name into something like "sinjun."

Feuchtwanger: — "foy-CHt-vahng-er"; sing the *ng;* do not put another *g* sound in front of the *er.*

Forsyte Saga: — "for-sight' sah'-ga."

Gide, André (French author): — "zheed."

Gondola: — accented on the first syllable.

Gosse, Sir Edmund (English poet and critic): — one syllable, rhymes with *joss.*

Guiterman: — his lecture manager recommends the following couplet:

> *There ain't no better, fitter man,*
> *Than Mister Arthur Guiterman.*

Haverhill (Academy): — "hay-vril."

Hergesheimer, Joseph: — (personal letter) "the *g* is hard; the end is *simer* and not *shimer.*"

Houghton (Mifflin): — (letter from the Boston office of the company) "*Houghton,* even within our own Board of Directors, is pronounced in two ways: in Boston it is pronounced *Ho-ton,* whereas in New York and in the South it is pronounced *How-ton.*"

Inge (the gloomy Dean): — (personal letter) "I rhyme with *thing* or *sting,* not with *twinge* or *cringe.*" Likewise for John *Synge,* the Irish playwright.

Irita (Van Doren): — (personal letter) "the word Irita is an entirely made up name with no excuse except that it pleased my parents' fancy. It is pronounced 'eye-ree'-ta.'"

Knopf: — (letter from the New York publishers) "every letter in the name *Knopf* is sounded, and the *o* is given the sound of *u* as in the word *much.*"

Kruif, Paul de: — rhymes with *strife.*

Krutch, Joseph Wood: — (personal letter) "the name is pronounced with the *u* long, as in *rooster.*" Our city readers, whose acquaintance with roosters may be limited, should rhyme it with *hootch,* like Sir Arthur *Quiller-Couch.*

Lagerlöf, Selma (Swedish writer): — "lah'-ger-luf" (*u* as in *urn*). The vowel sounds are similar to the corresponding ones in the Norwegian author's name, Ole *Rölvaag:* "rul-vahg."

Lehmann, Rosamond: — (personal letter) "I pronounce my name *Lay-man,* which is the only way I've ever heard it pronounced." Note that the Governor of New York not only spells his name with one *n* but pronounces it "lee'-man." Lake *Leman* (Geneva) is also "lee'-man."

Lenine: — a correspondent of *The Saturday Review* wrote that the correct pronunciation is not "le-neen'" or "le-nine'," but "len'-yin." However, "len'-nin" most nearly approximates the Russian vowel sounds and accent.

Liveright, Horace (New York publisher): — this sermon in two syllables is pronounced exactly as spelled.

MacKaye, Percy: — (in a personal letter, he tells me that he once wrote to a lady as follows, in reply to a similar inquiry):

> *Dear madam: I*
> *Am named MacKaye.*

Marquis, Don: — "Mark-wis."

Maugham, Somerset: — rhymes with *shawm.*

Maurois, André: — "more-wah."

Mazo de la Roche: — (personal letter) "my Christian name is pronounced with the *a* as in *May*. My surname is pronounced in the French manner."

Meynell, Alice: — rhymes with *kennel.*

N*obel* (Prize): — "no-bell'."

Notre Dame: — In America, "noter dame" (long *o*, long *a*) is right, my authority being this letter from Notre Dame, Indiana: "The name has been completely anglicized by the university community and the near-by residents. Only visitors now give the place its French pronunciation."

P*epys:* — Drinkwater advocates the pronunciation "peppis," while "peeps," "pips," and "peps" are admitted.

Porgy: — forget the old nursery rhyme when speaking of DuBose (hard *z* sound) and Dorothy Heyward's novel and play; their hero has a hard-boiled *g*.

Powys, John *Cowper:* — we are told to say "coo-per po-ess," which sounds distinguished, but hardly sensible, to American ears.

Pulitzer: — the *u* is sounded exactly as it is in the word *pull*, with slightly more emphasis on the first syllable than is given to the last two syllables.

R*epplier*, Agnes: — (personal letter) "in two syllables, with the accent on the first, as Rep'pleer."

Roosevelt: — in spite of repeated public announcements, a great body of Americans will doubtless continue the Coolidge-Hoover tradition by giving their successor also the double *o;* but both T. R. and Franklin D. are correctly known as "roze-velt"; use *v* rather than *f*, and squeeze the whole thing into about two syllables. As for *Delano*, it is still "dell'-a-no."

S*eumas* (O'Sheel): — rhyme it thus —

O'Sheel wouldn't blame's
If we called him "Shame's."

O'Sheel, before he "grew Gaelic," was simply James Shields. The pronunciation of other Gaelic names is as follows: "pad-ric coll-um" (*Padraic Colum*); "shawn" (*Sean* O'Casey); "pay-der" (*Peadar* O'-Donnell); and "lee-um" (*Liam* O'-Flaherty).

T*ietjens*, Eunice: — (personal letter) "We call it simply Tee'-jens."

Truslow (James T—— Adams): — (personal letter) "the *trus* sounds like *cuss*, and the second syllable is pronounced just like the word *low*. I have usually heard it broadcasted as if it were *Troozlow*, and clergymen seem to have a particular fondness for this pronunciation."

Tunney, Gene: — rhymes with *money*. Excerpt from personal letter: "I answer to *Tooney* only in Italy, because there it is correct."

W*alpole*, Hugh: — (personal letter) "the *Wal* is pronounced 'Wall' although Americans *will* not do so!"

Waugh, Evelyn: — "waw"! And when a British gentleman has *Evelyn* for a Christian name, he pronounces it "eev-lin."

Bobbs-Merrill, Milton Bradley, Brentano's, Cosmopolitan, Doubleday Doran, Ginn, Harcourt Brace, Harper, Heath, Houghton Mifflin, Little Brown, Longmans Green, Lothrop Lee and Shepard, David McKay, Macmillan, Nelson, Putnam, Schirmer, Scribner, and Stokes.

Aanrud, Hans.—On' rood.

Akeley, Delia.—Ake' ley, first syllable like ache.

Alexanian, Manoog Der.—Man ōg' (hard g) Der Al ex" an yon' (French nasal on final syllable).

Artzybashev, Boris M.— Art zee bat' shef.

Beebe, Charles William.—Bee' bee.

Beebe, Mabel Borton.—Bee' bee.

Bianco, Margery Williams.—Byan cō.

Bianco, Pamela.—Byan cō.

Benet, William Rose.—Ben' ay.

Berlic-Mazuranic, Ivan.—Ber' litch Ma zu-raan' itch.

Beuret, Georgette.—Bew ray'. (First syllable rhymes with pew).

Blauvelt, Anna La Tourette.—Blaw velt.

Borchgrevink, Carstens.—Borch grev' ink (Borch as in porch).

Bourne, Henry Eldridge.—Born.

Boutet de Monvel, Louis Maurice.—Boo tay' de Mon' vel.

Bouton, Josephine.—Boo' tun.

Burchenal, Elizabeth.—Accent first syllable, pronounced like birch.

Capuana, Luigi.—Ca pwan' a, Lwee' jee.

Cather, Mrs. Katherine Dunlap.—Rhymes with rather.

Collodi, C., pseud. (Lorenzini, Carlo).—Col lo' di (Rhymes with toady).

Colum, Padraic—Cō' lum, Padrik.

Coulomb, Charles Augustin.—Coo long (French nasal on final syllable).

Cowles, Henry Chandler.—Rhymes with coals.

Crothers, Samuel McChord.—Rhymes with bothers.

Dalkeith, Lena.—Dăl' keeth.

Deming, Mrs. Therese Osterhold.—Rhymes with hemming.

Dobias, Frank.—Do by' as.

Dombrowski, Baroness (K.O.S., pseud.)—Dom brow' ski.

Du Bois, Mary Constance.—Doo boyss'.

Du Chaillu, Paul Belloni.—Du shi' yu.

Dussauze, Alice.—Dew zas.

Duval, Elizabeth W.—Du val' (Last syllable rhymes with hall).

Eells, Elsie Spicer.—Just like the plural of eel.

Erleigh, Eva Violet (Mond) Isaacs, Lady.—Er lay'.

Fabre, Jean Henri.—Făbr.

Fanciulli, Giuseppe.—Fan choo' lee, Jew sep' pa.

Farjeon, Eleanor.—Far' jun, with not too short a last syllable—just a hint of the e before un.

Faulkner, Georgene.—First syllable rhymes with walk.

Francillon, Robert Edward.—Fran' sil on.

Fyleman, Rose.—File' man.

Ghosh, Sarath Kumar.—Gosh!

Gollomb, Joseph.—Goll' om.

Guerber, Helene Adeline.—Gur' ber (Gur as in gurgle, ber as in barber).

Haaren, John Henry.—Rhymes with barren.

Heyliger, William.—High lig' er (Rhymes with bigger).

Jagendorf, Moritz Adolf.—Ya gan dorf.

Jungman, Beatrix.—Jung' man.

Kaler, James Otis.—Kay' ler.

Kihn, W. Langdon.—Pronounced like keen.

Knipe, Mrs. Emilie (Benson), and Knipe, Alden Arthur.—Nipe, rhyming with pipe.

Lagerlof, Selma.—Lah' ger luv (hard g).

Lamprey, Louise.—Lamp' ree.

Larrieu, Odette.—Lar rew.

Lenski, Lois.—Len ski (as in Trotsky).

Lustig, Sonia.—Loos' tig.

McElroy, Margaret J.—Mack' el roy.

Meigs, Cornelie Lynde.—Megs (Rhymes with pegs).

Meyer, Zoe.—My' er, Zo ay'.

Mukerji, Dhan Gopal.—Mu kér jee.

Olcott, Frances Jenkins.—All' kut.

Pogany, Willy.—Po gan' y (Po as River Po; gan as in began; y as short i, almost not sounded).

Poulsson, Emilie.—Paul' son. (One of Miss Poulsson's translations, "Inger Johanne," should be pronounced: Inger—like singer— Yo han' na.)

Rihbany, Abraham Mitrie.—Ree baa' nee.

Riis, Jacob August.—Rees.

Rowe, Dorothy.—Rhymes with bough.

Spyri, Mrs. Johanna.—Rhymes with weary.

Squier, Emma-Lindsay.—Rhymes with tire.

Stefansson, Vilhjalmur.—Stef' en sun, Veel ya mur.

Stow, Edith.—Rhymes with flow.

Sublette, Clifford MacClellan.—Sub let, with equal accents on both syllables.

Szalatnay, Rafael D.—Zall at' nay.

Untermeyer, Louis.—Un rhymes with sun.

Walmsley, Leo.—First syllable rhymes with palm.

Wiltse, Sara E.—Wil' see.

Yonge, Charlotte Mary.—Young.

Youmans.—Rhymes with humans.

Zeitlin, Ida.—Zite' lin (First syllable rhymes with bite.)

Padraic Colum

from two saints

Patrick

and

Colum Cille (hard c)